INFRASTRUCTURE REGULATION:
WHAT WORKS, WHY AND HOW DO WE KNOW?

Lessons from Asia and Beyond

INFRASTRUCTURE REGULATION:
WHAT WORKS, WHY AND HOW DO WE KNOW?

Lessons from Asia and Beyond

Darryl S L Jarvis • M Ramesh • Xun Wu • Eduardo Araral, Jr.
National University of Singapore, Singapore

Editors

World Scientific

NEW JERSEY • LONDON • SINGAPORE • BEIJING • SHANGHAI • HONG KONG • TAIPEI • CHENNAI

Published by

World Scientific Publishing Co. Pte. Ltd.
5 Toh Tuck Link, Singapore 596224
USA office: 27 Warren Street, Suite 401-402, Hackensack, NJ 07601
UK office: 57 Shelton Street, Covent Garden, London WC2H 9HE

British Library Cataloguing-in-Publication Data
A catalogue record for this book is available from the British Library.

INFRASTRUCTURE REGULATION: WHAT WORKS, WHY AND HOW DO WE KNOW?
Lessons from Asia and Beyond

ISBN-13 978-981-4335-73-7
ISBN-10 981-4335-73-8

Typeset by Stallion Press
Email: enquiries@stallionpress.com

Preface

Infrastructure provision in the world over has undergone a series of profound changes in the last quarter century. Historically the preserve of the state, infrastructure provision is now increasingly a private sector affair. These changes reflect a confluence of concerns from fiscal constraints on states, public sector inefficiencies and bloated operating costs to ideational changes about the appropriate role of the state and market in the provision of infrastructure. While it would be inappropriate to conflate these developments with notions of the "decline of the state" or the "retreat of the state", clearly the rise of neo-liberal policy agendas and new public management approaches have made increasing levels of private sector participation a key feature of the infrastructure terrain.

These developments, however, are not unproblematic. Indeed, they raise a series of challenges, not least the issue of regulation and how to design, implement and operate effective regulatory regimes in a way that both protects public and private sector interests. Regulation is itself a highly-problematic affair, and getting right the design characteristics, institutional structures, modes of operation, consultation, and mechanisms for stakeholder participation in a way that produces optimal outcomes is no easy task. As this volume further suggests, the nature of these challenges are amplified in developing countries, where institutional endowments vary and institutional capacity is often constrained or severely impaired. Such a combination of issues presents both the state and private sector participants as well as regulators with a panoply of challenges that few could envisage when new public management models were foreshadowed a few decades ago.

This volume is a contribution to exploring these challenges. We have asked contributors to focus on the issues that confront regulators in three sectors, telecommunications, electricity, and water. While privatization of the telecommunications sector is now a well established practice across much of the world, this is less true for electricity and water where experiments with private sector participation are relatively nascent. It is, however, problematic to assume that the lessons of the telecommunications sector can be transposed entirely into the electricity and water sectors. Traditional constraints surrounding network economies of scale or the economics of deploying multiple networks have, to some degree, evaporated in the telecommunications sector with technological innovations in digital communications and the ending of the reliance on copper wire networks. The network economies for electricity and water provision remain, however, producing unique problems associated with regulating natural monopolies and ensuring quality service in the supply of critically important input factors necessary for human wellbeing, economic growth, and development.

To help grapple with the numerous issues that surround the regulation of electricity and water, and the series of problems that confront regulators, we posed a simple question to the contributors: *Infrastructure regulation: What Works, Why and How Do We Know?* The simplicity of the question has produced a series of responses as diverse as they are enlightening in their conclusions. These vary not just between different political environments but between developed and developing states, and between the unique institutional legacies that circumscribe the political and organizational spaces within which regulation and regulators are forced to operate. The broader lessons of the volume thus speak of the inherent diversity of regulatory experiences, and the myriad of models, governance mechanisms, and the outcomes that emerge. The notion of policy converge or indeed of a ubiquitous "regulatory state" finds little support among contributors to this volume. Policy diffusion is certainly operative, especially in developing states in Asia, and championed by multilateral development agencies, but the notion that policy diffusion is producing similar regulatory outcomes or broadly similar public–private market composition in electricity and water services is misleading.

This volume began as a conference held at the University of Hong Kong in March 2009, generously sponsored by LIRNEasia and support from its Director, Rohan Samarajiva, and funding provided by The International Development Research Centre (IDRC). In October 2009, a writers workshop in Sri Lanka helped to put the final touches to the manuscript and solidify the thinking of participants in the project. Professor Michael Howlett, Burnaby Mountain Chair in Public Policy, Department of Political Science, Simon Fraser University, Vancouver, Canada, acted as the workshop commentator and discussant on all the Chapters and provided invaluable advice and encouragement. His efforts in no small measure helped to enhance our thinking and the quality of the final contributions.

Generous support from LIRNRasia and IDRC made the writers workshop possible. Our special thanks go to Rohan Samarajiva and Sanchala Arangalage, of LIRNEasia, for their sustained support for the workshops.

We would also like to thank the Institute of Water Policy at the Lee Kuan Yew School of Public Policy for its financial support for the water papers appearing in its volume. Likewise, we would like to thank the *Water Policy* journal for allowing the reprinting of the water papers which first appeared in its 12th Volume.

Finally, there are always countless acts of assistance that help support a project such as this. Ian Holiday, Dean of the Faculty of Social Sciences at the University of Hong Kong has been a staunch supporter of the project from the outset. Jenyce Lim and Chris Koh of the Lee Kuan Yew School of Public Policy, National University of Singapore have been stellar in their efforts to support the production of the volume and provide technical assistance in the preparation of the manuscript. Equally, our thanks go to V. Sandhya of World Scientific, whose professionalism under stringent deadlines to see the volume through to publication has been much appreciated.

The Editors, August 2010

Contents

List of Contributors

Alberto Asquer is Assistant Professor in the Faculty of Economics of the University of Cagliari, Italy, where he teaches planning and organizational control. His research interests include regulation and regulatory reform of infrastructure industries, public policy making and implementation, and public management. His current work is focused on the political economy of liberalization, re-regulation, and privatization of public service industries. His recent publications include "Implementing Fiscal Decentralization: A Case Study of a Tax Agency in Italy" (Governance, 2010), "Regulatory Reform and Industrial Restructuring: The Cases of Water, Gas, and Electricity in Italy" (*Competition and Regulation in Network Industries*, 2010), and "The Regulatory Reform of Water Infrastructure in Italy: Overall Design and Local Variations" (*Water Policy*, 2010).

Alex Coram is Winthrop Professor of Political Economy at the University of Western Australia and has also been Professor of Political Economy at the Robert Gordon University in Scotland and Professor of Economics at the University of Massachusetts, Amherst. His main area of research is in theoretical political economy. He works on social choice theory, game theory, emissions abatement problems, public policy and welfare optimizing problems and nuclear energy.

Andrew B. Whitford is Professor of Public Administration and Policy at the University of Georgia, USA. His research on bureaucratic politics, political economy, and research methodology has been published in the *Administrative Science Quarterly, American Journal of Political Science, The Journal of Politics*, and the *British Journal of Political Science*. His book *Presidential Rhetoric and the Public Agenda: Constructing the War on Drugs*, co-authored with Jeff Yates, was published by The Johns Hopkins University Press in 2009.

Boyd Fuller is Assistant Professor in the Lee Kuan Yew School of Public Policy, National University of Singapore. His research focuses on the resolution of difficult water and environmental conflicts in Asia and North America and investigations on how to get reforms done in imperfect institutional environments. He has published on the negotiation and facilitation of complex conflicts in journals such as *Environmental Science and Policy*, *Negotiation Journal*, and *Water Policy*. He has also published several articles about the implementation of water and energy sector reforms by sub-national actors as national reforms struggle. He is also the co-founder of Consensus Building in Asia: A Network of Academics and Practitioners. His advanced negotiation class has convened and facilitated several dialogues on current policy issues in Singapore each year, involving stakeholders from various sectors.

Chalita Srinuan is a PhD Candidate at Department of Technology Management and Economics, Chalmerse University of Technology, Gothenburg, Sweden. She obtained her Master's Degree in Finance from the Faculty of Accountancy and Commerce, Chulalongkorn, Bangkok, Thailand (2005), with scholarship from the Walailak University, Thailand and her Bachelor's Degree in Economics is from Walailak University, Nakorn Si Thammarat, Thailand (2002). She was a lecturer at the School of Management, Walailak University from 2005–2008. Her research interest includes telecommunications policy and firm performance.

Darryl S.L. Jarvis is Associate Professor at the Lee Kuan Yew School of Public Policy, National University of Singapore, and a co-editor of this volume. His research and teaching interests focus on regulatory, political and investment risk in Asia. His recent publications include *ASEAN Industries and the Challenge from China* (Palgrave Macmillan), *Handbook of International Business Risk: The Asia Pacific* (Cambridge University Press), *International Relations and the Challenge of Postmodernism: Defending the Discipline* (Columbia, South Carolina: University of South Carolina Press); *International Relations. Still an American Social Science? Toward Diversity in International Thought* (Albany, New York: State University of New York Press), and *Post-modernism and its Critics: International Relations and the Third Debate* (Greenwood/Praeger). He has also contributed articles to *Regulation & Governance, International Relations, Journal of International Relations & Development, Politics and Society, Asian Survey, Global Society, History of Economics Review, Contemporary Politics*, and *The Australian Journal of International Affairs.* He is currently the recipient of a large multi-year grant investigating the role of regulatory risk in five of Asia's leading economies; China, India, Thailand, the Philippines and Indonesia.

David Ehrhardt is the Chief Executive of Castalia. He has advised on the reform and regulation of water utilities and other infrastructure for nearly 20 years. Qualified in law and economics, David has been called on to assess regulatory regimes, synthesize best practice, and develop new approaches for improving the performance of utilities. He has worked on water sector reform, regulation, and private participation in Australia, Armenia, Azerbaijan, Bulgaria, the Czech Republic, Guyana, India, Indonesia, Jamaica, Kenya, Lithuania, Nigeria, Paraguay, Romania, St. Lucia, Vanuatu, and elsewhere.

Ed Araral is Assistant Professor and Assistant Dean (Academic Affairs) in the Lee Kuan Yew School of Public Policy, National University of Singapore, and a co-editor of this volume. He received his PhD in Public Policy from Indiana University-Bloomington on a Fulbright PhD Scholarship. His research interest focuses on the political economy of institutions particularly property rights, decentralization, regulation, public bureaucracies, foreign aid, and common pool resources in developing countries in Asia. His dissertation on the study of institutions for collective action was one of the three finalists in the best dissertation prize of the International Society for New Institutional Economics. His research on institutions has also earned him a Fulbright PhD Award, Ronald Coase Institute Fellowship, George Stigler Center Fellowship, a US National Science Foundation Research Grant, International Water Management Institute research grant, and scholarship from the Workshop in Political Theory and Policy Analysis-Indiana University. He has published in top tiered journals such as the *Journal of Public Administration Research and Theory, World Development, Policy Sciences, Governance, Policy and Society, Journal of Economic Policy Reform,* the World Bank Working Papers Series and a number of articles in edited volumes.

Edouard Perard, PhD, is a Research Associate at Sciences Po Paris and expert on international organizations (OECD, UNCTAD, World Bank). He specializes in infrastructure economics, particularly in public-private partnerships and regulatory reform. He studied at Sciences Po Paris and at Yale University.

Erik Bohlin is currently Head and Professor in Technology Assessment at the Division of Technology & Society, Department of Technology Management & Economics at Chalmers University of Technology, Gothenburg, Sweden. He has published in a number of areas relating to the information society — policy, strategy, and management. He is Chair of the International Telecommunications Society; Chief Editor of *Telecommunications Policy;* Member of the Scientific Advisory Boards of *Communications and Strategies, Info, International Journal of Management and Network Economics, and Nordic and Baltic Journal of Information and Communication Technologies.* He obtained his graduate degree in Business Administration and Economics at the Stockholm School of Economics (1987) and his PhD from Chalmers University of Technology (1995).

Farid Gasmi is a professor at the Toulouse School of Economics (TSE), France where he is a member of the Atelier de Recherche Quantitative Appliquée au Développement (ARQADE) and the Institut D'Economie Industrielle (IDEI). Prior to joining the Toulouse faculty, he was a Member of Technical Staff at Bell Communications Research (Bellcore), NJ, USA.

He holds MS and PhD degrees from the California Institute of Technology (CalTech), CA, USA. His research interest and consulting activities are in the areas of industrial organization, regulation, and development as they apply to infrastructure sectors.

Hui Lin is a researcher at the Lee Kuan Yew School of Public Policy, National University of Singapore. Her current research focuses on political and regulatory risk and its impact on foreign direct investment in Asia, with special reference to the energy sector in China. She has co-instructed courses on Empirical Analysis for Public Policy and Public Management at the Lee Kuan Yew School of Public Policy.

Kun-Chin Lin is Lecturer at King's China Institute, King's College, London, and holds an affiliation with the School of Social Sciences and Public Policy. He obtained his PhD in political science from the University of California at Berkeley, and was a Leverhulme Postdoctoral Fellow in Contemporary Chinese Studies at the University of Oxford. Prior to joining King's, Kun-Chin was Assistant Professor of Political Science at the National University of Singapore. His research activities focus on the politics of market reform in developing countries, industrial organization and labour relations, federalism and public goods provision, energy policy and foreign direct investment, political risk analysis, regional and urban-rural distributive issues in transport network expansion, land usage, migration and urbanization. He is working on a book on the corporatization of large Chinese state-owned enterprises into shareholding concerns in the late 1990s, using the case study of national oil and petrochemical companies to examine the political and macroeconomic conditions that enabled a radical reorganization of the commanding heights, and the ensuing legacy of contentious state-market relations. He has also written on Asia-Pacific regionalism and China's changing role in international organisations, and begun a database tracking Chinese multinationals' investments around the world. He is an editorial board member of *Business & Politics.*

Laura Recuero Virto is an economist at the Africa and Middle East Team at the Development Center, Organization for Economic Cooperation and Development (OECD), Paris. Prior to joining the Development

Center in October 2008, she was a research associate at Télécom ParisTech in charge of the program on Telecommunications Infrastructure and Economic Performance in the Chair on Innovation and Regulation in the Digital Economy sponsored by Télécom ParisTech, Ecole Polytechnique, and France Télécom. Her professional experience includes Nortel Networks, the Centre National d'Etudes Spatiales (CNES) and the European Space Agency in the field of radio communications (mobile and satellite). She has collaborated with the World Bank Institute on the topic of regulatory institutions in Africa and Latin America, and with Vodafone on an analysis of cellular demand in South Africa. She has also collaborated with the Public Governance and Territorial Development Directorate at the OECD on budgetary institutions in OECD and Latin American countries. Laura holds a B.A. degree on telecommunications engineering and an MBA specializing international trade from the Polytechnic University of Madrid. She also holds a PhD in economics from Toulouse School of Economics.

Lyle Noakes is Winthrop Professor of Pure Mathematics at the University of Western Australia. He has a background in algebraic topology and differential geometry, and does research in applications to problems in approximation theory, classical mechanics, computer vision, and social science.

M Ramesh is Visiting Professor at the Lee Kuan Yew School of Public Policy, National University of Singapore, and a co-editor of this volume. Prior to joining in the Lee Kuan Yew School of Public Policy, he was a Professor of Social Policy at the University of Hong Kong, SAR. He has previously worked at the University of Sydney, University of New England, and Victoria University of Wellington, New Zealand. He specializes in public policy and governance in Asia. He is the author, co-author, or editor of Studying Public Policy (3rd Ed. 2009), *Transforming Asian Governance* (2009), *Deregulation and Its Discontents* (2006), *Social Policy in East and Southeast Asia* (2004), *Welfare Capitalism in Southeast Asia* (2000), and *The Political Economy of Canada* (1999). He has also published extensively in reputed international journals. He is the co-editor of *Policy and Society* as well as *World Political Science Review.*

Mika Purra is a Research Fellow at the Lee Kuan Yew School of Public Policy, National University of Singapore. His research focuses on investment risk in infrastructure and the operation of capital markets in Asia. He has wide experience in regulatory and transnational governance work within government, academia and the private sector. He has previously held positions with Goldman Sachs International, London, and with the Finnish Foreign Office, Helsinki as a trade negotiator. His current research focuses on investment risk and issues associated with the development of capital markets in Asia.

Nils Janson is a Senior Vice President at Castalia. He advises financial institutions, public and private utilities, regulatory authorities and governments on strategies related to restructuring, regulation, privatization, and financing. During his more than 15 yrs of professional experience, Nils has advised on the regulation and reform of the water sector and water utilities in Argentina, the Bahamas, Belize, Brazil, Jordan, Malawi, Mexico, Montenegro, Paraguay, Saint Lucia, Tanzania, and Uganda.

Paul Noumba is a senior infrastructure specialist in the Finance and Infrastructure division of the World Bank Institute. He is working in the areas of regulation, and policy support related to infrastructure sector reforms in developing countries. He joined the World Bank in 1998 as a telecommunications policy specialist in the Energy Mining Telecom Department. From October 2000 to March 2003, Paul was a regional coordinator for Africa in the ICT policy division part of the Global Information and Communications Technology Department. Before joining the bank, he worked as an economist with France Telecom Research and the Development Center (CNET) in Paris, and a lecturer and researcher in telecommunications and regulatory economics in the Ecole Nationale Superieure des Telecommunications de Bretagne (France). Between 1987–1992 he was the head of the economic analyses unit in the Ministry of Post and Telecommunications in Cameroon. He received a PhD in economics from University of Rennes 1 (France) in 1995, and a Masters in Telecommunications Engineering in 1987 from a French grande école.

Pratompong Srinuan is a PhD Candidate at the Department of Technology Management and Economics, Chalmerse University of Technology, Gothenburg, Sweden. He obtained his Master's Degree in Economics from the Faculty of Economics, Thammasat University, Bangkok, Thailand (2005), and his Bachelor's Degree also in Economics (second class honors) from Walailak University, Nakorn Si Thammarat, Thailand (2002). He has been Economist at the Policy and Regulatory Department, National telecommunications Commission (NTC), Thailand since 2005, and is now on leave. His research interest include telecommunication policy and anti-competitive behavior.

Puree Sirasoontorn is an Assistant Professor at Faculty of Economics, Thammasat University in Thailand. Puree holds a PhD in Economics from the Australian National University. Her research interests include economics of regulation, industrial organization, energy economics and ICT and telecommunication economics. Her experiences in the energy policy and regulatory field have been extensive, including research projects of energy tariff regulation in Thailand, implication of Energy Industry Act for Thai energy sector and Thai economic measures and policy on energy crisis. Recently her research interest extended to analysis of sectoral-level economic measures and policies on climate change. She also advises Energy Regulatory Board of Thailand on electricity tariff regulation. Puree serves as referee in various journals such as *Regulation & Governance*, *International Energy Journal* and *Thammasat Economic Journal* and occasionally writes newspaper columns on infrastructure reform and regulation.

Rajendra Kumar holds a PhD in international economic development and regional planning and an MCP from the Massachusetts Institute of Technology, an MTech from the Indian Institute of Technology in Delhi, and a BTech from the Indian Institute of Technology in Kanpur. Kumar is a senior officer in the Indian Administrative Service (I.A.S.). His current research interests are in examining how the potential of modern information and communication technologies (ICTs) can be harnessed for greater social, economic, and political development in developing countries. He has conducted research on assessing the social, economic, and governance impacts of ICT for development projects in India and their impact on the rural poor. His research also includes studies focusing on the role of the state in promoting innovations in ICT industries and strategies for enhancing Indian ICT global competitiveness.

Sunil Tankha is Lecturer in Public Policy and Management at the International Institute of Social Studies of Erasmus University Rotterdam in the Netherlands. His research is focused on economic and infrastructure development, and public sector and governance reform. He has worked on these issues in North and South America, Europe, Africa and South Asia. He holds a doctorate in Economic Development from the Massachusetts Institute of Technology, USA.

Wu Xun is Associate Professor in the Lee Kuan Yew School of Public Policy, National University of Singapore, and a co-editor of this volume. He specializes in the analysis and evaluation of policy reforms in developing countries, with emphasis on social and environmental sectors. His current research focuses on water governance, environmental valuation, power sector restructuring, anti-corruption strategies, comparative healthcare reforms, and integrated approaches to sustainable development. He teaches research methods for policy analysis, policy evaluation, cost-benefit analysis, environmental policy, and natural resource management. Wu Xun has been a consultant to the World Bank, UNEP, and International Vaccine Institute for a variety of assignments ranging from non-market valuation to integrated water resource management. Dr. Wu received his PhD in Public Policy Analysis from the University of North Carolina at Chapel Hill, USA.

CHAPTER 1

Regulating Infrastructure: A Review of the Issues, Problems, and Challenges

Ed Araral, Darryl S.L. Jarvis, M. Ramesh and Wu Xun

1. Introduction

The political economy of infrastructure provision has undergone profound transformation in the last quarter century. Historically, telecommunications, electricity, water, gas, railroads, ports, airports, and urban transport were the exclusive preserve of the state and operated as state monopolies. They tended to be vertically and often horizontally integrated, financed by the state and managed by bureaucrats. The involvement of the state in network utilities was seen as necessary to ensure rapid deployment of strategically important services to support economic development and promote national interests. In the last few decades, however, these views have eroded as governments across the world reformed infrastructure provision. The first wave of reforms centered around the privatization of state monopolies, most famously under the Thatcher government in the United Kingdom with the divestiture of British Telecom and British Rail, the unbundling of electricity and water sectors, and the sale of electricity generating facilities, sanitation and water supply infrastructure. Similar reforms were subsequently undertaken in many countries around the world (Thomas, 2006, p. 1974; Millán, 2006; Kessides, 2004, p. 3).

The reforms have not, however, been viewed as an end in themselves. The advocates of energy, water and telecommunications reform have had various rationales, but nearly all center around what Stephen Littlechild describes as the overreaching desire to "create new governance arrangements that provide long term benefits to consumers" (Littlechild, 2006, p. xvii–xviii). However, such a rationale is problematic. Governance by whom, for whom, and at what cost, are inherently complex questions and the institutional arrangements charged with effecting oversight are not easy configurations to establish or sustain. Michael Pollitt perhaps understates the problem when he notes that reform in the utilities sector is a complex business that requires not just a "commitment to competition and efficient regulation" but also the construction of a reflexive regulatory apparatus that is responsive "to emerging information and allows scope for mid-course adjustments" (Pollitt, 2008, p. xxxi). To these we could add the dimension of policy goals, administrative and legal structures, and the appropriate sequencing of reforms to ensure regulatory credibility and thus the sustainability of reforms. As the British experience taught us, privatization and the divestiture of state assets is but a first, and perhaps the easiest, step in a long sequence of initiatives that must be carefully calibrated, flexible, credible, sustainable, and perceived as such if the regulatory bargain that is struck is to sustain private sector participation, allow efficient operation of competitive forces, and deliver benefits to consumers (Thomas, 2006).

In addition to dealing with the relatively simple issue of incentive and market design, regulations need to address numerous complex problems. As Levy and Spiller (1994, p. 205) observe, the universe of regulation is divided between the design of regulatory incentives (utility pricing, subsidies, entry costs, market extensity, etc) and the design of the governance apparatus (institutions, administrative processes, review mechanisms, dispute procedures) that administers these incentives. Cost plus, rate of return, price cap and other variations on the design of regulatory incentives have produced multifarious models to allocate risk, determine who captures exogenous windfalls from technological innovations or efficiencies, and the allocation of unanticipated costs, revenues, and risks. Far from a simple econometric exercise, the history of such endeavors has been fraught with experimentation, unanticipated outcomes, and less than optimal results. Indeed, instead of enhancing economic efficiency or correcting the inefficiencies associated with state operated monopolies, real world experiences have highlighted the importance of *review, revision, flexibility*, and *modification* in regulations.

As the contributors to this volume highlight, such decisions about models of regulation, the sequencing of reforms and the operation of regulatory regimes occur within the context of specific political landscapes, institutional endowments, and, indeed, geographical attributes. While regulation and the design of regulatory characteristics might be viewed as the quintessential mechanism of sector reform, the economic geography of a sector defines market density, network deployment costs, returns, and thus the motivations that underlie investment decisions. No amount of tinkering of the regulatory apparatus can overcome the inverse relationship between the economies of network density and network deployment costs, for example. The physical characteristics of a state (market size, resource endowments — hydro, coal, gas, oil — the geographical distribution of energy demand — thinly distributed versus concentrated demand nodes — and the disbursement of population centers) impacts the nature of the energy market and thus the nature of competition that might reasonably be expected to develop (Correljé & De Vries 2008, p. 68). Thinly populated and geographically dispersed markets pose steep barriers to entry constraining competition; a fact equally true for water and the telecoms sectors. To these issues we can add the extent and rate of economic development, the institutional capacity and endowment of states, among others, as major determinants that shape the reform process and impact the regulatory outcomes. In all, far from a relatively homogenous or unproblematic process, reform and regulation of the utilities sector highlights a series of enduring problems, obstacles, constraints, and thus a diversity of experiences, outcomes, and lessons.

The complexities involved in infrastructure industries are now being recognized, with reform minded proponents more circumspect about the dynamics of the reform process, the problems of regulation and the benefits that may ensue. The World Bank, for example, one of the original proponents of privatization and unbundling in utilities sectors has recognized the difficulties of regulation in countries with low institutional endowments, noting that "regulating unbundled utilities is harder than regulating vertically integrated utilities," and that reform of this nature may have limitations in markets that are small in scale and scope (Kessides,

2004, p. 5; see also Yi-Chong, 2006). Unbundling, as the World Bank admitted, "is no panacea" and the economic geographies of markets is an important determinant of the limits beyond which privatization and private sector participation can play only a limited role (Kessides, 2005, p. 5). As the same World Bank report went on to note, privatization has been "oversold and misunderstood," in many cases producing less than optimal outcomes, in other cases outright hostilities and political protest.

In hindsight, such opposition and sensitivities were perhaps to be expected. Reform, privatization and the political act of divestiture of state assets provide fertile political terrains for opposition, especially if poorly implemented or implemented in environments that are less than transparent, seen to favor sectional interests, inefficient or corrupt. More generally, the act of reform itself and the on-the-ground changes to employment practices, pricing regimes, tariff review mechanisms, billing processes, and connection costs have proven obvious avenues for political contest. In more aggressive reform environments where cost recovery regimes have been implemented, affordability and equity of access issues have driven consumer backlash and generated heated political opposition.

These experiences explain the elongated spectrum along which reform of the utilities sector has progressed and in many cases stalled or failed to launch. If the success of the reform agenda is judged by the extent to which full privatization has occurred, wholesale or spot markets created, statutory independent regulators set in place, and state involvement in the sector withdrawn, then there are few examples of successful reform. Rather, the reform processes examined in the chapters in this volume display a preponderance of hybridized systems: a continuing strong state involvement in the utilities sector but with varying degrees of private sector participation. Rather than an unproblematic spectrum along which reform progresses, in many jurisdictions reform has been a start-stop, on again, off again affair, creating hybridized systems with unique characteristics and, as a result, a series of unique problems for effective regulation to be realized. Any attempt to understand the regulation of infrastructure has thus to grapple with the added complexity of regulation in hybridized environments — a feature that is particularly dominant in Asia. Powerful institutional legacies and the continued presence of entrenched state utilities, creates polycentric regulatory environments where issues of coordination, information asymmetries, organizational-bureaucratic competition, confusion over rule ownership or contestation, adds complexity and often deleteriously to the effectiveness of reform and regulation. While multilateral development agencies such as the World Bank and Asian Development Bank (ADB) have euphemistically denoted these problems as "sequencing issues," they more correctly speak to the larger political hurdles and domestic contexts within which reform and regulation have to be managed.

2. Organization of the Volume

Reforming infrastructure regulations involves more problems and potentially negative externalities than the early proponents of reform realized. Constructing competitive markets and regulatory governance systems to oversee these are complex tasks, and require adroit policy formulation cognizant of the limitations imposed by the sector's economic geography, and the regulators' planning, design, and implementation capacity if the reforms are to be successful and sustainable. This volume is a contribution to addressing these issues across three infrastructure sectors: telecommunications, electricity and water. The specific task of the volume is implied in its title: *Infrastructure Regulation: What Works, Why, and How Do We Know*? Each of the contributors reflect on the innovations adopted and the obstacles encountered during the course of reforming infrastructure regulations with the purpose of drawing broader lessons. As the contributions to this volume demonstrate, answering the questions implied in the title of the volume are more difficult than they first appear. Indeed, despite more than two decades of reform efforts and regulatory innovation, the overreaching lesson appears to be that there is no universally appropriate model for reform of network utilities, that no singular regulatory model can be transposed across multiple environments, and that the mechanisms of regulatory governance are often more specific to the domain in which they operate then generalizable beyond basic governance principles implied in accountability, participation, and transparency.

The volume is organized into three sections. Part I addresses the problems, issues, and perspectives in regulation focusing on regulatory design issues and outcomes in relation to the telecommunications sector. In Part II, the volume addresses electricity sector regulation and governance, and in Part III issues relating to water sector regulation and governance.

Part I: Telecommunications Sector Regulation and Governance

The economic and social significance of telecommunications in the contemporary world is broadly recognized. A widely quoted US National Academy of Sciences study in 2006 noted that while the sector accounted for only 1 percent of the American economy, it contributed 10 percent to the nation's economic growth. The sector's significance has strengthened particularly with the emergence of mobile and, subsequently, broadband technology. The declining cost and improving quality of mobile phones has been instrumental in fostering economic and social benefits unimagined as recently as the 1980s. Mobile telephony has now reached distant rural communities — by 2002, for example, the number of mobile subscribers exceeded fixed line subscribers — in ways no other technology has been disseminated since the advent of the steam engine and electricity. As a consequence, the material benefits and mode of commence available to the rural poor have been vastly expanded. The subsequent spread of the internet and the advent of broadband technology has likewise changed the face of commerce, vastly reducing the cost of communications and the ease of transaction across multiple geographical spaces and markets. These new technologies have enabled developing countries, of which India is the most spectacular example, to experience some of the highest economic growth rates in the world. In 2009, information and technology industries are believed to have contributed 6 percent to India's and 8 percent to the Philippines' GDP. Moreover, telecommunications form the basis for e-governance which has the potential to strengthen the public sector's efficiency, the mechanisms of accountability, and the modes via which the public is able to engage with government.

Telecommunication was the first networked infrastructure sector to be deregulated. The experiences of the sector, especially its methods of liberalization and privatization, thus casts a long shadow over other network industries. Prior to deregulation, telecommunications was regarded as a case of pure natural monopoly and, as such, heavily regulated and often owned by Ministries of Post, Telegraph and Telecommunications. With the decline in telegraph's significance and the separation of telecommunications from postal services, the telecommunications industry came to emerge as a key pillar of the modern economy. The subsequent removal and or relaxation of barriers to new entrants, often accompanied by privatization, further stimulated the industry. The lower prices and better service quality that followed deregulation of the telecommunications sector remains a key selling point for those proposing greater deregulation for all infrastructure industries. While in many respects telecommunications is a typical infrastructure industry, in other crucial aspects it is unique: mobile and internet technologies allow a level of competition in the industry that is simply not possible in most other networked infrastructure industries. For example, multiple telecommunications networks can be deployed because of technological innovations, network economies of scale are not fixed but now more elastic because of falling network deployment costs, and barriers to entry are now not driven so much by technological costs as political restrictions and considerations. While these features are atypical and do not represent the technological realities confronted in the electricity and water sectors, the experiences of the telecommunications sector continues to be a catalyst for approaching and examining deregulation and liberalization in other networked industries.

There is wide agreement that regulations and their implementation is a key determinant of the telecommunication sector's performance. There is less agreement over exactly what sort of regulations are the most appropriate for the telecommunications sector. The dispute is not over whether the regulatory regime should be more or less liberal but, rather, over the extent to which the government needs to be involved in the sector beyond establishing the essential market rules and letting competition determine the rest. Current debate in telecommunication regulations thus pertain to more complex issues. How should societies and regulators deal with the emerging convergence between fixed line and mobile telephony, broadband, VOIP, mobile TV and broadcasting? To what extent should new firms be allowed to enter the sector and bundle services? To what extent should dominant players be required to share backbone and network infrastructure? What should be the nature and form of accountability of telecommunication regulators and firms? And what is the meaning and significance of universal access to services in the current environment and how can it best be achieved?

Of all the issues confronting the sector, that of market entry, accountability, and consumer access are the most pressing as well as complex. The three chapters in section 1 of the volume discuss these issues in turn.

The chapter by Chalita *et al.* analyses the effects of changes in entry regulations on mobile telephone firms across a series of Asian countries. It finds a noticeable improvement in the sector's performance as a result of entry relaxation when accompanied by the existence of favorable macroeconomic conditions and an independent regulator. However, to realize the full potential of entry relaxation, the chapter points to the need for an independent regulator before entry restrictions are relaxed — the sequencing of regulatory reforms, in other words, remains a key determinant of regulatory and sector outcomes.

Judith Clifton and her colleagues assess the sector from a new, and broader, perspective: that of the consumer. Instead of focusing on the supply side, as is the case for most writings on the subject including Chalita *et al.*, they concentrate on the citizen–consumer, i.e. on the demand side. The traditional focus on supply is premised on the assumption that consumers are automatically well served in the presence of optimal regulations with regard to market concentration, market entry, and access to networks. Regardless of the theoretical merits of concentrating on supply conditions, the ultimate test for the success of any regulation is how its benefits are perceived by end users. The authors use stated and revealed preferences gathered from Eurobarometer and Household Budget Survey data to reflect on the performance of the telecommunications sector with respect to accessibility, affordability, service use, and consumer protection in the European Union. The chapter provides rich evidence on the diverse patterns of consumption and attitudes towards public services. They conclude with a plea for regulators to take consumers' preferences into account when designing regulatory regimes.

Gasmi, Naoumba and Virto cast their net far and wide in the following chapter and assess the performance of the telecommunications sector in 29 developing and 23 developed countries. Using a composite methodology that combines overall political variables with sector-specific "regulatory governance" variables, they find strong empirical evidence highlighting the importance of political and institutional contexts, especially in developing countries, for performance outcomes. Countries with stronger political accountability are found to perform better in terms of mainline penetration, cellular subscription, mainlines per employee, and prices. The chapter concludes with suggestions for greater emphasis on improving overall "good governance" rather than sector-specific reforms.

Part II: Electricity Sector Regulation and Governance

The foundations of the electricity industry go back to 1882 when the world's first central power station was established in Manhattan by the Edison Illuminating Company. The event set a trend that for the first half century of the electricity supply industry (ESI) which saw power generation, transmission, and distribution dominated by private firms. The extent of private domination diminished as the sector was nationalized in most parts of the world during the post-War period.

As Gratwick and Eberhard (2008, p. 3948) note, the rationale for progressive government involvement in the sector was fourfold. First, the network nature of the sector combined with economies of scale makes the industry a natural monopoly, paving the path for government intervention to help protect the public interest. Second, the scale of national electrification efforts, each requiring the deployment of extensive networks and large generating plants to capture economies of scale, required massive long term commitments of capital, with the state increasingly called on to act as financial guarantor and socialize the investment risk. Third, the burgeoning size and scope of the sector made state involvement a natural corollary. Effective coordination, standardization of service delivery and reliability, uniform pricing and equity of access issues, combined to involve the state as a means to enhance efficiency, reduce information asymmetries, and coordinate capacity development in line with demand requirements. Fourth, post-war energy intensive industrialization elevated the strategic importance of the sector, aligning the sector with national industrialization and development plans and progressively bringing the sector under central state planning. By the mid-1950s, the sector had thus been transformed with governments of all political persuasions seeing the sector too important to be left to the seemingly haphazard ways of private sector interests.

Vertical integration of the industry replete with government intervention into fuel source chains, coal transportation, electricity generation, transmission and distribution was a common outcome. While the United States, Japan and Germany opted for significant private participation in the sector, vertically integrated monopolies became the order of the day with the state involved through a strong regulatory and oversight presence (Gratwick and Eberhard, 2008, p. 3949).

In developing countries too, much the same trajectory was followed. From the 1950s through to the 1990s, electricity provision was dominated by the state. Indeed, strong state involvement in the ESI was championed by leading multilateral development agencies like the World Bank and seen as essential to the rapid deployment of energy infrastructure in support of economic development (Williams and Dubash, 2004, p. 411–412; Victor and Heller, 2007). In Asia, a core feature of state involvement was the formation of state-owned utilities predominantly organized as vertically integrated monopolies and overseen by large energy ministries and bureaucracies charged with energy planning (World Bank, 1993; Williams and Dubash, 2004, p. 414). Electrification schemes became synonymous with national development, commanding massive public resources and assuming iconic status as purveyors of national aspirations. In countries as varied as India, Thailand, South Korea, Indonesia, China, and the Philippines, bureaucracies overseeing the development of the electricity sector commanded a central place in the institutional and political fabric of the state, indeed often becoming large political empires unto themselves.

Since the early 1990s, however, this model has been progressively eroded with the private sector again increasingly involved in the ESI across a large swath of jurisdictions. Concerns about service quality, fiscal burdens, inefficiencies, and spiraling costs combined with ideational changes about the role of the state in the provision of infrastructure triggered a decade long series of reforms across the globe. By the end of the 1990s it was commonly accepted that private sector participation in the ESI was both desirable and necessary, and that the progressive reform of the sector via the introduction of performance and market based incentives, could deliver significant cost reductions, sector efficiencies, and increase network deployment and access in developing countries. Remarkably, by the end of the 1990s, over 70 countries had instigated sector reforms, progressively moving the sector away from public monopolies and toward private ownership coupled with publically regulated structures (Jamasb *et al.*, 2005, p. 1).

Unbundling of the ESI through the divestiture of generating assets, the introduction of private power producers (PPP), competitive tendering and procurement processes, and innovations in network operations have been the obvious forms of sector reforms. Equally, however, a small revolution has occurred in the mode and manner of regulation of the ESI, with the sector witnessing a general move toward the establishment of independent regulators charged with oversight, licensing, compliance, and review of the sector, and otherwise challenging the vertically integrated nature of the industry, the domination of state utilities and the large energy ministries and bureaucracies which have historically dominated the sector.

These reforms, of course, are ongoing. In Asia and further afield, there is no resolution to these experiments, the mix of public-private sector participation, and the manner and mode of oversight and regulation. Indeed, the reform process itself has thrown up a series of challenges and conundrums that remain as much unsolved as they were unanticipated. Questions about what models, forms, styles, institutional designs, and operational parameters produce what outcomes and in what order of magnitude and deliver what benefits to who have proven more problematic than reform minded proponents initially anticipated. Indeed, the broader project of trying to devise regulatory forms that produce superior outcomes while serving equally the interests of private sector participants and the general public remain as contested today as when first proposed. So too the institutional mechanisms of governance and making effective regulators and thus regulation, have equally been the subject of experimentation, on-going reform and innovation, with little sense that this project has been completed or the questions settled. And perhaps most importantly of all, such issues have proven doubly difficult in developing countries, where institutionally contested environments or inadequate institutional and analytical capacity have exacerbated the complexity of these questions and problems. When it comes to regulating electricity infrastructure, "what works" and what does not are likely to produce multifarious and contradictory conclusions.

It is not surprising, then, that "the evidence on the success of electricity reform is ... mixed" and particularly so for developing countries (Pollitt, 2008, p. xxvi). Much of this might be explained by the unfinished business of electricity reform. The reform process has not been a uniformly linear process of nations progressing along a continuum towards full liberalization. As Pollitt (2008) observes, "significant progress towards the maximum possible electricity reform" is observed in only a handful of countries "while reform progress has stalled at some intermediate stage in many more jurisdictions" (Pollitt, 2008, p. xxvii). In Asia, in particular, reform of the ESI sector is spotty, with a mix of institutional forms, different levels of private sector involvement and still dominant state utilities in operation. Constructing a simple narrative about where we stand with reform of the ESI is thus more difficult than it might first appear, with countries displaying different trajectories and mixes of private-public forms and methods of regulatory oversight. It might thus be more appropriate to describe regulation of the ESI in Asia as a "work in progress." Despite more than a decade of reform efforts, addressing some of the most elemental questions about sector reform outcomes, efficiency, modes of regulation and regulatory design, what works and what does not proves more difficult than ever to answer authoritatively.

The contributions in Part II of this volume, *Electricity Sector Regulation and Governance*, grapple with many of these questions, highlighting how problematic and perhaps premature are firm conclusions. If there is a common strand to the seven chapters in this section of the volume, it speaks to how particularistic are the institutional environments and political contexts in which the electricity supply industry is situated, and to the historical legacies each much grapple with as the process of reform is confronted. This conclusion is amply demonstrated in Chapter 5, where Darryl Jarvis looks at the labored process of reform in the Thai ESI which has ebbed and flowed amid political crisis, contestation, protest, and violence. While it would be unfair to take Thailand as representative of other developing countries, the analysis by Jarvis highlights the unique problems developing countries face in constructing credible regulatory governance mechanisms with sufficient capacity to oversee effectively a complex and highly politicized policy space such as electricity. If the problem of regulation resides significantly in getting right the mix of public and private interests that allocate risk, profit, and other externalities, equally Jarvis demonstrates it also lies in getting right the forms of regulatory governance necessary to make credible the commitments that governments make and the market extensity set in place for private sector participation. The problem, of course, as Jarvis highlights, is that there is no universally accepted road map on which to build effective regulators and regulatory institutions, not least for developing countries where traditions of administrative practice are often pre-formative or where historically strong state utilities command extensive political power.

These issues are fully exposed in Chapter 6 where Puree Sirasoontorn sets about a detailed examination of the regulatory substance of Thailand's enhanced single buyer model and the problems surrounding the regulation of tariffs in institutional environments where rule ownership, roles, and multiple agencies have overlapping jurisdictional control. Puree explores the practical implications of these regulatory designs on consumers by addressing the impact of an electricity tariff that is separated into two tariff steams; a base tariff and an automatic tariff adjustment mechanism. By tracing the incentive structure that emerges, who captures exogenous rents, and how windfall revenues are allocated Puree suggests that the enhanced single buyer model contains inherent flaws that discriminate against the Thai consumer, favoring the interests of ESI operators. More importantly, Puree is able to explore the ramifications of this model, the perverse incentives it generates and which lead, for example, to the development of excess capacity, and excess profits for industry operators.

Puree's main concern, however, is to suggest the development of alternative models and how a reconfigured design of the regulatory incentive structure using price cap regulation can ameliorate price distortions and perverse incentives. Simulating such a price cap regulatory system, Puree's analysis demonstrates the importance of revisiting the enhanced single buyer model and reforming the systems of oversight that administer this.

In Chapter 7, Kun-Chin Lin, Mika Purra and Lin Hui address the broader problems of constructing effective regulatory regimes and regulatory bodies in one of the world's largest electricity markets, China. As the second largest power market in the world, China will invest some USD$2 trillion dollars over the next 30 years in the ESI, with China's demand for power generation equipment alone likely to account for 32% of total global demand. China's phenomenal demand for energy is only matched by its ever increasing demand for effective planning, coordination, and regulation of the sector. Indeed, with demand for electricity growing at approximately 10% a year, and likely to double in the coming decades as China's industrialization deepens, China will require a massive expansion of its energy infrastructure if its developmental goals are to be realized and per capita electricity consumption increased to global averages. As Kun-Chin, Purra and Lin Hui argue, however, the institutional legacy of the National Development and Reform Commission (NDRC) which has historically overseen energy sector planning, has undercut new institutional initiatives such as the State Energy Regulatory Commission (SERC), otherwise established to introduce market and efficiency incentives, breakdown vested interests, and represent the interests of both ESI industry participants and consumers. China, like other developing countries, equally faces the challenges of vested SOE interests, particularly in the large 5 generating and transmission companies whose monopolistic control of the ESI has effectively hamstrung the prospects for the emergence of an integrated national energy policy. Such an outcome, Kun-Chin, Purra and Lin Hui argue, is producing inferior oversight capacity, diminished regulatory effectiveness, and potentially harbors longer term risks for satisfying the electricity needs of China.

The conclusion reached by Kun-Chin, Purra and Lin Hui is that institutional collusion among existing ESI providers and oversight institutions bears on the facility not just to plan and enact policy reform, but diminishes the implementation of reforms, new performance benchmarks and thus the prospects for successful reform outcomes. As the authors note, their analysis partly answers some of the key themes in this volume, not just in terms of what works, and why, but more importantly of what is feasible in highly contested political spaces where vested interests and inter-organizational rivalry impact efficient policy making and implementation.

In Chapter 8, Mika Purra addresses the ESI in Southeast Asia's largest economy, Indonesia. Indonesia's most recent past has been a tumultuous period of authoritarian rule, street violence in the wake of the Asian Financial crisis, and severe economic dislocation as foreign investment evaporated amid political protest and a full blown currency crisis. By contrast, Indonesia's most recent past has witnessed the emergence of a vibrant and flourishing democracy, with numerous calls for increased accountability, political transparency, and improved public administration to pursue much needed national reforms to enhance economic growth and development. Such calls are understandable. Eighty per cent of Indonesians still live below or slightly above the poverty line, only 60% of Indonesians enjoy access to electricity, and the informal sector of the economy tends to dominate the lives of most ordinary Indonesians.

Not surprisingly, getting energy policy right and embarking upon an effective electrification campaign has been seen as essential to the growth aspirations of Indonesia. As Purra observes, however, Indonesia also presents a case of substantial policy failure, poor levels of implementation, highly contested policy domains and poor levels of administrative capacity, pen ultimately leading to policy inertia and less than optimal policy or reform outcomes. Amid such constraints, reform initiatives in the ESI have been modest, with the underlying issues of electricity pricing, the introduction of new tariff mechanisms and incentive structures to allocate efficiency gains, lost amid an essentially dysfunctional bureaucratic culture that is unable to grapple with the institutional configuration that has dominated the sector for the last several decades. The lessons Purra identifies, then, reside not so much in the regulatory systems and modes of regulation necessary for reform, but how to ensconce reform and enable its implementation in an environment where reform is often thwarted at multiple junctures.

In Chapter 9, Rajendra Kumar addresses ESI reform in India, a country experiencing rapid growth in electricity demand and, in the process, experimenting with innovative reforms and regulatory models. Like other developing countries, India too has moved to liberalize the sector, recognizing the importance of foreign capital and investment as a means of closing the energy gap and increasing generating capacity. One of most significant reforms appeared in the 1990s, designed to create uniform institutional frameworks for independent power producers (IPPs) and encourage greater private sector participation in the ESI. As Kumar observes, however, multiple layers of governance and the vastly dissimilar administrative systems between Indian states produced dissimilar outcomes and performance in the sector. Kumar examiners these dissimilarities and the reasons for them by analyzing three states, Andhra Pradesh, Gujarat, and Tamil Nadu. Using legal, political, institutional and comparative economic analyses, Kumar assess the relative performance of IPPs in each state with reference to the literature on institutional economics to examine the interactions between political institutions, regulatory process and outcomes.

Kumar's analyses offer some sobering conclusions. First, no single regulatory process, model or incentive structure produces similar outcomes across all three states. Indeed, institutional design alone, replete with the manner by which profits, costs and risks are allocated, do not themselves determine performance. Second, intangible variables like leadership, trust relationships, and effective communication in some cases prove the overriding reasons that determine successful outcomes, even in the face of relatively poor regulatory models. Third, intervening political variables, especially the manner of politicization of the sector, irrespective of the regulatory system and its operation, can, but not in all cases, be the determining factor for performance in the sector. Kumar's analysis is thus unique in as much as it takes three very different case studies and demonstrates through the application of a uniform analytical framework how important is context. As Kumar observes, above all "an institutional 'fit' between the regulatory systems and the overall institutional endowment of the state in the political, legal, and economic contexts is extremely important to ensure success of the reforms and the IPPs."

Finally, Sunil Tankha in Chapter 10, and Junki Kim and Kyuhyun Kim in Chapter 11 attempt to grapple with the outcomes of conventional approaches to liberalization, the privatization of infrastructure, the emergent regulatory systems of oversight, and the outcomes associated with these models. Again, the conclusions are mixed with both chapters suggesting vicarious performance contingent on anomalous assumptions contained in orthodox approaches to liberalization and regulation, and the enormous challenges that effective regulation poses for governments of all types and capacities. The chapters by Tankha, Kim and Kim thus provide further evidence that performance outcomes of infrastructure regulation are far from uniform, that any conclusions we might draw about what works and how has to be heavily qualified as much by context, the political environment in which regulation occurs, as by the nature of the regulatory model, and the capacity of the agencies changed with oversight.

Part III: Water Sector Regulation and Governance

Water is unique among infrastructures: it is essential to life, local in supply, mysterious in information (asymmetry), and dull in technological innovation (Shirley, 2007). Water being essential to life and public health, and hence politically salient, has led most governments around the world to be directly responsible for its provision. Water is also dull in innovation. Compared with telecommunications and electricity where technological innovations have changed their natural monopoly characteristics, there is no equivalent in the water sector. These distinguishing characteristics have implications for the way the water infrastructure is provided and regulated.

To meet the vital need for water adequately, about 85% of water utilities worldwide are publicly owned and controlled. Public ownership, however, is not without its problems. Like other state-owned enterprises, they suffer from poor service quality, excessive staffing, and political interference. In addition, water and sanitation services are often priced at below cost-recovery level, creating enormous financial burdens for governments in developing countries. These problems have become widely manifested in the late 1980's, especially in developing countries.

The failure of public water utilities to expand service coverage and improve service quality prompted municipalities in many developing countries to turn to the private sector for investment capital, technical expertise, and efficiency improvement (Dosi and Easter, 2003). At the same time, private participation in the water sector is controversial and subject to intense debate. While private operators may be more efficient because of their profit motive, critics argue that profits are incompatible with public interest (Estache *et al.*, 2001; Birdsall and Nellis, 2002; Smith and Hanson, 2003). Others have held that water privatization compromises access to water as a basic human right and that it harms the welfare of the poor (Gleick *et al.*, 2004; Scanlon *et al.*, 2004).

The privatization of water in England and Wales in 1989 is considered as a catalyst in the rapid expansion of private participation in the water sector in the following decade (Marin, 2006). The early results were encouraging; raising hope among policy makers in developing countries that privatization might provide a viable solution for poorly performing public water utilities. By the end of 2000 at least 93 countries had experimented with water privatization in one form or another (Brubaker, 2001), and the population served by private operators in developing countries grew from 6 million to 94 million between 1991 and 2000. However, the period of tremendous expansion of private participation in the water sector didn't last long as the late 1990s were marked by renegotiation, termination, and cancellation of privatization contracts and projects. A World Bank database on infrastructure revealed that by 2002, 75% of contracts for water privatization in Latin America and the Caribbean had gone sour, experiencing either renegotiation or cancellation (Gómez-Ibáñez *et al.*, 2004). In Asia, the rate of water privatization has slowed considerably since the Asian financial crisis, as a number of high-profile water privatization projects have been abandoned or canceled due to disputes over water tariff increases (Hall *et al.*, 2004).

While much of the existing literature has focused on the rationale and merit of private participation in the water sector, more attention needs to be paid to the role of regulatory systems in improving the sector's performance. Given the unique characteristics of water supply, water sector regulation usually aims to 1) improve efficiency i.e. producing and delivering water at the lowest possible cost while ensuring that operators receive adequate returns on their investments; 2) improve equity i.e. the population have access to affordable quality service and 3) ensure environmental sustainability i.e. minimizing pollution and damage to the natural resource base. The major challenge is information asymmetry. As Shirley (2007) notes, consumers cannot fully assess water quality, utilities cannot cheaply determine quality of underground pipes while investors cannot cheaply see how well underground pipes have been maintained.

The first objective, improving efficiency, can be achieved using three regulatory instruments to determine the industry structure (i.e. the extent of competition in the industry): 1) promoting competition for the market; 2) competition in the market (also called yardstick competition); and 3) direct competition for specific services. Competition for the market involves operators competing for control of the market. These involve the use of regulatory instruments such as concession contracts, management contracts and lease agreements. Competition in the market — also known as yardstick competition — involves splitting the market into service areas covered by operators that do not compete directly but that can be compared by a regulator. Examples of these include Paris and Manila. Yardstick competition is often used to deal with the problem of information asymmetry and to ascertain cost information (Shleifer, 1985).

The second objective, equity, makes use of tariff regulation, performance incentives, community service obligations, fiscal transfer to utilities and targeted subsidies as policy instruments. Tariff regulation is often controversial because of its multiple and sometimes conflicting goals: cost recovery, economic efficiency, equity and affordability. Performance incentives and community service obligations are two common features of water concession agreements to provide access to poor households and peripheral urban areas.

Whatever industry or tariff structure is in place, the literature on optimal regulatory design calls for a politically independent public body to set rates and monitor performance based on objective and verifiable information, with a neutral and independent appeals process (Shirley, 2007). This raises an important question. Does having an independent regulator really matter to the performance of a water utility?

The collection of papers on water supply regulation in Part III of this volume, *Water Sector Regulation and Governance*, examine a number of important questions that have not been adequately addressed in the otherwise extant literature.[1] For instance, can regulation improve the performance of government-controlled water utilities? What is the role of regulatory agencies when concession contracts serve as a regulatory mechanism? How independent are water regulatory agencies and does it matter? What determines industry and market structure for water supply? What processes are needed to establish decentralized water regulatory institutions and what are the challenges associated with building those processes? What does it mean to have a successful regulatory

[1] The papers by Earthardt and Janson, Asquer, Perard, Tanka and Fuller, and Whitford *et al.* were earlier published in a special volume of Water Policy (2010). Permission by the journal publisher — *International Water Association* — is gratefully acknowledged.

scheme in allocating river water and how is success to be understood and measured?

Regulatory independence is a subject explored in Chapters 12 and 13. In Chapter 12, Wu Xun *et al.*, argue that there exist two intrinsic conflicts in the regulation of privatized water utilities under concession agreements. First, although concession agreements constrain the discretionary power of regulatory agencies, contract incompleteness, widespread and unavoidable in the water sector, calls for more extensive uses of discretionary power. Second, although contract renegotiations may undermine the efficiency gains achieved through competitive bidding processes, they suggest that the economic costs and political risks of terminating concession contracts can be prohibitively high.

Using the case of the water regulatory agency in Manila, which supervises a major water concession contract in Metro Manila, they assess the impact that these two tensions exert upon the effectiveness of regulations. Their analysis suggests that concession contracts were indeed relatively effective in curbing opportunistic behaviors on the part of the government and concessionaires in the earlier years following privatization. But the relevance and usefulness of these contracts as the primary regulatory mechanism has declined as the regulatory system moved tacitly toward discretionary regulation. They argue that more emphasis should be placed on transparency and performance benchmarking to improve regulatory effectiveness in the absence of regulatory independence.

In Chapter 13, Ehrhardt and Janson explore the question of whether regulation can improve the performance of government-controlled water utilities. The conventional literature has mostly examined the question of whether private participation combined with regulation can improve the performance of government controlled water utilities but little research has been done on whether regulation alone can improve performance. Their paper examines five water utility reform episodes in Latin America and the Caribbean. In each episode, a regulatory regime designed for private companies was applied to a government-controlled utility. Assessing performance across a number of indicators, the authors find that performance was as likely to deteriorate as to improve during periods of regulation of government controlled utilities. This contrasts with the evidence of improvement following reforms that combined regulation with private participation.

Ehrhardt and Janson's findings suggest that conventional regulation may be of little use in government controlled utilities. Conventional regulation is designed to prevent a profit-maximizing utility from raising tariffs above reasonable cost-recovery levels. Government controlled utilities, however, are not commercially motivated and face systematic incentives for short-termism in tariff-setting, so limiting monopoly profits is not usually the problem that needs to be addressed. The authors conclude that conventional regulation of a government-controlled utility is not useful in isolation. They argue, however, that regulatory tools can complement governance reforms. One approach may be to adapt conventional regulatory tools so as to help citizens judge utilities' performance, and thus be more effective in holding government to account for the performance of government-controlled utilities.

The political salience of water and its institutional implications is a topic explored by Whitford *et al.* in Chapter 14. Specifically, Whitford explores the macro institutional causes of disparities in access to clean water and sanitation. Using econometric analyses on a cross-country data set, he assess the impact of a number of political, economic, and social mechanisms on disparities in access to clean water and adequate sanitation. Whitford offers a series of vignettes using cross-national data from 2002 and 2004 to assess the effects of key institutional variables on the improvement of access to safe water and sanitation. The two key variables explored are 1) the country's commitment to "quality regulation" and the 2) country's long-term development path. They find that the evidence for the effects of these factors on expanding or contracting access to water and sanitation is mixed.

In Chapter 15, Alberto Asquer illustrates two important themes in water sector regulation. The first theme explores the choice of industry, market and contract structure in the water sector while the second explores the implementation of regulatory reforms. Using the case of Italy, Asquer finds that the implementation of water regulatory reforms, which lasted about 12 years, resulted in a new regulatory regime which combined selected features of public ownership, franchise allocation, and discretionary regulation. These reforms were implemented in different ways across the country, at the national and sub-national levels, resulting in different forms of organization and management of the water services at the local level. Asquer then attempts to explain why water regulatory reforms were designed as 'hybrids' between different regulatory 'models' and why, within a given regulatory institutional framework, water regulatory reforms may be implemented in different ways at the local level.

In Chapter 16, Alex Coram and and Lyle Noakes take on a different view of water, not as a service, but as a resource. They are particularly concerned with assessing the effectiveness of regulation across a river system. Such a system, they argue, is characterized by complex interdependencies among the various components of the hydrological system. Extraction of water at any one point in the river has a number of welfare and environmental impacts at a large number of other points. This raises a number of important regulatory questions. What does it mean to have a successful regulatory scheme in allocating river water? How is success to be understood and measured? How do we know that whatever regulatory scheme is in place is allowing the appropriate amount of water to be extracted at each point? If the regulator has to negotiate with various interests over pricing or water allocations what criteria should be used? To answer these questions, Coram proposes a welfare approach to measure the effectiveness of regulation across a river system using the case of the Murray Darling Riverbasin in Australia.

If the water source is a stock, such as a lake or a dam, it may be necessary to regulate it in a way that controls demand according to some criteria and set different prices for different users, such as agriculture and industry. It may also be necessary to have a regime that allows the amount extracted to vary inversely with the volume available. If the water source is a river system, it has different characteristics because it is a uni-directional flow in which upstream extractors are able to inflict damage on downstream interests. In this case it will be necessary to devise the criteria for measuring the effectiveness of regulation and to set regulatory standards in a way that takes into account these interconnections.

Perard also explores, in Chapter 17, the issue of independence of water regulatory agencies. Donors, and the literature on efficient water supply, routinely recommend the separation of regulation from production and provision. In reality, only a few developing countries are able to do this.

Using case studies from southern Mediterranean countries (Tunisia, Algeria, Egypt, Morocco and Jordan), Perard finds that (a) "independent" regulatory agencies have been set up only in a few countries and that a closer look at them confirm that they are rarely independent; (b) in all cases he examined, the management of water supply suffers from political interference and is overly centralized; and (c) while the corporatization of local operators has been legalized in most countries, few have implemented it.

There are two possible explanations for this, both of which need further testing. First, water supply is a politically salient good and therefore politicians are reluctant to give up effective control to an independent regulator. Second, water is a mysterious good (i.e. has significant information problems in terms of water quality, information about customers and information about hidden pipe networks) which gives the service provider informational advantages relative to an independent regulator. Thus, when the marginal transaction costs of having an independent regulator plus the political salience of water significantly outweighs its marginal benefits, there is little incentive to establish independent water regulatory agencies. This is one possible hypothesis why independent water regulators are more the exception rather than the norm.

Finally, in Chapter 18, Tankha and Fuller (2010) are concerned with the importance of processes in establishing decentralized regulatory institutions for water and the challenges associated with establishing those processes. While the argument on the importance of the learning process approach to local institution building was first suggested by Korten (1984), most aid agencies and academic literature still often assume that participation will follow once the organizations and rules supporting it are in place. Comparing case studies from Brazil and India, Tankha and Fuller find that water sector reforms are creating a market of informed demand for public participation, and a supply of services to aid both the participation process and the technical work that will ensue. However, they find that this market must be created using four strands of crucial processes: (1) creation of forums for public participation; (2) capacity building for both government and non-government stakeholders; (3) creating the institutional environment for administration reform; and (4) creating demand for "good" participation from the affected communities. They argue that as each of these strands gets developed, the market for services expands and consolidates. However, they find that in both India and Brazil, capacity building and administrative reforms are lagging, thus suppressing the demand for participatory reforms, a point illustrating the difficulty of participatory approaches to decentralized regulatory reforms.

References

Correljé, AF and LJ De Vries (2008). Hybrid electricity markets: The problem of explaining different patterns of restructuring. In *Competitive Electricity Markets: Design, Implementation, Performance*, Sioshansi, FP (ed.), pp. 65–94. Oxford: Elsevier.

Gratwick, KN and A Eberhard (2008). Demise of the standard model for power sector reform and the emergence of hybrid power markets. *Energy Policy*, 36, pp. 3948–3960.

Jamasb, T, R Mota, D Newbery and M Pollitt (2005). Electricity Sector Reform in Developing Countries: A Survey of Empirical Evidence on Determinants and Performance. World Bank Policy Research paper 3549.

Kessides, IN (2002). *Reforming Infrastructure: Privatization, Regulation, and Competition.* World Bank and Oxford University Press.

Levy, B and PT Spiller (2004). The institutional foundations of regulatory commitment: A comparative analysis of telecommunications regulation. *The Journal of Law, Economics, & Organization*, 10(2), pp. 201–246.

Marin, W (2006). *Altered Perception: Addressing the Real Water Crises.* Unlimited Publication, Indiana, USA.

Millán, J (2006). *Power Sector Reform in Latin America: Accomplishments, Failures and Challenges.* Inter-American Development Bank, Washington, D.C.

Pollitt, M (2228). Forward: liberalization and regulation in electricity systems — How can we get the balance right? In *Competitive Electricity Markets: Design, Implementation, Performance*, Sioshansi, FP (ed.), pp. xvii–xxxiv. Oxford: Elsevier.

Thomas, S (2006). The grin of the Cheshire cat. *Energy Policy*, 34, pp. 1974–1983.

Victor, D and TC Heller (eds.) (2007). *The Political Economy of Power Sector Reform: The Experiences of Five Major Developing Countries.* New York: Cambridge University Press.

Williams, JH and NK Dubash (2004). Asian electricity reform in historical perspective. *Pacific Affairs*, 77(3), pp. 411–436.

World Bank (1993). *The World Banks Role in the Electric Power Sector.* World Bank, Washington, D.C.

Xu, Y-C (2006). The myth of the single solution: Electricity reforms and the World Bank. *Energy*, 31, pp. 802–814.

PART I

Problems, Issues, and Perspectives in Regulation, Regulatory Design and Outcomes

CHAPTER 2

Infrastructure Regulation: What Works, Why, and How do we Know?

Judith Clifton, Daniel Díaz-Fuentes,
Marcos Fernández-Gutiérrez and Julio Revuelta

Public infrastructure services have been subject to dramatic regulatory reform since the 1980s in the European Union, particularly privatization, at the national level, and increased liberalization and deregulation, via the Single Market Programme. Despite this ambitious reform programme, there are signs that regulation is not always working. The Commission itself has recognised the limits of reform undertaken so far. Recently, it drew up a list of 23 sectors which were both crucial for economic growth and significantly "malfunctioning" in the Single Market. This list included major public infrastructure services — energy, gas, telecommunications and transportation. Work is ongoing to identify the causes of this "malfunctioning" and it is intended that new regulation will be implemented to improve this situation. As part of efforts to make these markets perform better, policy-makers are turning their attention to better understanding the consumer. Previously, regulation was usually based on that economic theory which assumed consumers were rational and selfish, but this is now being questioned using insights from Behavioural Economics. The Directorate General for Health and Consumers is moving towards a more eclectic approach to economics. In this light, this paper analyses regulatory reform of public infrastructure services from a user-consumer perspective. Stated (derived from *Eurobarometer*) and revealed (*Household Budget Survey*) preferences of consumers as regards public services are analyzed with a view to better understanding consumer behaviour. By contrasting stated and revealed preferences, new insight into consumer behaviour can be gained for use in the design of future regulation of infrastructure services in many countries world-wide. The new evidence generated can be used as a basis for the development of new consumer or user-related regulation.

1. Introduction

Most infrastructure regulation deals with the supply-side because it is usually assumed that regulation is working for consumers when competition among firms in an integrated market is being promoted. Independent Regulatory Agencies therefore tend to focus on providing well-functioning markets via policies to avoid market concentration, guarantee market entry and supervise licensing, use and access to networks, interconnection, prices and so on. What finally matters in the regulation of public infrastructure services, however, is the user. Despite this, knowledge about patterns of user behaviour vis-à-vis these services is often deemed of secondary importance, at best, or, at worst, ignored, in the design of regulatory regimes. While not using knowledge on user behaviour could constitute an important omission for any sector, it could be a particularly significant oversight in sectors which provide experience, credence or merit goods. In recent years, however, interest is growing in integrating user behaviour into regulatory design and implementation. The OECD (2007, 2008 and 2009), the European Union (DG SANCO, 2008), together with the governments of Australia (Australian Government Productivity Commission 2007 and 2008), the United Kingdom (Fletcher, 2008; Vickers, 2003) and the United States (Federal Trade Commission, 2007; Mulholland, 2007), increasingly coincide that regulation which considers only the supply-side is inadequate. These governments are increasingly paying attention to regulation from the demand-side as a complement to supply-side considerations. Knowledge of user satisfaction is a key means of understanding the impact of reform from the bottom-up, and provides insight into the dynamics of the user-service relationship. These insights may give rise to innovations in regulation, which better ensures that users are informed and empowered, thus better able to drive competition, quality and innovation.

In the light of the turn towards better understanding the user for regulation, this paper evaluates public infrastructure services and their reform from the user perspective. The second section of the paper analyses how and why a common European position on evaluating infrastructure services from the demand-side was forged during the 1990s. Latest thinking in the Commission and its implications in terms of policy design, particularly as regards its new emphasis on understanding consumer behaviour, is discussed. The main tools used to evaluate infrastructure services from the demand-side are described, including an analysis of the main improvements and limitations for the better understanding of the effects of reform on users. The third section contains the empirical analysis. In order to gain insight into user satisfaction with infrastructure services, the relevant data available is analysed in the case of Spanish consumers in the European context. It should be emphasised that the same methodological approach could well be applied to multiple countries around the world, this indeed being a future intention of the authors. Particular attention is paid to issues of universality, accessibility, affordability, service use and non-use, perceived importance of the services, consumer protection and so forth, all from the perspective of disaggregated data on users. Because stated preferences can be difficult to compare across cultures and countries and, in order to check these declarations, patterns of expenditure on these services are analysed through the *Household Budget Surveys* (HBS). Contrasting stated and revealed preference is an innovative methodology applied to user satisfaction. Standing back from the current approach to demand-side evaluation, the conclusions in the fourth section summarise what insights have been gained into the relationship between infrastructure services and users, and conclude that some of these insights could form a basis for improved demand-side regulation.[1]

---

[1] Acknowledgement is made to research financed by the Spanish Ministry for Science and Technology (ECO2008-06243). Future research will evaluate regulation using methodological presented here across all 27 Member States.

2. The Political Economy of Reforming Infrastructure Regulation

2.1. *From State to Market: Establishing Citizen Rights to Public Services*

Privatization, liberalization, deregulation and internationalization of enterprises that were previously organised as national monopolies for several decades raise complex questions about regulation for users (Clifton, Díaz-Fuentes and Revuelta, 2010). From a political economy perspective, regulatory reform shifts the old balance between winners and losers. In theory, consumers are set to gain from these reforms, due to expected price reductions and increases in service performance and choice, whilst labour may lose as working conditions are subject to more competition.[2] Usually, governments decide which policies they wish to implement and when in order to suit their political economy interests. An additional factor in the case of the EU is the issue of the Single Market, since liberalization and deregulation policies, as well as the introduction of new regulation in certain fields, "lock-in" national governments to European reform.

In the face of the dramatic reform of public services in the EU from the 1990s, the need to establish regulation from the user perspective was agreed, though views on what elements should be regulated and how was disputed. After some conflict, a typically "European compromise" emerged between two main positions, led in particular by France and the UK. Whilst the French position sought to regulate the user by establishing citizen rights or entitlements at the EU level inscribed in a charter or Directive, the UK remained optimistic about the capacity of the market to resolve problems, though conceded some minor measures may be required to protect consumers. From the beginning of the 21st century, the failure of the legal project to establish a Constitution for European citizenship sounded the death knell of the continental project. In any case, efforts were shifting away from finding legal solutions to finding economic solutions as regards regulating from the user perspective. This section

[2] See the outputs of the PIQUE (Privatization of Public Services and the Impact on Quality, Employment and Productivity) EC VI Framework Programme at http://www.pique.at/, Hermann *et al.*, (2007).

examines the contested development of demand-side regulation from the 1990s and explains the position reached at the beginning of the twenty-first century.

From the 1980s, as part of the Single Market Programme, the European authorities agreed to implement liberalization and deregulation of infrastructure services. Privatization, in contrast, was a national affair: some countries, such as the UK, had been early privatizers, though most Member States embarked on privatization programmes later on, from the 1990s (Clifton, Comín and Díaz-Fuentes, 2003 and 2006). As reform deepened and extended, however, pressure accumulated from representatives of the European political elite as well as from consumer and labour organizations due to their concern with the consequences of these reforms. These concerns crystallised around the fear that if the regulatory reform of infrastructure services was left unchecked, users could end up with services of a worse quality than before reform. Member States characterised by continental legal traditions, whereby universality, accessibility and non-discrimination were inscribed as citizens' rights, as well as numerous consumers' associations, and social partners, were particularly important representatives of this position.

Public services played an important role in the historical evolution and institutional building of the EU Member States, representing a different model to that found in the United States (Galambos, 2000). One important difference was legal: public services were defined distinctly and occupied different places in the legal systems and Constitutions of various countries. In France, Italy and Spain, citizens had enjoyed rights to public services since the 19th century. In other countries, such as Germany, the Low Countries and the UK, public services had a less marked place in the legal system, but were associated with specific obligations connected to the provision of public services (for instance, accessibility, quality and continuity). Though there were differences across the EU, there were also many common features in terms of the organization, ownership, regulation and development of public service regimes. Rationales for public enterprises were similar across Europe, such as the existence of natural monopolies, the strategic nature of goods or services, and social justice. Other important similarities in public service regimes across Europe included the kinds of activities that had been operated and managed by public enterprises, a resistance to allowing market forces to govern these activities, and the introduction of similar laws on how these services should be run (such as monopolies, concessions, exclusive or special laws). When public services had been provided by the State, citizens had a "voice" via a universal right to vote nationally and locally for a political manifesto, in which public services were always central. Politicians were accountable to citizens for public service provision. Under privatised ownership and market-driven rules, it was feared that commercial interests would be pursued over and above the public interest, which could negatively affect public service obligations, universal service, quality, price and continuity of supply, blurring who would be taken as accountable for these services (CEEP and ETUC, 2000). As firms in the communications, transportation, water and energy sectors became increasingly internationalised, fears were voiced by consumer associations and other NGOs that basic public services that were once understood to "belong" to the nation would now be owned and controlled by distant foreign interests motivated by short-term profits because of the principal-agent problem (Balanyá *et al.*, 2000). Considering much internationalization was by foreign national governments, another concern was geopolitics: in Europe, the main threat was Russia's perceived energy interests (Clifton, Comín and Díaz-Fuentes, 2007; Goldstein, 2007).

As privatization and liberalization of the infrastructure services gained ground, actors mobilised — led particularly by France and Belgium — to express their fundamental concerns. Whilst liberalization was a clearly defined policy, the nature and role of "Services of General Interest" or SGI[3] — which could be legible for state-aid and exemption from liberalization — was less clearly defined. In general, these actors were not against reform *per se*, however, they did insist that, whether public services fell to private or public hands, the user needed written guarantees about their rights, which should be included in a European Directive or Charter.

[3] "Services of General Interest" (SGI) is the official EU terminology for a range of public services. SGI is sub-divided into two categories: Services of General Economic Interest (including most public infrastructure services) and Services of General Interest (education, many health services, defence and so on). For a discussion see Clifton, Comín and Díaz-Fuentes (2005), Mangenot (2005), and Louis and Rodrigues (2006).

Jacques Delors, President of the European Commission (EC) was central when, in 1994, he commissioned two of the EU social partners, the "European Centre of Enterprises with Public Participation and of Enterprises of General Economic Interest" (CEEP), and the European Trade Union Confederation (ETUC) to draft a Charter for SGI as a basis for a Framework Directive, which was published six years later after multiple rounds of consultation (CEEP and ETUC, 2000, EC, 2003b, EC, 2004). This development was also championed by the European Parliament and supported by the German government (Prosser, 2005). The draft Charter urged for a "bottom-up" approach to social regulation. This draft put citizens — not users or consumers — at the centre of the document and argued that all citizens should be guaranteed rights to: equal access, no discrimination, continuously working, quality and adaptable services, universal provision, safety, fair pricing, efficiency levels that could be verified objectively, transparency, participation and democratic control. In this way, public services would be a foundation for a Social Europe characterised by solidarity, territorial and social inclusion, quality of life and a dynamic economy (Van de Walle, 2006). A logical extension of guaranteeing rights to public services was the establishment of a European citizenship, part of the objective behind the failed European Constitution.

2.2. *A European Compromise: Creating "Citizen–Consumers"*

Other EU actors, particularly business lobbies and the British and Dutch governments, argued that granting entitlements to citizens was unnecessary, and that liberalization should be allowed to work freely, though, as consumers, some forms of protection may need to be established. To counter the French-led proposals, they proposed a market-based one, much of which was influenced by New Public Management (Clifton, Comín and Díaz-Fuentes, 2005). While the continental position called for a charter or Directive to uphold citizens' rights, the UK and Dutch governments supported a service charter similar to those associated with New Public Management, as promoted by governments in Australia, the United Kingdom and the United States, as well as international organizations such as the OECD (McGuire, 2002). Though diverse in scope and objectives, most service charters emphasize issues about consumer empowerment and performance benchmarking. New Public Management basically suggests that market mechanisms can be introduced into business where privatization is not feasible or desirable. Though the concept New Public Management has been criticised as being over-stretched (Hood, 2001) it is often associated with techniques such as contracting out and downsizing: from the consumer perspective, users may pay charges in exchange for expecting good information about service performance, levels of satisfaction, and have channels to voice their discontent (Hirschman, 1970; Clifton, Comín and Díaz-Fuentes, 2005). There are several important differences between the "citizen-centred" and "consumer-centred" approaches (Clarke *et al.*, 2007), but perhaps the fundamental one is that the "continental" perspective addresses citizens (the entire population) whilst the "Anglo-Saxon" perspective begins with the point of consumption; there is little said about those who fall outside this market exchange.

As is usual in the EU, a compromise was sought to satisfy opposing positions. In Communications, such as EC (2000), the Commission attempted to "merge" the two main positions by using "citizen" and "consumer" almost interchangeably. It was argued that citizen and consumer rights were two sides of the same coin: consumers must be guaranteed a set of basic obligations by service providers, enjoy choice of supplier, receive a transparent and better service at a lower price. It was argued that citizen and consumer rights were compatible, and both helped to forge a stronger Europe in economic and social terms. Perhaps the Commission was trying to fudge the differences, because debate reached new peaks on the publication of the Green Paper of SGI in 2003 (EC, 2003b). The Green Paper elicited responses that revealed significant differences across the EU, with British and French policy-makers representing the most "extreme" positions. This Green Paper was concerned with whether user rights should take the form of a charter or Directive, and, if so, whether a single charter or a series of mini-charters for each kind of public service would be preferable. The British opposed the establishment of a single charter, while the French emphasised the need for a proper definition of SGI as well as a clarification that the Member States could use discretion in order to organise and fund them as thought fit (Prosser, 2005). The resulting White Paper, published two years later, was very cautious and only contained "soft" instruments as regards regulation for two main reasons. Firstly, due to the lack of consensus about the way in which user rights to these services should be regulated, and secondly, because overshadowing all these developments was the process whereby the European Constitutional Treaty was to come into force, granting rights to a long-awaited European citizenship. When the Constitutional Treaty was rejected and, as the EU entered an institutional crisis, the project to establish rights to these services linked to citizenship faded away quietly.

If, in the mid-1990s, it looked possible that a Directive could be passed that focused squarely on establishing citizens' rights to these services, it seems that the EU has quietly abandoned the aim of protecting citizens through "positive integration". Any rights to services will be guaranteed at the national level, or will be promoted by the European authorities through "soft" instruments (Clifton and Díaz-Fuentes, 2010).

2.3. *Evaluating Regulation: What do we Know, and How?*

From the 1980s, the rhetoric of reformist policy-makers centred on the ideas of augmenting choice and quality of infrastructure services for users. Paradoxically, systematic research on whether users are more satisfied after reform has not always been prioritised. Most policy has focused on supply-side concerns, and it is only more recently that attention is being paid to demand-side issues. Better information about users' opinions figures as a central aspect of this new approach.

The EC started to monitor public opinion from 1973, using standard survey techniques as a working tool in its policy-making process. Since then, special surveys which focused on specific topics were introduced — including user satisfaction with public services — as well as surveys by telephone and more qualitative approaches including the use of focus groups. Between 1997 and 2007, the surveys dedicated to exploring satisfaction with public services changed in terms of the focus of the survey, the questions posed, those surveyed and the process of inclusion/exclusion of those surveyed. For methodological reasons, the first survey, published in 1997, is not directly comparable to the proceeding ones, though from 2000 methodology is homogenous so results can be directly compared.

The first dedicated survey was *Eurobarometer* 47.1 (EC, 1997). This stands apart from the proceedings ones, because it centred on views of citizens in the face of the prospective exposure of public monopolies to competition. To this extent, it is the only survey of opinions about public services "before" they are subject to significant regulatory change or at a relatively early stage in regulatory reform, though regulatory change was already advanced in some Member States and relatively more advanced in telecommunications than in other public service sectors. There are two striking features of this survey (Clifton, Comín and Díaz-Fuentes, 2005). The first is that the 1997 survey is concerned with the opinions of "citizens" as opposed to "users": questions touch on what perceptions citizens have about the opening of monopolies up to competition as regards prices, access, quality, choice and consumer protection, as well as questions about what benefits they had already noticed. The influence of the continental approach is thus revealed: for instance, in the 121-page document, "citizen" is used 303 times. The other striking thing is the survey results: levels of citizen satisfaction depend heavily on (1) which country a citizen lives in and (2) which sector was being evaluated.

The proceeding surveys on satisfaction are more directed at user satisfaction. Thanks to the efforts by the Commission to deploy the same methodology, the surveys from 2000 onwards are directly comparable making the evaluation of satisfaction over time possible. Each of these surveys consists of in-depth analyses of consumer satisfaction with SGI, in the EU-15 (EC, 2000; EC, 2002), the new EU-10 (EC, 2003a) and the EU-25 (EC, 2005; EC, 2007b). EC (2000), EC (2002), EC (2003a) and EC (2005) measure satisfaction with access, price, information and other contract indicators for electricity, gas, water, fixed telephony, mobile telephony, postal services, urban transport and railways. EC (2007b) covers these sectors plus internet and banking.

There is one significant methodological difference, however, which mirrors the concerns in Europe over understanding consumer behaviour. In the 2000 and 2002 surveys, "non-consumers" were screened out of the survey results. The problem with this exclusion is that the results on satisfaction are biased as they do not include those who cannot afford them, do not have sufficient information about them, or do not want them for a variety of reasons. To a great extent, this policy reflected the influence of New Public Management's focus on the consumer. This policy was changed in the 2004 and 2006 surveys: here, the survey respondents were grouped into two categories at the outset: consumers and non-consumers of a given service. Both categories were analysed in order to gain a deeper understanding of what people consumed or not. Questions of access were stressed for both categories, and, once identified, non-consumers were surveyed further on issues such as accessibility, affordability-price, quality, consumer rights' protection and consumer relations. Non-consumers who potentially had service provision were asked about accessibility, affordability and knowledge of the quality and reliability of the services. In addition, for the first time, additional socio-economic variables of respondents were considered in the analysis, including gender, age, education, household composition and urbanisation. These efforts towards better understanding consumer behaviour, including the behaviour of "non-consumers" differed to the earlier attempt to learn about citizens' opinions. These changes reflect, again, a change of influence, in particular, the turn to better understanding consumption patterns in the first few years of the 21st century as discussed in the fourth section.

Now, while the *Eurobarometer* provides rich statistical data on citizens' opinions and perceptions as regards infrastructure services, they have not been used sufficiently in the design and implementation of regulatory policies to date. In addition, there has been a lack of empirical and analytical research to uncover what can be learnt about stated preferences as regards evaluating infrastructure reform. One exception includes Clifton, Comín and Díaz-Fuentes (2005) who analysed patterns in stated user satisfaction across the EU-25 for six services based on *Eurobarometers* 1997–2004. In addition, Fiorio *et al.* (2007), Bacchiochi *et al.* (2008) and Fiorio and Florio (2008) also used *Eurobarometers* to assess infrastructure reform based on stated preferences. These three pieces of research find that competition, but not privatization, has a positive effect on satisfaction, particularly as regards prices. Fiorio *et al.* (2007) highlight the complexity of the economic, social and institutional environment as a determinant of attitudes about these services. Fiorio and Florio (2008) conclude that institutional circumstances should be borne in mind in the design of regulatory policies, since it is misleading to suppose that a single, homogeneous regulatory framework will have the same results in different contexts.

The objective of research based on stated preferences is to empirically analyse questions previously studied exclusively from the theoretical perspective. This justifies the need to evaluate institutional aspects and the quality of public policy, as well as the net effect in terms of winners and losers (Frey and Stutzer, 2002). However, a large literature exists which points to the biases that may take place in the expression of stated preferences. This has led to scepticism as regards deploying data on user satisfaction as a means of improving the design of service regulation. Stated preferences have traditionally been compared with revealed preferences (user behaviour) as an instrument to explain consumer behaviour. The utility inference derived from real consumer behaviour has been dominant, due to its ascribed objectivity, when comparing comparatively household welfare from the economic point of view. Despite this, there is a lack of research on the evaluation of regulatory reform of infrastructure services, perhaps due to a lack of homogenous data at the European level. Recently, more attention has been paid to evidence of empirical anomalies in human behaviour which has led to a questioning that utility can be inferred from revealed preferences (Frey and Stutzer, 2002). This could be taken to imply that when regulation is evaluated from the demand-side, possible biases in user behaviour, which are of central concern to the new economic approach detailed in the next section, should be taken into account. Thus, stated and revealed preferences could be considered as complementary sources which, combined, will enrich an analysis of user behaviour.

2.4. *Implications for Designing a Regulatory Framework: New Regulatory Policies in the OECD and EU*

From the early years of the 21st century, new ideas gained importance among policy-makers in institutions such as the OECD, the EU, as well as several national competition agencies such as those in Australia, United States and the United Kingdom. Just as ideas derived from New Public Management diffused by the OECD and other organizations, particularly Anglo-Saxon governments, became influential within European authorities during the 1990s, in the first few years of the twenty-first century, Behavioural Economics was promoted by these same countries and organizations.

Using insights from psychology, behavioural economists critiqued the traditional view of *homo oeconomicus* consumers as rational, selfish and time-consistent individuals which underwrote an understanding of the act of consumption as a cost-benefit analysis resulting in the optimum choice for the individual. Though economists argued this was a useful approximation of consumer behaviour, other economists and psychologists argued that insights from psychology based on observation could help to refine this traditional approximation. In particular, insights from Behavioural Economics can try to explain why consumers do not always take optimum decisions. For instance, behavioural economists analyse ways in which people tend to discount the future whilst overemphasising the present ("myopia"), which may led to inertia: diets always start — tomorrow. In addition, Behaviour Economics argues that the way in which information is presented — or framing — can affect consumer behaviour. Experiments showed how pictures of a female associated with a product could significantly increase sales. Related to the presentation of information are default options. Depending on whether the default option is to automatically become — or not become — a member of a pension scheme could have significant consequences for peoples' future security, it was claimed. Moreover, choice or information overload may result in consumer boredom and non-consumption, or in electing the "wrong" product. Applying insights on information presentation to the infrastructures, research has shown that, frequently, when consumers switch provider, a great proportion opt for a package that makes them worse off (EC 2007a; DG SANCO, 2008). This could be explained by lack of information, information overload and other aspects of human psychology. Kahneman (2002) explained the phenomenon of "slow learning" which occurs not because people do not learn but because of the way information is processed. Behavioural economists also studied the ways in which social aspects such as peoples' level of education, gender, residence and age can affect their consumption decisions. Applying these insights to use of infrastructure services could shed light on why citizens do not always take optimal decisions. For instance, many consumers fail to switch provider when better alternatives are available. Other citizens′ behaviour vis-à-vis infrastructure could be explained using data on the social context or their social role.

Patterns in user behaviour could be useful in explaining how markets function. Now, it is argued that these insights could have important consequences for regulatory design. In this regard, from the practitioner perspective, one powerful suggestion is that rather than separating competition policy (supply-side) and consumer policy (demand-side) institutionally, these regulations could — and should — be combined. This is the policy of the new "Fair Trade Policy" at the UK Office of Fair Trading (Fletcher, 2008). By merging demand and supply-side regulation, aspects of consumer behaviour, such as inertia, limited memory, myopia, choice overload and so on can be addressed through better regulation.

DG SANCO, the European Union's newly established Directorate for Health and Consumers, argues that incorporating consumer behaviour into the design of regulatory frameworks for infrastructure could be a means of improving regulatory quality. Better understanding user behaviour as part of a demand-side consideration, combined with supply-side considerations, could all feed into a better, higher quality, regulatory policies. Improved regulation of these issues can help make consumers and non-consumers alike more knowledgeable about products and services, making them more "empowered", "active" and "confident" in the marketplace (Fletcher, 2008). Improving our understanding of consumer behaviour could mean consumers benefit more from the potential advantages of competition policy. From a political point of view, it should be noted that this solution is of interest to the Commission because, while it has historic competence in competition policy, it has much less competence and experience in consumer policy. An attempt to merge elements of consumer policy with competition policy could increase the Commission's competence in consumer policy.

Quietly, the previous approach to defending citizens' rights to public services was abandoned, whilst policy-makers turned to eclectic approaches to economics for sources of new insights into regulation. From 2006, the Commission undertook a review of the Single Market Programme in order to identify what was still not working as regards an integrated market. A list was identified of 23 sectors which were both important for the European economy and which displayed significant problems as regards obstacles to a Single Market. Unsurprisingly, all the main public infrastructure services were included on this list. As regards supply-side regulation, in-depth analysis was dedicated to quantifying characteristics such as market power, competition, prices, mark ups and so on, with the aim of reconsidering the optimum policy response (DG SANCO, 2008). However, this is also being complemented by a demand-side analysis, as the Commission, following the OECD, states that interactions between consumers and the market may exhibit problems that supply-side regulation alone will not fix. Thus, the Commission is seriously studying the benefits of demand-side regulation if analysis indicates this is required.

In order to signal increased attention to understanding the consumer, a new tool was launched from 2008, the "Consumer Market Scoreboard" (DG SANCO, 2008). The idea is to produce a highly visible and accessible document on an annual basis which charts aspects such as consumer use and satisfaction with products and services across the EU. Because the Commission had been producing detailed surveys and reports on satisfaction with infrastructure services since 1997, this approach and data has dominated the work done so far. In order to gather similar information on satisfaction for the other sectors, the Commission and DG SANCO have to coordinate the collection of national data on consumer satisfaction and behaviour from national authorities.

3. Exploring Patterns of Infrastructure Use

The main objective of this section is to empirically analyse consumer behaviour patterns vis-à-vis public infrastructure services. Data is derived from the *Eurobarometer* to assess use of services and explanations for use and non-use. Stated preferences are contrasted with revealed preferences through analysis of household expenditure patterns on these services. Contrasting in this way preferences constitutes an innovative way of evaluating infrastructure services from the demand-side. The main characteristics of the database sources for stated and revealed preferences are shown in Table 1. Here, stated preferences or citizen satisfaction with

Table 1: Comparison of data on declared satisfaction and observed patterns of consumption of selected infrastructure services in the European Union (2006)

	Stated preferences (Eurobarometer)	Revealed preferences (SHBS)
Sample size	1006	19435
Level of analysis	Individuals	Households
Main variables	**Individual characteristics**	**Reference person characteristics**
	Marital status	Marital status
	Education[1]	Education[1]
	Sex	Sex
	Status in employment	Status in employment
	Age[1]	Age[1]
	Nationality	Nationality
	Area of residence	
	Household size	**Household characteristics**
	Household type	Climate characteristics
	Political ideology	Area of residence
		Household size
	Service satisfaction	Household type
	Accesibility	Size of municipality
	Affordability	Population density
	Service importance[2]	NUTS1/NUTS2
	Ease to compare offers[2]	Total spending
	Consumer protection perceptions	Total income

(*Continued*)

Table 1: (*Continued*)

	Stated preferences (Eurobarometer)						Revealed preferences (SHBS)					
Use	93.44	61.13	91.95	81.21	73.86	35.19	98.47	56.38	95.34	82.82[3]	67.54[3]	31.03
Non use-related factors[4] Mean analysis	Age < 35 Urban area Self-employed	Rural area Age > 65 Low education	Age < 25	Age < 25 Rural area One-member households Unemployed	Age > 65 Low studies Small households	Age > 65 Low studies Rural area Small household	Age < 25 Foreigner One-member household	Rural area Age > 70 One-member household	Rural area Age < 30 Age > 70 1 or > 4-member household Low education	Age < 30 Foreigner One-member household	Age > 65 1 or 2 member household Low studies	Age > 65 Low studies Rural area One-member household

[1]Not exactly comparable
[2]Only in fixed telephony, mobile telephony and Internet
[3]95.2 % considering jointly fixed and mobile telephony
[4]Only individual and household characteristics
Source: Authors. Information is based on EC (2006) and INE (2006).

SGI are derived from the *Eurobarometer* (EC, 2006). These are compared with revealed preferences, or consumption patterns of particular services, derived, in this case, from the *Spanish Household Budget Survey* (*Encuesta de Presupuestos Familiares* or SHBS) of the same year (INE, 2006). Clearly, this analysis could be extended to the rest of the EU using the Household Budget Survey (EUROSTAT, 2009). Both surveys include data on the use of diverse services, including, for our purposes, electricity, gas, water, fixed and mobile telephony and internet services. The Spanish survey sample is 19,435 households, while the *Eurobarometer* sample is 1,006 individuals. Socio-economic characteristics which are comparable across the two surveys are marked in bold. There are some characteristics included in one survey but not in the other, such as political position (in *Eurobarometer* but not in SHBS), or total household income (in SHBS but not in *Eurobarometer*).[4] Whilst *Eurobarometer* indicates whether individuals state they use a service, SHBS reveals consumption through expenditure. Service use is revealed when the amount spent is positive.

A preliminary and important observation is that stated and revealed use for all six services is highly consistent. Electricity and water are universal services, fixed and mobile telephony are near-universal, whereas gas and internet are much less universal. Revealed use is higher than stated use for the universal or near-universal services, whilst stated use is higher than revealed for the two less universal ones. By comparing means, stated and revealed use can be calculated according to the most relevant control variables in the survey, thus identifying the most important factors explaining the non-use of services. These factors are listed by declining importance under each sector. There is also a high degree of consistency as regards factors explaining non-use. Age appears repeatedly as a significant factor. Lower educational attainment appears relevant for gas, mobile telephony and internet, while rural areas are relevant for gas, fixed phone and the internet. The over 65s are less likely to use mobile telephony, internet and gas; whilst younger people are less likely to use electricity, water and fixed telephony. Rural dwellers are less likely to use gas and internet, whilst

[4] Considerations of the climate have also been introduced to better understand consumption patterns of electricity and gas.

people with lower educational attainment are less likely to use mobile telephony and internet.

Using information on stated use of services, Table 2 analyses which factors best explain use of the six sectors. Both personal characteristics of the person surveyed, as well as their satisfaction with different aspects of service provision, are tested for their influence on service use. In order to do so, probit estimations and marginal effects of the following models are used:

$$Yi = \alpha + \beta Xi + \varepsilon i \quad (1)$$
$$Yi = \alpha + \gamma Zi + \varepsilon i \quad (2)$$
$$Yi = \alpha + \beta Xi + \gamma Zi + \varepsilon i \quad (3)$$

where:

Yi = Service use: 1 = Use, 0 = Non-use.

Xi = Personal control variables such as age, sex, educational attainment and so on as listed in Table 2.

Zi = Control variables about the services as regards: satisfaction with accessibility, satisfaction with affordability, perception of the services as being important, perception of the service as being very important, ease with which offers can be compared and satisfaction with consumer protection.

There are some striking findings as regards factors influencing service use. First, consistently, for all six sectors, satisfaction with accessibility is — by some margin — the leading *common* factor associated with service use. That is, the easier users perceive access to a given service, the more likely it is they will use that service. The second observation only concerns the three communications services since questions about how important the service in question is perceived for daily life was only asked of these, and was not a common question across all sectors. In all three cases, the more important these sectors are perceived to be for daily life, the higher the probability is that they will be used. The association between importance assigned to a service and use was even stronger than the association between accessibility satisfaction and use. Returning to common factors asked of all six services, the second common factor explaining use was satisfaction with price (affordability), though this was much less significant

Table 2: Marginal effects of significant variables in service use (2006)

Variable	Electricity *Coefficient*	Gas *Coefficient*	Water *Coefficient*	Fixed tel. *Coefficient*	Mobile tel. *Coefficient*	Internet *Coefficient*
Foreigner		–0.3067**				
Left					0.0717***	
Single						–0.1301***
Nostudies				–0.1202***		–0.0923**
Women			–0.0386*	–0.1003***		
> 65		0.1308***		–0.2171***		–0.1390***
Selfemployed		0.0394***	0.1137***	0.1341***		0.1561*
Unemployed						0.1493*
Student						0.1649**
Rural		–0.1367***		–0.1159***		–0.1843***
Householdsize		0.0533**				0.0423**
Children		–0.0886***				–0.0535**
Unipersonal		0.0344***				
Oneparent		0.3406***				
Tempjan				0.0117***		
Tempjuly		0.0214***	0.0083***		0.0099**	
Accessibility	0.4898***	0.6391***	0.4744***	0.2152***	0.3080***	0.2769***
Affordability	0.0339*	0.3466***	0.0567***	0.1106***	0.1289***	0.1648***
Important				0.3046***	0.3859***	0.2848***
Vimportant				0.1043***	0.2072***	
Easyoffer				–0.0621***		
Protection					0.0556*	

***, **, * indicates significance at 1%, 5% and 10%, respectively.

Source: Authors. Information based on EC (2006).

than accessibility satisfaction. More in-depth analysis is organised by sector.

Reinforcing the universality of electricity and water as shown in Table 1, personal characteristics intervene only weakly in explaining usage as provision is non-discriminatory. Satisfaction with accessibility to electricity and water is by far the leading explanation for use (48.98% and 47.44% respectively). Satisfaction with affordability comes second, though is much less important in explaining use (3.39% and 5.67% respectively). Gas services are provided to around 60% of households. As in the cases of electricity and water, the leading explanation for usage is satisfaction with accessibility (63.91%) followed by affordability satisfaction (34.7%). Associations with affordability are stronger than those found in the other five sectors. Personal characteristics of the respondents also matter: one-parent families or the over 65s are more likely to use gas (34.1% and 13.08% respectively) whilst negative associations are found for foreigners (–30.7%), rural dwellers (–13.8%) and two-parent families with children (–8.86%).

Fixed telephony services cover over 80% of consumers, mobile phones cover around 70% and the internet around 30%. In all three cases, perceptions that these services are either important or very important for daily life were strongly associated with probability of usage. For fixed phones, perceptions of their being important or very important and usage reached 30.46% and 10.43%; in mobile telephony this was 38.59% and for the internet this was 28.48% and 20.72%. As in the cases of electricity, water and gas, there are strong positive links between satisfaction with accessibility and usage, though this is weaker for communications services (21.52% for fixed, 30.8% for mobiles and 27.69% for internet). Satisfaction with affordability is more strongly associated with use than with electricity and water, though not than gas (11.06% for fixed, 12.89% for mobiles and 16.48% for internet). In contrast to water and energy, issues of satisfaction with provision and customer handling appear as significant in explaining usage patterns. Satisfaction with consumer protection in the mobile sector is positively associated with use of mobiles (5.56%). Personal characteristics influence use: the self-employed are more likely to use mobile (13.41%), fixed (11.37%) and internet (15.61%) communications. Students (16.49%), the self-employed (15.91%), and the unemployed (14.93%) are also more likely to use internet. Personal characteristics also affect usage in a negative direction: for fixed phones, these include rural dwellers (–11.59%) and females (–3.86%); for mobile phones, these are the over 65s (–21.71%) and those with lower educational attainment (–12.02), and for the internet, rural dwellers (–18.45%), the over 65s (–13.9%), singletons (–13.01%), females (–10%) and those with lower educational attainment (–9%).

Revealed use is derived from the SHBS (INE, 2006) as shown in Table 3. Average spending on the service in question of the population is measured (G_{ij}). Additionally, the variation coefficient of G_{ij} is calculated, in order to analyse the extent to which this is homogenous. Next, the average service expenditure by household users is calculated ($G_{ij} | G_i > 0$). The relative importance of G_{ij} / G_i is calculated in relation to total household expenditure, to discount the income effect. The absolute and relative importance is finally analysed by a comparison of means, according to the control variables in the SHBS. To estimate the factors explaining service expenditure, an Ordinary Least Squares regression is performed where the dependent variable is household expenditure on a particular service (G_{ij}) and the independent variables are regional (R_i), territorial (T_i), household type (H_i), characteristics of the bread-winner (S_i) or economic situation (E_i),

From the applied model:

$$G_{ij} = \alpha + \beta R_i + \gamma T_i + \delta H_i + \zeta S_i + \eta E_i + \varepsilon_i$$

where i = representative person and j = the service in question.

It is derived:

β, indicates regional differences in expenditure

γ, indicates differences related to territorial accessibility

δ, indicates differences according to household characteristics

ζ, indicates the effects due to characteristics of the bread-winner. These include: age, non-monetary effects of employment, non-monetary effects of education, etc.

η, indicates the effect of income, associated with levels of spending (G_i) and/or total income.

Table 3a: Estimations of effects on revealed spending

	Electricity	Gas	Water
Importance (average spending)	377.47	326.59	135.87
Spending CV	0.47	0.96	1.41
Average spending (users)	383.34	326.59	135.87
Regression results	β stand.	β stand.	β stand.
Income			
TOTAL SPENDING	0.464***	0.212***	0.375***
TOTAL INCOME			−0.017**
Sex		0.015**	
WOMEN RP			
Age			
AGE RP	0.028***	−0.026***	0.067***
RP < 25	−0.011***		
RP < 30		−0.033***	
Marital status			0.015**
SINGLE			
Nationality			
FOREIGN-RP	0.055***	0.025***	0.151***
EU-RP	0.027***	0.020***	−0.015**
Education			
Employment			
UNEMP-RP	0.013**		
SELFEMP-RP	0.033***		
Household type			
SIZE	0.052***	0.014**	0.039***
5MEMBERS	−0.026***		−0.013*
ONEPARENT	−0.017***		−0.012**
WOMAN > 65	0.029***		
TWO > 65		0.018**	−0.017***
Territorial	0.043***		
variables	0.032***	−0.028***	
SEMIPOB			
SCPOB			0.024***
URBANLUX		−0.030***	0.028***
URBANHIGH			−0.013*

(*Continued*)

Table 3a: (*Continued*)

	Electricity	Gas	Water
RURAL			−0.016***
MUN50000			−0.035***
MUN20000			−0.029***
MUN10000			
MUN > 10000			−0.061***
Regional variables			
NOREAST	−0.040***		
CATALONIA	0.133***	0.171***	0.261***
CVALENC	0.131***		0.092***
MADRID	0.168***	0.247***	0.225***
ANDALUCIA	0.177***		0.152***
CANARIAS	0.113***		
BALEARIC ISLANDS			0.045***
EXTREMADURA			0.032***
CLAMANCHA			0.023***
MURCIA			0.062***
TEMPJAN		−0.076***	

Source: Authors information based on INE (2006).
RP = Reference person.
***, **, * indicates significance at 1%, 5% and 10%, respectively.

Electricity represents an important part of household expenditure. Because spending is largely homogenous, there are large differences in the relative ease of purchasing electricity due to income differences. Despite this, stated affordability was not very strongly linked with usage (as shown in Table 2) because demand is inelastic. Higher expenditure is associated with dwellers of less densely populated zones, foreigners, the unemployed and self-employed, and the older a person the more they will spend on electricity. Less is spent by one-parent families. It also appears that spending is higher in large cities which suffer hot temperatures during the summer.

Expenditure on water is much lower than for electricity and is therefore quite affordable as demand is price inelastic. Variations in expenditure, however, are high due to differences in price and consumption

Table 3b: Estimations of effects on revealed spending

	Fixed telephony	Mobile telephony	Total telephony	Internet
Importance (average spending)	240.23	350.62	590.85	77.85
Spending CV	1.17	1.96		2.52
Average spending (users)	290.12	519.13	620.69	250.89
Regression results	β stand.	β stand.	β stand.	β stand.
Income				
TOTALSPENDING	0.321***	0.427***	0.480***	0.291***
TOTALINCOME		0.033***	0.024***	0.018**
Sex				
WOMENRP	0.022***	0.028***	0.026***	
Age				
AGE-RP	0.131***	−0.078***		−0.024**
RP < 25				−0.017**
RP < 30	−0.041***			
RP < 35		0.041***	0.039***	
Marital status				
SINGLE		0.020***	0.017***	
Nationality				
FOREIGN-RP	−0.027***	0.102***	0.081***	−0.018**
EU-RP	0.081***	−0.042***	−0.011*	0.039***
Education				
SECONDARY				0.018***
PREUNIV	0.022***	−0.012**		0.054***
PROFEDUC		−0.023***	−0.013**	0.037***
UNIV1	0.019***	−0.024***	−0.012*	0.053***
UNIV2&3	0.030***	−0.049***	−0.028***	0.081***
Employment				
LESS2OCC		−0.027***	−0.020***	−0.026***
NONOCC			−0.030***	
SELFEMPRP	0.029***		0.016***	
Household type				
SIZE	0.042***	0.073***	0.064***	0.070***
ONEMEMBER		0.048***	0.028***	0.025**
5MEMBERS	−0.023***			−0.037***
ONEPARENT	−0.015**			
WOMAN> 65	0.030***	0.031***		0.018**
TWO> 65				−0.025***

(*Continued*)

Table 3b: (*Continued*)

	Fixed telephony	Mobile telephony	Total telephony	Internet
Territorial variables				
SEMIPOB				−0.039***
SCPOB	−0.037***	0.020***		−0.058***
RURAL	−0.014**			
Regional variables				
CATALONIA	0.186***	0.026***	0.090***	0.099***
CVALENC	0.067***		0.031***	
MADRID	0.207***	0.035***	0.105***	0.062***
ANDALUCIA	0.132***	0.044***	0.088***	
CANARIAS		0.031***	0.031***	

Source: Authors information based on INE (2006).
RP = Reference person
***, **, * indicates significance it at 1%, 5% and 10% respectively.

patterns. Human geography is important as rural dwellers consume less than more urban zones. Communities in the south and east spend more. As in the case of electricity, increased age and being foreign are associated with greater expenditure, whilst one-parent families are associated with lower expenditure. Water services may be granted for free in some rural areas with abundant water resources, particularly in northern Spain. Smaller municipalities are associated with lower levels of expenditure of water.

Gas is a considerable expense for those households which use it. Expenditure is negatively related to households in rural and less populated areas, and also to increasing age. While greater expenditure on electricity is noted during the summertime, higher gas expenditure is noted for the winter (TEMPJAN). Households in Madrid and Catalonia spend more perhaps because networks are established in these large urban areas (as will also be seen for the internet).

Fixed telephony represents an intermediate expenditure between electricity and water, and variation is important. In contrast, expenditure on mobile telephony is very high: mobile phone-user households spend more on mobile telephony than any other of these services, though there is a large variation. In order to study consumer behaviour in depth, fixed and mobile telephony are analysed individually and together. There are some interesting non-monetary effects of education here as expenditure on voice telephony is related inversely to education: the higher the level of education received, the less spent. Moreover, the highly educated spend relatively more on fixed phones and relatively less on mobile phones. Likewise, the older a person, the more likely it is they will spend more on fixed phones and less on mobile phones. Younger users do just the opposite: relatively more is spent on mobile telephony, often, as a substitute for fixed. Rural households also substitute fixed for mobile phones. Foreigners also spend relatively more on mobile than on fixed telephony, though EU foreigners do not spend quite so much more. Singletons spend relatively more on mobiles. One-parent households also spend relatively less on fixed telephony though average on mobile telephony. Self-employed spend more on fixed. As has been shown in throughout the social history of telecommunications, women tend to spend more on this service than men.

Users' expenditure on internet services is intermediate relative to the other services and the variations are much higher than other sectors. There is a clear, positive, relationship between level of education attainment and internet use. Households with more educated inhabitants spend relatively less on voice telephony but relatively more on the internet. Rural dwellers spend relatively less as do households with less than two jobs. Increased age is associated negatively with expenditure on the internet. Non-EU foreigners spend less on internet and EU nationals more (a pattern reinforced by their expenditure patterns on fixed telephony).

4. Discussion and Conclusions

4.1. *Measuring Regulatory Outcomes and Effectiveness: What do we know?*

Mainstream approaches to the regulation of public infrastructure services which gained importance from the 1980s, such as New Public Management, promoted a consumer-centred policy design and evaluation. And yet for all the discussion of consumers, consumer and citizen satisfaction with these services was only marginalised in the design of regulatory policies. Little was therefore known about the effectiveness of these reforms from the citizen/consumer perspective. In the light of increased attention to supply-side considerations, as evidenced for instance in the importance assigned to insights from Behavioural Economics in policy-making, more interest is being shown by international organizations such as the EU, the OECD and national governments in combining supply-side with demand-side regulation.

This chapter sought to enquire what could be learnt from examining the demand-side for better regulation. Contrasting stated and declared preferences shows that both sources can be complementary, and their combination can provide a better understanding of user behaviour. Individually, stated and revealed preference-based analysis has limitations. Combining analysis of stated and revealed preferences consists of an innovative approach which helps to partially overcome these limitations. At the same time, information problems which occur in the policy-making process can be partially improved using this approach. And it is often these informational problems which affect the efficient functioning of the market in the cases of the infrastructure services. A better understanding of consumer behaviour can be used to improve regulation during the design and implementation stages. It should also promote increasing consumer confidence to take advantage of the potential benefits opened up by competition and liberalization. The empirical work here focused on the case of Spain in the context of the reform of EU-wide regulatory policies. This analysis is part of a wider research project focused on the evaluation of regulatory reform in different countries and regions.

4.2. *Implications for Regulatory Design: Effectiveness and Operation*

Results obtained underline the importance of evaluating regulatory reform of infrastructure services from the demand-side using a better understanding of consumer satisfaction and behaviour. Analysis based on stated preferences (*Eurobarometers*) shows that the most used services are electricity and water, followed by fixed phone and mobile phone. Gas and internet are less used services. In addition, variables related to service perception are the main factors explaining service use. The main factor is accessibility and, in the case of telecommunication services, also its perceived importance. Another relevant factor in all cases is affordability, although this has a lower incidence. Factors related to personal characteristics have a limited incidence on use: while some factors are relevant explaining use of some of the services, none are significant in all cases. Contrasting stated and revealed preferences reveals that both gas and internet are services exhibiting territorial accessibility problems. This problem does not exist in the case of water, since its lower cost is the reason for the lower spending in rural areas. Territorial accessibility is not a key aspect either in telephony services, as mobile phones increasingly substitute for fixed phone use and expenditure.

Revealed preference-based analysis shows relevant effects of individual related characteristics on expenditure on the universal services such as electricity and water. In general, a positive relation is observed between being a foreigner and expenditure on electricity and water, on the one hand, and between age and expenditure on water, on the other. In contrast, one-parent families are associated with lower expenditure on electricity and water. In telecommunications, where the possibility of choice is greater, fixed telephony expenditure is directly related to age. This holds even when mobile phone expenditure is included as an explanatory variable. Additional expenditure of between 2.4 and 2.6 Euros for each additional year is estimated. This age-related effect is greater in telecommunications than in the other services. Moreover, *Eurobarometer* data shows that the older a person is, the more likely they will exhibit a passive attitude towards telecommunications and more difficulty when comparing different offers between telecommunications firms. In addition, when fixed and mobile phones are considered jointly, an inverse relation is observed between expenditure and educational attainment. Annual savings in telecommunications are estimated at 33 Euros for people that have received further education, this saving increases to 36 Euros for graduates and to 77 Euros for those with advanced graduate studies. Educational attainment is not a relevant variable when explaining expenditure on services where there is less choice (electricity, water and gas). Moreover, *Eurobarometer* data shows that individuals with lower educational attainments claim they have greater difficulties when comparing different options available amongst telecommunications firms. They state also, in the case of mobile telephony, a more passive attitude towards the service, lower satisfaction with contract conditions and lower perception of consumer interest protection.

The importance of analysing and understanding consumer behaviour and its relation to individual and environmental variables is reinforced with other effects estimated. Firstly, inertia is important, through personal-related variables, explaining the use of substitutive services as fixed and mobile phones. Secondly, a family support effect is observed — there is less expenditure in households with a younger reference person — in the context of a Latino-Mediterranean Welfare State (Guillén & Álvarez, 2004). Last but not least, the incidence of personal attributes such as employment or marital status on individual preferences is observed, reflected in expenditure on some services. The results obtained show a relationship between expenditure and certain personal-related variables. Many of these patterns are consistent with those derived from stated preferences. These results show how psychological and socio-economic elements affect consumer behaviour vis-à-vis infrastructure services. This reinforces the argument that better understanding the consumer from this perspective can improve regulatory quality.

4.3. *Lessons for Regulators: What Works, What doesn't?*

Analysis of the development of infrastructure regulation over time, and the presentation here of results from an examination of revealed and stated preferences support the argument that regulators would do well to design and implement policies jointly based on competition policies (the supply-side perspective) in addition to consumer policies (the demand-side perspective). Improved regulation, as a result of better understanding consumers, could result in helping consumers benefit more from the potential advantages of liberalization and competition of services. Ideally, better regulation should diminish cases where citizens do not take the optimal decision when consuming these services, such as inertia to switch.

This paper has confirmed that homogeneous consumers do not exist. So, clearly, regulatory policies could have heterogeneous effects depending on the characteristics of the consumer in question. Estimated effects and recommendations derived from them should not be applied in the same way across all the services analysed here, though several common patterns are observed. Instead, regulators would do well to consider which of the findings from an analysis of the demand-side would best translate into an improvement in the quality of regulation. Interestingly, certain private firms have been quite alert to the fact that consumers are not homogenous, and are affected by the social context surrounding them. Commercial strategy by some fixed phone providers has started to offer special discounts to particular groups such as the unemployed or foreigners. Spanish Telefónica has a tariff called "We Help You," while Vodafone in Italy has a reduced tariff for foreigners. Clearly, these tariffs are not altruistic, rather, they implement price discrimination in order to avoid losing customers, particularly in the current times of crisis. In contrast, policy-makers are slow to implement new regulatory policies based on concepts such as consumer heterogeneity and behavioural dimensions. Indeed, the current crisis only emphasises the importance of consumer's social and economic situation, which understood dynamically, can affect consumption patterns. Regulators should move more quickly, with different objectives to firms, to address issues of service consumption from the demand-side in order to improve regulatory quality and service consumption.

References

Australian Government, Productivity Commission (2007). *Conference Behavioral Economics and Public Policy.* 8–9 August.

Australian Government (2008). *Productivity Commission Inquiry into Australia's Consumer Policy Framework.* Available at http://www.treasurer.gov.au/DisplayDocs.aspx?pageID=&doc=pressreleases/2006/133.htm&min=phc.

Bacchiocchi, E, M Florio and M Gambaro (2008). Telecom Prices, Regulatory Reforms and Consumers' Satisfaction: Evidence for 15 EU Countries. *Working Paper,* 2008–10, *Dipartimento di Scienze Economiche Aziendali e Statistiche, Università degli Studi di Milano.*

Balanyá, B, A Doherty, O Hoedeman, A Ma'nit and E Wesselius (2000), *Europe Inc: Regional and Global Restructuring and the Rise of Corporate Power.* London: Pluto Press.

CEEP (European Centre of Enterprises with Public Participation and of Enterprises of General Economic Interest) and ETUC (European Trade Union Confederation) (2000). *Proposal for a Charter for Services of General Interest.* Available at http://www.ceep.org/en/documents/ceep_projects_studies/charterSGI_En.pdf.

Clarke, J, J Newman, N Smith, E Vilder and L Westmarland (2007). *Creating Citizen-Consumers: Changing Publics and Changing Public Services.* London: Sage.

Clifton, J, F Comín and D Díaz-Fuentes (2003). *Privatization in the European Union: Public Enterprise and Integration.* Dordrecht: Kluwer.

Clifton, J, F Comín and D Díaz-Fuentes (2005). Empowering Europe's citizens? On the prospects for the charter of services of general interest. *Public Management Review,* 7(3), pp. 417–443.

Clifton, J, F Comín and D Díaz-Fuentes (2006). Privatization in the European Union: Ideological, pragmatic, inevitable? *Journal of European Public Policy,* 13(5), pp. 736–756.

Clifton, J, F Comín and D Díaz-Fuentes (eds) (2007). *Transforming Public Enterprise in Europe and North America: Networks, Integration and Transnationalization.* New York/London: Palgrave.

Clifton, J and D Díaz-Fuentes (2010). Evaluating EU policies on public services: A citizen's perspective. *Annals of Public and Cooperative Economics,* 81(2) pp. 279–306.

Clifton, J, D Díaz-Fuentes and J Revuelta (2010). The political economy of incumbent internationalization in the single market. *Journal of European Public Policy,* 17(7) (In print).

DG SANCO (2008). *How Can Behavioural Economics Improve Policies Affecting Consumers?* Conference held in Brussels, 28 November.

EC (1997). *Eurobarometer 47.0: L´Europe des Consummateurs, Les Citoyens face a l´ouverture a la concurrence des monopoles de services public.* Brussels: EC.

EC (2000). *Communication on Services of General Interest in Europe.* Brussels: EC.

EC (2002). *Eurobarometer 58: Consumers' Opinions About Services of General Interest.* Brussels: EC.

EC (2003a). *CCEB Eurobarometer European Consumers and Services of General Interest.* Brussels: EC.

EC (2003b). *Green Paper on Services of General Interest.* Brussels: EC. Available at http://www.europa.eu.int/eur-lex/en/com/gpr/2003/com2003_0270en01.pdf.

European Commission (EC) (2004). *White Paper on Services of General Interest.* Brussels: EC. Available at http://europa.eu.int/comm/secretariat_general/services_general_interest/docs/com2004_374_en.pdf.

EC (2005). *Eurobarometer 219.* Brussels: EC.

EC (2006). *Eurobarometer Special: Services of General Interest,* No 260, Wave 65.3. Brussels: EC.

EC (2007a). Communication from the Commission to the Council, the European Parliament and the European Economic and Social Committee, EU Consumer Policy strategy 2007–2013. Empowering Consumers, Enhancing Their Welfare, Effectively Protecting Them. Available at http://ec.europa.eu/consumers/overview/cons_policy/doc/EN_99.pdf. Accessed on 15 August 2009.

EC (2007b). *Eurobarometer 260.* Brussels: EC.

Eurostat (Statistical Office of the European Communities) (2009). *Household Budget Surveys.* Available at http://europa.eu.int/estatref/info/sdds/en/hbs/hbs_base.htm.

Federal Trade Commission (2007). *Behavioural Economics and Consumer Policy.* Conference sponsored by the Bureau of Economics Federal Trade Commission. New Jersey, 20 April.

Fiorio, CV, M Florio, S Salini and P Ferrari (2007). European Consumers's Attitudes on Services of General Interest: Accessibility, Price and Quality. Working Paper, 2007-04, Dipartimento di Scienze Economiche Aziendali e Statistiche, Università degli Studi di Milano.

Fiorio, CV and M Florio (2008). Do you Pay a Fair Price for Electricity? Consumers' Satisfaction and Utility Reform in the EU. Working Paper, 2008-12, Dipartimento di Scienze Economiche Aziendali e Statistiche, Università degli Studi di Milano.

Fletcher, A (2008). *What do Policy-makers Need from Behavioural Economists?* Unpublished paper delivered at the DG SANCO Conference. *How can Behavioural Economics Improve Policies Affecting Consumers?* Brussels, 28 November.

Frei, BS and A Stutzer (2002). What can economists learn from happiness research? *Journal of Economic Literature*, XL, pp. 402–435.

Galambos, L (2000). State-owned enterprises in a hostile environment: The U.S. experience. In *The Rise and Fall of State-Owned Enterprise in the Western World*, Toninelli, PA (ed.), pp. 273–302. Cambridge: Cambridge University Press.

Goldstein, A (2007). *Multinational Companies from Emerging Economies.* New York: Palgrave Macmillan.

Guillén, A and S Álvarez (2004). The EU's impact on the Spanish welfare state: The role of cognitive europeanisation. *Journal of European Social Policy*, 14(3), pp. 285–299.

Hermann, C, K Verhoest, M Andersson, T Brandt, I Hofbauer, T Schulten and C Thörnqvist (2007). *Varieties and Variations of Public-service Liberalisation and Privatisation in Europe.* Vienna: FORBA, Forschungs und Beratungsstelle Arbeitswelt.

Hirschman, AO (1970). *Exit, Voice, and Loyalty: Responses to Decline in Firms, Organisations, and States.* Cambridge MA: Harvard University Press.

Hood, C (2001). A public management for all seasons? *Public Administration*, 69(1), pp. 3–19.

INE (Instituto Nacional de Estadística) (2006). *Encuesta de Presupuestos Familiares.* Madrid: INE.

Kahneman, D (2002). Maps of Bounded Rationality: A Perspective on Intuitive Judgement and Choice, Nobel Prize Lecture, 8 December.

Louis, VJ and S Rodrigues (2006). *Les services d'intérêt économique général et l'Union européene.* Brussels: Bruylantm.

Mangenot, M (ed.) (2005). *Administrations publiques et services d'interêt général: quelle européanisation.* Maastricht: European Institute of Public Administration.

McGuire, A (2002). Service charters — Global convergence or national divergence? A comparison of initiatives in Australia, the United Kingdom and the United States. *Public Management Review*, 4(1), pp. 493–524.

Mulholland, JP (2007). *US perspective: Behavioural economics and the Federal Trade Commission*, Working Paper Series, Westport63 Consulting.

OECD (2007). *Roundtable on Demand-Side Economics for Consumer Policy Summary Report.* Paris: OECD.

OECD (2008). *Enhancing Competition in Telecommunication: Protecting and Empowering Consumers.* Paris: OECD.

OECD (2009). *Focus on Citizens. Public Engagement for Better Policy and Services.* Paris: OECD.

Prosser, T (ed.) (2005). *The Limits of Competition Law: Markets and Public Services.* Oxford: Oxford University Press.

Van de Walle, S (2006). The Impact of Public Service Values on Services of General Interest Reform Debates. *Public Management Review*, 8, pp. 183–205.

Vickers, J (2003). *Economics for Consumer Policy, Keynes Lecture in Economics*, 29 October, The British Academy. Available at http://www.britac.ac.uk/pubs/src/_pdf /vickers.pdf. (Accessed on 24 August 2007).

CHAPTER 3

Does Political Accountability Matter for Infrastructure Regulation? The Case of Telecommunications*

Farid Gasmi

Toulouse School of Economics (ARQADE & IDEI)
Université Toulouse 1 Capitole, France

Paul Noumba

The World Bank, Washington, DC, USA

and

Laura Recuero Virto

OECD, Paris, France

This paper discusses the link between political accountability, regarded as an important aspect of institutional design, and infrastructure regulation that has been emphasized in the recent literature on the role of institutions in economic development. We report on the findings and lessons drawn from an analysis of telecommunications data covering the period

* Corresponding author: farid.gasmi@tse-fr.eu. This paper is based on Gasmi *et al.* (2009). We thank participants of the conference on *Infrastructure Regulation, What works, Why, and How do we know?* Hong Kong, February 26–27, 2009, jointly organized by the University of Hong Kong, LIRNEasia, and The Institute of Water Policy of The Lee Kuan Yew School of Public Policy, Singapore, for useful comments on an earlier version. This version has benefited from the suggestions of the editors of this volume. All remaining errors are that of authors.

1985–1999 on two sets of countries; one comprising 29 developing countries and the other 23 developed countries. The main point higlighted by the analysis is that infrastructure regulation in any country cannot be independent of the institutional environment, in particular, the degree of political accountability that supports the country's institutions. The argument is demonstrated by means of an econometric estimation of dynamic panel data models that shows evidence of a significant effect of pro- political accountability factors on regulatory performance as reflected in measures of sector output and efficiency. Expectedly enough, this effect is found to be more pronounced in the developing countries data set. A key policy implication of this result is that efforts to enhance institutional quality and support politically accountable systems in developing countries should yield large benefits for infrastructure regulation.

Keywords: Infrastructure regulation; regulatory performance; political accountability.

1. Introduction

Over the past two decades, economic reforms have significantly affected the organizational and institutional landscape of infrastructure sectors including telecommunications, electricity, water, and the like. In developed countries, the main purpose of the reforms is to enhance the efficiency of these sectors that are traditionally organized as vertically integrated monopolies. The policy objective in these countries has then been to redesign the legal and regulatory framework so as to induce "proper" economic incentives, namely, incentives for operators in the infrastructure sectors to improve their cost efficiency, quality of service, and tariffs.

While the reforms conducted in developing countries follow the same principles, they differ in their implementation in at least two respects. First, even though there was clearly a room for improving the performance of infrastructure sectors in developed countries, the availability of service did not pose a fundamental problem. In contrast, in developing countries service was sometimes merely non-existent and, in the case of telecommunications, networks were not developed in large parts of the rural areas. Second, institutional design in developing countries was far more challenging than in developed countries. Developed countries typically needed to modernize an existing social and institutional fabric with a complex system of operating rules built over a long history of political and economic administration of market economies. This crucial experience was just lacking in developing countries. Beyond the fact that these countries with poor human capital endowments had to follow the industrialized world in the setting of totally new institutions, they had to reform their old inadequate administrative functioning rules.

After a period of implementation of policies of liberalization and privatization of some segments coupled with the creation of regulatory authorities, efforts have been made to improve the efficiency of these authorities. Independent regulatory authorities, capacity of human resources, and quality of regulatory governance in the sector are the three policy items that have mobilized much of these efforts. On the research front, however, both theoretical work on the optimal design of regulatory institutions and empirical work on the measurement of regulatory institutions' performance suggest that these specific items should not be considered independently from factors related to the governance of the economy as a whole. This paper is concerned with the relative weight of these sector-specific and economy-wide determinants of the performance of infratrsucture regualtion. It reports on an investigation of this issue in the case of telecommunications through econometric analysis of two data sets: one on developing countries and another on developed countries.

The determinants of regulatory performance have been discussed both in the theoretical and empirical streams of the literature on infrastructure industries regulation. We distinguish the two approaches. The first approach is conceptual in nature and inspired by political science. It argues that when thinking about regulatory performance, the relevant game is the one that takes place upstream at the (higher) level of politics (Spiller and Tommasi, 2005). The second and a more empirical approach emphasizes the impact of regulatory governance on performance (Cubbin and Stern, 2005b). Our view is that the relationship between political and regulatory structures and processes has to be given due attention when assessing regulatory performance. Hence, our study attempts to merge both approaches in order to incorporate some empirical elements into the debate on the relationship between political and regulatory institutions that has so far taken place at a conceptual level.

The empirical strategy adopted is based on a set of econometric regressions with special attention paid to variables that give some indications on the "degree" of political accountability that characterize the economic institutions of a country. How politically accountable an economic system is depends on the existence and the degree of implementability of "...a proactive process by which public officials inform about and justify their plans of action, their behavior and results, and are sanctioned accordingly" (Ackerman, 2005). We consider political accountability as a fundamental factor in the exercise of the link between political structures and regulatory processes and hence view its (political-game) equilibrium level as an important determinant of the regulatory process' performance. This leads to our hypothesis that, if all things are kept equal, "more" political accountability should enhance the performance of infrastructure regulation. A further conjecture that the empirical analysis allows us to test is that this hypothesis finds stronger support in the data on developing countries.[1]

This chapter is organized as follows. The next section describes theoretical and empirical arguments, developed in the recent literatures, on the design of institutions and on the evaluation of regulatory performance in infrastructure sectors. This section is by no means an exhaustive survey, but its goal is to show that there is a need to merge these two streams of the literature on regulatory institutions. Section 3 is devoted to the description of the data and a discussion of their general properties. Section 4 discusses the findings of our empirical analysis of the relationship between political accountability and the performance of infrastructure regulation. Section 5 summarizes the empirical results and discusses some policy implications. The appendix gives some standard summary statistics of the data.

2. Institutional and Regulatory Design and Outcomes — What Do We Know?

Recent contributions to the theory of the design of institutions and empirical work concerned with the measurement of their performance have

[1] From a normative perspective, since a better regulatory performance is expected to improve social welfare, this would suggest that marginal social benefit of political accountability is higher in developing countries.

brought to daylight the issue of the evaluation of the performance of regulation. Laffont (2005) provides some edifying thoughts on the design of regulatory institutions in developing countries.

Two approaches have been adopted to examine the determinants of regulatory performance and outcomes. The first approach is conceptual and analyzes the role of political structures and processes. The second approach is more empirical, and emphasizes the impact of the quality of regulatory governance. We briefly review the main arguments that arise in the two approaches and point to the need to develop a unified analytical framework. This paper is an empirical effort in this direction.

The first approach analyzes the relationship between political structures and processes and the conduct of regulation by emphasizing the need to open the black box of the organization and functioning of governments (Estache and Martimort, 1999; North, 2000).[2] In their analysis of the link between politics and regulation in the US, McCubbins *et al.* (1987) argue that by reducing the costs of monitoring and by sharpening sanctions, administrative procedures can give rise to an equilibrium in which compliance with the preferences of political agents is greater than it otherwise would be.[3] This relationship is further explored by Levy and Spiller (1994) in the telecommunications sector through an analysis of case studies. In particular, they evaluate the potential for political agents to manipulate the regulatory process. They find that sector performance can be satisfactory under a wide range of regulatory procedures as long as arbitrary administrative decisions can be restrained.

The link between the political and regulatory spheres is further analyzed by Spiller and Tommasi (2005) through the impact that the characteristics of political environments have on the ability of political agents to reach intertemporal cooperation. They argue that long-term

---

[2] By emphasizing the political game, this approach fits in the *New Institutional Economics* paradigm that takes its foundations in the precepts of transaction cost theory and positive political economy. This paradigm constitutes an important departure from the standard normative approach to public economics.

[3] Bottom-up "fire-alarm" monitoring through external agents affected by regulatory policies is a good example of a method that can reduce the informational costs of following the activities of agencies (McCubbins and Schwartz, 1984).

political cooperation is likely to lead to stable and flexible regulatory policies, hence, to effective regulation. This is particularly true when the agents with decision power have strong intertemporal relationships, policy and political moves are widely observable, good enforcement technologies are available, and the short-run payoffs from noncooperation are not so high. They further argue that less efficient regulatory rules resulting from a rigid regulatory context may in fact provide incentives for investment whereas granting discretion to the regulator may lead to arbitrary outcomes if institutional endowments are low.

Heller and McCubbins (1996) argue that incentives for investing in infrastructure industries are not credible within a given regulatory structure, unless there is a political context that makes them sustainable. Regulatory predictability is a key feature for gaining credibility and political institutions play an important role in enhancing this predictability. The higher the quality of the political and institutional environment, the harder it is to change regulatory structures and procedures. In particular, the more veto political players with effective authority there are, the easier it is to block policy change. The main argument of this line of policy research is that the more established political structures and processes, the higher the cost of institutional change, and the more efficient the conduct of regulation.

Let us now briefly review the empirical approach that emphasizes the role of regulatory governance. The fundamental belief that motivates much of this line of research that essentially deals with infrastructure industries is that good regulatory governance is a prerequisite to a proper functioning of the positive relationship between regulatory incentives and regulatory performance. This belief is based on the conjecture that "...regulatory agencies with better governance should make fewer mistakes, have their mistakes identified and rectified better and more quickly, so that good regulatory practice is more readily established and maintained" (Cubbin and Stern, 2000a).

The basic empirical implications of these hypotheses is that, thanks to the structuring and the practice of regulation it entails, e.g., as an independent regulator making transparent regulatory decisions, better regulatory governance increases supply capacity and enhances productive and allocative efficiency. In the case of telecommunications, these implications are typically tested in data collected on a set of developing countries observed during a given time period. Regulatory performance is measured by mainline penetration rates and/or mainlines per employee, and regulatory governance is captured in an index that aggregates a set of aspects related to the structure and internal organization of regulation (Gutierrez, 2003a).[4] Overall, when applied to telecommunications (Gutierrez, 2003b) and electricity (Cubbin and Stern, 2005a), the methodology yields a positive impact of regulatory governance on such regulatory output measures. For a survey of empirical studies on regulatory governance and performance in developing countries, see Cubin and Stern (2005b).

A typical contribution to this line of research starts from the global conceptual view that "...institutional quality is the dominant determinant of variations in long-term growth performance." (See Cubbin and Stern, 2005a and the citations thereof) However, when it comes to implementation, often it only accounts for micro dimensions of institutional quality embodied in what is referred to as the quality of regulatory governance. Our view is that this approach should substantially gain in richness by drawing lessons from the literature on the design of institutions discussed earlier in this section. We adopt a unified approach that — when evaluating regulatory performance, in addition to specifying variables of regulatory governance — explicitly incorporates variables linking political and regulatory structures and processes. In our analysis, the variables through which the interface between political and regulatory structures and processes is going to materialize are variables that are used to proxy the concept of political accountability as described in the introduction.

This approach assumes that limiting the use and sanctioning the abuse of political power should help disentangling regulatory processes from the opportunistic behavior of political agents.[5] The elections

[4] Our study as well as this study uses (indirect) outcome variables to measure regulatory performance. An alternative (more direct) assessment of regulatory performance entails conducting surveys to capture the quality of regulators' decisions which ultimately impact sector outcomes (see, for e.g., Correa *et al.*, 2008; Brown *et al.*, 2006). Such surveys do not exist but would definitely, if undertaken, provide a better indication of the performance of regulation in infrastructure industries.

[5] As noted by Spiller and Tommasi (2005), opportunistic behavior of politicians can be expected in infrastructure industries because of the important economic stakes involved.

mechanism should, in principle, ensure political accountability since citizens select representatives who hold bureaucrats and members of the judiciary system accountable for their behavior. However, this characteristic of elections is hard to satisfy since the electoral process suffers from important information asymmetries between elected politicians and citizens and lack of politicians *ex post* accountability. Privatization of government monopolies, liberalization, and the application of private management principles to state-owned entreprises, have been proven to improve political agents' accountability in a much more targeted way. However, when analyzing regulatory performance, beyond giving full consideration to such pro-accountability reforms as the above "marketization" policies, to the independence of the regulator, and to other factors related to the sector's regulatory governance, we think that it is also important to give due attention to other pro-accountability factors that are related to the governance of the economy as a whole. The implementation of this idea is central to our empirical study. The next section discusses about this.

3. Data on Regulatory Outcomes and Institutional Environment

This section gives a broad description of the data used in this study and discusses some of their general charcteristics. We have constructed and analyzed separately two data sets both covering the period 1985–1999, one on developing countries and another on developed countries.[6] The countries included in the data set on developing countries are: India, Sri Lanka, Malaysia, Pakistan, Thailand, Ivory Coast, Ghana, Kenya, Malawi, Tanzania, Uganda, South Africa, Jordan, Morocco, Argentina, Bolivia, Brazil, Chile, Colombia, Costa Rica, Dominican Republic, Ecuador, Guatemala, Honduras, Jamaica, Panama, Peru, El Salvador, and

[6] The choice of analyzing separately the two data sets reflects our attitude towards the issue that, when pooling them, we necessarily face the tradeoff between potential gains in estimates efficiency associated with data sample size and potential estimates inconsistency associated with high data heterogeneity.

Table 1: Variables and designation

Variable	Designation
Regulatory performance	
ml	Mainline penetration
cel	Cellular subscription
eff	Mainlines per employee
p_res	Monthly subscription to fixed
p_cel	Price of cellular
Local accountability	
reg	Regulatory governance index
Global accountability	
corruption	Corruption
bureau	Bureaucracy
law	Law and order
expropri	Expropriation
currency	Currency risk
institutional	Institutional environment index
checks	Checks and balances
Other variables	
priva	Privatization
comp_fix	Competition in fixed
comp_cel	Competition in cellular
rural	Rural population
density	Population density

Venezuela. Those included in the data set on developed countries are: Australia, Austria, Belgium, Canada, Denmark, Finland, France, Germany, Greece, Iceland, Ireland, Italy, Japan, Luxembourg, Netherlands, New Zealand, Norway, Portugal, Spain, Sweden, Switzerland, United Kingdom, and United States. For each of these countries, we have collected information on variables regrouped into the four categories: "Regulatory performance," "Local accountability," "Global accountability," and "Other variables." Table 1 gives the list of these variables along with their designation.

As indicated above, regulatory performance is measured by the level of output (mainline penetration or cellular subscription), efficiency (mainlines per employee), or price (fixed residential, cellular).[7] In view of the conceptual framework discussed in the previous section, we have regrouped variables that indicate the existence of political accountability into variables of "local" and "global" accountability that represent the quality of regulatory governance in the sector and political governance at the level of the whole economy respectively. Therefore, local accountability is captured in variables reflecting the degree of political and financial independence of the regulator, the level of transparency of accounts and regulatory decisions, the clarity of the allocation of responsibilities among institutions, the nature of the legal environment, and the degree of social participation in regulatory decisions.[8] The global accountability is captured in variables reflecting the quality of the institutional framework (government integrity, efficiency of bureaucracy, strength of courts and enforcement capacity, government commitment capacity, and currency risk) and the quality of the political process (strength of checks and balances).[9]

The variables in the group of other variables are introduced to control the effects that are deemed important when estimating the relationship between political accountability and regulatory performance. Given that the telecommunications sector has undergone significant market structure changes during the period under study, we have included some reform

[7] These outcome variables are indirect measures of regulatory performance based on objective data on regulated firms as opposed to direct measures based on subjective data reported by surveyed regulatory agencies.

[8] Our study contributes to the literature on the impact of the infrastructure industries reforms by extending the set of variables capturing regulatory governance. In that respect, it stands along the line of Gutierrez (2003b) and Holder and Stern (1999) who have constructed detailed indices of regulators' characteristics in Latin American countries for the telecom sector, and in Asian countries for the electricity sector, respectively. The importance of these dimensions for regulatory agencies to be sustainable has been repeatedly emphasized (Estache and Martimort, 1999). In our data samples, in 26 of the 29 developing countries and 21 of the 23 developed countries, the regulator has become independent at some point during the period under study.

[9] Both the empirical and theoretical literatures suggest that it is not so much the extent of democracy that is relevant to investors, but rather the ability of the government to credibly commit to a policy regime. The level of policy stability is captured here through an index that indicates whether there exists an "effective" number of checks and balances.

variables that indicate the privatization of the incumbent and the introduction of competition in fixed and cellular service as the liberalization of these segments has arguably had different market implications (Gasmi and Recuero Virto, 2009). During the period spanned by our samples both developing and developed countries, countries have been extensively engaged in reforms of their telecommunications industries formerly organized as state monopolies. In our data set on 29 developing countries, 18 of these countries have partially privatized their historical operator, 14 have introduced competition in the local fixed-line segment, and 24 have introduced competition in the cellular segment. In our data set on 23 developed countries, these figures are 20, 10, and 15 respectively. In both types of countries, the reforms have coincided with the introduction of new technologies that have significantly reduced costs and increased demand. We have also included in this group of control variables some country-specific demand features that indicate population (density) and its distribution (urban vs rural).

Table 2 presents the correlation coefficients between the variables representing regulatory performance and political accountability.[10] We see from this table that the correlation between the variables of regulatory performance and political accountability is generally stronger for developing countries compared to those of developed countries. This is much more

Table 2: Correlation coefficients (developing countries, developed countries)

		Regulatory performance				
		ml	*cel*	*eff*	*p_res*	*p_cel*
Global accountability	*Institutional*	(0.41, 0.63)	(0.65, 0.24)	(0.42, 0.22)	(0.23, 0.28)	(0.60, 0.01)
	checks	(0.34, 0.07)	(0.39, 0.04)	(0.36, 0.01)	(−0.01, 0.12)	(0.30, 0.24)
Local accountability	*reg*	(0.19, 0.43)	(0.57, 0.55)	(0.30, 0.05)	(−0.06, 0.01)	(0.61,−0.07)

Note: In any entry (a, b) of the table, 'a' represents the developing countries and 'b' the developed countries.

[10] Table A1 in the appendix provides some summary statistics of the data on the developing and developed countries.

evident when regulatory performance is measured by mainline penetration, cellular subscription, or mainlines per employee, and political accountability is captured by the strength of checks and balances. The same hold true when regulatory performance is measured by mainlines per employee and political accountability is captured by the regulatory governance index, and when regulatory performance is measured by cellular subscription or price of cellular and political accountability is captured by the quality of the institutional environment. We also note that, in both samples, the regulatory performance variables tend to correlate relatively "more"' with the variables that reflect the quality of the broad institutional environment than those that reflect the quality of regulatory governance in the sector.

It is interesting to examine the evolution of these variables over the period spanned by the samples. When measured by mainline penetration, cellular subscription, or mainlines per employee, regulatory performance has, on average, increased twice as much in developing countries than in developed countries. This relatively higher increase of output in developing countries most likely reflects the fact that the demand that was not met was considerably more important in these countries in the early part of period. In contrast, when measured by the monthly subscription to the fixed service, which has increased in both developing and developed countries, or the price of cellular, which has decreased, regulatory performance has improved noticeably more in developed countries. However, this conclusion should be moderated. First, the significantly higher increase of the monthly subscription to the fixed telephone service in developing countries might be due to the fact that policies of tariff re-balancing have been relatively more intense in these countries. Second, the significantly lower decrease of price of cellular in developing countries might reflect a relatively less mature and hence less effective competition in this segment of the market than in developed countries.

To conclude, we find that the quality of the institutional environment and the political process has shown a relatively higher improvement in developing countries during the period under study. However, it should be noted that these countries were considerably lagging behind on these two dimensions.

4. Does Political Accountability Affect Regulatory Performance?

As indicated above, our investigation of the effect of political accountability on regulatory performance relies on a set of regressions.[11] While the estimation of the coefficients of these regressions allows us to assess the (quantitative) impact of the political accountability variables on the regulatory performance variables, asking ourselves whether there exists a causal relationship between these variables will allow us to meaningfully interpret this impact. We, therefore, performed some causality tests.[12] Table 3 summarizes our findings on the existence of causal relationships in the two data sets analyzed.

Table 3: (Granger -) Causality relationships (developing countries, developed countries)

Regulatory performance	Local accountability	Global accountability	
	reg	*institutional*	*checks*
ml	(Yes, No)	(Yes, Yes)	(Yes, No)
cel	(No, Yes)	(Yes, Yes)	(Yes, Yes)
eff	(No, No)	(Yes, No)	(No, No)
p_res	(Yes, Yes)	(Yes, Yes)	(Yes, No)
p_cel	(Yes, No)	(Yes, No)	(No, No)

Notes: (1) In any entry (a,b) of this table, 'a' represents the developing countries and 'b' the developed countries.
(2) A "Yes" ("No") indicates that evidence of a causal relationship running from the accountability variable to the regulatory performance variable has (has not) been found.

[11] In these regressions, the dependent variable is one that measures regulatory performance and the independent variables that retain much of our attention are those that are used to capture political accountability. We apply the Differenced Generalized Method of Moments (DIF-GMM) method developed by Arellano and Bond (1991) for analyzing panel data and applied by Beck and Katz (2004) to Time Series Cross-Sectional data. A technical issue that we addressed prior to estimation is that of stationarity of the dependent variable. To address stationarity, we followed a method sugested by Blundell and Bond (1998, 1999). See also Arellano and Bover (1995).

[12] These tests combine the DIF-GMM estimation technique with a Granger-causality testing procedure developed in Holtz-Eakin *et al.* (1988) for panel data.

From Table 3 we see that, overall, the results support the proposition that in both developing and developed countries there exists a causal relationship between political accountability and regulatory performance. This is particularly true when political accountability concerns the institutional environment. The results also show that global accountability variables seem to be in a stronger causal relationship with regulatory performance than local accountability variables, and this is even more so in developing countries. Even though the empirical evidence of such relationships is admittedly stronger in the data on developing countries, we feel that the importance of the issue from a policy point of view warrants a careful analysis of the quantitative aspects of these relationships.

The preliminary analysis of the data performed so far sets the ground for a scrutiny of the relationship between political accountability and regulatory performance in the two data sets. In addition to bringing empirical evidence on the causal relationship between political accountability and regulatory performance, the Granger-causality tests provided us with information on the dynamic structure of this relationship. The end-product of this testing procedure is a list of potential variables to be included as regressors when estimating the quantitative impact of political accountability on regulatory performance. In order to minimize the risk of estimation inaccuracy, a serious threat in the context of dynamic data analysis which is ours, we made sure that, when needed, the variables used to measure regulatory performance, the dependent variables, were transformed so as to make them stationary. The next step was to run DIF-GMM regressions using political accountability regressors drawn from the set of variables that have "passed" the causality test and for both the developing countries and developed data panels.

Concerning the developing countries data, we find that, for any of the five variables used to measure regulatory performance, there is at least one variable used to represent political accountability that significantly affects it. Except when regulatory performance is measured by the monthly subscription to fixed, the sign of this impact is as expected, namely, the higher the degree of political accountability, the better the regulatory performance as reflected in higher output (increase in mainline penetration and cellular subscription), higher efficiency (increase in mainlines per employee), and lower prices (decrease in price of cellular).

The apparently counterintuitive case where we find that higher political accountability (less risk of expropriation for operators and stronger checks and balances) leads to a higher monthly subscription to fixed service might in fact only reflect the extent of tariff rebalancing that took place in developing countries during the early stages of the reforms. When we distinguish local accountability (regulatory governance) from global accountability, we find that the latter is more often found to have a significant impact on regulatory performance. Nevertheless, in the cases when it is found to be significant, the effect of regulatory governance on regulatory performance has the expected sign, namely, a better regulatory governance leads to a higher output and a lower price.

The results obtained with the data on the developed countries convey quite different messages and are generally less strong than those obtained with the data set on the developing countries. In fact, some reasonable regressions are found only when regulatory performance is measured by mainline penetration, cellular subscription, or monthly subscription to fixed. With respect to the impact of political accountability on regulatory performance, the results obtained with the data on developed countries are a positive effect of regulatory governance and checks and balances on cellular subscription and a monthly subscription to the fixed service that decreases when the currency risk to operators diminishes.

In both data sets, the time-specific effects are highly significant suggesting that the performance of regulation is also affected by important political and economic events that occured in a given country. We also find that the reform variables are endogenous in all the regressions except when regulatory performance was measured by cellular subscription and by the monthly subscription to fixed in the data set on developing countries, and by the monthly subscription to fixed in the data set on developed countries. These results are consistent with the idea that reforms are increasingly performance-based.[13]

These findings suggest that the local accountability — synonymous in this paper to regulatory governance — generally affects regulatory

[13] The endogenous nature of regulatory policies has been discussed in Gasmi and Recuero Virto (2009), Gutierrez (2003), and Ros (1999, 2003) among others.

performance in a significant way in developing as well as developed countries. This is not in the case of global accountability. In the data set on developing countries, we found that the quality of the political process and the institutional environment have a favorable impact on regulatory performance when the latter is evaluated by the level of output, price, or efficiency in the telecommunications industry. In contrast, in the data set on developed countries, while the quality of the political process has been found to have a positive impact on regulatory performance when the latter is measured by achieved output, the institutional environment showed an ambiguous impact when regulatory performance is measured by output and prices.

Table 4 summarizes our findings. In this table, the signs "+" and "–" respectively indicate a positive and a negative impact of the political accountability variable indicated in the column on the regulatory performance variable indicated in the row. The variable *institutional* which is an index reflecting the quality of the institutional environment, is constructed by aggregating five indices reflecting the extent of corruption in the country (*corruption*), the burden of the bureaucracy (*bureau*), the strength of the judicial system and the degree of observance of the law (*law*), the risk of expropriation through outright asset confiscation or

Table 4: Impact of political accountability on regulatory performance (developing countries,developed countries)

Regulatory performance	Local accountability	Global accountability	
	reg	*institutional*	*checks*
ml	(+, NA)	(NS, –)	(+, NA)
cel	(NA, +)	(+, NS)	(+, +)
eff	(NA, NA)	(+, NA)	(NA, NA)
p_res	(–, NS)	(+, –)	(+, NA)
p_cel	(–, NA)	(–, NA)	(NA, NA)

Notes: (1) In any entry (a,b) of this table, 'a' represents the developing countries and 'b' the developed countries.
(2) A "+" ("–") indicates that a positive (negative) and significant effect was found.
(3) "NS" indicates that no significant effect was found and "NA" stands for "not applicable."

imposed nationalization (*expropri*), and the risk of losses to operators due to exchange rate fluctuations (*currency*).

5. Conclusions and Lessons for Regulators

The quality of political institutions has long been emphasized in both academic and institutional literatures, as being a crucial determinant of economic performance. This paper has illustrated an approach that draws lessons from the recent conceptual literature concerned with the role of the economy-wide governance in the shaping of regulatory outcomes and feed them into the more empirical approach that directly examines the impact of sector-wide governance on regulatory performance. This "integrated" approach rests on the idea that political accountability is a key factor in the interface between political and regulatory structures. This approach is illustrated for the case of telecommunications in developing and developed countries by analyzing the impact of political accountability variables on regulatory outcome variables in two time-series-cross-sectional data sets.

Two sets of variables are used to capture political accountability: local accountability variables and global accountability variables. Local accountability variables include most of the features related to "regulatory governance," namely, unbundling of regulation from policy making, autonomy and independence of the regulator, accountability of the regulator, clarity in the allocation of mandates and attributes among government institutions, legal aspects, transparency of regulatory practices, and participation in the regulatory process. These variables are synthesized in a regulatory governance index. Global accountability variables include variables concerning corruption, bureaucracy, law and order, expropriation, currency risk, and checks and balances.

Using a data sample on developing countries and another on developed countries, the study measures the impact of these political accountability variables on some outcome variables variables meant to measure regulatory performance, namely, mainline penetration, cellular subscription, mainlines per employee, monthly subscription to the fixed, or price of cellular service. The analysis has shown a relatively weak effect of political accountability on the performance of regulation in developed countries and a clearer effect in the case of developing countries. This means that higher political accountability yields higher regulatory performance. What implications can one derive from such a finding for the telecommunications industry and, to some extent, for most of the infrastructure industries?[14]

During the last two decades, many developing countries have created regulatory agencies that mostly rely on advice provided by international financial institutions and international lawyers to implement these regulatory models. New regulatory institutions were, however, not tailored or customized enough to fit the local cultural, political and social endowments. This chapter stresses that this is an important requirement for success in developing new institutions. Furthermore, the study goes beyond most current analyses in the area by extending the focus of the analysis to what has been referred to as issues of global accountability which reflect the quality of political institutions.

Recent contributions have deepened the understanding of regulatory effectiveness along two dimensions. The first dimension is regulatory governance: a concept which is a bit broader than what the concept of local accountability discussed here encompasses. The second is regulatory substance: a concept which is meant to capture the way regulation is actually performed. Brown *et al.* (2006) have proposed a comprehensive evaluation process of the effectiveness of regulatory institutions. If implemented, this process will highlight not only the structural weaknesses but also the deficiencies stemming from the surrounding environment of regulation, in particular, the political environment.

It is, therefore, important to devise policy mitigation instruments that incorporate both of these dimensions. Unfortunately, common practices during the last decade or so have shown that donors' interventions are centered on structural issues. The analysis described in this chapter clearly advocates the definition of a set of instruments of effective intervention with the objective of achieving political accountability improvements in

[14] The results found for the telecommunications sector can be expected to hold in other infrastructures although this study calls for a careful account for the technological specificities of the other sectors.

the practice of infrastructure regulation. Indeed, building regulatory institutions in developing countries should be part of a broader strategy of "good governance" and not be considered, as it has been in the past years, only as a sectoral matter. The empirical analysis reported in this chapter has shown that it is important to take note of how regulatory institutions should be built in developing countries.

Building regulatory institutions in developing countries has proven to be more complex than initially thought. This chapter argued that regulatory governance is a necessary, but is not a sufficient condition for good regulatory performance. Political accountability affects the operational and decision-making aspects of regulatory institutions. Deepening the understanding of these inter-relationships calls for a better assessment of the political economy of infrastructure reforms as well as entail proper analysis and understanding of how political systems work. This calls for a greater integration of work undertaken by economists and political scientists while designing regulatory institutions. However, we need to take note that building new institutions requires time. Regulatory institutions in developing countries still need support. For development partners, this means a greater concentration of their efforts on countries where pre-conditions for success, including political ones, are relatively tangible.

Appendix

Table A1: Data summary statistics (developing countries, developed countries)

Variable	Designation	Obs.	Median	Std. Dev	Min.	Max.
REGULATORY PERFORMANCE						
ml	Mainline penetration	(435, 345)	(3.76, 47.49)	(4.96, 10.87)	(0.11, 14.52)	(22.36, 73.56)
cel	Cellular subscription	(431, 344)	(0.01, 2.55)	(2.09, 13.51)	(0, 0)	(15.96, 63.37)
eff	Mainlines per employee	(424, 345)	(53.06, 166.08)	(58.85, 57.53)	(7.78, 43.48)	(371.16, 358.76)
p_res	Monthly subscription to fixed	(256, 252)	(4.44, 4.70)	(4.23, 4.70)	(0, 5.60)	(21.29, 26.27)
p_cel	Price of cellular	(324, 192)	(0, 1.40)	(0.53, 0.86)	(0, 0)	(2.24, 4.95)
LOCAL ACCOUNTABILITY						
reg	Regulatory governance index	(435, 345)	(0, 0)	(4.60, 3.11)	(0, 0)	(13.5, 8)
GLOBAL ACCOUNTABILITY						
corruption	Corruption	(435, 345)	(5, 8.33)	(1.43, 1.37)	(1.66, 3.33)	(10, 10)
bureau	Bureaucracy	(420, 345)	(5, 10)	(1.86, 1.33)	(1.66, 4.5)	(10, 10)
law	Law and order	(435, 345)	(5, 10)	(2.06, 1.11)	(0, 5)	(10, 10)
expropri	Expropriation	(420, 345)	(7.35, 10)	(2.00, 0.66)	(2, 4.6)	(10, 10)
currency	Currency risk	(435, 345)	(6, 9)	(1.98, 1.16)	(1, 4)	(10, 10)
institutional	Institutional environment index	(435, 345)	(28.66, 47)	(7.10, 3.99)	(8, 25.26)	(41.16, 50)
checks	Checks and balances	(423, 345)	(3, 4)	(2.06, 1.62)	(1, 2)	(18, 16)
OTHER VARIABLES						
priva	Privatization	(435, 345)	(0, 0)	(0.32, 0.48)	(0, 0)	(1, 1)
comp_fix	Competition in fixed	(435, 345)	(0, 0)	(0.29, 0.42)	(0, 0)	(1, 1)
comp_cel	Competition in cellular	(435, 345)	(1, 0)	(1.10, 0.47)	(0, 0)	(3, 1)
rural	Rural population	(435, 345)	(49.82, 24.70)	(20.95, 12.73)	(10.95, 2.95)	(90.31, 62.84)
density	Population density	(435, 345)	(48.07, 94.59)	(79.39, 119.50)	(5.38, 2.01)	(330.34, 466.49)

Note: In any entry (a,b) of the table, 'a' represents the developing countries and 'b' the developed countries.

References

Ackerman, JM (2005). Social Accountability in the Public Sector: A Conceptual Discussion. Social Development Paper 82, The World Bank.

Arellano, M and SR Bond (1991). Some tests of specification for panel data: Monte Carlo evidence and an application to employment equations. *Review of Economic Studies*, 58, pp. 277–297.

Arellano, M and O Bover (1995). Another look at the instrumental variable estimation of error-component models. *Journal of Econometrics*, 68, pp. 29–51.

Beck, N and J Katz (2004). Time-series-cross-section Issues: Dynamics. Paper presented at the 2004 Annual Meeting of the Society for Political Methodology, Stanford University.

Blundell, R and S Bond (1998). Initial conditions and moment restrictions in dynamic panel data models. *Journal of Econometrics*, 87, pp. 115–143.

——— (1999). GMM Estimation with Persistent Panel Data: An Application To Production Functions. The Institute for Fiscal Studies Working Paper Series No. W99/4.

Brown, AC, J Stern and BB Tenenbaum with D Gencer (2006). *Handbook for Evaluating Infrastructure Regulatory Systems*. World Bank Publications.

Correa, P, M Melo, B Mueller, and C Pereira (2008). Regulatory governance in Brazilian infrastructure industry. *The Quarterly Review of Economics and Finance*, 48, pp. 202–216.

Cubbin, J and J Stern (2005a). Regulatory Effectiveness and the Empirical Impact of Variations in Regulatory Governance: Electricity Industry Capacity and Efficiency in Developing Countries. World Bank Policy Research Working Paper 3535.

——— (2005b). Regulatory Effectiveness: The Impact of Regulation and Regulatory Governance Arrangements on Electricity Industry Outcomes. World Bank Policy Research Working Paper 3536.

Estache, A and D Martimort (1999). Politics, Transactions Costs, and the Design of Regulatory Institutions. World Bank Policy Research Paper 2073.

Gasmi, F, P Noumba, and L Recuero Virto (2009). Political accountability and regulatory performance in infrastructure industries: An empirical analysis. *The World Bank Economic Review*, 23(3), 509–531.

Gasmi, F and L Recuero Virto (2009). The determinants of reforms and their impact on telecommunications deployment in developing countries. *Journal of Development Economics*, doi:10.1016/j.jdeveco.2009.09.012.

Gutierrez, LH (2003a). Regulatory governance in the Latin American telecommunications sector. *Utilities Policies*, 11, pp. 225–240.

—— (2003b). The effect of endogenous regulation on telecommunications expansion and efficiency in Latin America. *Journal of Regulatory Economics*, 23, pp. 257–286.

Heller, WB and MD McCubbins (1996). Politics, institutions, and outcomes: Electricity regulation in Argentina and Chile. *Journal of Policy Reform*, 1, pp. 357–387.

Holder, S and J Stern (1999). Regulatory governance: Criteria for assessing the performance of regulatory systems. *Utilities Policies*, 8, pp. 35–50.

Holtz-Eakin, D, W Newey, and HS Rosen (1988). Estimating vector autoregressions with panel data. *Econometrica*, 56, pp. 1371–1395.

Laffont, JJ (2005). *Regulation and Development*. Cambridge University Press.

Levy, B and PT Spiller (1994). The institutional foundations of regulatory commitment: A comparative analysis of telecommunications regulation. *Journal of Law, Economics and Organization*, 10, pp. 201–246.

McCubbins, MD and T Schwartz (1984). Congressional oversight overlooked: Police patrol vs fire alarms. *American Journal of Political Science*, 28, pp. 165–179.

McCubbins, MD, RG Noll and BR Weingast (1987). Administrative procedures as instruments of political control. *Journal of Law, Economics and Organization*, 3, pp. 243–277.

North, DC (2000). Institutions and the Performance of Economies Over Time. Paper Presented at the Second Annual Global Development Conference, Tokyo, Japan, December 10–13, 2000.

Ros, AJ (1999). Does ownership and competition matter?: The effects of telecommunications reform on network expansion and efficiency. *Journal of Regulatory Economics*, 15, pp. 65–92.

—— (2003). The impact of the regulatory process and price cap regulation in Latin American telecommunications markets. *Review of Network Economics*, 2(3), pp. 270–286.

Spiller, PT and M Tommasi (2005). The institutions of regulation: An application to public utilities. In *Handbook of New Institutional Economics*, Ménard, C and MM Shirley (eds.), pp. 515–543.

CHAPTER 4

Entry Relaxation and an Independent Regulator: Performance Impact on the Mobile Telecoms Industry in Asia

Chalita Srinuan, Pratompong Srinuan and Erik Bohlin*

Technology and Society Division,
Technology Management and Economics Department,
Chalmers University of Technology, Göteborg, Sweden

This chapter examines empirically the effect of entry relaxation on the performance of the mobile telephone firms and the role of regulators in the Asian countries of Hong Kong, Indonesia, Japan, Malaysia, Republic of Korea, Singapore and Thailand. Two hypotheses are tested: first, that the sector performance (as measured by mobile teledensity) improves after the entry relaxation and establishment of the independent regulator; second, that performance of incumbents declines after the entry relaxation. The sample in this study consists of 14 listed incumbent mobile network operators during 1990–2007. The data are collected from the International Telecommunication Union (ITU), the World Development Indicators Database (WDI), DataStream and websites of companies. The results show that the macroeconomic variables, entry relaxation and independent regulator variable have significant positive impacts on mobile teledensity. For the second hypothesis, the results show that entry relaxation does not affect the profitability of incumbent firms for either developed or developing countries during the study

* Corresponding author.

period, but it affects the operational efficiency and financing. Thus, if the regulatory structure is in place and on time, there will be potential benefits to the mobile telecommunication sector and consumers.

Keywords: Performance: entry relaxation: independent regulator, mobile industry.

1. Introduction

The initial stage of the telecommunications industry in most Asian countries started with the establishment of national telecom providers. The governments created state-owned enterprises to take responsibility for providing telecommunications services, in particular fixed telephony. The major reasons for having a monopoly telecom provider are economies of scale, economies of scope, and lack of funds.

However, the telecommunications industry has been reformed from the monopoly era to the competition and regulation era. This reform started when the liberalization agreement of the World Trade Organization's group on basic Telecommunications came into force. This liberalization agreement introduces the entry relaxation concurrent with a re-regulation by the independent regulator. The nations which committed themselves to follow an open-market policy have to provide the regulations in line with the reference paper including telecom licensing scheme, interconnection, and anti-competitive practice as well as establishing an independent regulator. Resulting from these regulations, new entrants can come into the market with lower barriers to entry. At the same time, incumbents in the market are forced to limit their dominant position.

One could call the necessary regulations a set of market entry regulations. The market entry regulation can induce competition in the telecom market. There are many empirical studies which reveal that relaxation of market entry is associated with significant improvements in teledensity and total factor productivity (Ros, 1999; Gutierrez and Berg, 2000; Wallsten, 2001a, b; Fink *et al.*, 2003; Madden *et al.*, 2003). Moreover, increasing competition after the relaxation induces lower prices (Stennek and Tangerås, 2008).

On the other hand, the market entry regulation affects the performance of incumbent carriers. A number of new entrants coming into the market will increase competition. It will impact the profit and structure of incumbents, even if they have an opportunity to move into a new market and develop services. The largest effect on incumbent carriers is a decrease in their monopoly profit, since their profits are derived from the prices which are set above marginal cost.

Many countries have experienced the entry relaxation, but New Zealand is one country which introduced entry relaxation in telecommunications without an independent regulator (Noam and Kramer, 1994). The lack of an independent regulator who monitors the extent and significance of competition in telecom markets appears to have some disadvantages. In 2000, New Zealand changed to the regulatory regime. Subsequently, the telecommunications commissioner was established in order to regulate telecommunications services in 2001.[1] This suggests that the regulation and regulatory body are still needed in order to ensure that the entry doors to telecom markets remain open and competitive opportunities are maximized. Therefore, it is interesting to investigate how the entry relaxation and independent regulator affect the performance of incumbents.

This chapter investigates the effect of the entry relaxation and the establishment of independent regulators on the performance of the mobile sector and carriers in the Asian mobile market during 1990–2007. The incumbent carriers in this study are chosen to represent a particular model of market reform as identified by Verhulst (2003). It focuses on three out of four identified models of market structure reform in Asia: privatization with full competition, privatization with phased-in competition and regulation, and liberalization without privatization. The last model, which is private sector participation without privatization or liberalization, was not included in this study, since carriers in the last models have limited access to capital markets and continue to be strong through state control. So, the incumbent carriers in the first three models were selected for this study.

The primary objective of the chapter is to determine whether entry relaxation impacts the performance of the mobile sector or not. It also considers the establishment of independent regulators prior to entry relaxation.

---

[1] Available at http://www.med.govt.nz/templates/StandardSummary_38607.aspx.

The expected results would suggest that building a regulatory body before entry relaxation should yield greater improvement and investment in the mobile phone sector because of the certainty and transparency of regulation. A second objective is to investigate whether the entry relaxation affects firm performance. Performance is measured by profitability, efficiency, output, employment and leverage. Since entry relaxation can foster competition and new entrants, the expected results would suggest that the incumbent firm performance will be worsened by the relaxation of entry.

This chapter is organized as follows. Section 2 provides a summary of the background on the relaxation of entry. The conceptual framework and testable hypotheses are described in Section 3. Section 4 presents empirical results. Conclusions are given in Section 5.

2. Background

The opening of Asia's telecommunication market began in the late 1990s. Japan was the first country which began the process of entry relaxation and then it spread to South Korea, Hong Kong, Singapore and ASEAN countries (Indonesia, Malaysia and Thailand). The entry relaxation of fixed-line services occurred first, followed by mobile phone service. It increased participation from private companies and it has been the keystone of telecommunications reform in this region. The development of the telecommunication industries in Asian countries varies (see Appendix I), depending on the state of economic progress and politics of the country, but it can be summarized as follows.

2.1 *Japan*

Until 1988, the former government monopoly, Nippon Telegraph & Telephone Corp. (NTT), was the sole mobile telephone service operator in Japan. Later, the Ministry of Posts and Telecommunications allowed competition. In July 1992, NTT mobile operations set up a separate subsidiary, NTT DoCoMo, to provide mobile communication services. Earlier in 1997, NTT was restructured under a holding company. In 1988, KDD (an international telecommunication firm) bought TeleWay Japan to enter the domestic long-distance market. In 1999, KDD announced a merger with DDI and IDO in order to provide mobile, domestic and international telecommunication service (Information and Communications in Japan 2000, p.11). Thus, Japan became completely liberalized at the end of the 1990s.

2.2 *Korea*

Korea began the liberalization process by legally privatizing the Korea Telecommunication Authority, which was renamed Korea Telecom (KT) in 1990. KT, however, acted as a monopoly agency for the government in building information infrastructure until May 2002, because the foreign players such as the US government and international organizations pressed the Korean government for liberalization and opening markets to foreign carriers (Jin, 2006). The Korean government revised the telecommunication law to introduce competition. Finally, KT privatized and foreigners became major shareholders in May 2002. Mobile service was first provided in 1984 by the monopoly supplier, Korea Mobile Telecommunication, which later was privatized in March 1997 and was renamed as SK Telecom (SK). Liberalization had a slow start in the initial stages and then gradually accelerated its speed in 2000 (Yoon, 1999).

2.3 *Hong Kong*

Historically, telecommunications in Hong Kong was not a market open to competition. Before 1995, local fixed-line telephony and external services in Hong Kong were provided on a monopoly basis. In the early 1990s, the Hong Kong Government recognized the economic and social importance of telecommunications. Later, the Office of the Telecommunications Authority, OFTA, the telecommunications regulator, was established by law in 1993. In 1995, the local fixed-telephony franchise of the Hong Kong Telephone Company ended in 1995 and the Hong Kong government seized the opportunity to introduce competition to the local fixed telecommunications network services (FTNS) market and mobile telephony. The external telecommunications market was liberalized from 1999 (Ure, 1998). Today, there is no pre-determined quota of licenses for any kind of telecommunications service operators. There is also no foreign investment restriction imposed on foreign entities owning telecommunications facilities or operating telecommunications services after the full liberalization in January 2003.

2.4 *Singapore*

In 1999, the Singapore government passed the Telecom Competition Code and lifted foreign equity limits on telecommunications infrastructure. At the same time, the government empowered the Infocomm Development Authority (IDA) to oversee the development and deregulation of the telecommunication market.[2] The mobile phone services market has been dominated by SingTel, MobileOne and StarHub, since 2000. Virgin Mobile was the first international carrier which was granted an operating license for mobile phone services. The liberalization process marked the most significant change in Singapore's telecommunication industry, years before the deadline originally agreed with the WTO (Hori, 2003).

2.5 *Indonesia*

Telecommunication service provision in Indonesia was monopolized by state-owned operators: the domestic provider PT Telekomunikasi Indonesia (TELKOM) and the international provider PT Indosat before 1995 (Lumanto and Kosuge, 2005). Development of the telecommunications infrastructure, particularly funding of the national backbone network, was financed primarily by the state, mainly through loans from the World Bank, the Asian Development Bank and through bilateral foreign assistance under the umbrella of the Consultative Group on Indonesia (CGI). However, loans from international agencies were reduced in early 1990 and totally stopped in 1995. Due to limited state funds, accelerated telecommunications development was achieved by the investments of local and foreign investors. This strategic decision was taken by the government to cater for market demand and to encourage industry growth. In 1995, the cellular market and value-added services were opened up to private operators. In the meantime, the privatization of state-owned companies was also launched (Asmiati, 2005). On July 11, 2003

[2] Available at http://www.ida.gov.sg/About%20Us/20060413182921.aspx

Indonesia's government established the Indonesian Telecommunications Regulatory Body (BRTI) to guard the public interest and to support the telecommunications business competition.[3] However, by the end of 2008, there were three large GSM cellular operators in Indonesia: Telkomsel, Indosat and Excelcomindo, and each had a national coverage license.

2.6 *Malaysia*

Liberalization brought about a fundamental change in the regulatory structure in telecommunications. For example, the Telecommunications Act of 1950 was amended to make Jabatan Telekom Malaysia (JTM) the regulatory authority for the sector, and the implementation of the Telecommunications Service (Successor Company) Act of 1985 paved the way for Syarikat Telekom Malaysia (STM, renamed Telekom Malaysia Berhad or TMB) to take over the provision of telecommunications services from JTM, which it did in 1987 (Painter and Wong, 2005; Singh, 2000). In November 1998, the Malaysian Government restructured the Ministry of Energy, Telecommunications, and Post (METP) into the Ministry of Energy, Communications and Multimedia (MECM). The MECM was replaced by the Ministry of Energy, Water and Communications (MEWC) on March 27, 2004 which was established following Malaysia's new cabinet line-up. However, the cellular sector had partial liberalization in 1999. TMB has faced competition from other operators in mobile phone services. Competition in the mobile services market increased with the entry of major operators such as Maxis, DiGi and TIME (Lee, 2002).

2.7 *Thailand*

Thailand has been among the slowest countries to liberalize, and needed to fully liberalize fixed telephony markets by 2006 following Thailand's commitment to the WTO (Hori, 2003). However, this process is still incomplete liberalization because of the political and economic problems faced by the country. Despite the absence of a fully liberalized market, competition already exists, for example, in the mobile phone and internet

---

[3] Available at http://www.brti.or.id/index_en.php?mod=site&site=about

markets. After the Telecommunications Development Master Plan was approved in 1997 and the independent regulatory body, the National Telecommunication Commission (NTC), was established in 2004, the mobile services intensified because of new market entries of international telecommunication companies (Mavichak, 2004). Orange, a European telecommunication operator, had expanded services in Thailand by joining Telecom Asia of the CP Group to provide mobile phone services under the new company called TA Orange (renamed Truemove). On 23 January 2006, the Thai Telecommunication Act (2006) became effective, raising the limit on foreign holdings in telecom companies to 49% from 25%. In 2008, AIS and DTAC were more than 49% owned by Temasek Holding (Singapore) and Norway's Telenor, both direct and indirect shareholders.

To summarise, Asian telecommunication markets, which have begun to undergo the entry relaxation, vary from country to country because of the difference in infrastructure and economic development. However, governments have without exception assigned a role to market liberalization and competition.

The telecommunications policy reforms undertaken by Asian governments combine, with some variations, three elements: a shift from public to private ownership, increased scope for foreign ownership (and/or control), and liberalization of entry into the industry. Governments have taken different views as to the degree of equity participation that they wish to maintain in the former state monopolies. Full privatization may be contemplated at a later stage in some of these countries, but it seems that many governments consider it prudent to maintain a certain level of equity participation in the sector for strategic reasons (Low and Mattoo, 1997). A summary of Asian mobile market indicators is shown in Table 1.

3. Measuring Regulatory Outcomes and Effectiveness: What Do We Know?

Data are sourced from two primary sources to test the effect of entry relaxation on the sector and firm performances. First, the International Telecommunications Union (ITU) compiles sector data on the mobile phone teledensity, GDP per capita, trade openness and competition. For trade openness, the data are from the World Development Indicators

Table 1: Asian mobile market indicator (2007)

Country	Characteristics and degree of liberalization	Entry restriction
Japan	Liberalization and privatization started in 1985 Shift from controlled liberalization to market-based competition since the end of the 1990s	Entry is not restricted
Korea	Four-cellular operators and 7 licenses after 1995	Partially liberalized. Government is proposing to raise the maximum investment by foreign companies to 49% from 20%, while maintaining the combined limit of direct and indirect investments at 60%
Hong Kong	Competition among five cell phone operators Liberalization of mobile service began in 2000	Entry is not restricted
Singapore	Partial privatization in 1993; a second cellular license and complete liberalization before the deadline originally agreed with the WTO	Entry is not restricted
Malaysia	Partial liberalization in 1990s	There are restrictions. Upper limit of foreign investment raised to 95% from 49% in August 2000
Indonesia	Partial liberalization in cellular, 1995	There are restrictions. Upper limit of foreign investment set at 49%
Thailand	Pledged full liberalization by 2006 to the WTO agreement	Upper limit of foreign investment set at 49%

Database (WDI). Finally, data on financial information for selected firms are from the mobile telecommunication sector in DataStream and homepages. The sample includes 14 incumbent carriers from 7 countries which consist of Japan, Korea, Hong Kong, Singapore, Malaysia, Indonesia and Thailand, liberalized over the period 1990–2007. All carriers are dominant providers of mobile service and listed on the stock markets.

For the econometric analysis, a panel data model is employed with the following function:

$$\ln Y_{it} = \beta_0 + \beta_1 X_{1it} + \beta_2 X_{2it} + \varepsilon_{it}, \quad (1)$$

where

Y_{it} dependent variables
X_1 regressors of macroeconomic variables not including the constant
X_2 regressors of regulatory variables not including the constant
β parameters
ε_{it} error term
I country-specific
t year

The first objective is to determine the effect of entry relaxation on sector performance. An econometric model is adapted from Gutierrez and Berg (2000) but with different dependent variables.

$$\ln(\text{sector performance}) = \beta_0 + \beta_1 \text{ Macroeconomic variables} + \beta_2 \text{ Regulatory variables} + \varepsilon_{it}. \quad (2)$$

In Equation (2), the mobile phone teledensity will be used as the dependent variable, as a proxy of performance of the mobile phone sector, while previous studies use main line teledensity. The independent variables are ln (GDP per capita) and ln (trade) which are measured by the sum of imports and exports over GDP and a dummy variable for financial crisis (year 1997) as macroeconomic variables. The authors also use the competition level and two dummy variables which are the relaxation of entry and the establishment of a regulatory body. These measures are expected to have a positive impact on mobile phone teledensity as previous studies (Galal and Nauriyal, 1995; Ros, 1999; Gutierrez and Berg, 2000; Wallsten, 2001a, 2002; Fink *et al.*, 2003; Li and Xu, 2002; Maiorano and Stern, 2007) except a dummy variable for financial crisis.

All variables are in natural logarithms in order to measure the elasticity of the variable, except for dummy variables. The expected impact of all independent variables is positive except the dummy variable for Asian financial crisis in 1997.

In addition, the endogeneity problem is tested since mobile phone teledensity and GDP are jointly determined by lag of GDP in this paper. There is a strong possibility of a correlation between GDP and error terms. GDP is one of the most important factors to determine teledensity, but many studies suggest that the ICT diffusion will directly influence the performance of the economy (OECD, 2003).

Hence, Equation (2) is estimated assuming that GDP is influenced by the lagged value of GDP as an instrumental variable.[4] The instrumental variable of panel data will solve the first equation by regressing the following equation:

$$\ln\text{GDP}_{it-1} = \alpha_0 + \alpha_1 * \ln\text{GDP}_{it-2} + v_{it-1} \quad (3)$$

Thus, the lagged value of the GDP is used (not the actual value) as the instrumental variable in Equation (2). In addition, variation in mobile teledensity by countries required that Equation (2) be modified. The alternative specifications considered are one-way Fixed-Effect (FEM) and Random Effect (REM) models. The FEM allows intercepts to vary by country at a point in time, while the REM considers country variation to be randomly distributed and uncorrelated with explanatory variables; the result is a complex error term (Madden *et al.*, 2004). However, Hausman's test is employed and confirms that the FEM is appropriate in this study. It means that there is a difference in the mobile phone teledensity across countries.

The last objective is to analyze the change in performance of sampled firms following the entry relaxation. The authors rely on five broad indicators of firm performance, namely: profitability, operating efficiency, output, employment and leverage which adapted from Megginson *et al.* (1994). These indicators are expected to decrease after the entry relaxation, except employment.

Following the standard methodology of Megginson *et al.* (1994), Boubakri and Cosset (1998) and D'Souza and Megginson (1999), this study determines the performance measures presented above for a period

---

[4] In order to fulfill the definition of instrumental variable, the lag of GDP has no covariance with the error term in Equation (2). Moreover, the lag of GDP should correlate with the suspected source of the endogeneity problem (GDP in our case).

of seven years (three years prior to the entry relaxation and three years after the entry relaxation, including the year of the entry relaxation itself). The differences of mean (median) before and after this period are computed for each performance measurement. The two-tailed Wilcoxon signed-rank test is used in order to assess the significance of performance changes.

4. Implications for Regulatory Design, Effectiveness and Operation

The final results of the estimation of Equation (2), which is conducted by two-stage least squares, report that GDP, trade openness, competition level and entry relaxation have positive effects on mobile penetration (see Appendix 2). These results are consistent with Fink *et al.* (2003) who assess the telecommunications reform in developing countries. They mentioned that mainline penetration had a positive relationship with per-capita GDP. Moreover, the results of Maiorano and Stern (2007) are similar to those of this study in that the GDP per capita and trade openness have a positive relationship with the mobile penetration rate.

The regulatory variables confirm that the competition level and the regulatory establishment also have positive impacts on mobile penetration. If the mobile phone sector has full competition and a regulatory body prior to the entry relaxation period, it will accelerate mobile penetration. The results are consistent with previous studies showing that competition drives the improvements in the sector (Ros, 1999; Fink *et al.*, 2003; Li and Xu, 2001; Wallsten, 2001a).

For the listed incumbent carriers' performance, comparisons of the mean (median) of operating changes before and after the entry relaxation period show that three ratios change significantly after the entry relaxation: employment, output and leverage ratio (see Appendix 2). A possible reason for an increase of employment may be high demand of consumers, so that the incumbent needs to expand its business result in more employment after the entry relaxation. This result is consistent with our expectation. The increase in demand may be supported by the increase in output. The result shows that the incumbent firms have higher real sales after entry relaxation. For leverage ratio, the entry relaxation reduces the total debt to total asset; it suggests that incumbent listed firms have more opportunity for funding through capital markets and foreign ownership.

However, the profitability ratio and efficiency change insignificantly. This study uses three ratios to measure profitability: return on sales (ROS), return on assets (ROA) and return on equity (ROE). The results show decreases in profitability after the entry relaxation period, but they are insignificant. Even the change in median of ROS increases after entry relaxation, but it does not affect performance.

The next measurement is efficiency, in terms of both sale and net income. The finding is that the efficiency in sale (median) decreases insignificantly. It may imply that the increase in employees in order to serve the demand growth in mobile services is the main cause of this result. It might reflect an unclear picture for the long run since the authors use only three years after the relaxation of entry. However, the effect should also occur in the long run, whereas the net income increases insignificantly. This result contrasts with our hypothesis that the efficiency of the incumbent's net income should be reduced. The economy of scale advantage of incumbent firms may be a reason why their net income still increases after the market is opened.

Since the selected firms come from different levels of economic development, this study divides the whole sample into two groups based on the definition of World Bank 2008 income group in order to investigate the effects in different groups of countries. These groups are so-called developed and developing countries, as shown in Appendix 2.

For the developed countries, which consist of Japan, Korea, Hong Kong and Singapore, the results reveal that both output and employment of listed incumbent firms increase significantly. These results, combined with the evidence on net income efficiency where the median NIEFF increases after entry relaxation (from 5,730.245 to 6,714.41), suggest that the customers continue to use and buy the services from the incumbents since they might not be sure about the new entrants' services. Moreover, the sale efficiency and profitability of these firms decrease insignificantly. Thus, the incumbent firms still have a business advantage after the relaxation of entry.

This study also shows a significant decrease at 1% level in the leverage ratio. The median TDTA decreases after the entry relaxation (from

0.50 to 0.26). It implicitly assumes that the incumbents have an alternative source of funds from the relaxation of capital market and foreign ownership.

For the developing countries — Indonesia, Malaysia and Thailand — the profitability ratio results are the same as in the developed countries. All three profitability ratios decrease insignificantly after the entry relaxation.

In contrast, measurements of efficiency, employment and leverage show significant change. Both measures of efficiency, sale efficiency and net income efficiency, reflect the demand for mobile phone services in a developing country. SALEEF and NIEFF increase in these countries.

The incumbent firms need more employees after the entry relaxation. The total employment increases after the entry relaxation (from 4,760 to 6,683). For the real sales, it shows a significant decrease at the 5% level. The median output decreases after the entry relaxation (from 849,598.1 to 560,726.4).

The firm's leverage ratio in developing countries shows that these firms use more debt for their funding at 10% significant level, which differs from the case of developed countries and the hypothesis.

5. Lessons for Regulators: What Works, What Does Not?

The findings show that the regulatory body and entry relaxation variables have a positive impact on mobile penetration. This suggests that the regulator has an important role of setting up a regulatory system outside government intervention in order to promote competition.

However, as Levy and Spiller (1996) note, the "credibility and effectiveness of a regulatory framework, and so its ability to encourage private investment and support efficiency in the production and use of services, vary with a country's political and social institutions." Thus, the mobile telecommunication performance will depend on how transparent the regulations are, and how well the regulator acts as neutral.

According to the results of this study, the relaxation of entry does not affect the profitability of incumbent firms significantly in either developed or developing countries during 1990–2007. But it affects the operating efficiency — net income, output and employment and financing or the leverage ratio of incumbents. This suggests that the incumbents try to prevent competition during the entry of relaxation. However, it is possible for new entrants to enter the market since they can offer new technology with lower cost of investment due to later competitive advantage. Then it may result in a merger and acquisition between incumbent firms in the near future in order to compete with the new entrants, and the market will become less competitive. Therefore, the necessary regulation is needed in order to create a competitive market and reduce the dominant position of incumbents.

6. Conclusion

This paper provides empirical evidence for the entry relaxation in the mobile industry in Asia (Hong Kong, Indonesia, Japan, Korea, Malaysia, Singapore and Thailand) during 1990–2007.

Firstly, the relationship between mobile penetration and macroeconomic variables — GDP and trade openness and regulatory variables which include the entry relaxation, competition level and the establishment of a regulatory body as dummy variables — was examined by using an econometric model. The findings show that macroeconomic variables have a positive impact on mobile penetration. Moreover, the regulatory variables improve mobile penetration. In particular, the independent regulator will play an important role of setting up a regulatory system outside government intervention in order to promote competition.

Lastly, results of the comparison between the pre- and post-entry relaxation show that the entry relaxation leads to reduction in financial and operating efficiency performance of incumbent listed firms in the selected countries even for developed countries. This emphasizes that the entry relaxation has effects on financial and operating performance of incumbent firms. For instance, it is not necessary for the incumbent who has a high market share to have high financial and operating performance. This result would be a good sign for regulators since the entry relaxation can create intense competition and the benefit will be to consumers and mobile phone users. However, the entry relaxation does not affect the profitability of incumbent firms significantly in either developed or developing countries. It suggests that the incumbents try to prevent competition during the period of entry relaxation. To ensure a level playing field, regulation and regulatory monitoring will be needed. Government and regulator should prepare the market conditions by introducing laws and regulations in order to facilitate new entrants. The new entrants can then enter the market with fewer constraints.

In addition, the relaxation of entry improves the macro-level of countries' competitiveness. It provides a positive impact for consumers and new entrants. Consumers will have a variety of services and products, and the competition level will drive prices down. At the same time, newcomers' ease of entering the market faces less restriction by foreign owners, which usually have the ability to invest. The incumbents need to improve technical and managerial efficiency in order to sustain growth momentum, since the entrants can manage to grow strong enough to exert competitive pressure on the incumbents (Yoon, 1999). If this statement is true, the relaxation of entry is a correct policy to promote a more competitive and efficient mobile industry.

More research is also necessary to verify and refine the other findings presented in this study. Comparing incumbent firms and new firms makes it possible to analyze several issues that have been addressed here. What will happen to the incumbents' performance in the long run? What is the difference between regulatory reforms in advanced countries and developing countries? What is the next step for regulators to make the market more efficient under the relaxation of entry? It will become possible to respond to these questions when more observational data become available after the policy is implemented.

Acknowledgements

We thank Gary Madden and Lennart Flood for valuable comments on an earlier version of this paper. We are also grateful to Au Man Ho, Former Director General of Telecommunications and Telecommunications Authority, Hong Kong for sharing the data and helping with some of the mobile operators' background in Hong Kong.

Appendix 1: Timeline for the Entry Relaxation in Selected Asian Countries

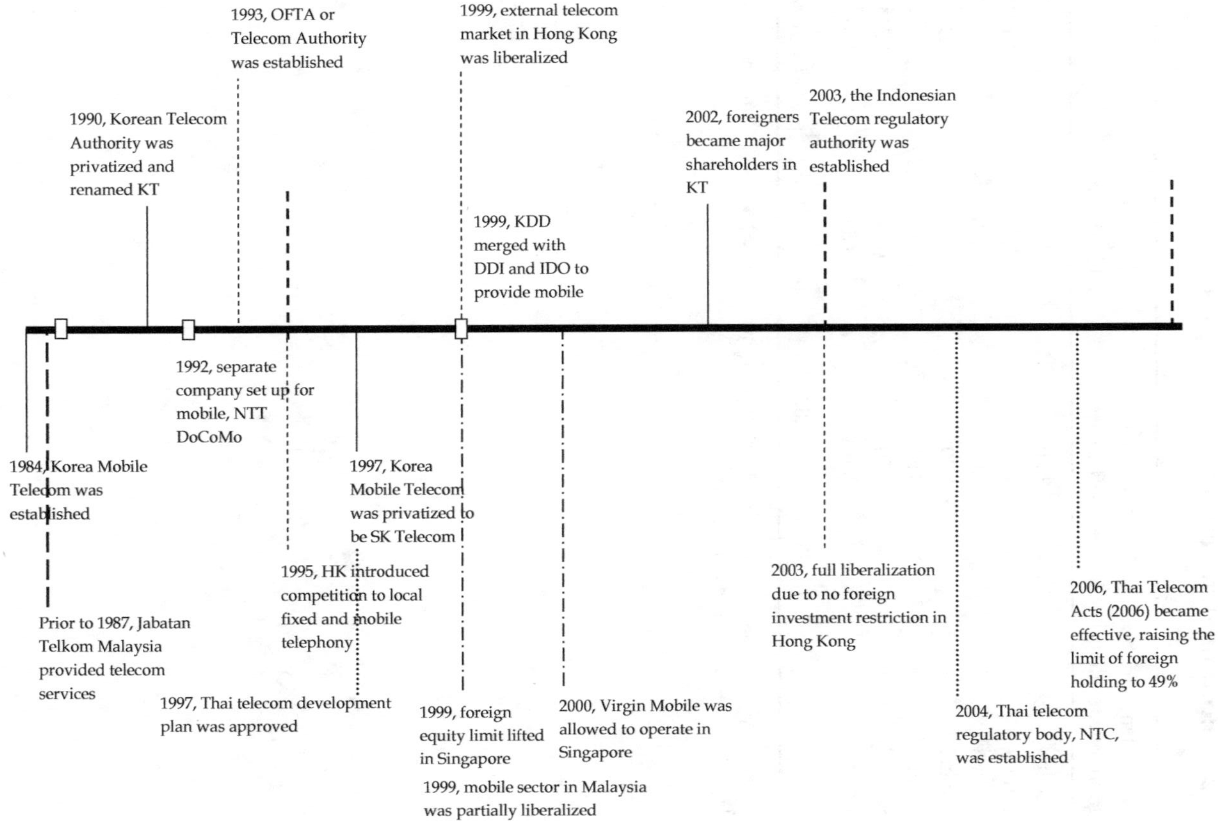

Appendix 2

A2.1 *Econometric results*

Dependent variable: ln mobile teledensity	Estimated coefficient	Standard Error	*t*-test
lngdp	2.80	0.60	4.73***
lntrade	4.90	0.60	8.10***
entryrelax	1.02	0.48	2.12***
comp2	1.29	0.33	3.95***
comp3	0.51	0.66	0.78
regbody	0.70	0.27	2.52**
yr97	0.30	0.34	0.87
	R-squared = 0.8337	Prob > F = 0.0000	No. of obs. = 101

Note: All specifications estimated by two-stage least squares (2SLS). *** and ** indicate significance level at 1% and 5% respectively.

A2.2 *Listed firm performances — full samples*

Variables	*N*	Mean before (Median)	Mean after (Median)	Mean change (Median)	Z-statistic for difference in median (after-before)
Profitability					
Return on sale (ROS)	41	0.10	0.16	0.62	–0.96
		(0.07)	*(0.08)*	*(0.01)*	
Return on assets (ROA)	41	0.05	0.03	–0.02	–1.30
		(0.042)	*(0.03)*	*(–0.02)*	
Return on equity (ROE)	41	0.04	0.04	0.01	–1.28
		(0.07)	*(0.05)*	*(–0.02)*	
Efficiency					
Sales efficiency (SALEFF)	41	460,216.80	162,000,000,000.00	161,999,539,783.20	1.005
		(284429.80)	*(220037.80)*	*(–64392.00)*	
Net income efficiency (NIEFF)	41	42331.78	82488.80	40157.02	1.131
		(4122.52)	*(6714.41)*	*(2591.90)*	
Output					
Real sales (OUTPUT)	41	19,300,000.00	18,200,000,000,000.00	18,199,980,700,000.00	4.340***
		(10,100,000.00)	*(2,300,000.00)*	*(12,900,000.00)*	

(Continued)

(*Continued*)

Variables	*N*	Mean before (Median)	Mean after (Median)	Mean change (Median)	Z-statistic for difference in median (after-before)
Employment					
Total employment (EMPL)	41	6,810.707	9,436.538	2,625.831	3.580***
		(2,947.00)	*(6,241.00)*	*(3,294.00)*	
Leverage					
Total debt to total assets(TDTA)	41	0.36	0.28	−0.09	−2.324**
		(0.47)	*(0.30)*	*(−0.16)*	

Note: ***, **, and * indicate significance level at 1, 5, and 10%, respectively.

A2.3 *Listed firm performances in developed countries*

Variables	*N*	Mean before (Median)	Mean after (Median)	Mean change (Median)	Z-statistic for difference in median (after-before)
Profitability					
Return on sale (ROS)	24	0.09	0.07	−0.03	−0.40
		(0.06)	*(0.05)*	*(−0.01)*	
Return on assets (ROA)	24	0.05	0.03	−0.02	−0.97
		(0.04)	*(0.02)*	*(−0.01)*	
Return on equity (ROE)	24	0.04	0.04	−0.01	−1.37
		(0.07)	*(0.04)*	*(−0.032)*	
Efficiency					
Sales efficiency (SALEFF)	24	624,588.90	163,000,000,000.00	162,999,375,411.00	0.31
		(409,74.007)	*(220,037.80)*	*(−189,709.20)*	
Net income efficiency (NIEFF)	24	6,457.03	67,914.15	61,457.12	1.77**
		(5,730.25)	*(6,714.41)*	*(984.17)*	
Output					
Real sales (OUTPUT)	24	17,900,000.00	7,730,000,000,000.00	7,729,982,100,000.00	3.60***
		(13,600,000.00)	*(28,300,000.00)*	*(14,700,000.00)*	

(Continued)

(Continued)

Variables	*N*	Mean before (Median)	Mean after (Median)	Mean change (Median)	Z-statistic for difference in median (after-before)
Employment					
Total employment (EMPL)	24	4,217.958	7,701.667	3,483.709	3.36***
		(2,564.00)	*(4,850.50)*	*(2,286.50)*	
Leverage					
Total debt to total assets (TDTA)	24	0.39	0.24	−0.15	−4.10***
		(0.50)	*(0.26)*	*(−0.25)*	

Note: ***, **, and * indicate significance level at 1, 5, and 10%, respectively.

A2.4 *Listed firm performances in developing countries*

Variables	*N*	Mean before (Median)	Mean after (Median)	Mean change (Median)	*Z*-statistic for difference in median (after-before)
Profitability					
Return on sale (ROS)	17	0.12	0.32	0.20	−0.63
		(0.18)	*(0.08)*	(−0.09)	
Return on assets (ROA)	17	0.06	0.04	−0.02	−0.80
		(0.03)	*(0.02)*	(−0.02)	
Return on equity (ROE)	17	0.03	0.05	0.03	−0.28
		(0.07)	*(0.05)*	(−0.02)	
Efficiency					
Sales efficiency (SALEFF)	17	228,162.20	161,000,000,000.00	160,999,771,837.80	1.33
		(13,111.52)	*(527,737.70)*	*(514,626.18)*	
Net income efficiency	17	92,978.49	111,638.1	18,659.61	−0.55
(NIEFF)		(2,388.67)	*(48,476.04)*	46,087.362	
Output					
Real sales (OUTPUT)	17	21,300,000.00	3,500,000,000,000.00	3,499,978,700,000.00	2.39**
		(849,598.10)	*(560,726.40)*	*(−288,871.70)*	

(*Continued*)

(*Continued*)

Variables	*N*	Mean before (Median)	Mean after (Median)	Mean change (Median)	*Z*-statistic for difference in median (after-before)
Employment					
Total employment (EMPL)	17	10,471.06 *(4,760)*	12,212.33 *(6,683)*	1,741.27 *(1,923)*	1.56*
Leverage					
Total debt to total assets (TDTA)	17	0.33 *(0.24)*	0.33 *(0.31)*	0.01 (0.07)	1.47*

Note: ***, **, and * indicate significance level at 1, 5, and 10%, respectively.

References

Asmiati, R (2005). Indonesia: Liberalization at the crossroad impact sector performance, teledensity and productivity. *Communications Strategies*, 58(2), pp. 61–80.

Boubakri, N and JC Cosset (1998). The financial and operating performance of newly privatized firms: Evidence from developing countries. *Journal of Finance*, 53(3), pp. 1081–1110.

D'Souza, J and WL Megginson (1999). The financial and operating performance of privatized firms during the 1990s. *Journal of Finance*, 54(4), pp. 1397–1438.

Jin, DY (2006). Political and economic processes in the privatization of the Korea telecommunications industry: A case study of Korea Telecom, 1987–2003. *Telecommunications Policy*, 30(1), pp. 3–13.

Fink, C, A Mattoo and R Rathindran (2003). An assessment of telecommunications reform in development countries. *Information Economics and Policy*, 15(4), pp. 443–446.

Galal, A and B Nauriyal (1995). Regulating Telecommunications in Developing Countries. World Bank Policy Research Working Paper No. 1520. Available at http://papers.ssrn.com/sol3/papers.cfm?abstract_id=569212[Accessed 24 May 2009].

Gutierrez, LH and S Berg (2000). Telecommunication liberalization and regulatory governance: Lesson from Latin America. *Telecommunications Policy*, 24(10–11), pp. 865–884.

Hori, N (2003). Developments of the IT revolution and informatization in East Asia. Economic and Social Research Institute Working Paper. Available at http://www.esri.go.jp/en/tie/ea/ea6-e.pdf [Accessed 24 May 2009].

Information & Communications in Japan (2000). InfoCom Research, Inc. Japan.

Lee, C (2002). Telecommunications reforms in Malaysia. *Annals of Public and Cooperative Economics*. 73(4), pp. 521–540.

Levy, B and P Spiller (1996). *Regulations, Institutions and Commitment: Comparative studies of Telecommunications*. Cambridge: Cambridge University Press.

Li, W and LC Xu (2002). Liberalization and performance in telecommunications sector around the World. *Journal of Comparative Economics*, 30(3), pp. 439–462.

Low, P and A Mattoo (1997). Reform in Basic Telecommunications and the WTO Negotiations: The Asian Experience. Available at http://www.netamericas.net/researchpapers/documents/low/Low2.wpf.doc [Accessed 15 Feburay 2010].

Lumanto, R and T Kosuge (2005). Telecommunications reform: Resolving performance problem in Indonesia. *Technology in Society*, 27(4), pp. 517–529.

Madden, G, SJ Savage and J Ng (2003). Asia-Pacific telecommunications liberalization and productivity performance. *Australian Economic Papers*, 42(1), pp. 91–102.

Madden, G, G Coble-Neal and B Dalzell (2004). A dynamic model of mobile telephony subscription incorporating a network effect. *Telecommunications Policy*, 28, pp. 133–144.

Maiorano, F and S Jon (2007). Institution and telecommunications infrastructure in low and middle-income countries: The case of mobile telephony. *Utilities policy*, 15(3), pp. 165–181.

Mavichak, V (2004). Telecommunication Sector: Moving towards Free Competition. Available at http://www.thailandoutlook.com/thailandoutlook1/download/special/telecom.pdf [Accessed 24 May 2009].

Megginson, WL, RC Nash and M van Randenborgh (1994). The financial and operating performance of newly privatized firms: An international empirical analysis. *Journal of Finance,* 49(2), pp. 403–452.

Noam, EM and RA Kramer (1994). Telecommunications strategies in the developed world. A hundred flowers blooming or old wine in new bottles? In *Telecommunications in Transition. Policies, Services and Technologies in the European Community.* Steinfield, C, JM Bauer and L Caby (eds.), pp. 272–286. London. Sage Publications.

Organization for Economic Cooperation and Development (OECD) (2003). Information and Communication Technologies: ICT and Economic Growth Evidence from OECD Countries, Industries and Firms, OECD Report. Paris.

Painter, M and S-F Wong (2005). Varieties of the regulatory state? Government — business relations and telecommunication reforms in Malaysia and Thailand. *Policy and Society,* 24(3), pp. 27–52.

Ros, AJ (1999). Does ownership or competition matter? The effects of telecommunications reform on network expansion and efficiency. *Journal of Regulatory Economic,* 15(1), pp. 65–92.

Singh, JP (2000). Institutional environment and effects of telecommunication privatization and market liberalization in Asia. *Telecommunications Policy,* 24(10–11), pp. 885–906.

Stennek, J and T Tangerås (2008). Competition vs. Regulation in Mobile Telecommunications. NET Institute Working Paper No. 08–09. Available at http://ssrn.com/abstract=1147677 [Accessed 28 September 2009].

Ure, J (1998). Hong Kong's telecommunications policy. In *Hong Kong Economy and Society: Challenges in the New Era.* Wong SL and T Maruya (eds.), pp. 39–60. Centre of Asian Studies, University of Hong Kong and the Institute of Developing Economies, Tokyo, Japan.

Verhulst, SG (2003). Introduction to Telecom Reform and Liberalisation: Policy and Regulatory Tools, Markle Foundation. Available at http://www.stanhopecentre.org/ict/materials/IntroTelecomReform.ppt [Accessed 24 May 2009].

Wallsten, SJ (2001a). An econometric analysis of telecom competition, privatization, and regulation in Africa and Latin America. *Journal of Industrial Economics,* 49(1), pp. 1–20.

Wallsten, SJ (2001b). Telecommunications investment and traffic in developing countries: The effects of international settlement rate reforms. *Journal of Regulatory Economics,* 20(3), pp. 307–323.

Wallsten, SJ (2002). Does Sequencing Matter? Regulation and Privatization in Telecommunication. World Bank Policy Research Working Paper No. 2817. Available at http://papers.ssrn.com/sol3/papers.cfm?abstract_id=304705 [Accessed 24 May 2009].

Yoon, C H (1999). Liberalization policy, industry structure and productivity change in Korea's telecommunication industry. *Telecommunications Policy,* 23(3–4), pp. 289–306.

PART II

Electricity Sector Regulation & Governance

CHAPTER 5

Risk, Regulation and Governance: Institutional Processes and Regulatory Risk in the Thai Energy Sector

Darryl S.L. Jarvis

Lee Kuan Yew School of Public Policy
National University of Singapore

Infrastructure provision around the world has undergone a series of profound changes in the manner of its financing and governance over the last 30 years or so. While the role of the state has diminished as a direct provider, builder and operator of infrastructure, its role as regulator and overseer has undergone substantial growth, increasing the regulatory burden on the state. While this transition has occurred relatively smoothly in developed country contexts, in developing countries the diffusion of the regulatory state has produced manifestly different forms of governance, stressing the regulatory capacity of existing and newly formed regulatory bodies. This chapter explores the impact and manifestations of regulatory diffusion in the context of the Thai energy sector and the governance mechanisms responsible for electricity generation, transmission and distribution.

Keywords: Thailand energy sector; institutions & regulation; regulatory risk; institutional endowment.

1. Introduction

In recent surveys of multinational firms, regulatory risk was rated 'the greatest strategic challenge facing global business.'[1] Indeed, despite traditional risks associated with treasury operations, currency exposure, competition and operational risks, survey respondents overwhelming rated 'political risk' as the greatest recurrent challenge to business continuity and profitability. We should, perhaps, not be surprised by this. If the spate of theorizing, voluminous academic literatures and empirical investigations about 'governance' over the last two decades have taught us anything, it is this: institutions matter. Institutions frame the risk environment; institutional processes can generate, moderate and amplify risk, download compliance costs and otherwise define market extensity and the parameters that mediate economic, social and political interactions.

Beyond these observations, however, further insights are more difficult. Precisely what institutional features matter, what specific institutional variables are at play in risk generation, and in what magnitude and priority they relate to governance outcomes or regulatory systems, remains contested. This makes for a strange paradox; a near universal embrace of 'good governance' as a key ingredient for economic growth, social welfare and optimal state-market outcomes, yet an inability to operationalise the concept in ways that make it transparent or readily transferable. Policy diffusion might be all around us and the transplantation of regulatory frameworks a feature of an emergent 'regulatory capitalism' (Levi-Faur and Jordana 2005, p. 191), yet the sense in which such diffusion relates to the adoption, building and operation of institutions and the emergence of 'good governance' remains elusive. As the Nobel laureate Douglas North noted recently, we perhaps know more about the surface of the moon than we do about the processes that lead to institutional formation, instantiation, institutional legitimacy, efficiency and probity, and their relationship to governance and regulatory systems.[2] Despite their importance, institutions

---

[1] See surveys at www.ey.com; DLA Piper "European Regulatory Risk Awareness Survey 2007" assessable at www.dlapiper.com

[2] Douglas North, address to the Lee Kuan Yew School of Public Policy, National University of Singapore, March 11, 2008.

remain enigmatic and the quest for 'good governance' a highly prized but often unrealized goal.

These questions and the relationships that undergird them are increasingly important in an era that David Levi-Faur (2005) characterizes as 'governance through regulation;' where the expanding neo-liberal agenda does not diminish the state's role but transforms it, indeed increases its importance under the *modus operandi* of 'regulatory capitalism' (see also Zhang and Thomas 2009, pp. 1–2). Increasing levels of private sector participation and an ever growing need to mobilize larger pools of private capital to fund infrastructure deployment — from roads, railways, information communications technologies (ICT) to energy and educational capacity — transforms the scope and role of government, often demanding more rather than less, or what Hood *et al.* (1999) describes as an 'explosive growth in investment in oversight.' In developed economies, this has produced contradictory tendencies; 'leaner and meaner' government which, in the case of the United Kingdom, for example, saw a 25% reduction in the number of civil servants between 1976 and 1996 but, for the same period, a relative explosion in staffing levels in regulatory bodies, growing by over 90% (Hood *et al.*, 1999, pp. 29–31; Levi-Faur, 2005, p. 20).

In the UK, as in other advanced economies this transformation has been relatively well accommodated. Highly evolved institutional capacities, long established procedural norms and practices, and deeply instantiated institutional legitimacy has allowed for effective governance adaptation. For theorists like Levi-Faur (2005), the conundrum that presents itself is thus little more than understanding the ubiquity of this process and how 'regulatory diffusion' and policy transfer transform the mode of governance in various juridical settings. Other theorists similarly approach the rise of regulatory capitalism in ubiquitous terms, but defined by the diffusion of global regulatory standards and codes that create over-reaching structures of regulation. Braithwaite and Drahos (2000, p. 3), for example, note the extent to which states outside of Europe and the US 'have become rule- takers rather than rule-makers,' where the regulatory standards and codes evolved by international organizations or consortia of public and private interests witness a diffusion of these standards into national contexts. In Australia, for example, many of the air safety standards 'have been written by the Boeing corporation … or … the US Federal Aviation Administration. Australia's ship safety laws have been written by the International Maritime Organization … its motor vehicle safety standards by Working Party 29 of the Economic Commission for Europe and its food safety standards by the Codex Alimentarius Commission in Rome' (Braithwaite and Drahos, 2000, p. 3). For such literatures, the conundrum of regulatory capitalism resides in the technocratic imposition of rules and the implications for democratic participation in rule formation; how these may benefit the interests of rule-makers, disadvantage rule takers, and the costs and issues associated with technical implementation of global standards, regulatory codes, and practices. For other literatures, the rise of the regulatory state is approached in more technical terms, focused upon regulatory design and the technical parameters of outcomes, costs, efficiencies, and optimality for sector participants (Jaffe and Stavins, 2007; Strausz, 2009).

Strangely absent from these literatures, however, are explicit attempts to theorize the institutional-regulatory nexus or examine it empirically. Institutions, while not ignored or theorized away, are simply assumed and their capacities, procedural systems, levels of instantiation, norms and practices, taken as given. Jordana *et al.* (Forthcoming, p. 9), for example, at various points conflate regulatory diffusion with institutional transplantation and adoption, neglecting issues of institutional capacity and the specific social and political contexts in which institutions are embedded — they are simply transplanted, capacities and all. Similarly, Levi-Faur (2005, p. 17; Levi-Faur and Jordana, 2005), while noting that 'regulatory capitalism sits quite comfortably' with neoinstitutionalist literatures, fails to make the linkage between institutional forms, institutional functionality and specificity, and the implications for the regulatory state in institutionally unique or impaired environments. There is, in effect, what Zhang and Thomas (2009, p. 331) describe as a 'reality gap,' where best practice and the regulatory and institutional models evolved in developed country contexts produce a singular policy prism that ignores the 'actual legal, administrative, political and economic processes that exist in low and middle income countries' (pp. 331–332). As they point out, the danger is that this leads to a 'one size fits all' approach that when diffused into developing country contexts is likely to produce 'perverse outcomes' or 'fatal remedies.' Regulatory reform and the emergence of regulatory institutions in developing economies face 'more and bigger difficulties than in developed countries," but the precise dimensions these take and the consequences that evolve remain mostly under explored and little theorized (Zhang and Thomas, 2009, pp. 331–332).

In this chapter, I suggest that the diffusion of the regulatory state and with it specific regulatory models and systems in developing country contexts, generate fundamentally different regulatory outcomes. Rather than a ubiquitous regulatory capitalism, variations in regulatory efficiency, differences in institutional endowments and the manner in which institutions are embedded in contested political and social domains, produces not only multifarious and unanticipated outcomes but often reductive oversight capacity. Further, I suggest that the unique institutional-regulatory interface that obtains in developing country contexts produces qualitatively different forms of regulatory risks, and, with them, a much wider and potentially more deleterious set of outcomes for both private sector participants and state interests.[3]

2. Theorizing Regulatory Risk

The purpose of economic regulation as Levy and Spiller (1994) famously remarked is to focus attention on the regulatory arrangements necessary to sustain private sector investment. Because of their unique characteristics, investments into utilities face a series of problems. Utilities, for example, are characterized by technologies that require large sunk investments into fixed infrastructure. The return on investment is largely captured by the requirements of economies of scale and scope, where the technology is unique because of the ubiquity of its distribution and consumption — we all demand access to electricity, water and telecommunications.

[3] While I do not address the methodological parameters of institutional analysis, I draw implicitly on the broader debates surrounding institutionalism in political science. See, for example, Hollingsworth (2000) and Hall and Taylor (1996). On the broader overreaching debate surrounding governance and conceptual approaches to institutional processes in governance outcomes see Kaufman *et al.* (1999).

Utilities investments also tend to be non-transferable. Utility assets have little value in alternative uses — they cannot be easily dug up and deployed to alternative sectors — and the exigencies of economies of density and network externalities make it largely uneconomical to deploy multiple networks (Spiller 1996, p. 423). Investments into such sectors thus tend to be captured by the exigencies of the technology, their size, scope and non-transferability. As Levy and Spiller note, 'what separates the utility sector from the rest of the economy is the combination of three features: specific investments, economies of scale and widespread domestic consumption' (Levy and Spiller 1994, pp. 202–204; see also Spiller 1996, p. 423; Stern and Holder, 1999, pp. 37–38).

These characteristics create specific risks for investors into the utilities sector. First, they make the sector inherently political. The relatively ubiquitous consumption of utilities (e.g., electricity, water, communications), make the issue of tariffs, tariff adjustments and review, open to interest group and political pressures, while the state divesture of assets through privatization and the pricing of utilities creates political agendas often accompanied by intensive political scrutiny. Second, because of economies of scale and scope, utilities investment and operation suffers from the 'whiff of monopoly,' fueling interest group pressures and often the mobilization of political resources against operators (Levy and Spiller, 1994, p. 424; Spiller and Tommasi, 2005, pp. 517–520). Third, sunk investments into fixed infrastructure are exposed to the perils of what Raymond Vernon (1971) termed the 'obsolescing bargain' problem, where the relative bargaining strength of the investor vis-à-vis the state declines post market entry. Once the investment is sunk, the problems of divestiture, tariff adjustment, the requirement for government approvals for market exit or transfer of ownership, increases the relative bargaining power of the state, enabling it to engage in rent seeking behavior or otherwise change the extensity of the market and impact investment returns (see Jarvis and Griffiths, 2007). Fourth, the large transaction costs associated with market exit, divestiture of sunk assets and redeploying investments elsewhere, means that utilities operators will 'often continue operating as long as operating revenues exceed operating costs,' effectively stranding the asset, generating stranded costs and depreciating the value of the sunk investment (Spiller 1996, pp. 423–424).

2.1. *Regulation to the Rescue?*

Government opportunism and the tendency of political constituencies to demand economic concessions or rents remain the greatest disincentive to private sector participation in utilities and infrastructure provision (Jarvis and Griffiths, 2007; ADB, 2009, p. 124). For governments to mobilize private sector investment they need to construct credible institutional arrangements that constrain their opportunism and balance the obsolescing bargain problem. Regulation, regulatory theory and practice, thus arise from this dilemma, where the design and operation of a regulatory regime is meant to ameliorate political risk, constrain the opportunistic behavior of government, decrease uncertainties for the investor, and provide frameworks that set in place administrative procedures for review and revision due to changed circumstances, unforeseen externalities, and disputation.

Such frameworks have become an increasingly dominant feature of the regulatory landscape of developed economies since the spate of privatizations of state utilities commenced in the late 1970s. These produced a series of regulatory models with most coalescing around the implementation of independent regulators; key agencies charged with oversight, administration, compliance, licensing, review and due process as electricity sectors where unbundled and private sector participation encouraged. Indeed, such regulatory systems became the preferred model of multilateral development banks and were identified as a key means of mobilizing private sector investment into resource poor countries and accelerating infrastructure provision. Throughout the 1980s and 1990s, countries in Latin America and Asia thus adopted a series of pro-market policies in utilities provision, commencing reforms in the sector by allowing the establishment of independent power producers (IPPs) and in many cases adopting variations on the regulatory models that had sprung up in Europe — notably the United Kingdom (Stern and Holder, 1999, pp. 33–35).

It would be wrong, however, to assume that the adoption of such regulatory frameworks in developing country contexts has mitigated the risks of opportunism, political risk, or the problems of creeping expropriation through rent seeking behavior (Bergara and Spiller, 1997, p. 16; Dassler, 2006). Constraining government opportunism and political risk is a function of both the regulatory regime and the institutional environment. Not all institutions are created equal and the manner of these variations creates a regulatory-institutional mix that lies at the heart of what we might term *regulatory risk.* Without effective institutions the *credibility* of the regulatory regime is degraded,

Levy and Spiller (1994) suggest the nexus of this regulatory-institutional mix can be divided analytically into two categories: *regulatory governance* and *regulatory incentives.* Regulatory incentives refer to the formal rules (often contractual) stipulating utility pricing, tariffs, subsidies, public service delivery and quality obligations, and associated economic costs and returns. As they correctly observe, 'the structure of regulatory incentives has been the central preoccupation of virtually all theoretical work on regulation.' As they further note and as this study will contend, 'such an emphasis is inadequate' (p. 205). Regulatory incentives are not advanced in an institutional vacuum; incentives are meaningless absent a credible commitment and the institutional means to extract these. Rather, this comprises the realm of *regulatory governance* defined as the 'mechanisms that societies use to constrain regulatory discretion and to resolve conflicts that arise in relation to these constraints' (Levy and Spiller, 1994, p. 205).

The choice of mechanisms available to societies, however, are themselves constrained by the 'specific institutional endowment of the nation' (North, 1990). These comprise its socio-political attributes; the means by which representation, rules, judicial process, informal norms and customs, and the constellation of social forces and administrative capabilities, impact, constrain, and enable institutional commitments (Levy and Spiller, 1994, p. 206; North, 1990). In other words, the institutional endowment 'both determines the form and severity of the regulatory problems and shapes the range of options available for resolving them' (Levy and Spiller, 1994, p. 205). Variations in the effectiveness of regulatory governance and the credibility of regulatory commitments thus derive from variations in the institutional endowment.

2.2. *Regulatory Risk*

Policy diffusion and transplantation of regulatory models into diverse institutional endowments can thus be expected to generate dissimilar regulatory outcomes and variations in regulatory governance. These variations lie at the heart of our notion of regulatory risk, where variations in the quality of regulatory design, regulatory tools, and regulatory institutions may generate a series of risks that detract from or degrade the credibility of the regulatory commitment (see also Henisz, 2002). These risks can arise at various points in the regulatory process. For example, the regulatory design can be flawed or imperfect, comprised of inadequate formalization of the rules, rule contradiction, poor rule clarity or confusion. The tools associated with regulatory incentives may be mispriced, inappropriately or poorly administrated, subject to manipulation, or otherwise poorly calibrated to balance public and private interests. The institutions associated with regulatory governance may be ineffectual or impaired, where the principles that undergird good governance (transparency and information symmetries, stakeholder participation, accountability and redress mechanisms, autonomy), are absent, unavailable or poorly practiced (see Spiller and Tommasi, 2005, pp. 524–529).

The combination of such attributes is endless (Correa, 2007; Dixit *et al.*, 2007, p. 7; Nakhooda *et al.*, 2007, p. 8). The point is that the presence of any contributes to a degradation of regulatory credibility, producing various regulatory risks that impact predictability and certainty in the sector, due process, and the right of redress (CEPA, 2005, pp. 20–25; Bertelli and Whitford, 2009; Globerman and Shapiro, 2002). Regulatory risk can thus manifest in countless forms; for example, the inability of the regulator to enforce rules and defend public and private interests; contestation of rule ownership leading to policy or rule making paralysis, confusion, or rule instability; regulatory implementation deficits creating governance gaps, inconsistency and lack of predictability, among many others.

Efforts to redress the extent of regulatory risks have invariably focused on bolstering the institutional endowment by engineering the degree to which proxy attributes of regulatory governance are present and practiced in regulatory institutions. The degree of transparency, the mode and practices via which information is shared, the method and manner of stakeholder engagement and participatory practices in regulatory processes, the means by which accountability principles are enshrined, and the degree to which institutional autonomy is balanced against regulatory discretion to protect against regulatory capture or political interference are all now standard measures of the governance capacity of regulatory regimes and, in turn, the extent to which they are impaired or absent serve as broad indicators of regulatory risk (see also Strausz, 2009, p. 2).

This chapter explores these issues in relation to the institutional endowment of the energy sector in Thailand; specifically, the electricity generation, transmission and distribution sector. Like many developing economies, Thailand has evolved an energy policy reflecting its desires to increase its energy security and lessen its dependence on external energy sources while rapidly deploying energy infrastructure to facilitate economic development. Part of this process has involved the imposition of new regulatory frameworks, largely adopted from models developed in the UK. Thailand thus represents an instance of regulatory diffusion of specific regulatory models, but in a developing country context where institutional processes are evolving and where institutional endowments and capacities remain truncated.

The chapter is organized into two sections. The first section surveys the Thai electricity sector, addressing the evolution of the regulatory regime governing the up-stream (generating) and downstream (distribution / transmission) sectors and the governance outcomes produced by an impaired and still pre-formative institutional environment. In essence, this section outlines the institutional endowment in which the Thai energy sector initially evolved but, more importantly, the legacy this set in place and into which reform efforts and an independent regulator have emerged. The second section addresses the outcomes of this institutional endowment vis-à-vis the interplay of historical legacies and newly evolved regulators, using the standard metrics of transparency, stakeholder engagement processes and systems of accountability as a means of understanding how specific institutional-regulatory contexts generate unintended regulatory outcomes and regulatory risk. As the paper attempts to demonstrate, the interplay between the historical endowments of Thailand's institutional environment and the emergence of new regulatory institutions creates an institutional — regulatory mix that, far from guaranteeing the success of the reform process and effective regulation, creates new tensions and political dynamics whose outcomes make regulatory governance problematic.

Critical to my analysis have been the perspectives gathered through fieldwork and interviews conducted with regulators and private sector participants in the Thai energy sector. Where requested, the identity of interview subjects has been protected.[4]

3. The Thai Electricity Sector

3.1. *Historical Background*

Electricity is a political commodity in Thailand. Electrification, roll out of generating and transmission infrastructure, and consumer and industrial access to electricity is intimately associated with the developmental plans and ambitions of the Thai state and its people (Williams and Dubash, 2004). Indeed, growth in the demand for electricity, increasing annually by 10% from the mid-1980s, has been a leading indicator of the country's rapid development as Thailand moved into energy-intensive industrialization in petrochemicals, manufacturing, steel and cement production, and expansion of upstream refinery capacity (Woo, 2005, p. 3). At the same time, rapid urbanization and favorable pricing policies made electricity comparatively inexpensive, promoting electricity energy substitution and a further expansion in generating capacity (Wattana *et al.*, 2008, p. 43). While the Asian financial crisis witnessed significant reductions in electricity demand in line with a contraction in economic activity, since 2001 growth in demand has returned, expanding annually between 3–7% and on April 24, 2007, achieving a record peak power demand indicative of continuing energy-intensive industrialization (EGAT, 2008, p. 7).[5]

The importance of electricity to Thailand's economic development has historically made for a strong state presence in the electricity sector, with three government-owned enterprises dominating power generation and distribution since the late 1960s: the Electricity Generating Authority of Thailand (EGAT), the Metropolitan Electricity Authority (MEA), and the Provincial Electricity Authority (PEA)(see Table 1). EGAT's inception

[4] Interviews were conducted in November 2008, between 26 and 30 January 2009, and August 2009.

[5] Electricity demand grew by its six fold between 1982 and 2002, with consumption growing from 16, 900 gigawatt-hours (GWh) to 108,400 GWh (Greacen and Greacen, 2004, p. 518).

Table 1: Thailand's electricity sector: 1968–1992

Utility	Inception	Mandate and functions
EGAT	1968	Sole agency responsible for electricity generation and transmission in Thailand; central planning of national electricity development; pricing and tariffs; direct power and electricity distribution to a few, key large consumers
MEA	1958	Responsible for distribution and all retail service functions (connections, meters, billing, maintenance) in key metropolitan areas such as Bangkok, Nonthaburi and Samut Prakan
PEA	1960	Distribution responsibilities for all other (predominantly rural) areas outside of Bangkok, Nothaburi and Samut Prakan

Source: Woo, 2005, p. 5; EPPO, Energy Sector Management in Thailand, p. 15.

in 1968 represented a decade long process of vertical integration, with the government merging several state-owned regional generating authorities to form a 'sole agency responsible for generation and transmission of electricity to the entire nation' (Wattana *et al.*, 2008, p. 44). Indeed, the creation of EGAT is itself a reflection of earlier forms of policy diffusion, with the World Bank and USAID strongly endorsing a single independent power agency as a condition for loans to finance infrastructure roll out.[6] The result was a triangulated and vertically integrated electricity sector, whose central role in powering Thailand's industrialization made the three power utilities not only politically strong but in effect self-regulating apart from financial requirements set by the *Ministry* of *Finance* (Wattana *et al.*, 2008, p. 48; Williams and Dubash, 2004; Greacen and Greacen, 2004, p. 519).

The institutional legacy this set in place should not be understated. By default, EGAT enjoyed a monopoly that constructed a series of powerful dynamics, vested interests, and control over substantial resources. Reform of any kind, whether in the modes of regulatory governance or attempts at creating stand alone oversight agencies beyond the reporting mechanisms

[6] As Supannika Wattana *et al.* (2008, p. 43) notes, for example, for much of the 1970s and early 1980s, the World Bank was EGAT's main source of external financing, creating a dependent relationship that saw EGATs adopt much of the policy architecture favored by the bank.

required at its inception, would henceforth invariably be seen as threats to these interests and likely incur the resistance of EGAT. By championing strong state agencies as the primary vehicles for electrification, EGAT became aligned with the domestic objectives of industrialization and economic growth, allowing it to enjoy prime place in the institutional fabric of Thai society.

3.2. *Early Reform Efforts in the Thai Electricity Sector: 1980–1989*

The rapid deployment of electricity capacity via centralized agencies like EGAT proved both highly successful and costly for Thailand.[7] Much of the capacity roll out was financed by external loans, with EGAT, MEA and PEA responsible for nearly half of all of Thailand's external borrowing between 1967 and 1971 (and as much as 37% between 1972–1976). Thailand's power utilities thus entered the energy crises of 1974 and 1979 with heavy debt burdens and a reliance on imported oil (required for electricity generation). The result was a tripling of the nation's external energy bill between 1979 and 1981 and a blow out in national debt, reaching 39% of GDP (Wattana *et al.*, 2008, pp. 44–45; Greacen and Greacen, 2004, p. 520).

By the early 1980s, state-led development through external financing thus became problematic, and in the case of electricity, highly politicized. Electricity prices rose dramatically off the back of higher energy costs and debt servicing, increasing 259% between 1979 and 1982. Political pressure to maintain low electricity tariffs and facilitate greater access to electricity among Thailand's rural and urban poor created contradictory pressures to appease domestic constituencies and set artificially low tariffs while attempting to address the rising debt burden of the utilities. In the face of bourgeoning public debt, Thailand was forced to seek emergency assistance from the International Monetary Fund (IMF) (in 1981, 1982, and 1985) and negotiate a series of conditional structural adjustment loans (SALs) from the World Bank. Part of the loan conditions required price increases for electricity and the privatization of state-owned enterprises in

[7] By 1981, for example, over 50% of Thai's had access to electricity (Greacen and Greacen, 2004, p. 519).

order to increase private sector participation and thus reduce public sector debt (Greacen and Greacen 2004, p. 520; Chaivongvilan *et al.*, 2008, p. 56).

By 1988, the government's 'White Paper on Enterprises' recommended the privatization of 41 of Thailand's 61 state-owned enterprises (by 2001). EGAT was classified a 'Class A state Enterprise' and earmarked for privatization through a three track process: first, partial privatization of EGAT through equitization and forced divestiture; second, the introduction of new industry players via the sale of EGAT's up-stream generating assets; and third, the procurement of power from privately operated independent power producers (IPP)(Woo, 2005, p. 6).

Despite emergent ideational change among domestic coalitions, in particular, an increasingly vocal and influential Thai middle class and a pro-democracy movement generally aligned with the interests of privatization or, at least, greater public accountability and transparency, the first efforts to privatize the utilities and liberalize tariffs failed. Labour unions, consumer groups, Thai nationalists and academics created a powerful coalition that, in conjunction with EGAT's vested interest in preserving the status-quo, succeeded in thwarting privatization initiatives. Disbanding such an embedded institutional arrangement as provided by EGAT, or the sense that alternative ownership models could or would produce superior outcomes in terms of tariff reductions, greater efficiencies or enhanced public service delivery, essentially misunderstood the deeply intertwined relationship between Thailand's rapid industrialization and relative poverty reduction, and the role that state agencies like EGAT were seen to have played in this process.

By the end of the decade, EGAT thus continued to enjoy a monopoly, but with mounting external debt and expanding infrastructure obligations. Thailand's explosive economic growth throughout the 1980s, for example, tripled electricity demand and resulted in electricity shortages and 'brownouts,' threatening the country's continued industrialization. EGAT was forced to roll out greater generating and transmission capacity amounting to over US$ 1 billion annually by the end of the 1980s, again mostly financed through concessional bi-lateral loans. By 1989–1990, EGAT's fiscal position was thus precarious, with some 57% of its annual operating budget forced to be set aside to service its foreign debt obligations

(US$1.168 billion in fiscal year 1989–1990) (Greacen and Greacen 2004, p. 520; Wattana *et al.*, 2008, pp. 45–46).

3.3. *The Diffusion of Privatization in the Thai Electricity Sector, 1990–1999*

Thailand's continued economic success in the early 1990s only exacerbated electricity capacity issues. Between 1985 and 1995, for example, Thailand was the world's fastest growing economy, with real GDP expanding annually by 8.4% (Greacen and Greacen, 2004, p. 521). With mounting generating capacity and transmission requirements EGAT's financing arrangements became increasingly problematic. By the early 1990s, the World Bank had put in place new electricity infrastructure lending policies, setting down conditions stipulating the establishment of market based regulatory regimes, the commercialization and corporatization of electricity sector agencies, and liberalization of the sector to facilitate foreign ownership and greater private sector participation (World Bank, 1993). As Wattana *et al.* (2008, p. 45) notes, 'the continuing pressures coming from international financial agencies in parallel with the rapid rise of electricity demand created a situation which saw private investment the best alternative.' At the same time, the successive administrations of prime ministers Chatchai Chunhavan (1988–1991), Anand Panyarachun (1991–1992) and Chuan Leekpai (1992–1994) commenced an extended period of pro-market reforms that would ultimately come to reconfigure the policy architecture and regulatory regime governing electricity.

The initial cluster of reforms, however, were tentative and essentially worked around the thorny issue of an entirely new regulatory regime or radically new ownership structure in the face of still powerful institutional legacies that constrained political options. Some of these reforms had commenced previously with the creation of the National Energy Policy Office (NEPO) in 1986 and formed as a secretariat to the National Energy Policy Council (NEPC) which reported directly to the Prime Minister's office. NEPO was headed by the influential and politically powerful Dr. Piyasvasti Amranand (1986–2002) with NEPO essentially driving energy policy in Thailand through the NEPC. Under Piyasvasti, NEPO became a strong proponent of market rationalism and privatization, lobbying the Prime Minister and cabinet for reform in the electricity sector as a means of addressing EGAT's precarious debt position (Greacen and Greacen 2004, p. 523; Electricity Governance in Thailand, 2006). Its invigorated role under the 1992 National Energy Policy Council Act, essentially made NEPO the most influential energy body in the country, assuming significant powers over all facets of energy policy, planning, and pricing.[8] In quick succession, NEPO secured technical assistance from the World Bank to assist in the privatization of the electricity sector and supported passage of amendments to the EGAT Act (1992), allowing private power producers (PPP) to enter the upstream generating sector.

Two PPP's subsequently came on line; the first in May 1992 with the formation of the 'Electricity Generating Company Limited' (EGCO), and the second in March 2000 with the formation of the 'Ratchaburi Electricity Generating Holding Public Company.' Both were initially formed as wholly owned subsidiaries of EGAT. Both EGCO and Ratchaburi would be floated on the Stock Exchange of Thailand (SET), raise funds via their initial public offering (IPO), tap capital markets and then purchase generating plants from EGAT as part of a forced divestiture. By breaking EGAT's monopoly on power generation and creating market competition in up-stream generation, the reforms aimed to lower generation costs and stem the tide of tariff increases under EGAT.

3.3.1. *Outcomes*

Thailand's first foray into electricity privatization produced contradictory outcomes. Far from perfect competition, EGAT retained significant interests in both EGCO and Ratchaburi. As recently as 2005–2006, for example, EGAT retains a 25% stake in EGCO and a 45% interest in Ratchaburi. As the sole purchaser of power from EGCO and Ratchaburi, EGAT's interests are conflicted. It retains a commercial interest in the profitability of EGCO and Ratchaburi and an ability to pass on supplier costs to end consumers. By one account, for example, EGAT pays as much as 20% more for power from EGCO than from other private producers (Greacen and Greacen,

[8] See 'National Energy Policy Council Act, B.E. 2535' (1992), Government Gazette, 109, Part 7, February 12, Kingdom of Thailand.

2004, p. 523). This incentivizes collusion and the prospects of agreed cost structures rather than competition with incentives to lower costs. As Woo (2005, pp. 6–7) observes, rather than competition 'there is an informal agreement between … [the] …companies not to directly compete for the acquisition of assets' that even extends to setting out 'their prospective spheres of influence for investment in neighboring countries.' More obviously, the nature of the power purchase agreements (PPAs) between EGAT, EGCO and Ratchaburi utilized a 'take or pay' contract, protecting PPPs from demand variations and downloading excess capacity risks to EGAT and in turn Thai consumers.

Most glaring, however, was the failure to develop new regulatory oversight authorities or innovate regulatory capacity concomitantly with privatization roll-out. EGAT retained a powerful role in the government structure and for all practical purposes enjoyed self-regulation. EGAT's reporting and accountability mechanisms, for example, amounted to little more than the preparation of annual accounts to the Ministry of Finance, with sensitive or commercial in-confidence agreements with PPPs remaining undisclosed. Privatization was essentially occurring in a regulatory vacuum, absent accountability, oversight, compliance and enforcement mechanisms surrounding competition, pricing, private sector participation or consumer protection. Privatization was itself seen as a form of regulatory innovation but absent institutional developments to administer the commercial parameters of this new environment. As far as NEPO were concerned, privatization would bring its own rewards — the institutional innovations could come later (Sirasoontorn, 2005, p. 3). The introduction of formal rules governing regulatory incentives or the instigation of new institutions to effect regulatory governance were thus strangely absent amid what was otherwise championed as energy sector reform.

The instigation of a series of IPPs while signaling some degree of liberalization in the upstream generating sector in Thailand also demonstrated how the reform efforts of Piyasvasti and NEPO were constrained by institutional legacies. Much of the 'reform' that occurred was confined to the policy realm, where political leaders accepted the need for private sector participation in generation, but generally shunned the broader and politically more challenging tasks of erecting new institutional arrangements or embarking on regulatory innovation. The institutional legacies which had seen resources and authority for electricity provision centralized in the hands of EGAT, essentially constrained the options available to reform minded bureaucrats or political elites, leaving EAGT relatively untouched if not commercially benefiting from the instigation of IPPs. More importantly, the failure to effect meaningful reform in the modes of regulatory governance left reform-minded constituencies without non-political mechanisms to break down EGAT's 'black box' operating mentality.

There was, however, one significant outcome of these efforts: control over Thailand's electricity policy had been firmly placed in the hands of the Thai bureaucracy. EGAT would no longer be the sole repository of electricity knowledge, policy and planning.

3.3.2. *Privatization amid Regulatory Opacity: The Introduction of IPPs*

The absence of a robust regulatory context defines much of Thailand's subsequent reform efforts in the electricity sector. The second track of privatization commenced in December, 1992, for example, saw the introduction of independent power producer (IPP) and small power producer (SPP) programs, designed to attract private foreign investment to build, own, and operate large and small scale power plants, enhancing generating capacity while reducing public expenditure commitments.[9] As before, IPPs and SPPs would enter into power purchase agreements (PPAs) with EGAT, the sole purchaser of electricity. Seven IPP concessions were granted in 1994–1995 to supply 6,345 megawatts (MWs) with commercial operating dates commencing between 1999–2003 (Woo, 2005, p. 7).

While the bidding process for IPP licenses was competitive, there was no regulatory mechanism in place to oversee governance in the sector in terms of the mediation of competitive pressures down the value chain to consumers and tariff prices. PPAs negotiated between the IPPs and EGAT, for example, operated on the basis of a regulated returns environment, guaranteeing returns on the basis of estimated IPP costs at the time of the granting of the concession. Any efficiency gains through technical innovation or lower operating costs were retained by the IPP (Wattana *et al.*,

[9] EGAT commenced purchasing power from large IPPs in 1999 and SPPs in January 1994.

2008, p. 47; Sirasoontorn, 2005). Similarly, oversight of the sector and the commercial practices of the IPPs and EAGT's fell to NEPO and NEPC, who, as Sirasoontorn (2005) observes, were not regulators *per se*, but architects of the policy environment with no surveillance, enforcement, or compliance capacities or mandated obligations in this regard. For investors in the IPPs, the absence of a formal system of regulatory oversight exposed them to the perils of a single purchaser (EGAT) relationship, changes in the policy preferences and agendas flowing from NEPO, and possible changing political coalitions driving energy policy at the Cabinet level via the NEPC. Rather than a consistent regulatory environment, Thailand's energy policy existed outside of an institutionally instantiated process defined by formal processes for review, stakeholder engagement and innovation. Regulatory governance in a sense was entirely absent, with energy policy contained in a highly circumscribed institutional setting, NEPO, and otherwise captured by an energy Czar, Piyasvasti. NEPO, Piyasvasti, and Thailand's electricity privatization agenda disappeared with the political winds of change.

3.4. *Winds of Change in the Thai Electricity Sector: Policy & Political Instability, 2000–2006*

After the Asian financial crisis (1997), the Thai government drew up and approved a 'Master Plan for State Sector Reform' in line with the letter of intent presented to the IMF as part of Thailand's bailout package (Electricity Governance in Thailand, 2006, p. 10).[10] The Master Plan outlined the 'basic guidelines, principles, practices and time frames for privatization plans, legal, regulatory and institutional changes' (Sirasoontorn and Quiggin 2007, p. 403; see also NEPO, 1999, p. 7). The plan called for the full privatization of the electricity sector similar to the 'power pool model' adopted in the UK. In essence, the sector would be 'unbundled,' separating out the generating, transmission and distribution sectors. At the generation end, EGAT's generating assets would be split into three separate generation companies, privatized and sold off. Each of

[10] Master Plan for State Sector Reform available at http://www.mof.go.th/sepc/sepcfn1.htm.

these generating companies would then compete in a 'power pool' selling power on a spot market where supply and demand would determine spot prices for electricity. EGAT would be morphed into a transmission company and retain sole national transmission rights and responsibilities. MEA and PEA, in the meantime, would each be split up into regulated electricity delivery companies and compete in the retail market. The power pool would commence functioning in 2003, instigating a period of competition in the electricity sector at both the wholesale and retail ends with EGAT solely responsible for transmission activities (EPPO, 2000). Concomitantly, the government would move to appoint an independent and all-powerful regulator similar to the UK model (Office of the Gas and Electricity Markets, UK) whose mandate would be to regulate competitive activities in the wholesale sector, oversee the natural monopoly created in the transmission sector by regulating transmission charges to IPPs, as well as regulate the limited competition expected to emerge in the retail distribution sector (Sirasoontorn, 2005, p. 3; Electricity Governance in Thailand, 2006, p. 9; EPPO, 2000; World Bank, 1999).[11]

While strongly supported by the Chuan Leekpai administration (1997–2001) as an effort to meet not only its obligations to the IMF, but fundamentally transform the electricity sector and address the precarious financial status of EGAT, the reform agenda was widely unpopular. EGAT opposed the reform initiative: EGAT unions feared job losses, Thai nationalists felt it would lead to the takeover of national assets by foreign interests, consumers feared it would increase power prices or lead to the advent of privatized monopolies, and the Thai press feared corruption or favoritism in the privatization process (Sirasoontorn, 2005, p. 3; Electricity Governance in Thailand, 2006, p. 9).[12] In the wake of the fallout and severe economic dislocation caused by the Asian financial crisis (1997–1998), popular sentiment in Thailand was increasingly suspicious of still further reform championed by international organizations or the value of imported foreign models. The Chuan government's reform efforts thus

---

[11] Greacen and Greacen (2004, p. 526) reports that NEPO commissioned the report outlining the reform recommendations at a cost of some US$10 million which was paid to a consortium of foreign management companies.

[12] "EGAT people in search of a future," *The Nation*, June 25, 1999.

became increasingly imperiled, indeed used by the populist politician, Thaksin Shinawatra, in his election bid to become prime minister (Electricity Governance in Thailand, 2006, pp. 9–10).

Soon after its election, the Thaksin administration (2001–2006) abandoned the power pool model. Behind this move lay a broader political agenda that aimed to transform state-owned enterprises into strategic entities that would fuel Thailand's subsequent growth and propel the country out from underneath IMF loan obligations and a languishing economy. Instead, Thaksin moved to create a 'register of capable state enterprises as public companies.' These companies would be incorporated, floated on the SET, stimulating investment in the still languishing Thai equity market and, in the process, generating significant financial resources that could be directed into needed expenditure programs (pay down of IMF loans, for example). Thaksin's aims were simple: turn SOEs like EGAT into 'national champions.' The move was a populist one which had the veneer of keeping Thai assets in Thai hands by imposing foreign equity ceilings or ownership limits (partial privatization) while also addressing a privatization agenda with the aim of improving competition and sector efficiencies (see Chirarattananon and Nirukkanaporn, 2006; Greacen and Greacen, 2004, p. 527; also Jarvis, 2002).

Most significant in the energy sector, however, was Thaksin's restructuring of the formal institutional mechanisms for energy governance. Soon after his election, Thaksin transferred the energy czar, Piyasvasti, out of NEPO and subsequently established a new Ministry of Energy (MOE) in 2002, renaming NEPO the Energy Policy and Planning Office (EPPO, 1997).[13] Under these new governance arrangements, electricity policy making roles were relocated directly into the Ministry, with EPPO downgraded and reporting to the Energy permanent secretary rather than to the Minister or cabinet. In doing so, the political clout of EPPO (compared to NEPO) was diminished, with energy policy now firmly controlled inside the executive and subject to direct political considerations.

These changes benefited EGAT, allowing it to emerge as a 'national champion' and, in the process, able to exert increasing influence over the

[13] The events surrounding Piyasvasti's relocation out of NEPO and his displacement as Thailand's energy Czar are contested. See Greacen and Greacen (2004, pp. 530–532).

MOE and to position itself strategically inside the reform debate. The new political climate called for strong Thai companies, 'champions' that would promote Thai enterprise and compete successfully against foreign companies. Thai nationalism latched on to Thai SOEs as potential saviors against foreign ownership and resentment toward organizations like the IMF and their perceived roll in the economic hardships Thailand had been forced to endure. As a result, EGAT enjoyed political support from the Thaksin administration which it leveraged to help guide reform of the electricity sector. The appointment of the Boston Consulting Group (BCG) in 2003 to prepare a new National Energy Strategy by the MOE, for example, was welcomed by EGAT who enjoyed a long standing relationship with the consulting house. In turn, the defacto advisory role that EGAT played in the subsequent recommendations prepared by BCG and adopted by the Thaksin administration, enabled EGAT to preserve much of the status quo.

The recommendations of the new National Energy Strategy called for the implementation of an Enhanced Single Buyer (ESB) model. The model deviated little from previously recommended models. EGAT would be privatized, preserve its monopoly over transmission and compete directly with IPPs in the generating sector. PEA and MEA would be corporatized and compete in the retail market. Finally, the ESB model called for the creation of a robust independent regulator with clearly defined rules, powers and resources in order to ensure enhanced competition and address monopolistic practices (EGAT, 2008). The policy was to be implemented by 2004.

Despite Thaksin's popularity, the privatization of EGAT proved politically difficult. Public hearings, union concerns and the increasing mobilization of civil society groups created a strong political constituency opposed to EGAT privatization (Thomas *et al.*, 2009, p. 27; Foran, 2006, p. 40). In particular, the September 2005 decision by the Thaksin administration to restructure and at the same time increase electricity tariffs, created a popular backlash. While the Thaksin administration sought to increase EGAT's revenues, improving its debt to equity ratio and thus share price when it listed on the SET, civil society and consumer groups thought the changed tariff structures unjustified and feared that the benefits of privatization would not accrue to Thai consumers (Electricity

Governance in Thailand, 2006, p. 13). There were also fears that the privatization process was not impartial and that those sitting on the privatization committee would perhaps improperly benefit from the privatization of EGAT. Despite attempts to appease opposition groups by announcing a freezing of the tariff regime for three years, the Confederation of Consumer Organizations submitted a petition to the Supreme Administrative Court to suspend EGAT's share offering. Subsequently, the Supreme Administrative Court ruled in favor of the petition, noting conflict of interest among members of the privatization committee and ordering a suspension of the share issue on November 17, 2005. The royal decrees allowing the privatization of EGAT were subsequently cancelled (Sirasoontorn, 2008; Chaivongvilan *et al.*, 2008, pp. 56–57).

4. Regulatory Diffusion: The Emergence of the Energy Regulatory Commission, 2007

The story of Thailand's electricity reform efforts does not end with the premiership of Thaksin. They were, however, abruptly interrupted by the military coup (September 2006) and the political machinations leading to the reinstatement of democracy in December, 2007. Ironically, despite 14 years of reform efforts it was amid the relative chaos of the post-coup period that legislators finally approved the creation of a regulatory regime with the adoption of the Energy Industry Act (December 2007). A new era had arrived in Thailand's energy sector.

The adoption of a formal regulatory model and with it an attempt to create a system of regulatory governance was a milestone in the evolution of Thailand's approach to energy sector governance. In part, this abrupt about face was a culmination of several factors. First, the abandonment of the 'national champion' model as a result of Thaksin's forced departure deprived EGAT of the political patronage it had previously enjoyed. The circuits of influence and political relations that stood EGAT in a relatively strong position vis-à-vis the reform agenda and boarder political attitudes toward the composition of the electricity sector had been abruptly interrupted. Indeed, the repudiation of the Thaksin administration reflected a strong political constituency that had mobilized against corruption and patronage, in the process marginalizing those individuals and entities that had been seen to be aligned with Thaksin and his political agenda.

Second, and perhaps ironically, the privatization agenda while largely usurped because of fears over corruption, conflicts of interest and due process, did not halt the allied reform agenda associated with the instigation of regulatory oversight in the sector and calls for greater accountability and transparency. Popular suspicions that cozy deals, patronage, and vested interests had driven the sector at the expense of greater efficiencies and the national interest created a political terrain that even the likes of EGAT was unable to resist.

Third, the importance of the energy sector (electricity, gas and oil) had been increasingly elevated by rising energy costs, concerns about energy security, and the sense that Thailand's energy resources should be managed for the national benefit. In part, a combination of civil society groups, popular sentiment favoring transparency and accountability, and the sense that mismanagement of the energy sector would have implications for national economic development proved an unstoppable tide of opinion that culminated in the adoption of the Energy Industry Act.

The Energy Industry Act created a single regulatory body, the Energy Regulatory Commission (ERC). Modeled on the UK's Office of the Gas and Electricity Markets, ERC's mandate is wide and varied. It includes the following (ERC, 2008; interview with ERC Chairman, Mr. Lavansiri and Commissioners, ERC, Bangkok, January 26, 2009):

- input and review of Thailand's national energy policy
- input and review of the Power Development Plan (historically the exclusive preserve of EGAT)
- review and comment on the investment plans of the electricity industry, the national gas procurement plan and the energy network system expansion plans
- development and implementation of customer service standards
- development and oversight of service provision standards
- surveillance, inspection and oversight of licensees in the upstream generation, transmission and distribution sectors
- development of regulatory codes and standards pertaining to industry operators

- establishment of stakeholder engagement processes and procedures
- development of conflict of interest guidelines for ERC board members
- development of regulations and criteria for financial contributions, disbursements and administration of the 'Energy Fund'
- oversight authority in respect of IPP and PPAs
- development of regulations and engineering safety standards in respect of industry operation and the certification of equipment / devices
- oversight and development of energy consumer protection protocols, including the appointment and operation of a 'Regional Energy Consumer Committees' (RECC's)[14]
- oversight and review of electricity tariffs and applications for tariff adjustment, including the development of a 'methodology' for tariff calculation
- oversight and responsibility for the security and reliability of the power system
- responsibility for promoting competitive practices in the industry.

Despite what appears far sweeping regulatory reform it would be wrong, however, to view this as a break with the past or, indeed, the instigation of a regulatory regime that is uncontested. Rather, the ERC has been inserted into a highly political terrain and is forced to operate astride a series of institutional legacies and in a political climate that is far from stable. This has implications for the type of regulatory governance regime the ERC might reasonably be expected to evolve. Indeed, it speaks to the constraints of an institutional endowment that makes problematic the ability to overcome uncertainty, provide credible regulatory commitments or erect effective regulatory governance mechanisms mediated through transparency, accountability, and autonomy.

[14] RECC's are, in turn, charged with addressing the petitions of consumers against generators, EGATs and power distributors as it impacts retail operations, mediating consumer complaints, the development and proposal of corrective measures to improve measures regarding energy provision in the regions, coordination with the energy industry operators in securing information petitioned by consumers and mediating consumer complaints with industry operators to improve service delivery.

4.1. *The Metrics of Regulatory Governance: Transparency, Accountability and Autonomy in Embedded Institutional Endowments — The Case of the ERC*

Thailand's institutional endowment is a contested domain of finely balanced social forces that position around the monarchy. They include the military, a strong and growing middle class predominantly located in Bangkok, an intellectual class focused around Bangkok's universities, an extremely wealthy but small elite whose diverse holdings in intermediate industries and agri-business has benefited from the country's rapid industrialization, and a large rural population consisting of mainly poor farmers and agricultural workers. The institutional fabric of Thai society makes for a series of cleavages that have often broken down, with the Kingdom reverting to military coups on numerous occasions. Not surprisingly, amid this highly contested political landscape the sense in which forms of regulatory governance are able to emerge is not just a matter of institutional development and the establishment of formal rules, but a much more problematic series of issues around institution building, institutional instantiation, balancing social forces and interests, and constructing mechanisms of governance virtually from the ground up.

Evidence of how problematic is this process can be seen since the inception of the ERC itself. The adoption of the Energy Industry Act (2007), for example, should not necessarily be interpreted as a vote of support for the ERC or its mandate. Successive post-coup administrations under Samak Sundaravej, Somchai Wongsawat, Chaovarat Chanweerakul, and Abhisit Vejjajiva between January 29 2008 and December 17 2008 were not immediately or strongly supportive of the establishment of an independent regulator (interview with Dr. Piyasvasti Amranand, former chairman of NEPO, Bangkok, November, 2008).[15] The passage of the Energy Industry Act can thus equally be explained in the context of

[15] In the wake of the military coup and the reestablishment of democracy, Thailand experienced political instability with four different Prime Ministers in quick succession: Samak Sundaravej (29 January 2008–8 September 2008); Somchai Wongsawat (2 September 2008–18 September, 2008); Chaovarat Chanweerakul (acting Prime Minister, 2 December 2008–17 December 2008); Abhisit Vejjajiva (17 December 2008–).

Thailand's continuing political machinations and political realignment in the post-coup era. As one commentator close to the ERC noted, the weakness of successive administrations, their need to carry core constituencies coupled with weakened executive authority in determining the legislative agenda probably allowed the Energy Industry Act to pass where previously vested interests would have delayed or modified it (interview, January, 2009). Evidence in support of this interpretation is not hard to find. Throughout 2008, for example, the Thai Cabinet was lukewarm to the ERC and seemingly adopted a go slow attitude, delaying approval of the ERC's budget and announcement of Commissioner salaries, in effect putting the ERC on hold during its first year of operation (interview, ERC Commissioners, Bangkok, November, 2008).

It is in this broader political climate and amid an institutional endowment that suffers from continuing social cleavages, unresolved political machinations and underdeveloped administrative capacity that the ERC is forced to operate and evolve effective regulatory governance in the energy sector. Clearly, such legacies place a series of constraints on the operating environment of the ERC which, combined with its own endowments and capacity, provides insights into how effective attempts to development regulatory governance will likely be. I examine each of these attributes briefly.

4.2. *Autonomy*

Autonomy is an important attribute for effective regulatory governance. It signals that political or special interest capture of the regulator is not possible and that the regulator will likely act in accordance with the regulatory principles of its mandate. Without autonomy, the credibility of the regulatory commitment is diminished.

The extent to which the ERC is autonomous, will enjoy fiscal autonomy over its budget and be able to control resources necessary to discharge its mandate, remains problematic. Historically, Thai governments have not been well disposed to stand-alone statutory agencies since they represent lost revenue streams. Prior to the creation of the ERC, for example, the MOE enjoyed a windfall from operator fees of Baht THB100 million (approximately US$ 2 million) per license. This now falls to the ERC whose income from license fees is estimated to be between Baht

THB500 to 600 million annually (approximately US$16 million) (interview, ERC Commissioners, January 26, 2009). Yet, in its first full year of operation (2008), the ERC was only able to issue interim operating licenses due to the failure of cabinet to approve full licensing autonomy, curtailing the ERC's budget revenues and capacity development in its first year of operation. Such irritants likely point to future contests between the ERC and future administrations. Under the current Energy Industry Act (2007), for example, the Minister for Energy and cabinet have ultimate approval authority over the ERC's budget expenditure including its operational plan and, under section 40 of the Act, the ERC is notionally required to return excess revenues above operational costs to the Ministry of Finance (Energy Industry Act, 2007, Section 9–8; Part 2, Section 40). The full intent of these clauses and how they might be interpreted and applied remains to be seen; what is obvious, however, is the interpretative space this leaves successive administrations to challenge the fiscal autonomy of the ERC and in the process its autonomy as a statutory regulator. Without budget autonomy and guaranteed revenue ownership, the prognosis for the ERC establishing its autonomy will be problematic (interview with Dr. Piyasvasti Amranand, former chairman of NEPO, November, 2008).[16]

There are also broader concerns about the level of autonomy the ERC will enjoy. Cabinet approval for the issue of regulations, for example, is required under the Act as are public hearings before regulations can be proclaimed (interview, Dr. Pallapa Ruangrong, ERC Commissioner, ERC, Bangkok, November, 2008). Further, in the discharge of its mandated duties to review and set tariffs structures, it is unclear where the lines of authority are drawn. Ostensibly these lie with the ERC, but when interviewed ERC commissioners indicated that the tariff review process was governed by guidelines issued by the NEPC, MOE and prevailing government policy, and that stakeholders like EGAT had significant interests as well. When asked about authority spheres and rule ownership, for

[16] At the time of writing, the ERC budget for 2009 had been approved. However, the details of this cannot be confirmed. Dr. Direk Lavansiri, Chairman of the ERC, indicated the ERC budget would approach Baht THB600 million for 2009 and that the operating budget for the organization would come entirely from license fees (Interview, January 26, 2009).

example, the Chairman and ERC Commissioners suggested these still had to be worked out; that the ERC was still in its early stages of development (Interview, ERC, Bangkok, January 26, 2008).

These blurred lines of authority are also evident in the consultative and bespoke relationships between the ERC, MOE, and EPPO and how each relates to the other in the operation of the regulatory regime. The process of policy review of the national energy plan, historically the preserve of NEPC and EGAT in terms of its 'future demand models,' will not likely be ceded by either organization easily, suggesting that the ERC might act more as a commentator than serious player in energy policy, compromising its ability to oversee energy security, quality of service delivery and energy security. Similarly, its ability to act as an impartial broker in tariff adjustment cases requires cross-institutional cooperation, information symmetries between commercial operators, EGAT, and NEPC, and political non-interference by the Minister for Energy and cabinet in what have historically been highly contested political decisions. While stipulated in the Act and thus notionally within the authority domain of the ERC, operationalizing the policy mechanisms that instantiate the ERC's role in energy policy, tariff adjustment, or the issuance of licenses, thus far remains undefined and unaddressed.[17] When asked, for example, how the ERC will inject itself into this policy space, establish its presence and effect inter-agency cooperation and policy coordination, ERC commissioners were only able to refer back to the black letter law of the Energy Industry Act, highlighting the fact that administrative norms or considerations about the broader project of instantiating the institution to ensure its regulatory effectiveness have not been considered. As the ERC Commissioners noted, they are currently focused on more tangible operational issues: construction of a mission and vision statement,

[17] These problems impact all levels of energy policy in Thailand. The relationship between EPPO, the Ministry of Energy, the permanent secretary for energy and the Cabinet, for example, reveal little policy coordination and an absence of policy consultation mechanisms. As the report on energy governance in Thailand noted, 'there is no ... defined mechanism that requires the executive to consult (EPPO) ... on major policy issues or to evaluate how the executive responds to recommendations/decisions of the agency' (Electricity Governance in Thailand, 2006, Section A: 15–16).

getting the web page up and running, and developing capacity (Interview with ERC Commissioners and Chairman, ERC, Bangkok, January 26, 2009). While the ERC's inception is thus a positive step forward, the highly contested and fluid nature of governance in Thailand's energy sector presupposes that this is still a sphere open to future contestation, where the authority, legitimacy and regulatory effectiveness of the ERC remain in doubt.

4.3. *Regulatory Capacity*

This gap between the creation of a regulator and its ability to regulate is perhaps the most obvious example of how problematic the institutional-regulatory nexus is in developing country contexts. Regulatory diffusion pen ultimately hangs on regulatory capacity (see especially Stern, 2000). As Gasmi *et al.* (2009, p. 2), observes, the fundamental role of liberalization and of regulatory reform has been to 'redesign the legal and regulatory frameworks so as to induce "proper" economic incentives ... namely, incentives for operators to enhance their offerings ... cost efficiency, quality of service, and tariffs." For developed countries, this has essentially involved a modernization 'of an already existing fabric of institutions with a complex system of operating rules built over a long history of political and economic administration of market economies' (Gasmi, 2009, p. 2). In developing country contexts, the question of institutional design or the diffusion of regulatory models, presupposes a much more complex set of issues that range from administrative capacity to human skill capacity (Stern, 2000, pp. 135–137).

Thailand's ERC is a case in point. After 15 months of operation, its administrative and regulatory function remains rudimentary. The breadth and scope of its mandate, for example, requires high capacity surveillance over market functions, the deployment of compliance and enforcement mechanisms, sophisticated analytical systems in the case of review and input to the Energy Master Plan, tariff adjustment claims, economic and social impact assessment, roll out of a host of regulatory standards, the development of an extensive network of representative regional offices, oversight and administration of the collection and disbursement of revenues to the 'Power Development Fund,' among other technical programs and oversight responsibilities.[18] In all, the ERC will require nine administrative departments to oversee all of its regulatory functions.[19]

The mandate is obviously extensive, yet the available capacity to meet these regulatory obligations is still formative. The organization is currently resourced with thirty staff, mostly non-technical administrative personnel, with ERC leadership provided by six full-time commissioners and a chairperson. The absence of personnel with technical ability in regulatory administration in the industry is notable, with the ERC currently negotiating the transfer of 10 staff from EPPO to help provide technical capacity to the organization (interview, ERC commissioners, January 26, 2009, Bangkok, Thailand).[20] Attracting and retaining technical and high capacity personnel, however, is a problem. While the ERC will be able to offer salaries twice those of public service pay rates, these still fall far short of remuneration standards available in the industry itself. There is thus little prospect for attracting candidates with industry experience or of preventing talent transfer to industry operators in the

---

[18] The Power Development Fund has multiple objectives. It is leveled against any utilities with a PPA greater than 6 MWs, and charged against production of natural gas, oil, diesel, coal, wind and solar power, biomass and hydro electricity generation. The fund compensates licensees who have provided services for underprivileged power consumers at below cost recovery rates; subsidizes rural electrification; pays for the rehabilitation of localities impacted by power plant operation; subsidizes the development of renewable energies; pays for public awareness campaigns in the use of energy; reimburses users under previous tariff formula who were overcharged for energy usage; and pays for the operation of the fund itself (Lavansiri, 2008).

[19] The ERC have announced the following administrative divisions: 'General Provisions, Regulatory Body for the Energy Industry Operation, Regulation of the Energy Industry Operation, Energy Consumer Protection, Utilization of Immoveable Property, Redress of Disputes and Lodging of Appeals, Competent Officials, Disciplinary Procedures and Punishment' (Lavansiri, 2008).

[20] It should be noted that it is not the practice in the Thai civil service for personnel to move between agencies or ministries. Thai Civil servants normally join a specific administrative arm or agency of the government and remain there for the duration of their career, gaining seniority through cumulative service (Interview with Kurujit Nakornthap, Director General, Department of Mineral Fuels, Bangkok, Thailand, January 27, 2009).

longer term. Most telling, however, is the 'map' to which the ERC commissioners are working in terms of developing ERC's capacity. The ERC's organizational structure, operational goals, and organizational needs appear to be mostly defined by external, private sector consultancies (notably the Boston Consulting Group and PriceWaterhouseCoopers) with little internal input into the adequacy of the targets, their impact or utility to the organization's structure, functions and operation. Indeed, the fact that PwC has been retained and appears to be the lead agency in the strategy and roll out of the ERC's capacity development is itself an indication of the paucity of internal capacity the ERC faces. Without adequate capacity, how the ERC will be able to manage and adjust accurately the regulatory incentive structure, effectively balance public and private interests, determine and price regulatory instruments appropriately, or set in place the appropriate regulatory tools remains problematic.

4.4. *Transparency & Accountability*

These capacity issues also impact the regulatory functions of the ERC in other less immediate ways. The diffusion of regulatory governance principles surrounding accountability, transparency and stakeholder engagement processes, for example, articulate in vastly different ways in countries where the institutional endowment is impaired or less developed. While the ERC have nominally adopted transparency and accountability principles as part of its legislated mandate in the Energy Industry Act (2007), the interpretation and intended practices surrounding these reveal highly perfunctory outcomes. ERC Commissioners, for example, indicated that the organization would be transparent through its web page, but 'sensitive information' would be excluded. What the parameters were for the listing or exclusion of information appeared to be at the discretion of the ERC Chairman and Commissioners. Transparency in the ERC context simply amounts to selected information being placed on its web page, with little appreciation that principles surrounding transparency might also extend to decision making processes, making transparent information sources, the analytical assumptions, tools, and methods used for decision making, and disclosing the consultative processes and information inputs and representations made by industry operators and other stakeholders.[21]

These same issues emerged with the notion of accountability, with the ERC Commissioners indicating they were accountable to the Minister for Energy and the cabinet and that once a year the ERC would present its budget to the Ministry of Finance. Yet, the commissioners struggled to identify the mechanisms of accountability, emphasizing that the most important compliance requirement they had was annual budget reporting and a parliamentary tabling of the ERCs annual activities — none of which had yet occurred (interview, ERC Commissioners, January 26, 2009, Bangkok, Thailand). ERC Commissioners also indicated they were accountable to their stakeholders, consumers and industry operators, but through what administrative mechanisms or engagement systems the Commissioners failed to identify.

Principles of transparency and accountability thus appear to articulate as purely perfunctory compliance obligations rather than being approached as regulatory tools that can further regulatory governance and performance though establishing the regulator's legitimacy or increasing industry understanding of the regulator's processes, decision making systems, and objectives.

Stakeholder Participation

Such attitudes were also evident in terms of stakeholder engagement processes, an otherwise critical tool for mediating conflicting sectional interests, constructing credible commitments, and legitimating the ERC and its regulatory authority. Indeed, actively involving stakeholders in the regulatory process is frequently cited as one of the most important elements for instantiating regulatory legitimacy, increasing information symmetries between regulators and regulatees, compliance outcomes, and

[21] In other jurisdictions, for example, transparency standards extend to the public disclosure of all communications, meetings, phone calls and other forms of representation between regulators, industry operators and stakeholders, to reduce the possibility of nefarious activity, collusion and thus increase the impartiality and perceived legitimacy of the regulator.

reducing regulatory risk through mediation and long-lead time signaling of regulatory changes (Cubbin, 2005; Spiller and Tommasi, 2005; Stern, 1997; ADB, 1995). Yet, the ERC's approach to stakeholder engagement was defined almost exclusively by its desire to defuse civil society and consumer advocacy groups opposed to tariff adjustment applications (Lavansiri, 2008; ERC, 2008; Interview, ERC commissioners, January 26, 2009, Bangkok, Thailand). Stakeholder engagement appeared to be confused with public relations and the management of vocal groups. More obviously, the only mechanism identified for stakeholder engagement was 'public hearings.' The sense in which stakeholder engagement might involve active participation of stakeholders in internal decision making, energy planning and the regulatory process was alien.

These issues are not purely academic for newly emerged regulators like the ERC. The adoption of a largely UK-based model and its infusion into the governance space of the energy sector in Thailand, holds potentially large risks absent a robust institutional base and strong administrative tradition on which to found it. The continuance of strong industry players like EGAT, for example, and the institutionalized monopolies it continues to enjoy in the transmission sector and over price determination for transmission rates, make for resilient practices that will be difficult to modify. Adding the ERC to this mix does not necessarily suppose the diffusion of a regulatory governance regime so much as the addition of another institutional player in an already highly contested and vexed governance environment. The establishment of the ERC is thus but a first step in a still highly fluid environment, the outcomes of which have yet to effect systems of regulatory governance in ways that lessen uncertainty, provide for greater predictability, or are able to instantiate regulatory credibility.

5. Regulatory Risk in Contested Environments

The history of reform efforts in the Thai energy sector betray the perils of institution building in developing country contexts. Regulatory and policy diffusion into environments where the institutional endowment is fragile and where rule making and authority structures are contested makes for inherent instability. Thailand's experiences bear this out. The policy environment has ebbed and flowed from one set of proposals and operating policies to another, held hostage to the whims of changing political coalitions, the vested interests of key players like EGAT, and key personalities inside agencies like NEPO. The result has been policy contestation, with energy policy increasingly politicized if only because of the lack of formal institutional forums / mechanisms to mediate competing social forces. As a result, the political arena has been the obvious and most productive environment in which to prosecute interests and influence energy policy. Indeed, for political elites, such a contested policy environment has made for highly motivated constituencies able to be mobilized and used to bolster political ends.

The risks that arise from this, however, have been all too obvious: the increasing politicization of energy policy debates, the use of litigious and juridical processes to adjudicate disputes and decide policy outcomes, and attempts by coalitions to capture policy processes and disenfranchise competing interests. In such a vexed environment, the policy outcomes adopted have been viewed as illegitimate, imposed, and unrepresentative of broader interests, in turn fueling further policy contestation or policy gridlock.

The creation of the ERC and the instigation of a formal regulatory regime should, under normal circumstances, go a considerable way to mitigating regulatory risk and balancing these contending social forces. However, as the findings of this article suggest, the ERC's ability to ensconce itself amid a highly contested environment and discharge its regulatory functions cannot be assumed. The impaired institutional base, porous administrative traditions, and capacity issues it faces may well end up not ameliorating regulatory risks but contributing to them through further institutional complexity and contested authority domains. These concerns speak to the larger project that economic regulation is meant to achieve. The three tiers of the regulatory matrix — regulatory design, regulatory incentives, and regulatory governance — cannot be assumed. If any one of these elements is impaired, then the issue of regulatory credibility is diminished. This appears to be happening in the case of Thailand. In interviews with senior executives and managing directors of international power generation companies, the message was near universal, exemplified by one regional manager noting 'it's a mess' (interview, August 18, 2009). When asked why, the interviewee responded with a laugh noting that on each visit to Thailand he always tries to take at least one ERC Commissioner to dinner, hoping to understand developments, directions, plans and policy in the pipeline. Of these conversations he offered the following observations; 'pointless, some are clueless, nobody has an idea where things are going and nobody agrees ...' (interview, August 18, 2009). The impression of several of the industry interviewees appeared to be that commissioners were travelling frequently to European and North American cities ostensibly to study regulatory governance systems, but most laughed and inferred it was obviously not impacting their work (interviews, August, 2009).

None of these impressions have aided the credibility of Thailand's regulatory system. Indeed, for investors into the Thai electricity sector, regulatory risk from policy instability and frequent policy changes has increased the risk premium, with investors demanding higher rates of return, stringent contractual indemnity, and in-built guarantees before committing investment capital — all of which has contributed to a higher cost environment for investors and end users alike. Indeed, one interviewee, a regional managing director of a large international generation company, noted that they continued to operate successfully in places like Pakistan without contractual issues and with predictability in terms of operating requirements and compliance standards. He compared this to Thailand, noting that Pakistan was easier and less risky! (interview, August 18, 2009). These observations appeared to center around what the interviewee identified as 'changing their minds,' where policy confusion or frequent policy changes has left investors disinterested. When questioned further about these risks, the interviewee explained that even the process of putting together bids or contemplating a strategy to engage the relevant stakeholders in Thailand was not worth the effort since it was likely to be the case that half way through any of these processes the 'game plan' would change (interview, August 18, 2009). As one executive of a large British multinational power provider noted of Thailand, 'it's in our too hard basket until they work out what they are doing' (interview, November, 2008).[22]

[22] Recent studies by Udayasankar *et al.* (2008), also finds that there is strong evidence to suggest that paucity in regulatory environments adversely impacts the corporate governance of firms, downloading costs to business as they try and navigate opaque environments with poorly regulated competition policies which impair or degrade firm governance capacities.

These observations speak to poor regulatory outcomes if, as Levy and Spiller (1994) noted, economic regulation is meant to construct regulatory arrangements able to sustain private sector investment through credible regulatory commitments. Clearly, this is not the view of interview subjects engaged for this research. Rather, regulatory credibility amid a still impaired political environment suggests that governance in the sector remains unpredictable, the autonomy of the ERC still unclear, and the attributes of transparency, accountability, and stakeholder participation far from realized as instruments for effective regulation.

6. Going Forward: Lessons

Thailand's experiences with regulatory reform in the energy sector reveals much about the perils and pitfalls of institutional change and the consequences for regulatory governance. These lessons fall into four broad categories.

First and foremost are the lessons for policy makers in developing country contexts. Policy diffusion and the adoption of regulatory models from vastly dissimilar environments is a problematic policy exercise. While international benchmarking and the tendency to emulate 'best practice' standards is now part of the policy makers lexicon and *raison d'etre*, the adoption of regulatory models and their transplantation into different institutional endowments can often produce unintended or even deleterious regulatory outcomes. Policy learning is not simply a process of policy emulation, and regulatory innovation and reform much more than regulatory diffusion and the transplantation of specific regulatory models. If Thailand's experiences teach us anything, it is the need for policy makers to calibrate regulatory reform with the institutional endowment, and to recognize that developing institutional capacity as an end in itself may yield much greater effectiveness with regard regulatory governance than the simplistic imposition of a new regulatory model.

Second, Thailand's experiences of regulatory reform in the electricity sector speak to the enduring problems of institution building. Institutions are complex sets of individuals, interests, rules, practices, and norms. They involve an array of relations between stakeholder constituencies and complex mediations as a means of not simply allocating resources, but instantiating agendas, practices, and behaviors to effect desired outcomes. In the case of Thailand, reform of the energy sector has been a dual process of reconstituting the institutional environment responsible for energy sector governance at the very highest political levels as well as a process of creating new institutions mandated to regulate energy (the ERC) on the ground. The flux this creates in the institutional environment makes for all manner of problems, complicating the environment in which regulators are forced to operate and in the process increasing the burdens and costs on regulators. The consequences for regulatory efficiency and the impact this may have on regulatory capacity can perhaps only be imagined rather than measured with any degree of precision. What is evident, however, is that radical policy innovation that both transforms institutional environments and creates new regulatory bodies generates exogenous factors that may end up increasing transaction costs rather than reducing them. Adaptation to new institutional terrains, developing new trust relationships between stakeholders and impacted constituencies, and developing transactional norms to facilitate the business of regulation generate added burdens — many of which new regulatory agencies may be ill equipped to manage.

Third, and relatedly, policy innovation of the regulatory apparatus and institutional environment can create all manner of rule confusion, reducing regulatory effectiveness and outcomes. The division of duties, responsibilities and the jurisdictional space that applies to the ERC, EPPO, the Ministry of Energy, and Ministry of Finance, is a case in point. At a recent meeting organized by the Asian Development Bank for electricity and water regulators in Thailand, for example, questions about specific areas of responsibility, jurisdiction and rule making authority had one ERC Commissioner repeatedly consulting the Legislation, admitting that it was not always clear who had specific authority over particular issues or if the ERC had jurisdiction to even consider certain matters (Bangkok, July 27, 2009). Rule confusion, contested rule making or, worse still, competition over roles and responsibilities, are key ingredients for poor regulation and inferior regulatory outcomes. This not only makes for an opaque regulatory environment but generates risks and costs for stakeholders as they try and navigate the regulatory terrain. Getting the institutional design right so that roles, responsibilities, and jurisdictions are clear and transparent should be an elemental concern for all regulators.

Fourth, reform of the institutional and regulatory environment in the Thai energy sector also highlights lessons about the appropriate mix between a regulator as an administrator and overseer of rules, standards, and practices, and the relationship between these activities and policy development. In the case of the ERC, its role in energy policy development as well as regulatory oversight of the sector is blurred, ostensibly engaging in both but in a manner that does not really define its relationship to energy policy formulation, the mechanisms for policy development between the Ministry, ERC and EPPO, or how policy roles are to be assigned. Again, institutional design is all important, requiring the transparent allocation of roles and responsibilities in order for effective regulation and policy development to be achieved.

These lessons are not exhaustive and speak more to a set of enduring problems rather than solutions. But in exploring them and highlighting the interplay between variations in the institutional endowments of developing countries, regulation, and the broader political environment within which transplanted regulatory models are often diffused, it is to be hoped that regulatory outcomes will be enhanced for the betterment of all.

Bibliography

Asian Development Bank (1995). *Governance: Sound Development Management.* August, Asian Development Bank, Manila.

Asian Development Bank (2009). *Infrastructure for a Seamless Asia.* Asian Development Bank & Asian Development Bank Institute, Tokyo.

Bergara, M, WJ Henisz and PT Spiller (1997). *Political Institutions and Electric Utility Investment: A Cross-Nation Analysis.* Program on Workable Energy Regulation (POWER), University of California Energy Institute, California.

Bertelli, AM and AB Whitford (2009). Perceiving credible commitments: How independent regulators shape elite perceptions of regulatory quality. *British Journal of Political Science*, 39, 517–537.

Braithwaite, J and P Drahos (2000). *Global Business Regulation.* Cambridge, UK: Cambridge University Press.

CEPA (Cambridge Economic Policy Associates) (2005). *PPIAF Mechanisms to Mitigate Regulatory Risk in Private Infrastructure Investments.* Washington, DC: Public Private Infrastructure Advisory Facility.

Chaivongvilan, S, D Sharma and S Sandu (2008). Energy challenges for Thailand: An overview. *Greater Mekong Subregion Academic and Research Network (GMSARN) International Journal*, 2(2), 53–60.

Chirarattananon, S and S Nirukkanaporn (2006). Deregulation of ESI and privatization of state electric utilities in Thailand. *Energy Policy*, 34(16), 2521–2531.

Correa, P (2007). What it takes to lower regulatory risk in infrastructure industries. *Gridlines,* Washington DC: Public Private Infrastructure Advisory Facility, Note Number 29, September.

Cubbin, J (2005). Regulatory Effectiveness and the Empirical Impact of Variations in Regulatory Governance: Electricity Industry Capacity and Effectiveness in Developing Countries. *World Bank Policy Research Working Paper 3535*, March, World Bank, Washington, DC.

Dassler, T (2006). Combining theories of regulation: Proposing a framework for analyzing regulatory systems worldwide. *Utilities Policy*, 14, 31–43.

Dixit, S, NK Dubash, C Maurer, and S Nakooda (2007). *The Electricity Governance Toolkit: Benchmarking Best Practice and Promoting Accountability in the Electricity Sector.* The Electricity Governance Initiative, World Resources Institute & Prayas Energy Group, Pune, India.

EGAT Act (1992). (Emendation to the 1968 EGAT Act), Generating Authority of Thailand Act B.E. 2511 (1968), Bangkok, Thailand.

EGAT People in Search of a Future. *The Nation*, June 25, 1999.

Energy Industry Act, B.E. 2550 (2007). 10 December, Bangkok, Thiland.

Electricity Generating Authority of Thailand (2008). *Thailand Power Development Plan*, 2007–2021. Report Number 912000-5104, System Planning Division, January, Bangkok, Thailand.

Electricity Governance in Thailand: Benchmarking Best Practice and Accountability in the Electricity Sector (2006). Health Systems Research Institute, Thailand Environment Institute, Conference of Consumer Organization, Palang Thai, and the World Resources Institute, Bangkok, Thailand.

Energy Policy and Planning Office [EPPO] (2000). *Electricity Supply Industry Reform and Thailand Power Pool.* Available at http://eppo.go.th/power/index.html [Accessed 15 January 2010.]

Energy Policy and Policy Office (EPPO)(1997). *Energy Sector Management in Thailand.* Ministry of Energy, Bangkok, Thailand.

Energy Regulatory Commission (2008). Office of the Energy Regulatory Commission (ERC), Bangkok, Thailand. Available at http://www.eppo.go.th/index-E.html.

Foran, T (2006). Thailand's Politics of Power System Planning and Reform. *M-Power Working Paper*-2006–2005, Mekong Power Project on Water Environment and Resilience, Unit for Social and Environmental Research, Chiang Mai University. Available at http://www.sea-user.org/mweb.php?pg=76 [Accessed 14 June 2010].

Gasmi, F, P Noumba and L Recuero Virto (2009). Political Accountability and Regulatory Performance in Infrastructure Industries: An Empirical Analysis. Paper presented to the Infrastructure Regulation: What Works, Why, and How do we Know Conference. University of Hong Kong, SAR, February 26–27.

Globerman, S and D Shapiro (2002). Global foreign direct investment flows: The role of governance infrastructure. *World Development*, 30(11), 1899–1919.

Greacen, CS and C Greacen (2004). Thailand's electricity reforms: Privatization of benefits and socialization of costs and risks. *Pacific Affairs*, 77(3), 517–541.

Hall, PA and RCR Taylor (1996). Political Science and the Three New Institutionalisms. Max-Planck-Institut für Gesellschaftsforschung, Cologne, Germany, MPIFG Discussion Paper 96 / 6, June.

Henisz, WJ (2002). The institutional environment for infrastructure investment. *Industrial and Corporate Change*, 11(2), 355–389.

Hollingsworth, JR (2000). Doing institutional analysis: Implications for the study of institutions. *Review of International Political Economy*, 7(4), 595–564.

Hood, C, C Scott, O James, G Jones and T Travers (1999). *Regulation Inside Government*, Oxford: Oxford University Press.

Jaffe, J and RN Stavins (2007). On the value of formal assessment of uncertainty in regulatory analysis. *Regulation and Governance*, 1(2), 154–171.

Jarvis, DSL. (2002). Problems and prospects in Thaksin's Thailand: An interim assessment. *Asian Survey*, 42(2), 297–319.

Jarvis, DSL and M Griffiths (2007). Learning to fly: The evolution of political risk analysis. *Global Society*, 21(1), 5–21.

Jordana, J, D Levi-Faur and XF Marin (Forthcoming). The global diffusion of regulatory agencies and the restructuring of the state. *Comparative Political Studies.*

Kaufmann, D, A Kraay and P Zoido-Lobaton (1999). Governance Matters. *Policy Research Working Paper 2196*, Development Research Group, The World Bank, Washington, DC.

Lavansiri, D (2008). Thailand's Energy Regulatory Commission: Vision and Mission. Presentation by the Chairman, 27 September, Portland, Oregon, USA, Palang Thai & A World Institute for a Sustainable Humanity (A W.I.S.H), Sponsored by Blue Moon Fund.

Levi-Faur, D and J Jordana (2005). Regulatory capitalism: Policy irritants and convergent divergence. *ANNALS of the American Academy of Political and Social Science* March, 598, 191–197.

Levi-Faur, D (2005). The global diffusion of regulatory capitalism. *ANNALS of the American Academy of Political and Social Science* March, 598, 12–32.

Levy, B and PT Spiller (1994). The institutional foundations of regulatory commitment: A comparative analysis of telecommunications regulation. *The Journal of Law, Economics and Organization*, 10(2), 201–246.

Nakhooda, S, S Dixit and NK Dubash (2007). *Empowering People: A Governance Analysis of Electricity — India, Indonesia, Philippines, Thailand.* World Resources Institute & Prayas Energy Group, Washington, DC.

National Energy Planning Office (1999) *Privatization and Liberalization of the Thai Energy Sector.* March 29, Thailand.

North, D (1990). *Institutions, Institutional Change and Economic Performance.* Cambridge: Cambridge University Press.

Sirasoontorn, P (2005). Fiscal Assessment of Partial Privatization: Case of Electricity State Owned Enterprise in Thailand. Mimeo, Faculty of Economics, Thammasat University, Bangkok, Thailand.

Sirasoontorn, P (2008). Tariff Regulation in Electricity Supply Industry in Thailand. *Discussion Paper Number* 0007, March 19, Faculty of Economics, Thammasat University, Thailand.

Sirasoontorn, P and J Quiggin (2007). The political economy of privatization in the Thai electricity industry. *Journal of the Asia Pacific Economy*, 12(3), 403–419.

Spiller, PT (1996). Institutions and commitment. *Industrial & Corporate Change*, 5(2), 421–452.

Spiller, PT and M Tommasi (2005). The institutions of regulation: An application to public utilities. In *Handbook of New Institutional Economics*, Menard, C and MM Shirley (eds.), pp. 515–543. Netherlands: Springer.

Stern, J (1997). What makes an independent regulator independent. *Business Strategy Review*, 8(2), 67–74.

Stern, J (2000). Electricity and telecommunications regulatory institutions in small and developing countries. *Utilities Policy*, 9, 131–157.

Stern, J and S Holder (1999). Regulatory governance: Criteria for assessing the performance of regulatory systems. An application to infrastructure industries in the developing countries of Asia. *Utilities Policy*, 8, 33–50.

Strausz, R (2009). Regulatory Risk under Optimal Incentive Regulation. SFB 649 *Discussion Paper* (2009–2006), Humboldt University, Berlin, Germany.

Thomas, S, D Hall and V Corral (2009). *Electricity Privatisation and Restructuring in Asia-Pacific*. Available at www.psiru.org [Accessed 14 June 2010].

Udayasankar, K, SS Das and C Krishnamurti (2008). When is Two Really Company? The Effects of Competition and Regulation on Corporate Governance. National University of Singapore, Business School.

Vernon, R (1971). *Sovereignty at Bay*. New York: Basic Books.

Wattana, S, D Sharma and R Vaiyavuth (2008). Electricity reforms in Thailand: An *Historical* Perspective. Greater Mekong Subregion Academic and Research Network (GMSARN). *International Journal*, 2(2), June, 41–52.

Williams, JH and NK Dubash (2004). Asian electricity reform in historical perspective. *Pacific Affairs*, 77, 411–436.

Woo, PY (2005). Independent Power Producers in Thailand. *Working Paper* 51, Program on Energy and Sustainable Development, Center for Environmental Science and Policy, Stanford University, California.

World Bank (1999). Thailand Power Pool and Electricity Supply Industry Reform Study (Phase 1: Final Comments of Independent Review Committee), Bangkok, Thailand.

World Bank (1993). *The World Banks Role in the Electric Power Sector*. World Bank, Washington, DC.

Zhang, YF and M Thomas (2009). Regulatory reform and governance: A survey of selected developing and transition economies. *Public Administration & Development* July, 29(4), 330–339.

CHAPTER 6

Electricity Tariff Regulation in Thailand: Analyses and Applications of Incentive Regulation

Puree Sirasoontorn

Thammasat University, Thailand

Under the enhanced single buyer model of the electricity supply industry in Thailand, tariff regulation is needed to prevent unfair pricing for consumers. Retail electricity tariff, comprising the base tariff and the automatic tariff adjustment mechanism, is regulated by multiple regulatory bodies. According to the rate of return approach, the Thai electricity base tariff regulations tend to favour electric utilities rather than consumers. In addition, the automatic tariff adjustment mechanism attaches greater importance to operators than to consumers, enabling the former to burden consumers with fuel and power purchases. The results of the adoption of the current regulatory regime are excess capacity in the electricity supply industry and excessive profits for the electric utilities. This chapter explores the tariff regulatory alternatives that could enhance the efficiency of electricity operators while providing benefits to consumers. Under price cap regulation, electricity tariffs are estimated with various *X* and *Z* factors. The results reveal that the simulated electricity tariffs under the incentive regulatory approach are lower than the tariff. It implies that if Thailand were to adopt price cap regulation, consumers would benefit from the lower tariff, whereas firms would be incentivized to increase efficiency.

Keywords: Electricity supply industry; incentive regulation; rate of return regulation.

1. Introduction

The electricity supply industry (ESI) in Thailand has essentially operated in a monopolistic manner. It consists of four main activities: generation, transmission, distribution and retailing. Transmission and distribution activities are characterized by natural monopoly, thus prompting regulation (Gans and King, 2000). Although generation and retailing can technically be competitive businesses, they are operated by the state-owned monopolists. From this structure and together with its importance as the backbone industry needed for economic and social development, tariff regulation to prevent unfair and unrealistic tariffs set by monopolistic operators is needed. In general, there are four economic goals in tariff regulation, of which two goals are for consumers — which are rent extraction and demand-side efficiency, and two are for operators — which are capital attraction and supply-side efficiency (Joskow, 1998). In practice, it is difficult to achieve all these goals at the same time. Setting goals in favor of either consumers or operators is not economically desirable. For instance, if the regulators set too high a tariff to attract investment (capital attraction goal), it would be unfair for consumers (rent extraction goal). In most of the cases, the regulators prefer to employ a supply-side approach. For example, if regulation could ensure efficient operation, resulting in lower costs of power generation, transmission and distribution (supply-side efficiency goal), it would indirectly benefit the consumers by charging a fair and reasonable price (rent extraction goal). Hence, the regulators would be able to achieve two goals from both sides at the same time.

In practice, there are two principal regimes of tariff regulation, namely 'rate of return regulation' and 'incentive regulation.' While incentive regulation is best known for providing incentive for operators to improve supply-side efficiency, rate of return regulation guarantees operators that all of the costs incurred will be covered. Under rate of return regulation, the rate of return is regulated to ensure that it matches exactly the cost of capital. According to Averch and Johnson (1962), this type of regulation provides a firm with incentives to over-capitalization or over-investment because the firms are guaranteed of the return for any investment they have made. In this regulatory approach, there is no incentive for the firms to pursue supply-side efficiency whereas the capital attraction goal is achieved.

On the other hand, under incentive regulation the regulators provide incentive to the firms to reduce costs and increase supply-side efficiency. There is no earning guarantee in this regulatory regime. In the real world, pure regulatory regimes are not feasible. All known regimes range from adopting high-powered incentive regulations such as pure price cap and revenue cap regulations to low-powered ones such as rate case moratorium and banded rate of return regulations (Rothwell and Gomez, 2003). The regulators in the developed and developing countries employ a combination of incentive regulatory methods in different ways. Some developing countries have adopted incentive regulation, in particular price cap regulation (Jamasb, 2006). The increasing popularity of this approach is due to the successful experiences in the UK and to the support of such international organization as the World Bank (Kirkpatrick *et al.*, 2005).

Thailand has employed rate of return regulation for decades and restructured its electricity tariff with the attempt to apply a combination of rate of return and incentive regulation approaches on its tariff in 2000 and again in 2005.

The concept of electricity tariff restructuring was based on goodwill. However, evidence shows that since 2000, on average, the electricity tariff has increased with time. Also, Thai state-owned electricity enterprises have enjoyed profits resulting from improved efficiency. One question that arises is whether the current electricity tariff in Thailand is regulated for social benefits.

This chapter aims to study and evaluate electricity tariff regulation in Thailand since 2000, which comprises the base tariff and the automatic tariff adjustment mechanism (F_t). It starts with a brief background on the ESI and tariff regulation in Thailand. Then evaluations of tariff regulations, including their problems and achievements, are discussed separately for the base tariff and the F_t. The next section proposes regulatory alternatives. The last section concludes the paper.

2. Background of Electricity Supply Industry in Thailand

The current structure of the ESI in Thailand since December 2003 is called the enhanced single buyer model. In this model, the state-owned enterprise (SOE), the Electricity Generating Authority of Thailand (EGAT), is a major power producer, a single buyer or monopsonist of electricity from private power producers and a natural monopolist in the transmission business.

With an attempt to promote competition in this industry, the government promoted private sector participation in the electricity generation business in the form of Small Power Producers (SPPs) and Independent Power Producers (IPPs) since 1992. Under the power purchase agreements, both SPPs and IPPs are required to sell electricity to EGAT, which it subsequently transmits to the distributors.

The distribution and retail activities are the responsibility of the other two SOEs, namely the Metropolitan Electricity Authority (MEA) and the Provincial Electricity Authority (PEA), in the areas under their respective jurisdiction. Essentially EGAT generates and supplies electricity to the MEA and PEA for further distribution to consumers.

Under the current structure, the majority of the consumers nationwide have to depend on the services of the three utilities: the EGAT, MEA and PEA, as there is no direct competition in their activities. The structures of operation and business of the ESI in Thailand take place in a monopolistic manner.

3. Electricity Tariff Regulation in Thailand

Due to the monopolistic nature of the ESI in Thailand, tariff regulation is needed to prevent unfair pricing for consumers. In Thailand, retail electricity tariff is separated into the base tariff and the F_t. Base tariffs have been restructured and revised for a number of times without any standard regulatory period but for various reasons, including economic, financial, social or even political reasons. The most recent base tariff restructuring was conducted in 2000 and 2005. The formulas of F_t were revised occasionally, ever since they were used for calculations in 1992. The recent restructuring was conducted together with base tariff in 2000 and 2005. Currently, F_t is reviewed every four months. This section will first discuss the roles of multiple regulatory bodies and stakeholders in the tariff determination processes. It then describes the electricity tariff structure and its determination.

3.1. *Multiplicity of Regulatory Bodies and Stakeholders in Tariff Determination Process*

During the period of study, there was no single, formal and independent regulatory body for the ESI in Thailand. There were a number of authorities acting as regulators at the policy and operational levels. On the one hand, the Ministry of Energy (MOE) and the National Energy Policy Council (NEPC) were responsible for energy policy, including setting the policy principle in determining the power tariff structure. The NEPC was also in charge of approval for the new tariff structure developed in 2000 and 2005. On the other hand, there was the Energy Policy and Planning Office (EPPO) under the MOE (formerly the National Energy Policy Office (NEPO) under the Office of the Prime Minister) which is responsible for tariff restructuring, tariff determination and tariff review of both base tariff and F_t. Henceforth in this paper, multiple regulatory authorities will collectively be referred to as 'regulators.'

Apart from permanently assigned authorities in charge of tariff setting, some committees, in which their members were from governmental agencies, electricity state-owned enterprises and various stakeholders, were appointed occasionally and temporarily to commission particular regulatory tasks.

For example, the Committees on Electric Power Tariff Restructuring had in 2000 comprised representatives from the NEPO, the Office of National Economic and Social Development Board (NESDB), the Comptroller-General's Department, the Public Debt Management Office, the Federation of Thai Industries, the Thai Chamber of Commerce, academicians, the EGAT, MEA and PEA.

In 2005, in order to restructure electricity tariff, the MOE appointed a Sub-Committee on Electricity Tariff Restructuring, chaired by Deputy Permanent Secretary of Energy. The Sub-Committee members comprised representatives from the EPPO; NESDB; the State Enterprise Policy office and the Public Debt Management Office under Ministry of Finance; the three public utilities: EGAT, MEA, PEA; the Federation of Thai Industries; the Thai Chamber of Commerce; academics and consumers.

The combination of representatives from governmental agencies, public utilities, industrial and residential consumers and academics was a good attempt to allow participation from various interest groups in the tariff determination process. However, the question that arose was to what extent their involvement were needed to balance the utilization of their expertise and the avoidance of regulatory capture.

3.2. *Objectives of Electricity Tariff Structure*

The tariff restructuring in 2000 and 2005 attempted to achieve the same objectives. As stated in the 2005 tariff restructuring reports:

> The objectives of the current electricity tariff structure determination are: (1) to have a tariff that best reflects the economic costs and to promote efficient use of electricity, in particular to encourage less consumption during the peak period of the power system, which will help reduce generation and distribution costs in the long run; (2) to secure the financial status of the three power utilities, which will enable future expansion of their operations; (3) to provide greater fairness for all power consumer categories by reducing cross subsidization from one consumer category to another; and (4) to devise a mechanism for the electricity tariff adjustment that is flexible and automatic, to be more in line with the changing fuel prices under the competitive market.

To achieve those objectives, the electricity tariff structure has been separated into the base tariff and the F_t. The base tariff consists of the bulk supply tariff representing the wholesale tariff which the EGAT charges the MEA and the PEA, and the retail tariff which the MEA and the PEA charge power consumers on a fixed basis during each regulatory period. In addition, power consumers have to pay for the F_t, which is reviewed and adjusted every four months.

3.3. *Base Tariff Determination*

In determining the base tariff, two main models: the long run marginal cost (LRMC) model and the financial model of each activity and each state enterprise are estimated — essentially, the long run marginal costs of each activity takes into account different time of use, losses in transmission, voltage levels and geographical locations, loss of load probability, to determine the capacity costs of generation, transmission and distribution systems. The costs of service provision for each individual customer category are also calculated. They are estimated with the main assumption that the generating capacity will be expanded to satisfy increasing power demand. This model relies on various assumptions such as the fuel costs, EGAT PROSCREEN marginal generation costs, investment plan, and operating expenses. The resulting marginal cost-based tariff — which varies with voltage levels and geographical locations — comprises energy charge and demand charge. While energy charge is calculated from the costs of generation and transmission businesses, including loss in the system and transmission cost apportioned to the peak and off-peak period, demand charge is calculated from the distribution costs.

In the financial model, the search for the base tariff to fully compensate the three utilities' financial burden incurred from investment and operating expenditures is done keeping in view operational and financial assumptions.

In this model, base tariff is derived from the revenue requirement of each activity and each of the state utilities, to ensure financial viability and capability to expand the power business in the future. In order to estimate the revenue requirement, explicit assumptions, particularly on fuel prices, inflation rates or consumer price index (CPI), efficiency improvement of each activity (*X* factor), investment plan, financial criteria, lump sum financial transfer, and remittances to the government are imposed.

The load forecast prepared by the Load Forecast Sub-Committee is used to develop the power development plan and transmission system expansion plan for the EGAT and the distribution system investment plan for the MEA and the PEA. Load forecasting for a moderate economic growth (MEG) scenario was used for the investment and operational plans in 2000. Owing to changes in demand, in 2005, the load forecast was scaled down at an average of 700 GWh per year from those forecasted under on MEG scenario. Hence, the investment plans for transmission and distribution activities are re-adjusted accordingly.

In addition, cash-based financial criteria are employed to estimate revenue requirement to ensure that sufficient revenue would be generated

Table 1: Financial criteria

	2000			2005		
	EGAT	MEA	PEA	EGAT	MEA	PEA
SFR (%)	≥25	≥25	≥25	—	—	—
DSCR (times)	≥1.3	≥1.5	≥1.5	≥1.3	≥1.5	≥1.5
D/E Ratio (times)	≤1.5	≤1.5	≤1.5	≤1.5	≤1.5	≤1.5
SM/L Debt (%)	—	—	—	—	—	—
ROIC (%)	—	—	—	8.39	4.8	4.8

Source: Electricity tariff restructuring reports, NEPO, February 2001 and EPPO, 17 October 2005.

to enable utilities to make further investments and pay back loans together with interests. The financial criteria employed since 2000 are shown in Table 1. Debt equity ratio (D/E ratio) has been capped at 1.5 times for all state utilities. Debt service coverage ratio (DSCR) was set at least 1.3 times for the EGAT and 1.5 times for the MEA and the PEA. Before 2005 self-financing ratio (SFR) was set at a minimum of 25% for all three firms. In 2005, return on invested capital (ROIC) was introduced and set at 8.39% for the EGAT and 4.8% for the MEA and the PEA. There are several reasons why ROIC for the EGAT is higher than those for the MEA and the PEA. First, by the time of conducting the 2005 tariff restructuring, the EGAT planned for the initial public offering in the Stock Exchange of Thailand in 2005 so that the ROIC would be attractive to investors. Second, investments in public service obligations such as the PEA's investment in remote rural areas or the MEA's investment in relocating the distribution lines to underground, will be directly subsidized by the government.

The revenue requirements are estimated to include the remittance rates to the government, income tax and dividends in the base tariff for various circumstances. As for the 2005 tariff determination, if the power utilities remain non-corporatized and non-privatized, the remittance rates would be set at 35% of the net profit for the EGAT and 40% for the distribution utilities. However, if the three state utilities were privatized, the income tax would be set at 30% of the net profit and dividends at 50% of the after tax net profit.

One important operational assumption is the X factor. In 2000, the X factors for the generation, transmission, and distribution and retail business were set at 5.8%, 2.6% and 5.1% per year, respectively. These *X* factors were also employed during 2005 tariff determination together with the coefficient of cost volume elasticity (CVE) of 0.8.[1] The ratio of the operating costs in the portion of non-fuel cost and power purchasing prices, to which these *X* factors and CVE are applied, has increased from 40% in 2000 to 48% in 2005.

Macroeconomic and market assumptions such as inflation rate, interest rate, exchange rate, and fuel prices, are also imposed in both the LRMC and financial models.

Thailand has adopted a uniform tariff approach that is applied nationwide for each customer category, for social and political reasons. To implement the uniform tariff, subsidization for certain customer categories, especially residential consumers, is required. This type of cross subsidization is implemented through direct financial transfers from the MEA to the PEA and sometimes from the EGAT to the PEA as shown in Table 2.

From the marginal cost and financial models, marginal cost-based tariff are rescaled to meet the estimated revenue requirements derived from the financial models of three utilities. For example, while determining the

Table 2: Financial transfers between state electric utilities during 2000–2008 (million baht)

Year	MEA to PEA	EGAT to PEA	Total
2001*	8,153	—	8,153
2002*	8,589	—	8,589
2003*	9,041	—	9,041
Oct–Dec 2003	1,677	880	2,557
Jan–Dec 2004	7,165	3,936	11,101
2005	9,083	—	9,083
2006	10,507	—	10,507
2007	10,728	—	10,728
2008	11,014	—	11,014

Source: Electricity tariff restructuring, NEPO, February 2001 and EPPO, 17 October 2005.

[1] It means that for each increasing sale unit, only 0.8 times the incremental costs per unit is allowed to be passed on to consumers.

2000 tariff, the energy charge was scaled to 115% of the marginal costs to ensure that the generation business met its financial requirements whereas the transmission charge was scaled to 70% of the marginal cost of transmission activity. The overall impact of the scalings was to increase tariffs relative to marginal costs at higher voltages and during off-peak hours and to reduce tariffs below marginal costs at lower voltages during peak hours.

The estimated tariff consists of the bulk supply tariff (BST) that the EGAT sells to both the MEA and the PEA, as well as the retail tariff. As a result, the average BST for October 2005-December 2008 has been set at 1.6648 baht/kWh, which is lower than the previous BST by 3.54%.

3.4. *Automatic Tariff Adjustment Mechanism*

The base tariff was estimated based on a number of assumptions, hence it cannot reflect in time the actual cost of the electricity business. Moreover, with the regulatory lag for five years — longer than international standards — there is potential for significant cost shocks to occur; potential for unanticipated demand growth leading to significant abnormal profits; and potential for unanticipated shocks affecting investment requirements that could have impact on the utility operations.

In order to have the actual costs reflected by the power tariffs and to reduce the impact of fuel price volatility on the power utilities' financial status, F_t was first introduced in 1991 and implemented in 1992.

Over the years the F_t formula has been revised from time to time so that it is in accordance with the changing economic situation, financial conditions of state utilities and regulatory objectives in Thailand. In 2000 the F_t was unbundled into generation, transmission and distribution and retail businesses.

At that time, the F_t formula included fuel costs and power purchasing prices from private power producers and foreign countries, changes in foreign exchange rate, changes in non-fuel operating expenditures, changes in marginal revenue, discrepancy charge between the expected and actual collection of the F_t in the previous period, and accumulated discrepancy of energy adjustment charge.

In 2005, the F_t formula was revised and simplified. It consisted of two components: constant F_t at 0.4683 baht/kWh and change in F_t or ΔF_t due to fuel costs and power purchasing prices differing from the constant F_t. The costs of fuel and energy purchase include fuel expenses of the EGAT power plants, and power purchase from private producers and neighboring countries such as Laos and Malaysia.

The revised F_t formula is claimed to be more beneficial to power consumers than the previous one because the consumers now bear only the fuel cost and power purchasing prices without having to bear the other financial burdens arising from different factors.

4. Thailand's Electricity Tariff Regulatory Outcomes and their Effectiveness

Electricity tariff regulation in Thailand was specially designed to fit the current structure of its ESI. Hence both natural monopoly activities (transmission and distribution) and competitive activities (generation and retail) are heavily regulated in order to ensure that consumers are least affected by the monopoly power of state utilities.

As discussed above, the base tariff and F_t structure are based on various assumptions. They have been modified occasionally but still relied on the hybrid regulatory approach which incorporates the rate of return regulation and incentive regulation.

The objectives of both electricity tariff determinations since 2000 are simultaneously to satisfy the rent extraction goal (i.e. to ensure the tariff genuinely reflects the economic costs); demand-side efficiency goal (i.e. to promote efficient use of electricity); capital attraction goal (i.e. to secure the financial status of three utilities); consumer–consumer distribution goal (i.e. to provide fairness across all power consumer categories by reducing cross subsidization from one category to another); and the tariff flexibility goal (i.e. to achieve a mechanism for electricity tariff adjustment). The tariff determination since 2000 has neglected the supply-side efficiency goal. It is a big challenge for regulators to achieve the aforementioned goals at the same time. For instance, in order to secure the financial status of the three utilities, the regulators need to set the tariff high enough to attract investment to achieve the rent extraction goal. It is important to prioritize these objectives and align tariff regulatory regimes in accordance with the development concerning regulation (Laffont, 2005).

The next section discusses observations on tariff restructuring approaches which include the base tariff and the F_t.

4.1. *Rate of Return Regulatory Approach and Base Tariff Regulation*

It can be seen that the current base tariff regulation, which attaches much importance to the financial status of the three utilities, is dominated by the rate of return regulatory approach. Such regulation favors the power utilities and works toward the capital attraction goal. The fact that the Thai regulators attach more importance to this kind of regulation than the incentive regulation deserves scrutiny.

First, the current practice of assuring investors of high returns has not provided investors with incentives powerful enough to improve performance efficiency and cost reduction. It might encourage over-capitalization, leading eventually to higher tariffs.

The second consideration is the appropriateness of the financial criteria and other assumptions governing tariff determination. One of the most important financial criteria is the ROIC. The EGAT was allocated a higher ROIC rate than its distribution counterpart. Moreover, the ROIC for the EGAT was set at 8.39% higher than the weighted average costs of capital (WACC) for each business, of 7.24% for power generation and 6.85% for the transmission business. The ROIC was adopted as a financial criterion rather than the WACC. In fact, the WACC could clearly reflect the cost of capital, which consists of the cost of debt and equity. Adopting the WACC as a financial criterion will give the utilities reasonable return to compensate for the costs incurred. An observation to be made here is whether employing the ROIC had given an unrealistic return to the state utilities.

Another observation made is that the ROIC calculation was based on the return of the average invested capital. The regulators used historical costs as the basis for the calculation of assets. The valued assets could be more than that which were necessary, or not directly related to the electricity businesses, thereby leading to asset over-valuation. To reduce the problem of excess capacity and over-engineering, the widely adopted method for asset valuation, called the depreciated optimized replacement cost method whereby the assets actually used in the operation are optimized, thus leaving out the excess capacity and unrelated assets, would be more appropriate.

Another financial issue is whether it is appropriate to include the remittance or dividend in the calculation of the base tariff. The current base tariff model incorporates remittances to the government and dividend into the revenue requirement of state utilities. Consequently the consumers are charged higher tariff so as to enable the three power utilities to send their remittances or dividend to the government.

4.2. *Application of Incentive Regulation to Base Tariff Regulation*

Incentive regulation was incorporated into tariff determination through the *X* factors and CVE. The *X* factors applied to non-fuel and non-power purchasing controllable operating costs for the generation, transmission, and distribution and retail businesses are 5.8%, 2.6% and 5.1% respectively. These *X* factors have been employed since 2000. The only difference between the imposition of *X* factors in 2000 and 2005 is that the proportion of non-fuel and non-power purchasing controllable operating costs have increased from 40% in 2000 to 48% in 2005. This warrants a number of observations.

First, the electricity business entails huge investments and highly uncontrollable operating expenses. Applying efficiency improvement parameters to non-fuel and non-power purchasing controllable operating costs creates negligible effects on operating cost reduction and subsequently total cost reduction. Table 3 shows a proportion of controllable operating costs applied with CVE and *X* factors to total operating costs are 4.9%, 3.2% and 3.8% for the EGAT, the MEA and the PEA respectively.[2] Therefore, although the regulators expected the operators to increase their efficiency in line with CVE and *X* factors, the gains

[2] They are calculated on the basis of 48% of the EGAT's operating costs applied with efficiency parameters, including operating expenses, transmission expenses and administrative expenses, representing 10.16% of its total operational costs; of the MEA's operating costs, representing 6.65% of its total operational costs; and of the PEA's operating costs consisting of distribution and supply costs, representing 7.85% of its total operational costs.

Table 3: Operating expenses ratios of the three utilities

Operating expenses	Operating expense ratio (%)
EGAT	
Total expenses	100
Fuel expenses	25.07
Operating expenses	74.93
Power purchase	57.73
Operating expenses*	4.11
Transmission expenses*	1.32
Administrative expenses*	4.73
Amortization of land right	0.17
Depreciation	6.55
MEA	
Operating expenses	100
Power purchase	80.89
Cross subsidy	8.14
Operating expenses*	6.65
Depreciation	4.33
PEA	
Operating expenses	100
Power purchase	93.14
Cross subsidy	−5.96
Distribution and supply cost*	7.85
Depreciation	4.97

Note: *Represents operating expenses using the *X* factor in the estimation.

from efficiency improvement were limited and unlikely to reduce the operating expenses as a whole.

These observations lead to the conclusion that the attempt to apply incentive regulation to operating expenses has not been effective enough. Besides, in spite of the significant success stories of incentive regulation elsewhere, the regulators still lacked the mechanisms that would enable the benefits, derived from the supply-side efficiency in the form of reduced costs or greater profits, to be carried over to the consumers in the form of reduced tariff, thus achieving the rent extraction goal. As a consequence, only the operators reap benefits from efficiency improvement.

It is interesting to note the method used to determine the X factor. Ideally, it needs to be up-to-date and incentive-oriented. In Thailand, the X factors have remained the same as those of 2000. With no revised estimation, they were unable to reflect the current efficiency level and could not provide a strong incentive for efficiency improvement in power utilities. In addition, it might have assisted firms in playing the regulatory game by over-estimating the operating expenses before efficiency improvement parameters are being imposed.

4.3. *Full Cost Pass-Through and F_t Regulation*

F_t was designed to pass on uncontrollable costs from operators to consumers. Although the F_t formula has been changed occasionally, the concept of full cost pass-through is still intact.

As for the F_t review in 2005, the constant F_t was set at 0.4683 baht/kWh, so the F_t would not be lower than 0.4683 baht/kWh except where ΔF_t is negative. In addition, this practice guarantees the operators that they could transfer the burden of fuel costs and power purchase to the consumers, resulting in a full cost pass-through, via ΔF_t.

F_t regulation should ideally be designed in a way to encourage the operators to enhance supply-side efficiency and power purchase efficiency. The full-cost pass-through ΔF_t failed to achieve supply-side efficiency. It might pave the way for collusion between the EGAT and private power producers and between the fuel buyers and sellers (Arizu *et al.*, 2004).

4.4. *Excess Capacity*

As discussed in previous sections, the current tariff regulation in Thailand is biased towards the rate of return regulatory regime rather than the incentive regulatory regime. The classic result of this rate of return regulatory regime is over-capitalization or over-investment in the electricity sector, which is sometimes referred to as the Averch and Johnson effect. Since the utilities are guaranteed with certain levels of rate of return, they might have more incentive to invest and expand their business. Considering the case of Thailand, as shown in Table 4, where the level of excess capacity maintained by the EGAT and private power producers in Thailand is well above the

Table 4: Peak demand, installed capacity and excess capacity in Thailand

Year[a]	Peak demand (MW)	Installed capacity (MW)[b]	Excess capacity (%)[c]
1997	14,506.3	16,964.9	16.95
1998	14,179.9	17,936.3	26.49
1999	13,712.4	19,100.7	39.3
2000	14,918.3	22,269	49.27
2001	16,126.4	22,004.8	36.45
2002	16,681.1	23,529.8	41.06
2003	18,121.4	25,422	40.29
2004	19,325.8	26,349.3	36.34
2005	20,537.5	26,450.2	28.79
2006	21,064	27,107.2	28.69

Source: EGAT

Note: [a]1997–2004 is budget year whereas 2005–2006 is calendar year. [b]Installed capacity of both the EGAT and private power producers who sell and transmit electricity to the EGAT transmission network. [c]Excess capacity is calculated from percentage of difference between installed capacity and peak demand to peak demand.

25% international standard. It reflects the under-utilization of installed capacity at an average of 34.36% per year since 1997. Although the higher excess capacity provides a more reliable and secured electricity system, the reliability is accomplished at a very high cost of excess capacity.

A further observation is that the levels of excess capacity has significantly been increasing since 1997 and has declined after 2000. The abrupt changes in excess capacity can be explained by the fact that the huge power plant projects had required planning in advance. Before the financial crisis in 1997, to serve the high growth rate electricity demand in Thailand, several power plant projects were approved. It took several years to finish building the plants whereas the growth rate of electricity demand after the financial crisis had declined unexpectedly and significantly. As a result, the excess capacity had increased, following from the old investment plan. The regulators attempted to re-adjust the forecast demands from time to time to reflect the actual demand as much as possible, in order to avoid the unnecessary investment. As a result, the excess capacity declined significantly from 41.06% in 2002 to 28.69% in 2006. Evidently, the fluctuation of excess capacity is the result of both regulatory discretion on investment to maintain service reliability, and the incentive contributing to over-capitalization induced by the rate of return regulation.

4.5. *Electricity Tariff*

As shown in Table 5, under the current regulatory regime, the Thai electricity base tariff and F_t has, since 1997, fluctuated from time to time, whereas the CPI has increased with time. Considering only the period of 2001–2006 in which the new tariff restructuring was in place, the data showed that on the average, the growth rate of the CPI was 2.66% whereas the growth rates of the indexed base tariff, F_t and total tariff were 3.97%, 16.77% and 4.99% respectively. These numbers showed that during that period, on an average, the growth rates of tariff have been marginally higher than the growth rate of the CPI. It implies that electricity users have paid for electricity at a marginally higher rate than their cost of living. Although rate of return regulation had heavily influenced electricity tariff determination, thus theoretically leading to setting tariff at cost, in reality the return on operation and investment costs, represented by ROIC, was over-estimated and the tariff determination process was intervened by political forces. As a result, electricity tariff was higher than what it should have been.

Table 5: Electricity tariff and tariff index in Thailand

Year	CPI	Base tariff (baht/kWh)	Base tariff index	F_t (baht/kWh)	F_t Index	Tariff (baht/kWh)	Tariff Index
1997	88.8	1.7	75.44	0.2793	126.86	1.9793	80.02
1998	96	1.6961	75.27	0.5023	228.14	2.1985	88.88
1999	96.2	1.6708	74.15	0.4088	185.67	2.0796	84.08
2000	97.8	1.8174	80.66	0.4534	205.92	2.2708	91.81
2001	99.4	2.273	100.87	0.2288	103.92	2.5018	101.14
2002	100	2.2533	100	0.2202	100	2.4735	100
2003	101.8	2.2475	99.74	0.2577	117.05	2.5052	101.28
2004	104.6	2.2426	99.53	0.3852	174.93	2.6278	106.24
2005	109.3	2.2428	99.53	0.4785	217.32	2.7213	110.02

Source: Bank of Thailand, EPPO and author's calculation.

The multiple regulatory bodies, particularly the Committees on Electric Power Tariff Restructuring and the F_t Sub-Committee, have discretionary power in setting both the electricity base tariff and F_t. For example, in October 2000, they agreed to incorporate the F_t from the previous month into a new, restructured base tariff while the new F_t was zero for three months. As a result, the base tariff jumped up from 1.6567 baht/kWh in September 2000 to 2.2751 baht/kWh in October 2000. However, the total tariff declined due to zero F_t.

The discretionary tariff setting regime had allowed politics to be involved in electricity tariff determination. A recent example is when the government planned to partially privatize the EGAT, the tariff restructuring in 2005 was urgently needed to prepare the EGAT for initial public offering (IPO). As a result of this restructuring, the total tariff rose from 2.9151 baht/kWh in September 2005 to 3.0014 baht/kWh in October 2005.

When comparing Thailand's electricity tariff with developed countries adopting incentive regulation, as shown in Table 6, Thai electricity tariff was relatively high. These countries have undertaken ESI restructuring and their regulatory frameworks and institutions have been established and developed for quite some time. Incentive regulation is applied to tariff setting for natural monopoly activities while wholesale tariff is not directly regulated but is determined by various electricity market mechanisms such as power pool, or bilateral contract.

Table 7 shows that when comparing Thai electricity tariff with that of ASEAN member countries, in 2005 Thai residential, commercial and

Table 6: Electricity tariffs in major countries (US dollar/kWh)

Country	Industrial users	Residential users
Australia	0.0609	0.0985
Canada	0.049	0.0676
South Africa	0.0218	0.0592
United Kingdom	0.1322	0.2205
United States	0.0613	0.1002
Thailand[a]	0.2329	0.2367

Source: Key world energy statistics 2007 by the IEA.
Note: [a]Average tariff in baht from the EGAT being converted by PPP conversion rate at 12.896 baht per US dollar in 2007.

Table 7: Average basic electricity tariff in ASEAN member countries in 2005 (US dollar)

Country	Residential users	Commercial users	Industry
Brunei Darussalam	8.92	7.47	7.441
Cambodia	12.02	15.015	12.975
Indonesia	2.81	3.76	2.715
Lao PDR	1.56	3.37	2.52
Malaysia	7.07	6.42	6.42
Myanmar	7.32	7.32	7.32
Philippines	7.25	7.075	7.42
Singapore	9.82	6.175	5.78
Thailand	5.51	5.265	5.09
Vietnam	5.19	8.525	7.865

Source: ASEAN centre for energy.

industrial electricity tariffs were lower than those in other countries at the same level of development such as Philippines, Malaysia and Singapore but higher than such countries as Indonesia and Laos in which electricity tariffs are still heavily subsidized.

4.6. *Performance of State Utilities*

The current mixture of regulatory regimes in Thailand also has some implications on the financial performances of the state utilities. On the one hand, that utilities earn excessive profits can be expected under hybrid regulatory regimes since the financial rate of return was over-estimated and state-owned enterprises had continuously improved their efficiency. On the other hand, due to political intervention and the adoption of discretionary tariff setting, utilities might experience losses.

As shown in Table 8, the three utilities have reaped huge net income from their operation since 2000. In 2005, the EGAT's net had income reduced significantly because it was preparing for IPO. The MEA and the PEA are also financially healthy.

However, although the regulatory framework was put in place from the beginning, regulators sometimes exercised discretionary power to freeze the F_t. For example, during February–May and June–September 2003, in order to freeze the F_t at 0.2612 baht/kWh, the EGAT was requested

Table 8: Financial performances of state-owned electric utilities

EGAT				
Year	Net income from electric operations (billion baht)	Return on equity (%)	Return on asset (%)	Debt equity ratio (%)
1999	−13.02	−20.62	−6.12	1.98
2000	31.29	16.49	4.64	1.77
2001	26.21	12.1	3.96	1.37
2002	36.13	19.52	6.91	1.09
2003	38.55	19.26	7.93	0.78
2004	35.52	16.16	7.52	0.59
2005	4.78	na	−0.04	1.05
2006	42.71	na	10.05	0.87

MEA				
Year	Net income from electric operations (billion baht)	Return on equity (%)	Return on asset (%)	Debt equity ratio (%)
1999	3.51	−3.83	−1.18	1.02
2000	3.58	8.38	2.54	1.09
2001	5.05	11.94	3.68	1.06
2002	3.93	10.54	3.48	0.91
2003	3.19	7.21	2.6	0.87
2004	5.68	9.86	3.86	0.77
2005	5.89	9.56	3.78	1.52

PEA				
Year	Net income from electric operations (billion baht)	Return on equity (%)	Return on asset (%)	Debt equity ratio (%)
1999	8.13	−14.30	−4.96	1.5
2000	7.42	12.52	4.26	1.56
2001	5.72	10	3.51	1.94
2002	6.06	10.07	3.53	1.92
2003	6.01	9.41	3.34	1.9
2004	5	7.48	2.61	1.98
2005	13.63	18.28	6.67	1.81

Source: Annual reports of EGAT, MEA and PEA.

to absorb fuel costs of 1.7 billion baht and 3 billion baht for the respective periods. This adversely impacted the financial status of the EGAT.

Moreover, as SOEs, these three utilities are required to remit their income to the government. Apparently, only the profitable EGAT has the capability to do so. In 2005, the EGAT's remittance to the government was the highest among all SOEs, amounting to 16.93 billion baht. Undoubtedly, that would have had an unfavorable impact on the financial status of the EGAT.

5. Implications for Tariff Regulatory Design

From the above analysis, it is obvious that the current tariff regulatory regime has given rise to a numer of concerns. These concerns include; regulatory governance due to the lack of a single regulatory body responsible for tariff setting, the possibility of regulatory capture due to the high degree of electricity operators' involvement in the tariff determination process, and regulatory substance in tariff setting that is biased towards the rate of return regulatory approach, leading to excess capacity and high profit for state utilities. This chapter does not aim to discuss solutions or find alternatives for all of these concerns, but will focus on alternatives for tariff regulatory approach from which consumers and operators would benefit.

Considering the specific context of developing countries, Laffont (2005) proposes that the regulatory approach adheres to the stages of development of the sector under discussion. As the ESI develops and the electricity system is established, usually characterized by excess capacity, ROR regulation that facilitates large scale investment should be discarded. As the development of the electricity sector continues, it will be optimal to move towards more powerful incentive regulation. Incentive regulation refers to regulatory regimes where the regulator delegates certain pricing decisions to the firm so that the firm is given an incentive to be more efficient and can reap profits earned from cost reduction (Vogelsang, 2002). The main objective of incentive regulation is to overcome the problem of supply-side inefficiency.

In the 1980s, incentive regulation was employed extensively in the United Kingdom to accompany privatization and liberalization in the public utility industries such as electricity, natural gas, water and telecommunications. In the United States, incentive regulation was first introduced in the telecommunication sector to replace ROR regulation in 1989. Since then incentive regulation has been widely adopted in other countries.

In practice incentive regulation is a form of regulation that gives incentives to lower rates or lower costs or to improve non price performance by weakening the link between regulated prices and the firm's costs which can be accomplished by increasing the regulatory lag.

Following Laffont and Tirole (1993), to show the link between ROR and incentive regulation, a typical model of regulatory scheme, based on historic cost and demand data, is:

$$TR = a + bC, \tag{1}$$

where TR is the actual (*ex post*) total revenue received, a is fixed payment, b is the fraction of cost borne by the firm, $0 < b < 1$ and C is *ex post* cost. It shows the relationship between revenue and costs based on parameters a and b, set *ex ante*. The incentive of a firm to minimize costs is inversely proportional to the fraction of cost, b. The two extreme cases of this linear regulatory scheme are:

- $b = 0$: The fixed price regulatory contract or incentive regulation; and
- $b = 1$: The cost-plus regulatory contract or ROR regulation with no regulatory lag.

When $b = 0$, the firm's total revenue is set to a, and the firm receives only a fixed fee. The firm is a residual claimant for its cost saving, and the fixed price contract is considered as an extremely high-powered incentive scheme.

When $b = 1$, the firm can recover the whole cost. The cost-plus regulatory contract is an extremely low-powered incentive scheme. The power of incentive regulation increases when the value of b is decreasing from 1 and approaching 0.

To increase the incentive to reduce cost, where b approaches 0, forms of high-power incentive regulation such as ROR regulation with infrequent rate cases or with a long regulation lag and revenue cap or price cap formulas with a long regulatory lag, can be undertaken.

Essentially, prices under incentive regulation are less sensitive to costs than those under ROR regulation. Under incentive regulation, the regulator periodically updates and adjusts the revenue requirement, caps and adjustment factors to eliminate excessive returns to the regulated firms. Therefore, prices do not change due to changes in cost. Under ROR regulation, a public rate hearing is required to change the regulated variables. Because rate hearings are often initiated by regulated firms, cost-related variables, particularly inflation, are important determinants of the frequency of reviews.

Incentive regulation has many variations in practice. The most important types are as follows:

5.1. *Price Cap Regulation*

Under fixed price regulation, the regulator defines *ex ante* a set of prices that the firm will be allowed to charge consumers for the services it provides. A price adjustment formula is tied to a prespecified set of economic indices and factors such as the inflation index and the productivity growth rate. The most common formula for price cap is,

$$P_t = [p_{t-1}(1 + i - X \pm Z)], \qquad (2)$$

where P_t is the maximum price that can be charged to the customers in year t, i is the inflation index, X is the productivity or efficiency factor and Z is the adjustment factor for unforeseen or external events including the effect of changes in tax rates and other government policies on the company's unit cost such as policies promoting energy conservation.

The X factor represents the increase in efficiency or productivity which leads to cost reduction in a firm. The inclusion of X into the price cap allows consumers to share the benefit of cost reduction from the increase in efficiency or productivity through the declining price. In the United States, this form of price cap regulation is called 'performance-based regulation' (Crew and Kleindorfer, 1996: 213).

5.2. *Revenue Cap Regulation*

Under fixed or pure revenue cap regulation, the firm's allowed revenues are set during a regulatory period. The amount of revenue allowed during the first year is adjusted in subsequent years according to a prespecified set of economic indices and factors. With the revenue cap, the firm is allowed to maximize profits during the regulatory period by minimizing total costs. Fixed revenue caps pass cost risk to the regulated firms, which means that the firm has to absorb any increase in costs and will be unable to pass such cost increases to customers. Under the fixed revenue caps, the firms can reduce the volume risk through price adjustment. The rate case then takes place and a new revenue cap formula is set for the new regulatory period. The general formula for revenue cap is,

$$TR_t = \{[TR_{t-1} + (CGA^* \Delta Customers)]^*(1 + i - X \pm Z)\}, \tag{3}$$

where TR_t is the allowed revenues in year t, CGA is customer growth adjustment factor (US$/customer), $\Delta Customers$ is the annual change in the number of customers, i is the inflation index, X is the productivity index and Z is the adjustment factor for unforeseen events (Rothwell and Gomez, 2003: 85–6).

With revenue adjustments in Equation 3, the firm can change the costs in accordance with changes in the variables in the formula. The measurement of inflation can be *CPI*, *RPI* or other price indices such as sector-specific industrial price indices.

The productivity growth rate, X, ensures that the customers receive a share of the expected enhanced productivity required by the firm. Examples of unforeseen events, Z, are increased taxes, changes in environmental taxes, natural disasters and so on. Z must include only the costs that can be forecasted with a reasonable rate of accuracy.

Both price and revenue cap create the same incentive for supply-side efficiency in order to maximize profit but provide different incentives for a firm to increase its sales.

Under price cap regulation, the firm has an incentive to maximize sales. The sales maximizing behavior of the firm can increase demand in the market which is achieved by advertising for new customers and for greater electricity use per customer. This runs counter to the encouragement of the demand-side efficiency goal to give incentives to consumers to utilize electricity efficiently. Yet under revenue cap regulation, a firm can choose the level of output and has incentive to minimize sales by increasing prices because its revenue is capped. Revenue cap regulation goes well along with the energy savings and demand side management program which aims at reducing electricity demand (Rothwell and Gomez, 2003: 87).

5.3. *Sliding Scale Regulation*

Under price cap regulation, there is a gap between the cost and price which leads to allocative inefficiency. Consumers will not gain from cost efficiency of the firm, as profits from cost savings belong to the firm.

Sliding scale regulation, sometimes called profit sharing regulation, allows the consumers to participate in the excess profit or profit shortfalls earned by a firm in the form of *ex post* refunds or a decrease in the price of future purchases (Vogelsang, 2002: 9).

Also, sliding scale regulation provides more incentives to a firm for reducing costs than ROR regulation, which transfers all the benefits from cost reduction to consumers by allowing the firm to share the profits.

The other form of sliding scale regulation is a banded rate of return regulation under which a sliding scale would adjust prices in the current rate case so that the allowed rate of return, *s*, at the new prices would be,

$$s = r_t + h(r^* - r_t), \tag{4}$$

where h is a constant number between 0 and 1, r_t is the realized rate of return at the tariff set in the previous rate case in year t and r^* is the target rate of return (Joskow and Schmalensee, 1986).

For implementation, the target rate of return is set and prices are expected to yield a realized rate of return equal to r^* for the firm. Then the sharing constant, h, must be selected. If $h = 1$, prices are always adjusted to give the firm the target rate of return and the firm would not have any incentive for being cost efficient because the profit obtained will be passed to consumers. If $h = 0$, the regulation is fixed price and, as a result, all profits and gains from efficiency belong to the firm, and all unexpected cost increases affect the firm alone. If $h = 0.5$, then unexpected profit and loss is shared between the firm and the consumers.

The banded rate of return regulation is a mechanism under which tariffs are adjusted to keep a utility's rate of return within a pre-specified

ROR band. If earning falls within the ROR band, rates are not changed and the firm can make a profit or loss depending on its efficiency.

5.4. *Yardstick Competition*

Even though the electric utilities operate in particular geographical areas and do not compete directly with each other, there are a relatively large number of utilities around countries such as the United States and internationally. If these firms operated in a single competitive market, the price charged by one firm will be determined by the costs of the competitors.

To simulate this process by basing a firm's prices on the cost of other comparable firms operating under similar conditions with the same production and demand functions, it would be a strong yardstick competition in which a firm's performance is evaluated by its rivals.

Under yardstick competition, the firm is rewarded based on its standing against how a set of similar firms perform (Shleifer, 1985: 326).

Assume there are N regulated firms. Let the total cost for the jth firm be C_j and let AC_i be the average of the C_j for all $(N-1)$ firms in this group, excluding firm i. Strong yardstick competition would be implemented by setting firm i's price equal to AC_i. The prices for the other firms are set in exactly the same manner. They are facing prices which are not based on their own cost. To make a profit, firms will try to reduce their costs below the average. This approach provides all firms with strong financial incentives for cost efficiency.

The problem of undertaking yardstick regulation is that regulated firms are not homogenous (Lyon, 1994: 14). It is difficult to determine which firms should be grouped together and the differences between the firms such as geology, population density, variation in customer base, consumption patterns and so on, which affect the costs, must be taken carefully. Simply comparing regulated firms' economic variables without accounting for differences in the factors that affect their operation is misleading.

Another means of yardstick regulation is to use benchmarking based on a hypothetical efficient firm, in which efficient cost is derived from the efficient long-run costs (Vogelsang, 2002: 9). Benchmarking with comparable firms is also employed together with price and revenue cap regulation.[3] Benchmarking applies to various regulatory variables such as capital costs and operating costs in order to create efficient costs as revenue requirement, efficient level of service quality, and *X* factor (Jamasb and Pollitt, 2001: 123).

5.5 *Rate Freeze*

Under rate freeze, rates for electricity services are kept constant for a fixed and prespecified period of time. The period between rate reviews is fixed in advance so it can create strong incentives for efficiency improvement and cost reduction. Compared with ROR regulation, under a rate freeze, the firm will retain the profits of any efforts to reduce costs for a certain period of time. However, rate freezes work only in the periods of slow unit cost growth. During the 1990s in the United States, multi-year rate freezes were the major options for many firms owing to slow input price growth. At present, multi-year rate freezes are employed as components of incentive regulatory plans (Lowry and Kaufmann, 2006).

5.6. *Incentive Regulation in Practice*

In a number of countries around the world, incentive regulation has been adopted in various forms as shown in Table 9.

As many countries have liberalized the electricity generation activity, they have engaged in regulatory reform, particularly in natural monopoly activities such as distribution business and adoption of incentive regulatory models. In Latin American countries, the most widely employed incentive regulatory methods are price cap regulation whereas in the European countries, revenue cap regulation is preferred.

Latin American countries are the first group of developing countries which restructured their ESI in the early 1980s and also explicitly adopted incentive regulation in natural monopoly activity and established agencies to enforce regulation. The choice of regulatory regimes in Latin American

---

[3] Jamasb and Pollitt (2001) provide a review of benchmarking methods adopted by regulators across countries and jurisdiction within one country.

Table 9: Application of incentive regulation in various countries

Country	Regulation Principle
European countries[1]	
Norway	Revenue cap regulation
Sweden	Revenue cap regulation
Denmark	Revenue cap regulation
Spain	Revenue cap regulation
Great Britain	Revenue cap regulation
Netherlands	Price cap regulation
United States of America[2]	
Missouri	Multi-year rate freeze
South Dakota	Multi-year rate freeze
Iowa	Multi-year rate freeze
New York	Multi-year rate freeze
Florida	Multi-year rate freeze
California	Revenue cap regulation
Maine	Revenue cap regulation
Massachusetts	Revenue cap regulation
Ontario	Revenue cap regulation
Mississippi	Benchmark regulation
Developing countries[3]	
Argentina	Price cap regulation
Brazil	Price cap regulation
Chile	Efficiency standard
Colombia	Price cap regulation
Peru	Efficiency standard
Bolivia	Price cap regulation and efficiency standard
El Salvador	Price cap regulation and efficiency standard

Source: [1]Viljainen *et al.* (2004); [2]Lowry and Kaufmann (2006); [3]Jamasb (2006).

countries was influenced by the advice of international consultants who assisted in the reform preparation (Estache *et al.*, 2003: 5). The most common suggested regime is a price cap, followed by a hybrid regime closer to price cap regulation than ROR regulation. In practice, incentive regulation incorporates different methods into single hybrid methods such as price cap regulation and efficiency standard.

In several European countries the electricity distribution sector has been reformed during the 1990s. Regulators have aimed to develop the regulatory models that promote cost reductions and assure that returns to investors and prices are reasonable. They have employed the various regulatory models based on revenue cap regulatory principles (Viljainen *et al.*, 2004).

In the United States, incentive regulation, known as performance-based regulation, has been adopted by new regulators in states like California, Massachusetts and Mississippi and a diverse groups of states and provinces, including Iowa, North Carolina, Florida, Ontario, and Oregon (Lowry and Kaufmann, 2006).

Incentive regulation has become an attractive alternative regulatory approach to ROR regulation in the US because its ESI has come to the end of a period of relative rate stability resulting from favorable operating conditions. Many firms have not made major power plant additions for more than a decade. Major additions represent a new source of risk for the firms such as volatile market prices for fuels, future changes in environmental and nuclear operating policies, vulnerability to change in transmission pricing policies and regulatory requirements for non-traditional, renewable generating technologies.

Due to these risks, a utility's generation capacity decisions may not be cost-competitive even if they represent good choices in the longer term. Therefore, the utilities are forced to file more rate cases. Frequent rate case filings are costly and time-consuming. Moreover, they do not enhance the efficiency improvement since the regulatory lag is shortened.

Incentive regulation enables firms and regulators to manage the rate case process more effectively and reduce these regulatory costs. At the same time, it provides incentives for utilities to manage their operating and capital costs more efficienctly.

6. Application of Incentive Regulation in Thailand: Case Study of Price Cap Regulation

The classic price cap regulation will be employed as an illustration of the application of incentive regulation to electricity tariff regulation in Thailand. It should be noted that this study does not aim to search for the best alternative for electricity tariff regulation in Thailand but aims to experiment and investigate price cap regulation, as a classic form of incentive regulation, and compare the estimated tariffs with the actual electricity tariff under current regulation in Thailand in the past years. The choice of application of price cap regulation is made based on the availability of data in Thailand.

The form of pure price cap is shown in Equation 2. P_t is proxied by tariff (baht/kWh) in period *t*. The inflation index is calculated based on the Consumer Price Index (CPI). In Thailand, the CPI is appropriately employed. Even though it does not reflect true input costs, it is more convenient and less costly than constructing an industry specific index which is not readily available.

6.1. *X Factor*

The *X* factor can be directly constructed by econometric methods or mathematical programming, based on the data available from the two distributors in Thailand: the MEA and PEA. An inherent difficulty in measuring the *X* factor is that regulated firms have private information about their operation which enables them to extract information rents.

In addition, issues of efficiency and productivity of firms under public ownership are politically sensitive in Thailand. It is possible that Thai distributors prefer to supply data in a way where the estimated *X* factors are favorable to them. Potential drawbacks are regulatory gaming between the regulator and regulated firms, and the unavailability of comparable firms.

Another problem is that in Thailand, only data from two distributors can be used for comparing efficiency. To obtain a more robust *X* factor, a larger database is required, hence international benchmarking is recommended.

While data on comparable firms from other countries can increase the amount of data, however the problems of comparability and data collection still exist. To solve the problems of firm comparability, again exogenous variables, including country's variables, such as the level of economic development, must be considered (Estache *et al.*, 2004).

Due to the unavailability of data, the other option for Thailand is to directly employ the *X* factor from the other regulators in developed countries and set it as a goal for Thai electricity firms.

Viljainen *et al.* (2004) reviewed the *X* factors in European countries and found that European regulators have set values, ranging from 1% to 3% whereas their Australian counterparts employed 1% to 2%. Sirasoontorn (2005) measured the technical efficiency of state-owned Thai electricity generation enterprises and found that Thai electricity generation firms are on the frontier and fully technically efficient, compared to other firms around the world.

The *X* factor is important for the application of price cap regulation. Setting the *X* factor too high will make it impossible for the firms to reach it whereas setting it at too low a value will fail to provide good incentives for performance improvement.

This study will directly employ the *X* factors from the developed countries. The case study of 1% and 2% of the *X* factors will be investigated.

6.2. *Z Factor*

Z factor adjusts the price for external developments that are not reflected in inflation and *X* factors. *Z* factor adjustments are needed to adjust price limits for the effect of changes in tax rates and other government policies, on the company's unit cost such as those performing to policies promoting energy conservation.

In Thailand, the government policies that affect the company's unit cost are in various forms, such as energy efficiency and renewable energy policies and changes in tax rates during 1997–1998.

Z factor of 1%, 2% and 3% will be employed to estimate tariff to represent the low- medium- and high-price adjustment respectively, to the external. A low *Z* factor adjustment case represents the case that government imposes the policies that does not affect unit cost of firms much, whereas a high *Z* factor adjustment case represents the case that the government aggressively imposes policies that affect unit cost significantly such as energy efficiency and renewable energy policies.

6.3. *Effect of Price Cap Regulation on Electricity Tariff*

Under price cap regulation, with the annual 1% and 2% *X* factor, electricity tariffs are projected with the 1997 actual tariff as the base year as

Table 10: Electricity tariff under the price cap regulation (baht/kWh)

Year	Actual tariff (baht/kWh)	CPI	% change of CPI	$X = 1\%$	% difference with $X = 1\%$	$X = 2\%$	% difference with $X = 2\%$
1997	1.9793						
1998	2.1985	96	8.1081	2.1200	3.7033	2.1002	4.6806
1999	2.0796	96.2	0.2083	2.1032	−1.1225	2.0626	0.8257
2000	2.2708	97.8	1.6632	2.1172	7.2571	2.0556	10.4678
2001	2.5018	99.4	1.6360	2.1306	17.4212	2.0481	22.1499
2002	2.4735	100	0.6036	2.1222	16.5549	2.0195	22.4784
2003	2.5052	101.8	1.8000	2.1392	17.1118	2.0155	24.2966
2004	2.6278	104.6	2.7505	2.1766	20.7296	2.0306	29.4083
2005	2.7213	109.3	4.4933	2.2526	20.8052	2.0813	30.7527
2006	3.0259	114.4	4.6661	2.3352	29.5768	2.1367	41.6126

Source: Author calculations.

shown in Table 10. The results show that with the application of price cap regulation, the lower electricity tariffs could have been offered to consumers if the electricity firms were incentivized to improve their efficiency. With a higher value for the *X* factor, the benefits from efficiency improvement to consumers in the form of lower tariffs have increased. The estimated tariffs under price cap regulation with 2% *X* factor are lower than the actual tariff throughout the period of study. Under price cap regulation with 1% *X* factor, the estimated tariffs are also lower than the actual ones throughout the period of study except in 1999.

When adding the *Z* factors into price cap formula in order to take into account the effect of other government policies on unit cost, with 1% *X* factor, the estimated tariffs are lower than the actual ones in the case of low and medium value of *Z* factors throughout period of study, except in 1999. If *Z* factor is as high as 3%, price cap regulation will result in higher tariffs than the actual ones. Under price cap regulation with 2% *X* factor, the estimated tariffs are lower in all cases except in 1999. The differences between actual tariffs and estimated tariffs under price cap regulation became increasingly significant with time. Moreover, electricity firms had tariffs growth rates exceeding that of the CPI, hence resulting in excessive profits.

Table 11: Electricity tariff under the price cap regulation: *X* factor = 1% (baht/kWh)

Year	Actual tariff (baht/ kWh)	% change of CPI	*Z* = 1%	% difference with *Z* = 1%	*Z* = 2%	% difference with *Z* = 2%	*Z* = 3%	% difference with *Z* = 3%
1997	1.9793							
1998	2.1985	8.1081	2.1398	2.7440	2.1596	1.8024	2.1794	0.8778
1999	2.0796	0.2083	2.1442	−3.0147	2.1857	−4.8530	2.2275	−6.6396
2000	2.2708	1.6632	2.1799	4.1697	2.2439	1.1997	2.3091	−1.6585
2001	2.5018	1.6360	2.2156	12.9191	2.3030	8.6308	2.3931	4.5442
2002	2.4735	0.6036	2.2289	10.9720	2.3400	5.7069	2.4554	0.7388
2003	2.5052	1.8000	2.2691	10.4068	2.4055	4.1455	2.5487	−1.7053
2004	2.6278	2.7505	2.3315	12.7099	2.4957	5.2932	2.6697	−1.5708
2005	2.7213	4.4933	2.4362	11.7011	2.6328	3.3617	2.8431	−4.2838
2006	3.0259	4.6661	2.5499	18.6670	2.7820	8.7683	3.0326	−0.2214

Source: Author calculations.

Table 12: Electricity tariff under the price cap regulation: *X* factor = 2% (baht/kWh)

Year	Actual tariff (baht/ kWh)	% change of CPI	*Z* = 1%	% difference with *Z* = 1%	*Z* = 2%	% difference with *Z* = 2%	*Z* = 3%	% difference with *Z* = 3%
1997	1.9793							
1998	2.1985	8.1081	2.1200	3.7033	2.1398	2.7440	2.1596	1.8024
1999	2.0796	0.2083	2.1032	−1.1225	2.1442	−3.0147	2.1857	−4.8530
2000	2.2708	1.6632	2.1172	7.2571	2.1799	4.1697	2.2439	1.1997
2001	2.5018	1.6360	2.1306	17.4212	2.2156	12.9191	2.3030	8.6308
2002	2.4735	0.6036	2.1222	16.5549	2.2289	10.9720	2.3400	5.7069
2003	2.5052	1.8000	2.1392	17.1118	2.2691	10.4068	2.4055	4.1455
2004	2.6278	2.7505	2.1766	20.7296	2.3315	12.7099	2.4957	5.2932
2005	2.7213	4.4933	2.2526	20.8052	2.4362	11.7011	2.6328	3.3617
2006	3.0259	4.6661	2.3352	29.5768	2.5499	18.6670	2.7820	8.7683

Source: Author calculations.

The evidence shows that the estimated tariff is sensitive to *X* and *Z* factors. Therefore, the regulator's discretion on choices of *X* and *Z* factors is necessary for the consumers to benefit from the price regulation while the firms would have been given the right incentive to improve their efficiency.

7. Conclusion: Lessons for the Regulators

This chapter studies and analyzes electricity tariff regulation in Thailand since 2000, which comprises the base tariff and the F_t.

The analysis shows that base tariff determination relies on a hybrid regulatory approach biased towards rate of return regulation. The attempt to employ incentive regulation has been made, but its effect on tariff setting is negligible. Incentive regulation through imposing *X* factor on operating cost was employed but the gain from efficiency improvement is limited and there is no mechanism to pass its benefits to consumers.

The consequences of adopting the hybrid regulatory approach together with regulatory capture in tariff determination process are excess capacity, increase in base tariff with time and excessive profits of the state utilities.

This chapter explores incentive regulatory alternatives such as price cap regulation, revenue cap regulation, sliding scale regulation and yardstick regulation, to provide incentives for efficiency improvement to state utilities and to ensure that consumers enjoy benefits from efficiency improvement.

The case studies on price cap regulation with various *X* and *Z* factors are investigated. The findings illustrate that during the period of study most of the estimated tariffs under price cap regulation are lower than the actual tariffs even in the case of adding the *Z* factor for the firms to take additional costs incurred from implementation of government energy policies into account. If the price cap regulation was adopted in Thailand, the consumers would have benefited from lower electricity tariff. Hence the choice of *X* and *Z* factors should be carefully made under the regulatory power's discretion.

However, given Thailand's unique ESI, the current tariff regulatory regime has its own merit. It was successful in providing stable, reliable and adequate electricity supply, particularly during the period of high and unpredictable demand growth, and this was the main factor contributing to favorable economic and investment environment in Thailand. Nevertheless, as economic and social conditions change, Thailand's tariff regulatory regime should be re-evaluated and re-designed occasionally.

Acknowledgment

I would like to thank Thailand Research Fund for New Researcher Grant on the Project of Electricity Price Regulation in Thailand: An Application to the Enhanced Single Buyer Model.

References

Arizu, B, L Maurer and B Tenenbaum (2004). Pass through of power purchase costs. Energy and Mining Sector Board Discussion Paper, Paper No. 10, World Bank, Washington DC.

Averch, H and LL Johnson (1962). Behavior of the firm under regulatory constraint. *American Economic Review*, 52, pp. 1052–1069.

Crew, MA and PR Kleindorfer (1996). Incentive regulation in the United Kingdom and the United States: Some lessons. *Journal of Regulatory Economics*, 9(3), pp. 211–25.

Estache, A, JL Guasch and L Trujillo (2003). Price caps, efficiency payoffs and infrastructure contract renegotiation in Latin America, *World Bank Policy Research Working Paper 3129*, World Bank, Washington DC.

Gans, JS and S King (2000). Options for electricity transmissions regulation in Australia. *The Australian Economic Review*, 33, pp. 145–160.

Jamasb, T (2006). Between the state and market: Electricity sector reform in developing countries. *Utilities Policy*, 14, pp. 14–30.

Jamasb, T and M Pollitt (2001). Benchmarking and regulation: International electricity experience. *Utilities Policy*, 9(3), pp. 107–30.

Joskow, PL (1998). Regulatory priorities for reforming infrastructure sectors in developing countries, Paper prepared for the Annual World Bank Conference on Development Economics, Washington, DC, 20–21 April.

Joskow, PL and R Schmalensee (1986). Incentive regulation for electric utilities. *Yale Journal of Regulation*, 4, pp. 1–49.

Kirkpatrick, C, D Parker and YF Zhang (2005). Price and profit regulation in developing and transition economies: A survey of the regulators. *Public Money and Management*. April, 99–105.

Laffont, JJ (2005). *Regulation and Development*, Cambridge University Press, Cambridge.

Laffont, JJ and J Tirole (1993). *A Theory of Incentives in Procurement and Regulation*. Cambridge, Massachusetts: MIT Press.

Lowry, MN and L Kaufmann (2006). Alternative regulation for North American electric utilities. *The Electricity Journal*, 19(5), pp. 15–26.

Lyon, TP (1994). Incentive regulation in theory and practice, In *Incentive Regulation for Public Utilities*, Crew, MA (ed.), pp.1–26. Boston: Kluwer Academic Publishers.

Parker, D and Kirkpatrick (2005). Regulating prices and profits in utility industries in low-income economies: Rate of return, price cap or sliding-scale regulation? *International Journal of Public Sector Management*, 18(3), pp. 241–255.

Rothwell, G and T Gomez (2003). *Electricity Economics: Regulation and Deregulation.* New Jersey: John Wiley & Sons Publications.

Shleifer, A (1985). A theory of yardstick competition. *RAND Journal of Economics*, 16(3), pp. 319–327.

Sirasoontorn, P (2005). Efficiency measures and regulation: Thai electricity generation. *Thammasat Economic Journal*, 23(1), pp. 38–81.

Viljainen, S, KLJ Tahvanainen, S Honkapuro and JP Lappeenranta (2004). Regulation of Electricity Distribution Business, Paper presented at Nordic Distribution and Asset Management Conference, Espoo, Finland, August.

Vogelsang, I (2002). Incentive regulation and competition in public utility markets: A 20-year perspective. *Journal of Regulatory Economics*, 22(1), pp. 5–27.

CHAPTER 7

Regulating Power without a Five Year Plan: Institutional Changes in the Chinese Power Sector

Kun-Chin Lin, Mika Purra and Hui Lin

The command economic bureaucracies governing China's power sector have struggled to meet the power demands of a rapidly growing domestic economy in the reform era. Aiming to reduce the politicization and direct administration of electricity generation, transmission and distribution, the central planners launched three major episodes of institutional changes in the reform era which culminated in the creation of an independent ministry-level agency — SERC — to oversee an oligopoly of restructured power companies in 2002. However, a new regulator operating in face of powerful state-owned firms is bound to open a new chapter in contentious politics. Resistance to an arms-length regulatory relationship has come from the bureaucratic and market levels.

We argue that the influential role of NDRC has undercut the institutional role and autonomy of SERC, while domestic players have been hampered in their growth strategies by lack of clarity in rules of competition. As a result, they have focused their efforts on crowding out the private sector and foreign investors, and lobbying around SERC for particularistic gains. We conclude by comparing the power sector to oil and petrochemicals, telecommunications, and transport sectors, deriving that even in a highly-authoritarian political environment, the domestic diffusion of regulatory institutions has manifestly produced different forms of governance with troubling implications for industry-specific regulatory bodies and peak associations.

1. Introduction

China has become the second largest electric power market in the world. It is predicted that the Chinese power industry will invest over US$2 trillion in the next 30 years, and that the nation's purchasing of power generation equipment alone will account for some 32% of the world's total.[1] Indeed, data based on the China Electricity Council (CEC) study indicated that by the end of 2009, China's total installed power capacity had reached 874 GW (gigawatt) (CEC, 2010). This represents an increase of 10.2% up from 2008 and reflects an average annual growth rate of 10.8% since 1949.[2] Per capita consumption is low at around 2,149 KWh (kilowatt hour) in 2006, suggesting that a massive expansion of power infrastructure would be necessary if China's consumption is to approach the global average. Meanwhile, according to the International Energy Agency's (IEA) *International Energy Outlook 2007*, rapid continual growth as well as rapid development in the country's transmission and distribution power supply capability is expected in China's power generation capacity (IEA, 2007). It is estimated that by 2030, China's power consumption will double up to 8,472 TWh (terawatt hour) and that the nation's power generation capacity will reach 1,775 GW.[3]

To counter these enormous expectations and support the development of China's electricity sector, the government launched a series of reforms at the end of the 1990s and early 2000 with a view to create a more dynamic power market structure and to establish a modern regulatory

[1] Meet and network with China's Electric Power business, *EP Shanghai 2009*, 8–10 July 2009, Shanghai International Exhibition Centre (INTEX), China. www.ceejay.com.hk/EP%20Shanghai%2009.doc.

[2] The average annual growth rate is calculated based on the total installed power capacity data from CEC: 1.85GW in year 1949; 874.07GW in 2009.

[3] China Power and Energy News, Issue No. 61, April 2009.

framework. The first time when China's electricity industry was subjected to legislative control was with the passing of the 1995 Electricity Law that guaranteed the development of the electric power industry and pledged to safeguard the legal rights and interests of investors, operators and users of electric power. It was a landmark legislation that set the next stage of reforms in 2002 with the creation of the State Electricity Regulatory Commission (SERC) to establish a coherent system for regulatory organization and to regulate the power sector. It also led in key regulations to supervize and regulate electricity-related issues such as pricing of electricity, and issuing and managing electric business permits that were promulgated in 2005, with a view to create a more balanced market. The reform process and the transformation of the market governing structures are on-going, and while progress has been promising, today they are mired in numerous unintended consequences and problems that dampen not only electricity development but also the efficient provision of electricity across the country.

While the institution of neoliberal governance reforms has been the mantra of governance development across a number of Asian countries since the 1990s, China's unique system of governance is remarkably different. Indeed, the emerging regulatory framework for China's power sector is best understood not as a unique local adaptation of Western models, but also as a historically contingent expression of the Chinese state transforming its own capacities — specifically, Beijing's ambitious project of state-led privatization and marketization of China's commanding heights since the mid-1990s. The central premise of this national industrial restructuring project is the dismantling of the command economic authority and exchange relations based on ministerial direct supervision of production units. Two decades of reform had made it clear that clunky planned output quotas, redistributive targets, policy-mandated credit allocation, and administrative price signals no longer fulfilled atleast the basic goals of industrial policies, public sector sustainability, and macroeconomic stability. The reforms established new ground rules, mandating the new state-controlled corporations to pursue commercial imperatives in response to dynamic market signals. Unquestionably, market considerations must be subjugated to the firm's overriding role in defending national interests through their intimate ownership and regulatory ties to political principals in Beijing. In this new political economic context, what constitutes national interests, and which actors interpret these interests, become points of contention and compromise, that affect the performance of new corporate institutions.

It is against this background that we present an evident case of institutional collusion that bears on the facility of the nation's electricity sector reformers to carry out planned structural changes with a view to diminishing the level of politicization in energy policy and administration, and to strengthen the sector's performance. In essence, it is an example of a centralized regulatory regime that inspite of reform policies, continues to display high-levels of overlapping regulatory authority and bureaucratic competition for rule ownership and rule formulation between the sector governing agencies. This partly answers some of the key themes in this book regarding regulatory outcomes and effectiveness, and even reflects the questions of what is feasible and why. As the newly established regulatory agencies fail to fulfill their statutory functions and responsibilities, the answer is not evident. Whether or not the reformed regulatory design works, remains an open question as conventional institutional structures and bureaucratic mechanisms, practices, and norms continue to dictate policy-making despite the reform policies.

A number of elements in this chapter validate our claims and explicitly depict the obstacles that face the reformers of China's electricity sector. First, the National Development and Reform Commission (NDRC), as the key bureaucratic arm of the Communist Party, has seriously challenged the institutional mandate of the SERC as it seeks a clearer rule-based market structure for China's electricity sector. In fact, the rules creation in the electricity sector has been notably undermined by the administrative dominance of the NDRC. Second, the absence of reliable rules mechanism for a competitive market has resulted in the crowding out of the private sector and foreign investors as the domestic state-owned power companies dominate the market with the backing of the NDRC. And third, the diffusion of regulatory institutions in a highly-authoritarian environment continues to produce remarkably different governance forms thus hampering the institutional roles of industry-specific regulatory bodies and interest groups across industry sectors.

Measuring Regulatory Outcomes and Implications for Regulatory Design

Generally speaking, the national interests that drive the overarching market considerations are embedded in the following operational principles:[4]

1) The centrality of state ownership: The State Assets Supervision and Administration Commission (SASAC) serves as the property manager of state owned shares in the corporatized state firms (Green and He, 2005). Domestic and foreign investors are accorded a minority shareholding presence in the public listings of these firms at home and abroad. The State Council plans to gradually sell off state-shares towards the tipping point of majority ownership control, contingent on the firm's fund raising needs and the stability of the domestic stock markets. Complete divestiture has been ruled out as an immediate option.
2) Regulation based on mediation of interests, not an arms-length approach: In contrast to the global template of privatization plans with legally delineated state regulatory functions and limited public-private partnerships, China has taken a path-dependent approach in seeking consensus among inter-governmental and emerging business interests in the policy-making process (Kennedy, 2005). The Chinese

[4] The following principles are summarized from the major findings of these representative studies: Fei, H (1998). *Zhongguo qiye zhuzhi zhanlue xingwei* (The Strategic Orientation of the Organization of Chinese Enterprises). Beijing: Jingji guanli chubanshe; Ross, G, L Song, S Tenev and Y Yao (2005). *China's Ownership Transformation.* Washington, DC: IFC; Lin, KC (2008). Macroeconomic Disequilibria and Enterprise Reform: Restructuring the Chinese Oil and Petrochemical Industries in the 1990s. *The China Journal,* 60, pp. 49–79; Lin, Y-M 2001. *Between Politics and Market: Firms, Competition, and Institutional Change in Post-Mao China.* Cambridge: Cambridge University Press; Nolan, P (2001). *China and the Global Economy: National champions, industrial policy and the big business revolution.* Houndsmill: Palgrave; Sutherland, D and L Ning (2009). "China's Business Groups after Three Decades of Economic Reform: Diversified Conglomerates or Focused Industrial Groups?" In *China's Three Decades of Economic Reforms,* Liu, X and W Zhang (eds.). London: Routledge; Wang, Y, Y, Wan and B Wang (eds.) (1999). *Guoyou konggu gongsi lilun yu shijian* (Theory and Practice of State-Controlled Shareholding Companies). Beijing: Jingji kexue chubanshe.

regulators neither captured by organized corporate interests nor autonomous in the sense of standing apart from the private sector, bargain with contending ministerial and corporate officials in an institutional landscape of "fragmented authoritarianism" (Liberthal and Oksenberg, 1988; Lieberthal and Lampton, 1992).

3) Fiscal stability for the central government: This constitutes a key justification for gradualism in reform and restrained competition and administrative price controls in utilities and key energy inputs in particular. Evidenced in the political resistance to adjust domestic prices for refined oil products in recent years, Chinese planners have shunned price instability that may come with the kind of Schumpeterian creative destruction if markets are truly liberalized and state-controlled corporations are vulnerable to fierce competition.
4) Recentralization of corporate governance: After two decades of enterprise reform based on decentralization of decision-making authority, financial controls, and property rights to sub-national state agents, Beijing spearheaded partial policy reversals starting in the mid- and late-1990s. Earlier policy innovations such as managerial contract responsibilities, had created attenuated principal-agent relations that generated considerable economic and fiscal losses for Beijing. In restructuring heavy industries in the past decade, central planners aimed to enhance control and financial returns through adopting highly-centralized organizational forms such as the multidivisional form (M-form) in oil and petrochemical sectors (Freeland, 1996).
5) Corporate restructuring that builds on existing strengths: As David Stark has pointed out in the Eastern European context, organizational adaptations in post-socialist economies find building materials from salvaging the institutional rubrics of the former system (Stark, 1996). Chinese enterprise reforms are also bounded by the existing organizational possibilities. In practical terms, new corporations must have roots in older bodies, such as the administrative monopolies in functional areas such as oil exploration and development, coal industries, or regional power grids. In the oil and petrochemical industries, the upstream and downstream companies were converted into national oil corporations through asset swaps that established some measure of integration in operation similar to Western majors.

6) Financial diversification: Historically, a serious drain and risk factor for the domestic commercial banks, is that the state-owned enterprises (SOE) have been corporatized with an eye towards obtaining liquidity from the domestic and foreign stock markets. There is also a fledgling corporate bond market (Shih, 2006). The impetus towards public listing took off in the 1990s with the rapid growth of these stock markets and politicized drive by provincial planners to list firms for expansion and merger and acquisition purposes. The central government has allowed foreign direct and portfolio investments in the new corporations, which have not generated significant impact on corporate governance and control by Chinese stakeholders.

These state priorities have resulted in fundamental constraints to market liberalization. State-controlled corporations have exerted a direct influence on the rules of competition as their dominating market shares, exclusive networks of upstream and downstream integration, and policy privileges virtually guarantee corporate viability and significant gains from oligopolistic collusion. Beijing had anticipated that industrial self-governance would go hand in hand with market expansion, supplying the regulatory mechanisms to obviate further socialist planning and administrative coordination. The economic rent from collusion would buffer the destabilizing experience of privatization, extending a lifeline to the numerous managers, workers and consumers who have long relied on subsidies from SOEs. Predictably, the regulatory framework typically falls short of reducing the potential for conflicts of interest, introducing transparency and procedural regularity of government, or preventing collusion between the industry and government agencies (Andrews-Speed *et al.*, 2000).

The transformation from administrative to corporate hierarchy in industrial governance across the Chinese commanding heights — including oil and petrochemical, airlines, telecommunications, banking, railroad, and power industries, etc. — has taken on varying institutional adaptations contingent on specific challenges in each sector (Chung, 2003; Lin, 2008). We focus on particular regulatory outcomes in the power sector, but will discuss them in comparison to outcomes in other sectors. The chapter is divided into four sections. The first section discusses the nuances of the Chinese regulatory state and lays out our argument in more detail. The second section assesses the evolution of China's electricity and shows the key developments and phases that have come to define its progress. The third section discusses the SERC's institutional standing in light of China's power sector reforms particularly since the 2002 power sector reform. And finally the fourth section, in conclusion, provides a comparative assessment of the regulatory approaches in China's most dynamic industrial sectors.

2. The Rise of a Regulatory State in China

The case study of the power sector addresses the current academic debate over the rise of the "regulatory state" in China (Lin, 2005; Pearson, 2005). Proponents of the regulatory state perspective predict that the SOEs will become market oriented as the central state sheds its meddlesome ownership role in most industries (Guthrie, 1999). They point to the scrapping of numerous old-styled line ministries and the creation of dedicated regulatory agencies staffed with new officials, original capacities, and institutional autonomies (ADB, 2003; Yang, 2004; Pei, 2005; Lin, 2006). However, this line of thinking lacks analytical separation for distinct functions and motivations of the national government towards public enterprises — in particular the complex dualities of its roles as a majority owner-cum-monopolist vs the regulator of industries, its short-term financial vs fiscal interests, and its economic-developmental vs politico-social objectives. Furthermore, a bird's-eye view tends to neglect adverse reactions from the management, workers, and local states as traditional stakeholders in SOEs.[5] Lastly, the claims of a rising regulatory state would appear to presuppose the reconciliation of independent and contending institutional interests within the State Council and ministries, which would be premature given the fragmented authoritarian structure that governs policy-making process and bureaucratic exchanges in Beijing. Whether or not the central government can successfully manage the shifting relations among various bureaucratic agencies and corporate groups

[5] For accounts of bottom-up reactions from local stakeholders in response to the restructuring of the oil and petrochemical industries in the late-1990s, see Lin, 2006 and Lin, 2009.

should constitute a paramount empirical inquiry. The present case study of the power sector holds up these criticisms.

The Chinese experience sheds light on comparative theories of re-regulation and new industrial policy, which propose bureaucratic and market failure causes for national regulators to step up their law-making and institution building efforts (Hira *et al.*, 2004; Rodrik, 2004; Hausmann and Rodrik, 2006; Vogel, 2006; Vogel, 1999). Intra- and inter-sectoral coordination imperatives equally important as a cause of re-regulation are as each industry maintains forward and backward linkages to other producers and consumers. The management of these collective action problems and spillover effects represents the core challenges for the autonomous bureaucracy in pursuing a coherence approach and effective adjustments to the overall national developmental strategy (Doner, 1992). However, these comparative regulation theories pay inadequate attentions, to the institutional risks in creating new regulatory bodies — the re-regulatory view downplays the independent effects of regulatory bodies from the power players that created them, and the new industrial policy perspective emphasizes the precondition of market and government failures to invite strategic industrial policy.

The China's context exposes the problems of these analytical biases. The initial state of Chinese reform of the power sector is not necessarily the government or market failure, which had been evident for a long time. Instead, the reform objective is precisely to redefine state-market relations before attempting to make the operations of the respective spheres perfect.[6] Equally importantly, the boundary of the public and the private is hardly clear enough for conventional analysis of relative capacities of the

[6] By implication, reform could generate short-term output growth, while producing little efficiency gains. A parallel strand of institutional analysis on industrial policy has been developed by Acemoglu, D and J Robinson (2008). The Role of Institutions in Growth and Development. *Working Paper No. 10, Commission for Growth and Development of the World Bank.* Washington, DC: World Bank. They attribute policy changes with no apparent growth impact to a "see-saw effect" in which expropriation threats, persistent populist demand for redistribution, de facto and de jure political power affect performance of economic institutions. See William Easterly's online critiques of this strand of new institutional economics, http://larrywillmore.net/blog/tag/william-easterly/

state or the market in industrial governance. In fact, this very ambiguity — captured by the partially privatized corporate entities — poses binding constraints on institutional reform and complications for the use of policy levers. Regulatory agencies, once created, also generate a set of risks and coordination problems for the regulators and stakeholders. We will focus on how the nominal autonomy of the new, ministerial-level power regulatory body has produced limited effectiveness against competing regulatory sources in the State Council, as well as the problems in containing corporate interests.

Placing industrial restructuring in a broader political context, we find that the primary driving force for reform and policy design, stems from the central dilemma of the Chinese party-state's self-preservation. Even when the Politburo and central bureaucratic elite attempt to build capacities for the long-run maintenance of the economic bureaucracy, it cannot prevent sub-national state agents i.e., regulators, local officials, state-appointed managers — from acting strategically for short-run gains at the expense of the overall design. In other words, reformers face a kind of time-consistency problem, from which the state would pull back from optimal reform policies in anticipation of unintended consequences during implementation. Some of the reform measures we examine in the power sector would seem half-baked, tentative, or broken up in sequence, not because of the reformers not knowing what they were doing but as they deliberately refrained from a coherent and complete sequence of changes that might produce a major backlash that combines fiscal, economic, and social disruptions. Of course, the evaluation of these risks can only be political. Hence, we also examine the elite political equilibrium behind regulatory choices, and its impact on the level of institutional and policy commitment (Acemoglu and Robinson, 2006; Acemoglu and Robinson, 2008).

We also place the notion of regulatory diffusion in a national context. Though, to a limited extent, foreign models of industrial organization and international lessons in privatization (as imparted by IGOs) have gained notable airtime in elite policy discourse, we do not feel that they shaped reform choices in a way that was predicted by institutionalist or constructivist theories of regulatory convergence. Instead, citations of foreign models mainly reflect domestic contentions of interests. Industrial organizational models serve as competing techniques of corporate control, with specific forms of organization generating desired consequences for a unique set of regulators and stakeholders. Longitudinal analysis shows that, overtime, these competing sets of interests outlast the usefulness of any particular institutions (Yeh and Lewis, 2004).

Here, we lay out what these interests are in China's power sector, and to what extent the current institutions have met their demand. We focus on the linchpin of the national regulatory framework — the SERC — that was created in 2002 as a supra-ministerial agency with a mandate stipulating a wide-ranging authority over power generation, transmission and distribution. SERC was the first non-financial, independent regulatory body in the post-command economic sense. An understanding of its political and institutional context helps us to anticipate the form and effectiveness of new regulatory agencies planned for transport, environment, energy, and other policy areas.

3. Long-term Reform Objectives — From State Monopoly to (Notional) Free Market Structure 1949–2009

The Challenge of Institutional Reform

In light of these evolutionary stages, the institutional reform of the China's power sector revolves around five core policy challenges involving complex coordination between the domestic market, industrial players, and bureaucracies at central and local levels:

1) Meeting China's growing energy demand, preferably through market determination: While acknowledging a clear need to invest in capacity expansion to align supply with demand, Beijing also faces chronic problems of managing energy usage cycles and the unequal distribution of power generation areas and consumption centers across China. The dynamics of the alternating shortage and surplus crises are complex and have not been systematically investigated, but are likely to be amplified by the local political distortions that produce boom-and-bust cycles in capital formation and local state protectionism and market fragmentation (Walton and Finn, 2005; Zhu and Li, 2003).

2) Promotion and regulation of competition in the absence of a functional market: In this case, the central state regulator acts to compensate for deficiencies in the market, in particular, with respect to energy prices and access to energy transmission networks. Refraining from unrestrained competition, Beijing defends concerns for collective goods such as, upgrading the power grids and energy delivery and service standards, across China's vast territories, and private goods such as stable prices for consumers and policy aids on technological upgrading and capitalization for the power companies (Xie, 2009; He, 2003).
3) Aligning upstream-downstream interests: Industrial analysts often point out conflicts of interests among coal producers, generators, and transmission and distribution companies. These businesses have traditionally come under different lines of administration, and remain weak, mediated by market forces. There is a common perception that competition in regional markets is likely to be ineffective, thus, price liberalization is likely to cause tremendous volatility. Instead, the State Council has occasionally intervened to promote long-term supply contracts between coal suppliers and power plants to improve risk management and profitability (Ng, 2008). It has also established guidelines for price increases and cross-regional differences, that attempt to spread the costs of rising inputs. These interventions keep Beijing at the center of a Catch-22 dilemma of reacting to failures of competition and being blamed for not pushing for liberalization.
4) Defining the functions and bureaucratic standing of the new regulatory body: Given the weakness of the SERC and the contentious government-business and central-local relations described below, top Chinese leaders have sought ways to add another layer of strategic governance of energy-related policies and industries. In 2005, the State Council established a National Energy Leading Group to serve as the highest political forum for addressing China's energy security issues, and also to provide a formal, unified governmental interface with the emerging corporate interests of the National Oil Companies (NOC). These developmental strategic and industrial governance functions have become disarticulated in March 2008

upon the State Council's establishment of the National Energy Commission (NEC) and the National Energy Administration (NEA). The former serves as a formally independent policy forum, and the latter, a supra-ministerial agency housed within the NDRC. In January 2010, the State Council established a NEC to take rein of strategic policy-making and coordination.[7] This move resurrected a supra-ministerial body on energy policy, which had been absent since the Energy Ministry was disbanded in 1993. The question about how the new commission would relate to SERC, with implications for the power relations in the bureaucratic field and redistribution of authority and resources, remains (Hafsi and Tian, 2005; Lan, 2007).

5) Assessing the effectiveness of the institutional changes: How do different stakeholders in the power sector perceive the desired regulatory outcomes of reform? What are the key indicators of success for the central regulators? Our analysis would attempt to make the feedback loop explicit that leads to the next round of reform.[8]

These challenges have been a distinct feature throughout the evolution of China's electricity sector particularly since the mid-1980s. In varying stages of state-led privatization they are indicative of the progressive policy changes that the government has been implementing on one hand, and of the intricate balancing act the government is forced to play in the creation of more competitive market to satisfy the power demand of the growing economy on the other. Until the 1990s, the development stages of the electricity sector aligned with the broader industrial policy undertakings of the Communist Party since 1949. For example, the government, through the monopolistic Ministry of Electric Power Industry (MEPI), provided electricity production and service as a vertically integrated monopolized utility from 1949 to 1985. In essence, the MEPI also

[7] China Sets up National Energy Commission. *Xinhua News Agency*, 2010 January 27.

[8] Dua, L, M Jie and S Jinchuan (2007). Assessing the impact of regulatory reforms on China's electricity generation industry. *Energy Policy*, 37(2), February 2009, pp. 712–720. They identified efficiency gains from regulatory reform and nonfuel material upgrades, but no significant gains from fuel supply changes.

functioned as the industry regulator overseeing all functions of power generation, transmission and distribution.[9] All infrastructure investment, production quotas, power allocation and pricing were in turn overseen and controlled by the State Planning Commisssion (SPC).

The command economic system ensured coherence between upstream and downstream interests even if the allocation and distribution of both coal and electricity remained under strict planning control. However, while the state monopoly reflected the minimal goals of the five-year plans, it struggled to meet the growing electricity demands of the Four Modernizations Strategy.[10] Power shortages and public dissatisfaction were prevalent across the country as electricity remained in short supply. Overall, the growth of the sector remained negative throughout the 1960s and 1970s despite the reforms (See Appendix 2.). Some contend that the electricity shortages in this period are largely attributed to the fundamental nature of the command economy that crowded out other sources of investment, independent power producers (IPPs), and all other feasible incentives for sustained and balanced power generation (Zhang and Heller, 2004).

From 1985 onwards a notable shift towards a more decentralized mechanism took hold, consistent with the general direction of enterprise and fiscal reforms. By initiating specific *Construction Funds,* the government encouraged the provincial and the local government to plan the financing of electricity generation. The purpose of these funds was to increase the incentives for local governments and the private sector to participate in electricity generation and ultimately meet the increasing power demands of Deng Xiaoping's *Reform and Opening up Policy.* In all, the

---

[9] The MEPI was rebranded on a number of occasions — Ministry of Fuel Industries (1949–1955); Ministry of Electric Power Industry (1955–1958; 1979–1992); Ministry of Water Resources and Electric Power (1958–1979).

[10] The Four Modernization Strategy, a part of Deng Xiaoping's reforms, was initiated in December 1964 by Premier Zhou En'lai. It sought to stimulate the growth of agriculture, industries, national defense, and science and technology. It was officially launched in December 1978 at the Third Plenum of the 11th Central Committee, by Deng Xiaoping who had assumed the leadership of the Party after Mao's death. This formally marked the beginning of the reform era.

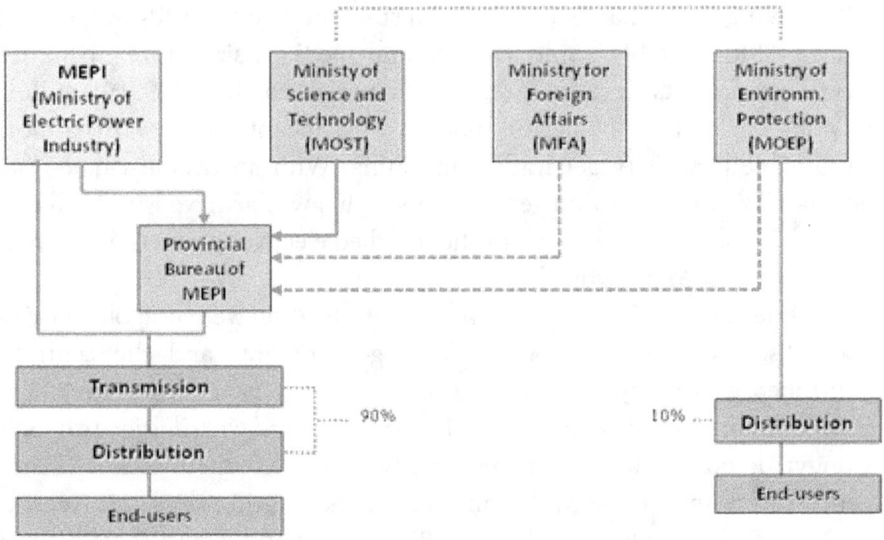

Chart 1: Electricity system after 1986 reform (1986–1996).

provinces were recognized as independent units responsible for the planning, regulation, and operation of their local and regional electricity utilities and encouraged to invest and create self-sustaining regional electricity markets.[11] Indeed, in 1985 the State Council for the first time allowed financing of power plants by provincial governments, private enterprises and even foreign investors (State Council, 1985). It was the first step towards exposing the power sector to competitive market forces and incentivizing state-appointed managers to respond to these forces. The regulatory authority was decentralized and the provincial governments were empowered to directly approve power projects that were 50MW or smaller in size (Zhang and Heller, 2004; Wirtshafter, 1990).

Even as the majority of transmission and distribution assets remained in the control of the central government, the proportion of state-owned generating assets was reduced to 46% by the mid 1990s with the remaining

[11] The principal of "Who is Generating Power Should Benefit from" is stated in the State Council Regulation No. 72, *Provisional Regulation on Encouraging Fund Raising for Electric Power and Multiple Rates of Power Tariff*, 1985.

54% staying in the hands of local governments and the IPPs (Wong and wong, 1998). Notably, some 84 large and medium sized foreign funded electricity projects were built during the period totalling US$19.4 billion in value. Essentially, the period marked a significant shift towards a more sustainable electricity generation in China. With an overall capacity of 236.54 GW, a nation-wide generation surplus was achieved by 1996 that ranked China second in terms of the installed electricity generating capacity and output in the world.

While, the positive effects of the decentralization were notable, the distinct discrepancies between the local governments and the centrally controlled grid companies also started to emerge at the same time. The grid companies, despite the agreed *Transmission and Distribution* principle (tongyi diaodu), often raised electricity tariffs for their state-affiliated generating plants all the while compressing the ongrid prices and volumes for the provincial plants and other IPPs (Zhang and Heller, 2004). These measures markedly undermined the implementation of the *New Plant, New Price* policy as well as the planned unification of transmission and distribution. Provincial protectionism as an emerging phenomenon also began to lay barriers for the opening of transmission and distribution channels to the IPPs from other provinces and regions.

The explicit adoption of market economy principles in China's electricity sector is recognizable from 1997 onwards. From 1997 to 2002, the government implemented measures to separate the daily running of commercial enterprises from government functions with the aim to reduce politicization and ministerial administration. With the establishment of the SPC the government created a monopolized state-owned corporation to control all facets of electricity business in generation, transmission, and distribution. The SPC's branches and subsidiaries also extended across the country to the regions, paving the way for the reorganization of the electricity market. To counter the local protectionist tendencies of provincial planners, who often blocked the uploading of generated capacity from neighboring provinces as well as the central government onto their transmission networks, the SPC received a mandate from the central government to overcome these regional power dynamics.

However, the establishment of the SPC only marked the beginning of a protracted process of fundamental, formal institutional changes that attempted to disentangle complexities in state-market relations. The electricity sector witnessed a wave of operational and administrative restructuring from 2002 onwards, of which, two specific changes are particular noteworthy. First, the State Council document No. 5 of 2002 partitioned the SPC by separating the power generating business from the grid transmission, in turn breaking up the socialist legacy of the integrated monopoly (State Council, 2002). The state-owned productive assets under SPC were subsequently dismantled and regrouped into five generating companies, namely the Huaneng, the Datang, the Huadian, the Guodian, and the China Power Investment Company. SPC's transmission and distribution assets were split into two grid companies roughly along the geographical lines; namely the State Grid Company (SGC), responsible for most of northern China, and the China Southern Grid Company (CSGC) covering the southern provinces. Finally, the administrative structure was fundamentally altered by the creation of an *independent regulator* for the power sector — the SERC — in 2003 (State Council, 2002). Endowed with the authorities to manage the state monopoly break-up, to oversee industry reforms, and to promote a competitive market structure of the power sector, the promise of SERC was ground-breaking as an institutional governance structure in China (State Council, 2003).

The reformed electricity market structure is depicted in Chart 2. It displays the parallel roles of NDRC, SASAC, and other relevant ministries alongside with the SERC in commanding the sector's industrial segments from generating to transmission and distribution. The seemingly promising structure, in place since 2008, does not clearly elevate the position of the independent regulator, but places SERC right back a midst of fragmented bureaucratic politics which demands compromises and resource exchanges among agencies with overlapping jurisdictions. One of the central questions that have plagued the electricity sector in particular, is the ability of the SERC to formulate national and regional policy responses to support the development and growth prospects of China's energy markets. As a matter of fact, the launch of regional competitive electricity markets in Northeastern China and other parts of the country has met with only marginal success predominantly due to inter-agency rivalries, regional politics, and the powerful position of the state-owned generating companies that continue to whittle the authority of the command economy in the provinces.

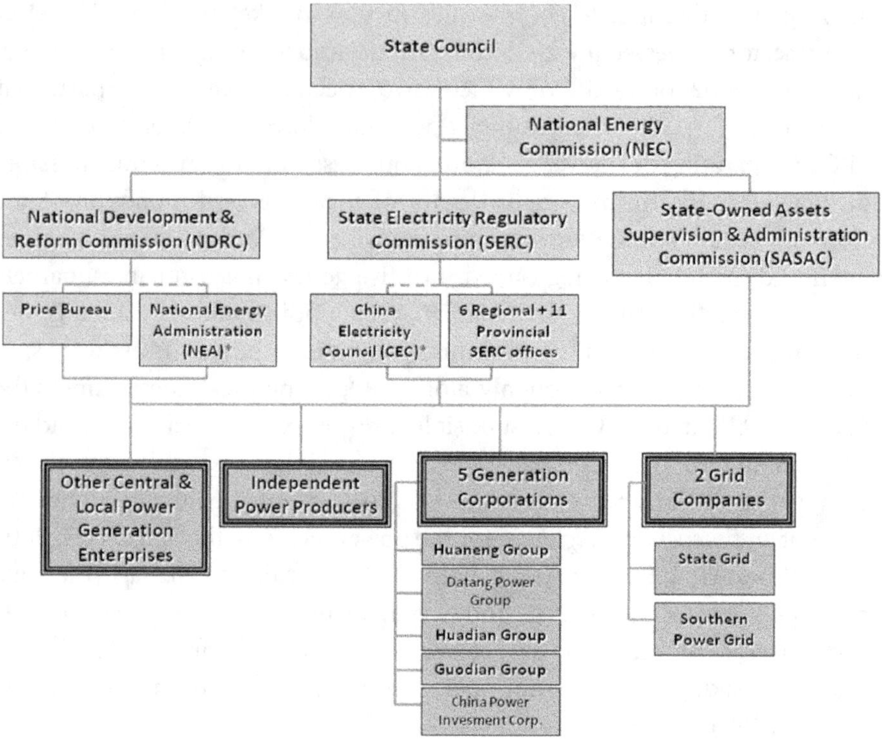

Chart 2: Electricity market structure after 2008 reforms.

Note: *CEC and NEA are independent organizations but under supervision of SERC and NDRC, respectively.

4. Between the Rock and a Hard Place: SERC's precarious institutional standing

Echoing the long-term reform objectives for China's power sector, with the 2002 electricity sector reform, the government sought to achieve multiple goals. It was keen to create a fair and a competitive power market structure with a wholesale market and independent regulation; to improve efficiency and lower costs; to optimize resource allocation and promote development and national grid interconnections; and to continue the rural electricity structural reforms (Zhang and Heller, 2004). To achieve these goals, the SERC was mandated with wide-ranging statutory powers that, in addition to the regulatory function, provided the agency with the authority to stipulate and enforce technical standards and propose tariffs and adjustments to government electricity pricing authority, and to investigate market violations (State Council, 2003). The mandated powers provided the agency with an authoritative statutory platform to oversee the electricity sector.

The promise of a competitive market marks a significant development to China's electricity sector and we refrain from passing judgment on either its failure or success. This would be premature in a transitional governance system whose institutions and normative governance structures are continuously evolving and maturing. Instead, as we acknowledge its shortcomings so far, our aim is to identify the challenges that the SERC faces in fulfilling its institutional mandate and in establishing a fully competitive electricity market to meet the country's growing energy needs. In essence, the shortcomings in the institution of the SERC and in the implementation of the competitive electricity market structures are palpable and in fact indicative of higher-level politicized capture among the China's governing elites. In effect, the execution of SERC's mandate is an on-going process that is dependent on the outcomes of a combination of essential elements in the electricity market. These elements culminate in four distinct explanatory factors that shed light on the underlying power structures that impede the fulfillment of a fully competitive energy market on one hand, and explain the intensification of an underlying struggle between the informal leverages of local governments and the new regulatory arms of the central government on the other.

a) *Power Politics within the State Council*

To begin with, the precarious institutional standing of the SERC and its inability to flex its wide-ranging formal mandates are best explained by the high-level of politicization of energy within the State Council. The power sector reforms including the institution of the SERC took form during the tenures of Zeng Peiyan (1998–2003) and Ma Kai (2003–2008) as the Chairmen of the NDRC.[12] Both individuals were strong proponents of

[12] Ma Kai joined the CPC in 1965 and has held various positions in the Central Planning function within the Party before becoming the NDRC Chairman in 2003. Zeng Peiyan in turn, while an equally long-running career within the Party, has a background as an electrical engineer and with Ministerial level appointments at the Ministry of Electronics Industry. He also held financial planning positions within the State Planning Commission before his tenure as the NDRC Chairman.

the power sector reforms and Ma Kai was a particularly strong proponent of the establishment of the SERC.[13] Their advocacy not only partly produced the decisive changes in the institutional structure in the 2002 reform, but also created the political conditions for the subsequent institutional standoffs and the dependence on high-level interventions in the form of a supra-ministerial leadership committee to push towards power reforms and mediate conflicting interests. Starting in 2010 that elite political impetus has taken the form of the NEC. Countercurrents are ever-present. Zhang Ping, the Chairman of the NDRC since 2008, has been less of a proponent of the decentralization of China's power sector and has openly preferred a stronger central government involvement in the key substantive and technical areas of energy administration.

Shifts in the balance of power within the State Council are one component against which we can interpret the slow structural development of China's power sector although it does constitute a decisive element. If we recall the ambitious agenda of responsibilities that the SERC has been trusted with, the uncertainty in political support from the highest political actors within the central government leaves the agency with a weak mandate regardless of its formal statutory position. Indeed, a careful breakdown of the major stipulated responsibilities of reform reveals the NDRC to be the dominant regulatory body in the power sector. In its function to organize the sector by establishing a coherent regulatory structure and exercising sectoral leadership through it regional branches, the SERC has been left with a weak practical, and an immediately usable authority. In the proverbial horse and cart analogy, SERC can only become a strong player if the domestic market is orderly and competitive, and only if regional corporate structures are strictly administered under central headquarters of the power and transmission companies. Either condition preexists. Furthermore, the NEA has taken the lead in power sector planning and promotion of new technologies along with approving new investments into the sector.[14] Generally speaking, it has become evident since the State Council reform in 2008 that the NDRC

[13] Interview with the National Energy Administration (NEA), 22 May 2009, and North China Electric Power University (NCEPU), 13 January 2010.

[14] Interview with State Power Economic Research Institute, Beijing, 20 May 2009.

has given up any of its authority, but instead has been increasing its stronghold of the power sector.

The surprising capture of the regulatory process by political and regulatory entities outside the independent power regulator extends to the realm of government-business relations. By statute, the SERC should be an effective regulatory and an oversight agency that is able to enforce transparency and accountability processes on the transmission companies. And while the SERC has been trying to establish these measures, it has little say over the actual outcome as the State Grid has no interest in introducing transparency in the pricing of electricity transmission. The NDRC in turn, does not provide the SERC with the essential information to improve transmission-related pricing problems nor allows it to establish mechanisms to scrutinize regional governance systems and institute accountability.[15] Furthermore, even if the SERC were mandated with the responsibility to issue licenses for market access including safety and standards certifications, the electricity market is far from being a leveled playing field — given the NDRC's controls and the market distorting role of the SOEs — to enable the SERC to fulfill this function.[16] In fact, licenses are issued by the NDRC as it maintains the power to decide whether or not a company can do business in the sector. Previously, as the NDRC also controlled power purchase agreements (PPAs) in contractual negotiations, its control of the electricity sector was unchallenged. That PPAs between power generating companies and central or provincial governments which have not been used since 1998, has made China's electricity an increasingly unpredictable and even inoperable environment particularly for foreign investors and power companies.[17]

b) *The Market Dominance of Power Companies*

With the dismantling of the SPC and the creation of the five SOEs and the two state grid companies, China's electricity governance dynamics were reshaped in ways that enforced a two-tier market structure. The five SOEs

[15] Interview with North China Electric Power University (NCEPU), Beijing, 13 January 2010.

[16] Ibid.

[17] Interview with Electricite de France (EDF), Beijing, 14 January 2010.

formed roughly 45% of the electricity market at the end of 2008 while remaining 55% remained divided between other central government and provincial power generating companies and private companies (See Chart 3. and Appendix 3.).[18] While the competition between the five SOEs has been intense, they have also been able to increase their overall national market share over other generating companies in the provinces. It stood at 49% at the end of 2009.[19] As the NDRC controls the generation

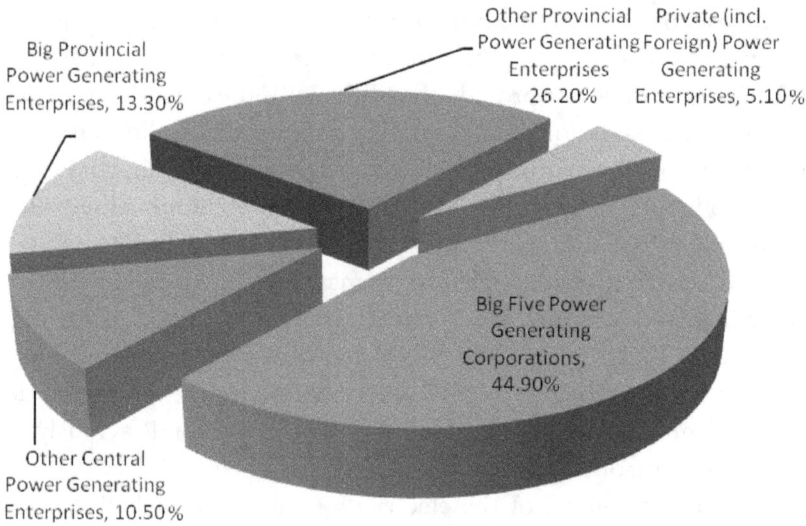

Chart 3: The composition of China's electricity market by market share in 2008.[20]
Source: SERC Annual Report 2008.

[18] From here on the abbreviation OGC (other power generating companies) is used to describe all other central and provincial government power generating companies and the private companies. The OGC specifically excludes the five SOEs.

[19] SERC Annual Report, 2009.

[20] The Big Five Power Generating Corporations, namely the five SOEs, are the China Huaneng Group, the China Datang Corporation, the China Guodian Corporation, the China Huadian Corporation, and the China Power Investment Corporation (PIC). Other Central Power Generating Enterprises (6) are the State Development and Investment Corporation, the Shenhua Group, the China Three Gorges Corporation, the China Resources Power Holdings, the China's Nuclear Power Group, the China Guangdong Nuclear Power Group Co., Ltd. Examples of the Big Provincial Power Generating Enterprises (17) are the Guangdong Yudean Group, the Zhejiang Energy Group, and the Shangdong Luneng Group.

price, also known as the regional benchmark, the other power generating companies are ill-equipped to seriously compete with the SOEs that enjoy favorable operating conditions from the NDRC. Furthermore, and even more strikingly, with wider national leverage, the SOEs have better access to coal whose price they can control and profit from by selling it to other power generating companies.[21] Finally, the NDRC also controls the transmission and distribution prices with almost non-existent transparency as to how the pricing mechanism is set up.[22] This provides the SOEs with a distinct advantage over provincial and private generating companies that are unable to provide long-term cost of production calculations.

The creation of a quasi-competitive market between the SOEs had the benefit of reducing investment costs into the generation side in particular and also of lowering operation costs. Investment cost into coal powered plant was reduced from 6000 yuan per kWh in 2000 to 4000 yuan per kWh today.[23] Whether or not the increased competition between the SOEs has resulted in overall efficiency gains for electricity is arguable, and in fact, our view is that it has significantly altered the power relationship between the central and regional governments on one hand and contributed to increased collusion between regional power market operators and the SOEs on the other. This collusion has been particularly striking with regards to both electricity and coal pricing.

In essence, while provincial power companies do not own distribution networks, they own inter-regional transmission systems and generation plants providing them with the ability to seek most beneficial power sharing deals with the SOEs. As the SOEs are known for their occasional non-compliance with NDRC imposed regulations, the collusion with regional governments and power companies is a predictable outcome.[24] They are politically well connected within the NDRC, providing them with significant freedom in their operations. And, in a system where the heads of the state-owned electricity companies are appointed and confirmed at

[21] Interview with NCEPU.

[22] Ibid.

[23] Ibid.

[24] Interview with Ximing Peng, Energy Specialist, World Bank, Beijing, 22 May 2009.

the highest-levels of government, namely the NDRC and the State Council, the authority of an independent electricity regulator can be seriously affected.[25] These obvious conflicts of interest, although not immediately visible to an observer, constitute a serious obstacle to the institution of competitive and balanced market mechanisms.

Even as the SOEs have been able to expand and increase their influence, the creation of the NEC in 2010 has failed to bring significant clarity to the governance structure of the sector.[26] In fact, the NEC has been unable to build authority over the NDRC and it is perhaps best viewed in light of the power sector reforms imposed by Zhang Ping, the incumbent Chairman of the NDRC, to deviate from the independent regulator model supported by his predecessors. The NDRC continues to impose the biggest hurdle to the development of competitive market structures as it refuses to surrender any of its powers to other agencies.[27] At this point, the SERC is the only voice supportive of the idea of integrating the NEA, the SERC and the planned Ministry of Energy to administer the sector without significant and overbearing oversight of the NDRC's.

c) *Upstream-Downstream Relations*

Apart from the political realities within the State Council and the market consequences of the SPC dismantling, a more illuminating component is the existing mechanism between the generation, transmission and distribution systems and the stronghold of the NDRC. It has the absolute power to approve transmission licenses in each province and to control the benchmark price for transmission across the country. Even if the institutional mandate grants the SERC with the authority to regulate national and provincial transmission and distribution systems, it is the NDRC that currently controls and determines the national transmission rates.[28] However, despite the centralized transmission licensing and pricing mechanisms, regional transmission price disparities distort the competitive landscape between power generating companies. In practice, it is the

---

[25] Interview with Zhao Jianfei, Caijing Magazine, Beijing, 20 May 2009.

[26] Interview with NCEPU.

[27] Ibid.

[28] Interview with World Bank official, Beijing, 13 January 2010.

Provincial Development and Reform Commissions (PDRC) that decides on the price of the transmission for pilot projects, thus providing the provincial governments with significant pricing powers. Only the issuance of certificates and licenses for regional small-scale power projects in generation and for transmission to grid companies is left to the SERC.

As the OGCs have a 51% share in the total national electricity generation capacity and the two state-owned grid companies buy the electricity from these national and private small- and large-scale power plants before selling it to consumers, any changes to this system are likely to have far-reaching consequences to China's electricity provision.[29] Recent policy changes however have allowed some of OGCs to sell electricity directly to provincial grid companies and to distribute it to end-users without the involvement of the state-owned grid companies. A few pilot projects of this nature currently exist and a greater number of such projects should eventually provide the SERC with the preconditions of significant scope and reduced transaction costs of the national market that it needs to exercise its market oversight authority.[30]

d) *Central local relations: local interests are narrowly pro-growth and protectionist*

In addition to the authority vacuum of the SERC, the regional implementation of the power sector reforms has only added to the number of challenges facing the sector. As one of the policy goals has been to adopt a competitive price mechanism (*jingjiashangwang*) for the benefit of the end-users, problems in the institution of the transmission reforms between the local governments and the SOEs have left some regions with disparate power systems. Despite the reform goals of distancing local power companies from their generation departments, some of the local companies have decidedly refused to do so. In some cases, the provincial companies have even gone so far as to increase their investments into power plants without seeking central government approval.[31]

[29] Interview with NCEPU, Beijing, 13 January 2010.

[30] Interview with World Bank.

[31] Interview with Asian Development Bank, Beijing, 13 January, 2010. Interview with World Bank.

Therefore, in direct violation of government policy, some grid companies have continued to operate their own power plants, hence stalling the overall reform process. And, even as regional companies continue to defy central government reform policies in relation to generation, the transmission sector has been experiencing a similar phenomena.[32] Despite being prohibited by law, private investments in the transmission sector have increased at the county-level as some governments have not been able to afford the maintenance and further development of their transmission networks.[33] Hence, unloading the financial burden of the local government by privatizing local state companies is not surprising, yet it is possible that these developments echo larger political and economic problems not only in the electricity sector but also in other industrial sectors. As the Electricity Law of 1995 allows only one power supply enterprise for each electricity service area, the transmission and distribution sectors have remained as natural monopolies.[34] In fact, power plants can only cooperate with a single grid company, either the SGC or the CSPG depending on the location, in order to deliver products in a given area.

And finally, even if the SERC and its local subsidiaries have been unable to fulfill their mandate in the creation of a competitive power market across the country, there are social tendencies that speak strongly in favor of granting the regions with the freedom to develop their local electricity markets. After all, disabling local governments from effectively developing their power markets for the benefit of local communities can prove to be counterproductive for the central government. While the economic benefits of regional power markets to the local governments may be against the tenets of communal welfare, the benefits to the local

[32] Interview with NCEPU and EDF, Beijing, 14 January, 2010.

[33] For example, a county government in Sichuan province sold its network system to the New Hope Group, a private enterprise among the top 500 Chinese enterprises, in 2002. See *The 21st Century Herald Business*, December 29, 2004, <http://www.nanfangdaily.com.cn/jj>. Similar situations have been found in Henan and Guizhou provinces.

[34] Article 25 of the 1995 Electricity Law of the People's Republic of China. The transmission sector has, in fact, experienced a transition of property rights at the county- and township-levels. Some county grid companies are now owned by either private enterprises or employees as shareholders. Author's interview with a chief of city power company on October 15, 2006.

governments are difficult to dispute. The Communist Party's "strategy of trading economic growth for people's consent to its absolute rule" may in fact eventually prove futile and it is in the power sector where this can become quite evident.[35] In preventing the regions from developing their local electricity markets, the central government, namely the NDRC, is also creating unnecessary obstacles for regional economic growth, which may, in time, contribute to social disparities and more wide-spread dissatisfaction over the government's policies.

5. Conclusion: Regulatory Capacities in Flux

We have presented an original case of regulatory framework in transition in the Chinese power sector, which has exhibited four institutional weaknesses:[36]

1) The independent ministry-level agency SERC's inability to serve as the primary signal-caller of the electricity market and locus of non-market activities of oligopolistic power companies since 2002;
2) A lack of progress in the industrial policy to resolve market imbalances manifesting in spouts of power shortages, chronic capacity underutilization, and relentless price pressures;
3) The power companies' own inability or unwillingness to internalize commercial risks through market- or contract-mediated relations with grid companies, coal producers, and consumers; and
4) Emerging patterns of discriminatory policies or collusion between provincial and local governments and power companies, which suggest anti-competitive dynamics.

Indeed, these weaknesses speak volumes about the problems being faced by not only China's policy-makers but also the power market more generally. Despite promising institutional reforms and restructuring

[35] Party needs to loosen is grip in China, International Herald Tribune, 2 March 2010.

[36] We hasten to point out that our conclusion is preliminary, as available evidence is far from adequate or reliable for rigorous data analyses. We plan to conduct further rounds of interviews with regulators, corporate officials, investors, and think-tanks and industrial associations refine our analysis.

efforts since 2002, the regulatory regime remains deeply centralized with overlapping regulatory authority and blurred lines of rules ownership between sector governing agencies. Based on the above observations, we can begin to identify dimensions along which we can measure variations in restructuring efforts across the Chinese commanding heights sectors. This also helps us to draw inferences from our narrative that specifically addresses the key. The following chart (Chart 4) proposes a first-cut analysis:

The above sectors share the general characteristics of natural monopolies with high sunk and lumpy costs and network externalities. In addition, their reform invariably prompts encompassing policy debates due to their national security considerations, developmental implications as complementary factors of production, and impetus for job generation and career recognitions for the politically ambitious. For the network industries, state intervention acquires an additional function in developing technical standards and operational rules to promote integration and interoperability. However, significant variations exist in the regulatory framework governing these Chinese industries. Interestingly,

Industry/ Regulatory Capacity	Electricity generation	Oil and petrochemicals	Telecommunications operators	Transport — roads, bridges, ports
Oligopolistic market structure	YES	YES	YES	YES
Independent regulatory agency, without ownership stake	YES	NO	NO	NO
Direct price setting by NDRC	YES	YES	NO (MII sets prices)	NO
FDI Restrictions	YES	YES (e.g. JV in retail stations)	YES (e.g. conditionalities on tech transfer)	NO

Chart 4: Comparing industrial regulation in the chinese commanding heights.

these variations center on the presence or absence of a central regulatory agency.[37]

Only the electricity producers fall under a nominal independent agency that maintains an arms-length relationship with the state-owned firms. Since 1992 the national oil and petrochemical corporations have reported directly to the State Council without the intermediation of an industry-specific agency. With the recent creation of the Energy Commission, both the power companies and national oil companies might find themselves operating under another level of political principal. The Ministry of Information Industry (MII) and Ministry of Transport (formerly Ministry of Communications) both hold significant property rights and financial stakes in the businesses under their jurisdiction, either through direct ownership of telecom operators or direct revenue collection on end-users and investment in infrastructure projects. Interestingly, the MII formerly competed with other players in gaining control of the telecom operators, and its consolidation of effective jurisdiction has actually handicapped telecom sector liberalization even as it has brought about a degree of market stability. Bureaucratic competition has not been an issue for the other three sectors, with the exception of the degree of intervention by the NDRC.

Direct price setting by the NDRC is seen in electricity — with the independent regulator — and in oil and petrochemicals — without a regulator. This reality is not due to the central government's lack of interest in liberalization. On the contrary, Beijing launched reforms with explicit intentions of giving oligopolies a chance to set prices. It was actually the failure of oligopolistic competition that has forced central regulators to resort to administrative prices (Lin 2008). Telecom and transport industries that remain embedded in ministerial control and ownership find ways to coordinate intra-sectoral price signals without

[37] One might argue alternatively that these industries display significant variations in network characteristics — transport and telecommunications infrastructures are highly local and regional in network density and distribution of nodes, whereas oil and petrochemicals and electricity arguably are essentially national in scope. Depending on the products and services included in our definition of the industries, one may also defect differences in the economies of scale, in collective good characteristics, and in the inherent tendency towards concentrated market structures. Regrettably we cannot provide thorough sectoral analysis here.

inviting third-party interventions. This is not to say that the resulting prices for the ministry-directed industries are closer reflections of market equilibrium forces and thus are more efficient – a quick glance at the various local fees and levies and exorbitant and persistent highway tolls should convince the reader otherwise.[38]

More generally, industrial self-regulation has failed in all sectors, despite government encouragements. For example, a State Administration of the Petroleum and Chemical Industries (SAPCI) was set up in 1998 to take up the administration of these strategic sectors in collaboration with newly-established state-controlled shareholding concerns (Arruda and Li, 2003). However, it proved too low in administrative status to adjudicate substantive disputes between CNPC and Sinopec and was disbanded in 2001 and replaced with a "service-oriented" peak association, the China Petroleum and Chemical Industry Association (CPCIA) (CPCIA, 2001). Formally under SETC supervision, CPCIA lost its aim after SETC's demise in 2003. CEC under SERC also seems weak, with the most notable function in sponsoring trade shows. No industrial associations exist in telecom operators and transport industries.

Another interesting dimension of difference lies in the role of certain stakeholders that could potentially play a governing function. Foreign portfolio and direct investors could have constituted a positive force in corporate governance, yet they have to do so. Their passivity can partly be explained by limitations on their shareholding and conditionalities on their ownership of assets. Western oil majors divested themselves of Sinopec and PetroChina shares soon after they obtained exclusive deals to build joint-venture retail stations and refineries with the Chinese oil companies. Provincial and local governments that have significant information advantage and welfare concerns over infrastructures have been kept out of key decision-making on industrial restructuring and strategic decisions of the new state-controlled firms. Lin (2008) has suggested that the dismal fiscal situations of local states, their profligate investment behaviors, and their local market protectionist tendencies under the previous period of decentralization in the 1980s and 1990s have discredited them in the eyes of the

[38] See Kennedy, S (2003). The Price of Competition: Pricing Policies and the Struggle to Define China's Economic System. *The China Journal*, 49, for a broader discussion of oligopolistic price setting.

central planners (Lin, 2008). There are certainly going to be management costs associated with local resistance to this recentralized governance approach, as we have noted in the electricity sector.

To a considerable degree, differences in the regulator-stakeholders relations in these four sectors are not deducible from the generic nature of the network industries, but are endogenous to the restructuring policy. For example, in the oil and petrochemical industries, the State Council fairly and effectively preempted provincial and local government interests in creating the national oil corporations, whereas the provincial interests were institutionalized in telecom as the Provincial Telecommunications Administrations under the Ministry of Industry and Information Technology. Provisions for transport projects are clearly delegated to provincial authorities, whereas provincial planners go against central mandates for promoting competition in entering into collusion with the electricity generators. Future research should focus on how central regulatory agencies interact with the quasi-federalist structure of Chinese administration to create opportunities for the representation of business interests at the sub-national level. For example, while the Ministry of Transport is a strong bureaucracy, its role is circumscribed by fiscal federalist constraints that place the financial burden of proposing and fundraising for road projects in the hands of provincial planners. Consequently, the politicized dynamics of competition and collusion mainly plays out at the local level. In contrast, while the SERC does not have any obligations or fiscal ties to local authorities, it also cannot govern the merging deals between provinces and power producers.

To conclude, we recall Andrew-Speed *et al.* (2000) who astutely observed a decade ago that, while the Chinese central government has lost or relinquished its vertical command and control, it is yet to take on new responsibilities in supervising or regulating horizontal, contractual relationships. The case study of the power sector and a cursory comparison to other sectors provide an illustration of the formidable challenges to the Chinese planners in achieving the basic functions of a regulatory state.

Appendix 1: Table of Phases and Characteristics of the Power Reform

Period	Stage	Generation	Transmission & Distribution	Critical Event & Policy	Outcome
1949–1984	State Monopoly	Ministry of Fuel Industries (1949–1955); Ministry of Electric Power Industry (1955–1978;1979–1992); Ministry of Water Resources and Electric Power (1958–1979)		Unification of goverment & business functions; state in charge of planning, business regulations, national assets management, infrastructure investmnet and production & operation of business enterprises	lack of diverse and sufficient investment; 20 year power shortage
1985–1996	Multiple funds	Ministry of Water Resources and Electric Power (1982–1988); Ministry of Electric Power; Provicial Power Bureaus; IPPs		Reform by the State Council: *Provisional Regulation on Promoting Pund Raising for Investment in the Power Sector & Implementing Different Power Tariffs* (1985)	participation of the local govenments & foreign investors in power but remain the old generation; management system
1997–2001	Speration of business from government	State Power Corporation (SPCo); provincial power companies: (e.g. Guangdong Power Co.; Tibet Power Co.; Hainan Power Co.; Mongolia Power Co.)		SPC established, separating the commercial enterprises from the government function	central government directly administrate SPC; local governments not completely follow the reform; absence of effective market mechanisms
2002–present	Marketization	Huangneng; Datang; Huadian; Guodian; China Power Investment Group	State Grid; Southern Power Grid	Reform policy in Dec.2002: *Scheme of the Reform for Power Industry* (doc. No. 5)	5 power generating co., 2 gird co. and 4 consultant & construction co.form by separating SPC; State Electriicty Regulaotry Commssion as an independent indutry regulator

Appendix 2: The Growth of National Electricity Generation Capacity (1949/1978–2008)

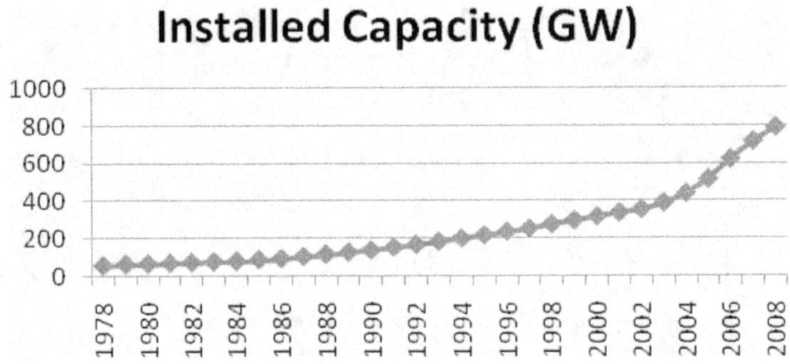

Source: CEC 2009.

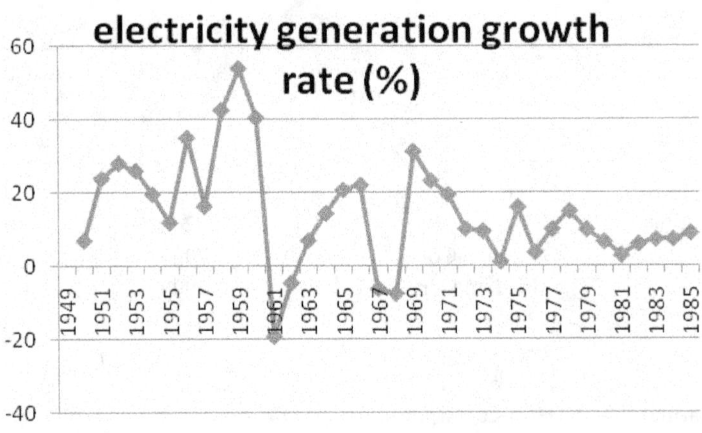

Source: CEC 2009, MEPI.

Note: Electricity demand: Since the opening up policy in 1978, the rapid economic growth has become one of the most important indictors of electricity demand in China. The national electricity generation quota generally reflects the Gross Domestic Product (GDP) in the FYP.

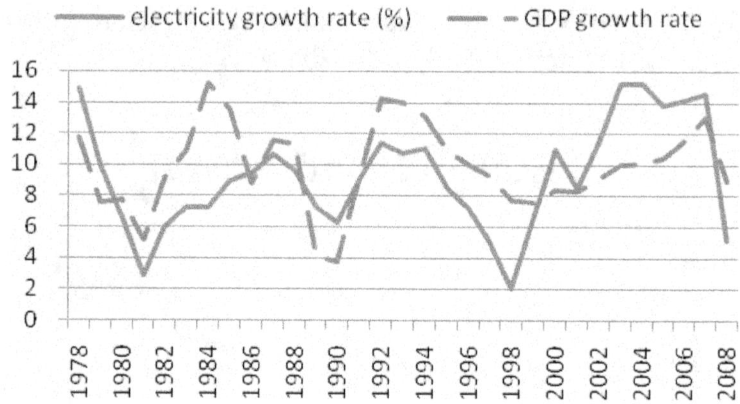

Data source: CEC 2009, WDI 2009.

Appendix 3: The Major Power Generating Enterprises by Share of the Total National Generation Capacity

Category	Company Name	Installed capacity (10MW)	Installed capacity (% of national total capacity)
Big Five Power Generating Corporations	Huaneng Group	8586	10.83%
	Datang Corp.	8242	10.40%
	Guodian Corp.	7020	8.86%
	Huadian Corp.	6908	8.72%
	China Power Investment Corp.	4571	5.77%
Central Power Generating Enterprises	Three Gorges Project Corp.	2108	2.66%
	Shenhua Group Co., Ltd	1850	2.33%
	China Resources Power Holdings Co., Ltd	1740	2.20%
	SDIC Electric Power Co., Ltd	1456	1.84%
	China Nuclear Industry Corp.	507	0.64%
	Guangdong Nuclear Power Corp.	438	0.55%

(*Continued*)

(*Continued*)

Category	Company Name	Installed capacity (10MW)	Installed capacity (% of national total capacity)
Big Provincial Power Generating Enterprises	Guangdong Yudean Group Co., Ltd	2105	2.66%
	Zhejiang Provincial Energy Group Co., Ltd	1860	2.35%
	Shandong Luneng Development Group Co., ltd.	817	1.03%
	Beijing Energy Investment Co., Ltd	688	0.87%
	Guizhou Jinyuan Co., Ltd	644	0.81%
	Hebei Construction Investment Co., Ltd	635	0.80%
	Henan Investment Co., Ltd	615	0.78%
	Jiangsu Guoxin Co.	517	0.65%
	Shengneng Co., Ltd	502	0.63%
	Shenzhen Energy Co., Ltd	497	0.63%
	Huayang Electric Power Co., Ltd	420	0.53%
	Hubei Energy Co., Ltd	419	0.53%
	Sichuan Investment Co., Ltd	370	0.47%
	Anhui Energy Co., Ltd	308	0.39%
	Guangxi Investment Co., Ltd	276	0.35%
	Jiangxi Investment Co., Ltd	270	0.34%
	Guangzhou Development Co., Ltd	262	0.33%

Source: SERC Annual Report, 2009 and the CEC Annual Report, 2009. At the time of writing, data on the "Other" Provincial Power Generating Enterprises that constitute 26.2% of the total national generating capacity is not available.

Appendix 4: Aggregate National Power Electricity Generation by Source — 2008

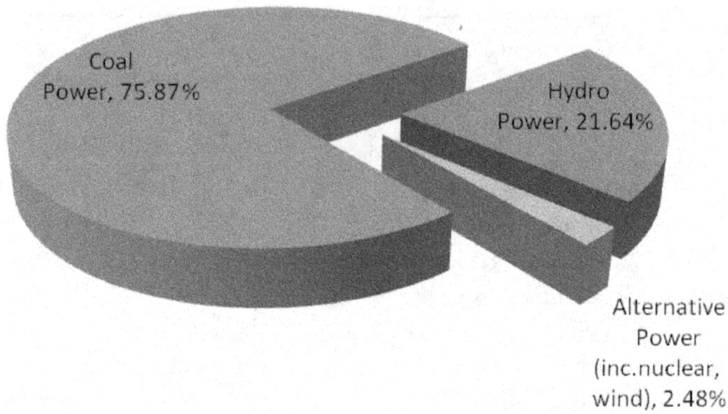

Source: SERC Annual Report 2009.

References

Acemoglu, D and J Robinson (2008). Persistence of power, elites and institutions. *American Economic Review*, 98(1), 267–93.

Acemoglu, D and J Robinson (2008). The Role of Institutions in Growth and Development. Working Paper No. 10, Commission for Growth and Development of the World Bank. Washington, DC: World Bank.

Acemoglu, D and J Robinson (2006). De facto political power and institutional persistence. *American Economic Review*, 96(2), 326–30.

Andrew, P and S Dow (2000). Reform of China's electric power industry. *Energy Policy*, 28, pp. 335–347.

Andrews-Speed, P, Dow S and Z Gao (2000). A Provisional Evaluation of the 1998 Reforms to China's Government and State Sector: The Case of the Energy Industry. *CEPMLP* doi: http://www.dundee.ac.uk/cepmlp/journal/html/vol4/article4–7.html.

Asian Development Bank (2003). Capacity Strengthening of PRC's National Development Planning Process (TA 4298). Manila: ADB.

Berg, S (2000). Developments in best-practice regulation: Principles, process, and performance. *The Electricity Journal*, 13(6), pp.11–18.

Bergara, M, JW Henisz and TP Spiller (1997). Political Institutions and Electric Utility Investment: A Cross-Nation Analysis, *Working paper, Program on Workable Energy Regulation*, University of California Energy Institute, CA.

Borenstein, S and J Bushnell (2000). Electricity Restructuring: Deregulation or Regulation? UC Berkeley: Competition Policy Center. Retrieved from http://www.escholarship.org/uc/item/22d2q3fn.

Chung, JH (2003). The political economy of industrial restructuring in China: The case of civil aviation. *The China Journal*, 50, 61–82.

Crew, MA and PR Kleindorfer (1986). *The Economics of Public Utility Regulation.* London: Macmillan Press Inc.

Cubbin, J and J Stern (2004). The Impact of Good Regulatory Governance on Electricity Industry Capacity and Efficiency in Developing Countries. *Regulation Initiative Working Paper No. 04/04,* City University, London.

Delmon, J (2009). *Private Sector Investment in Infrastructure: Project Finance, PPP Projects and Risks*, 2nd edn. Alphen Aan Den Rijn, The Netherlands: Kluwer Law International; Frederick, MD, Sold and distributed in North, Central and South America by Aspen Publishers.

Doner, RF (1992). Limits of state strength: towards and institutional view of economic development. *World Politics*, 44 (3), 398–431.

Downs, ES (2008). China's 'new' energy administration. A Commentary for *China Business Review*, November–December 2008, pp. 42–44.

Du, L, J Mao and J Shi (2009). Assessing the impact of regulatory reforms on China's electricity generation industry. *Energy Policy*, 37, pp. 712–720.

Dua, L, J Maob and J Shic (2007). Assessing the impact of regulatory reforms on China's electricity generation industry. *Energy Policy*, (37)2, 712–720.

Emily, Y and JI Lewis (2004). State power and the logic of reform in China's electricity sector. *Pacific Affairs*, 77, pp 437–465.

Freeland, RF (1996). The myth of the M-Form? Governance, consent, and organizational change. *American Journal of Sociology*, 102(2), 483–526.

Garnaut, R, S Ligang, T Stoyan and Y Yang (2005). *China's Ownership Transformation.* Washington, DC: IFC.

Glaeser, EL and A Shleifer (2003). The rise of the regulatory state. *Journal of Economic Literature*, 41(2), pp. 401–425.

Green, S and H Ming (2005). China's privatization ministry?. The state-owned assets supervision and administration commission. In *Exit the Dragon? Privatization and State Control in China*, Green S and G Liu (eds), pp. 176–177.

Guthrie, D (1999). *Dragon in a Three-Piece Suit: The Emergence of Capitalism in China.* Princeton: Princeton University Press.

Hafsi, T and Z Tian (2005). Changing Institutions: The Chinese Electricity Industry from 1980 to 2000. Working paper of École des HEC, Université de Montréal. doi. http://www.cerium.umontreal.ca/pdf/hafsi.pdf.

Hausmann, R and D Rodrik (2006). Doomed to Choose: Industrial Policy as Predicament. Working paper published online at http://reut-institute.org/Publication.aspx?PublicationId=2812.

He, X (2003). The Development and Status of the Power Grid in China, and International Cooperation for Grid Integration in Northeast Asia. A paper prepared for the *Third Workshop on Power Grid Interconnection in Northeast Asia*, Vladivostok, Russia, September 30–October 3.

Hira, A, D Huxtable and A Leger (2004). Deregulation and participation: An international survey of participation in electricity regulation.*Governance*, 18(1), 53–88.

Holburn, G and P Spiller (2002). Institutional or structural: Lessons from international electricity sector reform. In *The Economics of Contracts: Theories and Applications*, Bropusseau E and J-M Glachant (eds.). Cambridge University Press.

Hongping, F (1998). *Zhongguo qiye zhuzhi zhanlue xingwei.* (The Strategic Orientation of the Organization of Chinese Enterprises). Beijing: Jingji guanli chubanshe.

International Energy Agency (2007). International Energy Market Outlook 2007.IEA: Paris.

International Energy Agency (IEA) (2001). *Regulatory Institution in Liberalized Electricity Markets.*

Jacard, M (1995). Oscillating currents — the changing rational for government intervention in the electricity industry. *Energy Policy*, 23(7), pp. 579–592.

Jenenbaum, B (1992). Electricity privatization: Structural, competitive and regulatory options. *Energy Policy*, 20(12), pp. 1134–160.

Joskow, P (1989). Regulatory failure, Regulatory reform and structural change in the electric power industry. Paper provided by Massachusetts Institute on Technology (MIT), Department of Economics in its Working Paper Series with Number 516. Microeconomics, Washington DC: Brooking Institution, 321–336.

Kennedy S (2003). The price of competition: Pricing policies and the struggle to define China's economic system. *The China Journal*, No. 49.

Kennedy, S (2005). *The Business of Lobbying in China.* Cambridge: Harvard University Press.

Levy, B and TP Spiller (1994). The institutional foundations of regulatory commitment: A comparative analysis of telecommunications regulation. *Journal of Law, Economics, and Organization*, 10(2), pp. 201–46.

Li, BS and JP Dorian (1995). Change in China's power sector. *Energy Policy*, 23(7), p. 620.

Lieberthal, K and D Lampton (eds) (1992). *Bureaucracy, Politics, and Decision Making in Post-Mao China.* Berkeley: University of California Press.

Lieberthal, K and M Oksenberg (1988). *Policy Making in China: Leaders, Structures, and Processes.* Princeton: Princeton University Press.

Limin, D, M Jie and S Jinchuan (2009). Assessing the impact of regulatory reforms on China's electricity generation industry.*Energy Policy*, 37(2), 712–720.

Lin, KC (2005). Review of remaking the Chinese Leviathan by Dali L. Yang. *China Review International,* 12(2), pp. 578–587.

Lin, KC (2005). Review of Remaking the Chinese Leviathan by Dali, LY. *China Review International,* 12(2), 578–587.

Lin, KC (2006a). Disembedding socialist firms as a statist project: Restructuring the Chinese oil industry 1997–2002.*Enterprise & Society: The International Journal of Business History,* 7(1), 59–97.

Lin, KC (2006b). Review of China's Trapped Transition by Minxin Pei (published by Harvard University Press). *China Review International,* 13(2).

Lin, KC (2008). Macroeconomic disequilibria and enterprise reform: Restructuring the Chinese oil and petrochemical industries in the 1990s. *The China Journal,* 60, 49–79.

Lin, KC (2009). Class formation or fragmentation? Allegiances and divisions among managers and workers in state-owned enterprises. In *Laid-Off Workers in a Workers' State: Unemployment With Chinese Characteristics.* Gold, T, W Hurst, J Won and L Qiang (eds.), Houndsmill: Palgrave MacMillan.

Lin, YM (2001). *Between Politics and Market: Firms, Competition, and Institutional Change in Post-Mao China.* Cambridge: Cambridge University Press.

National Bureau of Statistics of China (2009). *China Statistics Yearbook 2008.* Beijing: China Statistics Press.

Ngan, HW (2009). Electricity regulation and electricity market reforms in China. *Energy Policy,* doi:10.1016/j.enpol.2009.06.044.

Nolan, P (2001). *China and the Global Economy: National Champions, Industrial Policy and the Big Business Revolution.* Houndsmill: Palgrave.

Pearson, M (2005). The business of governing business in China: Institutions and norms of the emerging regulatory state. *World Politics,* 57(2), 296–322.

Pearson, M (2007). Governing the Chinese economy: Regulatory reform in the service of the state. *Public Administration Review,* 67(4), 718–730.

Pei, M (2005). *China's Trapped Transition: The Limits of Developmental Autocracy.* Cambridge: Harvard University Press.

Pittman, R and VY Zhang (2008). *Electricity Restructuring in China: The Elusive Quest for Competition.* Economic Analysis Group (EAG) Discussion Paper, EAG 08–5.

Rodrik, D (2004). Industrial Policy for the Twenty-First Century. *CEPR Discussion Paper* No. 4767.

Rose, K (1995). *Planning versus Competition and Incentives: Conflicts, Complements, or Evolution? Regulation Regional Power System.* London: Quorum Books.

Shih, VC (2006). Partial reform equilibrium, Chinese style: Political incentives and reform stagnation in Chinese financial policies. *Comparative Political Studies* 20(10), 1–25.

Spiller, TP and M Tommasi (2005). The institutions of regulation: An application to public utilities. In *Handbook of New Institutional Economics*, Menard, C and M Shirley (eds.) US: Springer.

State Electricity Regulatory Commission (2008) Annual Report 2008. SERC, Beijing.

State Electricity Regulatory Commission (2009) Annual Report 2009. SERC, Beijing.

Stern, J and S Holder (1999). Regulatory Governance: Criteria for assessing the performance of regulatory systems: An application to infrastructure industries in the developing countries of Asia. *Utilities Policy*, 8(1), pp. 33–50.

Sutherland, D and N Lutao (2009). China's business groups after three decades of economic reform: Diversified conglomerates or focused industrial groups? In *China's Three Decades of Economic Reforms*, Li, X and W Zhang (eds). London: Routledge.

Vogel, S (1999). *Freer Markets, More Rules: Regulatory Reform in Advanced Industrial Countries*. Ithaca: Cornell University Press.

Walter, J and J Primeaux (1988). What can regulators regulate? The case of electric utility rates of return. *Managerial and Decision Economics*, 9(2), pp. 145–152.

Walton, J and T Finn (2005). Power Politics. *The China Business Review*, 32(5).

Wang, L and B Han (2009). Dynamics of mergers and acquisitions in the electricity industry in China: A social network approach. In *China's Three Decades of Economic Reforms*, Xiaohui, L and Z Wei (eds). London: Routledge.

Wang, X (2004). *Guanzhi Longduan: Longduanxinhangye de Zhengfu Guanzhi* [Regulate the Monopoly Industries]. Beijing: Zhongguo Shuili Shuidian Chubanshe.

Wang, Y, Y Wan and B Wang (eds) (1999). *Guoyou konggu gongsi lilun yu shijian* (Theory and Practice of State-Controlled Shareholding Companies). Beijing: Jingji kexue chubanshe.

Wirtshafter, RM (1990). Decentralization of China's electricity sector: Is small beautiful? *World Development*, 18(4), pp. 505–512.

Wong, J and CK Wong (1998). *China's power sector: Recent changes and scope for foreign participation*. Singapore: National University of Singapore Press.

Woo, CK, M King, A Tishler and LCH Chow (2006). Costs of electricity deregulation. *Energy*, 31(6–7), pp. 747–768.

Xu, S and W Chen (2006). The reform of electricity power sector in the PR of China. *Energy Policy*, 34(16), pp. 2455–2465.

Yang, D (2004). *Remaking the Chinese Leviathan: Market Transition and the Politics of Governance in China*. Stanford: Stanford University Press.

Yeh, E and JI Lewis (2004). State power and the logic of reform in China's electricity sector.*Pacific Affairs*, 77, 438–451.

Yeoh, BS (2004). Electricity in China: The latest reforms. *Electricity Journal*, 17, pp. 60–69.

Yueh, L (2011). *Enterprising China: Business, Economics and Law.* Oxford: Oxford University Press.
Zhang, C and CT Heller (2004). *Reform of the Chinese Electric Power Market: Economics and Institutions, Working paper No. 3, Program on Energy and Sustainable Development*, Stanford University, CA.
Zhu, S and X Li (2003). China powers up.*The China Business Review*, 30(3).
Zhu, S and X Li (2005). Electricity woes.*The China Business Review*, 32(5).

Laws Cited

Electricity Law of the People's Republic of China, Article 25 (1995).
Notice of the Issuance of State Electricity Regulatory Commission's Function, Organizational Structure and Staffing Requirements" or "SERC three settlements", Guofa [2003] No.7
State Council, Document No. 5 (2002).
State Council Regulation No. 72, Provisional Regulation on Encouraging Fund Raising for Electric Power and Multiple Rates of Power Tariff (1985).

News Cited

Aizhu, C (2008). China Eyes Power Grid IPO to Fund Upgrades.*Reuters*, Feb 5.
China Sets up National Energy Commission. *Xinhua News Agency*, January 27, 2010.
Lan, X (2007). Who'll Turn on the Lights? *Beijing Review*, http://www.bjreview.com.cn/Energy/txt/2007-11/30/content_87726.htm
Ng, E (2004). Power firms commit to coal price. *South China Morning Post*, January 14, 2004.
Ng, E (2008). Power Generation Plummets and May Struggle for Years. www.*ChinaStakes.com* , December 8, 2008.
Xie, X (2009). Capitalist Coal versus Socialist Electricity. *Energy Tribune*, July 21, 2009. Available online at: http://www.energytribune.com/articles.cfm?aid=2103&idli=3

CHAPTER 8

The Indonesian Electricity Sector: Institutional Transition, Regulatory Capacity and Outcomes

Mika Purra

Tenable infrastructure investing is based on a sound regulatory framework that can be relied on in the long-term. Competition, strong and reliable legal system, honoring of contracts, and favorable market-based government policies are just few of these essential components of an unwavering environment for infrastructure development. Since the Asian financial crisis, a wave of market reforms across Asia has sought to construct institutional governance mechanisms and processes that would correspond to these fundamental elements of a functional regulatory system. These reforms that have materialized in the privatization and liberalization of industrial sectors and in the institution of new governance processes across Asia have been palpable. Yet, the real success stories remain few and far between.

This chapter explores this phenomenon in the Indonesian electricity sector. Despite numerous and on-going attempts to reform, restructure and vitalize the sector, the sector continues to suffer from grave inefficiencies that bear on market participants' profitability, hinders overall economic growth, and maintains an untenable and uncertain environment for foreign investors. This chapter argues that despite the government's proactive policy measures to overhaul the sector governance, a real reform is held back by the relative weakness of the sector governing institutions on one hand and the entrenched and long-standing sector specific vested interests on the other. Essentially, it is these institutional realities that contribute to a dysfunctional regulatory environment in which both foreign and domestic investors operate in the Indonesian electricity sector.

1. Introduction

Assessing regulatory capacity and outcomes in a transitional economy with a relatively young democracy is a challenging undertaking. Yet, this is precisely the purpose of this chapter. A sound regulatory framework that supports sustainable infrastructure development is one of the essential components of economic progression for developing economies. Infrastructure investing stimulates economic activity and contributes to sustained economic growth and development in any given economy. Despite the positives, infrastructure development is no panacea for economic growth unless the underlying institutional governance structures and regulatory frameworks provide a balanced and a reliable market environment. In fact, in developing economies, institutional structures that support the formation of sound regulatory mechanisms are often weak, thus resulting in unpredictable regulatory environments that continue to challenge both domestic and foreign investors. Understanding complex regulatory structures and mechanisms constitutes a special challenge to market operators as they are based on institutional elements that are often poorly understood by the general public.

In this chapter, in order to assess the functioning of sector specific regulatory mechanisms, we examine the underlying institutional structures that delineate the utility of a regulatory system. Our focus is specifically on the evolution of governing institutions because, they essentially form and shape the regulatory environments through rules, policies and regulations, and where they intervene in and manipulate the vast number of social, economic and political interactions of a society. In other words, the effectiveness of the governing institutions is directly proportional to the efficacy of the regulatory design and regulatory outcomes. The body of knowledge on institutions, supports their societal relevance as largely responsible for structuring market environments including key industrial sectors such as infrastructure. Yet, given the extensive body of general knowledge on institutions, their character and, indeed, their impact on societies, it is surprising how little attention the existing literature pays to the effects of institutional processes on both governance and regulatory outcomes in such key sectors as infrastructure development (Levy and Spiller, 1996; North, 1990; Williamson, 1996). While the literature acknowledges the relevance of institutions, it provides few clues to the types of regulatory outcomes that may typically be associated with varying types of institutions.

With the rise of 'regulatory capitalism' where the division of labor between the state and the society has been transforming to the extent that state regulatory interventions across the globe are on the rise, questions regarding institutional uncertainty are increasingly important.[1] The interaction between the government's policy and regulatory functions and the private sector participation therein, has witnessed a dramatic change in the past decade with the private sector becoming more influential in policy-making. This is understandable in light of the consequences that government policy has on the long-term yield and profitability of private capital. Yet, whether positive or negative, the role of governmental oversight capacity in sectors from finance, healthcare, nanotechnology, to infrastructure has been steadily growing in form of both new or reformed institutions and regulations under the rubric of the rising regulatory state (Majone, 1997; Jordana and Levi-Faur, 2008; Loughlin and Scott, 1997). Indeed, it is the politics of regulation and regulation as a mode of governance that have become to define the intersection of the interest space between the government and the private sector.

Effectiveness of regulatory designs despite government's more active role under the rubric of "regulatory capitalism" is however not guaranteed. Even as number of examples from across the globe speak for the successful institution of regulatory mechanisms and specific legal frameworks for competitive and non-discriminatory markets, it is not always clear whether specific regulatory designs, particularly for

[1] See Levi-Faur, David 2005 and 2008 for in-depth analysis on *regulatory capitalism*.

infrastructure, are universally applicable.[2] Indeed, a number of Asian cases indicate that the pursuit of a neoliberal regulatory governance model across diverse industrial sectors sometimes fails as a readily adoptable model.[3] Significant variations in the implementation of sectoral reforms are discernible and in fact, the evidence unequivocally shows that the one-size-fits-all regulatory model runs into notable problems particularly in transitional economies with contested economic, political and social environments. What can we make out of this? If the applicable regulatory model differs from region to region and country to country, is it possible to discern the equitable factors that explain what works, what does not, and why? Moreover if the institution of novel governance mechanisms across the globe from advanced G8 economies to emerging mid-level economies has been so successful, why is it that many other countries, whether advanced, developing and/or emerging, fall short in their attempts to construct comparable governance mechanisms?

In this chapter, we explore these questions within the institutional environment of the Indonesian electricity sector. More specifically, we observe the role of institutions in shaping the electricity generation, transmission and distribution sectors. Characteristics of energy policy often associated with developing countries namely safeguarding energy sources and setting up energy infrastructure to support economic development are readily recognizable in Indonesia. Yet, the country also features a quality often found in transitional economies; over the years it has suffered from significant shortages in power generation and even today, it continues to display a palpable inability to rectify the situation. In light of the positive overall economic prognosis that it has enjoyed in this

[2] In Britain for example, the Office of Communications (Ofcom), the Office of the Gas and Electricity Markets (Ofgem), and the Financial Services Authority (FSA) with their wide and far-reaching statutory powers have been able to build solid reputations as decisive market authorities in their respective fields. In Brazil, the Electricity Regulatory Agency (Aneel) energy has been able to establish market authority in a relatively short period of time and continues to be an effective independent government agency in the energy sector.

[3] For example, see Jarvis, Chapter 5, Risk, Regulation & Governance, or Siratoorn, Chapter 6 Electricity Tariff Regulation in Thailand.

passing decade, the imminent energy problems it is facing are astounding. In fact, the Indonesian government, while otherwise lauded with progressive policies, is one of the few, if not the only government in the Asian region, that has failed to construct more modern regulatory frameworks or to adopt sound policies and mechanisms in support of the sector's development.

In line with the broader themes in this book, the study of the Indonesian electricity sector addresses the key question of why a specific regulatory design fails in a relatively dysfunctional institutional governance structure that is de-centred, fragmented, and frequently contested. In essence, instead of asking what works as a regulatory structure, the chapter reacts to *what does not* and *why*, and provides an illuminating case of a dysfunctional sector governance mechanism with contested institutional authority structures that display low levels of organizational probity. Moreover, a historical overview presents a fact rich narrative of a national governance framework that repeatedly falls short of expectations and serves as the validation to the essential question of *how do we know*.

This chapter has three sections. In the first section we evaluate the Indonesian electricity sector by narrating the development of the sector's governance parameters in both the upstream (generation) and downstream (transmission/distribution) sector on one hand and the governance outcomes in a centralized governance structure without an independent regulator on the other. In the second section we assess some of the fundamental obstacles that have continued to thwart meaningful reforms in the Indonesian electricity sector in the past two decades. We draw on essential components such as the Indonesian political system and its implications to the electricity sector, the proposed reform processes and their failure, and the very characteristics that continue to overshadow any serious plans to vitalize the sector. And in the third section we discuss the inherent sector specific problems that result in a challenging institutional governance structure with a contested regulatory mechanism. Essentially, the purpose is to show why, despite all the positive rhetoric to the contrary, the Indonesian energy sector has little tools for real reform, and how these reforms mostly end up in failure. By enhancing our understanding of institution specific governance dynamics, we are better positioned to assess the regulatory challenges that a specific governance system is prone to generate.[4]

2. The Indonesian Power Sector

2.1. *The Background: From Sukarno to Suharto and Beyond*

Maintaining an efficient nation-wide energy system is an enormous challenge for a country with the world's fourth largest population spread over a large archipelago of more than 6,000 inhabited islands. The struggle for proficient electricity supply has been a marked social characteristic in Indonesia since its independence from the Netherlands in 1949. Even as power shortages have been so evident throughout its history, the demand for energy has been steadily increasing in relation to its demographic and economic growth, both of which have seen relatively strong gains particularly in the past two decades.[5] With the GDP per capita of US$2,250, it is no surprise that energy has become a hotly debated political commodity in the country.[6] Even minor fluctuations in either gasoline or electricity prices have been prone to result in some degree of civil unrest and political turmoil, and forced the government to delicately balance its energy policies.

While the modernization of the power sector has been a specific goal of the government in the past decade since 1998, a historical narrative reveals repetitive attributes that have continuously stalled any serious efforts to reform the sector, thus causing significant harm to the state, its economy and the general public. These attributes manifest themselves in

[4] Much of the data for this analysis have been collected in numerous meetings and interviews with government agencies and private sector participants in the Indonesian power sector.

[5] The Indonesian population grew from 178mn in 1990 to 206mn in 2000, and reached 228mn in 2008. Despite the 1960s census and family planning policy, the Indonesian population is estimated to reach 315mn (235mn in 2009) by 2035. The GDP growth has been impressive in the past decade. It stood at USD 165bn in 2000 and reached USD 514bn in 2008. Source for both indicators: World Development Indicators (WDI), the World Bank Group, 2009.

[6] World Bank, 2009.

both institutional and legal arrangements that have defined the sector's functional parameters since the independence. First, the governance structure, largely based on the dominance of state-owned enterprises (SOEs), has been a recurring obstacle to any significant reform attempts by the government. And second, the government's central role particularly in the electricity sector was stipulated by the 1945 Constitution in which article 33 provides the government with the mandate and the power as the sole provider of electricity for the nation.[7] Essentially, the shift from Dutch rule to independence in 1949 established the crude governance foundations on which the Indonesian energy sector continues to rest.

In the decades following the independence, two periods of dictatorial rule, first by President Sukarno and his era of *Guided Democracy* (*1957–1966*) and subsequently by President Suharto and his era of *New Order* (*1966–1998*), saw numerous changes in the institutional governance structure through which the state and the principal industrial sectors including energy are governed. In rebuilding the country after its colonial Dutch masters, President Sukarno's national development plan had a strong leftist agenda that relied heavily on SOEs for the provision of the vital energy resources (Mortimer, 2006). And, as was commonplace at the time, most, if not all, commercial and social transactions were heavily influenced by Sukarno's socialist industrial policy that rendered the private sector, including foreign investors, largely dependent on the conditions agreed upon directly with the dictator.

Under the *New Order*, President Suharto's authoritarian government, instead, adhered to the principles of bureaucratization and corporatization of political and social organizations. While the government opened the economy by divesting some of the SOEs and encouraging foreign investment, the energy sector remained firmly in the hands of the government. Essentially, this meant that the sector was largely controlled by Suharto's closest allies and this partly contributed to the absence of a functional nation-wide energy policy. In other words, the *New Order*, despite the reforms in the 1990s, failed to a produce a coordinated national energy policy program that would have provided Indonesia with a sustainable

[7] The 1945 Constitution of the Republic of Indonesia, Chapter XIV, Article 33.

and efficient energy system. While the short-comings are evident even today, the absence of a coordinated energy policy has perhaps less to do with the inability of the government of Indonesia to design appropriate policy mechanisms and structures as it has to do with the legacy of political realities from the two dictatorial eras.

Notwithstanding the distinct ideological disparities between these two eras, the theme common to both periods is a discernible adherence to the principles of state-led industrialization. The history of the political economy of Indonesia is abounding with examples across various sectors where state-led industrialization has been a distinct method of economic growth (Hill, 1997). In the 1970s the state-led industrialization experienced an inefficient period and the primary engine for economic growth in the 1980s shifted largely towards export-oriented manufacturing. However, inefficient state-led industrialization in the 1970s did little to change the government's strategy in the power sector and it continued to adhere to a top-down governance authority structure through the two SOEs; namely Pertamina in oil and gas, and the PT PLN (Persero-Perusahaan Listrik Negara) in the generation, transmission and distribution of electric power.[8]

2.2. *The Evolution of the Institutional Governance Structure: From SOEs to a Liberalized Market Mechanism*

The central position of the SOEs has characterized the fundamental nature of Indonesian industrial policy and also shaped the character of the institutional governance form. In the electricity sector the PLN has wielded such enormous power that the history provides little, if any, evidence of coordinated and systematic energy policy conduct until the late 1990s. As a result, the lack of effective policy design and dysfunctional energy governance by the state largely culminate in the prevailing deficiencies in the nation-wide electricity provision. In essence, it has been an ill-conceived process long in the making and the absence of the most basic governance structures has only exacerbated the dilemma.

The decades-long institution of the Ministry of Energy and Mineral Resources (DEMR) is a fitting depiction of the disorganized manner in

[8] Interview with BABBENAS official, Jakarta, 25 March 2009.

which the institutional governance framework has evolved since the independence. The first department of energy was established only in 1978 prior to which the nation's energy policies had been managed and administered within the confines of a variety of government departments from geology, mining to industry. The first geology department was established in 1952 after which the organizational changes were numerous particularly under Suharto's regime in the 1960s.[9] While a degree of institutional stability begins to emerge with the transformation of the Ministry of Mining into the Department of Energy in 1978, the modern DEMR will not find a formalized institutional base until 2000. It provides the energy sector with a streamlined governance structure and effectively becomes the responsible agency for formulating and implementing policies in all energy related sectors including oil, gas, coal, and the electric power. [10]

A past timeline illustrates the disorganized manner in which the administrative governance mechanisms in the energy sector have emerged over decades. It is difficult to identify coherence or signs of systematic state planning when the key administrative agencies have been either absent or have frequently changed their institutional base. In such an environment, the emergence of a sustainable and well-functioning institutional governance mechanism is indeed an enormous challenge. However, despite a poor track record in developing and running an effective energy governance system, more systematic measures to reform and restructure the energy sector began to emerge in the mid-1980s with the overhaul of the country's age-old electricity law.

The Law Number 15 of 1985 Concerning Electricity Business qualifies as the first serious attempt to modernize the electricity sector and to strengthen the position of the State as the central energy agent.[11] The law sought to improve the operational parameters of the sector, i.e., by decentralizing the generation capacity and by proposing new ways of governance. For example, for the first time, the law allowed independent

---

[9] See Table 1 for the chronology of the evolution of the Ministry of Energy and Mineral Resources.

[10] Presidential Decree No. 2, 1999.

[11] Law of the Republic of Indonesia Number 15 of 1985 Concerning Electricity Business. From here on referred to as the 1985 Electricity Law.

Table 1: Chronology for the establishment of the Ministry of Energy and Mineral Resources (DEMR) — 1945–2000

Year	Organizational change
1945	Bureau of Mines and Geology established as the first institution in of mining. Its institutional base is in the Ministry of Welfare.
1952	Geology Department placed at the Ministry of Industry. It becomes the Central Bureau of Mines and Geology at the Ministry of Economy.
1957	Central Bureau of Mines becomes the Bureau of Mines and Geology at the Ministry of Trade and Industry.
1959	Ministry of Industry is split into the Ministry of Basic Industry and Miningand the Industry Department. Oil and natural gas is housed under the Ministryof Basic Industry and Mining.
1961	The government establishes the Bureau of Oil and Gas under the Ministry of Basic Industry and Mining.
1962	Bureau of Geology and Mining Department changed to the Directorate of Geology and Mining Directorate.
1963	Bureau of Oil and Gas Directorate placed under the authority of Assistant Minister for Mines and Mining Companies.
1965	Department of Primary Industry and Mining split into three departments, namely, the Department of Primary Industry, the Ministry of Mining, and the Department of Oil and Natural Gas.
1966	Department of Oil and Natural Gas is placed under the Ministry of Mining.
1978	Department of Mining becomes the Department of Mines and Energy.
2000	Department of Mines and Energy becomes the Ministry of Energy & Mineral Resources (DEMR).

power producers (IPPs) and electric cooperatives to supply electricity in the Indonesian electricity market; a function previously dominated by the PLN. Yet, despite the positives, the law still provided the PLN with the central authority to manage essential regulatory functions by allowing it to control the issuance of electricity business permits to the IPPs and the cooperatives.[12] Regardless, the law was a significant step that contributed to the opening up of the electricity market to the private investors.

[12] Article 7 of the Electricity Law 1985.

As is often the case with the implementation and enforcement of new legislative measures in Indonesia, the establishment of the first IPPs followed only in 1992; seven years after the passing of the 1985 Electricity Law. Even if the implementation and execution were slow, the law signifies the start of the structural reform that enabled the electricity sector to expand the national generation capacity in the 1990s. Still the law had little impact on the administrative governance structures under Suharto, and it was not until 2000 with the establishment of the DEMR that the sector finally found a formalized bureaucratic administrative and governance structure for energy.

Hence, the strong growth of the electricity sector during the 1990s has partly contributed to the partial opening of the market and the launch of the first IPPs in 1992. As the IPP market gradually took off, it was dominated by larger foreign enterprises that had received highly-favorable contract terms negotiated directly during with Suharto's regime. Indeed, with the signing of power-purchase agreements (PPAs) for 27 IPP operated power-plant projects, backed by foreign funds, the government was able to significantly increase the national electricity generation capacity. The share of the IPP generated electricity however remained marginal relative to the overall supply provided by the PLN. In the first five years of operation, the share of IPP generated capacity of the overall installed capacity amounted to a meager 834 MW of a nation-wide generation capacity of 21,000 MW in 1997.[13] Notably, the national generation capacity more than doubled between 1990 and 1997. It grew from 9,275 MW in 1990s to 20,000 MW in 1997 (See Appendix 1). The annual electricity growth rate prior to 1997 was at 15% while the power plant capacity growth was witnessing a growth of 13%. The rate of growth was promising and indeed desirable as the electrification ratio in the country was hovering only around 43%.[14] At the end of 2009, the PLN supplied roughly 25,000 MW of the total installed electricity generation capacity, while the share of the IPPs and cooperatives amounted to approximately 5,000 MW.

---

[13] Presentation by the Ministry of Energy and Mineral Resources officials, Jakarta, 6 April 2009.

[14] See Appendix 3 for an illustration of the electricity capacity growth.

2.2.1. *The asymmetrical catalysts of reform: the Asian financial crisis and the regime change*

The Asian financial crisis in 1997–1998 and the fall of Suharto's decades old regime in May 1998 are two interconnected events that precipitated a fundamental change in the Indonesian electricity sector. As the crisis swept across the region ravaging local currencies and depleting national monetary reserves, Indonesia suffered particularly severe losses to its currency and foreign investment flows. The consequences to the economy and the society were dire with massive lay-offs and high inflation that led to widespread civil unrest and forceful demonstrations against Suharto and his regime. In the face of mounting public pressure, Suharto finally stepped down in May 1998. But the damage had been done and the electricity sector suffered severely along with the broader economy.

Having negotiated the IPP contracts with dollar-denominated foreign funds during the 1990s, the government found itself in an increasingly deep financial quagmire as the crisis spread across Asia in 1997–1998. The depreciation of the rupiah against the US dollar combined with declining electricity revenues put both the PLN and the government into an insurmountable financial hole. Three distinct factors contributed to the government's financial dilemma. First, as the cost of power production had been gradually growing, the government was unable to raise electricity tariffs due to the sensitive political situation in the country. Second, the PLN had agreed to settle its commitments with the IPPs in US dollars which significantly worsened its ability to fulfill pending financial commitments. And finally, the PLN was also forced to supply its power plants with gas purchased in US dollars from the global markets. The financial losses to the government were enormous. From June 1997 to July 1998, the rupiah plunged 83% against the US dollar and the gross national product (GNP) lost an equal 83% of its value.[15]

A bad situation turned worse as the government had agreed to the PPA contract terms that guaranteed the IPPs an unusually high return on

[15] The Asian financial crisis ten years later: Assessing the past and looking to the future. Janet L. Yellen. Speech to the Asia Society of Southern California, Los Angeles, California, 6 February 2007.

their equity investment. This was as much the fault of the government as it was the fault of the PLN negotiators. The problems had been palpable. First, high-level politics had frequently left the PLN negotiators with nothing but prepared contracts to sign as Suharto had often personally agreed to the IPP contract terms with foreign statesmen including such heavy weights as Chancellor Kohl of Germany among others.[16] Second, as the PLN negotiators were predominantly engineers trained with limited commercial experience, they were often outmaneuvered in the contract negotiations by more experienced business negotiators from the IPP side.[17] And third, as the IPPs regarded the Indonesian energy sector as a high-risk environment, they were able to negotiate PPA terms that provided the IPPs with commitments for substantially high *return on equity* (*ROE*) as a margin of safety.

The natural outcome of the situation was that the IPP contract terms became unsustainable as the financial burden grew increasingly onerous for the government. The PLN was facing payments to the IPPs in the amount of US$133 billion over 30 years under the original PPAs.[18] As a result, the government had no choice but to suspend most of the contracts. The Asian financial crisis was a uniquely asymmetrical occurrence and heavily reflected the ROE commitments that the PLN had agreed to, however, these commitments would have been overly and unfairly burdensome even without the financial crisis. They also constituted a particularly untenable contractual structure in the reformist post-Suharto era.

The suspension of the IPP contracts had anticipated consequences. The IPP's legal recourse to remedy the breach of contracts by the PLN not only constituted a significant years long setback to the sector's development, it also created an additional financial burden to the government. For example, in 2001, the government agreed to pay US$260

---

[16] Asia Times, 22 June 2002.

[17] Ibid., The concept *return on equity* or *ROE* in financial parlance measures a corporation's profitability by revealing how much profit a company generates with the money shareholders have invested. Essentially, it is the amount of net income returned as a percentage of shareholders equity.

[18] Asia Times, 22 June 2002.

million to the US state-insurance firm Overseas Private Investment Corp (OPIC) as a compensation for the suspension of the Patuha and Dieng geothermal power projects owned by US firm Cal Energy.[19] And others followed.[20] Even during the Asian financial crisis, despite heavy losses and the high-cost of the IPP contracts, the government had honored its commitments to the IPPs thus preventing them from defaulting to their foreign debtors.[21] The measures were essential for the overall investor confidence and helped the government to resume negotiations with the IPPs on the basis of achieving lower ROI commitments and generally agreeing on more balanced contract terms for both parties.[22] And, as the PLN completed the construction of previously agreed transmission lines for the IPPs, hence facilitating the sale of their electricity to the PLN, the IPPs were able to walk out of the crisis relatively unfazed. In essence, this reflected positively on the sector and it generally alleviated investor's concerns about Indonesia as a high-risk environment.

2.2.2. *The institutional structure after 2000*

The fall of Suharto launched a new era of democratization of the political process and generally a more open and liberal political and social environment in Indonesia. Also known as the period of *Reformasi*, Indonesia has achieved notable changes in state institutions including the highest levels of the judiciary, legislature, and the executive office in the past decade.[23] Apart from the broader political and ideological goals of the Reformasi, much of the institutional reforms however, can be attributed to the policies imposed by the IMF in exchange for assisting the country in

---

[19] Asia Times, 22 June 2002.

[20] In the context of this research, it has proven difficult to gather and disclose the overall combined financial loss of all IPPs related legal cases, however, given the average size of the 27 IPP contracts, a fair estimate of US$ 2bn is likely not too far from the actual number.

[21] Ibid.

[22] Interview with Isworo.

[23] Since the fall of Suharto in 1998, which ended the three decades of the New Order period, Indonesia has been generally adhering to more open and liberal political and social principles. This is new democratic era in Indonesia has been called the period of *Reformasi* (Indonesian: "Reform").

the Asian financial crisis. The crisis hence precipitated the imposition of neoliberal reforms also in the Indonesian electricity sector.

The DEMR is largely the result of these IMF imposed reforms. By both official and unofficial accounts, it is generally regarded as the epicenter of administrative power in the energy sector. It proclaims to fulfill both the policy-making and the regulatory function and while the organizational changes have been promising, the picture is not evident from an operational perspective.[24] Notable discrepancy over the hierarchical administrative positions exists between the three DEMR departments. Given the sizable oil, gas and coal reserves that Indonesia has, both the Directorate General of Oil and Gas (MIGAS) and the Directorate of Mineral, Coal and Geothermal, are better supported by the government and well-resourced to formulate and implement policies in their respective sectors.[25] Essentially, both departments have been relatively effective in fulfilling their statutory mandates. This is supported by a track record of facilitating the issuance of mining and gas and oil exploration licenses for foreign companies in support of Pertamina's operations. The oil and gas sectors in particular, display relatively stable characteristics in terms of administrative governance processes as well as the general market conditions.

The position of the Directorate General of Electricity and Energy Utilization (DGEEU) is however arguably more contested. Due to the distinctive power position of the PLN, the electricity sector is also dependent on the administrative decisions by the Ministry of State-Owned Enterprises (MSOE), the Ministry of Finance (MOF) and the National Development Board (BABBENAS). This four-way agency structure makes the administrative process conducive to political manipulation and subject to inter-agency disputes. The MSOE oversees the shareholder interest of the state in the PLN, while the MOF is responsible for allocating government subsidies and loans to the electricity sector including the PLN. Furthermore, BABBENAS is responsible for the development planning of the energy sector and also possesses some jurisdiction over economic issues, natural resources and regional development.

---

[24] Interview with a member of the NEPC staff, Jakarta, 25 March 2009.

[25] Interview with NEPC staff.

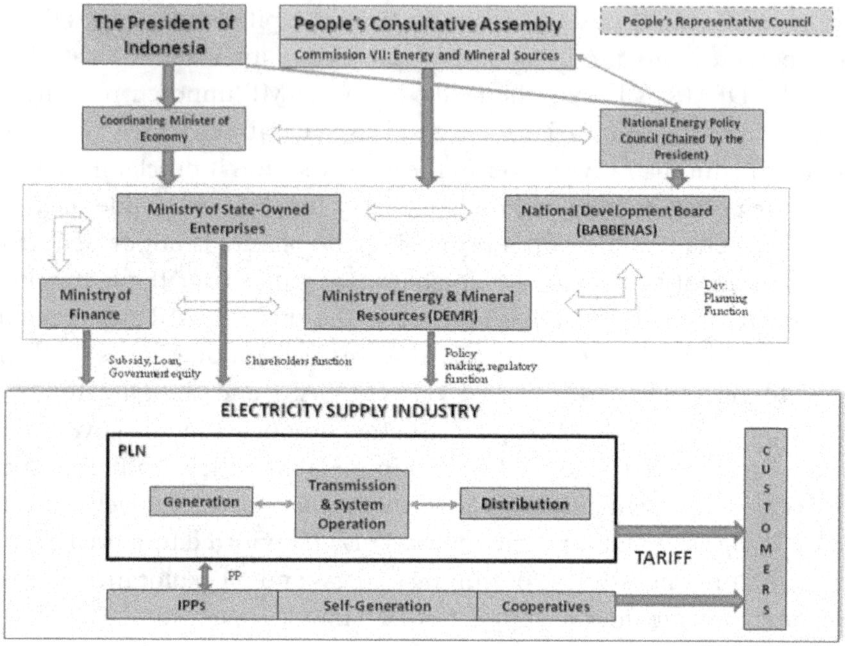

Figure 1: The institutional governance structure of the Indonesian energy sector.

The current two-layered governance structure that frames and governs the electricity supply market in Indonesia is depicted in Figure 1. Apart from sharing the generation business with the IPPs and cooperatives, the PLN is the monopoly provider of transmission, distribution and electricity supply. It is the sole buyer and seller of electricity in the power market, currently purchasing approximately 80% of the power produced by the IPPs.

Given the unique characteristics in the historical evolution of the Indonesian electricity sector and particularly the dominance of the PLN, the slow pace of the underlying institutional reforms and full commercialization are understandable. Over time, the pivotal position of the PLN and Pertamina as the nation's energy arms have left the government with little incentive or need to design all encompassing energy policies as the nation's energy needs have been channeled and processed through these two government-operated entities. A specific culture combined with established norms for policy design and policy execution did not have the opportunity to properly develop and mature.

Indeed, early steps towards reform and commercialization of the electricity sector were the direct results of the external pressure applied by multilateral agencies as opposed to domestically motivated and driven policy designs. The World Bank (WB) applied pressure on the Indonesian government and the PLN as early as the mid-1970s in order to kick-start the privatization of the electricity sector. Privatization was largely regarded as a better alternative to the continued foreign borrowing that the PLN was practicing to fund its inefficient electricity sector.[26] In essence, the granting of business licenses to private companies in the 1985 Electricity Law can be largely attributed to the efforts of the WB and the International Development Agency (IDA). Both agencies were adamant on imposing sector specific reforms after two decades of failed attempts to convince the government of the necessity of fundamental electricity market restructuring. The WB's frustration over the slow development of the sector and the loose lending practices of the PLN were prominent. It eventually threatened the government with non-renewal of its loan agreements unless the PLN took steps to open the electricity generation market to the IPPs and the electric cooperatives.[27]

3. The Chronic Indonesian Electricity Dilemma: Politicized Subsidy Scheme and the Inability to Transform

It is the efforts of the WB and the IDA in combination with the two asymmetrical events at the end of the 1990s that have shaped the reform of the Indonesian electricity sector since the 1970s and in the past decade. The governance structure that has been achieved can be described as progressive but by no means as a success, and the problems that remain are far-reaching and characteristic with past impediments to significant power sector reform. Indeed, while the change in political climate has been momentous and even fundamental, particularly in relation to institutional reforms, the spillover effects to specific industry sectors have been markedly less dynamic. Two explicit problems inherent in the Indonesian

[26] Interview with Parno Isworo, Principal, Prakarsa Ekatama Advisory, 23 March 2009. Between 1975–2008 Parno Isworo worked as a Finance Director for PLN.

[27] Ibid.

electricity sector emerge, that are often cited as fundamental obstacles to tenable long-term investing into the sector. First, the state heavily subsidizes electricity generation with a flat subsidy mechanism that results in an economically unviable market structure for IPPs, and second, the specific characteristics in the industrial governance culture, namely an unpredictable legal environment and heavy protectionism of national champions. Both issues result in an environment where foreign companies are often faced with highly-challenging operating environment where sunk costs can outweigh possible revenues in the long-term.

3.1. *The Unsustainable Highly Politicized Model: Artificially Low Electricity Tariff and PLN Subsidies*

Over time the biggest structural problems in the Indonesian electricity sector have been the low electricity tariffs and the high subsidization of the PLN. Together, they are responsible for an inefficient market structure that is also unreceptive to both foreign and domestic investment. With artificially low electricity tariffs, and the government subsidizing the bulk of electricity production costs, most foreign investors and power operators that have the potential to alleviate some of the acute electricity shortages in Indonesia, have kept their distance.[28] With the existing tariff levels, most power projects are financially unviable, particularly for many of the multinational power companies.[29] Yet, while the

[28] While most western based companies have largely shied away from the Indonesian electricity market, with the exception of few, Japanese companies such as the Mitsui and the Tokyo Electric Power Company and a number of Chinese investors have heavily invested in the sector. The Japanese companies have remained confident in the market particularly given the significant support they received from the Japan Bank for International Cooperation (JBIC). The JBIC has been able to negotiate indirect Indonesian government guarantee for power projects with the MOF.

[29] Interview with a multinational power company, Singapore, May 2009. In 2005, the basic electricity tariff in Indonesia US$ 1.50–4.11 cents per kWh for residential usage. By comparison, in Singapore the tariff was US$ 9.82 cents Malaysia US$ 5.40–8.73 cents and Cambodia US$ 8.41–15.62 cents per kWh. Indonesia historically had the lowest electricity prices in the Southeast Asian region for residential, commercial and industrial usage. While electricity prices have risen since 2005, the average tariff of US$ 7 cents kWh in 2009 is still the lowest in the region.

problem is clearly the subsidized market structure, the low GDP per capita is also a significant contributing factor for the electricity conundrum in Indonesia. The Indonesians can generally ill-afford higher electricity prices with the current income levels and attempts to do so have often resulted in undesired outcomes and even higher degree of politicization.

Indeed, any aspirations for serious price hikes have resulted in political turmoil that even contributed, at least by some degree, to the fall of Suharto's regime. At the time, PLN was largely blamed for failing to sell the idea of price hikes to the general public that ultimately resulted in large scale civil unrests. Having learned from this experience, and with PLN's improved public relations skills, the government repositioned itself for a renewed attempt at price hikes in 1999 as it acknowledged that the base rate for electricity was too low to yield sufficient return on capital (ROC) for the purposes of covering the cost of production.[30] The necessity of reform also precipitated the necessity of tariff increases and the government felt this could now be achieved without further public turmoil. This time, however, the controversy erupted as a result of the proposed 55% tariff increase that had been negotiated with an ADB-supported Working Group. In the Parliament, the proposed price hikes were met with substantial opposition and several NGOs were accused of favoring the price hikes (WRI and Dubash, 2002). In the end, the proposed price hikes ultimately failed without causing significant upheaval by the general public.

The degree of politicization of the tariff setting is perhaps best illustrated against the backdrop of heavy policy and advisory involvement by both the ADB and the WB. As noted earlier, their involvement in the energy sector stems back from as far as the 1970s. And indeed, this dialogue was equally intense in the late 1990s as the government set out to pursue reforms and tackle the electricity tariff structure. In the waning months of President Suharto's tenure, the government understood that the existing tariff structure was unsustainable in the long-term and

[30] ROC is a measure of how effectively a company uses either borrowed or owned money invested in its operations.

agreed, under pressure and guidance by the ADB and the WB, to a tariff that would cover 8% return of revalued IPP assets.[31] Moreover, to further depoliticize the tariff setting, the government had set up an automatic electricity tariff adjustment mechanism (ETAM) in 1994 that would adjust electricity tariffs based on the movements of four variables; namely inflation, exchange rates, fuel prices, and the level of power purchases.

In April 1998, the PLN told the government that the company would have to adjust the tariff to match prevailing market and business conditions by multiplying the tariff by 150%. The government responded by first declining the PLN's request and then by freezing the ETAM and replacing it with statistical tariff increase. These conditions were however agreed under the Suharto's final days. After the first tariff increase was announced on 4 May 1998, by 21 May Suharto was forced to step down. Effectively, the policy steps to retool the tariff mechanism had failed as a result of Suharto's resignation and the in-coming President Bacharuddin Jusuf Habibie lacked the political authority to adjust a higher tariff level. The PLN, however, managed to impose a tariff increase to the wealthiest consumers; for those who consumed more than 6,600 watts on an annual basis, without a notable backlash from the Parliament. Despite this controversial measure in 1999, the tariff level remained too low to cover the cost of electricity generation and as a result, the PLN found itself in an increasingly detrimental financial situation at the end of 2000.[32]

As the government showed little interest in the financial well-being of the PLN, their auditor, for the benefit of the shareholders, issued a disclaimer and renounced its financial commitments to the government. In order to improve the situation, the PLN approached the government with a five-step proposal. First, the PLN sought to increase the tariff level gradually with the goal of reaching full cost-recovery by 2005. Second, it sought to restructure all outstanding debt to the government. Through the crisis, the PLN successfully honored its financial commitments to its bond

[31] Interview with Isworo.

[32] Ibid.

holders and banks, only to default on its debt commitments to the government. Third, with the depreciation of the rupiah, the PLN wanted full freedom to revalue its assets. Slumping rupiah had made numerous assets on the balance sheet virtually worthless. Fourth, for the sake of leniency it sought a fundamental tax re-evaluation on how the government treats the company. And finally, the PLN wanted domestic gas incentives, which meant that government subsidies would be linked to gas prices rather than oil prices. The PLN viewed gas less transferable as oil and therefore the subsidies as better protected from abuse.[33]

The government agreed to PLN's proposals and proceeded with their implementation after Vice-President Megawati Sukarnoputri had become the President in 2001. Subsequently, after embarking on a sizable public relations campaign through various social networks including universities and women's networks, the PLN gradually increased the tariff. The electricity tariff was increased from 200 rupiah per kWh in 2000 to 600 kWh around mid-2003. The de-politicization of the tariff setting was, however, short-lived with the approaching presidential elections. In the fourth quarter of 2003, Megawati, in her bid to win re-election in 2004, reversed her decision to increase the tariff level, while her opponent, Susilo Bambang Yudhoyono, the in-coming President in 2004, was equally adamant about maintaining lower electricity tariffs.

Despite the set-backs in the re-politicization of the electricity sector, the PLN was still able to apply tariff increases on business-to-business basis. The Indonesian electricity tariff schedule had made this possible by allowing PLN to adjust the tariff for industrial and commercial entities. In essence, the electricity tariff for commercial purposes is less influenced by the political process than the consumer side. Hence, when the PLN endured losses due to higher oil prices in the mid-2000s, the company imposed cost-reflective tariffs for industry and commercial entities to discourage wide electricity consumption during peak-hours. It also applied a disincentive tariff for peak-load hours that encouraged businesses to operate outside peak-hours.[34]

[33] Ibid.

[34] Ibid.

While the politicization of the electricity tariff constitutes one of the central obstacles to any meaningful sector reform, a peculiar statutory feature in the Indonesian system is equally significant. Law 19 of 2003, paragraph 66 obligates the government to support SOEs if the government charges the SOE with a public service obligation. Effectively, the Law 19 of 2003 goes to the heart of the Indonesian electricity subsidy problem. While article 33 of the Constitution sets the state as the sole provider of electricity services, the obligation to support the SOEs according to the Law 19 of 2003 upholds a distinct duality that is ill-suited with the free market economy principles that the government of Indonesia generally seeks to abide by.[35] Unless there is a fundamental change in these archaic statutory principles of governance, it is difficult to foresee an energy market structure in Indonesia that is conducive to a sound investment environment for both domestic and foreign market operators alike.

Therefore, regardless of the subsidy conundrum, the prevailing market conditions together with the existing electricity governance structure, are chiefly responsible for the politicization of the electricity sector. The Indonesian electricity market is defined by a two-tier structure in which the real economic development is driven by large-scale industries and the supplementary economic development by small-scale rural entities that have, by and large, lacked sufficient sources of electricity even 60 years after the independence. In other words, due to insufficient electricity provision, Indonesia lacked a viable and innovative small business culture as a basis for sustained economic activity and growth. It is this duality of the economic structure that makes real progress in the Indonesian electricity sector an enormous challenge. The subsidization of the sector under these market conditions becomes a necessity, despite the government's attempts to maintain a clear distinction between the commercial and the private electricity market.[36] While the government sees that the two-tier market structure with franchised and competitive markets, could alleviate some of the political pressures in the electricity sector, it is also conducive to preserving the culture of national champions; a mind-set that is deeply engraved in Indonesia.

[35] Government of Indonesia, Law 19 of 2003, paragraph 66.

[36] Ibid.

3.2. *The Failed Launch of the (Reformed) Institutional Structure — From the 2002 to the 2009 Electricity Law*

Even if the institution of the DEMR in 2000 was a welcome development, it merely constitutes one component in a series of essential reforms that the Indonesian government was committed to after the Asian financial crisis. Further reforms were planned and the neoliberal policy designs imposed by the IMF had clear conditions. The government should a) restructure the power sector to improve efficiency and reduce the fiscal burden; b) establish the legal and regulatory framework to create a competitive electricity market; c) restructure the organization of the PLN; d) adjust electricity tariffs; and e) rationalize power purchases from private sector power projects (IMF, 2009). The government in its response to the IMF committed to initiating the organizational restructuring of the PLN by June 1999 and to enacting a new Electricity Law by December 1999.[37] While all this was promising, the restructuring became, by all accounts, an appallingly prolonged process that failed to materialize in the subsequent decade.

After three years of consultations between the government, the PLN and a small group of stakeholders, the proposed electricity sector reform materialized with the passing of the 2002 Electricity Law in September 2002.[38] The law addressed all of the IMF nominated key issues, including the notoriously controversial issue of PLN restructuring and practically set the foundation for an electricity market with open competition based on a multi-buyer multi-seller mechanism. The electricity supply, namely the monopoly of the PLN, was to be unbundled into generation, transmission and distribution markets, whereby generation would be based on full competition and the transmission and distribution would remain in the hands of the PLN.

Notably, the law also called for the establishment of a spot market and retail sales whereby power generators would be free to bid for the lowest price.[39] High-voltage (HV) and medium-voltage (MV) buyers would be

[37] Letter by Ginandjar Kartasasmita, State Coordinating Minister for Economy, Finance, and Industry, to Michael Camdessus, Managing Director, IMF, Jakarta, Indonesia, 16 March 2009.

[38] Government of Indonesia, Law No. 20/2002.

[39] Electricity Law No. 20/2002.

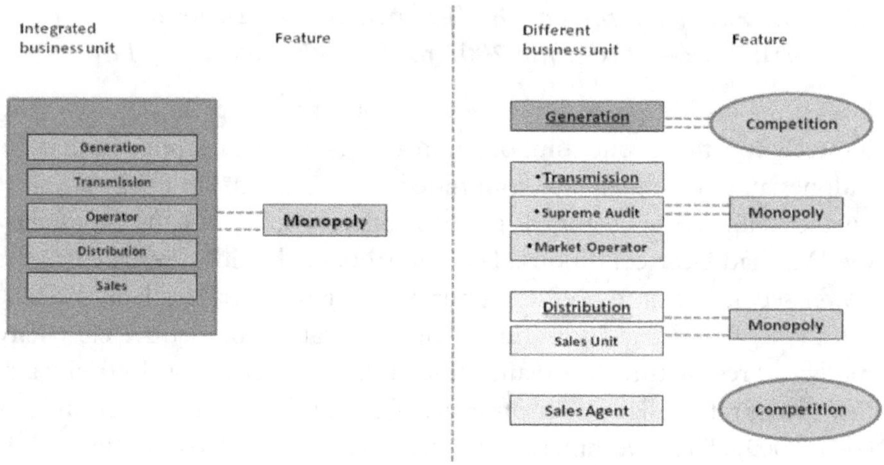

Figure 2: The structure of the power industry — Post 2002 reform.

able to buy electricity from suppliers other than the PLN at negotiated market price and the government would essentially maintain the regulation of the price of monopoly assets as well as the price to low-voltage (LV) customers. The planned Electricity Market Supervisory Body (EMSB) would regulate competitive zones as well as low-voltage (LV) retail, transmission, and distribution tariffs.[40] Even socially and environmentally beneficial measures were included. A clause to that effect required power producers to acquire a certain percentage of their generation capacity from renewable energy sources and provide a percentage of the generated electricity to the poor.[41]

3.2.1 *Outcome*

With the passing of the 2002 Electricity Law, the stage was set for a more dynamic electricity market structure with growing generation capacity through multiple power generators. The law would have allowed tariff setting through a natural mechanism of supply and demand and provide the consumers with multiple purchasing options for electricity. After

[40] Government Regulation No. 53/2003.
[41] Electricity Law No. 20/2002.

three years of continued negotiations, the statutory basis for the Indonesian electricity sector looked very promising. However, despite all the progress, the new legislation stumbled on the Indonesian constitution. The structure of the law, particularly regarding the PLN restructuring, was ruled in violation of the spirit of article 33. Privatizing and unbundling the PLN, with the intention of constructing competitive electricity markets, would have stripped the government of its authority and mandate to provide electricity for the nation. Article 33 provides that electricity is a public good, which under the constitution should be managed by the government.[42]

As a result, the Indonesian Constitutional Court in 2004 annulled the newly adopted law on the grounds that it was in direct violation of Article 33. As the law would have allowed an unregulated market price for electricity, it contradicted with the constitution's position that "all power supply should be in partnership with PLN, through the ownership of shares in a company or through a loan arrangement."[43] The constitution essentially had no objections to allow private power producers in to the market even if the government's share of ownership in any power plant was more or less than 50%; however on the condition that the government maintain ultimate authority for policy- and decision-making.

Given that the law had been in preparation for over three years prior to its adoption by the Parliament in 2002, it serves as a case in point of unpredictability of the Indonesian institutional environment. It prompts the question about the motives of the government to spend the time, energy and resources in preparing a comprehensive legislation only to see it falter on a fundamental legal issue. Frankly, any less than savvy legal expert should have picked up the legislative misalignment with the constitution. The evidence strongly suggests that the relative weakness of legislators in the newly democratized Indonesian parliament on one hand, and the lack of coordination between responsible government agencies combined with their weak capacity on the other, play a large role in the inability of the responsible agencies to foresee the associated constitutional problems with the 2002 Energy Law. Furthermore, the PLN, and particularly its labor

[42] Article 33 of the Indonesian Constitution.

[43] Ibid.

union, strongly opposed the law due to the privatization implications that it imposed on the company.[44] It is unclear whether the labor union posed any direct influence on the legal proceedings of the court system. However, this is a feasible possibility given the PLN's opposition to the privatization and the restructuring of the sector generally.[45] The combination of institutional capacity and the relatively strong market position of the PLN are indeed the two factors that often surface as the dominant explanatory variables in the retreat of the Indonesian electricity sector.

The implications of the annulment of the 2002 Law were damaging. While the IPP contract restructuring had been a major set-back to the sector, the effects of the annulment were even worse. It stalled any further progress and eventually contributed to chronic power shortages during the 2000s decade across the country, most notably in Jakarta.[46] The annulment meant that the electricity sector would revert to the statutory foundations set by the 1985 Electricity Law with the government controlling the electricity tariffs and the PLN operating as the single buyer and seller of all generated electricity. Given the highly-politicized manner of controlling electricity tariffs, the government has prevented the PLN from running its operations on a cost-recovery basis, thus greatly slowing down the roll-out of new generation capacity. In essence, the annulment contributed to the already dire financial situation of the sector, to which the PLN's financial predicament has only contributed.

Indeed, despite the government's on-going efforts to roll out accelerated programs to increase the generation capacity between 2004 and 2009, the PLN's track record has been modest at best.[47] In 2006, the government launched a phased-out program in order to increase the nation-wide generation capacity from 24,000 MW to 55,000 MW by 2015. In the first phase between 2006 and 2010, a PLN-run 10,000 MW accelerated plan would aim to build 35 power plant sites across the country; ten power plants in Java and the remaining 25 in other parts of the country; and in the second phase, the PLN would built an additional

[44] Interview with Dalimi.

[45] PLN Employees reject the electricity bill, *Antara News*, 7 September, 2009.

[46] Blackouts prompt Jakarta to consider having own plant, *Jakarta Globe*, 23 November 2009.

[47] Interviews with officials of the DEMR and the PLN, March 2009, Jakarta.

10,000 MW between 2009 and 2015. In the first phase, the increased capacity would predominantly consist of coal-fired power plants, but in the second phase, the capacity would be divided between gas, geothermal, coal and hydro-powered plants with geothermal producing close to 50% to the generated capacity. While PLN has been the predominant target of the government's accelerated plan, some 40% of the increased generation capacity in the second phase is estimated to originate from the IPPs.

The progress has been slow. By 2009, the overall national generation capacity had only increased from 6,000 MW to 30,000 MW and while construction is on-going and new plants are being launched, it is unlikely that the first phase will be able to meet its target by 2010 as only 60% of the targeted electricity projects had been completed by 2009.[48] In order to meet the capacity targets set out for the accelerated power programs by 2015, the PLN needs to find financing for the amount of US$17.3 billion for the second phase and despite recent advances to that effect, it is highly-questionable whether or not the PLN will be able to find financing for all of the planned 10,000 MWs.[49] The PLN has intended to finance 40% of the program with loans from agencies such as the WB, the ADB, JBIC, German financing institution KfW and even certain banks from Saudi Arabia. Their backing is essential as foreign commitment to the market with the existing electricity tariffs is questionable. The remaining 60% of the plan would be developed and financed by the IPPs. While a promising model, as it would reduce the monopoly position of the PLN, the prospects are not promising as even the current IPPs projects are facing significant financing problems.[50]

For the existing IPPs that renegotiated their PPAs with the PLN between 1998 and 2003, the annulment of the 2002 Electricity Law had little effect. The contracts signed with the PLN under the 2002 Law were deemed valid and the IPPs continued to generate and sell electricity to the PLN with the prevailing contract terms.[51] The Constitutional Court also

[48] Government to launch new coal-fired power plants, *The Jakarta Post*, 9 November 2009.

[49] In November 2009, Japanese enterprises along with the Japan International Cooperation Agency (JICA) committed a combined US$ 3.6 billion worth of loans to PLN.

[50] 50 IPP power plants face financing problems, *The Jakarta Post*, 3 November 2009.

[51] Government Decree No. 3/2005.

intervened by stating that all power projects would be carried out on the basis of a "partnership" with the PLN involving share ownership and shares even if the 1985 Law allows 100% private ownerships of the IPPs.

Undoubtedly, the setbacks during the past decade have been significant and the remaining challenges are equally discouraging for the electricity sector. On the positive side, the power industry has been adamant about securing the full commercialization of the sector, a goal that took an leap forward with the passing of the 2009 Electricity Law in September 2009.[52] The new law, under preparation since the annulment of the 2002 Law, again sets the legal foundation for the restructuring of the electricity sector. And indeed, one of the most outspoken proponents of the 2009 Law has been the MKI (Masyarakat Ketenagalistrikan Indonesia); an active industry group that has vigorously pushed the legislation forward and helped the government in drafting the Law.[53]

In light of these developments the overall prospects have appeared promising, yet they are unlikely to change or alter the position of the PLN by any meaningful degree. In fact, a closer scrutiny of the 2009 Electricity Law offers very little in terms of institutional reform or unbundling of the PLN. Instead, the Law firmly confirms the state as the controller of electricity supply and the PLN as the supplier, as stipulated in the constitution.[54] The biggest change is that the law allows provincial governments to issue regulations on electricity and permits for the supply of electricity to IPPs. It also allows a degree of freedom to provinces in the setting of the electricity tariffs.[55] These are all positive and decisive measures by the legislators to increase competition and dynamism in the sector, however, the PLN's central statutory role is still largely intact in the 2009 Law and unless this is changed, the monopoly structure will be difficult to alter. It appears that the only way to fix the recurring problems in the electricity sector is to change article 33 of the Indonesian constitution and allow the IPPs to enter the market without notable obstacles from the PLN either regarding pricing or selling of electricity.

[52] Interview with Isworo.

[53] Interview with members of the MKI, Jakarta, March 2009.

[54] Articles 3 and 4 of the Electricity Law No. 30/2009.

[55] Article 5 of the Electricity Law No. 30/2009.

4. The Nature of Institutional Governance: Uncoordinated, Dysfunctional, and Protectionist

In view of the different phases and characteristics of the Indonesian electricity sector; namely the Suharto era, the Asian financial crisis, the Reformasi, the monopoly of the PLN, low electricity tariffs and heavy subsidization, we can deduct distinct factors from these episodes that provide a sound reasoning to its intrinsic problems. As in any transitional economy, institutional problems often lead to difficulties not only in policy design and implementation, but particularly in rolling out and improving institutional resources and capacities in support of these reforms. In Indonesia, however, these problems are particularly striking. Between 1998 and 2009, the development of Indonesia's overall infrastructure has been substandard at best given the resources and the enormous size of the country and its economy.

By way of comparison, following the collapse of the Soviet Union in 1990, Estonia, a tiny Baltic state, was able to construct an effective electricity sector in less than a decade in the 1990s and has ever since successfully moved forward with the privatization of Eesti Energia, the state-owned electric company. Furthermore, in 1998 the three Baltic states, namely Estonia, Latvia, and Lithuania, formed BALTREL to undertake the "Baltic Ring" project that enables the three countries to share transmission of electricity and even sell it to the neighboring Sweden and Finland.[56] Estonia is small and certainly easier to govern than a country the size of Indonesia with all its special characteristics. However, Estonia and the Baltic states emerged from strict communist rule having had little, if any, experience with the functions and ways of a free market economy. Despite Suharto's corporatist and bureaucratic means of governance, Indonesia has largely adhered to the principles of free market economy since the 1970s, providing ample opportunities for more dynamic development of its industrial infrastructure including electricity provision. In fact, over the past two decades Indonesia has had numerous opportunities to improve its industrial infrastructure particularly given the substantial backing of the WB, the IDA, and the ADB, yet it continues

[56] See http://www.baltrel.com for more information on BALTREL.

to lack sufficient capabilities to do so. Why have most other transitional economies been able, despite similar problems, to construct relatively effective electricity sectors supported by a functional governance framework while Indonesia has not? Our view here is that the inherent problems in Indonesia have more to do with the lack of can-do must-do mentality and the entrenched vested interests by the elites that are highly protective against foreign competition.

Three distinct explanatory factors that arise from the narrative of the Indonesian electricity sector support this view. First, while the electricity sector and its governance functions have historically culminated in the central position of the PLN, the underlying governance structure has been a mishmash of ever-changing institutional structures that often fail to provide full clarity to the hierarchical authority lines between governing agencies. As a result, policy-design, implementation, enforcement, and oversight functions have often provided only weak institutional support to the sector. They not only frequently lacked a distinct clarity in terms of their institutional mandate, but also lacked a clearly distinguishable hierarchical structure. The lack of distinct authority lines, then, has allowed a certain level of governance capture at highest-levels of governance including the President and other key agencies institutions such as the CMEA and the MOF.

The existing institutional governance system has two distinct layers that control the electricity market. First, the interactions and linkages between the executive level agencies provide three separate channels of policy influence that effectually guide and dictate the administrative agencies, and are distinct from the DEMR and the parliamentary process. The President possesses the authority to stipulate policy measures by means of Presidential decrees and laws that carry enough weight to significantly shape sector specific governance functions. While the Coordinating Ministry of Economic Affairs (CMEA) fulfills the function of a normal government agency, it carries a specific role in the Indonesian system as one of the few high-capacity agencies that has the namesake function of coordinating and overseeing the functional parameters of the other ministries. The President effectually utilizes the CMEA as the key government agency for enacting policy measures particularly in the energy sector.

Traditionally, one of the central problems in the Indonesian energy governance system has been the lack of coordination of administrative duties on one hand, and overlapping regulations on the other.[57] To alleviate this problem, the Parliament initiated a new administrative mechanism to enhance the coordination of energy policies by establishing the National Energy Policy Council (NEPC) as an *independent* and permanent body.[58] The NEPC has been a welcome and a much needed development; however its ability to defuse the politicization in the electricity sector does not come without ambiguity. First, the council itself is a highly-politicized entity by design. While enhanced policy coordination efforts are undoubtedly beneficial, the NEPC is chaired by the President and co-chaired by the Vice-President. The Council members also include senior government officials and seven private sector stakeholders including the Chairmen of both, Pertamina and the PLN. With this composition, the NEPC is anything but free of the political process at the highest-level. And second, although eight of the Council members are selected by the Parliament, it does little good without a balanced and transparent decision-making structure; an essential bureaucratic feature that even still, two years after initiation, remains undecided within the NEPC.

The second layer consists of the administrative agencies driven by the political process. While other Asian countries such as China, the Philippines, and Thailand have managed to institute an administrative and governance mechanism based on a single agency structure with the statutory right for electricity oversight and management, the Indonesian system pertains to a more dispersed and a decentralized system. Surprisingly, despite all the notable democratic and institutional progress in the past decades, Indonesia still displays relatively strong notions of bureaucratization and corporatism, particularly in the energy sector. While the institution of the NEPC is one example of this, the notions of bureaucratization are also distinctly noticeable in the arrangement of the administrative mechanism on the whole.

---

[57] Interview with Rinaldy Dalimi, Secretary General, the National Energy Policy Council (NEPC), Jakarta, 25 March 2009.

[58] Government of Indonesia, Presidential Regulation No. 26 (2008).

In addition to improving the strength of sound parliamentary processes, the institution of the NEPC has been a positive development by the government in recent years. However, an effective parliamentary process does little good if the legislation that it deliberates and passes, is strongly influenced by the SOEs, such as the PLN. Can we really label the work of these agencies as progressive when legislative measures repeatedly protect a dysfunctional state-owned company that lacks sufficient capacities to develop an effective electricity sector? The NEPC is the first attempt by the government to tackle some of the serious energy governance deficiencies, but it leaves much to be desired in terms of institutional organization. And again, despite its wide mandate and the semi-democratic selection of its governing board members, it is still chaired by the highest executive in the government, namely the President; that provides little, if any statutory independence from the political process. And finally, while the sector governance has witnessed some level of progress, the statutory overlap between agencies continues to be a significant problem in that, it leaves the sector governing agencies vulnerable to institutional exploitation and political in-fighting.

Second, the capacity of the sector governing institutions constitutes another prominent obstacle to the meaningful development of the electricity sector. In addition to the low levels of statutory independence that the sector governing institutions display, human capital resources, appointment processes and stakeholder engagement processes appear alarmingly weak and with high-levels of procedural informality. The research has indicated serious flaws with respect to these capacities. Our questions varied from budgetary issues to hiring of new staff or making higher-level appointments, to engagement processes with stakeholders, and in each case the weaknesses are obvious.

With the exception of few government agencies, the electricity sector governing institutions, the DEMR in particular, suffer from such notable human resource deficiencies that the design, implementation, enforcement and oversight of essential policies and regulations is seriously embedded. As a result, the roll-out of infrastructure projects and their financing is obstructed by equal degree. A good example of this are, the continued efforts by the Indonesian government to invest in infrastructure development in sectors such as roads, bridges, and power plants, only to end up with little concrete results.[59] While the government has been proactive in terms of grand-design and financing of infrastructure projects, the responsible agencies are often poorly equipped to design and implement processes and mechanisms for project roll-outs.[60]

Furthermore, serious staffing problems that are often linked with budgetary issues, pay structures, and most notably hiring practices that appear to lack benchmarked criteria for formal qualifications exist.[61] Given the staffing related problems, the management of government infrastructure funds is habitually inadequate and substandard; and it is often the case that the funds remain under-used for most of the budget year due to flawed planning and failed execution of plans. The majority of the infrastructure funds are rolled out speedily prior to the end of the budget year so as to make at least "some use" of them.[62] Towards the end of the 2009 for example, the government had managed to utilize only 42% of the funds budgeted for infrastructure development for that year.[63] The urgency to roll out the remainder of the funds before the end of the budget year, then, often leads to poorly planned, inefficiently executed, and sometimes half-finished projects. Essentially, the institutional structure responsible for infrastructure roll-out suffers from severe shortfalls in planning, design, execution, reporting and follow-up; all problems that are mostly linked to the human resource capacities within the responsible agencies. Hence, from an operational perspective, the slow progress of the sector development since the 1980s is perhaps best viewed in light of the chronic lack of management capacity that has continued to plague the sector.

As regards to the budget, the DEMR, according to its top-level officials, is a well-funded and well-resourced department of the Ministry of

---

[59] Indonesia plans US$ 9.2 billion infrastructure bill in 2009, *Reuters*, 24 December 2008.

[60] Interview with an official from the Coordinating Ministry for Economic Affairs, Jakarta, 1 June 2009.

[61] Interview with the DEMR officials, Jakarta, 24 March 2009.

[62] Interview with Glendale Partners, Jakarta, 8 April 2009, and *Globe Asia*, Jakarta, 8 April 2009.

[63] Infrastructure Spending Spree Just Ahead, Indonesian Government Says, *Jakarta Globe*, 10 November 2009.

Energy that has the statutory right to design its budgetary needs and utilize these resources independently.[64] However, while the financial sources may exist, they can hardly be considered sufficient given that the DEMR employs 350 individuals with an annual budget of roughly US$1.9 million (2009). Provided that some 60% of that money is used for salaries, it would amount to US$3,250 annual average salary per employee; US$271 monthly income. Even for Indonesia, an average income in this range is low and certainly not sufficient to obtain and retain skillful individuals that are easily better off in the private sector. In addition to compensation, the lack of skillful and knowledgeable individuals is an equally serious problem. As technologies improve, even in the electricity sector with the roll out of smart grids and similar designs, the skills and knowledge to design, implement and manage will be increasingly important. The DEMR admits that one of the biggest problems it is facing is the lack of knowledge and foresight on how to steer the Indonesian electricity sector into the future.[65] It is also a problem to Indonesia's plans to gain more FDI and improve the energy infrastructure. In fact, the lack of skills is endemic, although the DEMR officials fail to specifically identify this.

While the lack of financial resources constitutes a considerable hurdle for achieving sustainable progress in the development of institutional human resources capacity, the DEMR also displays equally distressing characteristics in its hiring and appointing processes for new staff. On questions regarding these procedures, the DERM officials downplayed the importance of formal hiring processes and indicated that new officials are often recruited on an informal "good guy" basis.[66] This leads us to conclude that disregard for due process in hiring and appointing new staff within the DERM, and possibly within other central government agencies, is extensive. In essence, not only do we find a high degree of disregard but a complete absence of criteria for formal qualifications for potential employees. This point is particularly striking given that the DEMR is responsible for a highly-sensitive and important industrial sector.

---

[64] Interview with DEMR.

[65] Interview with DEMR.

[66] Interview with DEMR.

Finally, as the engagement with stakeholders is an essential element of any democratically governed system, we assume that also in Indonesia such mechanisms shall effectively be in place. Particularly from a foreign investor's perspective, clarity in stakeholder engagement processes adds to the element of confidence as market participants are able to track sector related developments that may affect their businesses and react accordingly. While the DEMR claims to consult stakeholders such as the PLN, the IPPs including the MKI, and consumer groups, very little evidence that would support the view of a sustained public stakeholder engagement exists. Instead, the DEMR admits that stakeholder engagement is based on an ad hoc system of "when the need arises," and further on a system that fails to provide adequate information to the stakeholders within an appropriate timeframe.[67] Furthermore, no formal mechanisms for dialogue, sharing of information, or even policy engagement exist between the DEMR and the regional governments. This is a major issue particularly in view of the weak capacity that both the DEMR and the regional governments display.

Regrettably, the system is plagued by a high-level of informality even as the DEMR considers itself as the chief regulator whose regulatory style is consultative instead of commanding.[68] Interestingly, as the DEMR claims to be engaged in regulatory implementation, it does not engage directly with the stakeholders on compliance issues. It does require an annual compliance report from stakeholders and claims to burden businesses with zero compliance costs with the current mechanism.[69] The agency has little influence or role in electricity pricing itself, yet it does act as the facilitator of policy initiatives that can emerge from both the government and the stakeholders. This puts the DEMR's role in a dubious light given its notions as the chief regulator. As a norm, the regulator is essentially the agency responsible for effectively monitoring a sector's development and for supporting it by providing and maintaining a balanced regulatory structure. This function should be filled by the regulator, the DEMR, not the government or the stakeholders. Instead, the

[67] Interview with DEMR.

[68] Interview with DEMR.

[69] Interview with DEMR.

DEMR emerges rather as a secretariat type agency much like the BABBENAS that fulfills the functions imposed on them by more powerful political forces.

We infer protectionism as the third explanatory factor that continues to dissuade the development prospects in the Indonesian electricity sector.[70] It is an ever-increasing phenomenon and pertains to a varied number of industrial sectors where SOEs operate. It has been a feature of the electricity sector and while the constitution supports economic nationalism, it is also deeply engraved in the Indonesian psyche; that national champions should be protected from foreign competition and that only the government can be trusted with energy provision. With the exception of the 2002 Electricity Law that set the foundation for the eventual privatization of the PLN, all the other legislative framework measures to shape the sector, including the 1985 and 2009 Electricity Laws, have been protective of the PLN's central position as the single provider of electricity. Furthermore, various drafts of the 2009 Electricity Law under preparation since the failure of the 2002 Law, have also sought to reduce foreign control of energy resources. For example, a proposed measure in the legislation would be required by the government to obtain approval from the House of Representatives before awarding contracts to foreign companies.[71] While this measure ultimately failed to materialize, it is nonetheless a notable indication of the nationalistic forces at play in the Indonesian energy sector.

Indeed, since the beginning of the Reformasi, the preparation and passing of any sector specific reforms have been invariably linked to the PLN, the PLN labor union, the judiciary, or the Parliament. Each of these entities has invariably emerged in opposition to any structural governance changes that would weaken the position of the PLN. And, all the measures used to oppose institutional reforms since then, do appear legitimate from both procedural and judicial perspective. However, in light of the recent occurrences regarding the role of Indonesia's "judicial mafias," their influence in the electricity sector cannot be ignored particularly in light of the

[70] Investors Steering Clear of Oil, Gas Bids Until Cost-Recovery Rules Ironed Out, Jakarta Globe, 25 November 2009.

[71] New energy law will 'reduce foreign control', *The Jakarta Post*, 27 April 2004.

sudden annulment of the 2002 Electricity Law in 2004. We have deliberately ignored the issue of corruption in this chapter due to the premise that the prevailing problems in the Indonesian electricity are mostly structural and capacity-related; however, the "judicial mafias" in the Indonesian system are an endemic problem that can affect the highest levels of government.[72]

5. Memo to Regulators — What Should They Know?

This chapter has provided an account of the outcomes of institutional and regulatory reform in the Indonesian electricity sector in view of the book's core questions, namely what works, why, and how do we know? It shows how the promise of neoliberal reforms in the Indonesian electricity sector is largely failing because the government is either unwilling or incapable of instituting real reforms. The former, unwillingness, would be unlikely given the country's pressing needs for electricity, although, as we have noted, the protectionist tendencies have a strong presence in the political system. The latter, incapable, is perhaps a more plausible explanation given the decades-long timeframe in which the Indonesian government, despite significant backing from multilateral agencies, has been unable to resolve the intrinsic energy problems of the country. Despite all the turmoil at the end of the 1990s, the evidence is clear that the problem lies largely in the execution and implementation of policy designs, not with corruption or inadequate financial resources. Since the 1990's, the country's electricity generation capacity has witnessed only modest growth as only 10,000 MW has been added to the overall nation-wide generation capacity, when in fact this capacity should have at least doubled in order to satisfy the growing energy demand.

As to the question about *why* the institution of functional regulatory framework is failing, the chapter lays out a feasible account. Hence, the legacy and nature of the political system preserves a highly-politicized, and hence dysfunctional, sector governance mechanism with repeated and deep-seated inefficiencies. The inefficiencies manifest themselves in an

---

[72] Yudhoyono Vows to Eradicate Indonesia's 'Judicial Mafia' in 100 Days, The Jakarta Globe, 6 November 2009.

institutional structure that continues to display high-levels of bureaucratization and corporatization, and thus generate uncoordinated and ineffective policy- and decision-making. Moreover, blurred statutory lines of authority between sector governing agencies are an additional element of a perplexing governance system. These mechanisms are largely responsible for poorly managed policy-making processes that obstruct an effective energy policy design and produce particularly harmful outcomes for the nation's electricity sector.

Two inter-connected explanations for the sector's problems then answers the *how do we know* in our narrative. First, the institutional political realities fail to support any reforms that the sector is faced with, and second, the PLN at the heart of the reforms, is an untouchable behemoth that is allowed to continue to dictate the future direction of Indonesia's electricity sector. First, ineffective inter-institutional cooperation is accentuated by considerable flaws in the institutional capacity of the sector governing agencies. We have depicted at least three such capacities in the context of this chapter. Financial and budgetary constraints constitute an explicit impediment to the development of institutional strengths in the form of human resources, skills development, statutory independence and functions, and institutional cooperation. And human resources, as we have noted, is a particularly momentous problem that often, and quite effectively, impedes execution and implementation of policies including their enforcement and oversight. This will be one of the biggest challenges facing the electricity sector in the following decade. Unless this situation is rectified by significantly improving the level of education in the country, it is unlikely that Indonesia will be able to meet the high expectations in terms of the much lauded future economic growth.

Furthermore, the improvement of stakeholder engagement, including regional governing agencies, will be of paramount importance in diffusing governance skills from the central government to the regions. The added benefit of this is that, foreign investors will feel more confident about directly engaging with the provincial governments and possibly contributing to the increasing flow of FDI into Indonesia. This is crucial for the electricity sector. Unless the capacity issue is seriously addressed by the central government, it is difficult to see significant improvement in the governance structure of the sector, not to mention the enhancement of the electricity generation capacity in the country. The institutional capacity of any governing institution is in direct correlation with the performance of the sector that it governs.

Secondly, the PLN needs serious reform. Unless the company is unbundled across sectoral lines as laid out in the 2002 Electricity Law, the economics of the Indonesian electricity sector will not be able to sustain an effective electricity infrastructure mechanism in the future. Signs of this have already emerged and with the existing capacities that the PLN possesses, the situation is likely to worsen. And, from the governance perspective, the new 2009 Electricity Law, in failing to address the issue of PLN, is insufficient as an underlying framework for achieving the country's electricity goals. Granted, the IPPs should eventually have more opportunities in electricity generation, but it does not change the fact that all roads still lead to the PLN. It is likely to dampen the investor interest, which it indeed has. And, even if the sector manages to implement the 2009 Law, if previous experiences are any guide, it will likely take years for any significant changes to take effect.

Finally, as per our findings regarding capacity, the PLN is no different in this regard. In addition to its financial predicament, the company has a serious lack of human resources capacity to operate its power stations and the grid system. While the company can be credited for its efforts to improve power provision, the existing resources are only sufficient to a certain degree. Furthermore, the accelerated 10,000 MW electricity programs include tens of small projects that are largely based on geothermal and renewable technologies. Indonesia, let alone the PLN, has no sustained experience in providing electricity to households or businesses from these sources. It is apparent that with the existing staff and skills resources, the company cannot cope with such large number of projects based on new and untested technologies. Finally, the PLN needs international support to overcome its resource deficiencies. The government's insulated policy approaches and protectionist views of the PLN are not conducive to helping the Indonesian electricity sector to meet its goals.

For a genuine reform to occur in the Indonesian electricity sector, the government needs to seriously address the capacity issue, find ways to improve the legal system, and implement policies that will gradually decrease the monopoly position of the PLN. For example, some of these goals could be achieved by streamlining PLN's operations. The biggest PLN operated power plants could be given to better resourced IPPs in order to increase competition in the sector. This would likely result in tariff hikes all the while improving electricity provision and creating a more dynamic electricity market. Equally, the government has to find ways to overcome the high-degree of politicization that continues to plague the sector. Otherwise, it is likely that the credibility of the Indonesian electricity sector as a sound investment target by private enterprises will continue to suffer on one hand, and that the impending power shortages will continue to constrain the country's economic growth on the other. Furthermore, in order to enable a shift towards renewable energy, the private sector needs support from both local and international agencies if the potential investors and numerous small-scale power projects are to find common ground.

Appendix 1: The Share of IPP Generated Electric Capacity of the National Electricity Supply Growth in Indonesia between 1995 and 2008 (in megawatts)

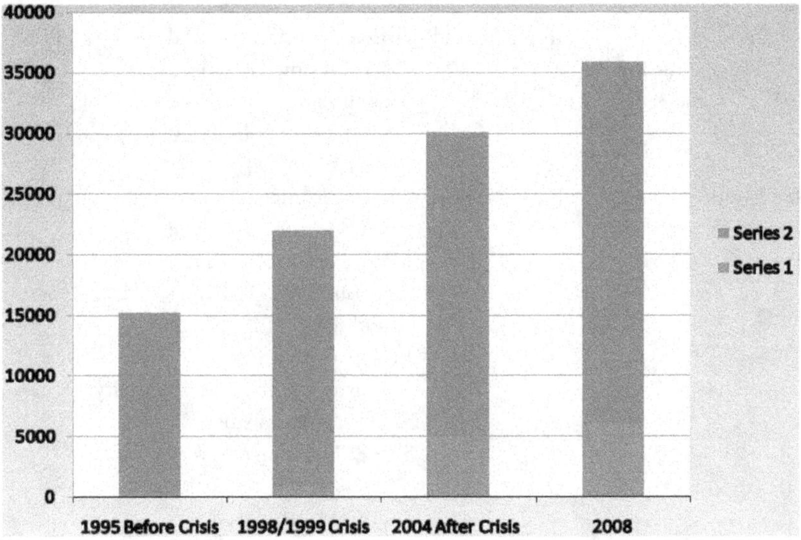

Subject	1995 before crises	1998/1999 crisis	2004 after crisis	2008
Electricity growth	14% p.a.	15% p.a.	6.6% p.a.	7% p.a.
Power plant capacity growth	12.9% p.a.	No growth	3.7% p.a.	4.8% p.a.
Investment	27% of demand from government	No investment	Government finance limited	Government and sector private
Electrification ratio	43%	53%	53.38%	65.15%

Source: Interview with DEMR, April 2009.

Note: Series 1: National Electricity Supply Growth by PLN.

Series 2: The Growth of IPP Generated Electric Capacity.

Appendix 2: Chronology of the Reform Phases in the Indonesian Electricity Sector

Year	Measure	Status	Characteristics	Agencies
1945	Indonesian Constitution — Article 33	Implemented	Article 33 authorizes and requires the government as the single provider of electricity for Indonesia state.	PLN
1985	Electricity Law No. 15/1985	Implemented	The government of Indonesia is responsible for regulating the electricity sector through the DEMR and the DGEEU. Private companies are allowed to participate in the electricity generation business. The PLN is single buyer of electricity and controls both transmission and distribution functions.	DEMR, DGEEU and PLN
1995	Small Power Producers Scheme (PSKSK)	Implemented	Scheme available to small power producers up to 30MW per project for the Java-Bali region and up to 15MW per project for regions outside the Java-Bali system.	DEMR, PLN
2002	Electricity Law No. 20/2002	Annulled	The law established a competitive electricity market by restructuring and unbundling the PLN, mechanism for adjusting electricity tariffs, rationalized mechanism for power purchase for the private sector and established a regulatory mechanism for the sector.	DEMR, PLN

(Continued)

(*Continued*)

Year	Measure	Status	Characteristics	Agencies
2002	Ministerial Decree No. 1122/K/30/ MEM Small-Scale Power Agreement	Implemented	Requires PLN to purchase electricity generated from on renewable energy sources by non-PLN producers for projects of up to 1 MW capacity. Institutions eligible to participate are cooperatives, and private and government companies. Sets purchase tariffs at 80 percent for medium voltage and 60 percent for low voltage of PLN's announced "Electricity Base Price," which is intended to be its marginal production cost at the point of gridline inter-connection of the renewable energy power plant.	DEMR
2006	Ministerial Regulation No. 2 on Medium Scale Power Generation from Renewable Energy Sources	Implemented	Extends the same price guidelines as MD No. 1122/ K/30/MEM for projects from 1 MW to 10 MW. Sets a minimum contract period of 10 years.	DEMR
2009	Electricity Law No. 30/ 2009	Passed in September 2009/ Implementation in process	PLN will no longer have a monopoly on supplying and distributing to end customers. IPPs will be allowed to do this as well, particularly in the regions, however, subject to a 'right of first priority' provided to state-owned companies (i.e. PLN).	DEMR, PLN

Appendix 3: The Functions and Responsibilities of the Power Sector Agencies in Regard to Sector Specific Laws

	Electricity Law of 1985	Electricity Law of 2002 (revised version of the 1985 Law under consideration in the Parliament)
Coordinating Minister of Economy (CME)	The CME has no direct involvement.	The CME monitors and coordinates the positions of relevant agencies in the preparation of the law, and informs the President appropriately.
Ministry of State-Owned Enterprises	The Ministry has overseen that the legislation corresponds to the interests of the PLN.	The Ministry oversees that the interests of PLN are take into account in the drafting process.
BABBENAS (National Development Board)	BABBENAS has been the central government agency in drafting the energy legislation during the Soeharto era. Since then its role has been reduced to a quasi think tank.	BABBENAS' role has been small. It has provided studies and thought leadership on the development of the Indonesian energy sector, but it has had no real effectual impact on decision-making. May assist in drafting and coordinating industry positions.
National Energy Policy Council (NEPC)	The NEPC will coordinate the positions of various agencies including the PLN.	The NEPC will coordinate the positions of various agencies including the PLN.
DEMR	Oversight, enforcement and compliance through DGEEU. DEMR has also been collecting legislative proposals for the revision of the 1985 Law.	Through the DGEEU, the DEMR is responsible for the drafting of the legislation, implementation, oversight, enforcement and compliance.
DGEEU	Mandated to oversee the implementation and compliance. Also responsible for executing the policies set by the Cabinet and the National Energy Policy Council.	The DGEEU is responsible for the drafting of the legislation, implementation, oversight, enforcement and compliance.

(*Continued*)

(*Continued*)

	Electricity Law of 1985	Electricity Law of 2002 (revised version of the 1985 Law under consideration in the Parliament)
Commission VII – House of Representatives	Responsible for coordinating andoverseeing the parliamentary legislative process and consult key agencies of the needed changes to the statutes.	Responsible for coordinating and overseeing the parliamentary legislative process and consult key agencies of the needed changes to the statutes.
Investment Coordinating Board (BKPM)	No role.	No role.

References

Baldwin, R, Cave M (1999). *Understanding Regulation: Theory, Strategy, and Practice.* Oxford: Oxford University Press.

Clark, E and R Tunaru (2005). The Evolution of International Political Risk 1956–2001. Paper provided by Money Macro and Finance Group in its Series Money Macro and Finance (MMF) Research Group Conference 2005 with Number 37.

Cook, P and M Minogue (2002). Introduction: Privatization, regulation and competition in developing countries. *Annals of Public and Cooperative Economics,* 73(4).

Ephraim C and T Radu (2005) The Evolution of International Political Risk 1956–2001. Money Macro and Finance (MMF) Research Group Conference 2005 37, Money Macro and Finance Research Group.

Gale, B (2007). *Political Risk & International Business: Case Studies in Southeast Asia.* Pelanduk Publications.

Gilardi, F (2002). Policy credibility and delegation to independent regulatory agencies: A comparative empirical analysis. *Journal of European Public Policy,* 9(6), pp. 873–893.

Hahn, R and C Cecot (2007). The economic significance of "insignificant" rules, regulation & governance, *Regulation & Governance,* 1, pp. 172–182.

Holmes, P (2004). The WTO and Domestic Regulation, Centre on Regulation and Competition, *Working Paper Series No. 78,* University of Manchester, UK.

Hutter, BM and CJ Jones (2007). From government to governance: External influences on business risk management. *Regulation & Governance,* 1, pp. 27–45.

International Energy Agency (1999). Electricity Reform: Power Generation Costs and Investment, OECD/IEA, Paris.

International Monetary Fund (2009). *Memorandum of Economic and Financial Policies (MEFP)*. Washington D.C.: International Monetary Fund.

Jaffe, J and RN Stavins (2007). On the value of formal assessment of uncertainty in regulatory analysis. *Regulation & Governance*, 1, pp. 154–171.

Jarvis, DS (2006) Conceptualizing, Analyzing and Measuring Political Risk: The Evolution of Theory and Method. Working Paper series RR4, Lee Kuan Yew School Public Policy, National University of Singapore.

Jarvis, DS (2009). Risk, regulation & governance: Institutional processes and political risk in the Thai energy sector. *Regulation & Governance*.

Jordana J, Levi-Faur D (eds) (2005). *The Politics of Regulation: Institutions and Regulatory Reforms for the Age of Governance.* Edward Elgar Publishing.

Jordana, J and D Levi-Faur (2008). *The Politics of Regulation: Institutions and Regulatory Reforms for the Age of Governance.* Cheltenham: Edward Elgar.

Kartasamita, G (2009) Letter by Ginandjar Kartasasmita, State Coordinating Minister for Economy, Finance, and Industry, to Michael Camdessus, Managing Director, IMF, Jakarta, Indonesia, March 16, 2009.

Knight, FH (2002). *Risk, Uncertainty and Profit.* Washington D.C.: Beard Books.

Levi-Faur D and J Jordana (2005). Globalizing Regulatory Capitalism. *Annals of the American Academy of Political and Social Science*, AAPSS, 598(1), 6–9.

Levi-Faur D and J Jordana (2005). Regulatory Capitalism: Policy Irritants and Convergent Divergence. *Annals of the American Academy of Political and Social Science, AAPSS*, 598(1), 191–197.

Levi-Faur, D (2002). Comparative Research Designs in the Study of Regulation: How to Increase the Number of Cases without Compromising the Strengths of Case-oriented Analysis? Centre on Regulation and Competition (CRC) Working Papers, University of Manchester, Institute for Development Policy and Management (IDPM).

Levi-Faur, D (2008). Regulatory Capitalism: Policy Irritants and Convergent Divergence, ANNALS, AAPSS, 598, March 2005.

Levi-Faur, D and J Jordana (eds.) (2005). The Rise of Regulatory Capitalism: The Global Diffusion of a New Order, The ANNALS of the American Academy of Political and Social Science Series.

Llewellyn, HD (2002). *The Handbook of Country and Political Risk Analysis*, 3rd edn., PRS Group, 2002.

Loughlin, M and C Scott (1997). The regulatory state. In *Developments in British Politics*, Dunleavy, D, A Gamble, I Holliday and G Peele (eds.), pp. 205–18. Basingstoke: MacMillan.

Majone, G (1997). From positive to the regulatory state: Causes and consequences of changes in the modes of governance. *Journal of Public Policy*, 17(2), pp. 139–169.

Minogue, M (2002). Governance-based analysis of regulation. *Annals of Public and Cooperative Economics*, 73(4).

Moran, M (2002). Review article: Understanding the regulatory state. *British Journal of Political Science*, 32(2), pp. 391–413.

Moran, TH (ed.) (2001). *International Political Risk Management: Exploring New Frontiers*, Washington, D.C.: World Bank.

MoranTH (ed.) (2001). *International Political Risk Management: Exploring New Frontiers.* Washington DC: World Bank.

Mortimer, M (2006). *Indonesian Communism under Sukarno: Ideology and Politics 1959–1965.* Equinox Publishing.

Nugroho, H, S Thamrin and G Hardjakoesoema (2005). Electricity Industry in Indonesia after the Implementation of Electricity Law Number 20/2002: Proposed Agendas to Support Implementation of the Law, A paper presented at the 28th Annual International Association for Energy Economics Conference, Taipei, 3–6 June 2005.

Ogus, A (2002). Regulatory institutions and structures. *Annals of Public and Cooperative Economics*, 73(4).

Ogus, A (2005). Towards Approriate Institutional Arrangements for Regulation in Less Developed Countries, Centre on Regulation and Competition, *Working Paper Series No. 119*, Institute for Development Policy and Management, University of Manchester, UK.

Parker, D (2002). Researching Economic Regulation in Developing Countries: Developing A Methodology for Critical Analysis, Centre on Regulation and Competition, *Working Paper Series No. 34*, University of Manchester, UK.

Peters, GB (2005). *Institutional Theory in Political Science: The New Institutionalism.* London: Continuum.

Pratomo, Y (2004). Power Sector Restructuring Program Under New Electricity Law, A paper presented in Bappenas-KKPPI Meeting, Jakarta 2004.

Sader, F (2000). *Attracting Foreign Direct Investment Into Infrastructure.* Washington D.C.: Foreign Investment Advisory Service (FIAS), The International Finance Corporation and the World Bank.

Satriya, E (2004). Indonesia's Energy: Regulation in Transition, A paper presented at the Indonesia National Energy Congress 2004, held by KomiteNasional Indonesia–World Energy Council, Jakarta, 23–24 November 2004.

Scott, RW (2001). *Institutions and Organizations.* Thousand Oak, CA: Sage.

Wargadalam, VJ (2004). Cogeneration in Indonesia: Current Situation and Prospects, Research and Development Center of Energy and Electricity Technology (EERDC), Ministry of Energy and Mineral Resources, Indonesia.

Wilkin, S (ed.) (2005). *Country and Political Risk: Practical Insights for Global Finance.* London: Risk Books.

World Bank (2009). World Development Indicators (WDI). The World Bank Group, Washington D.C.

WRI and NK Dubash (2002). *Power Politics: Equity and Environment in Electricity Reform.* Washington D.C.: World Resources Institute.

Yellen, JL (2007). The Asian Financial Crisis Ten Years Later: Assessing the Past and Looking to the Future. Speech to the Asia Society of Southern California, Los Angeles, California, 6 February 2007.

Laws Cited

Article 33(14), the 1945 Constitution of Indonesia.
Electricity Law of 2009 No. 30/2009. The Government of Indonesia (2009).
Electricity Law of 2002 No. 20/2002. The Government of Indonesia (2002).
Electricity Law of 1985 No. 15/1985. The Government of Indonesia (1985).
Government Regulation No. 3/2005. The Government of Indonesia (2005).
Government Regulation No. 53/2003. The Government of Indonesia (2003).
Law of the Republic of Indonesia No.19 of 2003 (paragraph 66).
Presidential Regulation No. 26.The Government of Indonesia (2008).
Presidential Regulation No. 26.The Government of Indonesia (1999).

News Cited

Allianz Global Investors (2008) Investors Brushing off Key Lessons from Financial Crisis. Harris Interactive.
Blackouts Prompt Jakarta to Consider Having Own Plant. *The Jakarta Globe*, 23 November 2009.
Government to Launch New Coal-Fired Power Plants. *The Jakarta Post*, 9 November 2009.
Investors Steering Clear of Oil, Gas Bids Until Cost-Recovery Rules Ironed Out. *The Jakarta Globe*, 25 November 2009.
New Energy Law Will 'Reduce Foreign Control'. *The Jakarta Post*, 27 April 2004.
PLN Employees Reject the Electricity Bill. *Antara News*, 7 September 2009
Under the Volcano: Indonesia's Electricity Woes. Asia Times, 22 June 2002.
Yudhoyono Vows to Eradicate Indonesia's 'Judicial Mafia' in 100 Days. *The Jakarta Globe*, 6 November 2009.

CHAPTER 9

Regulating the Independent Power Producers: A Comparative Analysis of Performance of Andhra Pradesh, Gujarat, and Tamil Nadu in India

*Rajendra Kumar**

New Delhi, India

Various states in India have vied with each other to attract Independent Power Producers (IPPs) to meet the ever growing demand for electricity, especially after the country embarked upon an ambitious economic reform program in the early 1990s. However, despite substantial efforts to create a uniform institutional framework for IPPs, the actual performance of various states in attracting and operationalizing them varies. In this chapter, I examine the performances of three states in India, namely, Andhra Pradesh, Gujarat, and Tamil Nadu, in attracting IPPs. As the institutional, legal, and economic contexts vary from state to state, comparing performances across states allows us to arrive at conclusions about the major factors that are relevant in influencing performance. Using secondary data and sources, I examine the differences in the institutional, legal, political, and economic environments that may account for contrasting performances of these states.

Andhra Pradesh has been a leader in power sector reforms in India, and has achieved considerable success in attracting IPPs. However, it has

* kumarr@alum.mit.edu

faced numerous obstacles due to high cost of power from the IPPs and has also faced protracted legal battles from them in this regard. Gujarat has been arguably the most successful in attracting and operationalizing IPPs through relatively low cost of the projects and low tariffs. Independent Power Producers in Gujarat have also succeeded in establishing efficient fuel linkages and have been relatively free from frequent political interference in negotiating tariffs and payments. Tamil Nadu succeeded initially in attracting a relatively high number of small IPPs. However, the weak financial position of the State-owned Electricity Board (SEB) has forced it to withhold full payments to IPPs for the power purchased. This resulted in making the state unattractive for IPPs.

The performances of the three states shows that while marked by a weak financial condition of the respective SEBs, and the political and institutional contexts in which IPPs operated, establishing efficient and cost was the key effective operations to their success in attracting IPPs.

Keywords: Regulation; performance; electricity; India; institutions.

1. Introduction

India has experienced a rapid increase in its power generation capacity after independence. The total installed capacity has grown from a mere 1,300 MW in 1947 to 1,52,148 MW in August 2009, excluding the captive capacity (Ministry of Power, 2009a). However, most of the additional capacity in the sector has been created by the state and central government agencies. The share of the private sector in the total installed capacity was only 25,618 MW (around 16.8%) in the same period. However, despite its limited share, the private sector, through IPPs, has played a significant role in providing additional generating capacity in India, especially after the country embarked upon an ambitious reforms program in the early 1990s. These reforms aimed at greater private sector participation and attracting foreign direct investment to meet growing shortages in electricity supply in the country.

The first major step in reforms in the sector was taken by the central government with the amendment of the old Electricity Supply Act of 1948 in 1991. This allowed 100% foreign ownership of generating plants and offered these owners guaranteed returns and generous investment incentives. In mid-1990s, several state governments also initiated their own reforms by unbundling their SEBs into separate generation, transmission, and distribution companies. The central government also enacted the Electricity Regulatory Commission Act in 1998 to allow for setting up of the central and state Electricity Regulatory Commissions that aimed at rationalizing the tariff structure, eliminating subsidies, and promoting private investment. Finally, the central government enacted the Electricity Act in 2003 that called for a single legislation aimed at ushering in the second generation reforms by replacing all the three old Acts. This Act eliminated licensing requirements and clearances for new generating plants and allowed the generators to sell electricity to any licensee or consumers directly. This Act currently provides broad institutional and a legal framework for IPPs in India.

As electricity is a 'concurrent' subject in the Indian constitution, states have a major say in regulating the policies and legal framework for IPPs within their territories. As the institutional, legal, and economic contexts vary from state to state, comparing performances across states allows us to arrive at conclusions about major factors that might be relevant in influencing the performance. In this chapter, I examine performances of three states in India, namely, Andhra Pradesh, Gujarat, and Tamil Nadu, in attracting IPPs within a comparative framework.

Using primarily secondary data and sources and employing a comparative multiple case study approach, I examine the differences in institutional, legal, political, and economic factors that may account for the contrasting performances of these states.

Figure 1 shows the location of these states in India.

The rest of the chapter is organized as follows: first, I present a broad analytical framework for regulatory systems that helps analyse the three case studies here. Then, I present the broad institutional and legal framework for the electricity sector in India and discuss specific provisions pertaining to IPPs. Next, I discuss the research methodology for this study and present the three case studies for this research in detail. Then, I present a comparative analysis of the three cases with specific focus on institutional, legal, and economic factors that might be responsible for

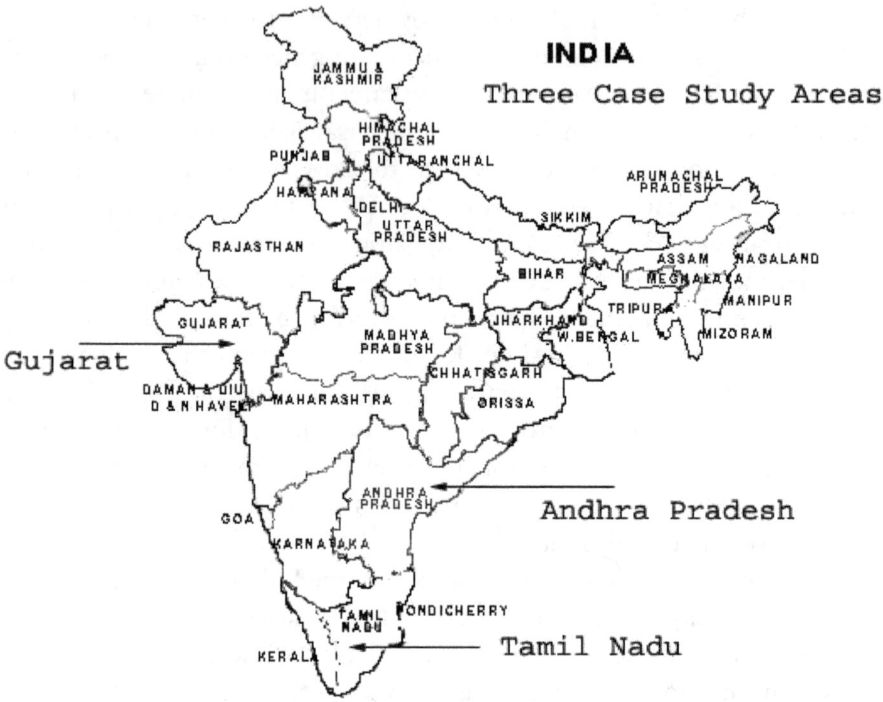

Figure 1: Map showing the three states where the case study was conducted.
Source: http://www.tourindia.com/htm/homepage.htm, modifications by the author.

differential outcomes in the three states with respect to the performance of the IPPs. Finally, I present conclusions.

2. Analytical Framework for Electricity Regulation in India

There exists a vast literature on regulation and regulatory systems. Debates regulation, regulatory reforms, and the relationship between the state and regulation are centered around themes such as rise of regulatory state (Majone, 1997), the regulatory society (Braithwaite, 2003), the post-regulatory state (Scott, 2004), and the notion of regulatory capitalism (Levi-Faur, 2005). While regulation took the form of command and control in the beginning, it has evolved over time to take the form of smart regulation (Gunningham and Grabosky, 1998) and the notion of a post-regulatory state where 'regulatory control is perceived as diffused through society with less emphasis on the sovereign state' (Scott, 2004: 165). Levi-Faur (2005) has argued that privatization is accompanied by an increase in delegation, proliferation of new technologies of regulation, formalization of inter- and intra-institutional relations and proliferation of mechanisms of self-regulation.

In this study, I primarily use two strands of literature to understand how regulation evolved and performed in these states. First, I use the literature on institutional economics to examine the interactions between political institutions and regulatory processes and its impact on the regulatory outcomes. In the wider literature on markets and regulation, the importance of institutions in efficient functioning of markets and economic outcomes has been well recognized (Williamson, 1996; North, 1990; Levy and Spiller, 1996). Levy and Spiller (1994) have argued that the success of any regulatory system depends on how well it fits with the country's institutional endowments and its prevailing institutions. They characterize the institutional environment by two main features: first, the presence of an independent and non-corrupt legal system, and second, the existence of checks and balances on the executive power. They argue that if the regulatory mechanisms are not aligned correctly with the prevailing institutions in a country and its institutional endowment, credible commitments will not be obtained and regulatory outcomes would be adversely affected. They further distinguish between regulatory governance that primarily focuses on the governance structure of the regulatory system, and regulatory incentives, that focus on the economic incentives, such as pricing, cross-subsidies, etc.

Stern and Holder (1999) extend this analytical framework and focus on regulatory processes to their study of regulatory systems. They identify six inter-related dimensions of regulatory governance that help in analyzing the performance of regulatory systems. These dimensions are: autonomy, accountability, clarity of roles and objectives, participation, transparency, and predictability.

The second strand of literature refers to "regulatory spaces" (Hancher and Moran, 1989). This framework basically focuses on the political, legal, and cultural contexts within which regulation is introduced, the evolution of the regulatory institutions within the broader national institutional framework, and regulatory processes that shape the interactions between the regulator, the state, and the utilities. Analyzing these aspects allows us to examine the contextual factors that are relevant to regulatory performance and to evaluate evidence of state capture of regulatory agencies (Stigler, 1971; Posner, 1974).

There have been significant studies on the nature of regulatory space in the Indian context. In particular, Dubash and Rao (2006) argue that the organizational space for the regulators in the case of Andhra Pradesh was shaped by three influential networks: the Indian Administrative Service (IAS) — highest ranked civil servants in India; technical professionals; and consultants. These networks have influenced the reforms process in several other states in India, particularly those where the initial impetus for reforms came from the donors. They argue that the regulators were deeply embedded within the larger networks of the IAS and the reforms were hardly regulator-driven and politically-independent. Instead, the reforms were a result of coordination between the regulator, the government, and the utilities.

In discussing the relevance of contextual factors and the nature of regulatory space, I also draw upon some of the key features of the post-regulatory state framework by Scott (2004). In contrast to the regulatory state where key mechanisms of control in regulatory systems are based on hierarchy and state law, the post-regulatory state invokes other non-legal mechanisms of control and non-state institutions, such as norms and practices in the community, rivalry or competition in organizational settings, and the capacity of institutional design in influencing behavior (Scott, 2004). This literature is relevant here as the regulatory processes in the electricity sector in these states were influenced, not only by the formal state created regulatory institutions and the legal framework, but also the informal influential networks of the IAS, the technical professionals, the donors, and the consultants.

3. Institutional Structure for IPPs in India

The electricity sector in India comes under the ‘Concurrent’ list in the Constitution, meaning that both the centre and the states have control over it through legislation. However, states have a major say in framing policies for the sector as the Electricity Supply Act of 1948 provided for heavy state involvement in the industry to achieve the goal of rapid industrialization of semi-urban and rural areas (Lamb, 2005; Tongia, 2003). In the following sections, I briefly discuss the major enactments in India that provided the broad legal and institutional framework for the development of the sector. For facilitating comparative analysis, I discuss the institutional framework in the pre- and the post-reforms periods separately.

3.1. *Pre-Reforms Period: Indian Electricity Act, 1911 and The Electricity Supply Act, 1948*

During the pre-reforms period, the electricity industry in India evolved under the broad institutional framework provided by two major Acts: the Indian Electricity Act in 1911 and the Electricity Supply Act, 1948. The Indian Electricity Act in 1911 was the first major step towards imparting a structure to an industry that was heavily fragmented and concentrated almost exclusively in urban areas at that time (Bhattacharya, 2003). This Act introduced the licensing system in the sector aimed at regulating the private licensees, which operated in the urban centers.

The Electricity Supply Act in 1948 propelled the industry towards state domination. This Act provided for the establishment of a Central Electricity Authority, vertically integrated state electricity boards (SEBs), and state power generating companies (Lamb, 2005). By the late 1950s, all state governments had established their own state electricity boards (Hansen and Bower, 2003). The major objective of this enactment was to achieve rapid electrification of the rural and semi-urban areas through state involvement. An amendment to this Act in 1956 further increased the scope of state involvement by increasing state control over the SEBs (Lamb, 2005). The results were disastrous. Massive subsidies in the sector (especially to agriculture) and the politicization of the SEBs led to huge losses and gaps in demand and supply. As the SEBs were unable to make huge investments required to meet the shortfalls in supply, the central government again amended this Act in the 1970s to allow for the establishment of central power generating companies, such as the National Thermal Power Corporation (NTPC) and the National Hydro-Electric Power Corporation (NHPC). These amendments also allowed for captive generation by industries to meet their growing demand.

3.2. *Post-Reforms Period: Amendments in 1991; Electricity Regulatory Commission Act, 1998; and The Electricity Act, 2003*

In line with the massive economic reforms program launched by the central government in 1991 aimed at liberalizing the economy, the electricity sector also witnessed a flurry of activities after 1991. The Electricity Laws Amendment Act, 1991 provided for 100% foreign ownership of power generating plants and offered guaranteed returns of 16% on equity, five-year tax exemption, and generous investment incentives. These IPPs could sell electricity to the SEBs at attractive terms through long-term power purchase agreements (PPAs). However, the capacity of the SEBs to make long-term commitments through PPAs was severely limited due to their huge operating losses and inability to predict their future earning potential (Lamb, 2005).

There was another important development during this period. In mid-1990s, due to mounting pressure from the World Bank, other lending agencies as well as several state governments also started their own reform programs by unbundling their SEBs into separate generation, transmission, and distribution companies. The impetus for these reforms was provided by the dire financial straits that the SEBs had pushed themselves into by the mid-1990s. A report by the World Bank in 1999 suggested that the losses incurred by SEBs on account of subsidized power to farmers and residential users was US$4.6 billion or roughly around 1.5% of the GDP at that time (The World Bank, 1999). The leader in state-level reforms during this period was Orissa, which enacted the Orissa Electricity Reform Act in 1995. This Act provided for the establishment of the Orissa Electricity Regulatory Commission and unbundling of the Orissa State Electricity Board. The World Bank approved the Orissa Power Sector Restructuring Project in 1996. In 1997, Haryana embarked upon a similar reforms program by passing the Haryana Electricity Reform Act.

In 1998, the central government enacted the Electricity Regulatory Commission Act to allow for setting up of the central and state Electricity Regulatory Commissions (ERCs) that aimed at rationalizing the tariff structure, eliminating subsidies, and promoting private investment. During 1998–2001, Andhra Pradesh, Uttar Pradesh, and Karnataka enacted their own state-level Electricity Reforms Acts. The World Bank supported reforms in all these states by approving projects specific to them.

The last piece of legislation in the electricity sector in India was the enactment of the Electricity Act in 2003. This Act of the central government brought about a single legislation, aimed at ushering in the second generation reforms by replacing all the three earlier Acts. This Act eliminated licensing requirements and clearances for new generating plants and allowed the generators to sell electricity to any licensee or to the end consumers directly. The main goal of the Act was to change the market from a single buyer to a multi-buyer and a multi-seller system (Lamb, 2005). The "open-access" regime envisaged in the Act was aimed at promoting competition in the sector and attracting IPPs. The Act also ended licensing requirements for captive power generation by any consumer (Lamb, 2005). However, though the Act removed entry barriers for new power generating plants; tariffs for sale by the generators was to be determined by the central (for the central generators that generate and sell power in more than one state) or the state ERC (for the generators within the state, except those falling under the purview of the CERC). The ERCs were required to maintain tariffs at predetermined levels for projects selected through competitive bidding.

The Electricity Act of 2003 currently provides the broad institutional and legal framework for IPPs in India.

4. Research Methodology

I mainly use qualitative techniques for this research. My main focus of research is to examine the differences in institutional, legal, political, and economic factors that may help in explaining the differential performances of the three states in attracting IPPs. I examine the three states in detail using a comparative multiple case study approach. This method focuses on inductive-iterative theory building (Eckstein, 1975; Ragin, 1987; Yin, 1994; Yin, 2003). This research tradition aims at building a theory based on empirical evidence through a close and intimate examination of the empirical reality. The selection of the three states as cases is based on a replication logic where cases are picked up based on either a literal replication or a theoretical replication or both (Yin, 2003). The criteria for selection of cases here are to select those cases that help in arriving at partially-controlled conclusions about the major factors that are relevant in influencing performance. These three states were selected as they fit well within these criteria. While both Andhra Pradesh and Gujarat have achieved considerable success in attracting IPPs, Tamil Nadu has lagged behind in comparison. While I use Andhra Pradesh and Gujarat as successful cases to build a theoretical framework for successful state-level policies in attracting IPPs, I use the relatively unsuccessful case of Tamil Nadu to help in generalizing the findings.

The data for this research comes mainly from secondary sources. These include official documents published by the three state governments and the central government regarding their policies for the electricity sector; published studies and scholarly research done in this field; statistical data and reports published by the government and the other governmental agencies, the industry associations, etc.; and reports and analyses published by the multilateral donor agencies, multinational private consulting firms, newspapers, magazines, etc. I also use primary sources of data for Tamil Nadu based on my own experience of working in the state as a senior government official in public policy and administration and interacting with a number of senior officials in the state electricity board over the past several years.

4.1. *Measuring Regulatory Outcomes and Effectiveness*

It is relevant to mention here the methods of assessment that I use in this research for measuring regulatory performance. I use both quantitative and qualitative methods in assessing regulatory performance. As the focus here is on assessing the performance of the states in attracting IPPs, I use the proportion of installed and operational generating capacity in the private sector out of the total installed capacity in the state as the main indicator of performance of the state. I use longitudinal analysis that focuses on the post-reforms period (after 1991) in analyzing the data as this is the most relevant period for assessing the impact of policy changes in these states in attracting IPPs. I also use qualitative indicators, such as emergence of disputes and protracted legal battles between the state and/or the regulator and the utilities, to assess performance.

5. Description of the Three Case Studies

The three states examined in this research offer us an opportunity to examine the factors that may help in explaining their differential performance in attracting IPPs. In the sections below, I discuss the performance of the three states in detail in attracting IPPs during the post-reforms period with specific focus on the institutional, legal, political, and economic factors that might be responsible for the specific outcomes in each of the cases.

6. Andhra Pradesh

Andhra Pradesh was an early leader in the development of the IPPs in India. Two of the original eight fast track IPPs in the country were located in this state. Both these companies (GVK and Spectrum) successfully established commercial operations. The installed capacity of power by the private sector in the state, including the renewable energy sources, was 2,126 MW (17.9%) out of the total capacity of 11,911 MW as of December 2008 (Ministry of Power, 2009b). The corresponding figures, excluding the wind energy sources, were 11,242 MW as a whole and 1640 MW (14.6%) in the private sector. In terms of performance, the state was ranked first in overall performance in the electricity sector among all the states in India in 2006 (CRISIL & ICRA, 2006).

6.1. *Reforms in the Electricity Sector in the State*

Andhra Pradesh was widely regarded as a leader in electricity reforms in the country during the late 1990s (Lamb, 2005; Dubash and Rao, 2006). The state enacted its own Electricity Reforms Act in 1998 that created the Andhra Pradesh Electricity Regulatory Commission (APERC), an independent regulator, and unbundled the State Electricity Board into separate generation, transmission, and distribution companies. APGenco was set up as the generation company, while APTransco was established as the transmission and distribution company. APTransco was further divided into one transmission and four distribution companies in 2000.

Scholars have pointed out some unique features driving the reforms in this sector. Unlike other states in the country, where the reforms were donor-driven and the political leadership played a supporting role, the reforms in Andhra Pradesh were led by the Chief Minister himself under a World Bank sponsored reforms program (Dubash and Rao, 2006). Here the government itself, under the leadership of the highest executive of the state, was leading the reforms program. This had several important institutional implications for the success of the entire process. As the government itself was driving the reforms, the regulators did not have to face a hostile government unwilling to implement politically unpalatable reforms, an experience that the state of Orissa faced to a significant extent (Dubash and Rao, 2006).

6.2. *Evolution of the IPP Scenario in Andhra Pradesh*

It is helpful to examine the development of IPPs in the state. As noted before, the state was an early leader in attracting IPPs. Both the early fast track MOU projects (GVK and Spectrum) were based on a cost-plus formula with no competitive bidding. The state later went for tariff bid projects, out of which two projects, Lanco Kondapalli and BSES/Reliance achieved commercial operations.

There have been several issues between the state government and the IPPs in the state. Scholars have noted the constant disputes between the government and the IPPs due to the relatively high fixed costs of the projects when compared to that of similar projects in the public sector, high-cost of the electricity produced, and the high rates of return provided to the IPPs (Lamb, 2005). These disputes led to renegotiations in two of the three high-profile IPPs in the state, GVK and Spectrum, while the third project, Lanco Kondapalli, pursued the disputes in court. Spectrum promoters were accused of massive financial fraud that led to huge escalations in the cost of the project (Lamb, 2005).

Here, it is important to note that despite all the contentious issues between the government and IPPs in the state, the latter continued to function and earn returns. How was this possible? One of the most important reasons for this was the necessity of power produced by IPPs to meet the growing power shortages in the state. While the projects themselves faced protracted negotiations, the state continued to buy the power produced by them out of necessity (Lamb, 2005).

6.3. *Conclusion*

Andhra Pradesh has performed creditably well in pushing reforms in the electricity sector. However, as noted before, its performance with respect to IPPs has been mixed due to a series of conflicts over cost and pricing issues. As can be seen from the analysis in the preceding sections, reforms in the sector in the state were led by a strong political leadership that was committed to bringing genuine reforms and improving the performance of the electricity sector. Institutional economics perspective shows that what possibly worked in this case was the overall political and institutional context within the state that allowed reforms to succeed in the sector as a whole. The framework of regulatory spaces shows that the reforms were politically-driven and came about as the result of coordination among the three entities that occupied the regulatory space: the regulator, the government, and the utilities. However, in the case of IPPs, the results were mixed due to relatively high-costs of power and the massive financial fraud that plagued one project.

7. Gujarat

Gujarat is among the most economically developed states in India. With a total installed capacity of 11,728 MW as on 31 December 2008, the per capita consumption of electricity in the state was over 1410 KWh during 2007–2008, over twice the national average (Government of Gujarat, 2009a). The total power generating capacity in the private sector in the state was 3,443 MW, amounting to 29.4% of the total generating capacity (Ministry of Power, 2009). However, taking the conventional sources of energy alone, the corresponding figures were 2,418 MW in the private sector out of a total of 9,814 MW (including the state share in the central sector) (Government of Gujarat, 2009b). In terms of performance in the electricity sector, the state has performed well and was ranked second in overall performance among all the states in India in 2006 (CRISIL and ICRA, 2009).

7.1. *Reforms in the Electricity Sector in the State*

Unlike Andhra Pradesh, Gujarat has been a late reformer in this sector. The state passed its reforms Act, Gujarat Electricity Industry (Reorganization and Regulation) Act, only in 2003. According to this Act, state electricity board was functionally unbundled into seven entities in 2005. However, the independent regulatory authority, Gujarat Electricity Regulatory Commission (GERC), was established in 1999 following the passage of the central Electricity Regulatory Commissions Act in 1998. The state ERC passed tariff orders and also announced charges for open-access consumers on a long-term basis in 2006.

7.2. *Evolution of the IPP Scenario in Gujarat*

Gujarat has been a late starter in the IPP space. Unlike Andhra Pradesh, the state did not have any of the original fast track projects. The state had seven IPPs with a total capacity of 2418 MW as of January 2009 (Government of Gujarat, 2009). The major IPPs in the state are Torrent Power with a capacity of 500 MW, Essar Power with a capacity of 300 MW, and GPEC Paguthan with a capacity of 650 MW.

Gujarat has been the most successful among the three states examined here in terms of cost of power produced by IPPs (Lamb, 2005). Fixed cost per MW was lower in the state and the state was also able to achieve reductions in tariff through renegotiations based on debt refinancing and altering fuel from naphtha to natural gas to reduce the variable costs (Lamb, 2005). The state government provided good support for these steps and politics appeared to have played a comparatively lesser role in this state (Lamb, 2005). Availability of new gas supplies through the state's own LNG terminals also facilitated the renegotiation process for changing the fuel from naphtha to gas during the crisis of 1999–2000, when naphtha prices shot up.

7.3. *Conclusion*

Gujarat, though a late reformer when compared to Andhra Pradesh, has been the most successful among the three states in attracting IPPs and has the highest installed capacity in the private sector. Unlike Andhra Pradesh, reforms were not driven politically and in the case of IPPs, politics seemed to have played a much lesser role. What seems to have driven the success of the state in attracting IPPs were relatively lower fixed costs of the projects and lower variable costs due to the availability of alternate fuel when the original fuel became relatively costly.

In terms of the analytical framework of regulatory structure and regulatory incentives, it is apparent that the regulatory incentives in the form of debt restructuring and reducing the variable costs by altering the fuel from naphtha to natural gas played an important role in the success of IPP projects in the state. Employing the regulatory spaces perspective, we can see that the reforms were not driven by the highest political executive in the state, as was the case in Andhra Pradesh. However, the state supported the regulator in renegotiations of the IPP projects for debt refinancing and ensuring the availability of the alternate fuel. Thus, the regulator played the lead role in this case in ensuring the success of IPP projects in the state.

8. Tamil Nadu

Tamil Nadu is one of the relatively more economically developed states in India and is widely known for its prowess in information technology and automobile sectors. The total installed generating capacity in the state as on 31 December 2008 was 9,676 MW, excluding the wind energy sources. Out of this, 1,165 MW was contributed by the private sector (Ministry of Power, 2009). However, if the wind energy sources are included, the total installed capacity jumps to 14,034 MW, out of which 5,434 MW was in the private sector. Thus, excluding the wind energy capacity, the state had the least installed capacity in the private sector among all the three states studied here. In terms of performance, the state was ranked 10th overall among all the states in 2006, down five places from its rating a year ago (CRISIL and ICRA, 2006). This ranking was far behind that of both Andhra Pradesh and Gujarat in the same year.

8.1. *Reforms in the Electricity Sector in the State*

Tamil Nadu was the last to start the reforms process among the three states examined here. Though it established its Electricity Reforms Commission in 1999 itself, the first chairman of the commission took charge only in 2002, i.e., after four years of passing of the CERC Act in 1998 (TNERC, 2009). The state has also not yet implemented the functional unbundling of its SEB as per the Electricity Act, 2003 (Government of Tamil Nadu, 2009). It also continues to supply free power to the farmers for agricultural purposes, a policy that has imposed huge subsidy burden on the SEB and has severely impacted its revenue generation capacity (CRISIL and ICRA, 2006). The state has also not been disbursing the full subsidy amount to the SEB as per its claims on free supply of power to the farmers.

Despite the heavy subsidy burden, the state took steps to support 'open access policy' and captive power generation to promote competition in the sector. Tamil Nadu Electricity Reforms Commission notified the policy on open access whereby consumers with a demand in excess of 10 MW could choose their supplier (CRISIL and ICRA, 2006). In November 2008, the state government also abolished the cross-subsidy charges for suppliers supplying electricity directly to consumers under the open access policy (Business Line, 2008). This step was aimed at easing the power crisis in the state. Under the state's captive power policy, captive power generators of more than 2 MW capacities could opt for banking scheme or power feed scheme by paralleling their generation units with the grid.

8.2. *Evolution of the IPP Scenario in Tamil Nadu*

Tamil Nadu was a slow starter in attracting IPPs. It did not have any of the original fast track IPPs in the country. However, it moved aggressively to attract IPPs in the mid 1990s and between 1998 and 2001, five of them achieved commercial production, though several more had been planned (Lamb, 2005).

IPPs in the state have faced a protracted battle with the SEB over payment issues. The SEB stopped making full payment to the IPPs for the power purchased from 2001, citing its own precarious financial condition (Lamb, 2005; Woodhouse, 2006). The SEB has been paying a uniform fixed tariff of only ₹2.25 per kWh for the power purchased from the IPPs, irrespective of the costs or the contracted rates. This move was supported by both the state government and the TNERC. The state government announced in the assembly in 2002 that it proposed to renegotiate the cost of power from the IPPs. The TNERC in its order stated "...TNEB to explore all possible options with concerned IPP generators at the earliest in order to optimize the cost of power purchase from IPP sources under the existing low interest regime. The TNEB should also strictly follow the principle of merit order despatch in its power procurement process" (TNERC, 2004:7–8). Though this policy was adopted as a temporary measure and the SEB promised to pay the arrears in full when its financial condition improved, it hit the private producers hard.

8.3. *Conclusion*

Tamil Nadu has been the least successful among the three states in both pushing reforms and in attracting the IPPs. The state has the lowest installed capacity in the private sector (excluding the wind energy sector) among the three states examined here. Free electricity to the farmers has been a very sensitive issue in the state and the political compulsions were too high to alter the status quo, despite an order by the state ERC in 2003 to levy a minimal charge on supply of electricity to the farmers. The precarious financial condition of the state EB also forced it not to pay the full cost of power to IPPs as per the contract agreement. Political commitment to reforms were low and, as the discussion in the preceding paragraphs suggest, this state also presents credible evidence of the undue influence of the government in the regulatory space, especially with respect to the payment dispute between the state EB and IPPs. The regulatory incentives to encourage IPP projects were also missing in this state.

9. Comparative Analysis of the Three Case Studies

The three cases examined in this research present contrasting pictures of their performance in ushering reforms in the electricity sector and, particular, attracting IPPs. Gujarat has been the most successful state among the three examined here, with the highest installed capacity and the least controversies with respect to costs of the projects and the power produced. Andhra Pradesh succeeded in implementing the reforms in the sector as a whole, however, its record with respect to attracting IPPs was not as successful. Tamil Nadu was the least successful among the three states in both implementing reforms in the sector as well as in attracting IPPs.

What were the critical factors that were important in ensuring the success of Gujarat in attracting IPPs? As noted before, politics seemed to have played the least role in this state during renegotiations with IPPs for revision of prices. The fixed costs of the Gujarat IPPs were also relatively lower compared to those in the other two states. Availability of alternate cheaper fuel also facilitated the renegotiations to bring down the prices without any additional costs being imposed on the IPP. From an institutional economics perspective, what ensured the success of the state was a good fit between the regulatory institutions, the regulatory processes, and the overall institutional endowment of the state, consisting of the prevailing political, legal, and economic institutions. Specifically, regulatory incentives in the form of debt refinancing and ensuring the availability of cheaper alternate fuel were very important in ensuring the success of IPPs. In terms of the regulatory spaces perspective, the reforms that ensured the success of IPP projects were led by the regulator with good support by the state government.

On the role of regulatory incentives in influencing regulatory outcomes, it is helpful at this point to draw upon the experiences from some other cases presented in this volume. Examining the case of Maharashtra state in India, Tankha (in this volume) has argued that regulatory innovation through partial privatization within the existing regulatory framework allowed the state electricity board to cut losses and improve supply. Drawing upon the experience of electricity tariff regulation in Thailand, Sirasoontorn (in this volume) also finds that regulatory incentives can play an important role in achieving the desired regulatory outcomes.

In the case of Andhra Pradesh, while the reforms in the sector as a whole succeeded well, it was not as successful in attracting IPPs. There were protracted disputes and litigations between the state EB and IPPs over fixed costs and the cost of power. There was also credible evidence of massive financial fraud in at least one project that increased the costs. In terms of the "regulatory spaces" perspective, the reforms in this case were led by the political leadership of the state, and not the regulator. Protracted disputes with IPPs and almost a total halt to the reforms process in the sector after the change of political leadership in the state in 2004 also acted as disincentives to further investments in IPP sector in the state (Lamb, 2005). From an institutional economics perspective, IPP sector in the state was a case of a mismatch between the regulatory systems and the overall institutional endowment of the state. Lack of regulatory incentives to make the operation of IPP projects attractive also contributed to their comparatively poor performance.

While discussing the case of Andhra Pradesh, it is relevant to mention the role of leadership. As noted before, this state was a leader in reforms in this sector as a whole, though its performance in attracting and operationalizing IPPs was mixed. The reforms in the sector were led by a strong political leadership under the personal supervision of the Chief Minister of the state himself who was committed to bringing genuine reforms and improving the performance of the electricity sector. Hence, while the overall political and institutional context within the state allowed reforms to succeed in the sector as a whole, in case of IPPs, the results were mixed due to a series of conflicts over the relatively high-costs of power and the massive financial fraud that plagued one project.

Tamil Nadu emerged as the least successful of the three states in this study in both implementing reforms in the sector as whole and in attracting IPPs. The state was the last among the three to start the reforms process. However, the reforms process in the state never got the required political support to succeed. The state EB was also financially weak due to a huge subsidy burden on account of free power to farmers. This forced it to stop making full payment to IPPs for purchasing power as per the agreement. In terms of the "regulatory spaces" perspective, the huge influence of the government in the regulatory arena was apparent when it succeeded in stopping full payment to IPPs. Thus, a weak regulatory structure combined with lack of regulatory incentives contributed to the poor performance of the IPPs in this state.

It is useful to briefly recapitulate the main points from the analysis of the three cases presented above using the institutional economics and regulatory spaces perspectives discussed earlier in this chapter. I present this comparative analysis in Table 1.

Why did Gujarat succeed so well in attracting and regulating IPPs while Tamil Nadu could not achieve similar success? Employing the analytical frameworks of institutional economics and regulatory spaces, we can see from the comparative analysis in the preceding sections and from Table 1 that the success of IPP projects in Gujarat was driven by strong regulatory incentives and a good overall institutional fit between the regulatory system and the political and governance institutions in the state. In Andhra Pradesh, though the reforms process itself went well due to the strong leadership of the highest political executive of the state, lack of adequate regulatory incentives led to protracted litigation between IPPs and the state. In at least one case, the role of IPP itself was dubious as it inflated the project cost due to financial fraud. The role of the regulator in the state in carrying out reforms was also weak as the Chief Minister of the state was himself driving the reforms.

In case of Tamil Nadu, as the analysis in the preceding sections shows, the reforms failed to succeed due to lack of commitment on the part of the state government. The regulatory structure in the state was also weak and there were no incentives for the IPPs to make their projects attractive. In terms of the regulatory spaces perspective, we can see that the role of the government was not supportive of the reforms and the regulator was weak in pushing reforms in the sector and making the IPP projects viable and attractive.

Table 1: Comparative Analysis of the Performances of the Three States in Attracting IPPs

Analytical Framework	Andhra Pradesh	Gujarat	Tamil Nadu
Institutional Economics Perspective			
Regulatory Structure and Governance	Relatively strong	Relatively strong	Weak
Regulatory Incentives	Weak	Strong	Weak
Overall Institutional 'Fit'	Relatively strong	Strong	Weak
Regulatory Spaces Perspective			
Role of Government/Political Institutions	Strongly supportive	Supportive	Not supportive
Role of Regulator	Weak	Strong	Relatively weak
Role of IPPs	Mostly negative	Positive	Neutral
Role of Political Leadership	Strongly supportive	Supportive	Not supportive

9.1. *Implications for Regulatory Design, Effectiveness, and Operation*

What are the implications of this research for regulatory design, effectiveness, and operation? As the experiences of the three states discussed in this study show, ensuring proper institutional 'fit' of the overall regulatory apparatus with the existing institutional endowment of the state is extremely important. Specifically, a proper regulatory and governance structure that ensures that the regulators can perform their task independently with adequate involvement of all the relevant stakeholders is extremely important. They also need to ensure that the regulatory incentives are designed in such a way to make IPP projects commercially viable. In terms of regulatory spaces, the regulators need to be provided with sufficient institutional autonomy to ensure that vested political interests do not encroach upon their territory in regulating the sector.

9.2. *Lessons for Regulators: What Works, What doesn't?*

What are the lessons that can be drawn from the three cases so far as the regulation of IPP projects is concerned? As discussed earlier, the role of regulatory and governance structures and regulatory incentives was extremely important in all the three cases. The states that ensured proper regulatory and governance structures and provided adequate regulatory incentives performed well in attracting and operationalizing IPP projects. Gujarat performed particularly well in this area. Andhra Pradesh had mixed success in this area due to lack of adequate regulatory incentives to make IPP projects viable. Lack of sufficient institutional autonomy for the regulator was another important reason for the relative failure of the state in IPP projects, though the reforms were led personally by the Chief Minister of the state. In case of Tamil Nadu, the state failed to provide sufficient institutional autonomy to the regulator and the incentives were highly-inadequate to make IPP projects viable. The SEB was making huge losses on account of free supply of power to the farmers and the reforms proved to be politically unpalatable to the political leadership in the state.

Here it is relevant to point out the inherent weaknesses in the regulatory system even in the successful case of Gujarat. As this research shows, the cost of the power produced by IPP projects was an important factor in ensuring their commercial viability. All the three states tried to renegotiate the projects to bring down the cost of the power produced. Gujarat succeeded well in this endeavor as it was able to negotiate debt refinancing and provide cheaper alternate fuel to the projects. However, resorting to renegotiations itself signaled weaknesses in the regulatory system and a disincentive to the potential investors as it implied that the sanctity of the power purchase agreement was open to question and the agreement itself could be opened at a later date.

This research suggests that an institutional "fit" between the regulatory systems and the overall institutional endowment of the state in the political, legal, and economic contexts is extremely important to ensure success of the reforms and IPPs. Regulatory incentives played a very important role in ensuring the success of IPPs. Wherever there was a mismatch or the regulatory space was monopolized by one of the stakeholders in the process, the reforms did not succeed.

10. Conclusion

This research shows that the political and institutional contexts in which IPPs operated, and establishing efficient and cost effective operations were the keys to success of the states in attracting IPPs. While Andhra Pradesh has been a leader in power sector reforms as a whole in India, it has achieved only mixed success in attracting IPPs. This was mainly due to the high-cost of power from IPPs that led to protracted legal battles with the state utilities. Gujarat has been arguably the most successful state in India in attracting and operationalizing IPP projects through relatively low cost of the projects and comparatively lower tariffs. IPPs in Gujarat also succeeded in establishing efficient fuel linkages and were relatively free from frequent political interference in negotiating tariffs and payments. Tamil Nadu initially succeeded in attracting a relatively high-number of small IPPs. However, weak financial position of the SEB owing to its huge subsidy burden due to the free supply of power to the farmers forced it to withhold on making full payments to the IPPs for the power purchased. The state also lagged behind in the reforms process. These factors resulted in making the state unattractive for the IPPs.

References

Bhattacharya, SC (2003). *Review of the Electricity Act 2003 of India*. Dundee: Center for Energy, Petroleum and Mineral Law and Policy.

Braithwaite, J (2003). *Meta Regulation for Access to Justice*, Paper presented at the General Aspects of Law (GALA) Seminar Series, University of California, Berkeley, 13 November.

Business Line (2008). *TN allows third party sale of private power*, Retrieved on February 2009 from http://www.thehindubusinessline.com/2008/11/10/stories/2008111050251500.htm.

Dubash, NK and N Rao (2006). *Emergent regulatory governance in India: comparative case studies of electricity regulation*, Paper presented at the Conference on Frontiers of Regulation: Assessing Scholarly Debates and Policy Challenges, University of Bath, UK.

CRISIL and ICRA (2006). *State Power Sector Performance Ratings 2006*. Retrieved on February 2009 from http://www.powermin.nic.in/indian_electricity_scenario/pdf/Final_Report_Rating.pdf.

Eckstein, H (1975). Case study and theory in political science. In *Handbook of Political Science, Vol. 7: Strategies of Inquiry*, Greenstein FI and NW Polsby (eds.), pp. 79–137. Reading, MA: Addison-Wesley.

Gunningham, N and PN Grabosky (1998). *Smart Regulation: Designing Environmental Policy*. Oxford: Clarendon.

Government of Gujarat (2009a). *Power Generation Policy 2009*. Retrieved on January 2009 from http://www.indextb.com/power-generation-09.pdf.

Government of Gujarat (2009b). *Power projects in Gujarat. Installed capacity of the state*. Retrieved on January 2009 from http://guj-epd.gov.in/epd_projects.htm.

Government of Tamil Nadu (2009). *Energy department. Demand no. 14. Policy note 2008–09*. Retrieved on January 2009 from http://www.tn.gov.in/policynotes/energy.htm.

Hancher, L and M Moran (1989). Organizing regulatory space. In *Capitalism, Culture and Economic Regulation*, Hancher, L and M Moran (eds.). Oxford: Clarendon Press.

Hansen, CJ and J Bower (2003). *The Political Economy of Electricity Reform: A Case Study in Gujarat, India*. Oxford: Oxford Institute for Energy Studies.

Lamb, PM (2005). *The Indian Electricity Market: Country Study and Investment Context. Working paper No. 48*. Stanford: Stanford University Program on Energy and Sustainable Development.

Levi-Faur, D (2005). The global diffusion of regulatory capitalism. *The ANNALS of the American Academy of Political and Social Science*, 598(1), pp. 12–32.

Levy, B and PT Spiller (1994). The institutional foundations of regulatory commitment: A comparative analysis of telecommunication regulation. *Journal of Law, Economics, and Organisation*, 10 (2), pp. 201–246.

Majone, G (1997). From the positive to the regulatory state. *Journal of Public Policy*, 17(2): pp. 139–67.

Ministry of Power (2009a), *All India Regionwise Generating Installed Capacity (MW) of Power Utilities Including Allocated Shares in Joint and Central Sector Utilities*. Retrieved on October 2009 from http://cea.nic.in/power_sec_reports/Executive_Summary/2009_08/8.pdf.

Ministry of Power (2009b), *Generation installed capacity (MW) of power utilities in states/UTs.* Retrieved on January 2009 from http://www.cea.nic.in/power_sec_reports/executive_summary/2008_12/9-10.pdf.

North, D (1990). *Institutions, Institutional Change and Economic Performance.* New York: Cambridge University Press.

Posner, RA (1974). Theories of economic regulation. *The Bell Journal of Economics and Management Science,* 5(2), pp. 335–358.

Ragin, CC (1987). *The Comparative Method: Moving Beyond Qualitative and Quantitative Strategies.* Berkeley: University of California Press.

Scott, C (2004). Regulation in the Age of Governance: The Rise of the Post-Regulatory State. In *The Politics of Regulation in the Age of Governance,* Jordana J and D Levi-Faur (eds.), pp. 145–74. Cheltenham: Edward Elgar.

Stern, J and S Holder (1999). Regulatory governance: Criteria for assessing the performance of regulatory systems. An application to infrastructure industries in the developing countries of Asia. *Utilities Policy,* 8(1), pp. 33–50.

Stigler, GJ (1971). The theory of economic regulation. *The Bell Journal of Economics and Management Science,* 2(1), pp. 3–21.

Tongia, R (2003). *The political economy of Indian power sector reforms. Working Paper No. 4.* Stanford: Stanford University Program on Energy and Sustainable Development.

TNERC (2009). *Commission's History.* Retrieved on January 2009 from http://tnerc.tn.nic.in/History.htm.

TNERC (2004). *Nellikuppam V Krishnamurthy Vs. ST-CMS Electric Power Company & others.* Retrieved on February 2009 from http://tnerc.tn.nic.in/orders/MP%20263%20Nellikuppam%20krishnamurthy.pdf.

Williamson, O (1996). *The Mechanisms of Governance.* New York: Oxford University Press.

Woodhouse, EJ (2006). *IPP Study Case Selection and Project Outcomes: An Additional Note. Working paper No. 59.* Stanford: Stanford University Program on Energy and Sustainable Development.

The World Bank (1999). *Meeting India's Energy Needs (1978–1999): A Country Sector Review,* Report No. 19972, Vol. 1.

Yin, RK (1994). *Case Study Research: Design and Methods.* Thousand Oaks: Sage Publications.

Yin, RK (2003). *Case Study Research: Design and Methods,* (3rd ed.). Thousand Oaks: Sage Publications.

CHAPTER 10

Partial Privatization and Nested Regulation: Institutional Choices in Public Sector and Regulatory Reform

Sunil Tankha

International Institute of Social Studies, Erasmus University Rotterdam

1. Introduction

The experience with orthodox approaches to infrastructure privatization and regulation has too often been unsatisfactory, particularly in electric power and water & sanitation, to be considered, as so many policy entrepreneurs of the time had characterized it, "an idea whose time has come" (e.g., Savas, 2000). This is particularly the case in developing countries where these policies had promised to simultaneously resolve inefficiency, corruption and underinvestment. Not only did privatization policies not resolve these problems, they created new problems which led to widespread dissatisfaction. Brazil abandoned power privatization in 2002, after it had led to extensive power rationing (Tankha, 2009). In Argentina, power companies, which had been privatized less than a decade earlier under frameworks hailed by the World Bank and orthodox policy analysts as exemplary, were re-nationalized (Baer and Montes Rojas, 2008). In Bolivia, privatization of water companies was reversed after only a few years as was done in Indonesia, the Philippines, and several African countries (Budds, 2003, Lobina and Hall, 2000). In India, tentative steps to involve power and water multinationals were fiascoes.

Several intellectual responses have appeared to explain the problems with developing country infrastructure privatization and regulation. The orthodox defense argues that infrastructure privatization was, in fact, a success and that inadequate communication of its benefits, especially to the poor, has been responsible for the negative perception surrounding it (Birdsall and Nellis, 2005). Another approach acknowledges that infrastructure privatization did not succeed because of a failure to implement properly generally-correct regulatory models and strategies (Parker and Kirkpatrick, 2005). A third approach criticizes privatization for allowing private interests to exploit power asymmetries in global economic relations to the detriment of developing countries (Hoff and Stiglitz, 2001).

In this chapter, I analyze regulatory failures in developing country privatization programs and conclude that arguments which say that the standard regulatory models are fundamentally good and need only to be "implemented correctly" are flawed. In fact, many of models underlying infrastructure privatization and regulation are of limited utility in developing countries and better implementation of these models is not only unlikely to happen given the political and economic constraints of their environments, but also unlikely to deliver satisfactory results. This is because the standard models overestimate the effects of market competition and underestimate the effects of investor-perceived risk in infrastructure investments in developing countries. In Sec. 3, I analyze problems with and alternatives to standardized privatization and regulation, in which nested and negotiated approaches are used to overcome the barriers which emerge when public service reforms are implemented in challenging institutional environments. I use the electricity industry to ground the research, illustrating the analysis with examples from two late-industrializing countries: Brazil and India. In Sec. 4, I present the implications of these two cases for regulatory design in infrastructure industries. Section 5 concludes.

2. Problems with Infrastructure Regulation in Developing Countries

Why has the regulation of privatized infrastructure systems proved so problematic in developing countries? To answer this question, let us re-visit the basic mechanics of regulatory processes. Infrastructure systems require strong regulation because the invisible hand does not work in these markets. Their characteristics — difficulty of entry and exist stemming from large sunk costs, economies of scale and scope, and information asymmetries — do not allow for free and fair competition. Moreover, increasing oligopolization in many large industrial sectors over the last few decades has complicated efforts to introduce free and fair competition even where technological developments have made it theoretically possible.

In the absence of effective competition, regulation has to curb two competing tendencies simultaneously, both of which emerge from the rational and self-interested assumptions which underlie human behavior in economic analyses. The first tendency is that selfish producers take advantage of market failures to price monopolistically. The second tendency is that self-serving public officials further their interests at the expense of private investors and operators.

The dominant approach to infrastructure regulation concerns itself with the financial implications of the regulatory contract and argues that the two above-mentioned tendencies can be curbed simultaneously by ensuring that the internal rate of return (IRR) of regulated companies approximates closely the weighted average cost of capital (WACC) employed by them. Regulatory failures are said to occur when IRR deviates from WACC. If IRR > WACC, it means that infrastructure operators are practicing monopolistic pricing at the expense of consumers and if IRR < WACC, it means that public choice is operating against investor interests, which will lead to under-investment and loss of consumer welfare in the long-run. Since the calculations for both the WACC and the IRR are fairly standardized, it is argued that applying this simple rule can lead to effective infrastructure regulation. The policy conclusion is that improving regulatory performance depends upon increasing the regulatory agencies' capacities, usually through increasing their funding and their independence from government, to accurately determine and enforce the setting of IRR = WACC .

This is a problematic tool to manage infrastructure regulation in developing countries. In advanced industrial countries, the cost of capital is low. In developing countries, it is not. Standard economic approaches posit that the cost of capital is a function of the risk embedded in the concerned investment. In infrastructure industries, the major risks embedded in the investment are (a) market risk and (b) regulatory or policy risk. The latter risks behave differently in developing countries, condemning them to more volatile infrastructure investment markets under scenarios of private, especially foreign, investment.

Market risks are generally low in infrastructure industries in both advanced industrial and developing countries as the demand for their output is stable and generally increasing. Regulatory and policy risks are also low in advanced industrial countries because the underlying elements that constitute policy and regulatory risks — currency markets, political orientation, government credibility and economic performance — are all stable. For this reason, the rates of return on regulated public utilities in developed economies have historically been low, not exceeding by much the cost of sovereign finance (Stigler and Friedland, 1962, Crew and Kleindorfer, 1987). Given that infrastructure industries are uniformly capital-intensive, low costs of capital translate into low prices for infrastructure services and, consequently, few losses of positive externalities.

The situation in developing countries is more complicated. Capital costs more in developing countries than in advanced industrial economies. This can be intuitively deduced from the fact that capital is scarcer in developing countries, and should therefore cost more. The standard approaches to pricing capital, however, does not dwell on its scarcity but on the risk involved in a project. Through this optic, capital is more expensive for developing countries' infrastructure investments because they involve higher levels of policy and economic risks. These risks are higher because of a combination of factors particular to developing countries such as (a) a tradition of controlling prices of utility services for social reasons instead of making direct cash assistance payments to the poor, (b) stronger unions and politicized public services, (c) new, weak and infrequently independent regulatory systems, (d) volatile political and economic conditions, and (e) an aversion to foreign ownership of core infrastructures.

Given that infrastructure industries are capital-intensive, it logically follows that the costs of providing infrastructure services will be much higher in developing countries than in advanced industrial economies if the standard reasoning of setting IRR = WACC is followed. This creates problems not only in terms of permitting developing countries to capture the externalities associated with infrastructure services, but also to address the not-unimportant redistribution concerns. Given the socio-economic characteristics of developing countries, especially in terms of distribution of income and poverty, and along with budget constraints, high prices of public services greatly complicate efforts to achieve necessary economic growth and social development objectives. The fact that the scarcity of capital has to be overcome by attracting foreign investment complicates matters even more, because the effects of currency risk and the higher transactions costs of foreign investment come into play.

In addition, the standard approach to determining the cost of capital, such as through the Capital Assets Pricing Model (CAPM), place a heavy emphasis on the country's debt levels in determining WACC, leading to wide disparities in capital costs in fundamentally similar economies. For example, Sirtaine *et al.* (2005) calculated the WACC for infrastructure investments in Brazil to be 14% and those in Mexico to be 4%. Indeed, according to their calculations, it was less risky to invest in Panama (8%) or Peru (9%) than in Brazil. Is investing in power project in Brazil three times as risky as investing in a similar project in Mexico? Has the investor who makes a 4% return on investment in Mexico made a better deal than one who makes an 8% return in Brazil?

The cost of capital estimated by the standard models used by regulatory systems thus does not depend on the policy orientation of the host government or the credibility of its policies (although it does have a big impact on the investor's decision to invest or not). It depends almost wholly on levels of debt, especially external debt. This approach is intuitively defensible: the more indebted an entity, the more likely it is to be unable to honor its financial obligations. Therefore, lending to the entity or investing in it is a riskier proposition and a higher return is logically demanded. But while the orthodox approaches to infrastructure regulation are internally logically coherent and superficially persuasive, they lead to some unexpected and disruptive consequences in developing countries.

The shortcomings of these models can be illustrated through the development of two scenarios: the death spiral and the infrastructure investment Ponzi. We begin by assuming that a developing country government initially, in its keenness (or desperation) to access finance and investment, agrees to pay high returns for both debt financing and investment in regulated public services. Once the government has agreed to this bargain, the following scenarios may play out:

Scenario One: The Death Spiral

Having committed to high rates of return and privatization in exchange for renewed access to capital markets, the government takes a decision to reduce its fiscal outlays and increase the real prices of public services to pay for these commitments. It can reduce fiscal outlays primarily by cutting discretionary spending, which is usually in the social sectors such as health, education, pensions, etc. These cuts will be deeply unpopular and unsustainable in a democratic system, which means either the government will abandon fiscal austerity or be voted out. This unpopularity explains the leftwards movement of electoral results in South America and the subsequent reversals of many privatization efforts such as in the water sector in Bolivia. In the unlikely event that the government is able to maintain fiscal austerity, the impact on the domestic macro-economy may be contractionary if private spending does not pick up substantially. If private spending does not compensate and economic growth does not accelerate rapidly, the government's revenues will fall and it will be unable to meet its financial commitments and will default. Prior to default, it will probably attempt to devalue its currency to increase exports and foreign exchange earning. For the investor in privatized public services this would lead to immediate and large losses. If its contract with the government pegs utility rates to the dollar, then a devaluation of the domestic currency will lead to a politically-unsustainable increase in already-high utility bills and the contractual protections for the investor will be abrogated. If the contract with the government does not peg utility rates to the dollar, then the difference between the investor's earnings in the local currency and debt service payments in hard currencies will widen and lead to large and persistent losses.

Scenario Two: The Infrastructure Investment Ponzi

Here, the government avoids making fiscal cuts in order to maintain social peace and reduce potential opposition to reforms, and meets its obligations by using newly-reopened capital markets to borrow again. As new debt is sought by governments with historically high debt levels, investors must be remunerated with high returns. Unless a combination of income from privatization proceeds and economic growth serve to reduce overall levels of public debt, interest rates will start to climb again, and will climb even faster if emerging and transitional nations' capital markets are volatile. Eventually, the debt servicing will become unsustainable and a moratorium or default will have to be adopted by the borrowing country. Investors who had entered early in the reforms cycle will have made handsome returns by the time the system breaks down, their high returns being paid in to a great extent by the funds provided by investors who come later.

Both these scenarios were realized in Latin American countries such as Argentina and Brazil. In the latter, for example, despite a privatization program that yielded billions of dollars, public debt actually went up as soon as the *Real* was introduced, indicating that high interest rate payments made to foreign investors to persuade them to buy Brazilian companies and hold Brazilian public debt would eventually become unsustainable (see Fig. 1).

Any regulatory contract based on these principles is therefore unlikely to be stable and enforceable. The fact that investors did not make these

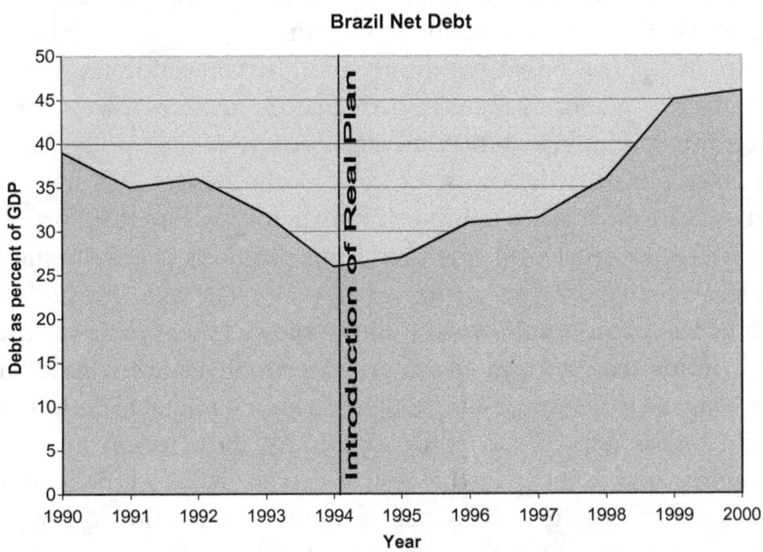

Figure 1: Brazil Net Debt 1990–2000.

astronomic returns putatively estimated by CAPM is then blamed on the quality of regulation. In spite of the economic crisis in Brazil, returns on capital in power projects in Brazil were comparable to returns on US power project in almost all years between 1998 and 2005, although this was considered deeply unsatisfactory because it was below the levels estimated by the standard capital assets pricing models (Rocha *et al.*, 2007). Moreover, none of the losses indicated in the paper were caused by regulatory malfeasance or shortcomings but by the collapse in currency markets in financial turmoil of 1997 and 1998.

The standard orthodox recommendations, a process of complete privatization of infrastructures in developing countries, which would include concessions and long-term leases of the entire network, were thus flawed. They contained a distribution of power which was not only asymmetric but also temporally unstable. Most analysts contend that developing countries did not privatize because of ideological convictions but because their hands were forced by deteriorating fiscal positions and credit constraints (Ramamurti, 1992), or in other words in precisely those conditions under which cost of capital would be very high for them. In contrast, private investors had access to large amounts of capital, not enough to finance the sum total of infrastructure needs in developing countries but certainly enough to enter strongly into the most promising markets. Moreover, the infrastructure firms based in advanced industrial economies were facing stagnant growth and revenues in their mature home markets. They were attracted to developing country markets because of their potential to generate large profits, which was the case partly because private investors could increase efficiencies but more importantly because these firms could get capital at low cost while the precarious positions of developing countries, exacerbated by the refusal of agencies like the World Bank to continue lending to state-owned utilities, allowed them to drive hard bargains in terms of capital remuneration. More problematically, these bargains had a long shelf life and even though a country might make substantial moves towards reform and policy credibility, these would not translate into appreciable declines in the cost of capital in the immediate future. Although infrastructure firms held a dominant position during initial contract negotiations, their long term positions were less secure because of the large amounts of sunk costs related to infrastructure investments. This made them vulnerable to government opportunism in the future. Because investors felt vulnerable to government opportunism, not only did they demand higher returns to compensate for this risk, but also they would try to front-end their returns so that their initial investments could be recuperated as quickly as possible, before government opportunism would expropriate them or limit their returns (Wells and Gleason, 1995). Perversely, investor attempts to protect themselves precipitated the very policy reactions they feared. The higher the returns that investors demanded and the higher the prices consumers had to pay, the lower became the support for these reforms and the higher became the eventual socio-political opposition to them (see, for e.g. Tankha, 2009). It was not so much regulatory lacunae or weaknesses in regulatory institutions which failed privatization and deregulation but rather a fundamental incompatibility in the objectives of the main stakeholders that caused the fiascos. Claims that these could have been avoided had the regulatory institutions been stronger are naïve. No democratic country's administration can allow power and water prices to double in the space of a few months, regardless of what is stated in the concessions contract with private investors.

Thus, the orthodoxy's mantra of "implemented correctly" has no meaning other than vague calls for actors to "behave" not according to their own selfish rationalities as underpin market models but according to the frameworks required by orthodox models of infrastructure market systems to function. They do not resolve the problem of the high costs developing countries have to pay for infrastructure services under their models and they provide no particular institutional innovation, or control mechanism to compel societies to pay this cost in the long-run. Moreover, the institutional and structural prerequisites required for the smooth functioning of orthodox recommendations do not exist in developing countries, and if they did, so many of the underlying problems of state provision would be solved that the need and urgency of privatization and other reforms would become moot. Finally, there is no evidence that the putative competition and economic growth that was to accompany such reforms have been realized other than, in the case of Brazil, for example, a short consumption led growth cycle caused by price stability in the immediate aftermath of the introduction of the *Real*. Indeed, the end of the inflationary cycle in Latin American is the signature and significant achievement of the orthodox reforms program.

After deconstructing the orthodox conceptualization of privatization and liberalization with or without the elusive and as-yet unidentified "correct implementation" of what is at best an inadequate solution and at worst a recipe for disaster, are we still left in an equally unsatisfactory state: i.e., a return to the state-owned utilities of twenty years ago with their inefficiencies, their corruption, their inflexibility and lack of creativity in solving urgent social problems? To some extent, it is inevitable that we must take a step back towards this unsatisfactory state-of-affairs in order to seek, construct and experiment with new approaches. And it is to begin exploring these approaches to which this paper now turns.

3. Two Illustrations: Power Sector Reforms in Brazil and India

Brazil and India present two contrasting approaches to power sector reform. The former first enthusiastically pursued and then forcefully retreated from an orthodox reform agenda. The latter timidly and tentatively experimented around the margins of an orthodox reform strategy while attempting to reform its public sector power companies. Regulatory problems arose in both cases, and their different responses demonstrate the range of options and strategies with which developing countries are experimenting in order to be able overcome infrastructure supply gaps.

3.1. *Brazil: Transformational Reforms and a Return to the Past*

In 1995, the Cardoso administration amended Brazil's 1988 Constitution to permit private investment and operation of public services. Electric power company privatization quickly followed. It was an integral part of an ambitious economic restructuring program through which the Cardoso administration hoped to break the cycle of high inflation and economic stagnation that had plagued Brazil for over a decade. The main features of this program were (a) the adoption of a new currency, the *Real*, pegged to the US dollar, to fight inflation and the credibility problem, (b) lowered import duties to stimulate competition in the domestic market, thus also pressuring local producers to price cheaply and not contribute to inflation, and (c) large scale privatization of infrastructure firms to reduce public deficits, pay down the debt and to create an inflow of foreign exchange which would in turn help the government maintain the currency peg.

When privatization began, Brazil's power sector was already mostly unbundled. For historical reasons, power generation was concentrated in four large federal firms and in a four vertically integrated firms owned by the wealthier states of São Paulo, Minas Gerais, Parana, and Rio Grande do Sul. Power distribution companies were generally owned by their various state governments. Brazil began power privatization with its distribution companies, reasoning that (a) private investment in power generation would be more forthcoming if the distribution companies were to be privatized first, thus obviating the need for federal government guarantees on power purchase agreements, (b) distribution companies were generally more inefficient and politically manipulated than the generation companies, and (c) state governments were fiscally less responsible than the federal government and it would thus be expedient to reduce their ownership of the large firms through which they practised profligacy and patronage.

Distribution companies were auctioned as 30-year concessions and the post-privatisation regulatory structure adopted by the Brazilians modelled closely on the British system of price caps. The privatization of distribution companies was initially very successful; most of them fetched handsome premiums over their minimum reserve prices. Within two years, a majority of the power distribution in the country transferred to private hands. The government then began to prepare the federal generation companies for privatization.

The power sector reforms program stalled after financial crises in Asia and Russia in 1997 and 1998. Investors withdrew massively from emerging markets and while Brazil tried to stanch the outflow by offering extremely high interest rates, even at the cost of massively increasing its public debt, it was unable to maintain the *Real* and was forced to devalue the currency in 1999, shortly after Cardoso was elected to a second term as President.

Brazil had managed to persuade investors to accept concessions contracts which specified retail power tariffs in the local currency, offering high initial utility rates as an incentive. After the devaluation, investors, who had borrowed heavily in overseas markets to finance the purchase of the power distribution concessions, started running huge losses. Pressure mounted on the Brazilian electric power regulator, ANEEL, from all sides. Investors wanted ANEEL to massively increase tariffs so that their losses could be controlled; consumers and the political opposition wanted tariff relief as the economy began to stagnate; the Cardoso administration wanted the regulator to manage the crisis while limiting damage to investor sentiment.

In the meantime, the generation sector was largely ignored. The Cardoso administration had practically paralysed the federal generation companies' investment programs even though Brazil was facing tight electric supply markets, and indeed, this was the primary reason publicly proffered for the privatization of its power infrastructure. The investment programs were paralysed partly because the administration intended to privatize these firms, and partly to keep the public sector deficit and borrowing requirements under control.

The depreciation of the *Real* was not the only reason that private investors were little interested in generation sector investment. A more problematic issue was the lack of policy clarity on the regulation and governance of the wholesale power markets. This lack of policy clarity stemmed from the fact that the standard models of wholesale power markets and their regulation threatened a brusque and sustained increase in wholesale power prices.

This was because the most common versions of wholesale power markets were based on market clearing models in which a central dispatch authority solicits bids from power generators and dispatches them in order of merit — cheapest to most expensive — until all the power demand is satisfied. The last, most expensive, power dispatched is the market clearing price, which is received by all the producers whose power is dispatched. In other countries, it was subsequently discovered that this system lent itself to gaming, where generators with some degree of market power would deliberately take out cheaper plants in order to drive the market-clearing price higher and earn rents on the power produced from their lower cost plants. In Brazil, the problem was even more fundamental. Almost 90% of the power produced and consumed in Brazil comes from large dams, whose operating costs are very low. In addition, a significant number of these hydropower plants had already amortized their capital costs. Following standard market governance models would lead to one of two equally undesirable scenarios.

In the first scenario, in the case of abundant power availability, if the low-cost hydropower plants established the market clearing price by bidding their marginal costs as the standard model required them to do, it would establish such a low market clearing price that investment in new plants would not be financially viable.

In the second scenario, in the case of restricted power availability, if the market clearing price were to be established by high cost thermal power plants bidding their marginal costs, then the low-cost hydropower plants would earn very large rents and the average price of power would shoot up tremendously. Calculations released by the government later revealed that this would have led to a doubling of the rates at which wholesale power would be traded under market-clearing conditions (Ministerio de Minas e Energia, 2002).

Again, the regulatory model being pursued in this case was internally coherent and defensible by falling upon standard commodity market clearing arguments, which formed the basis of the neoclassical (or neoliberal) reform recommendations then in vogue. It was, however, neither politically feasible nor economically desirable. Having already committed the country's power consumers to paying a high price for electricity in order to provide the high returns that distribution sector investors had demanded, the Cardoso administration was in no position to accede to these demands from potential investors in the generation sector. Moreover, as electricity is a basic input into all modern economic activities, high power prices were threatening to reignite inflationary pressures.

At the same time, turning their backs on a regulatory model they had been attempting to implant over the past five years was not politically attractive. The administration was confronted with two choices: it could either auction the utilities based on the assumption that the market clearing prices would prevail, thus actualizing the future rents accruing to the amortized generation infrastructure, or it could signal that some form of price controls in the generation sector would be imposed, with the result that potential purchasers of the generation companies would bid lower amounts for the firm. On the one hand, the administration would have preferred to maximize its earnings from the privatization of the generation companies; on the other hand, electricity rates were already at high levels, increasing steadily, and threatening renewed inflation.

Investors perceived that the administration could not credibly commit to either of these policy options. If the administration were to signal free markets in generation with only a light regulatory touch, and investors did bid high for the firms, there would be substantial incentive for the government to reverse the policy in the future, especially if a new political party reached power. If the government did intend to introduce price controls, they were not announcing any credible mechanisms as to how that would work. Moreover, it seemed unlikely that the government would allow politically prominent firms such as Furnas and Chesf to be sold for low prices. Indeed, in the end, only the smallest of the four federal generation companies, Eletrosul, was sold and only one investor bid for it, offering the minimum reserve price.

In the meantime, the paralysis of generation investment led to an increasing precariousness in the security of power supply in Brazil and in 2001, after weak rains that failed to sufficiently recharge the reservoirs of the hydropower dams, President Cardoso was forced to declare an emergency power rationing in which almost all classes of customers were required to reduce their power consumption by up to 20%. The rationing lasted 10 months and had severe repercussions on the finances of the sector as well as on the Brazilian economy.

In the aftermath of the rationing, the currency depreciation, and the economic stagnation of the country following these crises, a political opening appeared for the Workers Party to catapult Lula da Silva to the Presidency in the 2002 elections. The Lula administration abandoned privatization and market-based deregulation and implanted a New Model for the Brazilian power industry, which returned the industry to the basic organizational philosophy which had underpinned it during its period of rapid expansion between the 1950s and 1970s. During this period, Brazil had reasserted state control over the power sector, which had hitherto been dominated by two North American firms. It invested heavily in large hydropower projects but maintained efficiency and discipline by first establishing several federally and state owned power companies with overlapping jurisdictions and then having them compete with each other for each new large power development project. In this manner, inefficient public sector power companies would not win in the competition for new projects and would be eventually subsumed into their more efficient counterparts.[1]

[1] It is beyond the scope of this paper to provide a detailed analysis of the new Brazilian power sector organization. For a detailed description and analysis of the various organizational models of the Brazilian electric power system, see Tankha (2010).

In 2003, this competition for projects rather than competition in markets was recreated by the New Model. The government established a new state power planning agency, the EPE, to which distribution companies were required to submit projections of their power requirements. EPE would then solicit bids from power generators, awarding to the lowest bidder 30-year power purchase agreements which specified both the amount of power to be supplied on an annual basis and the fixed rate at which it would be remunerated.

The advantages of this model are (i) it allows public and private generation companies to compete on an equal footing, (ii) it does not predefine a high rate of return for power companies, allowing public sector companies to underbid private investors if the latter demand too high rates of return, (iii) it eliminates predatory and volatile pricing in power markets by, sensibly, establishing stable long-term rates, and most importantly, (v) it allows lower-cost energy from existing plants and new, higher-cost energy to trade in separate markets without contaminating each other. An early criticism of such single-buyer models was that by disallowing competition in retail markets, proper signals for real-time value of electric power would not be sent out, limiting long-term investment in the industry. But liberalized real-time wholesale markets had required distribution companies and large power consumers to purchase hedging contracts to lock in power rates, establishing the very kinds of derivative markets which are subject to manipulation and have been thoroughly discredited by the recent financial sector scandals.

3.2. *India: Form over Substance: Nibbling at the Margins*

For many decades now, the Indian power sector has been unable to keep up with the country's electricity demand because of inadequate revenues and inefficient operations. It provides a classic example of a sector trapped in a low-level equilibrium with (i) politically imposed and "populist" tariffs resulting in the utilities being starved for cash and unable to finance adequate network expansion or regular maintenance, (ii) political interference in the bureaucratic structures which manage the power companies resulting in corruption and uninspired management, which has led to high levels of power losses and unchecked power theft, and (iii) a reluctance on the part of civil society to pay higher prices for what is extremely poor service. The power supply situation in the country has deteriorated over the last decade as strong economic growth has led to an increasing gap between power demand and supply, a situation which would have been even worse had industries not compensated for the shortfall in service by building their own captive power plants. It is estimated that about 30% of the new power in India now comes from captive power plants (Ministry of Power, 2008).

In response to the inefficiency of the sector and continuing power shortages, the Government of India has enacted a number of new policies aimed at reforming the sector, the latest being the 2003 Electricity Act. In form, the power sector reforms policies follow the standard prescriptions: the establishment of independent regulatory agencies, unbundling of the generation, transmission and distribution functions which were integrated in the state-level Electricity Boards (SEBs) and eventual de-regulation of wholesale and retail markets. The Electricity Act 2003, which focused on unbundling, followed an earlier reform legislation, the Electricity Regulatory Commission Act of 1998, which had established the legal framework for creating independent electricity regulatory commissions at the central and state levels, a process guided by the World Bank in order to facilitate private sector participation (PSP) in and, eventually, the privatization of the state-owned electricity companies in India.

However, the agenda to shift the bulk of power sector investment responsibilities to the private sector has not advanced much. An early effort to invite PSP through the show-piece Dhabol Project was a fiasco. In 1997, the Maharashtra State Electricity Board (MSEB), one of India's wealthiest states, signed a power purchase agreement with the Enron Corporation Despite being part of a select group of fast-track projects which received Central Government guarantees, Enron obtained not only a guaranteed 16% return on investment but also, by vertically integrating the project by taking responsibility for its fuel supply, an even higher profit outside regulatory purview (Mehta, 2000; Srinivasan, 1996; Purukayastha, 1995). The company's aggressive negotiating strategy did not pay much attention to the fact that the wholesale power rates MSEB would have to pay Enron were much higher than the retail rates MSEB charged its own customers. Even the World Bank had argued against the project. Enron may have expected that the price differential would at best motivate the state government to implement an electricity tariff hike or at worst that the state or central government would step in with their guarantees. As it transpired, the project generated huge amounts of controversy, and was repeatedly canceled and renegotiated among accusations of graft and unethical behavior by all involved parties — Indian government officials, Enron, and the US diplomatic officials which backed the company's claims.

The Enron fiasco was not an isolated problem in the attempts to introduce PSP in electric power infrastructure in India. A few years later, a World Bank guided restructuring and privatization exercise in the Indian state of Orissa also failed. After the Dhabol fiasco involving the now-defunct Enron Corporation, which indicated that investment in even IPPs could become problematic, and the withdrawal of AES from power distribution in Orissa, it became clear to both domestic policymakers and foreign investors that the Indian power sector was not ready for large-scale sector participation.

With the failure of the first phase in PSP, power sector reforms in India, like public sector reforms in general, remain both difficult and slow. Reviews of the Indian power sector reform efforts conclude that they have been unsatisfactory, with poor performance in commercial and technical parameters of service, including financial stability, energy deficit and peak power shortages, and transmission and distribution (T&D) losses (Sharma *et al.*, 2005). Most analyses indicate that the principal problems lie not as much in the central sector generation companies as in the state electricity boards (Banks *et al.*, 1998; Dossani, 2004; Singh, 2004; Sharma *et al.*, 2005; Dubash and Narsimha Rao, 2008). While the former improved their technical performance steadily and considerably since the early 1990s — for example, in 1992–93, the plant load factor of central sector thermal power plants was 62.7% but by 2001–02, this had increased to 74.3% and reached 86% by 2007–08 (Ministry of Power 2008) — the financial and technical performance of state electricity boards remained poor. Within the state electricity boards, the critical area of reform is the distribution sector. With "populist" tariffs, high T&D losses and low bill collection efficiency in the distribution sector, the revenue stream from customer to distribution companies to generation companies is dysfunctional because of which investments in the generation sector also remain stunted.

In response, the 2003 Act focussed on unbundling the sector, separating out the generation, transmission and distribution functions into different companies. Unbundling of power sector companies has been recommended by many, including the World Bank, as a means of facilitating competition, but the Indian government's motivations in unbundling were very different. It has commonly been found that public sector enterprises tend to perform better at tasks which are more engineering oriented (such as power generation) than those which require more soft-skills such as customer service (e.g., power distribution) (see, for example, Tendler, 1968). It is this latter category of tasks which tends to require a larger labor force relative to output, which often translates into over-staffing and a locus for trade union opposition to orthodox reforms. These tasks represent also the arenas in which populist politics manifest themselves more strongly, such as in the case of tariff controls, because they are the point at which the state as a provider of services interacts directly with the citizens. Moreover, in terms of controlling corruption in an environment only weakly conducive to reforms, it is easier to reduce information asymmetries and implement better management information systems in areas like power generation where the infrastructure is not spread out and where transactions are on average larger and more routine. By unbundling generation from distribution, Indian policymakers aimed at two objectives. First, by isolating the better-performing generation sector from the distribution sector, they hoped to prevent the financial contamination of the former. This goal has also been furthered by rationalization of wholesale power rates by electric power regulatory agencies, irrespective of the level of subsidies offered to final consumers, so that the generation sector is not burdened by unremunerative tariff policies. Instead, distribution companies must alone bear the financial burden of these policies. Second, by preventing the generation sector from subsidizing the non-performing distribution sector, policymakers hope to create transparency regarding the true areas of inefficiency in the power sector and, consequently, to concentrate pressures for reforms upon the distribution sector.

This policy is only a first step in overcoming the low-level equilibrium that exists in the sector. It has created an environment which, albeit weakly, facilitates reform initiatives by separating better-performing parts of the system to prevent their contamination and to focus efforts on finding an exit from the low-level equilibrium in which the Indian power industry is trapped. In itself, the new policies are not sufficient to force through actual reforms.

Let us now turn to an interesting institutional innovation in one of the state electricity boards which takes a different approach to the regulatory question of providing policy credibility and safeguards to private investors while maintaining public control over public utility prices. Like other state electricity boards in the country, MSEB was plagued by inefficiency and political interference. Despite its relatively wealthy status, there was an increasing gap between demand and supply, the inability of the state government to substantially increase investment outlays and the predication of the release of central government funds upon meaningful reforms being undertaken by MSEB.

Given the requirements of the 2003 Electricity Act, the threat of reduced central funding for power projects and the fact that Maharashtra had not added to its installed capacity in the previous five years, MSEB was unbundled in 2005. The corporatization and unbundling of MSEB into generation, transmission and distribution firms followed form more than substance. There is still substantial political involvement in the running of the various companies, with the managing directors of the three companies reporting frequently to the state energy minister. The members of the boards of directors of these firms are also appointed by the government. Nevertheless, unbundling and associated reforms had some impact on performance parameters including profits, electricity losses, consumer base, and collection of dues in all three of the MSEB subsidiaries. Transparency has also increased and a certain degree of functional autonomy ceded, if only because there is now a certain degree of pressure on these companies to report healthy financials.

On the regulatory side, the state government established the Maharashtra Electricity Regulatory Commission (MERC), a quasi-judicial body responsible for determining tariffs (as well as for resolving disputes among the stakeholders). The procedures followed by MERC are fairly straightforward. The Government of India had specified in its 2003 Electricity Act the rates of return that power companies ought to earn on their equity. For generation companies, the target rate was 16% and for distribution companies this rate was between 14 and 16%. After calculating the asset base of the company, MERC arrives at an Annual Revenue Requirement (ARR) for the company. The next step involves estimating the amount of power supplied to different classes of customers and the relative rates of cross and direct subsidies that are to be provided to each category of customer. Based on this information, MERC determines the applicable tariffs for each category. The compilation of the information obtained from the power companies and the tariff determination is subcontracted to a private consulting firm which physically locates its consultants full-time in the MERC offices in Mumbai. It should also be mentioned here that MERC and its sub-contractor accept at face value the information provided by the MSEB companies and neither has the capacity to independently verify the information provided (personal communication to author by MERC representative, October 2008).

In reality, adherence to this textbook model of regulation is irrelevant. Power prices are politically determined and ex-post justified. A high-level MERC official, when queried about why rates were not being increased more in order to allow MERC's distribution arm to make the required rates of return responded that the consumer could not be punished for the company's inefficiency. Further inquiries did not lead to any clarity about what prices were appropriate for an efficient company or what levels of efficiency were considered adequate.[2]

Privatization of MSEB-Distribution, though it may be argued as desirable for increasing investment and efficiencies, is infeasible even if it is contemplated by the political establishment. There is still a political impasse over power tariff subsidies, which account for over 50% of tariffs and with over 75,000 employees, trade union opposition to privatization of MSEB is strong and assertive. The state's most attractive market, the city of Mumbai, is supplied power by a municipally-owned undertaking — the Bombay Electric Supply and Transport Corporation (BEST) — which has maintained a reputation for efficiency and good service, and neither the municipality nor its customers feel any need to privatize it. The next attractive market, the fast-growing suburbs of Mumbai, is supplied by the Bombay Suburban Electric

[2] Personal communication with MERC personnel, October 2008.

Supply Corporation (BSES) and this was sold to the Reliance Group in 2003. These are the very desirable markets as they incorporate a high number of commercial and higher-income residential users. The MSEB-Distribution territory, however, incorporates all of the state's rural areas, smaller and medium-sized towns and has comparatively a much lower-income clientele, which makes it both a riskier and a less remunerative market.

With outright privatization ruled out as an option and with difficulties in maintaining increases in efficiency gains, particularly in problematic areas, MSEB-Distribution devised a new strategy to push reforms further. The strategy, in broad terms, was to turn over to a private company the worst-performing of its 40 circles in operational and, more importantly, financial terms and see if they could turn it around. The circle chosen for this experiment was Bhiwandi, where poor service, power theft and non-payment of bills were rampant.

Given the high levels of losses and the slow pace of reform, in January 2007, MSEB turned over the Bhiwandi circle to a private operator in the form of a Distribution Franchise. A quasi-concessions contract was signed between MSEB-Distribution and the private company by which the latter granted exclusive rights to take over MSEB-Distribution's infrastructure on a "right to use" basis and supply power to the circle for a period of 10 years. As part of the franchise agreement, MSEB-Distribution would supply power at designated input points as per its power supply and load shedding schedule (which is based on the directives issued by MERC). The contenders for the franchise were required to bid on the price they would be willing to pay per unit of this power.

Although the MSEB did attempt, and to a certain extent had succeeded in improving its technical and commercial performance in Bhiwandi — it managed to reduce AT&C losses from 73% 2001–02 to 56.4% by 2005–06 — the circle continued to drain cash. To improve operational efficiencies, the concessionaire followed the same technical procedures which had been initiated by MSEB-Distribution, which were to install more meters and better equipment to reduce losses by more accurately identifying power flows. The difference was that the private operator was much quicker in squeezing further gains. It brought AT&C losses down to 37% and T&D losses down from 38.95% when it took over the franchise, to 19% by June 2008. It reduced the transformer failure rate from 44% to 9%. Collection efficiency increased from 66% to 89%. The company reduced the proportion of un-metered consumers from almost 50% to about 10% and increased the proportion of billed consumers from 46% to 87%. It also opened multiple billing-cum-collection centers to facilitate cash collection. According to a company source, the circle has now become "profitable," whereas under MSEB the circle was making losses to the tune of US$ 7 million annually.

Earlier attempts to involve the private sector in distribution, especially at the non-metro level, had proved problematic. In the state of Orissa, a similar arrangement was tried via a management contract but was abandoned after a six month trial period. Two problems had emerged. First, the public sector employees were assigned to the private operator with deteriorating terms of service and they challenged this in the courts. Second, the private operator found the assets too deteriorated and decided not to continue its involvement in the company (Banks *et al.*, 1998).

The Bhiwandi experiment sidesteps these and three other major barriers to the privatization of distribution companies: badly defined distribution zones, lack of independence of regulators, and controversies over justifiable rates of return.

Lack of information about the status of the infrastructure and asset valuation causes problems when investors claim to have overpaid for an asset and then try to renegotiate for a higher price, as occurs in a majority of infrastructure concessions. This problem is sidestepped in Bhiwandi because the ownership of the assets is never transferred to the franchisee. It is interesting to note that in the case of the Bhiwandi franchise, MSEB-Distribution did not charge any fees to transfer the right to use its assets to the franchisee. In effect, the franchisee gets to use the MSEB-Distribution infrastructure free of charge. Not charging for the assets reduced the amount of investment risk for the franchisee, which facilitates further investment in the sector. However, this subsidy does not appear to have any direct costs because MSEB-Distribution was making an operational loss of about Rs. 2.5 crores per month from its assets in Bhiwandi.

Defining distribution zones can lead to problems if the wealthiest zones are privatized and the financially weak areas are left under the state's responsibility, which makes the financial situation of the state-owned enterprise even worse. In Bhiwandi, the opposite was done, with the most inefficient and unprofitable sector being handed over to the private operator. In fact, the selection criteria adopted by MSEB-Distribution prioritizes areas of high electricity losses for franchising, although it does not contemplate franchising predominantly rural circles because of their low potential to generate revenue for the franchisee.

The issue of regulatory independence is also sidestepped for the time being because the regulator does not directly regulate nor has direct oversight over the profits of the private operator. Since the franchisee signs its contract with MSEB-Distribution, it is the latter which is supposed to monitor the franchisee's performance. Obviously, since the franchisee is nested within MSEB-Distribution, the service standards established by MERC for the distribution company also apply to the franchisee. The rates received by the private investor are the same as those that MERC awards MSEB-Distribution. Assuming that this principle is followed, the private company, which is putatively more efficient than the state-owned enterprise, should stand to make an attractive return even if the distribution company itself is making losses. Other advantages of this system are that consumers can be satisfied that they are being charged what they would have been had the system not been privatized while investors are assured that government opportunism will have financial repercussions also on the public sector enterprises. The disadvantage of this system is that assuming the regulator could correctly identify the cost savings by the private operator, these are not passed on to consumers.

Labor resistance is avoided because no MSEB-Distribution employees will be fired in response to the franchising, and indeed some 100 of them are receiving a higher remuneration without losing any of the privileges of public sector employment. Moreover, in terms of promoting efficiency, this form of public-private comparison has strengthened the ability of reformist management at MSEB-Distribution in bargaining with the labor unions for more performance improvements. If the labor does become more efficient in MSEB-Distribution, it consolidates its position against privatization; if it does not, it strengthens upper management in transferring more circles to private operation. As such, if regular and significant efficiency gains continue to be made, it would not even be necessary to expand the distribution franchise program much more.

4. The Implications for Regulatory Design

The desirability of private investment and operation of core infrastructures such as water & sanitation and electric power depends critically upon the institutional arrangements and regulatory systems in which they will be embedded. In the power sector, a standard textbook model of unbundling and real-time competition in wholesale markets, and subsequently retail markets has been a staple of orthodox approaches to sector reforms. In most systems of a certain size, unbundling delivers substantial managerial benefits in terms of monitoring costs and performance, even though these come at the cost of some scale economies and co-ordination problems. Competition, however, occurs more efficiently at different levels and over different time-scales than those recommended by orthodox prescriptions. In developing countries, where regulatory institutions are weak in terms of credibility and personnel, less complicated and more transparent forms of competition deliver better value in practice even though theoretical models describing ideal systems tend to look better on paper.

In the Brazilian case, we saw that it proved impossible to insert an internally logical but outwardly weak market structure and regulatory system based on the orthodox recommendations. When rationing was imposed upon the Brazilian power sector in 2001, many analysts criticized the government for privatizing too slowly, arguing that mixed state and private ownership can never work. Instead, since 2003, when a hybrid ownership approach was made official policy, the industry has continued to attract funding and increase capacity to keep up with demand. It has also permitted public-private competition, which serves as a useful guide to regulators trying to determine whether or not private investors are taking advantage of their bargaining power. This form of public-private competition is not new; the FDR administration in the United States had established the Tennessee Valley Authority and other federal power projects partly as a counterweight to private power companies who were exercising market power and insisting on the maintenance of high rates for electricity even though technological developments and scale economies had lowered their costs considerably (Granovetter and McGuire, 1998; Brown, 1980). Rather than the hybrid approach, it was the theoretically pure model of the recent privatization era which could not adapt itself to the exigencies of real-world developing country situations.

In the Indian case, we saw that practitioner approaches to solving intricate social problems are different from the grand transformative approaches of hegemonic institutions because they are limited in their capacity to shape institutions to suit their solutions. They are forced to innovate around the margins of institutional constraints, taking advantage of semi-porous institutional boundaries in order to construct new solution sets that respect institutional constraints yet seek to manipulate them in order to introduce modifications and see if they hold. It is an evolutionary rather than revolutionary strategy. It is difficult to come up *apriori* with theoretical models to describe them; a more fruitful approach is to study such innovations qualitatively, construct cause-effect and means-end analyses of the solutions and then relate them to possible theoretical development.

The distribution franchise model developed in Maharashtra is a good example of a practitioner's response to pressures for reform within an institutional environment which is not conducive to such reforms. Its structure was not deduced from theoretical considerations, but evolved out of a practitioner's attempt to create a space for reform and devise a system capable of yielding significant gains. The principal features we found in this arrangement are that it is (a) negotiated, (b) sequential, and (c) hybrid. The Bhiwandi distribution franchise indicates that some of the new forms of private sector participation that are being instituted are more negotiated and relational in nature, and facilitate ongoing cooperative behavior because of a better alignment of interests of the principal stakeholders. A mutually beneficial accommodation was negotiated among all the principal stakeholders, and it is difficult to define any clear losers. The fundamental implementation strategy is sequential, building upon successes and learning from experience. The arrangement is a hybrid between a concession and a management contract.

The reader will notice the lack of contractual guarantees. The literature on privatization and regulation emphasizes the creation of more complete contracts and protection for investors. In most developing countries, credible policy commitment at the outset of a reform program is clearly unlikely and writing more precise contracts gains no intrinsic advantage. This also indicates that domestic firms, which have better tacit knowledge of local socio-political conditions, are more likely to enter such markets than foreign investors.

In both Brazil and India, local experiments cognizant of the particularities of their situation have generated innovative solutions that work. Their operating principle has not been to make the case fit the theory, but to adapt theoretical knowledge to construct customized institutional and regulatory systems that deliver investment and efficiency at affordable prices. An overemphasis on market clearing, theoretically if not in practice, has dominated the discourse over regulatory structures and regimes. The two cases described here indicate that the original objectives of regulation, keeping services satisfactory and prices low should be the true measures of regulatory performance.

5. Conclusions: The Lessons for Regulators and Reformers

Traditional approaches to regulation have been dominated by mechanistic principles that focus mostly on bringing about an approximation of IRR to WACC. Institutional issues, when addressed, are approached mostly to facilitate these mechanistic principles rather than pragmatic practicable alternatives to achieving the ends of higher levels of infrastructure service delivery at low prices. These mechanistic principles are inappropriate for developing countries, and often unworkable in them. Adherence to such principles in developing countries means that regulatory agencies will often be condemned to act in a reactive manner and to following form rather than substance. Moreover, adherence to these principles also facilitates predatory capitalism, which is socially unsustainable. Demands for high rates of return to compensate for the riskiness of infrastructure investments in developing countries often leads to investors making high returns in the initial stages of reform and then threatening to walk away if governments do not compensate them for losses in subsequent periods, which is a vivid example of privatizing profits while socializing risks and losses.

A different, promising alternative to infrastructure regulation in developing countries functionally focuses on the relational aspects of the regulatory bargain, crafting each bargain with a negotiated approach. Such approaches offer the principal benefit of being customized to the realities, needs and idiosyncrasies of each situation, cognizant of the desires and abilities of the major participants and stakeholders.

Such approaches also indicate, though do not necessarily require, that participants be on relatively homogenous scales of knowledge and bargaining power. This does not necessarily exclude the multinational firms that have been at the centre of infrastructure controversies in developing countries but severely curtails their scope in favor of domestic enterprises. This, in turn, is more likely to deliver on developmental objectives, which underpin the success of any large private sector investment-based intervention in developing country economies and thereby to lead to a more sustainable regulatory bargain. In both Brazil and India, domestically-owned firms are taking the lead in power sector investments, which is a radical departure from the foreign-investment and operation based sector reform strategies these countries originally pursued.

What do the two very different cases of power sector reform and regulation attempts tell us? First, light regulatory approaches based on overseeing basically free markets are seldom desirable in infrastructure industries. Free markets always clear, but they do not deliver the desirable combinations of prices and supply, and they have important consequences for the overall economy if the industry being deregulated is systemically important. Electric power is one of the systemic industries in modern industrial economies. Stiglitz (2009) makes a similar point and elaborates it in the context of the global financial industry. Second, competition is a useful organizing principle for regulators seeking to promote gains in efficiency and welfare, but price competition in retail markets is possible in very few infrastructure sectors and where it is possible, it requires knowledgeable consumers and vigilant regulators. These inputs are often in scarce supply in developing countries and should not be taken for granted. Third, economic models are too simplistic to be relied upon to guide regulatory practice in the real world; a more useful approach would be to learn from experience and follow an incremental approach based on what has worked in the past. Similarly, practitioner driven experiments are important learning tools. Fourth, standard regulatory models yield expensive capital in developing countries. Fifth, partial privatization that enables comparison between public and private sector firms is valuable as a regulatory tool. Sixth, this leads to a nested approaches in which PSP is embedded into existing public sector structures in order to reduce risks, political and regulatory, for both consumers and investors.

These alternative models too have their limitations. They may remain vulnerable to public choice action by politicians. In Brazil, the political authorities might force the public sector generation firms to bid unreasonably low to obtain power projects, undermining the purpose of public-private competition. In India, unions may mobilize more strongly as more circles are franchised, and may block further franchises. Like the earlier privatization models, these too will undoubtedly be sensitive to economic growth as economic slowdowns will limit the ability and willingness undertake further financial reforms and low growth may dissuade investors.

References

Baer, W and G Montes-Rojas (2008). From privatization to what went wrong with privatizations in Argentina? *Oxford Development Studies*, 36(3), pp. 323–337.

Banks, J, D Bowman, TP Gross and J Guy (1998). The private sector: Cautiously interested in distribution in India. *The Electricity Journal*, June 21–28.

Bartram, J, K Lewis, R Lenton and A Wright (2005). Focusing on improved water and sanitation for health. *The Lancet*, 365(9461), pp. 810–812.

Bayliss, K and T McKinley (2007). Privatizing Basic Utilities in Sub Saharan Africa: The MDG Impact, UNDP Research Brief No. 3. January.

Birdsall, N and J Nellis (2005). Privatization reality check: Distributional effects in developing countries. In Privatization Reality Check: The Distributional Impact of Privatization in Developing Countries, N Birdsall and J Nellis (eds.), (Washington DC).

Brown, D (1980). *Electricity for Rural America: The Fight for REA*. Westport, CT: Greenwood Press.

Budds, J (2003). Are the debates on water privatization missing the point? Experiences from Africa, Asia and Latin America. *Environment and Urbanization*, 15(2), pp. 87–114.

Crew, M and P Kleindorfer (1987). *The Economics of Public Utility Regulation*. Cambridge, Massachusetts. MIT Press.

Dossani, R (2004). Reorganization of the power distribution sector in India. *Energy Policy*, 32(11), pp. 1277–1289.

Dubash, NK and D Narsimha Rao (2008). Regulatory practice and politics: Lessons from independent regulation in Indian electricity. *Utilities Policy*, 16, pp. 321–331.

Granovetter, M and P McGuire (1998). The making of an industry: Electricity in the United States. In *The Law of Markets*, Callon, M (ed.), 147–173. Oxford: Blackwell.

Hoff, K and J Stiglitz (2001). Modern economic theory and development in frontiers of economic development. In *Frontiers in Development Economics: The Future in Perspective*, Gerald MM and JE Stiglitz, (eds.), 389–459. World Bank.

Lobina, E and D Hall (2000). Public sector alternatives to water supply and sewerage privatization: Case studies. *International Journal of Water Resources Development*, 16(1), pp. 35–55.

Ministerio de Minas e Energia (2002). Comite de Revitalizacao do Modelo do Setor Eletrico, Relatorio de Progresso no. 2. Brasilia: MME.

Ministry of Power (2008). Annual Report. New Delhi: Government of India.

Parker, D and C Kirkpatrick (2005). Privatization in developing countries: A review of the evidence and the policy lessons. *Journal of Development Studies,* 41(4), pp. 513–541.

Power Finance Corporation Limited (2008). Report on the Performance of the State Power Utilities for the Years 2004–05 to 2006–07. Government of India, New Delhi.

Purkayashta, P (1995). The Enron caper. *Economic and Political Weekly,* 30(16), pp. 857–859.

Ramamurti, R (1992). Why are developing countries privatizing. *Journal of International Business Studies,* 23, pp. 225–249.

Rocha, K, F Camacho and G Braganca (2007). Return on capital of Brazilian electricity distributors: A comparative analysis. *Energy Policy,* 35(4), pp. 2526–2537.

Savas, E (2000). *Privatization and public-private partnerships.* New York: Chatham House Publishers/Seven Bridges Press.

Sharma, AK and E Vohra (2008). Foreign direct investment in the electricity sector: The Indian perspective. *The Electricity Journal,* 21(7), pp. 63–79.

Sharma, DP, PS Chandramohanan Nair and R Balasubramanian (2005). Performance of the Indian power sector during a decade under restructuring: A critique. *Energy Policy,* 33, pp. 563–576.

Singh, A (2006). Power sector reform in India: Current issues and prospects. *Energy Policy,* 34, pp. 2480–2490.

Savedoff, WD and PT Spiller (eds.) (1999). *Spilled Water: Institutional Commitment in the Provision of Water Services.* Washington, DC: Inter-American Development Bank.

Sirtaine, S, ME Pinglo, JL Guasch and V Foster (2005). How profitable are private infrastructure concessions in Latin America? Empirical evidence and regulatory implications. *Quarterly Review of Economics and Finance,* 45(2–3), pp. 380–402.

Stigler, G and C Friedland (1962). *What can regulators regulate — The case of electricity. Journal of Law and Economics,* 5.

Stiglitz, J (2009). Regulation and failure. In *New Perspectives on Regulation,* Moss D and J Cisternino (eds.). Cambridge, MA: The Tobin Project.

Tankha, S (2009). Lost in translation: Interpreting the failure of privatization in the Brazilian electric power industry. *Journal of Latin American Studies,* 41(1), 59–90.

Tankha, S (2010). Planning for power: Lessons from three generations of Brazilian electricity reforms. In *Reasserting the Public in Public Services: New Public Management Reforms,* Ramesh M, E Araral Jr. and X Wu (eds.), pp. 178–196. London: Routledge.

Tendler, J (1968). *Electric Power in Brazil: Entrepreneurship in the Public Sector.* Cambridge, MA: Harvard University Press.

Wells, LT Jr. and SG Eric (1995). Is foreign infrastructure investment still risky? *Harvard Business Review,* September-October, pp. 44–55.

CHAPTER 11

The Electricity Industry Reform in Korea: Lessons for Further Liberalization

Junki Kim and Kyuhyun Kim

Graduate School of Public Administration, Seoul National University

In January 1999, the Korean government announced a plan to split the generation unit of Korea Electric Power Corporation (KEPCO) into six subsidiaries with further plans for restructuring and privatization. Although privatization plan has been delayed indefinitely due to changes in the political environment, the originally planned was completed in 2001. This study analyzed how these generating units have performed since the restructuring using financial and operational indices. Although the restructuring had little impact on the prices of electricity, liability and profitability ratios were positively affected by the electricity sector reform. It was also found that the prices of fuels, government intervention, and the management capability were important variables affecting the performance of the sector. There are some important policy issues that need to be dealt with prior to further restructuring and privatization. In particular, policy-makers need to pay close attention to the declining reserve ratio, physical investments and maintenance costs. They also need to find right incentive schemes that encourage generators not only to save costs but also find environmentally sound investment plans.

1. Introduction

In the past decade, the electricity sector reform has speeded up and numerous reform programs have been implemented in various parts of the world. As of June 2006, 14 countries have completed electricity sector restructuring programs while 60 countries are undergoing some form of electricity sector reform programs (Sioshansi, 2006). Reform-minded nations often benchmarked earlier reform models to suit their own needs and circumstances and the electricity sector reform in Korea also proceeded in the context of global reform.

From 1961 until 2001, Korea's sole electricity power utility was Korea Electric Power Corporation (KEPCO). Set up as a state monopoly, 21% of its shares were sold to the public in 1989 while the rest were kept in the hands of the state. After the currency crisis in 1997, the Korean government devised a plan to reform the electricity sector to boost its efficiency. The plan was structured in three phases: the first step involves spinning off and privatizing the generation sector to create a competitive electricity market based on Cost-Based Pool (CBP). The second phase was restructuring and privatizing the distribution sector to induce a two-way bidding pool market. The third phase was opening the electricity market for free competition in all phases of the sector. Taking the British reform program into account, the generation unit of KEPCO was split into six subsidiary companies: Korea South-East Power (KOSEP), Korea Midland Power (KOMIPO), Korea Western Power (WP), Korea East-West Power (EWP), Korea Hydro & Nuclear Power (KHNP), and Korea Southern Power Co (KOSPO) in April 2001. This essentially meant that the remaining KEPCO unit was turned into a transmission and distribution monopoly.

But the plan to privatize generating units and the following restructuring and privatization of distribution sector was delayed indefinitely when President Roh came into power in 2003. The current market structure poses numerous problems. First, there exists imperfect competition among the generation companies as KEPCO owns generating units and it is in their best interests to maintain tight control over them. This also implies that competition among generating units are incomplete at best. Second, the system leaves opportunistic intervention by the state as it still owns KEPCO. It might be in their best interest to impose revenue maximization objective on KEPCO. Third, the current rate structure provides little incentive for generators to opt for environmentally sound generating plans. This is because fuel cost saving objective is stronger than other social obligations under the current system.

This study seeks to analyze the consequence of the current electricity system and thereby derive important policy implications for future course of institutional reform. This study also seeks to identify problems with the current market structure and is likely to find solutions at terms of market structure at various levels of electricity industry.

2. Backgrounds

In recent years, the objective of Korea's energy policy has shifted from ensuring a stable supply of energy to achieving sustainable development, largely due to rapidly changing internal and external conditions. In order to maintain high economic growth in the 1970s and 1980s, Korea's energy policy evolved around crude oil which was relatively cheap compared to other energy sources. However, the two rounds of oil crises in the 1970s and 1980s significantly influenced the national economy and new policies have been pursued since the 1980s. It called for diversifying energy sources and expanding energy infrastructures. The diversification plan called for increasing reliance on nuclear power as a major element of electricity production while rationalization plan was pursued in the coal industry to raise reliance on relatively inexpensive imported coal.

From the late 1990s, restructuring of the energy sector was pursued in full-scale with a policy goal of introducing competition in electricity and natural gas markets which were previously considered as natural monopolies. Furthermore, initiatives forwarded by the United Nations Framework Convention on Climate Change have strengthened environmental regulations. As a result, sustainable development has emerged as the focal point of Korea's energy policy.

Prior to the restructuring of the electricity industry, KEPCO enjoyed a monopoly status over power generation, transmission/distribution, and sales.[1] The government lifted entry barriers that virtually made it

---

[1] Information recomposed from www.kpx.co.kr.

impossible for independent power producer (IPPs) to operate in the market. In April 2001, the government allowed competition on the supply side in the current CBP market, while monopoly was maintained on the demand side. Given its current structure, the CBP market was competitive to the extent that, generators competed with each other. Moreover, since the Korean power system is maintained on a single national grid, there was no regional trading market where a single power trading market was required to coordinate and manage energy supply and demand across the whole country.

The current Korean electricity system is based on the CBP concept since the market price reflects the actual generation cost. Under the pool system, all generators are obliged to submit the details of their production costs which are independently checked and approved by the Generation Cost Assessment Committee (GCAC). Using this information, Korea Power Exchange (KPX) prepares a Price Setting Schedule and calculates the marginal price (SMP) based on the principle of minimizing the system variable cost. The market price is composed of the system marginal price (SMP) and capacity payment (CP). Capacity payment is the price paid to a generating unit that has declared its availability during the day. Price cap is imposed on the energy price of base load generating units such as coal and nuclear energy. SMP is determined as the most expensive generation available for the trading period in the Price Setting Schedule. After real-time dispatching, settlement for the energy produced takes place based on the market price:

$$\text{Settlement} = \text{Output} \times \text{SMP} + \text{Capacity} \times \text{CP} + \text{Other Payments}$$

3. Theoretical Framework

There are several studies that examine the results of electricity sector reform. Pollitt (1997) categorizes empirical studies on electricity sector reform into four groups: 1) ones that use financial and physical indicators; 2) ones that look at labor productivity measures or total factor productivity (TFP); 3) ones that use frontier methodologies; and 4) ones that are based on social cost benefit analysis of electricity privatization.

The first method is the simplest approach. Yarrow (1992) develops a counterfactual scenario which assumes that the British electricity sector had not been privatized and compares that with those of the actual results. Branston (2000) further improves the model and conducts counterfactual price analysis on the British electricity privatization case. The result is that the reform had minimal impact on prices. Duncan and Bollard (1992) analyze the impact of the reform of the government control of Electricity Corporation of New Zealand. Rocha *et al.* (2007) analyze the financial return on capital of Brazilian electricity distributors, and he concluded that the return on equity in Brazil was systematically negative until 2003.

In the second category, Bishop and Thompson (1992) analyze changes in the labor or TFP growth rates as a result of the 1983 Energy Act which sought to introduce limited competition into the electricity generation industry. Haskel and Syzmanski (1992) examine the impact of the implementation of divisional management structure in the UK in 1983. Plane (1999) estimates the TFP of Côte d'Ivoire Electricity Company (CIE) and finds that productive efficiency improved due to privatization.

The third category uses cross-sectional data to examine the comparative performance of privatized firms with that of state-owned firms. For instance, Hawdon (1996), using cross-sectional data for developing countries, finds that privatized firms performed better than state-owned electricity firms in terms of productivity efficiency. Berg and Jeong (1991) analyze the effects of the introduction of incentive regulation in the US and suggest that relative inefficiency was not reduced by the incentive regulation focused on plant utilization and thermal efficiency. Cullmann and Hirshhausen (2008) provide a cross-country efficiency analysis of electricity distribution companies in the East European transition countries of Poland, the Czech Republic, Slovakia, and Hungary. The results suggest that privatization had a positive effect on technical efficiency in the four countries that were examined.

The fourth method measures the impact of privatization on the society as a whole. Jones *et al.* (1990) outline the methodology, and Galal *et al.* (1994) apply it to 12 privatization cases. Newbery and Pollitt (1997) also apply the methodology to the privatization case of Britain's CEGB. In addition, Oliveira *et al.* (2004) measure the gains and losses of the shareholders, board members, fuel suppliers, consultants, equipment suppliers, service-providers, consumers, government, and regulators created by the British ESI regulatory system. They conclude that the reform is overall beneficial although the result is different among different stakeholders. Toda (2007) measures the welfare impacts of the electricity generation sector reform in the Philippines. The author finds that consumers and investors were net gainers, while the government lost due to decline in revenues. In addition, the author finds that pollution worsened after the ownership change.

In contrast to previous studies, this study examines the impact of the restructuring program by utilizing various financial data. In particular, we analyze financial and physical performance of the generation sector.[2]

3.1. *The Analysis of Financial Statements*[3]

Financial statements are the starting point of our analysis. Financial reports often contain information on income, cash flows, and assets and liabilities as well as supplementary data that, although not included in the statements themselves, enable users to interpret the financial status of the organization in question or to make adjustment of corporate performance (such as financial ratios) to make them more comparable, consistent over time, and more representative of the economic reality.

3.1.1. *The Analysis of Liability*

A firm's debt level is crucial to its long-run viability and growth. A firm can incur obligations in various ways; some of them are the results of the firm's operating activities while others result from its financing decisions. The former are characterized by exchange of goods and services for the later payment of cash (or vice versa), whereas debts arising from financial decisions generally involve current receipts of cash in exchange for later payments of cash. Both forms of debts are generally reported on the balance sheet.

---

[2] A social cost benefit analysis tends to better evaluate the overall aspects of the performance; however, it is hard to apply this to partial electricity industry reform cases. And the analysis of labor productivity is not adequate in this case because labor productivity is often affected by the total number of labor as employees in KEPCO are transferred to the generation companies.

[3] Recomposition of White *et al.* (2003).

Liability can be estimated by the current ratio[4] and the debt ratio.[5] Lenders and creditors assess the ability of a firm to meet its current obligations. That ability depends on the cash resources available as per the balance sheet date and the cash to be generated through the operating cycle of the firm. Current ratio compares the levels of cash resources with current liabilities as the measure of cash obligation. Long-term debt and solvency analysis evaluates the level of risk borne by a firm, changes over time, and risk relative to comparable investments. A higher proportion of debt relative to equity increases the riskiness of the firm.

The ideal current ratio is said to be above 200%. If KHNP is excluded in our data (KHNP has a different scale from the other generation companies), the current ratios range from 31% to 112% (See Figure 1).

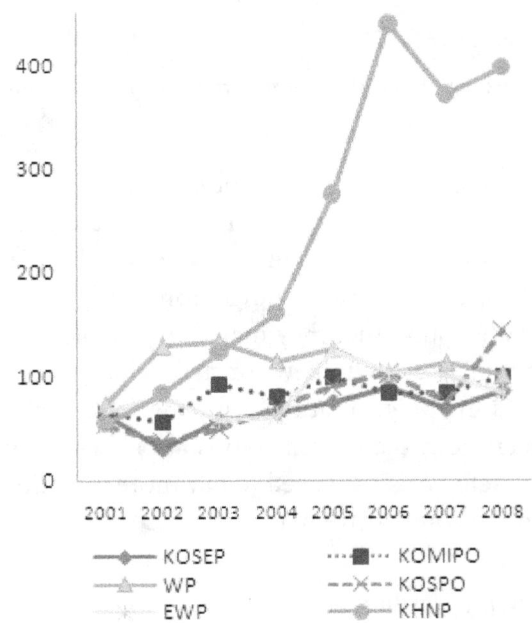

Figure 1: Current ratios of the generation companies (Unit: %)

[4] Current Ratio = Current Assets/Current Liabilities.

[5] Debt Ratio = Total Debt/Total Equity.

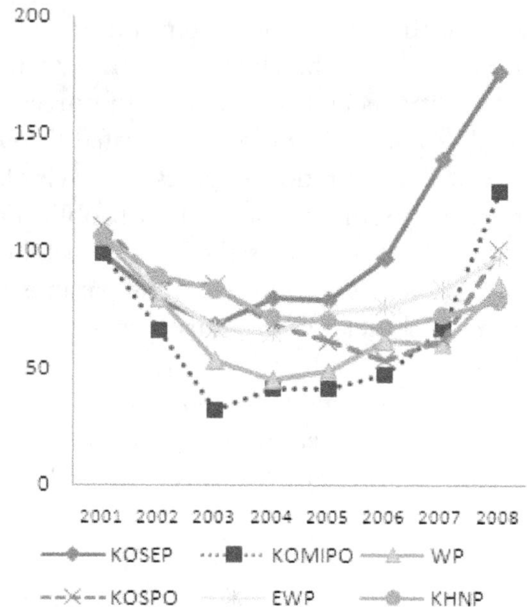

Figure 2: Debt ratios of the generation companies (Unit: %)

Although the ratios are lower than the industry standard, it does not mean that the companies are at a risk since they receive a stable cash revenue from KEPCO in the current system. Meanwhile the ideal debt ratio is under 100%. The actual debt ratios range from 32% to 139% (See Figure 2 and Table 5). It was found that they maintain a stable debt level although the ratios are on the rise due to new constructions of power plants.

The liabilities of the generation companies are well managed under the current system. But the current ratios are likely to improve with the future structural reform as they need to pay more attention to their financial structure in the competitive markets.

3.1.2. *The Analysis of Profitability*

Equity investors are concerned with the firm's ability to generate, sustain, and increase profits. Profitability can be measured in several different ways. First, the return on investment (ROI) measures profits to the investment required to generate them. ROI measures the relationship between profits and investment required to generate them. The ratio on profits to sale residual returns to the firm per sales dollar.

The return on assets (ROA)[6] compares income with total assets. It can be interpreted in two ways. First, it measures management's ability and efficiency in using the firm's assets to generate profits. Second, it reports the total return accruing to all providers of capital, independent of the source of capital. The return on total stockholders' equity (ROE)[7] excludes debt in the denominator and uses either pretax income (after interest costs) or net income. Both ROA and ROE reflect the firm's capital structure. Creditors and shareholders provide the capital needed by the firm to acquire the assets used in the business. In return, they receive their share of the firm's profits. ROA measure returns to all providers of capital. ROE measures returns to the firm's shareholder and is calculated after deducting the returns paid to creditors (interest). The equity shareholder can earn higher returns by "leveraging" the investment provided by the debt holders as long as the returns earned by the company's assets (ROA) are greater than the cost of debt. Operating margin[8] is the relationship between the firm's costs and its sales. The ability to control costs in relation to revenues enhances earnings power.

In actual analysis, we found that ROAs are usually lower than those of other industries. The average ROA of the generation companies ranges between 3% to 7%, and the average for the last 3 years near 4% (See Figure 3 and Table 6). It is extraordinary to find their ROAs under 5%. It is expected their ROAs will improve due to increased depreciation in the future.

ROE is an important summary measure of a firm's profitability and the return on investment. It captures many facets of a firm's operating, investment, and financing characteristics. Given its importance, it is worthwhile to ask whether current ROE can be used to forecast future ROE levels. A related question is whether abnormally high-levels of profitability can be expected to continue into the future. Penman (1991) provides some insight into these questions: (i) in the short-term,

---

[6] ROA = Net Income/Average Total Assets.

[7] ROE = Net Income/Average Stockholders' Equity.

[8] Operating Margin = Operating Profit/Sales.

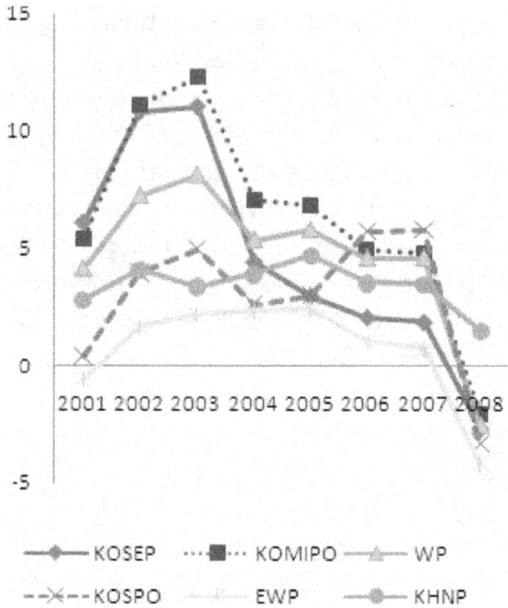

Figure 3: ROAs of the generation companies (Unit: %)

approximately five years (except for extreme portfolios), current levels of ROE persist into the future; (ii) over the long-term, ROEs tend to revert towards an average "economy-wide" ROE; (iii) although there is a trend towards the mean, the portfolio rankings persist. That is, the portfolios with higher (lower) ROE tend to have higher (lower) ROEs in the future.

We found that the ROEs of the generation companies move in similar patterns as shown in Figure 4. ROEs varied much during five years, and it shows a steady upward movement recently. But the ROEs of EWP and KOSEP are even lower than the base rates. These firms need to improve their efficiency for future course of action.

The operating margin is an index that shows the profitability of operating capital. The operating margins of 5 companies using fossil fuels sharply decreased in 2004 due to the electricity price decrease (see Figure 5). The reason for the sudden fall in price was that the operating profits of the electricity companies were deemed too high in 2003

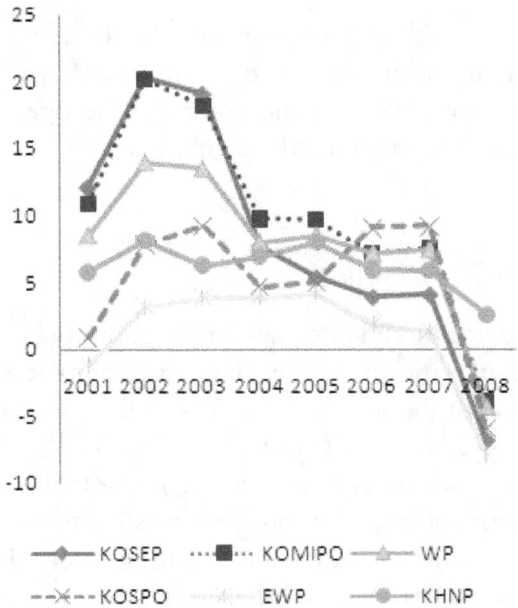

Figure 4: ROEs of the generation companies (Unit: %)

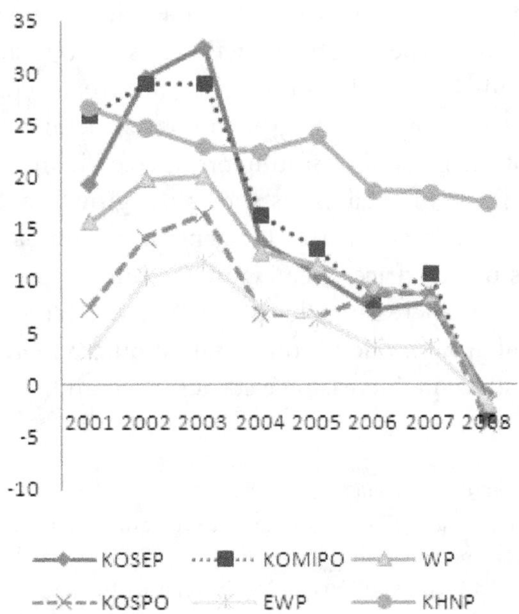

Figure 5: Operating margins of the generation companies (Unit: %)

and the government decided to lower the price. In terms of overall trend, the operating margins are decreasing continuously with the increasing price of fuels since 2004. On the contrary, the operation margin of KHNP has remained consistently high as the price of uranium was kept low.

3.1.3. *The Analysis of Growth*

The analysis provides useful information about future income, sales, costs, and profit. Growth ratio shows the company's ability to remain competitive in the market or the sustainability. The indices often used include the growth rate of sales,[9] operating profit,[10] net income,[11] and the assets.[12]

The Growth rate of sales is also an important index to assess a company's growth potential. It is possible to estimate the investment, efficiency, and competency of the company with the index. It was found that the growth rates of sales decreased sharply in 2003 (see Figure 6). And the rates are fluctuating with the addition of new power plants. In addition, the growth rate of operating profit needs to be carefully interpreted for electricity companies in Korea because the price of electricity is determined by the government. The growth rates of operating profit have negative values in 2004 (see Figure 7). The rates are dependent on changes in fuel and electricity prices. The growth rates of net income moved similarly to those of the rates of operating profit (see Figure 8).

The growth rate of total assets shows the growth of the investment. The growth rates of total assets of the generation companies are dependent on changes in fuel prices (see Figure 9). But the growth rate of total assets of KOSEP is increasing sharply since the addition of new power plants. The total growth rate of total assets should remain consistent as it needs to respond to the increasing electricity demand.

---

[9] Growth Rate of Sales = (Current Sales–Last year's Sales)/Last year's Sales.

[10] Growth Rate of Operating Profit = (Current Operating Profit-Last year's Operating Profit)/Last year's Operating Profit.

[11] Growth Rate of Net Income = (Current Net Income-Last year's Net Income)/Last year's Net Income.

[12] Growth Rate of Assets = (Current Assets-Last year's Assets)/Last year's Assets.

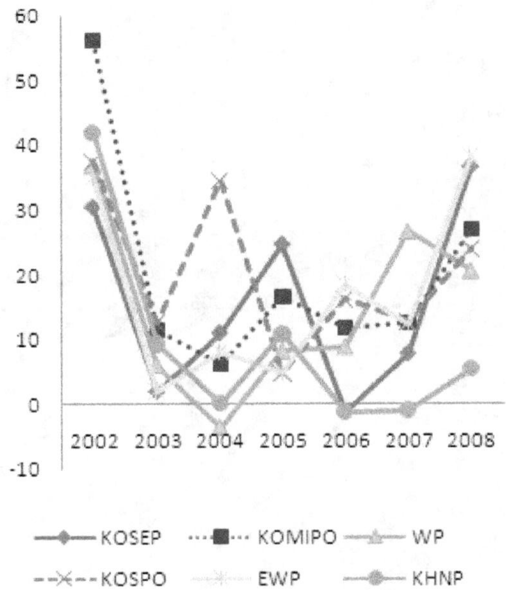

Figure 6: Growth rates of sales of the generation company (Unit: %)

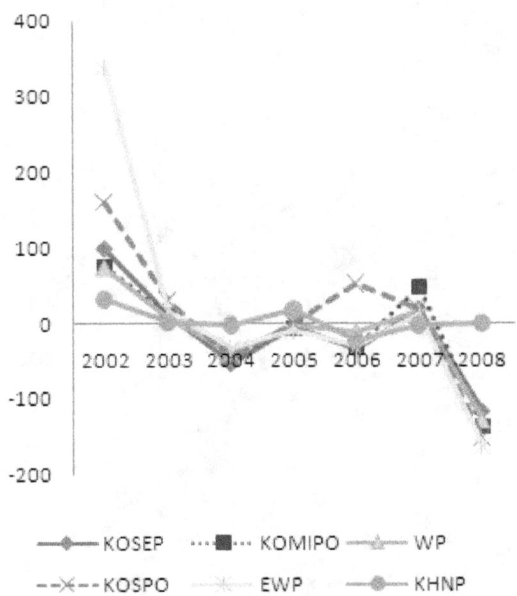

Figure 7: Growth rates of operating profit of the generation company (Unit: %)

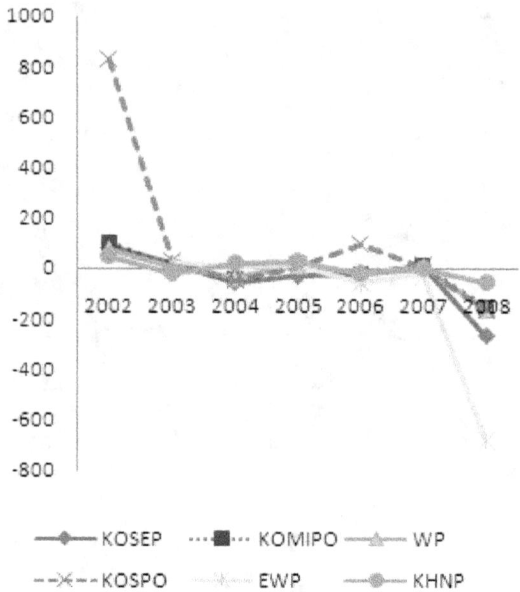

Figure 8: Growth rates of net income of the generation company (Unit: %)

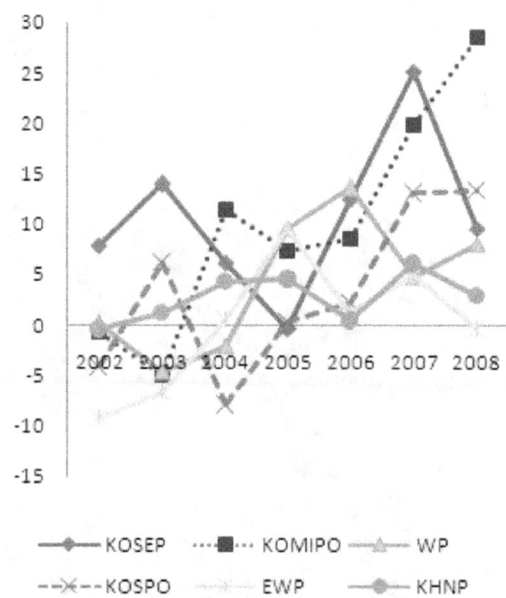

Figure 9: Growth rates of total assets of the generation company (Unit: %)

In summary, the price of fuels and the price of electricity had significant impact on the generation companies. Increases in fuel prices put downward pressure on operating incomes of generators while government influenced the generation companies' profit by setting the price of electricity. But the effects were different for different companies as their mix of generating capacity and operating strategies were different.

3.2. *The Regression Analysis*

We conducted regression analysis. The dependent variables that are included are prices and financial indicators. Independent variables are also taken from earlier studies and a dummy variable which is 1 for periods after the reform of electricity sector and 0 for period before it.

In terms of previous studies, Yarrow (1992) conducted a price analysis to examine the performance of the British electricity privatization. Branston (2000) renewed the methodology and executed a counterfactual price analysis of British electricity privatization. Branston's approach is similar to that of Yarrow's where the cost of electricity has been split into the three components shown in Eq. (1):

$$P_t = F_t + N_t + \Pi_t \tag{1}$$

where P_t is the relevant price (per kWh) of electricity in the year t; F_t the 'fossil fuel costs' per unit (kWh) of electricity sold in the year t; and N_t comprises 'non-fossil fuel costs' (per kWh) in the year t; and Π_t the 'profits' (per kWh) in the year t. This model is suitable for the examination of the Korean electricity reform since the proportion of nuclear generation is high in Korea and implicit profit regulation is imposed upon KEPCO. As a result, there use three independent variables including F_t, N_t, and Π_t.

Equation (1) uses the weighted unit cost of coal, gas, and oil generated electricity to calculate an estimate of the cost of fossil fuels per unit of electricity generated. However, Eq. (1) does not take the electricity generated from other non-fossil fuel sources such as nuclear or hydro into account. Equation (2) fully incorporates such limitations:

$$FF_t = (X_t \times C_t) + (Y_t + G_t) + \ (Z_t + O_t) \tag{2}$$

where FF_t is the fossil fuel costs per unit (kWh) of electricity sold in the year t; X_t the proportion of electricity sold in the year t generated using coal; C_t the unit (per kWh) fuel cost of coal generated electricity in the year t; Y_t the proportion of electricity sold in the year t generated using gas; G_t the unit (per kWh) fuel cost of gas generated electricity in the year t; Z_t the proportion of electricity sold in the year t generated using oil; and O_t is the unit (per kWh) fuel cost of electricity generated using oil in the year t.

To calculate the unit fuel cost of electricity generated from different fossil fuels, the formula Yarrow and Branston used can be applied to each of the fuel:

$$I_{it} = \frac{P_{it} \times Q_{it}}{QE_{it}}$$

where I_{it} is the unit fuel cost of electricity generated using fossil fuel i in the year t; P_{it} the unit price of fuel i in the year t; Q_{it} the quantity of the fuel i used in the year t; and QE_{it} is the quantity of electricity generated using fuel i in the year t. Equation (4) is then used to calculate the costs of the fossil fuels per unit of the electricity sold and not just the costs of the fossils fuels per unit of electricity generated by those fossil fuels, as was carried out in Eq. (2):

$$F_t = \frac{FF_t \times QEF_t}{QET_t}$$

where F_t is the fossil costs per unit (kWh) of electricity sold in the year t; FF_t the fossil costs per unit (kWh) of electricity sold in the year t which was generated using fossil fuels; QEF_t the number of units of electricity (kWh) sold in the year t which was generated using fossil fuels; and QET_t is the number of units of electricity (kWh) sold in the year t.

Although we do not conduct counterfactual analysis, these equations are useful for converting data. Without these conversion procedures, the fuel cost factor is likely be overestimated.

To analyze the impact of the electricity restructuring on the efficiency of electricity industry, several indices are used in this analysis. In the model I, the price of electricity is used as the dependent variable and the

Table 1: The regression result of model I

Dependent variable	β	t value	p-value	R^2	Adj-R^2	F Value	Pr > F
Price of electricity	−0.44389	−0.41	0.6955	0.7298	0.5947	5.4	0.0385

Note: The independent variables are price of fossil fuel, price of non-fossil fuel, profit, and electricity restructuring. β is the estimated coefficient of the dummy variable, electricity restructuring. The independent variables are standardized.

independent variables include the price of fossil fuel, the price of non-fossil fuel, the profit of KEPCO, and the electricity reform. The last independent variable is a dummy variable that reveals the impact of electricity restructuring. All units of the data are US cent/kWh and the period of our analysis is from 1997 to 2006.

In model II, the financial indices are used as a dependent variable, and the independent variables include the price of fossil fuel, price of non-fossil fuel, and electricity restructuring. The financial indices are calculated from consolidated financial statements of KEPCO which contains financial information about generation companies. We analyze the data for a period from 1997 to 2006.

In model III, the price of electricity is added to the independent variables of model II, and the dependent variables are the same. The price of electricity affects the financial indices since it influences the profits of these companies. The price of electricity needs to be controlled, because it is determined by the government. This model detects the impact of the restructuring excluding the effect from the electricity price changes.

The result from model I shows that electricity sector reform did not have a significant impact on the price of electricity. This can be interpreted in two ways. One possible explanation is that the price regulation set by the government limited the impact of the electricity sector reform and the other is that the price could already be at an optimal level.

The results of model II are slightly different. The current ratio shows a sign of positive impact from the restructuring. It shows that the current ratio has increased since the restructuring. And the debt ratio has had a

Table 2: The regression results of model II

Dependent variable	β	t value	p-value	R^2	Adj-R^2	F Value	Pr > F
CR[a]***	17.4158	5.1	0.0014	0.9754	0.9684	138.73	<.0001
DR[b]*	−44.4345	−2.27	0.0576	0.5907	0.4738	5.05	0.0439
ROA**	1.36965	2.69	0.031	0.5396	0.408	4.1	0.0662
ROE	1.96893	1.84	0.1085	0.3296	0.1381	1.72	0.2467
OM[c]***	5.99062	5.08	0.0014	0.8516	0.8092	20.09	0.0013
GRS[d]**	−6.52656	−2.64	0.0333	0.5572	0.4307	4.4	0.0578
GROP[e]	−7.3385	−0.86	0.4186	0.6811	0.59	7.48	0.0183
GRNI[f]	1.22026	0.04	0.9709	0.1913	−0.0398	0.83	0.4756
GRTA[g]*	−14.5186	−1.93	0.0951	0.3955	0.2228	2.29	0.1717

Note: The independent variables are price of fossil fuel, price of non-fossil fuel, and electricity restructuring. β is the estimated coefficient of the dummy variable, electricity restructuring. The independent variables are standardized.

Significance Levels: * $p < 0.1$, ** $p < 0.05$, *** $p < 0.01$.

[a] Current Ratio. [b] Debt Ratio. [c] Operating Margin. [d] Growth Rate of Sales. [e] Growth Rate of Operating Profit. [f] Growth Rate of Net Income. [g] Growth Rate of Total Asset.

Table 3: The results of model III

Dependent variable	β	t value	p-value	R^2	Adj-R^2	F Value	Pr > F
CR[a]***	16.98836	4.42	0.0045	0.9759	0.9639	81.01	<.0001
DR[b]	−34.2606	−1.92	0.1027	0.7382	0.6073	5.64	0.0352
ROA*	1.10798	2.38	0.0545	0.7023	0.5534	4.72	0.0508
ROE	1.40793	1.45	0.196	0.5756	0.3634	2.71	0.1378
OM[c]***	5.88485	4.42	0.0045	0.8532	0.7799	11.63	0.0065
GRS[d]*	−5.96425	−2.2	0.0699	0.5878	0.3817	2.85	0.1271
GROP[e]	−5.36653	−0.57	0.587	0.7039	0.5558	4.75	0.0501
GRNI[f]	−8.19882	−0.24	0.8205	0.283	−0.0754	0.79	0.5423
GRTA[g]	−11.7551	−1.52	0.1799	0.5044	0.2566	2.04	0.2105

Note: The independent variables are price of fossil fuel, price of non-fossil fuel, price of electricity, and electricity restructuring. β is the estimated coefficient of the dummy variable, electricity restructuring. The independent variables are standardized.

Significance Levels: * $p < 0.1$, ** $p < 0.05$, *** $p < 0.01$.

[a]Current Ratio. [b]Debt Ratio. [c]Operating Margin. [d]Growth Rate of Sales. [e]Growth Rate of Operating Profit. [f]Growth Rate of Net Income. [g]Growth Rate of Total Asset.

positive impact too. The debt ratio has decreased since the electricity reform. The index of liability has improved. It seems that KEPCO tried to enhance its liability, preparing for further liberalization.

The indices of profitability also have positive values. ROA and operating profit have significant results while ROE remains insignificant. The ROA and operating profit increased sharply after the restructuring (see Figure 12), but the ratios decreased due to the price increase of fuel since 2004. If the effect of price increase is eliminated, the impact of electricity reform is positive in terms of profitability. This implies that the restructuring brought about some positive impact on the efficiency of the companies' operation.

The growth rate of sales and total assets are the significant indices among growth indices. Growth rate of sales of electricity is affected by the economic growth, so the result does not have substantial meaning in this study. Also, the growth rate of total assets has a negative impact of the restructuring. It means the reform of electricity industry gave a negative impact on the investment.

The results of model III also have some significant outcomes. Although the debt ratio is no more significant, the liability of the company is still improved. Means at the reform still positively affected the liability of the company when the effect from the price changes of electricity is excluded.

The ROA is still significant at the 90% significance level, and the operating margin is significant at 99% significance level. The ROA's significance level is decreased, because the increases of electricity price can explain the changes of profit. However, the restructuring still has a positive effect on the profitability of the company. The indices of growth are insignificant except the growth rate of sales. But it is also not easy to concluded the reform has not affected the indices of growth. The indices of growth should be monitored continuously.

In conclusion, the reform of electricity did not benefit consumers since price is tightly controlled by the government but it impacted generating companies in several financial dimensions. Although the liability indices worsened due to increasing uncertainty surrounding operating enivornment, profitability measures were improved by the restructuring.

4. Implications for Regulatory Design, Effectiveness and Operation

4.1. *Imperfect Competition among the Generation companies*

KEPCO was split into six generation companies including KNHP and they produce 95% of electricity in Korea (see Table 16). They are competing with each other in an oligopoly market structure with KEPCO playing an important coordinating function. The low-level of competition and government intervention are causing inefficiencies in generating companies. Also, there are some indications that they are collaborating with each other since the current reserve margin is too low. If the reserve margin is too low, an oligopoly company can use oligopoly power more easily. Almost all countries that went through successful electricity reform had a reserve margin above 20% but current reserve margin of electricity in Korea is only 7.2% (Toda, 2005).

However, it is also hard to compare the current margins to because, the earlier ones the scale of electricity capacity is different. Maintaining 20% of reserve margin will require additional capacity investments in the current electricity market. At this stage, it seems that we need to study about the adequate reserve margin required in the system more carefully.

4.2. *The Cross-subsidization Among Users*

Regional Electricity Company is the one that has the privilege of supplying more than 70% of the regional electricity demand. The current pricing structure of electricity in Korea is based on a cumulative system where the maximum rate is 11 times higher than the minimum rate which causes severe cross subsidization among users. In this case, if a regional electricity company buys electricity at low price and sells the electricity at a high price, then other regional consumers are at a disadvantage (see Figure 10).

4.3. *Restructuring and Regulatory Deign*

There exist regulatory and operating uncertainties that are associated with incomplete restructuring. The current regulatory structure is based on the assumption that the electricity industry as a whole will be turned into a

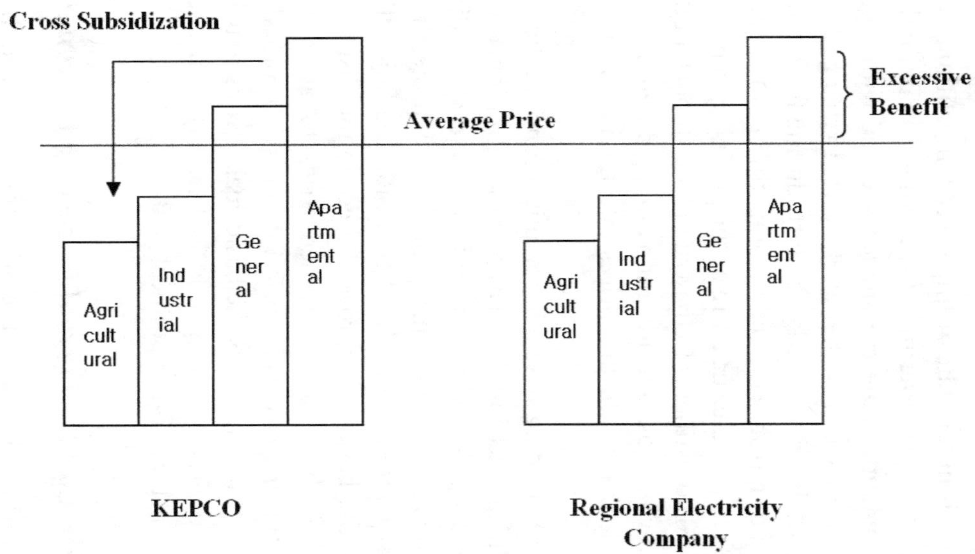

Figure 10: Cross subsidization under a regional electricity company

Note: Regional electricity companies usually supply the electricity only to general and apartment.

British model of competitive and a deregulated system. However, the current industry structure neither enjoys the advantages associated with vertical integration nor the advantages of the competitive system.

As the restructuring of the distribution sector is being delayed, the benefits of a two-way bidding system are not being fully realized. In other words, the electricity market is not smoothly working by the law of demand and supply but is in the state of imperfect competition.

The improvements that the government is seeking to make in the electricity market should include some measures associated with regulating the downstream industries. Recently, the Korea Power Exchange is making an effort to improve the electricity market by introducing further deregulatory measures aimed at introducing more competition in the generator level as well as changes in the rate structure of the pricing system. In addition to making technical adjustments to the system, it is important that the current policies of allowing cross-subsidization among different users and not fully incorporating changes in fuel prices into the rate structure are created.

Even more, KEPCO's pricing system is not quite economically rational as it is affected by political decisions, such as price stabilization, economic growth, or protecting low-income bracket, and allows cross subsidization. Of course, price stabilization, economic growth, and protecting low-income bracket are very important political goals. But the rationalization of electricity price is the basis to improve the economic distortions in whole energy market. While the government tries to achieve many national goals by controlling electricity price, it is easy to miss the efficiency of the electric industry, which is the basic goal of restructuring. To achieve the purpose of the restructuring, it is the best way to promote the most suitable means to achieve other political goals.

4.4. *Conflict between Cost Saving and Preserving Environment*

To save fuel costs and ultimately reduce the price of electricity in the long-term, the regulators need to expand the base load generators. Base load generation includes units that generate electricity from coal and nuclear energy sources. The cost of base load tends to be much lower than that of other generating units, and the price of current pricing system reflects which generator has generated the last unit of electricity critically. In essence, the proportion of base load to the total supply is the key factor of the electricity reform. Because the scale of the investment required for the construction of base load units tends to be substantially large, the regulators are often required to promise a more structured incentive to potential investors.

However, this needs to be balanced by the environmental factors as base load units including coal- and oil-powered stations tend to harm the environment seriously. In addition, nations are required to reduce emission of greenhouse gases from 2008 as stated in the Kyoto Protocol. This implies that both cost saving and environmental considerations need to be taken into account when making both short- and long-term investment plans. Because of the time lag in building power stations, the current level of base load production is difficult to change in the short-term. Investing in alternative energy sources in the long-term is a must for the sustainable growth of the nation. The cost of alternative energy is high at this point, but it is likely to decrease as the technologies evolve.

5. Conclusions

This study analyzed the overall impact of the electricity reform in Korea and reviewed the current issues in the electricity sector in Korea. The analysis of financial ratios found that the price of fuels and the price of electricity affected the performance of generation companies. It is difficult to expect the operation of generators to improve dramatically with a partial reform because opportunistic governmental intervention prevents the electricity market from fully realizing deregulatory and structural adjustments made. Moreover, we found that the restructuring program had different a impact on generating companies. Depending on the competency of the management, companies have responded differently to the reform program.

The analysis of the impact of the electricity reform generally showed positive results. Although the price of electricity has not fallen significantly, the liability and profitability indices showed positive changes. It appears that the intervention of government reduced the effect of restructuring on the price of electricity. The indices of profitability (especially

ROA and operating margin) have shown positive signs. More specifically, ROA (increased 1.1% in model III) and operating margin (increased 5.9% in model III) improved after the restructuring. We have also found that generating companies were successful in reducing their operating cost.

In addition, we found that the growth potential of the industry as a whole was declined, although it is hard to interpret that the effect is substantial since the data has an outlier. Also, the decrease in the growth rate of assets implies the decrease in investments. If the investment shrinks continuously, the reduced effect of depreciation cost will, in turn, increase the short-term profit. This may have caused the improvement in profitability measures. A continuous fall in investments is likely to have a detrimental effect on the industry in the long-run which in turn, may require regulatory intervention or changes in the rate structure so that generators make rational investment schemes.

For further liberalization, there are several problems in the electricity market in Korea. The current electricity market in Korea is an oligopoly with a single buyer. There are numerous possibilities that the market structure could cause critical problems in future. For instance, the generation companies can use their oligopoly power because the electricity reserve margin is currently quite low. It is quite hard to decide which reserve margin is optimal for the future but it certainly merits further studies. In addition, the regional electricity company is causing numerous problems under the distorted pricing system. The cumulative pricing system enables policy-makers to cross subsidize each other, causing severe misallocation of resources. These problems can only be solved by the institutional level changes.

There are problems which are derived from the unfinished business of restructuring. As the introduction of competition in power distribution is being delayed, the deregulatory and structural adjustment made in the power generation sector is being offset by distortions in other sectors. In addition, we need more discussions on the optimal level of base loads and the future course of action since there are trade-offs involved in terms of cost saving and future environmental costs. We need to be smart about designing incentive for future investment in generating units as it has future implications not only on costs but also on environmental issues.

References

Bacon, RW, and J Besant-Jones (2001). Global electric power reform, privatization, and liberalization of the electronic power industry in developing countries. *Annu. Rev, Energy Environ*, 26, pp. 331–59.

Berg, S and J Jeong (1991). An evaluation of incentive regulation for electric utilities. *Journal of Regulatory Economics*, 3(1), pp. 45–55.

Bishop, M and D Thompson (1992). Regulatory reform and productivity growth in the UK's public utilities. *Applied Economics*, 24(11), pp. 1181–1190.

Branston, JR (1999). The Price of Independents: An Analysis of the Independent Power Sector in England and Wales, Mimeo. L'institute, The University of Birmingham.

Branston, JR (2000). A counterfactual price analysis of British electricity privatisation. *Utilities Policy*, 9, pp. 31–46.

Bunn, D and K Vlahos (1989). Evaluation of the long-term effects on electricity prices following privatisation. *Fiscal Studies*, 10(4), pp. 104–116.

Bunn, DW (1993). Evaluating the effects if privatizing electricity. *Journal of the Operational Research Society*, 45(1), pp. 367–375.

Burns, P and T Weyman-Jones (1994). Productive Efficiency and the Regulatory Review of Regional Electricity Companies in the UK, Regulatory Policy Research Centre, Discussion Paper No. 1.

Comnes, GA, EP Kahn and TN Belden (1996). The performance of the US market for independent electricity generation, *The Energy Journal*, 17(3), pp. 23–39.

Cullmann A and C Hirshhausen (2008). Efficiency analysis of east European electricity distribution in transition: Legacy of the Past?, *J Prod Anal*, 29, pp. 155–167.

Duncan, I and A Bollard (1992). *Corporatisation and Privatisation: Lessons from New Zealand*. Auckland: Oxford University Press.

Galal A, L Jones, P Tandon and I Vogelsang (1994). *Welfare Consequences of Selling Public Enterprises — An Empirical Analysis*. Oxford: Oxford University Press.

Haskel, J and A Sanchis (1995). Privatisation and X-inefficiency: A bargaining approach. *Journal of Industrial Economics*, 43(3), pp. 301–321.

Haskel, J and S Szymanski (1992). The Effects of Privatisation, Restructuring and Competition on Productivity Growth in the UK Public Corporations, *Working Paper No. 286*, Queen Mary and Westfield Department of Economics.

Hawdon, D (1996). Performance of Power Sectors in Developing Countries — A Study of Efficiency and World Bank Policy using Data Envelopment Analysis, *Discussion Paper, No. 88*. Surrey Energy Economics Centre

Hewlett, JG (1996). Economic and regulatory factors affecting the maintenance of nuclear power plants. *The Energy Journal*, 17(4), pp. 1–31.

Hope, E, L Rud and B Singh (1993). Market for Electricity: Economic Reform of the Norwegian Electricity Industry, *Working Paper No. 12* SNF, Oslo.

Hunt, L (2003). *Energy in a Competitive Market*. Edward Elgar.

Jones, LP (1994). Appropriate Regulatory Technology: The Interplay of Economic and Institutional Conditions. *Proceedings of the World Bank Annual Conference on*

Development Economics, 1993: Supplement to The World Bank Economic Review and The World Bank Research Observer. Washington, D.C.: World Bank, 1994, pp. 181–204.

Jones, LP, P Tandon and I Vogelsang (1990). *Selling Public Enterprise. A Cost-Benefit Methodology.* Cambridge, Mass.: MIT Press.

Kirshen, DS, G Strbac (2004). *Fundamentals of Power System Economics.* Wiley.

Murray, B (1998). *Electricity Markets.* John Wiley & Sons.

Newbery, DMG and MG Pollitt (1997). The restructuring and privatisation of Britain's CEGB — Was it worth it? *Journal of Industrial Economics,* 45(3), pp. 269–303.

Plane, P (1999). Privatization, technical efficiency and welfare consequences: The case of the Côte d'Ivoire Electricity Company(CIE). *World Development,* 27(2), pp. 343–360.

Pollitt, MG (1995). *Ownership and Performance in Electric Utilities.* Oxford: Oxford Institute for Energy Studies/ Oxford University Press.

Pollitt, MG (1997). The impact of liberalisation on the performance of the electricity supply industry: An international survey. *The Journal of Energy Literature,* III (2).

Prandini, A (2007). Good, BETTA, best? The role of industry structure in electricity reform in Scotland. *Energy Policy,* 35, pp. 1628–1642.

Rocha, K and F Camacho, G Bragaça (2007). Return on capital of Brazilian electricity distributors: A comparative analysis. *Energy Policy,* 35, pp. 2526–2537.

Rothwell, G and T Gomez (2003). *Electricity Economics-Regulation and Deregulation.* Wiley-Interscience.

Sioshansi, FR and W Pfaffenberger (2006). *Electricity Market Reform — An International Perspective.* Elsevier.

Stickney, CP, PR Brown and JM Wahlen (2004). *Financial Reporting and Statement Analysis* — A Strategic Perspective. Thomson.

Thomas, S (1996a). The privatization of the electricity supply industry. In *The British Electricity Experiment. Privatization: The Record, The Issues, The Lessons,* Surrey, J (ed.), pp. 40–66. London: Earthscan.

Thomas, S (1996b). The development of competition. In *The British Electricity Experiment. Privatization: The Record, The Issues, The Lessons,* Surrey, J (ed.), pp. 67–94. London, Earthscan.

Toda, N (2005). Development of Japanese Model in the Liberalization of Electricity Market. at paper presented International Conference of KDI for Electricity Restructuring, June 20–21.

Toda, N (2007). Welfare impacts of electricity generation sector reform in the Philippines. *Energy Policy,* 35, pp. 6145–6162.

Warkentin, D (1998). *Electric Power Industry — In Nontechnical Language.* PennWell.

White, GI, AC Sondhi and D Fried (2003). *The Analysis and use of Financial Statements.* Wiley.

Yarrow, GK (1989). Privatisation and economic performance. *Carnegie-Rochester Conference Series on Public Policy,* 31, pp. 303–344.

Yarrow, GK (1992). *British Electricity Prices Since Privatisation.* Oxford: Regulatory Policy Institute.

PART III

Water Sector Regulation & Governance

CHAPTER 12

Regulatory Independence and Contract Incompleteness: Assessing Regulatory Effectiveness in Water Privatization in Manila

Xun Wu, Loit Batac† and Nepomuceno A. Malaluan‡*

**Lee Kuan Yew School of Public Policy, NUS, Singapore*
†Institute of water Policy, NUS, Singapore
‡Action for Economic Reforms, the Philippines

Two intrinsic conflicts are present in the regulation of privatized water utilities under concession agreements, the leading form of private sector participation (PSP) in urban water utilities in developing countries. First, although concession agreements constrain the discretionary power of regulatory agencies, contract incompleteness, widespread and unavoidable in water sector, calls for more extensive uses of discretionary power. Second, although contract renegotiations may undermine the efficiency gains achieved through competitive bidding processes, the economic costs and political risks of terminating concession contracts can be prohibitively high. This chapter assesses the impacts that these conflicts exert upon regulatory effectiveness by examining major regulatory decisions that were made after the water supply and sanitation services in Metro Manila were privatized in 1997. Our analysis suggests that concession contracts indeed were relatively effective in curbing opportunistic behaviors by the government and by concessionaires in the earlier years following privatization. But the relevance and usefulness of these contracts as the primary regulatory mechanism has since declined as the regulatory system tacitly moved towards discretionary regulation. We argue that more emphasis should be placed on transparency and performance benchmarking to improve regulatory effectiveness in the absence of regulatory independence.

1. Introduction

Private sector investments in urban water utilities have been declining in recent years. The World Bank's Private Participation in Infrastructure (PPI) database shows that the number of new private sector participation (PSP) projects in urban water utilities in 2009 was the lowest since 1995 (Figure 1). More important in the present context, the rate of decline for concessions, accounting for nearly 64% of all PSP projects in urban water utilities from 1990 through 2009, has been much more rapid than the rates for other forms of PSP, such as management contracts, leases, and Greenfield projects. The size of investments committed to concession projects has also declined sharply, from about US$1.6 billion in 1995 to about US$152 million in 2009. New concession projects tend to

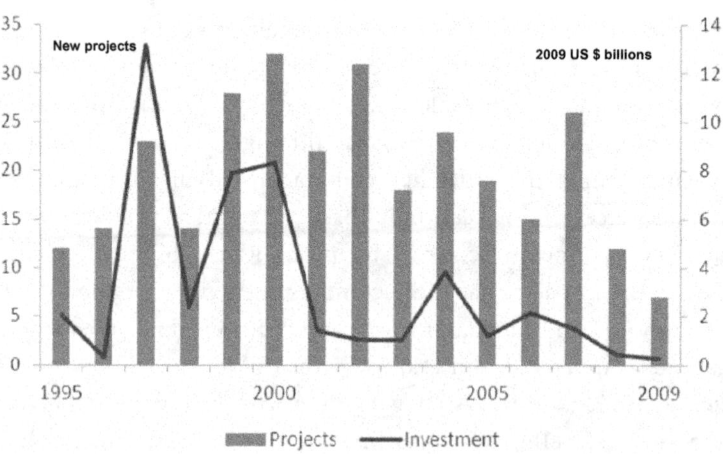

Figure 1: Private sector participation in water utilities 1995–2009.
Source: The World Bank and PPIAF, PPI Database

be highly-concentrated in a few countries such as China and Chile (Marin and Izaguirre, 2006).

Although the recent decline in PSP in urban water utilities by concession might be merely a short slump due to the recent global financial crisis, some recent high-profile cases of early terminations of concession projects — in Puerto Rico in 2003, in El Alto and La Paz, Bolivia, in 2005, and in Buenos Aires, Argentina in 2006 — have been worrisome, especially given that these projects had been in operation for a long period before termination, thus, raising concerns about the long-term sustainability of concession projects in water sectors in developing countries. Examination of these failures points to two intrinsic conflicts in the regulation of privatized water utilities under concession agreements. First, although concession agreements constrain the discretionary power of regulatory agencies, contract incompleteness, widespread and unavoidable in the water sector, calls for more extensive uses of discretionary power. Second, although contract renegotiations may undermine the efficiency gains achieved through competitive bidding processes, the economic costs and political risks of terminating concession contracts can be prohibitively high. The ability of regulatory systems to navigate these conflicts plays a central role in determining the success or failure of concessions in urban water utilities.

This chapter assesses the impacts of these conflicts upon regulatory effectiveness by examining major regulatory decisions made after water supply and sanitation services in Metro Manila were privatized in 1997. A regulatory office (RO) was established as a part of the concession agreements between Metro Manila Water and Sanitation Service (MWSS) and two private concessionaires, and its regulatory role envisioned at the inception of privatization was quite straightforward — to monitor the enforcement of concession agreements — and thus, required limited discretionary power, as mechanisms for tariff adjustments were supposedly clearly specified in the contracts. However, events that followed, have demonstrated that the tasks facing the RO are anything but straightforward. Although the design of the contracts followed best practices at the time, it soon became clear that the contracts were incomplete. Some critical terms, such as the rate of return, were left unspecified, prompting constant battles between the RO and concessionaires about their interpretations. More importantly, the financial calculations conducted by the concessionaires during the bidding process proved to be grossly overoptimistic in the wake of the Asian financial crisis, which occurred right after the concessions took effect. With inadequate regulatory capacity and limited regulatory independence, the RO was compelled to find workable solutions to these challenging problems through regulatory actions (Groom *et al.*, 2006).

The predicaments facing the RO in Metro Manila are not unique to regulatory agencies tasked with regulating privatized water utilities under concession agreements in other countries. Thus, its experience may offer valuable lessons for policymakers and regulators elsewhere. First, concession projects are common: during the very recent time frame we studied (and not counting projects canceled during that interval) there were about 278 water concession contracts in active operation, serving 160 million consumers in developing economies alone. Many of these have been under stress due to dif-ficulties in dealing with conflicts in implementing their contracts (Public-Private Infrastructure Advisory Facility, 2010), and lessons from Metro Manila's water privatization experience may help avoid major pitfalls. Second, much of the literature on water privatization around the world, based on case studies, has centered around a debate on the merits of water privatization as a measure of policy reform. Insufficient attention has been paid to the role of regulatory systems in shaping the success or failure of water privatization in a given context. The experience from Metro Manila suggests that the success of water privatization efforts may critically depend upon the performance of regulatory systems. Third, the challenges facing the RO in Metro Manila highlight several fundamental shortcomings of so-called best practices in the design of regulatory systems for PSP in water sector through concessions. Here again, the experience in Metro Manila may point to areas requiring new thinking and creative ideas.

2. The World's Biggest Water Privatization Deal

In January 1997, in what was known as the world's largest water privatization deal, competitive bidding was held to privatize MWSS, a government corporation responsible for water supply and sewerage service to all Metro Manila, as well as to a number of municipalities

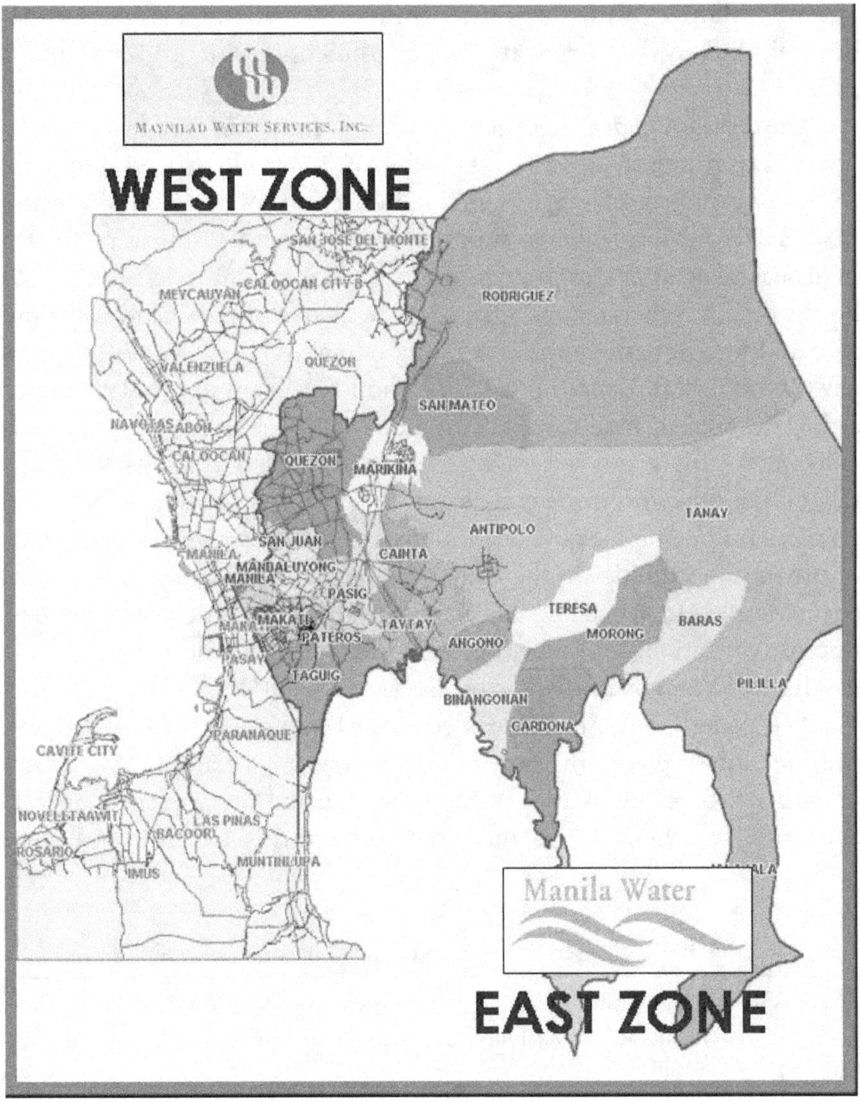

Figure 2: Concession areas.

in adjacent provinces of Rizal and Cavite. The service areas of MWSS were divided into two zones: the concession contract for the West Zone was awarded to Maynilad, a joint venture between Suez Lyonnaise des Eaux and Benpres Holdings Corporation (controlled by the Lopez family); Manila Water, a joint venture formed by United Utilities, Bechtel, and Ayala Corporation, won the concession contract for the East Zone.

The decision to privatize the water supply and sewerage service in Metro Manila was primarily driven by the failure of MWSS to expand service coverage to a rapidly growing population. By the time of privatization in 1997, MWSS had only been able to supply water to about two-thirds of residents in its service areas and to provide sewerage connections to less than 10% of households. In general, its services could be characterized by low water pressure and intermittent supply, operating on an average for only 16 hours a day (David, 2000). Unaccounted-for or non-revenue water (NRW) stood at as high as 60% of total water distributed (Table 1). To make things worse, with water supply and sewerage service priced below costs, MWSS had to rely on periodic government subsidies to service its debts, placing a heavy financial burden on the government. Inspired by the success of privatization of urban water utilities in the United Kingdom and Argentina, policymakers in Metro Manila decided that water privatization in their own area could improve operational efficiency, increase investments in the water sector, and end the need for government subsidies (David, 2001).

The Water Crisis Act was passed in 1995 to pave way for water privatization, allowing the government to privatize any or all of the segments, operations, or facilities of MWSS. Modeling the best practices in other countries, in 1996, MWSS increased water tariffs by 38% and cut its

Table 1: MWSS service compared to other major Asian cities, 1996

City	Population (millions)	Water availability (hrs/day)	Water coverage (% of population)	Non-revenue water (NRW) (% of production)	Staff/1000 connections
Manila	10.6	16	58.7	63	9.8
Singapore	3.0	24	100	7	2.0
Hong Kong	6.3	24	100	36	2.8
Seoul	10.6	24	100	35	2.3
Kuala Lumpur	1.4	24	100	36	1.4
Bangkok	7.3	24	82	38	4.6

Source: Second Water Utilities Data Book, Asian and Pacific Region, Asian Development Bank, October 1997.

workforce by 30%, aiming to boost private sector interest in participating in water privatization and to demonstrate the political commitment of the government (Dumol, 2000; Fabella, 2006). The decision to privatize MWSS was embraced wholeheartedly by international financial institutions. The Asian Development Bank (ADB) provided a technical assistance (TA) grant in 1995 worth US$582,000, to assist MWSS in promoting privatization activities, and the International Finance Corporation (IFC) of the World Bank acted as the transaction advisor for the design phase of the privatization process (David, 2000).

Two requirements were stipulated for the bidding process. First, each potential bidder or consortium had to be composed of a "local sponsor" with majority control and an "international operator" with expertise and a proven track record in the provision of water sector services. These criteria reduced the number of potential bidders from more than 50 to only four. Second, on the advice of IFC consultants, the service areas in Metro Manila were divided into two zones as described above, and it was stipulated that these two zones could not be awarded to a single concessionaire, in order to promote yardstick competition (David, 2000).

The bidders were required to submit a technical proposal that focused on service obligations and other technical requirements, and to state a rate bid expressed as a percentage adjustment to the prevailing MWSS rates. All four consortia met the minimum technical requirements in their technical proposals; the consortia with the two lowest rate bids, Maynilad and Manila Water, won the concessions for West and East zones, respectively. Both concession contracts were to last 25 years, and the targets for improvement in supply continuity, drinking water quality standards, wastewater treatment, and water and sewerage coverage (Table 2). The winning bidders took over MWSS operations on 1 August 1997.

Two outcomes that emerged from the bidding process have since posed significant challenges for the regulatory system over the ensuing years. The first is that local partners in the winning consortia are linked to Lopez (in the West Zone) and Ayala (in the East Zone), two of the top three family conglomerates in the Philippines, both with considerable financial and political clout in the country (Fabella, 2006). The financial health of these conglomerates may have significant impacts on the stability of the national economy, something the regulators have to take into consideration in their regulatory decisions for the metropolitan water concessions.

Table 2: Water Supply, Sanitation, and Sewerage Coverage Targets for the West and East Concession Areas

	MAYNILAD WATER SERVICES, INC. (West Zone)				
	2001	2006	2011	2016	2021
Water Supply*	87	97	97	98	98
Sanitation**	43	46	43	39	27
Sewerage**	16	20	21	31	66
	MANILA WATER COMPANY, INC. (East Zone)				
	2001	2006	2011	2016	2021
Water Supply*	77	94	94	94	95
Sanitation**	38	32	27	24	19
Sewerage**	3	16	51	52	55

*Expressed as a percentage of the population in the designated city of municipality at the time of the target (excluding users who are connected to a piped source of water other than from the MWSS system). For areas designated by the cities or municipalities as depressed areas, these targets may be met by the installation of one public standpipe for each 475 people.
**Expressed as a percentage of the total population in the designated city or municipality connected to the Concessionaire's water system at the time of the target.
Source: Concession agreement.

The second outcome stemmed from the extremely low-bids offered by the two winning consortia at the outset, especially the bid by Manila Water that won the East Zone (which was equivalent to merely one-fourth of MWSS tariffs) (Table 3). Although the low-rates obtained through competitive bidding were hailed as an indication of the great success of the privatization process, they became a major source of tensions between the RO and the concessionaires because of the enormous pressure for tariff increases that arose in the wake of the Asian financial crisis. Fabbela (2006) suspects that the winning bidders may have bid very aggressively due to considerations outside the water sector, as both the Lopez and Ayala families were heavily involved in real estate in Metro Manila.

3. The Design of the Regulatory System: Structure and Regulatory Independence

According to the concession agreements, the bid rates were to be established as the standard rates on the date on which the concession agreements

Table 3: Summary of the rate bids

MWSS rate per cubic meter, pre-privatization		PhP8.56
	Percent bids	Peso bids
WEST ZONE		
Ayala-International Water	28.6333	PhP2.5140
Benpres-Lyonnaise des Eaux	56.5922	4.9688
Aboitix-Compagnie Generale des Eaux	56.8800	4.9941
Metro Pacific-Anglian Water	66.8998	5.8738
EAST ZONE		
Ayala-International Water	26.3886	2.3169
Benpres-Lyonnaise des Eaux	62.8800	5.5209
Aboitix-Compagnie Generale des Eaux	64.5080	5.6638
Metro Pacific-Anglian Water	69.7888	6.1275

Source: Mark Dumol, The Manila Water Concession: A Key Government Official's Diary of the World's Largest Water Privatization, The World Bank, July 2000.

took effect, and any subsequent adjustments to tariffs could only be made on the basis of the following considerations:

1. The percentage change in the consumer price index for the Philippines;
2. Any extraordinary price adjustment allowed on the basis of circumstances such as amendments in service obligation, changes in law affecting cash flows, extraordinary currency adjustment, or problems in MWSS project commitments that would materially affect the financial performance of the concessionaire; and
3. Adjustments approved in periodic rate rebasing exercises, to be based on evaluation of the expenditure and operational performance of the concessionaires.

The RO, established as a part of the concession agreements, consists of a chief regulator and four deputy regulators, each responsible for one of the four functional departments — technical, financial, customer service, and administration and legal matters — and has about 60 employees (Figure 3). According to concession agreements, persons previously or currently affiliated with MWSS or the two concessionaires are barred from appointment to office in the RO. The RO is financed by concession fees

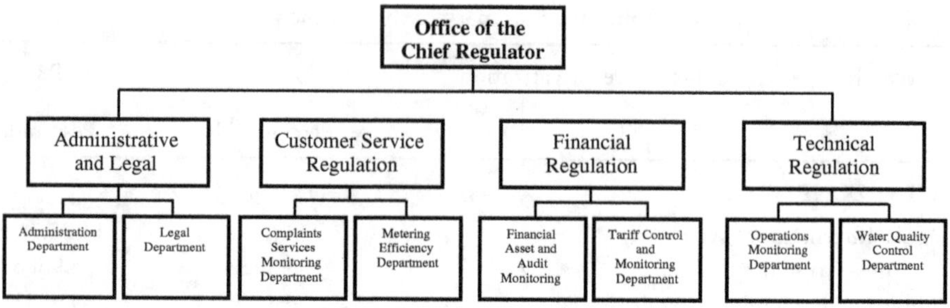

Figure 3: Organizational chart of the Regulatory Office (RO).

Source: MWSS Regulatory Office.

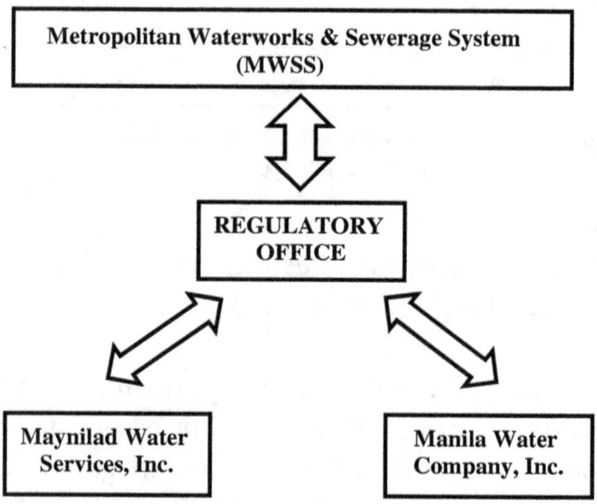

Figure 4: Regulatory system.

made by the concessionaires, so that it is financially independent of the state treasury (Fabella, 2006). These clauses were meant to provide the RO with some degree of independence.

Because the types and mechanisms for tariff adjustments are well-specified in the concession agreements, the scope of discretionary actions by the RO supposedly is very limited. According to the concession agreements, the RO's two key responsibilities are to implement the concession agreements' provisions on rates and to monitor and implement their information, reporting, and audit provisions. Essentially, the RO would be functioning as the guardian of the concession agreements.

Beyond the concession agreements, the regulatory power of the RO is confined by three features of the regulatory system for water privatization in Metro Manila. First, because it was established by virtue of the concession agreements, the RO has no legal or statutory independence (Fabella, 2006). The option of setting up an independent regulatory agency by legislation was initially contemplated by the government, but it was anticipated that more than a year would be required to complete the legislative process and build the political compromises necessary for passing the legislation, a delay that could potentially undermine the entire privatization process.[1] Instead, a "semiautonomous" RO was introduced as an "intermediate step."[2]

Second, after the concessionaires took over, RO did not become independent from MWSS, the asset owner and contracting party for the concession agreements. Regulators are appointed by the MWSS Board of Trustees (MWSS-BOT), which must also approve all RO budgets. More importantly, RO decisions require the approval of the MWSS-BOT, which holds the veto power for any regulatory decisions that the RO might render (Fabella, 2006). Because of this arrangement, the RO has never been regarded by concessionaires as a neutral body that can provide them a fair hearing.[3]

Third, the Appeals Panel, an arbitration body created under the concession agreements to settle disputes that cannot be resolved through consultation and negotiation, also exercises regulatory functions of an appellate character. It is composed of three members, including a chairman appointed by the International Chamber of Commerce, one representative nominated by the concessionaires, and another by the RO. The Appeals Panel can overrule the regulatory decisions made by the RO, and its decisions are considered final.

The regulatory system described above, opens the door for political interference while creating considerable tensions and conflicts between the RO and the concessionaires. The MWSS-BOT is composed of nine members, all appointed by the president of the Philippines. The ultimate

---

[1] Based on an interview with Dr. Felipe Medalla, former Cabinet Secretary for Socio-Economic Planning and Director-General of the National Economic and Development Authority (1998–2001).

[2] Based on an interview with a senior official in the RO.

[3] Based on an interview with Dr. Felipe Medalla.

decision-making power granted to the MWSS-BOT, along with its composition, paves way for political influence in regulatory decisions, as endorsement from the president and the cabinet is a critical factor in determining key regulatory actions.[4] One conspicuous flaw in the regulatory system is the lack of consumer representation in the MWSS-BOT.

Under this regulatory system, the roles of the RO remain unclear. On one hand, it is mandated to monitor compliance with rules and terms specified in the contracts, but on the other hand, it is also tasked with altering these same rules and terms when contract agreements are being renegotiated between MWSS and the concessionaires (Ehrhardt *et al.*, 2007). The conflicts between these two roles not only weaken the RO's credibility and legitimacy in dealing with the concessionaires but also lead to considerable confusion even among staff within the RO itself (Landingin, 2003).

4. Determination of Appropriate Discount Rate (ADR) and Contract Incompleteness

The first serious challenge to the RO as a newly-established regulatory agency came much earlier than expected. In March 1998, less than a year after MWSS was privatized, Manila Water requested a rate increase of P3.23 per cubic meter (an enormous amount, considering its bidding rate) under the Extraordinary Price Adjustment (EPA) clause in the concession agreement. This petition was triggered by two "extraordinary circumstances": the substantial devaluation of the peso following the Asian financial crisis, and the drastic reduction of available water in the Angat Reservoir that supplies 97% of Metro Manila's water needs resulting from extreme droughts due to the El Niño phenomenon in 1997–1998. Two critical provisions lay at the heart of Manila Water's proposal for the rate increase: an Appropriate Discount Rate (ADR) of 18%, and a front-loading of the recovery of losses on account of extraordinary circumstances over the first four years.

The RO acknowledged the extraordinary circumstances but found that the calculations in Manila Water's proposal were not in compliance

[4] Based on an interview with a senior official in the RO.

with the concession agreement. First, the front-loading of recovery of losses over the first four years was disallowed under the concession agreement, which clearly states that the impacts of any such adjustment should be spread out from the charging year up until the end date of the contract. Second, the 18% ADR in Manila Water's application was substantially higher than the ADR implied in its original bid (which was 5.2%, according to RO's calculation) and therefore, allowing such an adjustment in the ADR would be equivalent to granting Manila Water, the opportunity to scale down the commitment it had made in winning the concession agreement in the bidding process, and thus, would potentially undermine the integrity of the bidding process. On these considerations, the RO granted P0.04 per cubic meter, or only 6% of the increase sought by Manila Water.

Unsatisfied with this decision, Manila Water brought the case before the Appeals Panel in September 1998. According to Manila Water, the 5.2% rate of return in its bid was based on "unleveraged equity"; i.e., no debt was taken on. Antonino Aquino, the CEO of Manila Water at the time, argued that the ADR should be based on "the market-based weighted cost of capital" to account for the cost of borrowing, not on unleveraged equity, and that the Asian financial crisis has "made the ADR higher than what it might have been in the past."[5] However, interestingly, Manila Water had voluntarily lowered its requested rate increase from P3.23 to P0.52 per cubic meter by the time it took the case to the Appeals Panel (Fabella, 2006).

The dispute over ADR was fueled in part by an ambiguity in the contract that left both positions arguable. The concession agreement defines ADR as follows:

> "Appropriate Discount Rate" means, at any time, the real (i.e., not inflation adjusted) weighted average cost of capital (after taxes payable by the concession business). In determining the Appropriate Discount Rate, the Regulatory Office *shall* apply conventional- and internationally-accepted methods, and in particular, shall make estimates of the cost of debt in domestic and international markets, the cost of equity for utility businesses in the Philippines and abroad

[5] Quoted in Raj Chtrani, "Lessons from Philippines Water Privatization," *Asian Water*, July 1999.

> and shall make adjustments to such estimates to reflect country risk, exchange rate risk and any other project risks. The Regulatory Office, at its sole discretion, *may* consider the Concessionaire's rate of return, either stated or implied in its bid, in determining the Appropriate Discount Rate.

The second sentence of the provision can be used to support Manila Water's position, but the last sentence is in line with the position espoused by the RO. The Appeals Panel ruled that the correct ADR should be current-market-driven, as argued by Manila Water. The position taken by the Appeals Panel suggests that more importance was attached to the word *shall* in the second sentence instead of the word *may* in the last sentence. However, the panel computed the market-driven ADR to be 9.3% higher than the rate implied in the contract but lower than what was applied for by Manila Water; the allowed adjustment was P0.18 per cubic meter from the charging year to the end of the contract. The RO subsequently launched a petition with the Court of Appeals, but the Appeals Panel's decision was upheld.

Regulators may have been disappointed at the final outcomes of the conflict with Manila Water with regard to determination of ADR, but the incident in fact vindicated the RO's role, despite its many noticeable shortcomings, as a vital actor in regulating the concessions. The credibility of the RO as a guardian of contracting agreements was strengthened as a result. Reflecting on key lessons from the lengthy and costly process in the determination of ADR, Aquino stressed the importance of the concessionaires' establishing a good working relationship with the RO, instead of treating it as an adversary and relying on the Appeals Panel to solve disputes.[6]

5. The Contract Amendments and the Real Costs of Contract Renegotiations

Even if Manila Water, in the East Zone, could forgo an acceleration in cost recovery to offset peso depreciation in the wake of the Asian financial

[6] Based on an interview with Mr. Antonino Aquino.

crisis, Maynilad in the West Zone did not have that luxury. First, depreciation of the peso affected Maynilad much more deeply than it affected Manila Water. Based on an assumption that higher investment per capita would be required by the East Zone compared to the West Zone, the debts inherited from MWSS (mostly denominated in foreign currencies) had been allocated at a 90:10 ratio between the West Zone and the East, such that a disproportionately high-percentage of the financial impacts of peso depreciation fell on Maynilad in the West.

Second, Manila Water was able to make some critical adjustments in response to the financial crisis, such as considerably scaling down the capital expenditure plan based on its bid. However, Maynilad, had been more aggressive initially in making capital investments to meet service expansion as specified in the contract agreement; but these capital expenditures had failed to improve the concession's operational efficiency and its financial condition (Wu and Malaluan, 2008). For example, the NRW had actually increased after Maynilad took over the West Zone (Regulatory Office, 2002).

Third, Benpres, the local partner in Maynilad, was under financial stress. In 2000, Benpres reported net losses of P353 million, causing significant concern among banks targeted by Maynilad for financing. As a result, Maynilad was not able to close a US$350 million term loan which it desperately needed to weather the storm of the Asian financial crisis.

Fighting for its financial survival, Maynilad pinned its hope on accelerating the recovery of its foreign exchange losses, which had accumulated to P2.664 billion since 1997. In October 2000, Maynilad filed a petition for an accelerated EPA, similar to the one requested by Manila Water two years earlier. The RO rejected this proposal, as such adjustment is specifically prohibited in the concession agreements, and it only granted Maynilad an EPA of P0.26 per cubic meter to spread out the impacts of peso depreciation over the remaining duration of the contract. Maynilad was in despair, declaring *force majeure* on 8 March 2001, on the ground that none of its concerns was substantially addressed by MWSS or the RO, and it unilaterally decided to stop paying concession fees. The concession agreement for the West Zone was on the verge of cancellation.

The RO considered its regulatory discretion to be bounded by the concession agreements, but this was the not the case with MWSS, the asset owner, as well as its political master, which considered contract cancellation to be politically unacceptable.[7] An *ad hoc* team in MWSS was set up to negotiate a solution to the standoff, and on 5 October 2001, MWSS and Maynilad agreed to amend the concession agreement (Amendment No. 1), allowing Maynilad to increase its tariff by P4.71 per cubic meter in order to accelerate the recovery of its foreign exchange losses within a period of 18 months, instead of spreading it over the term of the contract. In addition, targets for expansion were also adjusted downward in the contract amendment so that the two concessionaires could reduce their capital expenditure requirements in the early years of operation. The big winner emerging from Amendment No. 1 was Manila Water, which saw its tariff raise from P5.10 to P9.37 per cubic meter by symmetric treatment without incurring any damages to its public image.

Although Amendment No. 1 seemed to be imperative to avoid a termination of the contract agreement between MWSS and Maynilad, in retrospect, the two parties would have been better off had the contract terminated when Maynilad stopped paying its concession fee. Although Maynilad was able to secure rate increases to fast-track the recovery of its foreign exchange rate losses through contract renegotiations, the tariff increase granted by the first amendment failed to save the financially troubled firm, primarily because, some fundamental problems internal to the firm, such as inefficient operations and bad investments, remained unsolved (Chiplunkar *et al.*, 2008). In December 2002, Maynilad filed a notice of termination of its concession contract, blaming the lack of efforts by the government to cooperate with the firm in sustaining its operation in the West Zone, and sought the reimbursement of more than US$303 million that it claimed to have invested. Bankruptcy was formally declared in November 2003, after an international arbitration panel ruled in favor of MWSS. Court documents showed that Maynilad had accumulated unsecured liabilities of P17.4 billion against recoverable assets of only P2.4 billion. In 2005, Maynilad was turned over to MWSS under a so-called debt-for-equity swap, in which Benpres relinquished its shares to MWSS and other creditors in exchange for unpaid concession fees and debts.

[7] Based on an interview with a senior official from the RO.

The public sector and consumers also suffered dearly in the fallout from Maynilad's collapse. The government was blamed for conceding too much to the demands of the financially-troubled concessionaire during contract renegotiations. The unpaid concession fees had accumulated to more than P6.8 billion by the end of 2003, forcing MWSS to assume short-term loans to service the debts. Most importantly, West Zone consumers were also at the losing end of the chain. About 80% of the population had received continuous service by 2001, but half of these customers suffered from intermittent service by 2005, when the contract was terminated (Marin, 2009). Eventually the costs of contract cancellations would be shouldered by the consumers for many years to come.

Although the RO had initially tried to defend the integrity of the concession contracts, it eventually played a supporting role in MWSS-BOT actions during the contract renegotiations, providing tariff computation for alternative scenarios. As the designated regulatory agency and the only agency with technical expertise and capacity in regulatory decisions, the RO — willing or not — found its responsibilities extending beyond the roles intended for it at the inception of privatization. The regulators came to realize that the effectiveness of their work was (and is) not only measured by the extent to which the original contract agreements are enforced, but also assessed by whether they can find "workable" solutions in changing circumstances; contract agreements should thus be regarded as living documents rather than a bible.[8]

Although contract renegotiations may seem imperative given changing circumstances and the high-costs of contract termination, the contract renegotiations that occurred in this case exposed some weaknesses in the design of the regulatory system. First, the institutional arrangements, along with rules and guidelines for contract negotiations, were not specified, resulting in both ad hoc decisions and long delays in conflict resolution. For example, the acceleration of recovery of losses from peso depreciation was granted for Maynilad, yet a similar request by Manila Water had been rejected two years before. Second, the credibility of the regulatory agency in dealing with the concessionaires was undermined by

[8] Based on an interview with a senior official in the RO.

the concessionaires' ability to bypass and undercut the RO's rulings by lobbying with politicians. Regulatory independence embedded in the design of the regulatory system, failed to protect the regulatory agency from opportunistic behaviors on the part of the concessionaires. Moreover, although the funding arrangements for financing the RO through concession fees paid by concessionaires might indeed make the agency independent from the state treasury, the financial dependence on concession fees could create a bias against contract termination.

6. Rate Rebasing Exercises and Changing Regulatory Roles

The regulatory mechanisms applying to the two concessionaires in Metro Manila represent a hybrid of cost-of-service regulation and price-cap regulation (Fabella, 2006). The concession agreements may have been able hold the concessionaires accountable to their bidding rates for the first five years, with tariff adjustments permissible only for inflation and other extraordinary circumstances. But the tariff levels and their structure are subject to review every five years, for rate rebasing exercises, to ensure that concessionaires' operating and capital expenditures are efficiently and prudently incurred and also recoverable over the term of contract, and that they earn a reasonable rate of return (the ADR). The determination of "efficiently and prudently incurred" expenditures and "reasonable" rate of return requires an extensive and judicious use of discretionary powers that is no different from Anglo-American regulatory systems featuring discretionary regulation.

According to the concession agreements, the RO holds the discretion to conduct its first rate rebasing exercise 10 yrs after the inception of concession agreements, which would have allowed plenty of time for the agency to develop the necessary regulatory capacity. Indeed, regulatory capacity was quite weak in the first few years after privatization. The regulators did not have any background experience in water regulation other than a seminar they attended on water regulation 1997, in Florida.[9] However, as a part of the contract amendment negotiated between MWSS

[9] Based on interview with a senior official in the RO.

and the concessionaires, the RO was obligated to conduct the first rate rebasing exercise on 1 January 2003. Ready or not, the agency had to take on the challenges.

The RO contracted UPecon Foundation, a corporate arm of the University of the Philippines School of Economics, to conduct this first rate rebasing exercise. The decision to outsource a major regulatory function, due in part to the RO's inadequate regulatory capacity, was more importantly intended to lend credibility to the rate rebasing in view of the RO's lack of independence. The rate rebasing team was headed by Felipe Medalla, a respected academic from the University of the Philippines. Medalla is also a prominent figure in the political scene, having served his term as Cabinet Secretary for Socio-Economic Planning and Director-General of the National Economic and Development Authority from July 1998 to January 2001. UK-based Thames Water International Services was subcontracted to conduct technical analysis, and Zambrano & Associates, an Ecuador-based law firm, was selected to deal with legal matters.

Medalla and his team were confronted with immense challenges in the undertaking. First, the concession agreements themselves were incomplete and vague in many respects. For instance, although a schedule of coverage targets existed, the contracts contained no definition of coverage. Nor was NRW, an important parameter in the rebasing exercise, covered in the service obligation section of the concession agreements. Second, benchmarking was essential to distinguish between expenditures that were incurred "efficiently and prudently" and those that were not, but information about efficiency levels of large water utilities elsewhere was either unavailable or not comparable for Metro Manila.[10] Third, the information required of concessionaires for rate rebasing was not clearly specified in the concession contracts, and technical submissions by the concessionaires were not standardized. Despite numerous requests made by the rate rebasing team, Maynilad did not submit crucial technical information.

The rate rebasing team developed a formula based on its interpretation of the parameters of the concession agreement, essentially benchmarking the concessionaires against financial models used in the

[10] Based on an interview with Dr. Filipe Medalla.

bidding process. On the basis of calculations conducted by the rate rebasing team, the RO recommended a tariff of P17.00 per cubic meter for Manila Water, slightly lower than the P19.54 per cubic meter requested, and P26.75 for Maynilad, in this case substantially lower than the P34.72 per cubic meter requested. The disparities in tariffs requested and granted, primarily reflected disallowances in the concessionaires' opening cash positions as well as projected future operating expenditures and capital expenditures. The disallowance amounted to P2.77 billion for Maynilad, compared to only P643 million for Manila Water, which suggests that the rate rebasing team regarded Maynilad's operations as grossly inefficient (Table 4).

Not surprisingly, the RO's decisions on tariff adjustments were accepted by Manila Water but acutely contested by Maynilad, which argued (via the concession contract's first amendment) that major bid assumptions had been superseded by unanticipated exogenous factors and that the bases for disallowances in future cash flows were not specified in the concession agreements. After several failed attempts at reconciling the differences, Maynilad took the case to the Appeals Panel, which ruled in favor of the RO. Maynilad was given a lifeline through the first amendment, but MWSS-BOT and its political masters did not actively intervene on its behalf, not only because of public pressures but also because there were clear indications that Maynilad was looking for a way out. By holding the concession accountable for its commitments, the first rate rebasing accelerated the eventual downfall of Maynilad.

Overall, the first rate rebasing demonstrated both the strengths of the concession contracts as regulatory mechanisms and the effectiveness of the RO in enforcing them. The disallowances imposed on Manila Water, the more efficient operator, indicated that the RO was able to exert pressures on private sector operators in a monopoly position, in order to improve efficiency. The strategy of dividing MWSS service areas into two zones, which had been introduced during the design phase of the privatization plan, seemed to have paid off as benchmarking, allowed the RO to defend its technical assessments more rigorously against various accusations made by Maynilad. The rate rebasing also provided financial incentives for concessionaires to make necessary investments. The significant rate increases awarded to Manila Water allowed the firm to improve

Table 4: Summary of recommendations for Manila Water and Maynilad

	Manila Water initial submission (March 2002)	Final recommendation (October 2002)	Maynilad initial submission (March 2002)	Final recommendation (October 2002)
ADR for historical cash flows	9.30%	8.80%	10.40%	10.40%
Disallowance on historical cash flows	PhP0.00	PhP0.64 billion	P0.00	PhP8.45 billion
Opening cash position per m^3	PhP1.83	PhP1.80	PhP8.22	PhP2.97
ADR for future cash flows	9.30%	10.40%	15.70%	10.40%
Future OPEX (net of tax) per m^3	PhP6.47	PhP5.01	PhP8.24	PhP6.33
Future CAPEX per m^3	PhP5.76	PhP3.79	PhP6.44	PhP5.43
Tariff implication (weighted average all-in tariff throughout concession life)	PhP19.54	PhP17.00	PhP34.72	PhP25.58

Source: UPecon Foundation, Rate Rebasing Exercise Final Report, December 2002.

its performance in NRW reduction and service expansion substantially. On 18 March 2005, Manila Water was listed on the Philippine Stock Exchange as the first IPO in the Philippines after the Asian financial crisis.

However, the completion of the first rate rebasing exercise, fundamentally altered the regulatory roles of the RO, which had used the concession agreements as its primary regulatory mechanism in dealing with the concessionaires as well as with other key stakeholders. Although the expansion targets and other service obligations specified in the original contracts might still be enforced, the tariff adjustments necessary for achieving those targets would be subject to discretionary decisions by the RO, based on "efficiently and prudently" incurred expenditures and a "reasonable" rate of return for concessionaires. How to exert pressure upon concessionaires to continuously improve efficiency without a competitive bidding process became a new challenge for the RO.

The RO has responded to this challenge by introducing a system of key performance indicators (KPIs), and business efficiency measures (BEMs). These measures established baselines that could be referred to subsequent rate rebasing exercises and also enabled the agency to monitor concessionaires' performance continuously so as to avoid politically costly showdowns during rate rebasing exercises (Table 5). The concessionaires have embraced these changes wholeheartedly, because staying on track with KPIs and BEMs minimizes the possibility of major surprises during rate rebasing exercises. Most importantly, any potential adjustments to KPIs and BEMs can be made through negotiations with the RO behind the scene on an incremental basis, rather than enforced reconciliations of differences during politically-charged rate rebasing exercises. In practice, the targets for KPIs and BEMs were primarily based on proposals made by the concessionaires and in that sense might be presumed "realistic and feasible."[11]

As expected, the second rate rebasing exercise, conducted in 2008, was much less eventful than the first. Medalla, who played an advisory role in the 2008 rate rebasing exercise, found that the second rate rebasing was "many times easier" than the first one, because the assessments of

[11] Based on an interview with a senior official from the RO.

Table 5: Manila Water's KPIs and BEMs performance, 2003 and 2004

Key Performance Indicators					
	Measurement	**2003 Target**	**2003 Actual**	**2004 Target**	**2004 Actual**
WATER SERVICE					
Domestic Connections	Number of household connections	466,563	515,237	485,211	556,089
	Number of water service connections	381,272	396,778	396,029	425,802
Continuity of Water Supply	24-hour water availability as % of coverage	100% by 2007	83%	100% by 2007	89%
Pressure of Water Supply	Average psi	7	9.6	7	9.6
Water Quality at Plant Outlet	% compliance with PNSDW limits on a monthly basis	100%	100%	100%	100%
Water Quality in Distribution	% compliance with PNSDW limits on total coliforms	95%	99%	95%	99%
Sampling	% compliance with PNSDW parameters on a monthly basis	100%	100%	100%	100%
SEWERAGE AND SANITATION SERVICES					
Domestic Connections	Number of sewered connections	25,918	26,742	26,138	29,406
Sanitation	Number of septic tanks emptied	7,200	11,130	14,600	17,674
Wastewater Effluent Standard	% compliance with DENR standards and parameters	BOD (50mg/L)	Reached all 5 targets	BOD (50mg/L)	Reached all 5 targets
		COD (100mg/L)		COD (100mg/L)	
		TSS (70mg/L)		TSS (70mg/L)	
		Oil and Grease (5)		Oil and Grease (5)	
		Coliform (10,000 MPN/100mL)		Coliform (10,000 MPN/100mL)	
BUSINESS EFFICIENCY MEASURES					
INCOME					
Billed Volume	MLD	782	767	814	825
Revenue Collection Rate	Actual Receipts as % of Sales	95%	99%	95%	101%
OPERATING EXPENSES					
Labor	Labor Headcount and Cost	1,516 and PhP698 M	1,516 and PhP622.5 M	1,528 and PhP724.3 M	1,532 and PhP677.6 M
Power	Power Consumption and Cost	82.4 MwH and PhP468 M	60.3 MwH and PhP484 M	83.7 MwH and PhP484 M	61.9 MwH and PhP353.1 M
Total	Total Operating Expenses	PhP1,848 M	PhP1,603 M	PhP1,942 M	PhP1,777 M
NON-REVENUE WATER					
Non-Revenue Water	Liters per connection per day	1,792	1,595	1,618	1,137
	NRW as % of water production volume	51%	20.70%	49.10%	43.40%

Source: Manila Water International Offering Circular, 28 February 2005.

performance were based on target KPIs and BEMs that had been continuously monitored by the RO. The regulators, on their part, found no major cause for disallowances; in fact Manila Water was even rewarded for surpassing its targets.[12] As a result of this highly-"successful" rate rebasing exercise, all MWSS and RO employees were rewarded with huge bonuses.

The second exercise exposed some potential flaws in the design of the regulatory system. First, although discretionary regulation is required for rate rebasing exercises, the regulatory system is not provided with the independence imperative for discretionary rulings. Second, some challenges stemming from the RO's changing regulatory roles after the first rate rebasing did not receive sufficient attention. The determination of KPIs and BEMs does potentially offer the RO an opportunity to exercise its regulatory discretion, but because the RO's mode of operation has not moved beyond the monitoring roles specified in the concession contracts, this opportunity has not been fully-utilized. Ultimately, the agency has not been equipped with the regulatory capacity necessary to support discretionary regulation. Determining "efficiently and prudently" incurred expenditures and "reasonable" rates of return for concessionaires would be challenging tasks even for regulators in developed countries, and it must be remembered that the RO was established primarily to monitor basic, not discretionary, enforcement of the contracts.

7. Contract Extension and Political Interference

Political inference is almost a given in the regulatory system for water privatization in Metro Manila, as all members of MWSS-BOT, the ultimate decision-making body in the regulatory system, are political appointees confirmed by the president of the Philippines. In a democratic system such as the Philippines, such political interference may be offset by other political forces. For instance, although Maynilad was able to extract favorable terms from MWSS in its original rehabilitation plan in 2003 (commonly known as the Second Amendment to the concession contract) through the support of former President Gloria Macapagal-Arroyo, the plan was not

[12] Based on an interview with Dr. Felipe Medalla.

approved owing to pressures from opposition politicians and civil society, forcing Benpres and its partner to take larger losses than had been hoped. A recent regulatory decision to award the concessionaires an extension of their contract agreements for another 15 yrs, however, has demonstrated that political interference can be outright destructive for regulatory decisions that are highly-technical and will have long-term impacts.

Manila Water has began seeking contract extension once it became listed on the Philippine Stock Exchange in 2005, because its share price will naturally come under tremendous pressure as the expiration date of its concession contract approaches. The firm submitted in 2007 a proposal for extension during the second rate rebasing exercise, scheduled for 2008, but this was dismissed outright by the RO on the basis of a clause in the concession contracts that requires the rebidding process to be conducted when the contracts expire, i.e., in 2022. Moreover, after having battled with concessionaires on numerous occasions over interpretations of the terms in the contracts, regulators also felt that some key provisions and costly omissions can only be adequately redressed through contract revisions which may not be possible within the existing contract period. For example, the existing contracts do not cap the rate of return, the key to the cost-of-service regulation in rate rebasing exercises, an oversight which has led to disputes regarding interpretations of ADRs.[13] The justifications provided by the RO in rejecting the contract extension proposal would seem perfectly sensible to scholars and practitioners familiar with the regulation of network infrastructure where monopoly is inevitable.

Manila Water could not have found better chances for reopening the discussion of contract extension than those that emerged after the second rebasing exercise. Amid financial crisis and looking towards an election year, President Arroyo made it clear to MWSS that no tariff increase recommended through the second rate rebasing exercise could be implemented in 2009. However, postponing the implementation of rate increases, would make it very difficult for the concessionaires to meet their operation targets; this was especially so for the new, post-crash Maynilad, which inherited sizeable debts and other financial obligations from its

[13] Based on an interview with a senior official in the RO.

predecessor. To make things worse, MWSS had to meet a mandatory requirement to accelerate the expansion of sewerage coverage in Metro Manila and several towns in Rizal and Cavite, in compliance with a landmark decision made by the Supreme Court of the Philippines to clean up Manila Bay. Such an expansion would require substantial investments from the concessionaires in a short period of time, which would make tariff spikes inevitable.

Given the political climate, Manila Water strategically framed the required investments as a part of stimulus package and proposed to MWSS that its concession contract shall be extended for another 15 yrs, so that the investment costs could be spread over a longer period to prevent price hikes and rate adjustments that could be deferred at later dates. Maynilad, a reluctant partner of Manila Water on the contract extension proposal, had initially considered taking legal actions against the MWSS decision to postpone rate increases recommended in the second rate rebasing exercise; now it saw no viable option but to go along with Manila Water on the proposal for extension.

The RO was not persuaded by these arguments, and made its position known to the public. The regulators argued that the extension of concession contract for Maynilad was especially unacceptable, as the company has yet to prove itself as an efficient operator and extending its contract could lead to significant long-term costs for consumers. However, concerns for efficiency and long-term impacts for consumers were overshadowed, by short-term political considerations for the President Arroyo and her cabinet that forced the MWSS-BOT to give reluctant approval to contract extension despite vigorous resistance from the RO. Contract extension was awarded to Manila Water in December 2009 and to Maynilad in April 2010.

The decision to extend concession contracts without a rebidding process clearly demonstrated the shortcomings in the design of the regulatory system regarding protection of long-term public interests from opportunistic behaviors on the part of politicians and concessionaries clearly. Holding the public hostage in their fear of rate increases, the concessionaires and political forces then in power were able to work together to advance their respective agendas at long-term expense to the public in an area in which political risk of interference might be low due to its highly-technical nature. The RO's regulatory expertise could have played a more decisive role in averting such an outome had the agency been endowed with more regulatory independence.

8. Conclusions

Water privatization in Metro Manila was highly-controversial in 1997 when water supply and sanitation services were privatized, and more than 10 yrs later, public perceptions and scholarly opinions regarding water privatization continue to be sharply divided. Supporters of water privatization point to the significant increase in coverage, the reduction of nonrevenue water (NRW) distribution, and improvement in water quality as evidences of success (Infrastructure Advisory Services, 2010; Wolf, 2007), but critics argue that water privatization has largely failed due to substantial rate increases, the collapse of one of the two concessionaires (Maynilad), and shortfalls in coverage against concession agreements (Freedom from Debt Coalition, 2010; Water for the People Network Asia, 2006; Esguerra, 2003; Bernhardt, 2005; Hall *et al.*, 2004). However, despite voluminous literature on water privatization in Metro Manila, little is known about the role of the design and evolution of the concomitant regulatory system in determining the outcomes of the privatization. Our analysis of major regulatory decisions since 1997, when privatization was instituted, has attempted to shed some light upon this critical aspect.

Our analysis suggests that the challenges facing the RO in dealing with privatized water utilities under concession contracts were grossly underestimated in the design of the regulatory system, in both the contexts of contract in completeness and of almost inevitable contract renegotiations. First, institutional arrangements, along with rules and guidelines for contract negotiations, were not specified, which resulted in confusion in regulatory responsibilities, inconsistency in regulatory decisions, and opportunistic behaviors by the concessionaires. Second, the RO's regulatory independence was not structured carefully in light of the political environment in which the regulatory system was situated. Rushed by the need to complete the privatization process in one year (as mandated by the Water Crisis Act of 1995), framers of the regulatory system made compromises that deprived the RO of statutory independence and crippled the ability of the regulatory system to protect consumer interests against the potential abuse of political and corporate power. Third, the complexities of shifting regulatory roles over time were not given sufficient attention, which resulted in large gaps between the RO's regulatory capacity and its increased regulatory discretion after the first rate rebasing.

Against the backdrop of these systematic flaws in the design of the regulatory system, the RO's overall effectiveness as a guardian of the concession agreements in the initial years after water privatization, was respectable. The case against Manila Water regarding determination of the appropriate discount rate (ADR) demonstrated the RO's strong commitment in protecting the integrity of the concession contracts. The collapse of Maynilad, cited by opponents as evidence of the failure of water privatization in Metro Manila (Water for the People Network Asia, 2006; Freedom from Debt Coalition, 2010), can in rebuttal be interpreted as a success for the RO in weeding an inefficient operator from the system. The substantial disallowances handed down to the concessionaires in the first rate rebasing exercise, demonstrated the RO's strong will and ability to hold concessionaires accountable for the commitments made in their original bids.

In comparison, RO's performance in recent years points to an urgent need to reexamine its regulatory mechanisms and capacities as the regulatory system has tacitly shifted towards discretionary regulation. Although the RO and MWSS have proclaimed the second rate rebasing exercise to be a general success, the regulatory mechanisms employed may entail high-risks of regulatory capture. The second rate rebasing's reliance on a system of KPIs and BEMs as the dominant regulatory mechanism, along with the RO's failure to apply intensive scrutiny to the target KPIs and BEMs proposed by the concessionaires, raises concerns about the agency's effectiveness in exerting pressures on concessionaires to improve efficiency by harnessing the potential of discretionary regulation.

It might be impractical to overhaul the entire regulatory system, but our analysis provides insights into two potential remedies within the existing system. First, a fundamental shortcoming in the current regulatory system is that the RO's limited independence in regulatory decisions is overpowered by the dominance of a single political actor: the president of the Philippines, who appoints members to the MWSS-BOT. Greater transparency in the making of regulatory decisions might provide the RO with an operating environment in which, other key stakeholders can be brought in to balance the influence of the dominant political actor. A high-level of resistance to the decision to extend the concession contracts in 2009 might have surfaced had a technical analysis of the ramifications of contract extension been made available to the public and to civil society groups.

Second, the RO's ability to benchmark the performance of the two concessionaires has become increasingly important as the regulatory system moves towards discretionary regulation. It is essential that the RO step up its efforts to address both information gaps and the shortfall in technical expertise. Innovative thinking is required to exploit the opportunity of having two concessionaires at hand to promote yardstick competition, as the RO did successfully in the first rate rebasing. Establishing an operational linkage to the National Water Resources Board, especially in the area of standardization of information collected from water utilities, would be fruitful in strengthening the RO's regulatory capacity by broadening the scope of yardstick competition.

References

Bernhardt, D (2005). Manila: A success story turned sour. In *Limits to Privatization: How to Avoid Too Much of a Good Thing*, Weizsäcker, EU, O Young and M Finger (eds.), p. 25. London: Earthscan.

Chiplunkar, A, C Duenas and M Flor (2008). *Maynilad on the Mend: Rebidding Process Infuses New Life to a Struggling Concessionaire.* Manila: Asian Development Bank.

David, C (2000). MWSS Privatization: Implications on the Price of Water, the Poor, and the Environment. *Philippine Institute for Development Studies: Makati City, Philippines.* Available on line at http://dirp4. pids. gov. ph/ris/pdf/pidsdps0014.pdf.

Dumol, M (2000). *The Manila Water Concession: A Key Government Official's Diary of the World's Largest Water Privatization.* World Bank Publications.

Ehrhardt, DE, GJ Halpern and S O'Connor (2007). Economic Regulation of Urban Water and Sanitation Services: Some Practical Lessons. *Water Sector Board Discussion Paper Series* 9.

Esguerra, J (2003). *The Corporate Muddle of Manila's Water Concessions.* London: WaterAid and Tearfund.

Fabella, R (2006) Shifting the Boundary of the State: The Privatization and Regulation of Water Service in Metropolitan Manila. *Centre on Regulation and Competition (CRC) Working papers.*

Freedom from Debt Coalition (2010, March 24). *FDC lambasts ADB, World Bank, multilateral banks for encouraging water privatization.* Retrieved August 10, 2010, from Freedom from Debt Coalition: http://www.fdc.ph/index.php?option=com_content&view=article&id=482:fdc-lambasts-adb-world-bank-multilateral-banks-for-encouraging-water-privatization&catid=36:advocacy-on-water&Itemid=88.

Hall, D, V Corral, E Lobina and AR Motte (2004). *Water Privatization and Restructuring Asia Pacific.* Changmai: Public Services International.

Infrastructure Advisory Services (2010). *Success Stories, Infrastructire Advisory — Philippines: Manila Water.* Washington D.C.: International Finance Corporation.

Landingin, R (2003, February 7). *Loaves, Fishes, and Dirty Dishes: Manila's Privatized Water Can't Handle Pressure.* Retrieved on 17 August 2010, from The Center for Public Integrity: http://projects.publicintegrity.org/water/default.aspx?act=ch&nsid=Philippines.

Marin, P (2009). *Public-Private Partnerships for Urban Water Utilities: A Review of Experiences in Developing Countries.* World Bank Publications.

Marin, P and AK Izaguirre (2006). Private participation in water: Toward a new generation of projects? *GridLines,* (14), p. 1–4.

Montemayor, CA (2005). Possibilities for public water in Manila. In *Reclaiming Public Water: Achievements, Struggles and Visions from around the World,* Balanya *et al.* (eds.). Amsterdam: Transnational Institute and Corporate Europe Observatory.

Public-Private Infrastructure Advisory Facility. (2010). *Private Activity in Water and Sewerage Declines for Second Consecutive Year.* Washington, D.C.: The World Bank Group.

Water for the People Network Asia (2006). *Water Privatization in the Philippines: Creating Inequity in People's Access to Sufficient and Potable Water.* Quezon City: Water for the People Network.

Wolf, C (2007). *Manila Water: Privatizing Regulated Services in a Developing Country.* Cambridge: Judge Business School, University of Cambridge.

Wu, X and NA Malaluan (2008). A tale of two concessionaires: A natural experiment of water privatisation in Metro Manila, *Urban Studies,* 45(1), p. 207.

CHAPTER 13

Can Regulation Improve the Performance of Government-Controlled Water Utilities?

David Ehrhardt and Nils Janson*

This chapter provides evidence for whether or not regulation can improve the performance of government-owned water utilities. While other studies have examined whether private participation combined with regulation can improve the performance of government-controlled water utilities, there has been little research on whether regulation alone can improve performance.

This chapter examines five case studies on water utility reform in Latin America and the Caribbean. In each case study, a regulatory regime designed for private companies was applied to a government-controlled utility. Assessing performance across a number of indicators, the evidence shows that performance was as likely to deteriorate as to improve during periods of regulation of government-controlled utilities. This contrasts with the evidence of improvement following reforms that combined regulation with private participation. The findings suggest that conventional regulation may be of little use in government-controlled utilities. Conventional regulation is designed to prevent a profit-maximizing utility from raising tariffs above reasonable cost-recovery levels. Government controlled utilities, however, are not commercially motivated and face systematic incentives for short-termism in tariff-setting.

* Corresponding author. *david.ehrhardt@castalia-advisors.com*

Therefore, limiting monopoly profits is not usually the problem that needs to be addressed.

We conclude that, conventional regulation of a government-controlled utility is not useful in isolation. However, regulatory tools can complement governance reforms. One approach may be to adapt conventional regulatory tools so as to help citizens judge the performance of the utilities. Such an approach would help to increase government accountability for the performance of government-controlled utilities.

Keywords: Regulation; governance; water utilities; government-control.

1. Introduction

There is growing interest in whether or not conventional economic regulation can improve the performance of government-controlled water utilities. Since the bulk of city-dwellers in the world rely on government-controlled utilities for their water supply, the performance of such utilities is a vital policy issue.

This issue is acute because government-controlled water utilities typically perform poorly. While some do well — those in Singapore, New Zealand, the Netherlands and Australia are notable examples — most offer only inadequate coverage, intermittent supply, and non-potable water. For example Araral (2008) found that, in India, water provided by government-controlled utilities on an average are available for only 5 hrs a day in 21 major cities.

Networks, commercial operations and staffing are generally inefficient, wasting natural and financial resources. For example, a study of 50 water utilities in 19 countries in Asia by McIntosh and Cesar (1997) found that the average non-revenue water (a widely-used measure of efficiency, which measures wasted water due to leaks, theft, unbilled consumption and inaccurate metering), accounted for 60%. According to a more recent survey by the Asian Development Bank (2007), average non-revenue water for 40 water utilities in Southeast Asia accounted for 28%. At the same time, tariffs seldom cover the full cost of service, meaning that water utilities are a burden on government finances and the taxpayer. According to estimates by the World Bank (Komives *et al.*, 2006), only 30% of utilities globally, and only 50% of utilities in developed countries, generate sufficient revenue to cover operation, maintenance and partial capital costs.[1]

The combination of vital importance and chronic problems has created intense interest in ways to improve the performance of government-controlled utilities in developing countries. Bringing in private capital or managers to government-controlled utilities, in a variety of private-participation models, has been a prominent reform option. Private water utilities have existed in the USA, France, the UK and elsewhere for over 100 years. Private participation as a way to turnaround under-performing government utilities started to be promoted in the late 1980s, with Chile, Guinea and England and Wales among the pioneers. Since 1991, the World Bank has supported the implementation of over 660 private participation projects in water and sanitation.[2]

While controversial, there is now good evidence that private participation is indeed effective in improving poorly-performing government-owned utilities. A World Bank paper by Gassner *et al.* (2007) conducted an empirical assessment of private sector participation (PSP) in water distribution in developing countries.[3] The econometric study analyzed a panel of 141 water utilities with PSP and 836 state-owned enterprises (SOEs) in 71 developing and transitioning countries. The dataset covered two decades ranging from 1973–2005. The results of the study compared PSP and SOEs on a number of performance indicators. The study found that none of the indicators that were examined, deteriorated under PSP, and that privately operated utilities outperformed SOEs in labor productivity and operational efficiency. In particular, the study found that the average number of residential water connections increased by 12%, residential coverage in sanitation services rose by 19%, and hours of daily water service increased by 41%. These effects — differences in

---

[1] Data for 132 cities were assessed. [EXPLAIN/CHECK: HOW IS THIS RELEVANT?] [It is correct that 'The tariff is estimated for a consumption level of 15 m^3 per month' is not relevant. I have deleted this statement].

[2] http://ppi.worldbank.org/explore/ppi_exploreSector.aspx?sectorID=4

[3] The global sample included developing regions as defined by the World Bank, which are East Asia and Pacific, Europe and Central Asia, Latin America and Caribbean, Middle East and North Africa, South Asia and Sub-Saharan Africa.

averages between the pre-PSP and the post-PSP period — occurred over five years or more, and are over and above the change for similar SOEs.

Almost all reforms involving private participation in water distribution have also involved the introduction of some form of regulation. Given the controversy and difficulty of introducing private participation in water, this has naturally raised the question of whether regulation alone, without private participation, could improve the performance of underperforming government-controlled utilities.

A number of jurisdictions have moved to regulate their government-controlled providers using regulatory models patterned after those that were used for private utilities. Examples include the States of Victoria and New South Wales in Australia, the island of Jamaica, and Scotland in the UK. Still, most jurisdictions continue to simply rely on public sector ownership and governance of the utility — examples include: New Zealand, Barbados, Indonesia and Uganda. As yet, there is little evidence as to whether or not regulation of the sort typically applied to private firms actually helps to improve the performance of government-owned utilities.

To shed light on the question of whether or not regulation alone can improve performance, we have developed five case studies of water utility reform in Latin America and the Caribbean. The case studies all share the following characteristics:

- A regulatory regime was developed in anticipation of private participation in the utility;
- The utility then reverted to government control (four cases), or the envisaged private participation transaction was never completed (one case);
- The regulatory regime developed for the private participation transaction was then applied to the government-controlled utility.

What makes this set of cases particularly interesting is that the regulatory regime in all cases was a fully-fledged, conventional system, in sense that it was developed in the anticipation that it would apply to a privately managed company. Most other cases of regulation of government-controlled utilities involve regulatory regimes developed in the expectation that they would apply to government-owned utilities. Arguably, in such cases, the regulatory designers may have taken less care than they would in a truly private transaction, or adapted the approach to take account of the fact that the utility was government-owned. Therefore, these cases, provide a distinctive opportunity to test the proposition that a regulatory regime of the sort commonly recommended for a privately managed utility can be used to improve the performance of a government-controlled company.

In the following section (Section 2), we present the five cases studies, analyze their results, and summarize our findings. Evidence from these cases shows that regulation has done little to boost performance of the government-controlled utilities.

In Section 3, we suggest that integrating regulatory tools into an overall governance reform approach is likely to be more effective than simply applying regulatory systems designed for private utilities to government-owned utilities.

2. The Case Studies

The five case studies presented in this section are:

- Belize Water Services Ltd (BWS) in Belize;
- Agua Y Saneamientos Argentinos (AYSA) in Buenos Aires, Argentina;
- Guyana Water Incorporated (GWI) in Guyana;
- Empresa de Servicios Sanitarios de Paraguay (ESSAP) in Paraguay;
- The Water and Sewerage Authority (WASA) in Trinidad and Tobago.

For each case we describe the institutional reforms that were implemented and the resulting application of regulation to a government-controlled utility. We then examine the change in performance of the utility under the combination of government ownership and conventional regulation. Following our presentation of the five cases, we conclude with our analysis and findings resulting from the case studies.

To assess the change in performance, we look at four indicators that are commonly used to judge the efficiency and financial health of water utilities:

- Network efficiency, as measured by the percentage of Non-Revenue Water (NRW), i.e., water which leaks away, is stolen, or is otherwise consumed without being paid for;
- Labor efficiency, as measured by number of staff per 1,000 active customers;

- Operating cost recovery, as measured by operating revenues as a percentage of operating costs;
- Average tariff-level, which is calculated by dividing the revenue from water sales by the volume of water sold.

We focus on these indicators not just because they are some of the common measures of performance, but because they are what one would expect a good quality regulatory system to be able to affect. OFWAT in the UK and the Regulatory Office in Manila, for example, have set NRW reduction targets for the private utilities in their jurisdictions, and have been successful in driving improvements on these measures. Labor productivity has also increased in most privately managed, regulated utilities.

Setting tariffs so that a utility can cover its reasonable costs is generally taken as the most basic regulatory objective. The combination of the cost recovery indicator and changes in the average tariff allow us to see if the regulatory regimes in the countries considered are achieving this objective. Ideally, the analysis would also include data on changes in service levels. Unfortunately, data on service levels was not available on a reliable and consistent basis for the cases studied.

2.1. *Belize Water Services Ltd (BWS) in Belize*

In 2001, the Government of Belize created Belize Water Services Ltd. (BWS), vested it with the assets and liabilities of the previous government-owned utility, granted it a 25-yr license, and sold 83% of the shares in BWS to the private water operator Cascal B.V. (Cascal). Four years later, the Government repurchased Cascal's shares in BWS. As a result, the Government owns 83% of BWS's shares (with the Social Security Board owning 10% and the general public having purchased the remaining 7%) and has the right to appoint seven of the eight members of BWS' Board of Directors.

2.1.1. *Changes in Ownership Have Limited the Regulatory Framework*

The Public Utilities Commission (PUC), which was established in 1999, is responsible for regulating BWS. As a part of the regulatory framework, the

PUC should approve BWS' tariffs on a 5-yr basis. BWS' tariffs should be set at a level that ensures a 12% rate of return. BWS can apply to the PUC to increase its tariffs in line with inflation and other indexation factors annually. The PUC last completed a full tariff review for BWS in 2004, when the company was in private control.

Since the government resumed control of the company in October 2005, BWS has not applied for an annual tariff increase in line with indexation factors — the last increase was in May 2005. BWS has not applied for a tariff increase because its Board, with the Government as the majority shareholder, has instructed BWS not to do so. Consequently, the PUC estimates that tariffs are 10 to 12% lower than they should be (given allowable increases for inflation and pass-through costs).

2.1.2. *Tariff Level does not Permit BWS to Undertake Necessary Capital Expenditures*

Table 1 shows that between 2002 and 2005, when Cascal was in control of BWS, the company made rapid gains in key efficiency indicators such as NRW and labor productivity. Thereafter, when BWS returned to Government ownership and control, the efficiency increases essentially stopped. The increase in operating efficiency, combined with tariff increases in 2004 and 2005, improved the utility's operating cost recovery ratio substantially. However, the cash flow generated from operations has not been sufficient for the company to repay its existing debt. Nor can the utility make the substantial investments required to meet the coverage and

Table 1: Operating and financial indicators for BWS (2002–2007).

Year	2002	2003	2004	2005	2006	2007
Ownership	Priv	Priv	Priv	Priv/Govt	Govt	Govt
Non-revenue water	52%	54%	43%	39%	40%	38%
Employees per 1,000 connections	6.7	6.1	5.8	5.3	5.4	5.3
Operating cost recovery ratio	126%	141%	146%	154%	162%	162%
Average tariff (B$/1000 US gallons)*	12.1	13.5	14	14.2	14.2	14.2

* This is the average effective rate for consuming 3,000 US gallons per month (264.2 US gallons ¼ 1m^3).

quality of service goals expected of it, especially in the area of wastewater treatment.

In summary, the water sector in Belize has a well-developed regulatory framework that the Government, as the majority owner of BWS, has decided to circumvent. As a result, the lack of financial capacity to invest may jeopardize BWS's substantial gains in operating efficiency and its ability to meet coverage and quality of service goals.

2.2. *Agua Y Saneamientos Argentinos (AYSA) in Buenos Aires, Argentina*

In March 2006, 13 years after it had awarded a 30-yr concession contract for providing water and wastewater services to the metropolitan area of Buenos Aires to a private company, the Government of Argentina terminated the concession contract and created AYSA, under private company law, to provide the services that had been concessioned. The Government capitalized AYSA with an initial equity contribution of 150 million pesos (equivalent to about US$ 50 million). In exchange for this equity contribution, the Government owns 130,000 of the company's 150,000 shares. All these shares are denominated as Class A shares and represent 90% of the company's social equity.[4] AYSA's Board of Directors consists of five members, four of whom are designated by the Government as the Class A shareholder and one by the Class B shareholders.

2.2.1. *The Government Adapts Prior Regulatory Framework for AYSA*

Shortly after terminating the concession contract, the Government established a new regulatory framework that was largely based on the one in place during the concession with the private company. The underlying principle was that AYSA would operate through a concession contract that would be applied by an independent regulator (or in the case of the new framework, three separate bodies responsible for regulating and planning).

[4] The other 20,000 shares, denominated as Class B shares and which represent 10% of the company's social capital, are owned by the ex-employees of Obras Sanitarias de la Nación who had purchased shares in Aguas Argentinas.

The three main components of this revised regulatory framework are:

- A concession contract, expiring in end-2020, between AYSA and the Ministry of Federal Planning, Public Investment and Services (MFPPIS);
- The designation of a dependency of the MFPPIS as the entity with primary regulatory authority over the concession;
- A regulatory entity (ERAS — Entidad Reguladora de Agua y Saneamiento) and a planning agency (APLA — Agencia de Planificacion), both created out of the previous regulatory agency (ETOSS — Ente Tripartito de Obras y Servicios Sanitarios)[EXPLAIN THESE ACRONYMS]. ERAS and APLA are effectively advisory bodies to the MFPPIS.

Despite the apparently comprehensive nature of this regulatory framework, what portion of its cost of service AYSA is supposed to recover through its tariffs and how the Government intends to ensure the financial sustainability of AYSA is unclear. In fact, the company's tariffs have not been increased since January 2002, despite large increases in costs.

2.2.2. *AYSA's Efficiency is Deteriorating*

AYSA's relatively good operating efficiency has decreased since it was created in 2006, as shown in Table 2. In 2007, it reported a NRW level of about 36%, labor productivity of about 1.5 employees per thousand customers, and a collection rate of about 95%. However, between 2006 and 2008 its operating costs nearly doubled. This doubling of its operating costs, in combination with tariffs that have not been increased since, has led to a drop in operating cost recovery levels from about 105% in 2006 to about 70% in 2008.

Table 2: Operating and financial indicators for AYSA (2006–2008).

Year	2006	2007	2008
Ownership	Priv/Govt	Govt	Govt
Non-revenue water	36%	36%	36%
Employees per 1,000 connections	1.5	1.5	1.55
Operating cost recovery ratio	104%	96%	70%

Despite AYSA's poor financial situation, it is embarking on an ambitious capital expenditure plan to increase water coverage from about 80 to 100%, and sewerage coverage from 60 to 85% by 2011. These investments are also expected to improve some deficiencies in the quality of service, such as low water pressure. This plan — estimated by the company at about US$ 2,000 million [PLEASE SUPPLY IN NUMERALS TO AVOID AMBIGUITY OVER US/EURO BILLION] over the period 2008 to 2011 — is based on the expectation that the Government will provide subsidies to cover the required capital expenditures.

In summary, despite an apparently comprehensive regulatory framework that includes three separate entities with some responsibilities for planning and regulating AYSA, the company is not financially sustainable because its tariffs are too low. Therefore, AYSA depends on subsidies from the Government to cover its operating and maintenance costs as well as any capital expenditures.

2.3. *Guyana Water Incorporated (GWI) in Guyana*

In the early years of this decade, the Government of Guyana embarked on an ambitious program to improve the country's water systems. The government-owned utility supplying the capital, Georgetown, was merged with the government-owned utility supplying the rest of the country. The merged utility was established under general company law as Guyana Water Incorporated (GWI), with 100% of its shares owned by the Government.

An international tender was held to select a specialist water operator to manage GWI. In November 2002, the UK company Severn Trent Water International (STWI) was awarded a 5-yr performance-based Management Contract.

Since GWI was to be privately managed, the Government decided that it should be regulated in a way that the private utilities are generally regulated. Guyana already had a PUC, which had been created as the independent regulator of the telecommunications and electricity sector in 1990, and now operates under the 1999 Public Utilities Commission Act (Act 10, 1999). The PUC's remit was extended to the water sector in 2003. It was given the responsibility for regulation of tariffs, service quality and expansion, and the handling of customer complaints. GWI was issued a license giving it the right to operate, and specify the service standards that it must achieve.

Under STWI management, GWI made some gains. Hours of service started to improve. The utility filed a rate application with the PUC and a 10% increase — less than that sought — was approved in 2005.

Unfortunately, the gains made were well below the levels envisaged in the management contract. As a result, the Government terminated the management contract in February 2007.

After the contract was terminated, the Government appointed a new Chief Executive to run GWI. The regulatory regime, and GWI's corporate form, remained unchanged from what had prevailed earlier under the management contract.

In the two years since it became a government-controlled, conventionally-regulated utility, there is no evidence that GWI has been able to improve on any of the key indicators. NRW figures are unreliable, as neither bulk supply nor consumption are properly metered, but observers believe that the utility has not managed to make any significant improvements. As a result, Labor productivity has declined. (See Table 3).

Financial information is unreliable as GWI's accounts continue to be prepared late, and are heavily qualified by the company's auditor.

Table 3: Operating and financial indicators for GWI (2002–2008).

Year	2002	2003	2004	2005	2006	2007	2008
Ownership	Govt	Govt	Govt	Govt	Govt	Govt	Govt
Management	Govt	Priv	Priv	Priv	Priv	Mixed	Govt
Non-revenue water*		61%	66%	66%	72%	65%	65%
Employees per 1,000 active customers			3.8			3.08†	4.3
Operating cost recovery ratio‡		66%	57%	68%	40%	40%	40%
Average tariff (G$/m^3)			35	38	38	38	38

*2003–2005, Halcrow Review estimates; 2006, GWI estimate; 2007 and 2008, DFID Review estimate.

† August 2007 Management report.

‡ GWI calculations from the 2007 10-yr turnaround.

Notes: Some figures estimated from discussions with management and donors, due to lateness and unreliability of GWI accounts.

However, indications are that operating cost recovery has not improved. Tariffs remain well below the costs. Moreover, GWI continues to breach the service standards specified in its license.

In summary, after the utility reverted to government control, performance gains slowed or went into reverse. The regulator did not act to enforce service standards, and the utility did not apply for further tariff increases, even though these were manifestly required.

2.4. *Empresa de Servicios Sanitarios de Paraguay (ESSAP) in Paraguay*

In 2000, the Government initiated a program to reform the water sector in Paraguay. The reform included a law that allowed for the privatization of the government-owned water utility (ESSAP — Empresa de Servicios Sanitarios de Paraguay),[5] and a law that established a new legal framework for the sector and created a regulatory authority (ERSSAN — Ente Regulador de Servicios Sanitarios). However, in 2002, the Congress approved the Law 1932, which prohibited the privatization of ESSAP. As a result, the Government continues to own 100% of ESSAP's shares. Therefore, the regulatory framework established in anticipation of having a private company owning and controlling ESSAP applies to a government-controlled utility.

The new legal and regulatory framework created ERSSAN as the regulatory authority responsible for economic regulation of ESSAP and all other water and sewerage providers in Paraguay. However, the Government did not take the steps required to implement this regulatory framework as intended in the law. For example, the Government did not prepare the concession contract between itself and ESSAP that would have provided for ERSSAN's regulation of ESSAP. Without this concession contract, ERSSAN's role was largely eliminated and the Government, as the company's owner, effectively retained control over setting the company's

[5] ESSAP was created from the previous government-owned water utility (CORPOSANA — Corporación de Obras Sanitarias) and incorporated as a company under private law. The company is responsible for providing water and sewerage to all municipalities with a population greater than 10,000.

tariffs. Tariffs were therefore not increased at a time when the company would have required significant increases in internally generated cash to meet its existing financial obligations.

2.4.1. *ESSAP's Financial Obligations Limit any Possibility for the Company to Make Required Capital Expenditures*

In anticipation of the privatization of the company, the Government increased ESSAP'S tariffs in 2002. This increase in tariffs contributed to an improvement in the company's operating cost recovery level from about 131% in 2002 to 174% in 2003. However, without any further tariff increase after 2002, the operating cost recovery level fell to 154% by 2005. However, this seemingly high-operating cost recovery level, did not generate sufficient cash from operations. This happened because, at the time of ESSAP's creation, the Government established a financial obligation to itself in the form of a canon payment that was equal to about 60% of the company's operating revenues. As a result, the company was unable to plan and carry out the investments necessary to increase its efficiency, improve its poor service (frequent water shortages every summer), and increase its falling coverage levels (amongst the lowest in Latin America at about 80% in water and 40% in sewerage). In fact, between 2002 and 2005, the company invested less than US$5 million. In comparison, the estimated investment requirements for improving the company's quality of service and meeting the Government's coverage goals was approximately US$30 million over a 3-yr period (see Table 4).

In summary, following the cancellation of the process to privatize ESSAP, the Government failed to implement the comprehensive legal and regulatory framework that had been developed for the water sector. As a result, ESSAP has not had the financial capacity to make the required investments to improve its poor service and increase its low coverage levels.

2.5. *Water and Sewerage Authority (WASA) in Trinidad and Tobago[CHECK 'this is correct]*

In 1994, the Trinidad and Tobago Government decided to delegate the management of WASA, the islands' water statutory authority.

Table 4: Operating and financial indicators for ESSAP (2000–2005).

Year	2000	2001	2002	2003	2004	2005
Ownership	Govt	Govt	Govt	Govt	Govt	Govt
Non-revenue water				50%	50%	50%
Employees per 1,000 connections					5.6	5.2
Operating cost recovery ratio	130%	151%	131%	174%	166%	154%
Average residential tariffs (US dollar/m^3)*	0.48	0.41	0.34	0.31	0.33	0.32

* This is the average tariff for a residential customer that consumes $15m^3$ per month. In local currency terms (Paraguayan Guaranis—PGY) the rate was increased 17% from 1,681 PGY/m^3 to 1,966 PGY/m^3 in September 2002. The variations in US dollars are due to variations in the exchange rate between the US dollar and Paraguayan Guarani. From 2000 to 2005 the Paraguayan Guarani depreciated by about 76% against the US dollar.

The Government's purpose was to improve service quality, with particular reference to reliability and upgrading of the utility's infrastructure. A five-year management contract was concluded with a subsidiary of Severn Trent, the UK water company.

This was intended to be the first step towards a longer-term arrangement for private operation of the island's water system. In preparation for this longer-term PSP arrangement, the Government established the Regulated Industries Commission (RIC) by Act No. 26 of 1998. The RIC was given regulatory jurisdiction over the electricity and water sectors.

As it turned out, the Severn Trent team was not able to achieve the goals set in the management contract. When the contract ended in 1999, the Government decided to bring the utility back under government management, rather than proceed with the planned longer-term private participation arrangement. However, even while bringing the utility back into government control, the Government persevered with the regulatory regime created in anticipation of continued private participation.

Bearing in mind that the Government decided not to continue with private participation in light of the disappointing state of the utility at the end of the management contract, improvements in WASA's performance were clearly requried, and expected. However, in WASA's eight years as a government-controlled utility, operating under a conventional regulatory regime, no such improvements are in evidence (see Table 5).

Table 5: Operating and financial indicators for WASA The tariff reported is the domestic tariff only. However, tariffs for other customer categories have also not changed.

Year	1999	2000	2001	2002	2003	2004	2005	2006	2007	2008
Ownership	Govt	Govt	Govt	Govt	Govt	Govt	Govt	Govt	Govt	Govt
Management	Priv	Govt	Govt	Govt	Govt	Govt	Govt	Govt	Govt	Govt
NRW	45%	45%	45%	55%	55%	55%	55%	55%	55%	55%
Employees per 1,000 active customers	11	10	10	11	12	13	15	16	16	16
Operating cost recovery ratio	67%	63%	63%	59%	45%	45%	43%	42%		40%
Average domestic tariff (TT$/m^3)	1.75	1.75	1.75	1.75	1.75	1.75	1.75	1.75	1.75	1.75

Source: http://www.ric.org.tt/consultations/WASA/2008/Wasa%20BP%202008%20Complied.pdf.

Unaccounted water is estimated at 55%, and has been constant at that level since 2002. This is an estimate only, as the absence of bulk meters and customer meters means that actual consumption — and therefore losses — is not measured. Pilot loss reduction studies indicate that unaccounted water is in fact higher than 60% in some regions.

High system losses have resulted in water scheduling, with some areas in the country, receiving supply for less than 48 hrs per week. To respond to these frequent supply interruptions, most consumers have installed water tanks, which are replenished each time supply is provided to an area.

Labor efficiency has deteriorated, with the utility now employing 16 staff for every 1,000 connections, where previously only 10 were needed. Revenues covered only 63% of operating costs at the beginning of the period, and this figure has deteriorated steadily to the point that revenues are now only 40% of operating costs.

At the beginning of the period, WASA's tariffs were low by regional standards, and had not been increased for eight years. Despite this, and WASA's worsening financial position, tariffs have remained constant over the period.

In summary, the regulator has not been able to make WASA reduce costs, nor has it increased tariffs towards cost recovery levels for eight years. The regulator initiated a tariff review in December 2007. Till now this has not resulted in any ruling. However, it is possible that the situation may change when the ruling is eventually issued.

2.6. *Case Studies Analysis and Findings*

Table 6 summarizes changes in performance of the utilities while operating as conventionally-regulated government-owned companies, according to the four key indicators:

- *Network efficiency.* While BWS managed to continue the program of improvements started under private management, water losses remained high at AYSA, GWI and ESSAP, and actually worsened noticeably at WASA;
- *Labor efficiency.* ESSAP managed to slightly improve labor productivity, BWS remained constant, while AYSA, GWI and WASA all had declining labor productivity;
- *Operating cost recovery.* Reflecting their ability to control costs, ESSAP and BWS show some improvements in operating cost recovery, although not sufficient to cover the utilities' financial obligations. AYSA started the period able to cover its operating costs, but by the end of the period, tariffs were only sufficient to pay 70% of the operating costs. WASA started the period with operating losses, and these losses grew steadily. GWI had the lowest-level of cost recovery, and has not improved under government-control;
- *Average tariff level.* Since none of the utilities are able to cover their full costs, and cannot even cover their operating costs, tariff increases might be considered. However, due to lack of autonomy or authority to request tariff increases, none of the utilities studied, has increased tariffs during their period of government-control and conventional regulation.

Table 6: Overall summary of changes in performance. For each indicator, the table shows how many of the five utilities got better, how many stayed the same, and how many got worse, over their period of operation as a conventionally-regulated government utility. The bottom line in the table sums the total number across all the indicators.

Performance	Better	Same	Worse
Network efficiency (Non-revenue water %)	1	3	1
Labor efficiency (employees per 1,000 active customers)	1	1	3
Operating cost recovery (%)	2	1	2
Average tariff	0	5	0
Total (indicators)	4	10	6

The overall impression is of stagnation and regress. Among the five cases and four performance measures, half registered no change, four were improved, and six got worse.

It should be borne in mind that none of the utilities were doing well at the beginning of the period considered. In four cases, the government had taken back control of the utility from a private firm because of perceived problems. In the case of ESSAP, the government had been planning a public–private partnership to address the utility's performance problems, but Congress prevented it from implementing it. Clearly improvements were needed, and one might have assumed that a conventional regulatory system could have helped to deliver them. But this did not happen.

3. Regulatory Tools to Improve Governance

The lack of improvements in the case studies may seem to be surprising. Why did regulation alone not deliver the desired result of improving utility performance? Why the marked contrast to the experience of regulation combined with private participation?

With regard to the first question, we believe that the regulatory frameworks in place did not contribute to improving the performance of these utilities once government ownership resumed because of the persistent inability of government-owned utilities to obtain tariffs that recover costs. The constant theme emerging from the case studies is that the government utilities did not have the autonomy or authority to request tariff increases. Without any requests for tariff increases, regardless of how necessary they were, the regulatory framework was impotent. Therefore, we believe that the performance of the utilities considered would not have deteriorated even further without regulation.

With regard to the second question, the findings can be explained by the fact that conventional regulatory systems are designed to apply to profit-seeking firms. Conventional regulation works by channeling private, profit-seeking incentives towards publicly beneficial ends. By limiting tariffs to reasonable cost levels, and only adjusting them with a lag, regulation gives the private firms, an incentive to increase efficiency, because the resulting cost savings translate into higher profits. Regulators can also rely on profit-seeking firms to ask for tariffs that are above cost-recovery levels. Consequently, the focus of conventional regulation is on limiting tariffs to no more than reasonable cost recovery levels.

Conversely, most government-controlled firms do not seek profits. Managers in the utilities in our five case studies were not rewarded for making profits, nor punished for making losses. On the contrary, they may have been incentivized by the political system to increase certain types of cost, for example, to employ more staff. Similarly, the government-controlled utilities surveyed did not seek tariff increases. The dominant incentive was the political one of keeping tariffs low. As a result, the utility did not file for a tariff increase in any of the cases, and in three of the five cases, cost recovery fell.

Clearly, conventional regulatory designs cannot be relied upon to improve the performance of government-controlled companies. But in such cases this does not mean that the tools of regulation are of no value. Rather, it means that those tools must be used in new ways — ways that take into account the real incentive structure of the utilities to which they are applied.

In the remaining part of this section, we:

- analyze key governance problems that lead to utility under-performance (Section 3.1);
- analyze how regulatory tools may be used to improve governance (Section 3.2).

3.1. *Governance Problems and Utility Under-Performance*

The continued underperformance of the utilities in the case studies can be explained by their dysfunctional incentive structures, which in turn are a product of their poor governance arrangements. Better governance, then, is the key to better performance.

Public utilities can perform well if the accountability systems and incentives that drive them are well-designed. Figure 1 from the World Bank (2008) provides a generic framework for sector governance that can be used both to diagnose the short-comings of actual governance frameworks, and to design ways to improve them.

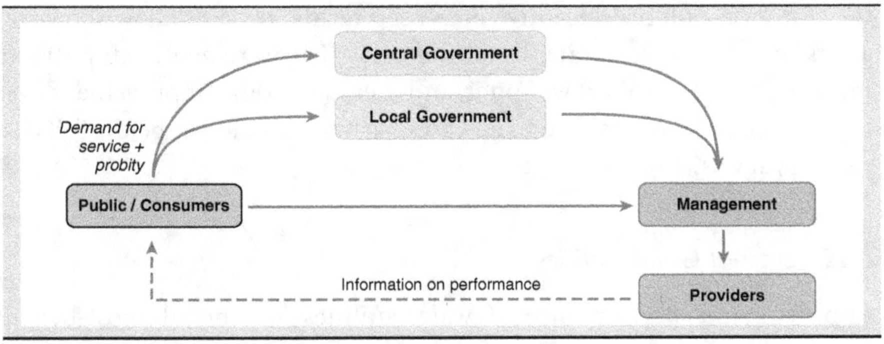

Figure 1: Governance framework. Dashed lines indicate a 'long route' of accountability needed when providers are not directly accountable to the public/customers. The short route of accountability refers to a situation where customers are able to directly seek redress from providers.
Source: World Bank, 2008.

The basic logic is that water providers have a monopoly power, and so product market competition is not enough to make them accountable to customers. Instead, a 'long route' of accountability is needed. In this 'long route,' the public turns to the government to ensure that good water services are provided at a reasonable cost. The government in turn ensures that the water provider meets public expectations. In principle, this system should be able to deliver good services, and it indeed does, in countries such as New Zealand and the Netherlands.

Though, all too often, the accountability links shown in Fig. 1 do not work properly. Three common problems are short-termism, interest group politics, and corruption.

3.1.1. *Short-termism*

Politicians focus on giving the public what they want before the next election, not in the medium term. Since water networks are long-lived and respond slowly to changes in how they are managed, short-termism can be disastrous. For example, most customers would prefer to pay a bit more and get a decent service. But because tariff increases are felt now, while the improvements they fund typically take a minimum of three years to be felt, the common political incentive is to keep tariffs low and allow the water assets to slowly deteriorate. In all the cases that were analyzed, NRW (a measure of asset quality) was poor, and there was some improvement over the period. only in one case In all cases, tariffs stagnated at below full cost recovery levels.

3.1.2. *Interest Group Politics*

Improving the performance of water utilities is generally cost-benefit justified, but not Pareto efficient. In other words, unlike in a Pareto efficient outcome where all will be winners, reforms of water utilities generate losses for some. The potential losers include consumers with illegal connections who are made to pay for water, and workers who are surplus to requirements and let go.

The poor state of many government-controlled water utilities can be explained by the political incentive to use the utility to court the support of particular groups. Networks are expanded into marginal electorates to win votes, regardless of whether or not the investment is economically justified. Public utility employment decisions may be driven by providing patronage to supporters. Indeed, in three out of the five case studies, the number of staff employed per 1000 active connections, increased during the period of combined government-control and conventional regulation.

3.1.3. *Corruption*

Public utilities control substantial resources. Those who control the utilities may seek to transfer these resources from public purposes to personal and party-political ends. Staff responsible for metering, billing and collections may facilitate illegal connections in exchange for bribes from the consumers — bribes that are often shared up the management chain, hence creating a systemic incentive to preserve illegal consumption.

Similarly, procurement of capital works, equipment and supplies is another common way for public resources to be transferred to private and political ends. The winners of these contracts are required to pay the staff responsible for them, or to make campaign contributions to the political party in power, in order to secure the contracts (Halpern *et al.*, 2008).

Indeed, Estache and Kouassi (2002) estimated that if corruption in water utilities could be eliminated, cost reductions of about 64% could be achieved. However, corruption benefits a small group of relatively powerful people. The costs of corruption are dispersed widely and borne largely by less powerful people. As a result, the governance structure of many utilities supports corrupt activities, rather than trying to root them out.

3.2. *Using Regulatory Tools to Improve Governance*

Of course, it is not new to observe that regulation and governance must work hand-in-hand. It is sometimes asserted that the best way to achieve this is to make government-owned utilities mimic private utilities. In this section we first explore this approach, observing that while it can work in certain situations, the case studies show that its application may be much more limited than it has often been assumed to be (Section 3.2.1). We then describe ways in which regulatory-like tools can be used to create more effective, but distinctly public sector governance arrangements (Section 3.2.2).

3.2.1. *Regulation Combined with Mimicking Private-Sector Governance has Limited Application*

Many countries have adopted 'corporatization' as a kind of 'privatization-lite' — an attempt to get the observed benefits of private management of commercial organizations, while avoiding some of the political costs of actual privatization. The New Zealand government pioneered this approach in the second half of the 1980s. It worked relatively well in New Zealand, was taken up by a number of state governments in Australia, and in time, also began to be recommended in developing countries.

While there are many forms of corporatization, in essence, the idea is to make a government-controlled firm behave like a private firm. This includes, giving it a separate legal identity, the right to spend the revenues it generates, an accrual accounting system, and a board of directors. It also includes giving the firm commercial objectives. For example, New Zealand's corporatization statute mandates that state-owned enterprises should make profits comparable to private firms.

Where the commercial mandate is effective — in the sense that board and management of a utility genuinely place profitability above political objectives — conventional regulation should help in improving performance. Managers will seek to boost profits, and so will try to keep tariffs above cost-recovery levels, while limiting their costs. They will also try to provide good service in order to avoid financial penalties for breaching regulatory standards. The State of New South Wales in Australia is among the jurisdictions which has taken this approach the furthest. The Independent Pricing and Regulatory Tribunal (IPART) regulates Sydney Water and a number of other corporatized water utilities in the State, and is generally said to make a significant contribution to improving their performance.

The achilles heel of the corporatization model depends on government-owned utilities being able to 'role-play' that they are private, and government ministers being able to role-play that they are shareholders. In New Zealand and Australia, this role-playing has worked. But it only seems to work in societies where there is a solid understanding of how company governance works, and a general belief that government should be an enabler, not a manager. Even in New Zealand, the initial zeal for profit-seeking, and arms-length relation between state-owned enterprises and governments, has decayed considerably in the two decades since the model was introduced.

The five case studies nicely illustrate the limits to applying the 'corporatization plus regulation' model in other social and political contexts. In all the five cases, the utility was a separate corporate entity. In four of the five cases it was incorporated under private company law. Yet in none of the five cases did the utility exhibit clear commercial incentives.

The reality is that, in the case study countries, the role-playing that the 'corporatization plus regulation' model requires is an alien concept. In Guyana, Belize and Trinidad, for example, applying for a tariff increase is a decision made by a political directorate, not the management or board of the utility. In fact, other board functions, such as appointing the Chief

Executive and approving the capital expenditure plan, are also made by the Cabinet.

A regulatory regime designed for profit-seeking firms is unlikely to be a good fit where the governance structure does not provide commercial objectives, to the utilities. What could work better in such a scenario?

3.2.2. *Regulatory Tools to Strengthen Democratic Accountability*

As we have seen, the governance structures of government-controlled utilities are generally quite different from those of privately-managed utilities, and have distinctive weaknesses. When citizens demand good services from the governments that control their utilities, but cannot get the governments or utilities to deliver, it means that something is wrong with the long-route of accountability. Either citizens cannot make governments do what they want, or governments cannot make government-controlled utilities to deliver. Fundamentally, the flaws in the accountability system are those that allow the problems of short-termism, interest group politics and corruption to persist.

Common flaws in the accountability system include information asymmetries, lack of capacity, and difficulties in making credible commitments. After analyzing these flaws, we suggest a few ways in which regulatory tools may be used to help overcome them.

Information asymmetries and lack of transparency. Citizens and the decision-makers that they elect, may not know what level of service is possible, and so have no benchmark against which to assess the level of service they are getting. In particular, they lack reliable information on what level of service should be reasonably possible at a given cost, and hence they cannot make cost-benefit trade-offs. They remain hostage to utility managers who assert that the service being provided is the best that can be achieved with the resources available.

Citizens and their elected politicians may also not know the actual levels of service being provided. Basic information like hours of supply and the percentage of the population served is lacking in many systems.

Finally, the quantity of government support to the water utility is usually hidden. The losses that the utility makes are concealed in deteriorating assets and accumulating debt burdens. Government support, rather than being transparent, may be spread across multiple capital programs and irregular bail-outs when the debt burden becomes unsustainable. In Guyana, for example, GWI is unable to pay its electricity bill, so it accumulates arrears to the state-owned power company, which the Government periodically clears. When no one has a clear view of the quantity of public resources that the water utility is consuming, citizens, politicians and officials simply cannot judge whether the resources are being well-deployed or not.

Not knowing the resources being deployed, or the results that should be attainable with those resources, or even the results actually attained, citizens are unable to hold their governments accountable, and governments are unable to hold their utilities accountable.

Difficulties in making credible commitments: Even if citizens had a clear understanding of the current situation, and about what is possible, that might not be enough. Politicians might promise to take a long-sighted view, but still cave into short-term incentives to keep tariffs low as an election approaches. Utility managers might sign up to reduce corruption but still seek to profit from kickbacks on construction contracts when they return to their offices. In other words, existing governance systems for government-owned utilities make time-consistent commitment, difficult. People make commitments, but will soon find it is in their interest to renege.

How regulatory tools can help: To overcome information asymmetries and transparency problems, three regulatory tools may be useful.

- *Benchmarking*: Regulators like OFWAT (in England and Wales) benchmark water utilities against each other to establish reasonable cost levels as an input to setting price caps. For a government-controlled utility, an agency that could provide benchmarking information understandable by citizens and their elected officials, might help with accountability by giving people a better idea of what is possible in the way of service and efficiency, and how well their own utility is doing. A number of countries, including the Philippines and Indonesia are trying this out. The World Bank's International Benchmarking Network for Water and Sanitation (IBNET) provides a global compilation of performance indicators.

As yet, however, these efforts suffer from problems regarding the reliability of the data, and the limited attention paid for making sure that it is accessed and understood by citizens and elected officials;

- *Reliable third-party analysis of achievable quality and cost combination*: Most regulatory processes involve analysis of utility business plans to ensure that the services are provided at a quality and cost that citizens prefer, and to optimize the trade-off between cost and quality. In the case of private utilities, the resulting service levels and tariff limits are then imposed on the company. In the case of government-controlled utilities, the real value of such an exercise may be useful in helping citizens and elected decision-makers to understand what is reasonably possible. For example, in a situation where the government effectively controls tariff levels, what is needed may not be an agency to limit tariff increases, but one which publicizes the likely medium term consequences — in the form of deteriorating assets and service — of failing to increase tariffs;
- *Performance contracts*: Accountability becomes easier when there is an agreement on what should be achieved, and reliable monitoring of whether or not it has been achieved. Relatively simple performance contracts, in which utility managers commit to government and the public to reach certain targets provided they are allowed to charge certain tariffs and receive other agreed support, could help here. While somewhat similar to the concession contracts used as the basis for regulation in Argentina and some other countries, the performance contract would differ in one crucial regard. It would not be legally enforceable between arms length parties, but rather, a basis on which citizens could judge whether or not their government is delivering (and vote accordingly), and governments could judge whether or not the utility management team is performing, and reward or replace them accordingly. One example is Sociéte Nationale d'Exploitation et de Distribution des Eaux (SONEDE), a statutory water body in Tunisia which has operated under such contracts since 1992. Another is the National Water Sewerage Company, which is a statutory body in Uganda that has also signed multi-year performance contracts (Baietti *et al.*, 2006).

Overcoming the problem of credible commitments within a government-controlled system is more difficult than providing information. In some cases, a government may overcome short-termism in tariff decisions for government-controlled utilities by delegating tariff-setting to an independent body. The Office of Utilities Regulation in Jamaica, for example, established its credibility as a telecommunications regulator, and was then able to order water tariff increases that were grudgingly accepted by the public. The Independent Pricing and Regulatory Tribunal (IPART) in New South Wales has been able to do the same. The Regulated Industries Commission in Trinidad has initiated a tariff review of WASA, so it will soon be known if it is able to achieve the tariff increase needed or not.

The limits to this approach also need to be considered. As a simple matter of mechanics, the regulatory regime needs to allow the regulatory authority to initiate tariff reviews on its own motion. Most conventional regulatory regimes — like those in Guyana and Belize — assume that the utility will apply for tariff increases. In these cases, government-controlled utilities have simply not applied for increases which they were entitled to. More fundamentally, where a regulatory body lacks popular legitimacy, governments likely to ignore or overturn their rulings to increase tariffs.

Finally, even if an independent regulatory body is successful in increasing tariffs, it may not do so well in making the utility to reduce its costs. In Jamaica, for example, the National Water Commission continues to be inefficient even as it is awarded even higher tariffs. The Office of Utilities Regulation, like other regulators of government-controlled utilities, can do very little. Since the Office does not manage the company, it cannot intervene directly, for example to lay-off surplus staff, change procurement practices, or introduce a NRW education campaign. At the same time, the conventional regulatory tool of finding a utility for non-compliance, or limiting tariffs to a level that covers only reasonable costs, does not work since it is ultimately the tax-payers who suffer the losses, not the utility's managers.

4. Conclusion

In conclusion, our five case studies show that the conventional regulation may be of little use in improving the performance of government-controlled water utilities. The problem is that conventional regulation does not address the governance problems that lie at the root of government-controlled utilities' performance problems.

Most obviously, the decision to apply for a tariff increase for a government-controlled utility typically lies with the government. Governments face systematic incentives for short-termism in tariff-setting. For this reason, none of the five government-controlled utilities in the cases studied, applied for a tariff increase, even though in all cases such an increase was needed.

More subtly, regulation cannot overcome the problems of corruption and interest group politics that drive up costs in government-controlled utilities. And because most government-controlled utilities are not commercially motivated, there is no inherent incentive for managers to reduce costs. Regulators may cap prices at no more than cost-recovery levels, or fine utilities for non-compliance, but the losses that the utility makes as a result will not make the utility's managers worse off, but simply be passed on to tax-payers.

It follows that the regulation cannot be applied to a government-controlled utility in isolation, but rather should be designed to support complementary governance reforms. A commonly advanced model has been to corporatize government-controlled utilities, give them commercial objectives, and then impose conventional regulation. This has worked to some extent in Australia, and in New Zealand's electricity sector. However, the evidence from the cases reviewed is that, corporatization as a governance reform only works in a limited set of circumstances. In all five cases, the utility was a corporate entity with formal commercial objectives, but these legal forms did little to limit the substance of direct government control for political ends.

A promising approach may be to apply some of the tools used by conventional regulators directly to improve governance. Poor governance stems in large part from citizens and elected officials being unable to judge whether the services being provided by the utility are the best that can be achieved with the resources available. Tools that could help include benchmarking, independent expert analysis, and reporting against agreed performance contracts.

Delegating decisions on tariffs and other regulatory questions to an independent body could help to overcome short-termism in tariff setting in some cases. But for this to work, the independent body must be able to initiate the tariff review itself, and must command popular respect. Even in cases where an independent body can help to keep tariffs in line with costs, it may not be able to keep costs down to reasonable levels. Other governance reforms, such as performance pay for managers, may well be more powerful than regulation, in improving the performance of government-controlled water utilities.

References

Araral, E (2008). The political economy of urban water in India and Southeast Asia. Presented at *3rd International Conference on Public Policy, Center for Public Policy*. Indian Institute of Management, Bangalore, India.

Asian Development Bank (2007). *Data Book of Southeast Asian Water Utilities 2005*. A partnership between The Southeast Asian Water Utilities Network and the Asian Development Bank. http://www.adb.org/documents/Books/SEAWUN/SEAWUN-Data-Book.pdf.

Baietti, A, W Kingdom and M van Ginneken (2006). Characteristics of Well-Performing Public Water Utilities. *Water Supply & Sanitation Working Notes No. 9*. World Bank, Washington DC.

Estache, A and E Kouassi (2002). Sector Organization, Governance and the Inefficiency of African Water Utilities. *Policy Research Working Paper 2890*. World Bank, Washington DC.

Gassner, K, A Popov and N Pushak (2007). An empirical assessment of private sector participation in electricity and water distribution in developing and transition countries. World Bank, Washington DC.

Halpern, J, C Kenny, E Dickson, D Ehrhardt and C Oliver (2008). Deterring Corruption and Improving Governance in the Urban Water Supply and Sanitation Sector: A Sourcebook. *Water Supply & Sanitation Working Notes No. 18*. The World Bank, Washington DC.

Komives, K, V Foster, J Halpern and Q Wodon (2006). *Water, Electricity and the Poor: Who Benefits from Utility Subsidies?* The World Bank, Washington DC.

McIntosh, A and Y Cesar (1997). *Second Water Utilities Data Book: Asian and Pacific Region*. Asian Development Bank, Manila.

Wagenheim, K, Editor/Publisher (1995). *Trinidad & Tobago: Water utility contract. Caribbean Update*, 11(5). New Jersey, US.

World Bank (2008). *Improving Governance and Fighting Corruption in the Water Supply and Sanitation Sector. Dissemination Note, Water Sector Board*. The World Bank, Washington DC.

CHAPTER 14

Effects of Regulatory Quality and Political Institutions on Access to Water and Sanitation

*Andrew B. Whitford**, *Helen Smith*† *and Anant Mandawat*‡

**School of Public & International Affairs, The University of Georgia, USA*
†*Princeton in Asia Fellow, Indonesia*
‡*Yale School of Medicine, USA*

This paper assesses the impact of regulatory quality, along with a number of political, economic, and social mechanisms, on disparities in access to clean water and adequate sanitation. We offer a series of vignettes using cross-national data from 2002 and 2004 to assess the effects of key institutional variables on the improvement of access to safe water and sanitation. The evidence is mixed for the two key variables of a country's commitment to "quality regulation" and the country's long-term development path as expanding or contracting access to water and sanitation.

Keywords: Access; sanitation; drinking water; disparities; poverty; regulation.

1. Introduction

Numerous recent studies have sought to show how the ability of the environment to sustain life depends on how humans interact in markets,

* Corresponding author. E-mail: *aw@uga.edu*.

polities, and societies. Most studies work on the presumption that societies should move away from older ways of engaging with the environment to new (and presumably better) ways of doing things (Dresner, 2002; Fullan, 2004; Bell and Morse, 2003; McDonough and Braungart, 2002; Doppelt, 2003; Edwards and Orr, 2005). One consequence of this debate is that policy analysts often focus on finding growth patterns that improve the economy and quality of life and still maintain a quality environment. Yet, the 1992 Rio Declaration on sustainable development also argued that "Human beings are the centre of concern for sustainable development. They are entitled to a healthy and a productive life in harmony with nature" (United Nations, 1993). Two of the most important linkages between the environment, development, and human health are access to clean drinking water, and the ability of communities to manage waste flows back into the environment through improved sanitation (Esrey, 1996).

Clean water and sanitation have been the central concerns of the public health movement for centuries (Beaglehole and Bonita, 1997). Access to safe drinking water and sanitation now stand among key known hazards or barriers that block communities from moving out of poverty and low-levels of development; moreover, these hazards are often accentuated — not mitigated — by rapid economic development (Corvalán *et al.*, 1999). Then, the central problem for many countries, is to supply access to water, a resource that stands in contrast to other environmental indicators like air quality because it is a survival requirement whose costs cannot be externalized. International organizations also see its importance; access to clean water and improved sanitation is important for achieving all of the United Nations Millennium Development Goals (MDG) outlined by organizations like the World Health Organization and the United Nations Children's Fund (UNICEF). For example, clean water and access to sanitation reduce water-carrying and health care burdens (often for women) and free labor to devote to economic and personal development. They lower child morbidity and mortality rates. Higher-level goals, like progress in education coverage, economic development, and health care, all depend on access to clean water.

In this chapter we focus on one key indicator as a possible cause of the degree of access in a country to clean water and sanitation: the "quality" of regulation in the country. We focus on this concept because it is a "low-dimensional" representation of the degree to which regulation supports active investment by the private sector. Important evaluators of economic development focus on the presence of regulatory quality as a marker of economies that are moving forward in the search for growth. For example, the World Bank has argued that a high-quality regulatory environment makes it amenable for businesses to contract; prominent economists say that the perceptions of regulatory quality are the important causes of economic growth, productivity, per capita income, and foreign direct investment for countries (Acemoglu *et al.*, 2005).

The presence of regulatory quality, though, is a function of the perceptions that the firms hold about the government and its commitment to specific policies with regard to the market. Firms perceive high-levels of regulatory quality if the regulatory burden that they bear is not excessive (or the tax burden is too distortionary) and the returns that they anticipate are sufficient to encourage investment and market entry. We build on this approach by focusing on how perceptions work. We examine whether or not expert informants perceive that the government's approach is market-unfriendly or excessive (e.g., in price controls, bank supervision, foreign trade, or business). Our approach here is built on a number of other papers, and is preferred because, it helps us to compare developed and developing nations (Bertelli and Whitford, 2009; Chinn and Fairlie, 2007).

The purpose of this chapter is to quantitatively investigate several possible foundations for access to clean water and improved sanitation, as measured across countries with varying geography, development patterns, social customs, and political arrangements. We are primarily concerned with testing hypotheses about regulatory quality of political institutions, levels of economic development, and the organization of society across a wide array of countries. We investigate the impact of attributes of political regimes such as the presence of parliamentary and presidential systems, representation systems like proportional representation, and the presence of federalism; we also assess the extent to which democratization increases access to water and sanitation. A number of recent studies argue that democratization causes nation-states to shift patterns of providing and preserving social benefits, but few assess the contribution at the levels that this chapter addresses. As noted above, our key measure of the shape of the political regime is the extent to which the country is perceived as having a high-quality regulatory regime.

We recognize that economic development, specifically the roles of a country's level of wealth (measured as per capita Gross Domestic Product), and its historical development path (whether the country's legal system has English origins) can influence the degree of access that the populations have, to improved water and sanitation.

We fully describe the rationale behind assessing the impact of these potential mechanisms below, but highlight here, the potential impact of the country's approach to regulation as of strong interest to those worried about the provision of these crucial public services. This chapter necessarily takes an aggregate or "high-level" view of potential mechanisms. Our data are measurements of the extent to which the public is provided with either improved water sources or improved sanitation, which we then disaggregate into rural and urban provision. We assess both overall disparity (what percentage of a country's population is served) and the disparities for these rural and urban populations.

The central contribution in this chapter is our use of cross-country statistical analysis of regulatory and political variables as major contributors to the access that people have, to improved water and sanitation. This approach stands in stark contrast with the vast majority of other papers on this set of social outcomes. We use a wide array of in-country experiences so that cross-country inferences tell us what regulatory environments contribute. The standard approach in these kinds of studies is the use of specific cases and/or the use of narrative explanations. Those approaches certainly have value, but here we suggest that our approach gives us the ability to center our investigations on causal factors that generally do not vary in a given country. This is important because the work of the United Nations and other interested non-governmental organizations usually comes down to statements that one country is doing well with regard to these metrics while another is lagging. The use of cases and narratives cannot generally help to answer the question of why we observe those disparities. For these reasons, our approach here is a unique contribution among the chapter represented in this book, and helps answer broader questions posed in a wide array of venues where analysts debate the ways to address these kinds of disparities.

Many of the potential causes listed below do not vary within country, although some certainly differentially affect different communities. Most are impossible for the decision-makers to change in the short-term. Thus, here the approach is largely "structural" in that we assess how these larger (macro) political, economic, and social structures affect the provision of water and sanitation. Perceptions of regulatory quality are different because governments can change behaviors that then change those perceptions. Perceptions are then indicators of a complex of behaviors that describe the government's interactions with the market. They offer insight into a "lever" in the search for improved social outcomes, whereas the other attributes investigated here represent "brakes".

Our data come from United Nations data assembled to help assess countries' performance towards meeting the MDG drinking water and sanitation targets (UNICEF, 2008). Our data come from two time periods (2002 and 2004) in order to limit the impact of a single measurement point in time on inferences about the impact of the mechanisms described earlier. We review a series of graphical and statistical discussions of these relationships, and then briefly describe multivariate regression results that assess the robustness of the bivariate results that were first reported.

Our view is that the gap in the literature on safe water access and sanitation is worrisome. No known papers address the impact of these political, economic, and social attributes on water scarcity, one of the most important areas for policymakers who are active in social development. The purpose of our chapter is to help fill this gap.

This chapter is organized as follows. The first section will discuss the key factors that this chapter assesses as potential causes of access to clean water and improved sanitation. Next, we briefly discuss our measurement strategies. In the third section, we review the results of the graphical and statistical approaches that we employ. Finally, we discuss our theory, data, test, and the implications of our results for our understanding of access to clean water.

2. Foundations

The central problem in meeting international development goals is determining the differences in reaching and serving rural versus urban populations. The MDGs lay out targets whose purpose is to lead countries closer to meeting the economic and social needs of their populations, but the MDGs imply specific services for specific populations that are often not met (de Janvry and Sadoulet, 2005). This is because of the mismatch between interventions and the locations of populations within countries; de Janvry and Sadoulet (2005) show that 25% of the World Bank's lending portfolio goes to rural development while 75% of world poverty is rural, that these are three times as many rural poor as urban poor worldwide, and that the incidence and depth of poverty are higher in rural areas. They see three themes as defining current development policy regarding this disparity: the use of income transfers for enhancing rural welfare, limits for reducing rural poverty through aggregate income growth, and migration to metropolitan areas as a main policy instrument.

On the policy analysis side, it is notable that most of the work done has centered on solutions to urban water availability problems, often for good reason (Bartlett, 2003; Allen *et al.*, 2004, 2006; Hanchett *et al.*, 2003; Pathak, 1999; Heller, 1999; Rheingans *et al.*, 2006; Altaf, 1994; Joardar, 1998; Martinez *et al.*, 2008; Choguill, 1999; Thompson *et al.*, 2000). Urban and peri-urban areas hold large numbers of people, are noticeable, and represent at-risk populations for disease and other problems associated with urban poverty. Water and sanitation are continuing concerns in urban areas. In this chapter, our purpose is not to dispute the necessity of serving urban populations: instead, we want to better understand the disparities in service provision among rural and urban populations, and investigate the degree to which the factors we detail below are associated with limiting or expanding service provision in these two different public service arenas.

The complaints of policy analysts like de Janvry and Sadoulet center on special needs in rural populations that are perceived as being neglected. In contrast, the litany of studies listed above on urban water needs show that most of our understanding mechanisms for handling water disparities come only in the urban public service provision sector. The problem we see is one of the limitations in inference: that we only learn by comparing mechanisms' performance across sectors, and that we only learn within sectors by comparing across places with varying social, political, and economic characteristics.

For these reasons, the data we employ center on cross-national comparisons of water and sanitation availability for rural and urban populations. Central issues in analyses of clean water and sanitation provision are variable definition and data availability. For instance, consider the 2008 UN-Water Global Annual Assessment of Sanitation and Drinking-Water (GLAAS), which seeks to provide a global and a comprehensive report on a periodic basis to help policymakers better understand the sanitation and drinking-water sectors (World Health Organization, 2008). This in-depth report complements the ongoing WHO/UNICEF Joint Monitoring Programme for Water Supply and Sanitation (JMP), the primary way in which the UN monitors the MDG target for water and sanitation. The JMP constructs estimates of coverage levels for each country that are disaggregated between sanitation and drinking water, and between urban and rural areas.

Our data come from the 2002 and 2004 JMP estimates for a wide array of countries. Differences exist between JMP coverage estimates and country-reported coverage estimates, usually based on whether different levels of "improvement" in water or sanitation facilities should be included in a given category (World Health Organization, 2008: 12). Those differences come because of the overall purpose of the JMP: to provide estimates that are globally comparable and represent a "best fit" to the trend in improvement or degradation that is occurring at the country-level. In contrast, the GLAAS offers measures that are perhaps more in-depth in specific countries (responding to those countries' concerns that the JMP underestimates the extent of provision of water and sanitation services), but does so by only examining a relatively small number of countries. We may lose some fine measurement resolution at the individual country-level, but our purpose is best served in this chapter by enhancing our coverage of many different types of countries with varying social, economic, and political institutions.

3. Measuring Regulatory Outcomes and Effectiveness: What Do We Know?

Next we turn to describing the key variables that we examine here graphically and statistically, as potential mechanisms underpinning the variation observed across countries in the provision of water and sanitation services to the overall population and their rural and urban subpopulations.

3.1. *Political Institutions and Behaviors*

Our first key indicator is the "quality" of regulation in the country. As noted above, we start with this concept because it is a "low-dimensional" representation of the degree to which regulation supports active investment by the private sector. Essentially, firms perceive high-levels of regulatory quality if the regulatory burden that they bear is not excessive (or the tax burden is too distortionary) and the returns that they anticipate are sufficient to encourage investment and market entry. The World Bank has argued that a high-quality regulatory environment is valuable if it makes it amenable for businesses to contract. Economists argue that perceptions of regulatory quality are fundamental to the long-term trajectory of economic growth, productivity, per capita income, and foreign direct investment (Acemoglu *et al.*, 2005). Our approach is built on the how perceptions work — on whether the government's approach is perceived by expert informants as market-unfriendly or excessive (e.g., in price controls, bank supervision, foreign trade, or business), and helps account for comparison problems between developed and developing nations (Bertelli and Whitford, 2009; Chinn and Fairlie, 2007). We offer the following hypothesis:

H1: Greater provision of water and/or sanitation is positively associated with stronger perceptions that the state engages in quality regulation of the market.

Our data come from the World Bank's Governance Indicators estimate of each country's "regulatory quality". This measure is fully described in the Technical Appendix.

We next offer the hypothesis that a country's level of democratization is positively associated with a country's commitment and ability to attain access to clean water and sanitation. A number of studies have asked whether democracies are more environmentally committed than non-democracies (Congleton, 1992; Midlarsky, 1998; Torras and Boyce, 1998; Barrett and Grady, 2000; Gaston and Fredriksson, 1999; Gleditsch and Sverdrup, 2002; Neumayer, 2002; Grafton and Knowles, 2004). These studies mostly argue that the free speech and press rights associated with democracies make citizens more informed about the importance of the environment and ways to alleviate environmental and public health stresses. Armed with this knowledge, citizens of democracies will place greater pressure on their government for positive environmental policy. There is strong evidence from social service provision that the democratic regimes are more likely to serve underrepresented populations, as seen in the cases of both literacy (Brown and Hunter, 1999) and even electric power provision (Brown and Mobarak, 2009).

However, we also recognize that the same individual liberties that lead to greater environmental commitment can also lead to greater environmental stress. The key to whether democracies are better able to commit to clean water access will be the balancing of the desires of the citizens and businesses in a democracy. Some studies assess this relationship because of the selection of cases from only industrialized democracies (Scruggs, 1999; 2003). Most studies of democracy find a positive effect, but many are limited to policy outputs. Others find varied support for improved environmental outcomes, usually in the case of air and water pollution levels or for land set-asides. While much of the debate has occurred over the measurement of democracy, we are equally troubled with the lack of attention to the effect of democracy on aggregate environmental outcomes. Consideration of the adoption of particular policies is a useful route of inquiry, as is gaining knowledge of the effect of democracy on individual policy outcomes. Yet, aggregate information is much desired in statements about access to clean water. Is democracy a prerequisite? Are inferences about the role of democracy policy-specific? We offer the hypothesis:

H2: Greater provision of water and/or sanitation is positively associated with higher levels of democratization.

Our data come from the Polity IV estimate of each country's level of democratization. This measure is also fully described in the Technical Appendix.

Our third political regime variable is the constitutional choice to have a federal system. On one hand, a number of studies have asked whether federalism is associated with lower environmental quality, which suggests that access to safe drinking water and sanitation would also be lower (Lowry, 1992; Scruggs, 1999; Eser, 2002; Helland and Whitford, 2003; Rabe, 2004; 2005). The answer appears to depend on context. Within countries, it is clear that states can make policy choices that lead to lower levels of environmental protection. The vertical delineation of tasks often makes the coordination and execution of environmental policy difficult. Environmental problems do not necessarily respect political boundaries, so national implementation might be more effective. The core hypothesis in much of this literature is that, aggregate environmental protection suffers from a "race to the bottom" when more active states push through stringent environmental laws, but other states (catering to capital and business interests) loosen their environmental regulations in response to perceived flight risk. Of course, we note that the increased power of capital may not be a by-product but instead an intentional outcome for federal systems that intend to be "market-preserving" (Weingast, 1995). While there is evidence that states vary in terms of environmental and thus public health commitment, other analyses show limited differences (but those studies have rarely addressed federal systems in less developed areas). We assess this claim in a set of countries with varied social, economic, and political features by offering this hypothesis:

H3: Greater provision of water and/or sanitation is positively associated with federalism.

Our measure of "strong federalism" comes from the Database of Political Institutions, and is described in the Technical Appendix. "Strong federalism" refers to states for which regional and local political leadership is directly elected.

Next, we turn to three narrow hypotheses about specific representation structures in the political regimes of the countries under study. We note that a number of important studies focus on the roles of proportional representation (PR) and single-member plurality (SMP) systems in organizing how citizens individually and collectively are represented in the government; for example, Persson and Tabellini (2003) argue that majoritarian systems provide direct accountability for politicians (e.g., reducing opportunities for corruption), and that relegating political competition to a small number of candidates in each district gives political outsiders few opportunities to challenge incumbents. Powell (2000) argues that proportional representation systems generally outperform plurality systems when translating votes into either majority governments or coalitions close to the median voter. This gives us a theoretical expectation that PR may be more responsive to minority interests, such as those underserved by public services like the provision of clean water and sanitation. We offer the following hypothesis:

H4: Greater provision of water and/or sanitation is positively associated with proportional representation.

Our data on proportional representation systems also come from the Database on Political Institutions.

Our next two narrow hypotheses focus on the broad institutional distinction between presidential and parliamentary regimes. The centralization of power under presidential arrangements does not distribute power as widely as the legislative authority does, wielded by the leadership in parliamentary systems, (Mainwaring, 1995; Shugart, 1999). While in presidential systems, both the party leadership and the chief executive must approve legislation, the president controls certain rents independent of a legislative check. This unconstrained authority over the creation and distribution of rents may make presidents less likely to represent underrepresented constituencies (like the ones we observe in our data here) than are prime ministers (Baldez and Carey, 1999). Parties are stronger in parliamentary systems, and checks are weaker because, parties in presidential systems are not required to organize to form governments. Additionally, the uncertain timing of elections may act to constrain parliamentary leadership due to the constant threat of no-confidence votes and subsequent dissolution. We note, though, the argument that presidents are elected from a national constituency, providing a direct line of accountability between principal and agent (Lijphart, 1984; Mainwaring, 1995; Shugart, 1999; Cox and Morganstern, 2001; Persson and Tabellini, 2003). We focus on the first rationale, though, in offering two hypotheses:

H5a: Greater provision of water and/or sanitation is positively associated with parliamentary systems.

H5b: Greater provision of water and/or sanitation is negatively associated with strong presidential systems.

We note that the omitted case here is weak presidential systems — those in which an assembly selects the president; in contrast, in strong presidential systems the president is directly elected to office. Our data on presidential and parliamentary systems also come from the Database on Political Institutions.

3.2. *Economic Attributes*

We know that other factors may contribute to a country providing access to clean water and sanitation, including a country's development path. The Porter hypothesis claims that environmental progress can be achieved without sacrificing competitiveness; yet, sustainability is not directly caused by increased GDP (Porter and der Linde, 1995). Esty and Porter (2001) show that strong environmental performance is positively correlated with competitiveness and national income, they also show that there are dramatic differences in environmental performance among different countries at similar economic levels. Related is the debate over whether there is an inverted U-shaped relationship between national income and pollution (Grossman and Krueger, 1995), although evidence for that relationship is limited in large samples and very specific policy outcome measures (Stern, 2004).

Below, we provide evidence about the impact of GDP on access to water and sanitation. We know that greater provision of water and/or sanitation is positively associated with higher levels of national income. Our data come from the Penn World Tables, and are measured as per capita GDP (accounting for purchasing power parity) (Heston *et al.*, 2009). We also calculate the natural log of this measure due to high skew. The details are presented in the Technical Appendix.

Our focus in this chapter is on broader potential causes that are related to institutions, so we assess whether historical development paths affect the provision of these public services — specifically, whether common law and the support of property rights are positively or negatively correlated with access to clean water. Property rights not only allow for security of contract and capital, but also lead to rapid economic growth and decreased access to clean water (Acemoglu *et al.*, 2000; La Porta *et al.*, 1999). Our hypothesis is:

H6: English origins are associated with lower levels of access to clean water and/or sanitation.

Our data on English origins comes from Acemoglu *et al.* We investigate only the impact of English origins (and not the impact of having origins in other countries such as France or Germany) due to the focus on the development literature on this factor.

4. Distributions of Types of Access

Figure 1 shows the distributions for three ways of looking at disparities in the provision of improved water sources: to (a) the total population; (b) the rural subpopulation; and (c) the urban subpopulation. The data shown here in the top two panels of Fig. 1 are from 182 countries measured at two time points (2002 and 2004); the third panel includes data from 188 countries, using the United Nations data described earlier.

The countries that scored "100" for the percentage of the total population served by improved water include some expected ones (e.g., Norway, Switzerland, Cyprus), and perhaps some unexpected ones

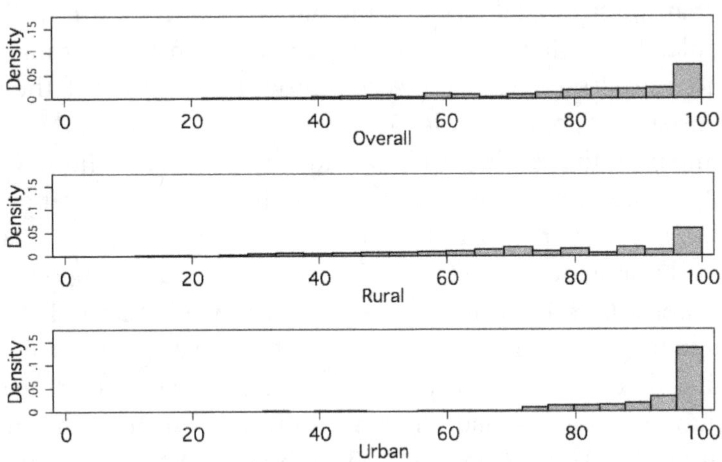

Figure 1: Access to improved water source.

(e.g., Saint Kitts and Nevis, Uruguay, Lebanon). The three lowest scores in the overall population data for this measure are Afghanistan (13%), Ethiopia (22%), and Somalia (29%). The mean percentage for the data shown in the overall population panel is 81.8%, with a standard deviation of 18.8%; Fig. 1 shows a clear left skew in the distribution.

The rural population panel shows a much thicker left tail for the distribution in the middle panel of Fig. 1. The countries that scored "100" for the percentage of the rural population served by improved water again include some expected countries (e.g., Austria, Switzerland, Germany), and perhaps some unexpected countries (e.g., Belarus, Tonga, Niue). The three lowest scores in the overall population data for this measure are Afghanistan (11%), Ethiopia (11%), and Romania (16%). The mean percentage for the data shown in the overall population panel is lower than the overall level reported above (74.4%), with a larger standard deviation of 22.8%; again, Fig. 1 shows a stronger left skew in the distribution.

The third panel in Fig. 1, for the urban subpopulation panel, shows a much thinner left tail for the distribution. The three lowest scores in the overall population data for this measure are Afghanistan (19%), Somalia (32%), and Chad (40%). The mean percentage for the data shown in the overall population panel is much higher than the overall level reported above (91.6%), with a smaller standard deviation of 12.3%. Figure 1 shows that the strong left skew in the distribution comes from the rural subpopulation — that the urban subpopulation in the vast majority of countries is well-served by access to improved water. Indeed, the median for the urban subpopulation is 97% covered.

Comparing the results in Fig. 1 with those in Fig. 2 shows the three populations' access to improved sanitation. In this case, the left tails of all three distributions are much thicker than those in Fig. 1. The average for the overall population is 66.0%, while that for the rural subpopulation is much lower (56.9%) and for the urban one much higher (78.7%). Note that though all three measures are lower than that for water provision, indicating that this good is rare across the countries. The three lowest scores in the overall population data for this measure are Ethiopia (6%), Afghanistan (8%), and Chad (8%). The three lowest scores in the urban subpopulation are Congo (14%), Afghanistan (16%), and Ethiopia (19%).

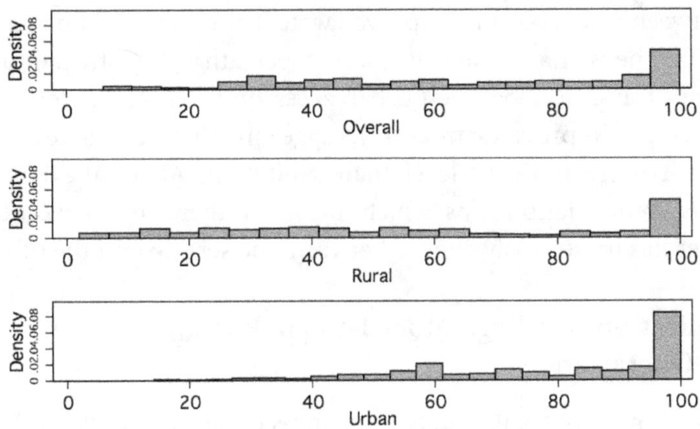

Figure 2: Access to improved sanitation.

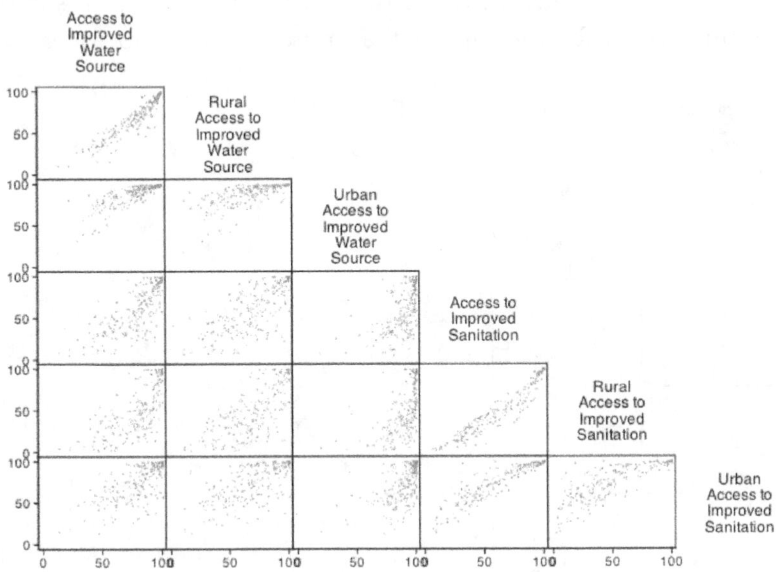

Figure 3: Relationships between disparities.

The three lowest scores in the rural population data are Congo (2%), Eritrea (3%), and Chad (4%).

Figure 3 shows how these six measures relate to one another. Note that for a number of relationships, we see a curvature rather than straight lines (e.g., between rural access to improved water source and urban access), indicating that one is attained at much faster speed than the other. Others show strong clustering (e.g., between urban access to improved water source and urban access to improved sanitation), suggesting that water access is attained at a much more uniform level than sanitation. All of the panels show upward-sloping relationships, which mean that there are no overt tradeoffs: one never has to expressly choose between one service and the other.

5. Implications for Regulatory Design, Effectiveness, and Operation

Next, we turn to assessing the relationships described above in the discussion of our individual hypotheses. We first discuss the evidence about the role of the regulatory environment by showing a graphic of the relationship and then assessing early statistical evidence. Figure 4 shows the scatterplot matrix for the case of the improved access to water sources

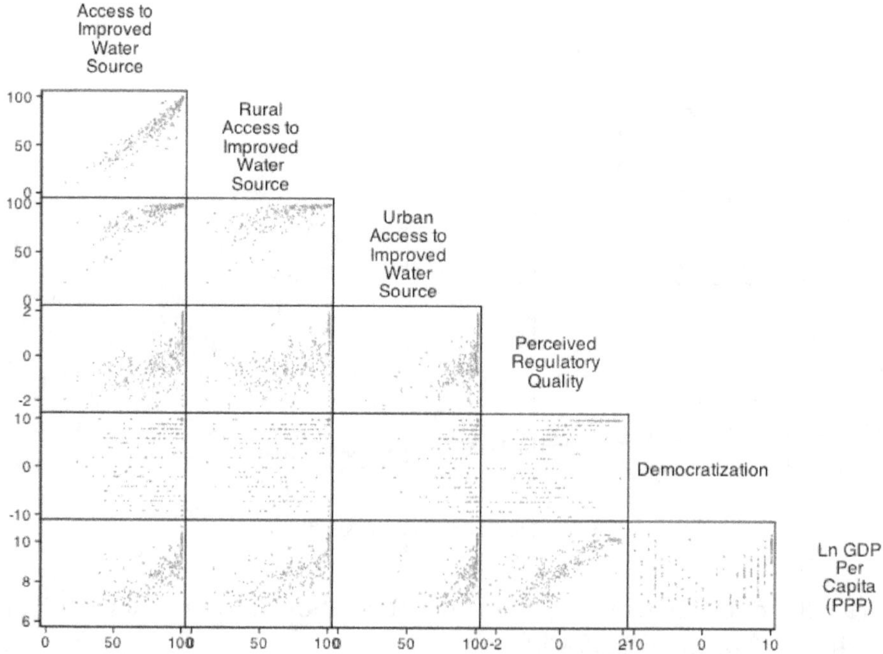

Figure 4: Relationships between disparities in access to improved water source and potential causes.

Table 1: Correlations

	Rural Improved Sanitation	Rural Improved Water Supply	Urban Improved Sanitation	Urban Improved Water Supply
Regulatory Quality	0.555***	0.549***	0.531***	0.505***
Democracy	0.343***	0.374***	0.291***	0.325***
Ln GDP Per Capita	0.754***	0.706***	0.743***	0.570***

Notes: * indicates significance at better than 0.05.
** indicates significance at better than 0.01.
*** indicates significance at better than 0.001.

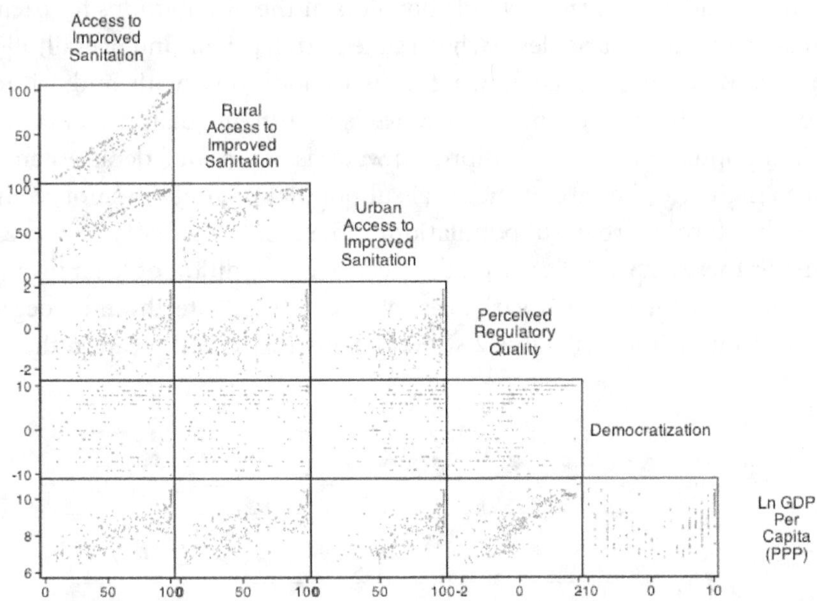

Figure 5: Relationships between disparities in access to improved sanitation and potential causes.

(measured for our three different populations); Table 1 shows the correlations. The scatterplot matrix suggests a positive relationship, and the estimated correlations are 0.549 (rural water) and 0.505 (urban water) (overall water is omitted since the measure is itself a blend of the two subpopulations). Figure 5 shows graphic for sanitation, and Table 1 shows the estimated correlations to be roughly the same as that for water. On its face, this appears to provide evidence that water and sanitation outcomes are positively related to perceptions of the quality of the regulatory regime across a wide array of countries.

In contrast, Figs. 4 and 5 show slightly upward-sloping but noticeably more diffuse relationships between democratization and our six dependent variables. Table 1 shows correlations in the 0.30–0.40 range, suggesting a weaker relationship between these outcomes and democratization. In some ways, it is useful to note any relationship here, but the contrast with regulatory quality remains important.

Next we review the relationships between our measures of access to water and sanitation and our remaining political institutional variables. Figures 6 and 7 show side-by-side boxplots of the distributions for each of our six dependent variables; each variable (rural, urban, and overall, all for water and sanitation) is shown for two conditions: with and without strong federalism. The simple inference is that the median percentage for overall population access to improved water is higher in federal systems; it is also higher in the case of the rural subpopulation, but does not seem to be higher for the urban subpopulation. Table 2 shows difference-in-means tests for these six variables given the treatment condition of federalism; all tests account for unequal variances by calculating Satterthwaite's degrees of freedom for the test. Table 2 shows a higher expected mean in the case

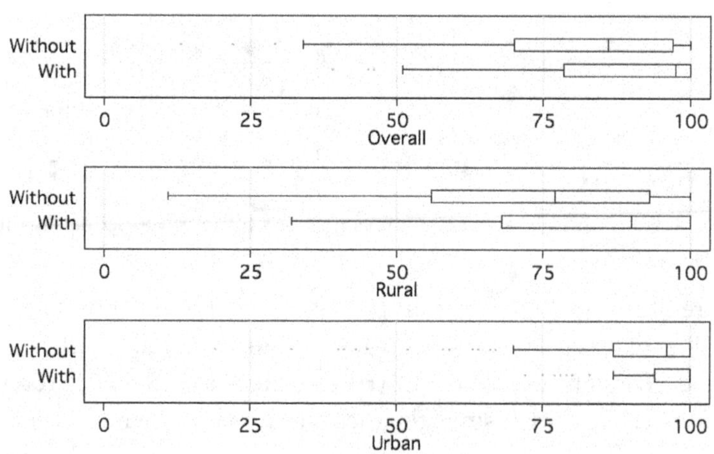

Figure 6: Disparities in access to water, by strong federalism.

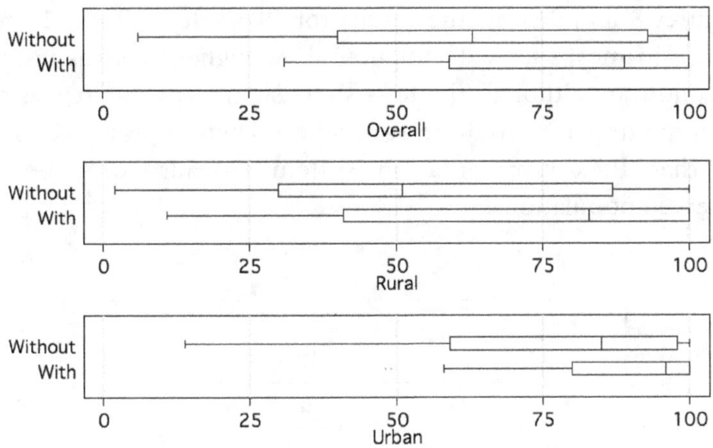

Figure 7: Disparities in sanitation, by strong federalism.

Table 2: Difference of Means Tests

	Rural Improved Sanitation	Rural Improved Water Supply	Urban Improved Sanitation	Urban Improved Water Supply
English Origins	5.596	4.229	2.425	0.646
PR	4.390	4.960*	5.471**	3.401**
Parliamentary	21.461***	14.731***	13.020***	6.230***
Presidential	−20.747***	−18.067***	−12.480***	−4.977***
Federalism	13.095**	8.148*	10.275	4.732***

Notes: * indicates significance at better than 0.05 (two-tailed test).
** indicates significance at better than 0.01 (two-tailed test).
*** indicates significance at better than 0.001 (two-tailed test).

of the rural subpopulation in the strong federalism condition (by 13.1% points); the urban population mean percentage is expected to be 4.7 points higher. The impact of federalism appears higher in the case of removing rural disparities than urban ones. Figure 7 shows the estimated differences in the case of sanitation, with rural differences even greater in the case of strong federalism; urban means are also expected to be higher, but that difference is not estimated to be statistically significant.

Figures 8 and 9 show the results for PR's effects; Table 2 shows the difference-in-means tests. The figures show higher medians in the treatment condition, although the tests show significant differences only for water supply and improved rural sanitation. There appears to be some evidence that PR's representation system spreads some benefits to underserved populations.

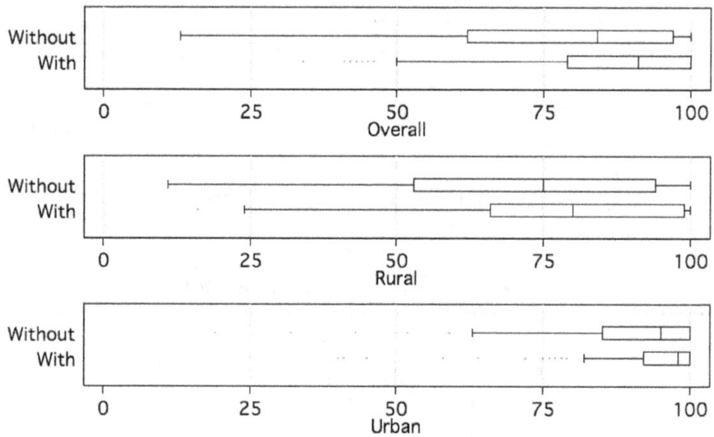

Figure 8: Disparities in access to water, by PR.

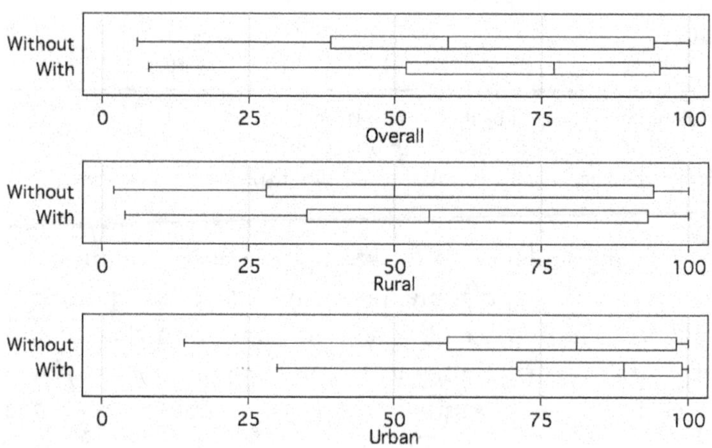

Figure 9: Disparities in sanitation, by PR.

Figures 10 and 11 show the results for having a parliamentary system; Figures 12 and 13 show the results of having a strong presidential system. Table 2 shows the difference-in-means tests. The figures show higher medians in the treatment condition for parliaments, and roughly the same reduction in medians for having a strong presidential system. The tests show significant differences for all sub-populations and for both water

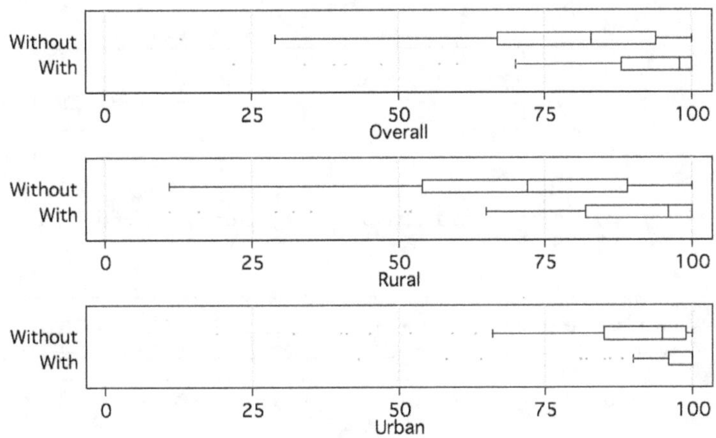

Figure 10: Disparities in access to water, by parliamentary system.

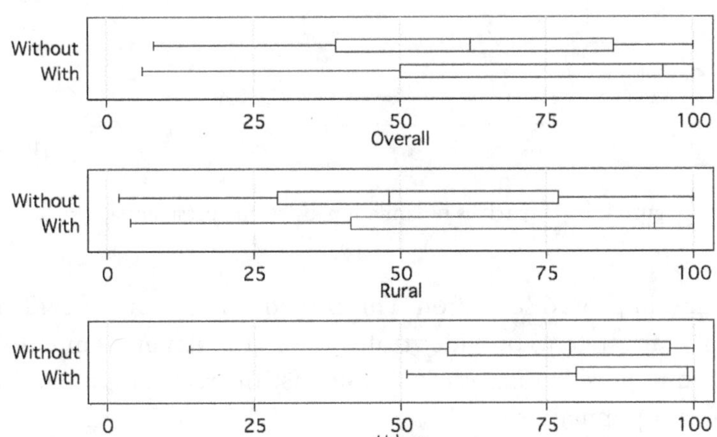

Figure 11: Disparities in sanitation, by parliamentary system.

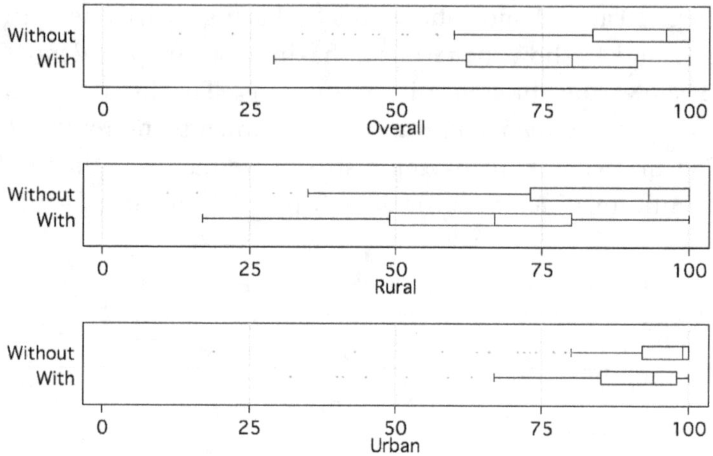

Figure 12: Disparities in access to water, by strong presidential system.

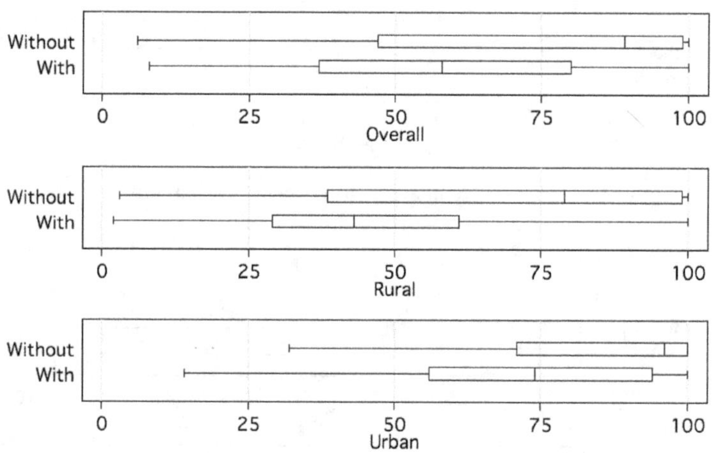

Figure 13: Disparities in sanitation, by strong presidential system.

supply and improved sanitation. This provides a measure of evidence that parliamentary systems provide greater access to water and sanitation when compared to presidential systems. Note that the real gains are in the cases of rural sub-populations.

Does this mean that political institutions and outputs are the most important drivers of access to clean water and improved sanitation? In contrast, Figures 4 and 5 show a fairly strong upward-sloping relationship between GDP and access to water and sanitation. The estimated correlations reported in Table 1 range between 0.57 and 0.76, indicating strong associations. The effects of our second "development path" variable, English origins, are shown in Figures 14 and 15. The graphs indicate no significant differences, although the difference-in-means tests in Table 2

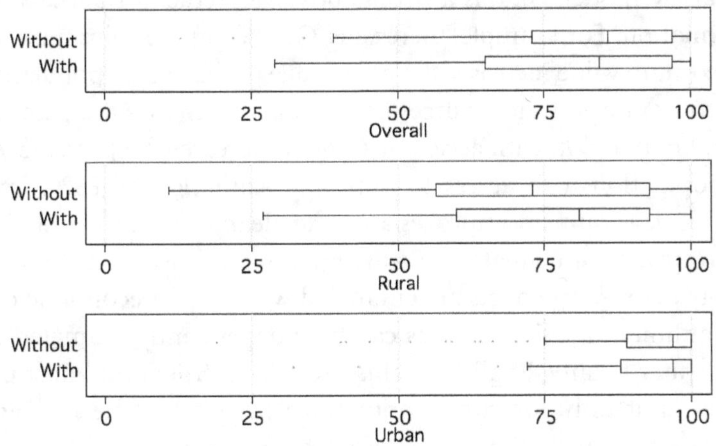

Figure 14: Disparities in access to water, by English origins.

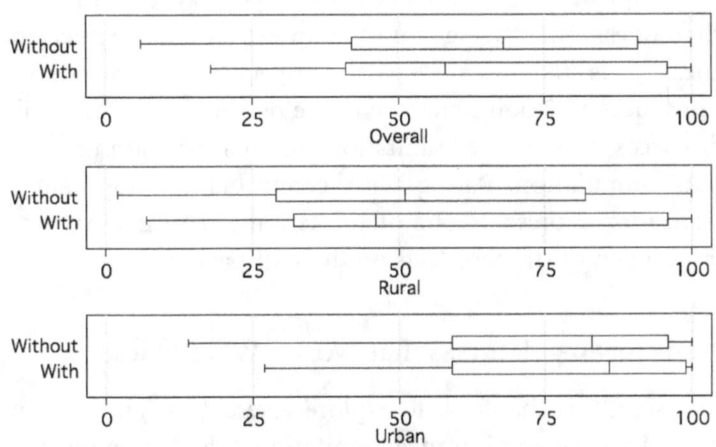

Figure 15: Disparities in sanitation, by English origins.

show slight positive (but not statistically significant) impact. In general, though, GDP seems to be a strong and important predictor of the degree to which countries mitigate urban and rural disparities in clean water and sanitation provision.

Are these results robust to multivariate analyses? Those analyses, which are not presented here due to space limitations, provide useful guides for interpreting the results shown earlier. The key findings are as follows. In a multivariate model, GDP is a strong, positive predictor of access to water and sanitation. For example, increasing GDP from the minimum value to the maximum value increases the percentage of the overall population with access to improved water sources by 56%; and increases the percentage of the rural population with access by 60%. It increases the percentage of the rural population with access to improved sanitation by 88%. Improved economic development improves access to clean water and sanitation.

Perceptions of regulatory quality are not a robust predictor of access, probably because its effects are entangled with that of economic development (although its direct effects can be independently estimated). In the case of water quality, English origins provide an 8% point boost in access to water (but only for rural populations). No other mechanisms have robust associations in the case of clean water access.

In the case of access to improved sanitation, the only additional robust association is the impact of democratization. Democracies are more likely to provide improved sanitation services — especially for rural populations, and urban ones, too. Moving from the lowest-level of democratization to the highest-levels still does not have the impact of economic development. It only produces a 17 point increase in the percentage of the rural population with access to improved sanitation, and half of that in the case of the urban sub-population. Along with economic development, though, democratization represents one of the few mechanisms explored in this chapter with demonstrable effects on these disparities.

6. Lessons for Regulators: What Works, What Doesn't?

The purpose of this chapter is to explore several possible foundations for access to clean water and improved sanitation. We offer an investigation of these foundations using data with access to improved water and sanitation, as measured across countries with varying geography, development patterns, social customs, and political arrangements. We test hypotheses and investigate the impact of attributes of political regimes such as the presence of parliamentary and presidential systems, representation systems like proportional representation, and the presence of federalism; we also assess the extent to which democratization increases access to water and sanitation.

We provide some evidence that (as other recent studies also do) democratization causes nation-states to shift patterns of providing and preserving social benefits. Our final measure of the shape of the political regime is the extent to which the country is perceived as having a high-quality regulatory regime; we do not find robust evidence that regulatory quality improves access.

Our primary finding is that economic development, specifically the roles of a country's level of wealth (measured as per capita GDP), builds the foundation on which countries can expand service provision. There is some evidence that historical development path (whether the country's legal system has English origins), plays a direct role here, but it is likely that the role is really indirect — that English origins support broader economic development, which then filters down to sub-populations through expanded access.

We believe that our real contribution is to move the discussion about mechanisms to the world of real data that come from the United Nations and assembled to help assess countries' performance towards meeting the MDG drinking water and sanitation targets. We believe that the gap in the literature on safe water access and sanitation — that no known papers address the impact of these political, economic, and social attributes on water scarcity — puts policymakers in a tough position when deciding about mechanisms to pursue this sort of social development. Access to safe drinking water and sanitation now stand among key known hazards or barriers that block communities from moving out of poverty and low-levels of development; but the evidence here is that the reverse may be true — that the key lever to be pulled is economic development for countries who want to supply access to water.

Technical Appendix

This appendix describes variables collected for the countries included in this study. Much of our data was generated by projects at the World Bank: The Database on Political Institutions (DPI) and the Governance Matters database. The former offers cross-country data chronicling the political institutions of 177 states whereas the latter measures perceptions of governance in 213. The data stem from work performed by Beck *et al.* (2001) and Kaufman *et al.* (2003). The variables that we employ are catalogued below. The DPI was updated in 2008. The data are available at: http://econ.worldbank.org/WBSITE/EXTERNAL/EXTDEC/EXTRESEARCH/0,,contentMDK:20649465~pagePK:64214825~piPK:64214943~theSitePK:469382,00.html.

Proportional Representation. This variable describes whether or not a state uses proportional representation to elect all or a portion of its legislators. A political system is coded "1" if either chamber of the legislature is elected based on the percent of votes received by their party and/or if Beck *et al.*'s sources specifically refer to the system in question as "proportional". The state is coded "0" if these conditions do not apply. N/A is recorded if the Legislative Index of Electoral Competitiveness for the country is 4 or lower, meaning that there is competition for seats, albeit in a one-party system. Source: Beck *et al.*, 2001.

Parliamentary or Presidential Systems. This variable designates political systems as either presidential, assembly-elected presidential or parliamentary. The system is coded presidential (0) if a single executive is elected by popular vote. Additionally, a system is coded presidential if the chief executive is elected by an assembly and can only be recalled by a two-thirds vote or dissolution of the assembly. The system is coded "1" if the assembly elects, but cannot recall the chief executive. Finally, in cases where both a president and prime minister exist, a system is deemed presidential only after passing a three-part test. First, the president must be able to veto legislation while the parliament may only override if it possesses a super majority. Second, the president must be allowed to appoint and dismiss cabinet ministers (including the PM) and to dissolve parliament. Third, Beck *et al.*, classify a system as presidential (0) if the available data does not clarify the executive's abilities on the first two counts, yet Beck *et al.*'s sources still refer to the president as the key decision-maker.

The system is coded as parliamentary (2) if the preceding conditions do not hold. We distinguish between systems with fully independent presidents (1) and others, including parliamentary systems and those where the assembly names the president. Source: Beck *et al.*, 2001.

Polity. The Polity variable consists of a score assigned to each country based on the level of democracy vs. autocracy within its political system. These distinctions are based on the general "openness" or "closedness" of political institutions as determined by Polity IV scholars through examination of numerous indicators such as the constraints on the chief executive, the regulation and competitiveness of participation, the openness of executive recruitment, etc. Scores are generated by subtracting aggregate "autocracy" from "democracy" to create a range of −10 to 10 with 10 being the most democratic and −10 the most autocratic. Source: Polity IV data set developed by Gurr *et al.* (2005).

Ln GDP per Capita. This variable records the natural log of each state's per capita GDP for each year in the database. GDP per capita is US$ 2000 and is adjusted for purchasing power parity. Source: Penn World Tables (Heston *et al.*, 2009).

Federalism. This variable describes whether the state or provincial governments are locally elected. The measure records a zero if neither the local executive nor the local legislature is directly elected by the population that they govern. The data point is coded as a one, however, if either is directly elected and the other is indirectly elected. Finally, a score of two for this variable signifies that both local executive and legislature are directly elected. Finally, in cases where multiple tiers of sub-national government exist, Beck *et al.*, consider the state/provincial level to the highest-level. We only code those with a score of "2" as being a strongly federal system. Source: Beck *et al.*, 2001.

English Origins. An English origin dummy variable is generated to reflect legal attributes such as judicial vs. legislative precedent, rights to private property, and the general rights of the individual relative to the state. As the literature identifies the impact these aspects of a legal system have on institutional performance we feel that it is appropriate to include them in our model regarding the control of corruption. In general, English legal systems are coded as "1" for former colonies and all others are coded as zero in keeping with La Porta *et al.*'s data on the subject. Source: La Porta *et al.*, 1997.

Regulatory Quality. Our variable is from the World Bank's Governance Matters data collection, which includes multiple year measures for six primary areas of governance in almost 200 countries. These "benchmarks" are meant to illuminate the core themes that contribute to the economic growth across disparate countries and across time. The six indicators are: Voice and Accountability, Political Stability and Lack of Violence, Government Effectiveness, Regulatory Quality, Rule of Law, and Control of Corruption. Since 1996, multinational organizations have used these measures for studying the key themes in governance and the ways that the citizens react to the state and its behaviour. Variables are constructed by estimating a measurement model that summarizes data provided by 17 different organizations as detailed in the appendix (Table A1). We employ data collected in 2002 and 2004. Our focus is the regulatory quality dimension that "includes measures of the incidence of market-unfriendly policies such as price controls or inadequate bank supervision, as well as perceptions of the burdens imposed by excessive regulation in areas such as foreign trade and business development" (Kaufman *et al.*, 2003).

Appendix

Table A1. Concepts Contained in Perceived Regulatory Quality Variable

Source	Concept Measured	Years
African Development Bank	Trade policy	2000–2005
	Competitive environment	2000–2005
	Labor Market Policies	2000–2005
Asian Development Bank	Trade policy	2000–2005
	Competitive environment	2000–2005
	Factor and products markets	2000–2004
Bertelsmann Transformation Index	Price Stability	2004–2005
	Competition	2004–2005
	Competitive Environment	1996, 1998, 2000

(Continued)

Table A1. (*Continued*)

Source	Concept Measured	Years
Business Environment and Enterprise Performance Survey	Information on the laws and regulations is easy to obtain Interpretations of the laws and regulations are consistent and predictable	2002–2005
	Unpredictability of changes of regulations	2002–2005
	How problematic are labor regulations for the growth of your business?	2002–2005
	How problematic are tax regulations for the growth of your business?	2002–2005
	How problematic are custom and trade regulations for the growth of your business?	2002–2005
		2002–2005
Country Policy and Institutional Assessment	Factor and Products Markets	1996, 1998, 2000–2003
	Competitive Environment	1996, 1998, 2000–2005
	Trade Policy	1996, 1998, 2000–2005
Economist Intelligence Unit	Unfair Competitive Practices	1996, 2002–2005
	Price Controls	1996, 2002–2005
	Discriminatory Tariffs	1996, 2002–2005
	Excessive Protections	1996, 2002–2005
	Discriminatory Taxes	1996, 2002–2005
European Bank for Reconstruction & Development	Price liberalisation	1996, 1998, 2000–2005
	Trade & foreign exchange system	1996, 1998, 2000–2005
	Competition policy	1996, 1998, 2000–2005
	Commercial Law Extensiveness	1998, 2000–2002
	Commercial Law Effectiveness	1998, 2000–2002
	Financial Regulations: extensiveness	1998, 2000–2002
	Financial regulations: effectiveness	1998, 2000–2002

(*Continued*)

Table A1. (*Continued*)

Source	Concept Measured	Years
Global Insight's DRI/ McGraw-Hill	Policies Non-Tax: Regulations — Exports	1996, 1998, 2000–2005
	Policies Non-Tax: Regulations — Imports	1996, 1998, 2000–2005
	Policies Non-Tax: Regulations — Other Business	1996, 1998, 2000–2005
	Policies Non-Tax: Ownership of Business by Non-Residents	1996, 1998, 2000–2005
	Policies Non-Tax: Ownership of Equities by Non-Residents	1996, 1998, 2000–2005
Global Insight's Business Conditions and Risk Indicators	Tax Effectiveness	2002–2005
	Legislation	2002-2005
Heritage Foundation/ Wall Street Journal	Regulation	1996, 1998, 2000–2005
	Government Intervention	1996, 1998, 2000–2005
	Wages/Prices	1996, 1998, 2000–2005
	Trade	1996, 1998, 2000–2005
	Foreign Investment	1996, 1998, 2000–2005
	Banking	1996, 1998, 2000–2005
Institute for Management Development	The exchange rate policy of your country hinders the competitiveness of firms.	2002–2005
	Protectionism in the country negatively affects the conduct of business.	1998, 2000, 2002–2005
	Competition legislation in your country does not prevent unfair competition.	1996, 1998, 2000, 2002–2005
	Price controls affect pricing of products in most industries.	1996, 1998, 2000, 2002–2005
	Legal regulation of financial institutions is inadequate for financial stability.	1996, 1998, 2000, 2002–2004

(*Continued*)

Table A1. (*Continued*)

Source	Concept Measured	Years
	Foreign financial institutions do not have access to the domestic market.	1996, 1998, 2000, 2002–2003
	Access to capital markets (foreign and domestic) is easily available.	2002–2005
	Ease of doing business is not a competitive advantage for your country.	2002–2005
	Financial institutions' transparency is not widely developed in your country.	2002–2005
	Customs' authorities do not facilitate the efficient transit of goods.	1998, 2000, 2002–2005
	The legal framework is detrimental to your country's competitiveness.	1998, 2000, 2002–2005
	Foreign investors are free to acquire control in domestic companies.	1998, 2000, 2002–2005
	Public sector contracts are sufficiently open to foreign bidders.	1998, 2000, 2002–2005
	Real personal taxes are non distortionary.	1996, 1998, 2000, 2002–2005
	Real corporate taxes are non distortionary.	1996, 1998, 2000, 2002–2005
	Banking regulation does not hinder competitiveness.	1996, 1998, 2000, 2002–2005
	Political system as obstacle to development.	2002–2005
	Labor regulations hinder business activities.	1998, 2000
	New Legislation restricts competitiveness.	2004
	Subsidies impair economic development.	2004–2005
	Ease to start a business.	2004–2005
Merchant International Group	Unfair Trade	2002–2005
	Unfair Competition	2002–2005

(*Continued*)

Table A1. (*Continued*)

Source	Concept Measured	Years
Political Risk Services	Investment Profile	1996, 1998, 2000, 2002–2005
PriceWaterhouseCoopers	Regulation	2000
World Business Enterprise Survey	Regulations on Starting New Businesses	1998, 2000
	Price Controls	1998, 2000
	Regulations on Foreign Trade	1998, 2000
	Foreign Currency Regulations	1998, 2000
	General Uncertainty about Regulations	1998, 2000
World Economic Forum — Global Competitiveness	Administrative regulations are burdensome	1996, 1998, 2000
Survey and African Competitiveness Survey (GCSA)	Tax system is distortionary	1996, 1998, 2000, 2002–2005
	Import barriers as obstacle to growth	1996, 1998, 2002-2005
	Competition in local market is limited	1998, 2002–2005
	It is easy to start company	1998, 2002–2004
	Anti monopoly policy is lax and ineffective	1996, 1998, 2002–2005
	Cost of tariffs imposed on business	1996, 1998, 2002–2004
	Government subsidies keep uncompetitive industries alive artificially	1996, 2002-2003
	Domestic banks are protected from foreign competition	1998
	Barriers to entry in banking sector are very high	1998
	Interest rates are heavily regulated	1998
	Private sector participation in infrastructure projects is not permitted	1998
	Costs of uncertain rules, laws, or government policies (GCSA)	1998

(*Continued*)

Table A1. (*Continued*)

Source	Concept Measured	Years
	Tranfer costs associated with exporting capital as an obstacle to business (GCSA)	1998
	General uncertainty on costs of regulations as an obstacle to business (GCSA)	1998
	Openness of public sector contracts to foreign investors (GCSA)	1998
	Policies for dividend remittances as obstacles to development (GCSA)	1998
	Dominance of state owned or state controlled enterpriese (GCSA)	1998
	State interference in private business (GCSA)	1998
	Regulatory discretionality (GCSA)	1998
	Price controls as an obstacle to business develpoment (GCSA)	1998
	Regulations on foreign trade as an obstacle to business develpoment (GCSA)	1998
	Foreign currency regulations as an obstacle to business develpoment (GCSA)	1998

References

Acemoglu, D, J Simon and JA Robinson (2000). The colonial origins of comparative development: An empirical investigation. *American Economic Review*, 91(5), pp. 1369–1401.

Acemoglu, D, J Simon and JA Robinson (2005). Institutions as the fundamental cause of long-run growth. In *Handbook of Economic Growth*, Aghion, P and S Durlauf (eds.). Amsterdam: North Holland.

Allen, A, D Julio and P Hofmann (2004). Governance and Access to Water and Sanitation in the Metropolitan Fringe: An Overview of Five Case Studies. Presented at the Urban Governance, Diversity and Social Action in Cities of the South, N-Aerus Annual Conference, 15–16 September 2004, Barcelona, Spain.

Allen, A, D Julio and P Hofmann (2006). The peri-urban water poor: Citizens or consumers? *Environment and Urbanization*, 18(2), pp. 333–351.

Altaf, MA (1994). Household demand for improved water and sanitation in a large secondary city: Findings from a study in Gujranwala, Pakistan. *Habitat International*, 18(1), pp. 45–55.

Baldez, L and JM Carey (1999). Presidential agenda control and spending policy: Lessons from General Pinchet's Constitution. *American Journal of Political Science*, 43(1), pp. 29–55.

Barrett, S and K Graddy (2000). Freedom, growth, and the environment. *Environment and Development Economics*, 5(4), pp. 433–456.

Bartlett, S (2003). Water, sanitation and urban children: The need to go beyond 'improved' provision. *Environment and Urbanization*, 15(2), pp. 57–70.

Beaglehole, R and R Bonita (1997). *Public Health at the Crossroads: Achievements and Prospects.* Cambridge, United Kingdom: Cambridge University Press.

Beck, T, G Clarke, A Groff, P Keefer and P Walsh (2001). New tools in comparative political economy: The database of political institutions. *World Bank Economic Review*, 15(1), pp. 165–176.

Bell, S and S Morse (2003). *Measuring Sustainability: Learning by Doing.* Sterling, VA: Earthscan Publications Ltd.

Bertelli, AM and A Whitford (2009). Perceiving credible commitments: How independent regulators shape elite perceptions of regulatory quality. *British Journal of Political Science*, 39, pp. 517–537.

Brown, DS and W Hunter (1999). Democracy and social spending in Latin America, 1980–92. *American Political Science Review*, 93(4), pp. 779–790.

Brown, DS and AM Mobarak (2009). The transforming power of democracy: Regime type and the distribution of electricity. *American Political Science Review*, 103(2), pp. 193–213.

Chinn, MD and R Fairlie (2007). The determinants of the global digital divide: A cross-country analysis of computer and internet penetration. *Oxford Economic Papers*, 59, pp. 16–44.

Choguill, CL (1999). Community infrastructure for low-income cities: The potential for progressive improvement. *Habitat International*, 23(2), pp. 289–301.

Congleton, RD (1992). Political institutions and pollution control. *Review of Economics and Statistics*, 74(3), pp. 412–421.

Corvalán, C, K Tord and KR Smith (1999). Health, environment and sustainable development: Identifying links and indicators to promote action. *Epidemiology*, 10(5), pp. 656–666.

Cox, GW and S Morgenstern (2001). Latin America's reactive assemblies and proactive presidents. *Comparative Politics*, 33(2), pp. 171–189.

De Janvry, A and E Sadoulet (2005). Achieving success in rural development: Toward implementation of an integral approach. *Agricultural Economics*, 32(s1), pp. 75–89.

Doppelt, B (2003). *Leading Change Toward Sustainability: A Change-Management Guide for Business, Government and Civil Society.* Greenleaf Publications.

Dresner, S (2002). *The Principles of Sustainability*. Sterling, VA: Earthscan Publications.

Edwards, A and DW Orr (2005). *The Sustainability Revolution: Portrait of a Paradigm Shift*. Gabriola, BC: New Society Publishers.

Eser, TW (2002). *Evaluation and the Appropriate Policy Level under the demands of sustainability*. Available at http://www.raumplanung.uni-dortmund.de/rwp/erra2002/cd-rom/papers/073.pdf.

Esrey, SA (1996). Water, waste, and well-being: A multicountry study. *American Journal of Epidemiology*, 143(6), pp. 608–623.

Esty, D and ME Porter (2001). Ranking national environmental regulation and performance: A leading indicator of future competitiveness?. *World Economic Forum*, The Global Competitiveness Report 2001, pp. 78–101.

Fullan, M (2004). *Leadership & Sustainability: System Thinkers in Action*. Thousand Oaks, CA: Corwin Press.

Gaston, N and PG Fredriksson (1999). The importance of trade for the ratification of the 1992 Climate Change Convention. In *Trade, Global Policy, and the Environment*, Fredriksson, PG (ed.). Washington, DC: The World Bank.

Gleditsch, N-P and BO Sverdrup (2002). Democracy and the Environment. In *Human Security and the Environment: International Comparisons*, Page EA and M Redclift (eds.). London: Edward Elgar.

Grafton, RQ and S Knowles (2004). Social capital and national environmental performance: A cross-sectional analysis. *Journal of Environment & Development*, 13(4), pp. 336–370.

Grossman, GM and AB Krueger (1995). Economic growth and the environment. *Quarterly Journal of Economics*, 110(2), pp. 353–377.

Gurr, TR, MG Marshall and K Jaggers (2005), *Polity IV Project: Political Regime Characteristics and Transitions, 1800–2003*. Available at http://www.systemicpeace.org/polity/polity4.htm.

Hanchett, S, Akhter, S, Khan, M Hoque, Mezulianik, Stephen and V Blagbrough (2003). Water, sanitation and hygiene in Bangladeshi slums: An Evaluation of the WaterAid–Bangladesh urban programme. *Environment and Urbanization*, 15(2), pp. 43–56.

Helland, E and A Whitford (2003). Pollution incidence and political jurisdiction: Evidence from the TRI. *Journal of Environmental Economics and Management*, 46(3), pp. 403–424.

Heller, L (1999). Who really benefits from environmental sanitation services in the cities? An intra-urban analysis in Betim, Brazil. *Environment and Urbanization*, 11(1), pp. 133–144.

Heston, A, Summers, R and B Aten (2009). *Penn World Table Version 6.3. Center for International Comparisons of Production, Income and Prices at the University of Pennsylvania*. Available at http://pwt.econ.upenn.edu/.

Joardar, SD (1998). Carrying capacities and standards as bases towards urban infrastructure planning in India: A case of urban water supply and sanitation. *Habitat International*, 22(3), pp. 327–337.

Kaufman, D, A Kraay and M Mastruzze (2003). Governance Matters III: Governance Indicators for 1996–2002. In *World Bank Policy Research Working Paper*. Washington, D.C.

La Porta, R, F Lopez-de-Silanes, A Shleifer and R Vishny (1997). Legal determinants of external finance. *Journal of Finance*, 52(3), pp. 1131–1150.

La Porta, R, F Lopez-de-Silanes, A Shleifer and R Vishny (1999). The quality of government. *Journal of Law, Economics, and Organization*, 15(1), pp. 222–279.

Lijphart, A (1984). Measures of cabinet durability: A conceptual and empirical evaluation. *Comparative Political Studies*, 17(2), pp. 265–279.

Lowry, WR (1992). *The Dimensions of Federalism: State Governments and Pollution Control Policies*. Durham, NC: Duke University Press.

Mainwaring, S (1995). Presidentialism, multipartyism, and democracy. *Comparative Political Studies*, 26(2), pp. 198–228.

Martínez, J, Mboup, G, Sliuzas, R and A Stein (2008). Trends in urban and slum indicators across developing world cities, 1990–2003. *Habitat International*, 32(1), pp. 86–108.

McDonough, W and M Braungart (2002). *Cradle to Cradle: Remaking the Way We Make Things*. New York: North Point Press.

Midlarsky, MI (1998). Democracy and the environment: An empirical assessment. *Journal of Peace Research*, 35(3), pp. 341–361.

Neumayer, E (2002). Do democracies exhibit stronger international environmental commitment? A cross country analysis. *Journal of Peace Research*, 39(2), pp. 139–164.

Pathak, B (1999). Sanitation is the key to healthy cities — A profile of Sulabh International. *Environment and Urbanization*, 11(1), pp. 221–230.

Persson, T and G Tabellini (2003). *The Economics Effects of Constitutions*. Cambridge, MA: MIT Press.

Porter, ME and C van der Linde (1995). Toward a new conception of the environment-competitiveness relationship. *The Journal of Economic Perspectives*, 9(4), pp. 97–108.

Powell, GB (2000). *Elections as Instruments of Democracy: Majoritarian and Proportional Visions*. New Haven, CT: Yale University Press.

Rabe, BG (2004). *Statehouse and Greenhouse: The Emerging Politics of American Climate Policy*. Washington, D.C.: Brookings Institution Press.

Rabe, BG (2005). Power to the States: The Promise and Pitfalls of Decentralization. In *Environmental Policy: New Directions for the Twenty-first Century*, Norman J. Vig and Michael E. Kraft (eds.). Washington, D.C.: CQ Press.

Rheingans, R, Dreibelbis, R and M Freeman (2006). Beyond the millennium development goals: Public health challenges in water and sanitation. *Global Public Health*, 1(1), pp. 31–48.

Scruggs, LA (1999). Institutions and environmental performance in seventeen western democracies. *British Journal of Political Science*, 29(1), pp. 1–31.

Scruggs, LA (2003). *Sustaining Abundance: Environmental Performance in Industrial Democracies*. New York: Cambridge UP.

Shugart, MS (1999). Presidentialism, parliamentarism, and the provision of collective goods in less-developed countries. *Constitutional Political Economy,* 10(1), pp. 53–88.

Stern, DI (2004). The rise and fall of the environmental Kuznets Curve. *World Development,* 32(8), pp. 1419–1439.

Thompson, J, IT Porras, E Wood, JK Tumwine, MR Mujwahuzi, M Katui-Katua and N Johnstone (2000). Waiting at the tap: Changes in urban water use in East Africa over three decades. *Environment and Urbanization,* 12(2), pp. 37–52.

Torras, M and JK Boyce (1998). Income, inequality, and pollution: A reassessment of the environmental Kuznets Curve. *Ecological Economics,* 25(2), pp. 147–160.

UNICEF (2008). *Meeting the MDG Drinking Water and Sanitation Target.* Available at http://www.unicef.org/wes/mdgreport/index.php.

United Nations (1993). *Agenda 21: The United Nations Programme of Action from Rio.* New York: United Nations.

World Health Organization. (2008). *UN-Water Global Annual Assessment of Sanitation and Drinking-Water (GLAAS): 2008 Pilot Report.* Available at http://www.who.int/water_sanitation_health/glaas_2008_pilot_finalreport.pdf.

Weingast, BR (1995). The economic role of political institutions: Market-preserving federalism and economic development. *Journal of Law, Economics, and Organization,* 11, pp. 1–31.

CHAPTER 15

The Regulation of Water Infrastructure in Italy: Origins and Effects of an 'Hybrid' Regulatory System

Alberto Asquer

University of Cagliari, Italy

Water infrastructure regulatory systems are occasionally characterized by the combination of selected features of alternative models of regulation, such as public ownership, discretionary regulation, and franchise regulation. Issues regarding why these combined or 'hybrid' systems appear, and what level of performance they achieve, arise. An instance of such 'hybrid' regulatory system is the one resulting from the implementation of the 1994 water reform in Italy, which largely resulted in the allocation of water franchise to local government fully or majority-owned water firms subject to price regulation in a two-tier regulatory system. The analysis shows that the water regulatory system in Italy was affected by both the behaviour of sub-national governments and incumbent water firms during the implementation process as well as the regulatory system statutory design. The performance of the water regulatory system is relatively disappointing in various dimensions. This case study suggests some theoretical and practical implications on the implementation and the effects of regulatory reforms which set up 'hybrid' regulatory systems.

1. Introduction

The field of water infrastructure is often characterized as being dominated by at least three main models of economic regulation: public ownership, franchise regulation (often characterized as a French model), and discretionary regulation (often referred to as an English & Welsh or Anglo-Saxon model) (Gómez Ibáñez, 2003; Ballance and Taylor, 2005; Rouse, 2007). In several countries around the world, regulatory reforms of water infrastructure which aimed to move away from public ownership have often imitated the distinctive features of the French or the English & Welsh models. Instead, in some countries, regulatory regimes have developed quite peculiar institutional and organizational traits. In Germany, for example, water infrastructure regulation is characterised by public-private partnerships and persistent forms of local public ownership of water firms. Such institutional and organizational variety is important, because it allows to explore how alternative systems of water infrastructure regulation work and whether and why they can deliver better performance.

One 'natural experiment' which has been relatively little researched so far, took place, in the last 15 years, in Italy. In 1994, the Parliament of Italy passed Act 36/1994, a piece of legislation which provided a reform of the water regulatory system aimed at deeply reconfiguring the institutional and organizational structure of the water industry in the country. Until then, water had been largely regulated through public ownership of water supply, sewage, and wastewater treatment firms, which were owned by either the central government, or the regions, or mostly local governments, resulting in a quite fragmented industry structure which counted more than 23,500 operators (ISTAT, 1991). The 1994 water reform aimed to consolidate the water management systems into a limited number of water districts and to tender out water management concessions to firms which would provide water supply, sewage, and wastewater services 'under one roof' (so-called 'integrated watershed management') and carry out infrastructure development. The 1994 water reform also provided that water firms should be financially self-sufficient by applying tariffs set by local regulatory authorities which would cover operating and depreciation costs and yield a fair return to the capital invested.

The regulatory design provided by the 1994 water reform included selected features of both franchise allocation and discretionary regulation models. Similarly to the French model, water firms would be awarded franchises for the provision of water services at the local-level. Likewise to the English & Welsh model, water tariffs would be set by regulatory authorities according to a price-cap formula. Some peculiar features, however, characterized the 1994 water reform. Unlike the regulation of the water industry in France, in Italy water franchises would be necessarily awarded by new entities established by associations of local governments at the local-level rather than by any single local government. While the English & Welsh system provided one independent regulator, the Italian one was organized in a two-tier system composed by a national regulator, which would set the general tariff-setting rules, and local regulatory authorities, which would implement the rules by setting and monitoring water tariffs.

The water regulatory system set up in Italy by the end of the implementation of the water reform in 2006 was partially different from the original design. Rather than opening up the water industry to competitive forces through the call for tender offering competitions for franchise allocation, most of the newly-established local regulatory authorities directly granted the water franchise contracts to local government fully or majority-owned water firms. Taking into account that the local regulatory authorities were set up by local governments, this behaviour resulted in the water firms being regulated by entities which were controlled by the same owners of the water firms themselves. This structure of the water regulatory system contained a sort of 'built-in' conflict of interest of local governments, which could hardly reconcile competing objectives concerning financing infrastructure development on one hand, and containing water tariff increases to avoid irritating the local communities, on the other. This conflict of interest had repercussions on the performance of the water regulatory system, as we shall see.

This study aims to address the questions of why the water regulatory system in Italy came to take the shape of an 'hybrid' regulatory system and how well it performs. These questions are answered by analysing the episode of the implementation of the water reform in Italy in the period 1994–2006 and by providing an assessment of the resulting water regulatory system. The analysis of the implementation of the water reform will show that particular context conditions favoured the diversion of the water reform implementation towards the award of water franchise to local government fully or majority-owned water firms. The assessment of the performance of the water sector will show that, in terms of infrastructure development, the new regulatory system delivered relatively modest results.

This research will also contribute to a broader scholarly interest apart from explaining and assessing the water regulatory system set up in Italy, namely understanding how 'hybrid' water regulatory systems work and what are their advantages and limitations. Scholarly works on the design and performance of water regulatory systems (Gómez Ibáñez, 2003; Ballance and Taylor, 2005; Rouse, 2007; Groom *et al.*, 2006) devoted some attention to those systems which combine selected features of different 'models'. Differing from these works, this study places a particular emphasis on the process through which a water regulatory system is put into place. Rather than focusing on the deliberate design choices made in the making of regulatory systems, the perspective followed here is that the design of a regulatory system may be affected by the political economy of implementing the regulatory reform of a particular infrastructure policy arena.

The rest of the chapter is organized as follows. Next section will recall the scholarly literature on water infrastructure regulation and outline the intended contribution of this chapter. Section 3 will describe the institutional arrangement for water infrastructure regulation provided by Act 36/1994. Section 4 will narrate the implementation of the 1994 water reform in Italy in the period 1994–2006. Section 5 will analyse the episode through the lenses of a simple sequential game theoretic model. Section 6 will discuss how to measure the regulatory outcome and effectiveness of the 1994 water reform. Finally, Section 7 will discuss the implications of this study for regulatory design, effectiveness and operation of water infrastructure reform, and Section 8 will outline some lessons for regulators.

2. The Regulation of Water Infrastructure

As in many other fields of human activity, the regulation[1] of water infrastructure is generally justified on both social and economic basis. Social regulation is concerned with the protection of the public interest, in terms of environmental preservation, safety, consumer protection, and achievement of social objectives. Instead, economic regulation is concerned with providing a substitution for competition in relation to natural monopolies (Ogus, 1994). Economic regulation aims to fix market failure by means of rules and organizations that set, enforce, and change the allowed tariffs and service standards for service providers. Hence, regulating water infrastructure satisfies social needs, such as the supply of safe drinking water and the working of sewage services, and provides a remedy to the natural monopoly of the water industry.[2]

---

[1] Regulation can be defined in many different ways. In a much-quoted work, for example, Baldwin *et al.* (1998) identify three general meanings for the notion of regulation. First, regulation refers to "the promulgation of an authoritative set of rules, accompanied by some mechanism, typically a public agency, for monitoring and promoting compliance with these rules." Second, regulation can be understood as "all efforts of state agencies to steer the economy." In this broader sense, regulation includes any form of governmental intervention, such as direct ownership, taxation, subsidies, and redistribution, and any kind of intervention carried out by state agencies. Third, regulation can be viewed as any kind of mechanism of social control, by whomsoever exercised. In this even broader sense, regulation takes place through any system of influence of behaviour, either intentional or unintentional, either carried out by the state or any other agent. The term 'regulation' is commonly understood as the various forms of intervention of the government in the economy and the society. As such, the term 'regulation' includes diverse kinds of regulatory activities as those carried on by independent regulatory agencies as well as those performed through direct governmental interventions. It is in this 'medium-range' scope of its meaning that the term 'regulation' will be used in this study.

[2] The water industry is often characterized as an instance of natural monopoly *par excellence.* Although what are the features that define a natural monopoly are variously defined, it is commonly acknowledged that the water industry is characterized by the presence of high-capital intensity and economies of scale in each segment of the industry (i.e., water collection, transport, storage, distribution, sewage collection, and sewage treatment), which makes it not economically advantageous to duplicate the asset base (Noll *et al.*, 2002; Spulber and Sabbaghi, 1994); the presence of high-sunk costs of the infrastructure assets and of installed excess capacity, which raise the barriers for entry into the industry

The need for regulation of water infrastructure is widely-acknowledged. Instead, less consensus exists on *how* exactly the water industry should be regulated (Ballance and Taylor, 2005). Different countries in the world have pursued different models of regulation of the domestic water industries. In the 1980s, evidence of government failures to directly manage water services led to a favourable climate for considering how to make market competition and private sector initiative compatible with the achievement of social goals. Since then, the ideas of getting the private sector involved in financing and managing water infrastructure (as well as the idea to require customers to pay for the full cost of water services) have greatly affected water policies worldwide (Winpenny, 2003). No definitive answer to the question of how water industry should be regulated, however, has been achieved. Recently, some authors have again called for the need to search for better governance and regulation of water services (Rees *et al.*, 2008).

The scholarly literature on water infrastructure regulation has identified at least three models for regulating the water industry, namely (from the most pervasive presence of the public sector to the least) public ownership, public franchise allocation, and discretionary regulation[3] (Gómez

---

(Ballance and Taylor, 2005); the limited geographical size of the market, due to high-cost of transport and the environmental unfriendliness of concentrating impacts in single points (Massarutto, 2007); the presence of externalities which are not reflected either in the cost of production or in the price for the consumers; and the presence of information asymmetries which arise because the consumers cannot easily assess the quality of supplied water or sanitation services.

[3] At least a fourth model is generally acknowledged, namely private ownership in conjunction with liberalization and regulation of access, prices and quality. The particular technical features of the water industry, however, make full liberalization of access to the industry practically unfeasable. Regulation through private ownership in conjunction with liberalization and regulation of access, prices and quality builds on the expectation that the mechanism of competition and the contestability of the market (Baumol, 1982) put enough pressure on the business companies to pursue the public interest. This kind of regulation is expected to bring several benefits, in terms of incentives to improve cost-efficiency, encouragement of investments, and innovation of service provision (Rees, 1998; Beecher, 2001; Cowan, 1993; Littlechild, 1986). However, this kind of regulation cannot work if the incumbents raise high barriers for entry and if the customers suffer too much asymmetry of information and uneven bargaining power with respect to the firms. Moreover, recent evidence of slowing down investment programmes in privatized British water companies has led to question the long-term viability of private ownership of water infrastructure (Massarutto, 2007).

Ibáňez, 2003; Ballance and Taylor, 2005; Rouse, 2007). Regulation through public ownership of monopolistic water companies builds on the expectation that mechanisms of political control and accountability lead to the pursuit of public interest goals (Tenbüken, 2006; Swann, 1988; Waterson, 1988). Regulation through public ownership is the most direct and pervasive form of intrusion of the government in the economy. It provides that the private sector can be partially involved when selected activities are contracted out to business companies under public supervision (Gómez Ibáňez, 2003), or when private investors are allowed to own minority shares of water public companies (Massarutto, 2007).

Regulation through public franchise allocation consists of the government awarding a concession to a business company, usually through competitive tendering, for managing water services in monopoly conditions (Ogus, 1994). By making business companies compete for access to the field (Demsetz, 1968), this kind of regulation is expected to make them reveal the lowest tariff at which they are willing and able to manage water services. After the award of the concession, the government monitors the business companies' compliance with the concession contract (e.g., expected performance standards) and eventually appeals to courts to enforce penalty provisions. Regulation through public franchise allocation is expected to bring several benefits, in terms of reduction of information asymmetries, credibility of the contractual commitments, and incentives to improve cost-efficiency (Ballance and Taylor, 2005). This kind of regulation, however, is also exposed to potential pitfalls, for example in terms of difficulty for the government to second-guess consumer preferences when writing the concession contract, risk of incompleteness of the concession contract, and distortion of the incentives to invest according to the criteria for asset transfer valuation at the end of the franchise period. Moreover, the extent to which water franchise markets are really competitive is questionable, as little evidence has been collected so far of any business companies challenging the incumbents in water franchise tender offers (Massarutto, 2007).

Finally, discretionary regulation consists of a regulatory agency having the power to unilaterally set business companies' tariff and service standards. In this kind of regulation, the legislation broadly states the general principles that the regulatory agency must follow when setting tariff and service standards, but it leaves the detailed decision criteria unspecified in order to allow some discretion for the regulatory agency. When making the actual tariff and service standard decisions, the regulatory agency can flexibly take unforeseen circumstances concerning the industry and the business companies into account. Discretionary regulation is expected to bring the benefits of allowing flexibility to unilaterally fill the details of the regulatory arrangement and of providing incentives to improve cost-efficiency. However, this kind of regulation is also exposed to potential pitfalls, for example in terms of difficulty for the regulatory agency to second-guess consumer preferences, the risk of capture of the regulatory agency by special interests, and the need for information for assessing the business companies' performance. Recent evidence of difficulties in measuring and assessing water business companies' performance (Merrett, 1997; Amato and Conti, 2005, Massarutto, 2007), in particular, led to questioning the limits of yardstick competition and other forms of benchmarking.

Within the variety of water infrastructure regulatory systems in the world, those set up in France and England & Wales usually are recognized as exemplar instances of the public franchise allocation and discretionary regulation models, respectively. In France, the water regulatory system is, by and large, one of the franchise allocation with a significant involvement of private companies (e.g., Veolia Water, Suez-Lyonnaise des Eaux, and Société d'Aménagement Urbain et Rural — SAUR). In England & Wales, the 1989 water reform led to the privatization of 10 River Water Authorities and the adoption of a system of discretionary regulation centred on the price-cap water tariff setting mechanism. However, rather than faithfully reproducing these models, several water infrastructure regulatory systems in various countries in the world combine selected features of these models in original ways. Then, an issue arises, concerning whether and how selected features of different water infrastructure regulatory models can be effectively combined. Some authors (Gómez Ibáñez, 2003; Groom *et al.*, 2006) discussed various reasons for which such 'hybrid' regulatory systems might work well or not. However, additional research is needed, in order to provide empirically grounded explanatory arguments for why 'hybrid' regulatory systems are put into place and what performance they deliver. This kind of knowledge is useful for understanding if we can design more effective regulatory systems by entirely replicating the given regulatory models or by combining selected features of some of them.

This study will analyse the case of the water regulatory system implemented in Italy in the period 1994–2006. The research design of this work is a single case study method, which has well-known strengths and limitations (Ragin and Becker, 1992; Stake, 1995; Yin, 1994). On one hand, the method allows to gain a deep historical understanding of the case by getting closer to the participants' perspective and providing a thick description of their social interactions. It is usually regarded as a research design particularly suited to researching complex social phenomena which need to be understood as wholes, rather than dissected into sets of isolated cause-effect relationships.[4] On the other hand, the single case study generally raises concerns about the limits of the external validity of the research findings. To some extent, these limits can be overcome by locating the case study within a broader collective research effort aiming at developing 'limited historical generalizations' (Ragin, 1982) about the research issue, i.e., theoretical propositions which are grounded on the historical evidence of cases whose validity holds, at least provisionally, for a certain type of appropriately qualified phenomenon. Therefore, the findings of this case can be put to more fruitful use comparing the implementation of the regulatory reform in Italy in the period 1994–2006 with other instances of water infrastructure regulatory reform. On the whole, the nature of this case study is exploratory anyway, as it aims to shed some light on the emergence and performance of 'hybrid' regulatory systems in the water industry, as exemplified by the case of the water regulatory system in Italy.

[4] On the merits of case studies in researching infrastructure regulation, Gómez Ibáñez (2003: 13–14) argued: "Cases are also valuable because they allow one to examine how the interplay of economics, politics and institutions affect regulatory commitment and performance. Some researchers have tried to examine this interplay using large data sets, and their results are reported here. However, few such data sets exist, and they capture only a portion of the many variables that might be involved. To appreciate how regulation works in practice, there is simply no substitute for examining the evolution of a specific concession contract or the history of a particular regulatory agency."

3. The Design of the 1994 Water Reform in Italy

During the course of the 1980s, increasing financial pressures led to a decline in water infrastructure development in Italy. Rising interest rates, inflation, and central government caps placed on water tariff increases, diminished the investment capacity of water firms. Growing stress on public finance, which culminated in the 1992–1993 financial crisis, and the termination of the '*Cassa per il Mezzogiorno*' (a special programme for funding infrastructure development in the southern regions of the country) led to a sharp reduction of public funds available for infrastructure development. However, new investments in water infrastructure were much needed, in order to comply with the rising environmental protection and water quality standards set by EC directives. In face of this situation, the national association of local government-owned water and gas firms, Federgasacqua, lobbied for a reform of the whole water industry based on the principles of integrated watershed management, comprehensive water resource preservation and planning of water use, cost-effectiveness, and increased water tariffs.[5]

At that time, evidence of relatively poor water service performance had been provided by the national statistics office (*Istituto Nazionale di Statistica*, ISTAT). Through a survey conducted in 1987, ISTAT had discovered that most of the country's population suffered from relatively poor water services, supply shortages, leakage, unreliable service, and pollution (ISTAT, 1991). For example, the survey showed that more than 45% of the population experienced interruptions in water supply and was not served by sewage networks and treatment of water discharges. The share of population affected by poor water services was particularly high in the southern regions of the country, where unreliable service and lack of proper sanitation affected more than 70% of the population.

---

[5] The issue of reforming the water sector was fully articulated at the 1989 national conference of Federgasacqua, which took place in Bologna on 20–22 November 1989. Among the members of Federgasacqua, gas firms were reputed to achieve better performance than the water ones in terms of financial self-sufficiency and customer service. In the 1989 Federgasacqua conference, the performance of gas firms set a benchmark standard which water firms were arguably expected to match.

Instead, the northern and central regions were mainly affected by inadequate wastewater treatment of the industrial and civil use of water. The survey also showed that the water sector was highly fragmented — it counted about 5,500 entities which managed the drinkable water supply, 7,000 which managed sewage services, and 11,000 which provided water treatment — totalling 23,500. Most of the water supply service was directly managed by the local governments (about 34.5% of water), local government-owned water firms (24%), local governments' consortia (18.5%) and other public bodies (17.7%) owned by either the regional or the central governments. Privately owned business firms played a relatively marginal role in the water industry (supplying about 4.5% of water).

The making of the water reform was initiated by the member of the parliament (MP) Giancarlo Galli of Christian Democrats in 1992. After a few years' parliamentary works, the reform was eventually issued on 19th January 1994 (Act 36/1994). The design of Act 36/1994 built on a few key principles (Citroni *et al.*, 2007). In order to reduce the fragmentation of the industry and allow water firms to achieve economies of scale, water services should be comprehensively organized and managed in relatively large territories (so-called *Ambiti Territoriali Ottimali*, that is, Optimal Territorial Areas or OTA). In order to better coordinate the stages of the water management cycle, all the segments of water services (i.e., water catchment, distribution, sewage, and wastewater treatment) should be managed 'under one roof' by only one water firm. In order to improve the entrepreneurial management of water firms, planning and control functions should be separated by those of operational management and service delivery (the former being assigned to local regulatory authorities and the latter to the water firms). Finally, in order to allow water firms to achieve financial self-sufficiency, water tariffs should cover the full cost of the water services (i.e., including investment depreciation and return to capital invested).

[6] The 'entities' included departments of the local governments (directly managing water services), consortia of local governments, local government-owned water firms, regional government-owned water firms, central government-owned water firms, and privately-owned business firms.

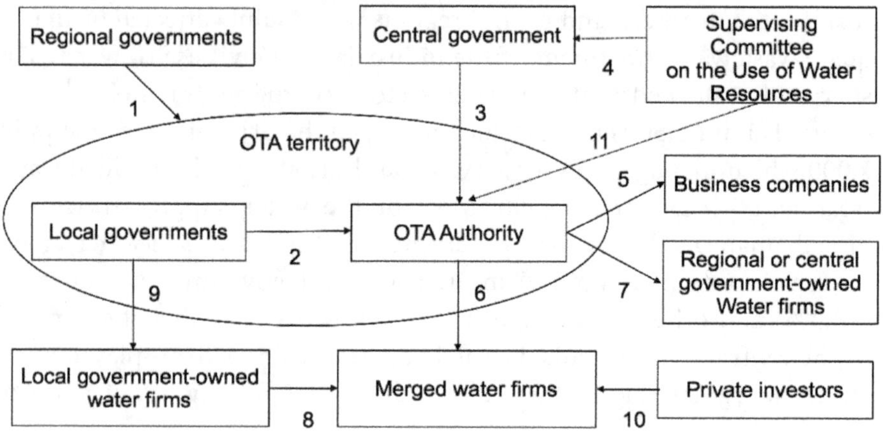

Figure 1: The institutional design of the 1994 water reform

The institutional arrangement of the new regulatory system provided by Act 36/1994 can be schematically represented in Fig. 1. The regional governments were required to design the OTA territories, in which water services would be comprehensively managed, and fill details concerning the establishment of the OTA authorities and the award and management of the water franchises (Arrow 1). Within each OTA, the local governments would establish the OTA authorities (Arrow 2). The OTA authorities would issue infrastructure development and tariff plans taking into account the criteria issued by the Minister of Public Works (Arrow 3), and proposed by the Supervizing Committee on the use of Water Resources, a semi-independent central regulatory authority (Arrow 4). The OTA authorities would award water franchises either through tender offer competitions between business companies (Arrow 5) or direct assignments to public sector water firms (Arrows 6 and 7). Public sector water firms were those that were owned by either the central or the regional governments (Arrow 7), or those that were formed through the merger (Arrow 8) of previously fragmented water firms owned by the same local governments of the OTA (Arrow 9). The merged water firms could be partially (minority or majority) owned by private investors (Arrow 10). Finally, the Supervizing Committee on the Use of Water

Resources would monitor the regulation and management of the water services in the OTAs (Arrow 11) and regularly report to the Parliament and the public.

4. The Implementation of the 1994 Water Reform in Italy (1994–2006)

After Act 36/1994 came into force, in January 1994 the regional governments started calling local governments to participate in making the laws required to transpose the national water legislation to the regional-level. In particular, local governments were expected to assist the regions in the definition of the territorial boundaries of the OTAs and of the forms of cooperation for pooling the water planning and control functions together. Instead, the local governments did not get actively involved because they claimed that they could not anticipate the net benefits of alternative organizational arrangements of the future water regulatory regime. They complained that the Act 36/1994 did not specify several details of the new regulatory system, which the central government was expected to fill. Since the central government kept delaying the issue of these regulatory details, the regional and local governments could not progress in implementing the water reform.[7]

In 1996, the Minister of Public Works of the Romano Prodi government, Antonio Di Pietro, realized that the regions had delayed in implementing the infrastructure development programmes funded by the 1994–1999 EU Community Support Framework (CSF), an EU programme for infrastructure development. Concerned with the risk of losing the appropriation of the 1994–1999 CSF funds, Di Pietro urged the regions to speed up planning and construction projects, including those in the water sector. Because most of the regions did not make any further progress, in 1997 Di Pietro's successor, Paolo Costa, started the

[7] Evidence on local governments' rationales for not collaborating with the transposition of the water reform was indirectly provided by the yearly reports to the Parliament of the Supervizing Committee. These yearly reports provide a detailed and periodical account of the implementation of the 1994 water reform.

procedure for commissioning the regions which had defaulted implementing the 1994 water reform. The activation of the commissioning procedure, which would spoil the regions of their competences on water policy, led some regions to speed up the transposition of the water reform and to approve regional laws within a few months. However, most of the regions still proceeded relatively slowly in accomplishing the transposition task.

In October 1997, the Parliament approved Act 344/1997, which budgeted public funds for an urgent investment programme for sewage and wastewater treatment systems. Act 344/1997, which was intended to comply with the 91/271/CE directive on sewage and wastewater treatment, provided that, in those regions which had not established the OTAs yet, these jurisdictions would be equalled to the territories of the provinces. This provision made local governments to care about the definition of the OTAs, as the authoritative definition of these jurisdictions had been negatively perceived as a break of their autonomy. In 1998, the transposition of the water reform was set as a requirement for accessing additional funds of the 2000–2006 CSF for financing water infrastructure development for the southern regions of the country, which promptly accelerated the passing of the regional laws. By the end of 1999 almost all of the regions had completed the transposition process (Fig. 2).

After the regions transposed the water reform, local governments were required to centralize their water planning and control functions into new regulatory agencies called OTA authorities (*Autorità di Ambito*). After the first OTA authorities were established in Tuscany and Lazio in 1996, other local governments slowly proceeded to set up these local regulatory authorities, whose total number only boomed from 1999 onwards. After their establishment, the OTA authorities started drafting water infrastructure development and tariff plans by trying to accommodate conflicting pressures from the incumbent water firms, which were interested in expanding the infrastructure base, and from local governments, which rather cared about containing water tariff increases in order to not alienate the favour of the local communities because of expensive water bills. Following the approval of the plans, the OTA authorities proceeded to award water franchises. The first of such awards took place on 1st June

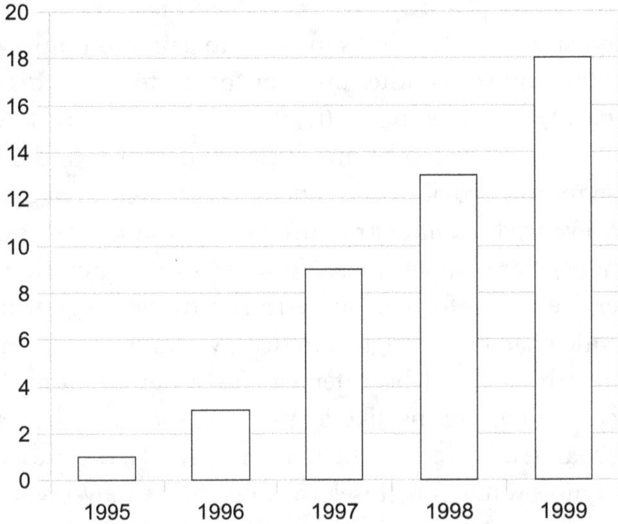

Figure 2: Number of regions which transposed the water reform, per year

Source: Yearly report of the Supervizing Committee on the Use of Water Resources, 1996–2000.

1999 in the OTA "Alto Valdarno" based in Tuscany, whose authority assigned the water franchise to the mixed public-private ownership company Nuove Acque (formed by 37 local government with minority shares held by Suez-Lyonnaise des Eaux, the utility firm controlled by the local government of Genoa AMGA, the banks Monte dei Paschi di Sienna and Banca Popolare dell'Etruria e del Lazio, and a local association of small business firms Iride).

During the 1990s, relatively few OTA authorities came to approve water infrastructure development and tariff plans and award water franchises. Rather than making the OTA authorities progress in implementing the reform, some local governments directly awarded the franchises to local government-owned water firms in order to exploit some exemption clauses which the 1994 water reform provided for the benefit of the incumbents. Various local governments tried to strengthen the position of their water firms by making them reincorporate as public limited companies (whose statutes granted more freedom of action from local government councils than other local government-owned organizational forms to the firms), diversify into related business area, and restructure through acquisitions and mergers in order to gain economies of scale.

From 2001 onwards, the number of water franchises awarded increased sharply. In December 2001, the Parliament passed Act 448/2001 (Budget Law), which contained, in article 35, a reform of the local public services. The reform provided the general rule that local public services of industrial relevance (i.e., infrastructure services) should be contracted out through tender offer competitions. However, special provisions applied to the water services: the reform conceded an exemption regime for the water franchises which had been assigned to firms without any tender offer competition, and which could be extended for a period from 3 to 9 years (provided certain conditions, like floating the shares of the water firm in the stock exchange). Moreover, the reform allowed a transitory regime for directly assigning water franchises to water firms fully-owned by all the local governments included in the OTAs within 18 months from the passing of the reform. After the passing of Act 448/2001, several OTA authorities speeded up planning water infrastructure development and tariff plans and awarding the water franchises.

A few years later, in September 2003, the government issued another reform of the local public services (Legislative Decree No. 269), which originated from the need to prevent an infraction procedure from the EU Commission concerning some provisions of the 2001 reform which contrasted with the EU directives on public sector contracts. The 2003 local public services reform restated the general rule that local public services should be assigned through tender offer competitions. However, the reform also provided that the local public service concessions could be directly assigned to mixed public-private ownership companies in which the private partner was chosen through tender offer competitions, or to firms which were fully-owned by the public authorities serviced by the same firms, and which were tightly controlled by the public authorities as close as their own divisions (so-called 'in house' water firms).

After the 2003 local public services reform, several OTA authorities started assigning the water franchises in accordance to the new rules, in particular to 'in house' water firms, which rapidly became the most common water service provider in the country. The award of water franchises to 'in house' water firms, which the European Court of Justice had ruled a legitimate way of organizing local public services in 1999,[8] allowed local governments to retain control of the firms which were restructured through the merger of various incumbent local government-owned water firms. As the direct award of water franchises to 'in house' water firms prevented opening up the water industry to competition, in December 2004 the Minister of the Environment Altero Matteoli issued a couple of directives which intended to limit the award of water franchises to 'in house' water firms and to mixed public-private ownership firms. Instead, most of the OTA authorities ignored them. By the end 2006, water franchises had been awarded in 67 OTAs, out of 92 which had been established in the country (Fig. 3).

In 2006, the implementation of the 1994 water reform came to the end. On 23rd October 2000, the EU Commission had issued directive 2000/60/CE on the preservation and safeguard of water resources. The transposition of the directive into the Italian legislation started in October 2001, when the government proposed a reform bill to the Parliament, and terminated on 3rd April 2006, when the Berlusconi government issued Legislative Decree 152/2006. Legislative Decree 152/2006 established eight water districts in the country, whose authorities would be charged of responsibilities on the preservation and protection of water resources. Moreover, the decree abrogated Act 36/1994, therefore it terminated the implementation of the 1994 water reform which had been conducted over the previous 12 years. However, the economic regulatory institutions of the water sector kept operating according to the water franchises which had been awarded by the OTA authorities.

---

[8] The 'in house' arrangement had been ruled legitimate by the European Court of Justice in the case C-107/98 Teckal vs. local government of Viano (Italy) on 18 November 1999. The case originated from the appeal of Teckal, a business company, against the direct award of heating services for certain municipal buildings from the local government of Viano to a fully-local government-owned business company. The Court ruled in favour of the local government, on the basis that the local government can contract out the local public service to a third party, juridically distinct from itself, without any tender offer competition and in derogation to sector-specific rules, if the local government is able to exercise a control analogous to the one on its own departments on the entity, and the other entity delivers most of its services to the controlling local government.

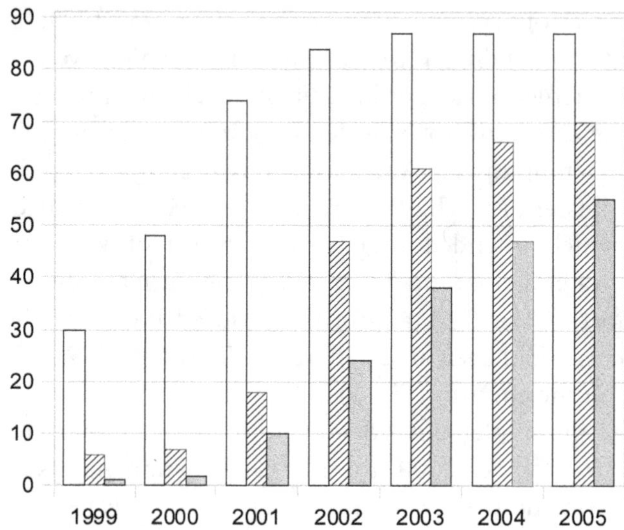

Figure 3: From left to right, histograms show the number of OTA authorities established, the number of water infrastructure development and tariff plans approved, and the number of water franchises awarded

Source: yearly report of the Supervising Committee on the Use of Water Resources, 2000–2006; BlueBook 2006.

5. The Analysis of the Water Reform Implementation in Italy (1994–2006)

The implementation of the water reform in Italy is an episode which has attracted considerable attention by various scholars in the field of political science, economics, and water management (Goria and Lugaresi, 2002; Muraro and Valbonesi, 2003; Anwandter and Rubino, 2006; Massarutto, 2007; Citroni *et al.*, 2007; Carrozza, 2008). These works already contribute to explaining the rationale and effects of the water reform design choices and the behaviour of implementers and target groups during the water reform implementation process. Instead, the analysis conducted here is mainly concerned with explaining why the water regulatory system in Italy came to take the shape of an 'hybrid' regulatory system. A case will be made for arguing that the political dynamics of the implementation of the water reform affected the particular combination of selected features of various regulatory models which came to form the overall regulatory system of the water industry in the country. Then, the case of the water regulatory system implemented in Italy shows how 'hybrid' regulatory systems may emerge from the decisions made during the implementation phase of the reform rather than from deliberate regulatory reform choices.

The water reform statute (Act 36/1994) required that the new regulatory system would be put into place by carrying out a specified sequence of activities. These activities included the transposition of the national water legislation to the regional-level, the establishment of the OTA authorities, the approval of water infrastructure development and tariff plans, and eventually the award of water franchises. Each of these activities required that implementers made decisions concerning how and whether to carry out the implementation tasks. In an overly simplified form, the sequence of 'decision points' during the course of the implementation process can be pictured as in Fig. 4. In the first decision point (transposing the water reform into the regional legislation), the regions could choose whether or not to transpose the water reform or to refuse or postpone

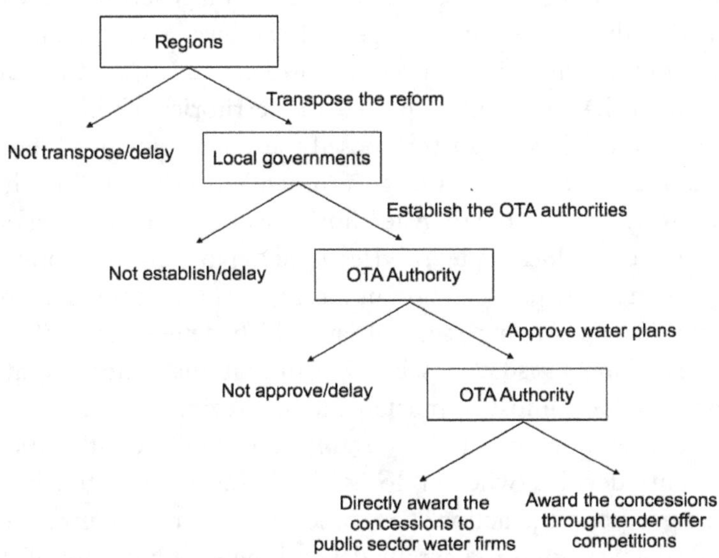

Figure 4: A simplified sequential model of the implementation of the 1994 water reform

the action. After the water reform came into effect, the regions generally delayed transposing the national water legislation while local governments did not collaborate to define the OTA territories and the central government deferred issuing some additional regulations concerning the criteria for the definition of the OTAs in particular. The behaviour of the regions can be understood because of the political uneasiness to pass regional laws which could be later contradicted by central government regulations and which did not take local governments' voice on the regulation of the local water industries into account. Instead, by postponing the transposition of the national water legislation, the regions could shift the blame for not accomplishing this implementation task on the delays of the central government to issue the required regulations and the lack of collaboration of local governments to define the OTAs.

In the late 90's, various regions started to progress in transposing the national water legislation to the regional-level. In 1996, the Minister of Public Works, Antonio Di Pietro, threatened to commission the regions which had not issued the regional laws defining the OTAs yet. Since most of the regions persisted to delay the transposition process, in 1997 Di Pietro's successor, Paolo Costa, started the commissioning procedure against the defaulting regions. In 1997, the central government, which was concerned with speeding up sewage and wastewater treatment works in order to comply with EU environmental directive 91/271/CE, authoritatively defined that the OTAs equalled the territories of the provinces in those regions which had not transposed the water reform yet. Local governments reacted to the central government's decision by turning their attention to redefining the OTA territories, as they generally regarded the organization of the local water services as falling in their own competences. Having gathered the participation of local governments, the regions eventually speeded up passing regional law which defined the OTAs in the respective regional jurisdictions. By 1999, the national water legislation had been incorporated almost completely into the regional ones.

In the second decision point (establishing the OTA authorities), local governments decided whether to establish the OTA authorities or to refuse or postpone the action. For some years after the definition of the OTAs, local governments generally delayed the establishment of the OTA authorities. If local governments established these entities, they should also have transferred their water planning and control functions to them and make them award the water franchises — which a few if any of incumbent local government-owned water firms could be qualified to receive. Instead, by delaying the reform, local governments allowed their water firms the time needed to restructure themselves through mergers and acquisitions in order to qualify for being awarded the water franchises later on. Local governments started to establish the OTA authorities when they understood that they could retain control on local water services by means of their ownership of relatively large water firms which would manage water provision in whole OTAs rather than in the territories of local governments only. Although the early OTA authorities were established in 1999, only from 2001 onwards the number of OTA authorities established in the country steadily increased as more and more local government-owned water firms fit the requirements to be awarded the water franchises.

In the third decision point (planning water infrastructure development and tariffs), the OTA authorities could decide whether to carry out drafting and approving water infrastructure development and tariff plans or to refuse or postpone the action. Initially, these planning efforts were carried out by some OTA authorities mostly based in the southern regions of the country, as they were required in order to appropriate additional funds of the the 2000–2006 CSF. Instead, most of the OTAs in the centre and in the north of the country initially delayed accomplishing these planning tasks because their local governments generally showed a modest interest to make the OTA authorities progress in a process which would eventually lead to award the water franchises. However, local governments later started to make the OTA authorities speed up the planning efforts when they perceived the opportunity to exploit the exemption and transition regime provided by the 2001 local public services reform for preserving the position of their incumbent water firms. Had the OTA authorities kept delaying approving the plans, they would have missed the transitory period and would have been later compelled to tender out the water franchises, rather than directly awarding them to local government fully- or majority-owned water firms.

Finally, in the fourth decision point (awarding the water concessions), the OTA authorities could decide whether and how to award the water franchises. Until 2001, a small number of OTA authorities mostly located in the central regions of the country accomplished this task. Until then, local governments generally preferred that the OTA authorities delayed the franchises award, because local government-owned water firms were not yet 'ready' to undertake water service provisions in relatively larger territories than they used to manage. When the 2001 local public services reform offered the possibility to directly award water franchises through exemption and transition regimes — rather than making tender offer competitions — then local governments made the OTA authorities speed up the franchises award. From 2001 onwards, the number of water franchises awarded increased sharply and kept rising in each of the following years. Had the OTA authorities kept delaying awarding the water franchises, they would have been later required to accomplish this task by selecting water firms through tender offer competitions — an outcome which could make local government-owned water firms lose the management of local water services because of the competition of multinational firms. Later on, the passing of the 2003 local public services reform even allowed the OTA authorities to directly award water franchises to fully local government-owned ('in house') water firms.

On the whole, the analysis shows that the new regulatory system of water infrastructure in Italy resulted from the sequence of decisions that various actors made during the implementation process. The national water legislation provided the general institutional design for setting up the new regulatory system, but the decisions made during the implementation of the reform partially reshaped the regulation of water infrastructure in a particular way. The resulting regulatory system of water infrastructure in Italy incorporated features of franchise allocation and discretionary regulation models (e.g., the award of water franchises and the application of the criteria for water infrastructure development and tariff setting, issued by the Supervizing Committee, by the OTA authorities), but it also largely preserved widespread public ownership of water firms. Then, the features of such a 'hybrid' regulatory system, originated from decisions made in both designing and implementing the water regulatory reform.

6. Measuring Regulatory Outcome and Effectiveness: What Do We Know?

How well does the new regulatory system of water infrastructure in Italy perform? One way to answer this question is to assess the extent to which policymakers' main explicit objectives of the 1994 water reform, namely reducing the fragmentation of the sector and increasing investments in water infrastructure, have been achieved. On the whole, the set up of the new water regulatory system in Italy resulted in higher concentration of the water industry and in relatively modest achievements in terms of infrastructure development. According to the 2007 Report to the Parliament of the Supervizing Committee on the Use of Water Resources (March 2008), water franchises were awarded in 67 of the 92 OTAs provided by the regional laws (i.e., about 79% of the country's population was affected by the new regulatory system). In these 67 OTAs, water franchises were awarded to 102 water firms, while in the other 25 OTAs, in which no water concessions have been awarded, water services are still provided by an uncertain number of hundreds (possibly thousands) operators. The concentration process led to the formation of relatively large operators, such as Acea based in Rome (serving about 7m users), Acquedotto Pugliese in Puglia (4.5m), Hera in Bologna (2m), Smat in Turin (2m), Iride in Genoa (1.9m), CAP in Milan (1.7m), and Abbanoa in Sardinia (1.6m).

However, the amount of water infrastructure investments carried out by these larger operators fell behind expectations. According to a survey of 53 OTAs conducted by the Supervizing Committee in 2007, in the first 3 years of water management under the new regulatory system, the surveyed water firms carried out about €2.12 billion investments per year, a figure which is less the amount originally expected in the OTA plans (€4.38 billion) and than the amount of investments needed to comply with the current EU pollution and quality standards (which was estimated to be about €3 billion per year for about 10 years; ASTRID, 2008). From a sample of 27 OTA plans, the Supervizing Committee also showed that water firms mostly financed infrastructure development through self-financing (45%), EU funds (21%), corporate debt (14%) and equity (11%). With respect to the planned financial structure of these OTA plans, water firms seemed to experience difficulties in financing through corporate debts, while they tended to still largely rely on public funds (i.e., EU funds and equity provided by the local governments, which still retain large shareholdings of water firms). One of the *plausible* reasons for the lack of funding from private sources is that the water firms still charged relatively low tariffs, at least in comparison to other cities in the EU (e.g., water tariffs in Italy range between 0.56–0.75 €/m^3, in Spain 0.78–0.90 €/m^3, in France 1.93–2.72 €/m^3, in Germany 2.87–4.30 ¤/m^3, and in the UK 2.08–4.39 €/m^3; ASTRID, 2008), and therefore water investments provided relatively little return to capital invested and failed to attract private investors. The conflict of interests built in the current water regulatory regime in Italy (e.g., the local governments being both the owners of water firms and the owners of the OTA authorities awarding the concessions) might be the causal source for keeping private investors at bay (Anwandter and Rubino, 2006).

The new regulatory system of water infrastructure in Italy exhibited various weaknesses, in many other respects. The 2008 report to the Parliament of the Supervizing Committee and a 2008 report issued by the think tank ASTRID, highlighted some of the water regulatory system's critical features. These reports argued that the OTA authorities lacked substantive powers for monitoring and controlling water firms, which could enjoy information asymmetries and better qualified competences and skills; that the water firms, on the whole, exhibited relatively modest return on equity, high-leverage, and difficulties to access corporate finance funds; that the OTA plans showed incomplete data, little coherence between strategic plans and operational programmes, unreliable and overoptimistic forecasts, and loosely defined provisions for reviewing the plans; that the OTA authorities and the water firms often seemed to collude in drafting loosely designed franchise contracts, particularly in those cases where both the OTA authority and the water firm were owned and controlled by the same local governments; and finally, that the water industry attracted less private funds than originally expected, mostly because of the reluctance of public authorities to give away ownership of water firms and of the relatively low tariff levels.

On the whole, the new regulatory system of water infrastructure in Italy resulted in changes of the structure of the water industry (e.g., less fragmentation) but not in the desired changes of the behaviour of water firms. Incumbent public sector water firms found the way to preserve their dominant positions in the water industry or even strengthen it by merging into larger operators and expanding the service areas. Larger water firms might achieve economies of scale and undertake more infrastructure development programmes than smaller ones, but, by the terms of the performance assessment recalled above, generally water firms in Italy missed carrying out the expected or required investment programmes. Stronger evidence is needed, but, without being subject to any competitive pressure or to regulation by truly independent regulatory agencies, incumbent water firms may be negatively affected by organizational slack, overmanning, and rent-seeking behaviour (Rees, 1998). Some efforts have been made to set up an association of the OTA authorities (ANEA) which promotes the diffusion of 'best practice' in the water professional community on issues such as cost monitoring, contractual design and management, and performance benchmarking. However, the regulatory governance of water infrastructure remains fundamentally affected by a special kind of 'regulatory capture' (Stigler, 1971; Posner, 1974), because generally the same local governments play the roles of the owners of both the local regulatory authorities, which contract out and enforce the water franchise concessions, and the regulated water firms.[9]

7. Implications for Regulatory Design, Effectiveness, and Operation

The regulation of water infrastructure resulting from the implementation of the 1994 water reform in Italy presented 'hybrid' traits between public ownership, the 'French' and the 'English & Welsh' models (Anwandter and Rubino, 2006). Similarly to the French system, the local OTA authorities

[9] In many instances of implementation of the water reform in Italy, the franchise allocation and the discretionary regulation models, which presuppose an institutionally-built divergence of interest between the franchisor/regulator and the franchisee/regulated, have been substantially neglected. The most illustrative case is the one which took place in the OTA "Sarnese Vesuviano" in Campania, where it is the same OTA Authority established by local governments to own 51% of the local water firm, GORI S.p.A., which has been awarded the water franchise.

contracted out the management of water services and investment programmes through franchise contracts. Similarly to England & Wales, water tariff is subject to price-cap regulation according to the criteria set by a national regulatory authority. However, differently from the French system, water franchises were usually granted to local government fully- or majority-owned water firms rather than to business companies selected through tender offer competitions, and differently from the English & Welsh system the water tariff is set by local regulatory authorities and written in the franchise contracts rather than being subject to discretionary scrutiny by a national regulatory (anyway, the OTA authorities do not enjoy any power compared to the English & Welsh water regulator, OFWAT). To some extent, the Italian water industry has some similarities to the German one, because of the emergence of public sector fully- or majority-owned multi-utility firms at the regional scale, which often diversified their activities into various related infrastructure business areas.

The analysis of the case suggests that these 'hybrid' features of the regulatory system of water infrastructure in Italy resulted from the political economy of the process of implementing the 1994 water reform as well as from the deliberate water reform design choices. The regulatory institutions, organizations, and tools resulted, in particular, from the efforts of local governments to implement the water reform in such a way as to retain control of the local water industries by protecting the position of their incumbent water firms. This finding suggests that 'hybrid' regulatory systems may originate from the decisions made during the implementation of a new regulatory system, rather than from intended design choices. This claim partially qualifies the argument put forward by Groom *et al.* (2006), who highlighted that 'hybrid' regulatory systems arise because of the policymakers' efforts to grasp the benefits of different regulatory 'models' (e.g., the French and the Anglo-Saxon ones). Rather than seeing the design of regulatory systems which borrow from different 'models' as a result of a deliberate attempt to strengthen regulation, this analysis suggests that 'hybrid' regulatory system can also result from the behaviour of actors in implementing the regulatory reforms. Then, the combination of regulatory models can simply 'fit' the political economy of the water domain, in particular if it results from the efforts to preserve the stakes of the incumbent firms in the infrastructure industry. In the case analysed here, for example, local governments were able to retain ownership and influence on the water firms rather than effectively separating the policy-making, regulatory, and operational functions.

The assessment of the performance achieved by the new water regulatory system in Italy poses some cautionary notes on the effectiveness of 'hybrid' regulatory systems. Groom *et al.* (2006) pointed out that the combination of public ownership with other kinds of regulatory models (such as franchise allocation and discretionary regulation) can promote more accountability, better transparency, and higher performance. However, the insights that we can gain from the case of the water regulatory system implemented in Italy suggests that the combination of selected features of different regulatory models may not necessarily strengthen regulatory performance. On the other hand, it seems that in 'hybrid' regulatory systems one regulatory model may prevail over the others, whose features may be formally adopted but substantively made irrelevant. In the case of the water regulatory system implemented in Italy, for example, water firms remained largely regulated through public ownership, while franchise allocation was not generally conducted on competitive basis and discretionary regulation was fundamentally undermined by the weakness of the regulatory authorities. The result of this uneven combination of different models can make 'hybrid' regulatory systems unable to outperform 'pure types' regulatory models and rather overburdened by unnecessary administrative tasks.

However, these insights into the establishment and effectiveness of 'hybrid' regulatory systems need to be appropriately qualified. The process and outcome of setting up 'hybrid' regulatory systems may be affected by particular context factors which either facilitate or impair the working of the combined regulatory mechanisms. The case of the water regulatory system implemented in Italy, for example, is characterized by the large number of implementers and units of target groups involved in the reform process (i.e., the water reform affected about 8,100 local governments and 23,500 water firms), by the inherent conflict of interest of local governments (i.e., local governments were both owners of the water firms and the local regulatory authorities), by the constitutionally sanctioned competences of sub-national governments on local public services (i.e., local governments ultimately decided how water service provisions should be organized), by the influence exercised by the EU (i.e., the central government was concerned with implementing EU directives on environmental standards and EU infrastructure development programmes), and by the relative stability of water service provision technology (i.e., incumbent water service providers were modestly threatened by other operators on the ground of technological innovation). Such types of context factors may contribute to enhance the complexity of implementing infrastructure regulatory reform, to increase the odds of diverting the regulatory system from the original design, and to undermine the effectiveness of the combined regulatory mechanisms.

8. Lessons for Regulators: What Works, and What Does Not?

The analysis of the case of the water regulatory system implemented in Italy suggests a few recommendations for designing and managing regulatory systems of infrastructure industries. At least two pieces of advice can be highlighted here, concerning the effectiveness and the implementation of 'hybrid' regulatory systems, respectively. First, policymakers and regulators should take into account that 'hybrid' regulatory systems may hardly attract private investors if regulatory governance does not ensure that they receive an adequate return on investments and that they do not incur the risk of regulatory opportunism. In the case of the water regulatory system implemented in Italy, for example, water tariffs were set by the local regulatory authorities (OTA authorities), which could take into consideration local governments' concern with keeping tariffs relatively low in order to avoid irritating local communities rather than private investors' interest to get return from the investments. In this case, the presence of multiple regulatory mechanisms did not result in a regulatory governance which provided more safeguards to private investments. The lack of some fundamental requisites for the well-functioning of franchise allocation and discretionary regulation — namely, competitive tender offers and truly independent regulators — weakened the credibility that public ownership did not expropriate the return to investment in water infrastructure. Then, it seems that more attention should be placed on the coherence between the various component parts of the regulatory system, rather than on the adoption of formal regulatory institutions borrowed from different regulatory models.

Second, policymakers and regulators should also pay attention to the political dynamics of putting new regulatory systems into place. As shown in the case of the water regulatory system implemented in Italy, an infrastructure regulatory reform may be significantly reshaped during the course of the reform implementation process. Particular context factors, such as the multi-layered governance system and the presence of a large number of implementers and units of target groups, may increase the odds that the regulatory system is diverted from the original design. 'Hybridization' of the regulatory system may be a consequence of such a type of implementation of regulatory reforms in which the central government is not able to steer the implementers to closely comply with the original regulatory reform design and in which implementers, instead, introduce novel features into the regulatory system. In the case of the water regulatory system implemented in Italy, for example, a 'hybrid' regulatory system resulted from the opportunity for local governments to retain control of local water industries by making the OTA authorities directly award water franchises to incumbent local government-owned water firms rather than to business companies selected through tender offer competitions. In this case, the central government could not steer the decisions about the award of the water franchise made by the OTA authorities, as constitutional constraints and favourable contemporaneous events at the EU level (i.e., the 1999 ruling of the European Court of Justice) limited the extent to which the central government could affect local governments' choices. Instead, political oversight of the central government on the implementation of the regulatory reform seems to be important in order to maintain consistency between the regulatory system put into place and the original regulatory design.

Anyway, the 'hybridization' of the regulatory system may be a reasonable price to pay for the achievement of ancillary policy goals. In the case of the water regulatory system implemented in Italy, for example, the implementation of the water reform also led to a significant reorganization of the water industry. By the end of the water reform implementation episode in 2006, the number of water firms operating in the country had reduced from about 23,500 to just 102 firms which served about 79% of the population, plus an uncertain number of operators (hundreds, possibly thousands) in those local areas where the regulatory reform had not been fully implemented. Taking policy-makers' objective to reduce the fragmentation of the water industry into account, to some extent the implementation of the water reform resulted in a partial success. However, the consolidation of the water industry could take place because of favourable institutional factors that provided the possibility to protect the position of the incumbent local government-owned water firms in the reformed local water industries to local governments. Possibly, the consolidation of local government-owned water firms would not have happened, if local governments could not preserve their control on the local water industries. Local governments' control on the local water industries, in turn, could have been put at risk, if the design of the regulatory system had not included public ownership as a legitimate model for regulating the local water services. Then, policymakers and regulators need to also take into account what are the policy priorities to pursue, and whether or not the implementation of a new regulatory system offers some scope for bargaining a compromise on satisfactory reorganizing as well as re-regulating the infrastructure industry.

References

Amato, A and Maurizio Conti (2005). *The Economics of the Water Industry: Technology, Ownership and Efficiency.* Milan: Franco Angeli.

Anwandter, L and Piero Rubino (2006). *Rischi, incertezze, e conflitti d'interesse nel settore idrico italiano: analisi e proposte di riforma.* Materiali Unità di Valutazione degli Investimenti Pubblici. Roma: Dipartimento per le Politiche di Sviluppo.

ASTRID (2008). *Infrastrutture e servizi a rete tra regolazione e concorrenza. Le infrastrutture idriche.* Associazione per gli Studi e Ricerche sulla Riforma delle Istituzioni Democratiche e sull'innovazione nelle amministrazioni pubbliche. Rome.

Baldwin, R, C Scott and C Hood (1998). *Regulation: A Reader.* Oxford: Oxford University Press.

Ballance, T and A Taylor (2005). *Competition and Economic Regulation in Water: The Future of the European Water Industry.* IWA Publishing.

Baumol, WJ (1982). Contestable markets: An uprising theory of industry structure. *American economic Review,* 72(S), pp. 1–15.

Beecher, JA (2001). Privatization, Monopoly, and Structured Competition in the Water Industry: Is there a role for regulation? In *Umweltaspekte einer Privatisierung der*

Wasserwirtschaft in Deutschland: Dokumentation der internationalen Fachtagungvom 20 und 21, Holzwarth F and A Kraemer (eds.). Berlin: Books on Demand.

Carrozza, C (2008). La riforma italiana dei servizi idrici. Modi locali di governo fra continuità e rottura. *Rivista Italiana di Politiche Pubbliche*, 1(April), pp. 5–36.

Citroni, G, N Giannelli, A Lippi and S Profeti (2007). Chi governa l'acqua? Regolazione, potere locale, e arene di rappresentanza nella governance del servizio idrico integrato. SISP Conference, Catania, 20–22 September.

Cowan, S (1993). Regulation of several market failures: The water industry in England and Wales. *Oxford Review of Economic Policy*, 9(4), pp. 14–23.

Demsetz, H (1968). Why regulate utilities? *Journal of Law and Economics*, 11(April), pp. 55–66.

Gómez Ibáñez, JA (2003). *Regulating Infrastructure: Monopoly, Contracts, and Discretion.* Harvard University Press.

Goria, A and N Lugaresi (2002). *The Evolution of the National Water Regime in Italy.* Milan: Istituto per la Ricerca Sociale-Ewareness.

Groom, E, J Halpern and D Ehrhardt (2006). Explanatory notes on key topics in the regulation of water and sanitation services. *Water Supply and Sanitation Sector Board Discussion Paper Series*, paper no. 6. World Bank.

ISTAT (1991). *I servizi idrici in Italia.* Rome: Istituto Nazionale di Statistica.

Littlechild, S (1986). Economic regulation of privatized water authorities and some further reflections. *Oxford Review of Economic Policy*, 4(2), pp. 40–67.

Massarutto, A (2007). Liberalization and private sector involvement in the water industry: A review of the economic literature. *Munich Personal RePEc Archive*, paper n. 5864.

Merrett, S (1997). *Introduction to the Economics of Water Resources: An International Perspective.* Rowman & Littlefield.

Muraro, G and P Valbonesi (eds.) (2003). *I servizi idrici tra mercato e regole.* Rome: Carrocci Editore.

Noll, RG, MM Shirley and S Cowan (2002). Reforming Urban Water Systems in Developing Countries. In *Economic Policy Reform: The Second Stage*, Krueger AO (ed.). University of Chicago Press.

Ogus, A (1994). *Regulation: Legal Theory and Economic Theory.* Oxford University Press.

Posner, RA (1974). Theories of economic regulation. *Bell Journal of Economics*, 5, pp. 335–358.

Ragin, CC and HS Becker (1982). *What is a Case? Exploring the Foundations of Social Inquiry.* Cambridge University Press.

Rees, JA (1998). Regulation and private participation in the water and sanitation sector. *Natural Resources Forum*, 22(2), pp. 95–105.

Rees, JA, J Winpenny and AW Hall (2008). *Water Financing and Governance.* TEC Background Papers No. 12. Global Water Partnership.

Rouse, MJ (2007). *Institutional Governance and Regulation of Water Services.* IWA Publishing.

Spulber, N and A Sabbaghi (1994). *Economics of Water Resources: From Regulation to Privatization.* Kluwer Academic Publishing.

Stake, RE (1995). *The Art of Case Study Research.* London: SAGE.

Stigler, GJ (1971). The theory of economic regulation. *Bell Journal of Economics & Management Science,* 2(1), pp. 1–21.

Supervising Committee on the Use of Water Resources (2008). *Report to the Parliament on the State of Water Services.* Rome.

Swann, D (1988). *The Retreat of the State: Deregulation and Privatisation in the UK and US.* Prentice-Hall.

Tenbücken, M (2006). *The Regulation of Network Infrastructure in the New European Union.* PhD Dissertation. Universität Konstanz.

Waterson, M (1988). *Regulation of the Firm and Natural Monopoly.* Blackwell Publishers.

Winpenny, J (2003). *Financing Water for All.* Report of the World Panel on Financing Water Infrastructure.

Yin, RK (1994). *Case Study Research: Design and Methods.* London: Sage.

CHAPTER 16

Measuring Effectiveness of Regulation Across a River System: A Welfare Approach

Alex Coram and Lyle Noakes

1. Introduction

Social scientists, governments, and policy analysts concerned with the management of water resources are increasingly becoming aware of the fact that there may be complex interdependencies between the various components of hydrological systems and that extraction at any one point may have a number of welfare and environmental impacts on a large number of other points. This has led to a shift in emphasis from simple efficiency in extraction to more complex questions of how to regulate extraction in order to produce outcomes that satisfy the objectives of system-wide management. For a regulatory authority responsible for allocating water through pricing, or some other mechanism, this raises a number of fundamental questions. Among these are those of what it means to have a successful regulatory scheme. How is success to be understood and measured? How do we know that whatever regulatory scheme is in place is allowing the appropriate amount of water to be extracted at each point? If the regulator has to negotiate with various interests over pricing or water allocations, what criteria should be used?

The question of appropriate regulatory regimes and how to measure the success of regulation are, in many ways common throughout this collection. In the chapter on water by Ehrhardt and Janson, for example, it is argued that regulation in all sectors needs to be designed to ensure that the services that can are provided are 'the best that can be achieved with the resources available' (Chapter 13). We also see similar problems in the regulation of electricity and telecommunications. In the chapter by Clifton *et al.* it is argued, for example, that regulation needs to be better designed to take the interests of consumers, and the fact that these may vary, into account (Chapter 2). A similar call for redesign of regulation focused on consumer welfare is found in the chapter by Sirasoontorn (Chapter 6).

As has also been pointed out in other chapters in this collection the different types of infrastructure have unique features which affect the type of regulation appropriate and the standards of what counts as success.

In the case of water, the regulator has to deal with standard problems, such as efficiency in distribution, investment in infrastructure, and ensuring optimal levels of provision in the forms which the apply to this particular good. In addition, there is another level of concern for the regulatory regime that take different forms according to whether extraction and distribution is from a stationary water source or from a flow.

If the water source is a stock, such as a lake or a dam, it may be necessary to regulate in a way that controls demand according to some criteria and set different prices for different users, such as agriculture and industry. It may also be necessary to have a regime that allows the amount extracted to vary inversely with the volume available.

If the water source is a river system, it has different characteristics, because it is a uni-directional flow in which upstream extractors are able to inflict damage on downstream interests. In this case, it will be necessary to devise the criteria for measuring the effectiveness of regulation, and to set regulatory standards, in a way that takes these interconnections into account. It is this problem which is of concern here.

More specifically, this chapter is concerned with the problem of finding the appropriate means of assessing the effectiveness of regulation across a river system, considered as a whole, when benchmarked against some standard of global optimality. This should be distinguished from a second sort of problem that also arises. This is, how should effectiveness of regulation be assessed when benchmarked in terms of efficiency of usage or access to resources? We know quite a bit about these questions and aspects of it are discussed in the chapters by Asquer (Chapter 15) and Ehrhardt and Janson (Chapter 13). However, we know very little about the first question.

In order to study the problem, it will be assumed that the planning agency stipulates that water is to be allocated across the system in a manner that maximizes welfare. This will be justified in more detail below. In this case, the criteria for measuring, at least benchmarking, effectiveness is given to the regulator.

What makes the problem difficult for the regulator, is that it needs to work out what allocation would meet the planner's condition at each point on the river in order to construct the appropriate programme. It is this specific problem that we address in this chapter.

In what follows, we discuss some progress we have made in providing the information needed to solve this problem in Coram and Noakes (2009). We show how it could, in principle, be solved and how the proposed solution might be implemented.

Because of the complexities of the problem, this chapter is more abstract than others in the collection. Nonetheless these complexities are instructive. They serve to illustrate the point that different sorts of infrastructure may have unique characteristics and that these may need to be analyzed in a new theoretical framework, rather than simply applying off-the-shelf technologies.

We set out the chapter as follows. In Sec.1 we specify the problem in more detail. In Sec.2, we look at the implications for attempting to assess welfare. In the Sec.3, we discuss some of the lessons that can be drawn from the model.

2. Measuring Regulatory Effectiveness

2.1 *The Problem of Assessing Effectiveness for a River System*

The planner may wish to use welfare maximization as a basis for assessing effectiveness because it provides a means of solving a number of unique problems associated with river systems. The most important of these are that, unlike other infrastructural goods such as electricity and telecommunications, [1] water is not a produced good, and [2] extraction at any one point impacts differentially at all other points.

These characteristics raise a number of questions around the issues of scarcity and fair allocation. In many cases, and perhaps increasingly, resource allocation is likely to be contested. For this reason, a regulatory regime based on precedent, or purely economic returns, is unlikely to be seen as fair or appropriate. In particular, late comers and those who have not historically been large users, or whose interests have not been previously considered, may be particularly aggrieved by any allocation that does not take their interests into account. Such problems can only be exacerbated where water flows across state borders.

The issues raised by interdependence and scarcity can be illustrated by looking at the Murray-Darling Basin in Australia. The Murray-Darling Basin catchment is over a million square kilometers. The stated objective of the Murray-Darling Basin Commission is to implement an 'Integrated Catchment Management' policy (Murray-Darling Basin Commission, 2001) for this entire system. This is to be done by setting targets for catchment health that are intended to protect urban users, to protect those who use the river for irrigation, to protect other environmental and economic assets and to protect the health of the system as a whole by imposing an end of catchment area target on flows at the terminal point, however defined.[1] In this case, effectiveness of the regulatory system is linked to satisfying the legitimate claims of the various groups with a stake in the system. Unfortunately, the criteria proposed by the Commission are mostly directed at the question of capacity building. It says little about developing a clear set of protocols or models of interaction that might provide a set of principles that could be used to inform regulation or to judge how well the regulatory regime has decision-making and discussions between the different interests within catchments. In addition, it is also necessary to show how the catchment approach can be extended to the system as a whole. There are, for example, considerable problems in setting targets for catchment health. Not only is it difficult to work out how environmental and economic demands are to be reconciled, but there is also considerable difficulty presented by the fact that end point targets for one catchment area are starting point flows for a downstream catchment. This

[1] There are 13 catchment management authorities.

means that it is not only necessary to deal with different environmental and economic priorities within catchments but it is also necessary to deal with different priorities between catchment areas.

In a similar manner, the National Water Commission in Australia has interpreted effectiveness in terms of meeting demands of various interests and has called for a 'nationally consistent approach to water planning' that is able to settle 'the trade-offs between competing outcomes for water systems, based on the 'best available science.'[2] This again raises questions about the criteria to be used to determine the consistency between different sorts of users and across different geographical regions.

Another example is the Colorado River Basin in the US. The Colorado catchment area is about half the size of the Murray-Darling catchment. Water usage is controlled by an agreement which splits the river system into an Upper Basin and a Lower Basin with a guaranteed allocation of water to the lower basin states and to Mexico under a treaty signed between the US and Mexico. However, it appears, with emerging demands exceeding the capacity of the river and increasing environmental concerns that many current agreements may need to be renogotiated (Colorado River District; Gelt, 1997).

If we take a broader perspective, the problem of establishing a consistent set of standards for water allocation seems even more severe. Many of the world's largest rivers such as the Nile, the Amazon, the Congo and the Niger run through multiple independent states.[3] If, as predictions indicate, water shortages are likely to increase in coming decades, the problem of managing the river, and its tributaries as a system and determining the gains and losses to different interests will become urgent.

What makes a welfare maximizing approach a reasonable solution to these problems is that, it provides a way of making an assessment of the impact of allowing more or less water to be removed at one point on all other points in the system which meets the criteria of consistency and

---

[2] National Water Commission. Water planning in Australia position statement. April 2008. http://www.nwc.gov.au

[3] Among the major rivers that are within a single state are the Yangtze, the Yellow, and, effectively, the Mississippi.

is defensible to various demands. It also has the advantage of being a well-established theoretical concept.

Before proceeding, it must be stressed that we do not claim that a calculation of welfare would, in any sense, provide anything more than a rough guideline for measuring the effectiveness of regulation. We say rough because this calculation is hampered by the fact that, among other problems, we do not have any non-contested inputs for the utility functions of various interests. These may themselves be part of the negotiation over regulation.

On the other hand, we do believe that such a criterion has the advantage of forcing the regulator to adopt a programme that attempts to achieve a consistent set of outcomes across the system, even though the specific regulations may vary from point to point. This has the advantage of forcing a system-wide view. At the least, it forces some consistency on the regulator in that, it would not be permissible to vary the utility functions for the same group of interests at different geographical locations without good cause.

In what follows, we consider the problems faced by the regulator in programme design and in determining a standard for effectiveness.

2.2 *The Regulator's Problem*

The regulator's problem is to obtain sufficient insight into what it would mean to maximize welfare at each point in the system in order to get the information it needs to deploy, and assess the effectiveness of, its instruments and this is approached in the following manner. It is assumed that the interests of the various legitimate stakeholders can be captured by aggregating their welfare functions. This, of course, leaves open a number of questions about how these functions are approximated and what sort of claims about relative utility are considered acceptable, although it is not considered that disagreement about such matters would be any more fierce than disagreement about any attempt to compare gains and losses. Such issues might themselves, be the subject to some negotiation or agreement between the appropriate parties. For the purposes of this chapter we leave these issues to one side. It is assumed that there are a number of agents who wish to extract water in different intervals throughout the entire system for agricultural, industrial or other purposes, and that there are others who value the water for recreational or other pursuits, or gain aesthetic benefit from it, or attach an environmental value to water flows. It is assumed that extraction imposes a cost on recreational and environmental users, or on the community, by reducing water levels, increasing the build up of toxins, causing damage to wild-life and fisheries and the like. Floods and other situations where it might be desirable to reduce the level of the river are ignored.

If we wanted to move the analysis even further in the direction of realism, it would be necessary to add dams and other means of storing and controlling water into the complex. This would also give the manager the option of holding back, or increasing, the flow at various points. In this case we would have what is known as a distributed parameter system. It might be thought of as a problem with a two dimensional dynamic given by the volume of water at each point at each time. In this case, the manager would be able to control the extraction of water at each point and the flow of water over time. This problem is reasonably challenging and could produce some interesting and useful analysis. However, for time-being, we wish to focus on the problem of the optimal rate of extraction at each point with the major complication being the interdependencies across the system.

This problem is complicated by the fact that extraction at any point will have an impact on all other interests and this impact will be different according to the location of the interest. In order to get some idea of this, take a preliminary look at Fig. 1. This illustrates a system of rivers S made up of n interconnected rivers. Any continuous flow of water that terminates at the sea, or in a lake, or marsh, or wherever, and any flow that terminates on another path, is thought of as a separate river. Each river is labeled as $\sigma_i \in S$ where i is the index $i = 1, ..., n$. It is assumed that rivers

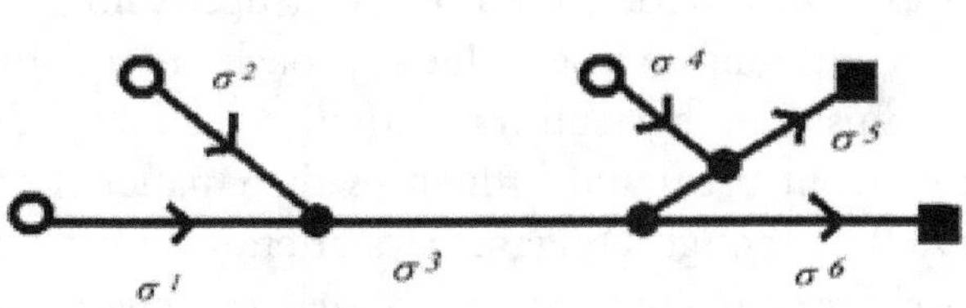

Figure 1: Example of a river system

collect or lose, water as the result of rain, evaporation or seepage along their way in the normal manner.

It is obvious that water extracted at any point on river σ_i will affect all interests downstream on river σ_i and all down stream interests on rivers into which σ_i flows. What is slightly less obvious is that, extraction of water at any point in σ_i will also affect the value of water in upstream rivers. This is because a unit of extraction from σ_i will reduce the flow of water into the terminating river for σ_i. This, in turn, will increase the value of water at every upstream point on that river.

For example, take a unit of extraction on river σ_4. This will affect the value of water at each downstream point on σ_I and σ_5. It will also increase the value of water at the node, or terminal point given by the junction of rivers σ_3, σ_5 and σ_6. This then affects the value of water at all points on these rivers.

By way of contrast note that, if there were only a single river, the manager would only have to calculate welfare along a single continuous flow and this would look like a standard optimization problem. What we now have is something like a problem of optimizing across several different flows simultaneously. Because of the interconnections between the flows, this cannot be solved by breaking the river up into discrete rivers or treating it as a sum of rivers.

Yet another difficulty is that, there will be jumps in the amount of water at points where rivers intersect. Unless this type of problem can be dealt with, it is difficult to see how it is possible to determine the optimal rate of extraction across the entire system.

These difficulties have so far not received much attention in the literature. The few studies that have treated a river as a flow in order to consider allocation problems have only considered the problem under restricted conditions, or for flows between discrete points. The paper by Quiggin, for example, models the impact of upstream users on downstream users by adopting an asset value approach in order to examine the way in which upstream agricultural activities may degrade water supplies for subsequent users and influences their patterns of production (Quiggin, 1988). Although Quiggin pays attention to the more general problem of welfare across the system analyzed, he only studies the system for a small set of discrete points without any intervening river junctions.

Other studies which have treated a river as a flow such as those by Weber (2001), for example, have also been limited to discrete number of points with no intervening junctions. There are no detailed explorations of the optimal programme across a complete system with continuous inflows and outflows at every point and multiple points of intersection between rivers. This problem was raised and described by Coram (2006) but not solved.

It might be thought that these problems could be avoided and an effective regulatory regime, in at least a narrow sense of one that maximizes efficiency, could be established by introducing some mechanism that combined property right and a market for permits at each point on the river.[4] In this case, it might be expected that each agent will pay for the value of the water at the point at which it is to be used and this would establish the efficient price at that point.

In general, this type of approach will not work if the criteria for effective regulation is tied to what satisfies the interests of different parties as understood in terms of their welfare. One difficulty is that, some interests will not be easy to represent in a market. Examples here are those that use the water for recreational or other pursuits, or gain aesthetic benefit from it, or attach an environmental value to water flows. In addition, the unidirectional ordering of agents along a flow means that the value of water at each point will be different and normal assumptions about market conditions and independence of traders will not hold.

In order to give a simple introduction to the problem in Fig. 1, and to illustrate what has been said about markets for rights, we consider the model for a single river. For this example we drop the super-scripts to ease the notation.

2.3 *Example. A Single River*

The river is thought of as a line, say the horizontal $\sigma := \{\sigma_1 \cup \sigma_3 \cup \sigma_6\}$ in Fig.1, with an initial point and a terminal point. Without loss of generality,

[4] The literature on rights is substantial. See for example, Burness and Quirk (1979), Booker and Young (1994), Free bairn and Quiggin (2006), Kanazawa (1991) and Weber (2001).

let the length of the river be one unit. Represent this by the interval [0, 1]. It is not possible to sensibly talk about the volume of water at a point, since there would be no water in a slice through the river of thickness zero, but we can speak about the volume of water in an interval. To do this partition σ into arbitrarily small intervals of length *dt* and let each internal be represented by a point *t*. Now, we can say that the amount of water in the river in the interval represented by the point $t \in [0, 1]$ is given by $\bar{x}(t)$. The volume of water in the interval around zero, that is $\bar{x}(0)$ is given. In order to save repeating 'in the interval around' we simply say *t* in what follows. Note that, $\bar{x}$ is a simple function, i.e., a function that is constant on every interval *dt*. In order to smooth things out, construct the continuously differentiable function $x: [0, 1] \rightarrow R$ that interpolates $\bar{x}(t)$ at every point *t*. We can now make *x* approximate $\bar{x}$ as closely as we wish by choosing *dt* sufficiently small. It suffices to concentrate on *x* in what follows.

Water will flow into the river at every point due to rainfall and run off from the land and also be lost in every interval due to evaporation, seepage and the like. Using the same argument as before, let the amount gained and lost at a point *t* in some standard unit of time, say one minute or one day as long as it is kept constant, be given by $a(t)$. Since these inflows and outflows happen at every point, it is assumed that *a* is a continuously differentiable function of *t*.

It is assumed that water can be extracted in any interval along the river and the amount extracted around the point *t* is $u(t)$ These points would, in practice, be presumed to be at a distance apart, represented by the distance between the points of intake of farms and towns, although this distance may be lessened by the fact that a single farm or town might extract water at several intake points and extraction at a single point will intake water over a wider interval. For the purposes of the model, it is assumed that there is no loss in approximating these discrete points by points that are arbitrarily close together. This means that we can treat $u(t)$ as a piecewise continuous function $u: [0, 1] \rightarrow R$. This is assumed to be, continuously differentiable almost everywhere.

When extraction is taken into account, we have complete data on the state of the river and the change in the volume of water per unit of time at every point along the river can now be written as

$$\dot{x}(t) = g(a(t), u(t)) \tag{1}$$

where $\dot{x}$ is the rate at which the volume of water is changing in the interval around the point t per unit of time.

For simplicity let

$$g := a(t) - u(t).$$

It is assumed that the welfare of each interest can be represented by a single payoff function. This function would, in general, be different for each interest. Agricultural users will all have the same payoff function and this may be different from those who wish to use the water for recreational purposes, for example. In order to deal with questions about pollutants and the quality of return flows, it is assumed that the quantity of water in the river can be used as rough proxy. Inflow of a pollutant, for example, could be taken as a reduction in the quantity of water available for other interests. If the problem is extended to multiple users, the reduction in the quantity of water may be different for users of different types.[5] One way to do this is to let the payoff for interest k be f_k and then write a payoff function at each point t in the system as $f(t) = \sum f_k(t)$ where f can be thought of as a composite function made up of the sum of all interests we might wish to include in the model. This gives $f: R^2 \rightarrow R$ where

$$f := f(u, x)$$

where it is assumed that f is concave in all its arguments and continuously differentiable and, since the water is valuable, $\partial f/\partial x > 0$ for all t.

To get the welfare of all agents the values f are summed at each point along the river. This sum is represented by the integral of f. This means that in order to determine the amount to be extracted at each point, it is necessary to choose the $u(t) \geq 0$ that maximizes

$$J = \int f dt$$

[5] It would be possible to extend the analysis to the case where there is one or more types of pollutant that cannot be represented in terms of the volume of water in the river. In this case, it would be necessary to specify the problem in terms of the appropriate state and control vectors. This is left for subsequent research.

evaluated between *0* and *1* at every point subject to the dynamics of the river given in Eq. (1).

In order to solve this problem form the Hamiltonian equation

$$H = f + \alpha\,(a - u)$$

where $\alpha(t)$ is what is known as the costate variable in optimization theory.

We can now use the Pontryagin principle to solve the problem (Macki and Strauss, 1982). This says that, if a solution exists, it must satisfy

$$\partial f / \partial u - \alpha = 0$$

and $\alpha(t)$ must be an absolutely continuous function with

$$\dot{\alpha} = -\,\partial f / \partial x$$

and $\alpha\,(1) = 0$.

It follows from the assumption that $\partial f / \partial x > 0$ that $\alpha > 0$ and α is decreasing for all $t < 1$.

It is also possible to interpret $\alpha\,(t)$ as the value, or price, of the water at point *t*. This means that, in the optimal programme the price of the water must be decreasing at each point. It follows that, if a market for rights produces a uniform price across the system, it cannot maximize welfare.

It might, of course, be possible to have a market with the purchase and sale of water at each price restricted to a particular location. In this case, we would need to know how optimal it is to extract at this point and hence need to solve the original problem of an optimal allocation.

An alternative would be to devise a bidding mechanism for water permits that forces the price at each point to incorporate the damage inflicted on downstream users. One possibility would be to design a mechanism such that, if an upstream agent bids for water, downstream agents damaged by the extraction could block the bid and force up the price to reflect this damage. This type of scheme is discussed in Weber (2001) and Coram (2006). In general such schemes are complicated and involve large transaction costs. In addition, it is difficult to incorporate the interests of non-extracting agents.

This completes our single river example and we now consider the implications of our approach for designing a system-wide scheme.

3. Implications for Regulatory Design: The Model for the Entire System

3.1 *The Problem of Junction Points*

The problem is solved for the complete river system by modifying the idea underlying the analysis of a single river to take the complications caused by interconnections into account. In this case, the problem now has a payoff function along the entire river system and it is necessary to optimize across all flows simultaneously. However, this cannot be done in a straightforward way. This is because multiple rivers may flow into and away from a node, and there are multiple termination and commencing points. It follows that the amount of water at any node will depend on the solution to optimization problems at other parts of the system. This means that it is not possible to start at a terminal point and use backward induction as might be done in a standard dynamic programming problem. In addition, we also have to deal with the problem of jumps in the water volumes at points where rivers intersect.

It might be thought that jumps in the volume of water at junctions between rivers could be dealt with by setting up a fictitious market and working in terms of purchases and sales between rivers at these points. This is an established technique in the literature (Seierstad and Sydsaeter, 1987: 194–210). If the price were given, as well as the function that determined the change in the amount of stock for a given outlay, it would be possible to calculate the optimum amount to be bought or sold at any junction between rivers from the shadow price for the resource. The amounts derived from this fictitious transaction would then correspond to the desired inflows or outflows.

This technique won't work for a system of rivers, since price is not exogenous. This means that the payoff function for the purchase of water from a tributary at a junction, and the function for the change in stock, are not well-defined and there is insufficient information to solve the problem in this way. In other words, price depends on the solution to a prior optimization problem which itself depends on price.

It might also be thought that these problems could be avoided altogether by dealing with the interconnected system in terms of network optimization theory. A glance at Fig. 1. would suggest this approach. Unfortunately, although the idea is attractive, it won't work. The main barrier is that network optimization can only deal with gains and losses at nodes where two or more arcs meet. This means that it cannot deal with gains and losses along any river in the system, or with extraction at any points other than at a junction between rivers (Trick, 1996).

What this means is that we have no alternative but to devise a method for dealing with the value of water at junctions between rivers in terms of the welfare optimization problem. In technical terms, what this problem amounts to is indeterminacy in the system of differential equations that describe the flow of water through the system. This is created by the fact that there is missing information on the end points at internal junctions.

In what follows, we show how the Pontryagin principle can be used to provide this information.[6]

3.2 *Outline of the Solution*

The system of n interconnected rivers is described by letting the functions $x(t)$ and $u(t)$ carry the same idea as before but they are now designated with a super-script to indicate which river they belong to. In this way, the change in the volume of water per unit of time at every point along river σ^i can now be written as:

$$x^i\,(t) = g^i(t) \tag{2}$$

for $i = 1, \ldots, n$ where $g^i := g^i\,(a^i, u^i)$ with a^i is now defined along σ^i.

In the same way, the payoff function for extracting water in an interval around t in σ^i can be written as:

$$f^i := f^i\,(c^i\,u^i, b^i\,x^i)$$

[6] For an accessible introduction to the Pontryagin principle see Kamien and Schwartz (1991). For something more mathematically rigorous see Macki and Strauss (1982).

where $f^i = \Sigma f_k^{\,i}$ is again thought of the composite function and the constants c^i, b^i take account of the normalization of length to give $t \in [0, 1]$.

We also want to add a few more complications that have not been dealt with in the single river model. The first is that the water at a terminal point on the system may have some value. Water that flows into the sea or marshes, for example, may have economic value for its affect on fish stocks or coastal areas or it may have value to environmental interests. If the water flows across state boundaries, as it does in many of the world's major rivers including the Colorado, water will have a value for the next political jurisdiction. These cases are dealt with by attributing a scrap value to a final termination point. This is written for each river as $\psi^i x^i(1)$.

It also seems reasonable to assume that there may be lower limits on the amount of water that must be retained in the river at each point and there may also be limits on the amount of extraction. Even though the target for the average flow of water through the river might be satisfied, it might be damaging to both commercial interests and environmental interests if the river were to be allowed to be dry over intervals. Similarly, too rapid a rate of extraction at some point might be environmentally damaging.

Another important set of constraints that is not dealt with is, constraints on fluctuations in extraction over time. This is analogous to the problem of storage and release in the distributed parameter problem mentioned earlier.

With these additions to the model, the welfare maximizing problem is to now choose the vector u at every point that maximizes

$$J = \Sigma \int f^i \, dt + \psi^i x^i(1)$$

subject to the dynamics in Eq. (2), the constraints on extraction, and the endpoint conditions where the summation is between *1* and *n* and the integral is between *0* and *1* as before. It will be noted that J is the type of integral function discussed in the single river example, but is now summed across all rivers.

In order to proceed, we need some assumptions that are reasonable in practice, but have not been explicitly stated. It is assumed that the problem has a unique solution and that all the required boundary condition problems can be solved for the differential equations. It is also assumed that optimal solutions are unique locally. Finally, it is assumed that the optimal solutions are continuous with respect to variations in their parameters.[7]

3.3 *The Main Theorem*

This problem cannot be solved head on, as in the single river case, and what we do is reduce it to a set of sub-problems that have a local solution and then use these solutions to get the global allocation. The idea is to get an initial value for water at each node while holding everything else constant and then use this to calculate the value of water at another node and so on with an improvement in the values at each calculation. By progressively iterating across the entire system, we can improve the information we have at each stage. Provided that these improvements converge, and it turns out that they do, we can approximate the welfare optimizing extraction to any degree of accuracy we desire.

In order to reduce the problem in the required manner, it is assumed that there are K nodes in the system and write a node as n^k. Each subsystem is specified around the rivers flowing into and out of a node n^k and is written $\langle n^k \rangle$ as in Fig. 2.

Write the algorithm used to iterate the solutions as F where F is constructed such that $J(F(u)) \geq J(u)$ with equality only when u is locally

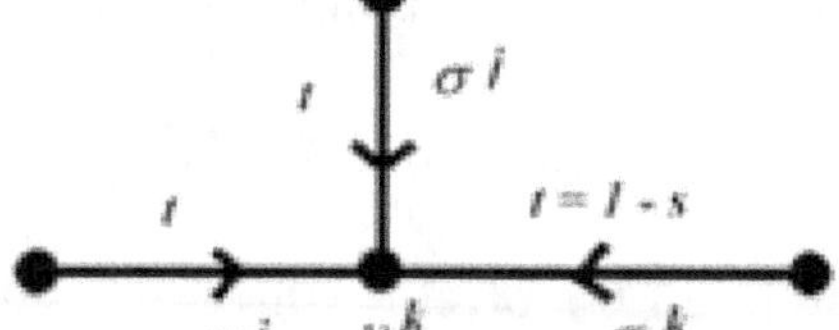

Figure 2: Example of a subsystem $\sigma^i \cup \sigma^j \cup \sigma^k = \langle \eta^k \rangle$

[7] This assumption would be expected to hold, except in pathological cases where the two point boundary condition problems generated may not be solvable. See Noakes (1998) for a discussion of this and for a development of computational algorithms.

optimal everywhere. What we need to show about convergence is given in the following theorem which corresponds to Theorem 2 in Coram and Noakes (2007).

Theorem. If it is possible to solve the optimization problem for each $\langle n^k \rangle$ in the system, then using F to iterate across all nodes will cause $F(u) \to u^*$ where u^* is the unique solution to the optimization problem for S.

This is all we need since, from Theorem 1 in Coram and Noakes (2007), it is possible to solve a subset of S for each $\langle n^k \rangle$.

It is one thing to say that a problem can be solved in principle and another to actually solve it. For most real systems, we would expect that rivers would have to be approximated and solved numerically.

From a practical viewpoint it can be shown that, given the size, and routine nature, of each local problem, the computational demands are small for a reasonably specified f. The appropriate routine could be implemented using any commercially available package that deals with optimal control such as MISER 3 or MATLAB.

It would be anticipated that the costs of implementing such a programme are well within the budget of most water management authorities.

4. Lessons for Regulators

What does a policymaker faced with practical problems of designing a regulatory regime and measuring the effectiveness of regulation, draw from this type of abstract theoretical analysis? There seem to be at least four points.

1. The most general lesson, and one that occurs throughout this volume, is that the problem of constructing a benchmark against which the effectiveness of regulation can be measured is far from simple and may require innovative thought for different sorts of infrastructural good.
2. Where the regulation problem concerns allocation from a river system, the uni-directional nature of the flow and the fact that, unlike say electricity, water is not produced, creates some unique measurement

difficulties. These are not found in many other goods, nor in allocating a given stock of water to consumers. In particular, standard measures of effectiveness, such as efficiency in provision, or amount provided, may be inappropriate. In this case, the regulator may have to consider effectiveness relative to, at least some rough idea of, welfare at each point in the system.

3. Despite the difficulties that rivers present, it is possible for a regulator to carry out the calculations of a welfare based approach to the extent necessary to provide useful guidelines for assessing the effectiveness of the instruments used.
4. If it were thought too difficult to solve the welfare programme, the approach would still provide the regulator with a useful way of thinking about effectiveness. It would also provide a useful framework for designing instruments that ensure consistency of treatment and for negotiations over regulation.

References

Burness, H and J Quirk (1979). Appropriate water rights and the efficient allocation of resoures. *American Economic Review*, 69, pp. 25–37.

Booker, JF and R Young (1994). Modeling intrastate and interstate markets for Colorado River water resources. *Journal of Environmental Economics and Management*, 26, pp. 66–87.

Chakravorty, U and U Chieko (2003). Basinwide water management: A spatial model. *Journal of Environmental Economics and Management*, 45, pp. 1–23.

Colorado River District. http://www.crwcd.org/. Accessed on 9 May 2009.

The Colorado River. http://www.water.utah.gov/interstate/thecoloradoriverart.pdf. Accessed on 9 May 2009.

Coram, A (2006). The optimal allocation of water along a system of rivers: A continuous model with sequential bidding. *Australian Journal of Agricultural and Resource Economics*, 50(3) and *Corrigendum*, 51(1), p. 112.

Coram, A and L Noakes (2009). The optimal extraction of water along an arbitrarily configured river system. *Australian Journal of Agricultural and Resource Economics*, 53(2), pp. 251–64.

Freebairn, J and J Quiggin (2006). Water rights for variable supplies. *Australian Journal of Agricultural and Resource Economics*, 50(3), pp. 295–312.

Gelt, J (1997). Sharing Colorado River Water: History, Public Policy and the Colorado River Compact. http://ag.arizona.edu/AZWATER/arroyo/101comm.html. Accessed on 9 May 2009.

Kamien, M and N Schwartz (1991). *Dynamic Optimization: The Calculus of Variations and Optimal Control in Economics and Management.* Elsevier. New York.

Kanazawa, M (1991). Water quality and the economic efficiency of appropriate water rights. In The *Economics and Management of Water and Drainage in Agriculture,* Dinar A and D Zilberman (eds.). Boston: Kluwer Academic.

Macki, J and A Strauss (1982). *Introduction to Optimal Control Theory.* New York: Springer-Verlag.

Murray-Darling Basin Commission (2001). Integrated Catchment Management in the Murray-Darling Basin 2001–2010. *Murray-Darling Basin Ministerial Council.* ACT. (9 May 2009).

Noakes, L (1998). A global algorithm for geodesics. *Journal Australian Math.Soc.,* (Series A) 64, pp. 37–50.

Quiggin, J (1988). Murray river salinity — An illustrative model. *American Journal of Agricultural Economics,* 70(3), pp. 635–645.

Seierstad, A and K Sydsaeter (1987). *Optimal Control Theory with Applications.* Elsevier. North Holland.

Trick, M (1996). *Network Optimization.* http://mat.gsia.cmu.edu/classes/networks/networks.html

Weber, M (2001). Markets for water rights under environmental constraints. *Journal of Environmental Economics and Management,* 42, pp. 53–56.

CHAPTER 17

Private Sector Participation and Regulatory Reform in Water Supply: The Southern Mediterranean Experience

*Edouard Perard**

Institut d'Etudes Politiques de Paris and
Fondazione Eni Enrico Mattei

The aim of this study is to examine the institutional organization of the water sector. The Mediterranean area provides diverse examples of water sector organization. This chapter focuses more particularly on two aspects of the water sector organization: the recent introduction of private sector participation and the institutional framework. Five countries have been reviewed in detail: Tunisia, Algeria, Egypt, Morocco and Jordan. The chapter analyzes institutional arrangements of the water sector for each of these countries, It not only presents the theoretical legal framework but also the practice. It shows that "independent" regulatory agencies have been set up only in a few countries. However, a closer look confirms that these regulatory agencies are rarely independent. The study also reveals that in most of the countries, the management of water supply suffers from political interference and is overly centralized. Experience with corporatization has also been limited. While the corporatization of local operators has been legalized in most countries, only

* Email: edouard.perard@sciences-po.org. Sciences Po. 27 rue Saint-Guillaume 75337 Paris Cedex 07 France.

few have implemented it. Experience with private sector participation in water supply has been relatively positive and therefore expected to expand in the future.

Keywords: Private sector participation: regulation: privatization: water: Middle East: North Africa, Mediterranean region.

1. Introduction

Water is like no other commodity in the sense that it is most essential to human life. It is also essential to economic growth and poverty reduction. About 18% of the world's population lacks access to improved water supply (UN Millennium Project, 2005). According to the World Health Organization, 1.6 million deaths per year can be attributed to unsafe water and lack of sanitation.

In the Mediterranean region (MEDA), the combination of aridity, foreign dependency, misallocation of water resource, climate change, rapid expansion of cities and escalating human demand for water, make water supply a primary issue for health, economy and poverty reduction.

The aim of this study is to examine the institutional framework of the water sector in MEDA countries and to review the recent development of private sector participation in this context.

The study is organized as follows. The first part presents the experience with private sector participation in water supply the MEDA region. The second part reviews institutional arrangements of the water sector in a group of five countries of the Mediterranean region (Algeria, Egypt, Jordan, Morocco and Tunisia), chosen for their economic homogeneity. The third part deals with the development of a water sector scorecard and the application of this monitoring tool to the group of countries. The methodology of this scorecard, developed in this study, has been adopted and expanded at the OECD to create the database "OECD Water At Glance" which examines water supply and sanitation infrastructure in developing countries. Based on the experience of the different countries in reforming the organization of the water supply sector, the fourth part of the study suggests institutional reforms for Algeria, Egypt, Jordan,

Morocco and Tunisia and concludes on the future development of private sector participation in water supply in these countries.

2. The Experience with Private Water Provision in the Southern Mediterranean Region[1]

2.1. *Regional Overview*

Private sector participation in water services is relatively recent in the Mediterranean region. The first public-private partnership was introduced in 1992 for the wastewater of Cairo. Countries of the MEDA region can be classified into three categories depending on the percentage of population delivered by the private sector.

The most "active" group includes Morocco, Jordan and Algeria. Jordan has the largest share of private water supply in the region: about 40% of its population receives drinking water from a private provider (as of December 2006). Private water operators have been present in Morocco, Jordan and Algeria respectively since 1997, 1999 and 1999.

The second group consists of countries where private sector involvement in water supply is low, but the private model is expected to increase in the coming years. It comprises of Egypt, Lebanon and Turkey.

The third group is constituted by Tunisia, the Syrian Arab Republic, Cyprus and Malta, where private provision is quasi-inexistent.

The map (Fig. 1) presents the percentage of population served by the private sector for each country of the MEDA region.

2.2. *Detailed Outlook of Private Involvement in Water Services*

There are different possible forms of private sector participation in water delivery: from the minimum involvement, the service contract to the full divestiture.

[1] This research project was conducted in 2006–2007. Therefore, this part of the study presents the experience with private sector participation in water supply as of December 2006. An update on recent developments from 2007 to 2009 is presented in Appendix.

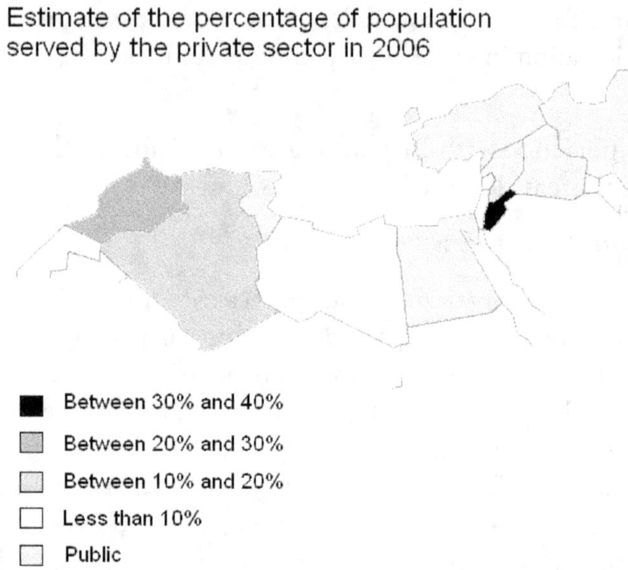

Figure 1: Private sector participation in water supply in the MEDA region

Source: Perard (2006).

The seven major types of private involvement are the service contract, the management contract, the lease contract ("Affermage"), the Build-Operate-Transfer (BOT) contract, the concession contract, the joint venture contract and the divestiture.

Under a service contract, the participation of the private sector is very limited. It provides technical and administrative tasks, such as repairs, meter reading or payment collection. The private sector does not bear any commercial risk regarding water supply. The contract period rarely exceeds one or two years. This contract is adapted to all situations even when the regulatory framework is particularly weak.

Under a management contract, the private sector takes over operation and management responsibilities. However, legally, the user remains, the client of the public entity. The private contractor is paid on a "fee per unit" basis defined in the contract: per volume of water sold, per number of connections and other management and operational tasks. The duration of the contract is usually three to five years and the private company does not bear commercial risks regarding water supply.

The lease contract differs from the management contract in the sense that the private company assumes the legal responsibility for operating the service in exchange for payments for the use of the fixed assets. Users become direct clients of the private contractor, which bears a much more important part of commercial risks. However, it is not in charge of the capital investment. In exchange for greater risks, the leaseholder receives a part or the totality of water revenues. The duration of the contract is usually of 10 to 12 years.

Under a Build-Operate-Transfer contract, the private sector is in charge of designing, building and financing a new investment project. It also has to operate and maintain it for the concession period and then hand it over to the public sector. This mechanism has the advantage of not increasing the sovereign debt. This type of contract is usually used for construction of water production and desalination plants and the sale of bulk water to the public provider rather than for water distribution. Currency risks and the significant length of legal negotiation increase the cost of projects financed under a Build-Operate-Transfer contract.

The concession contract is similar to the lease contract, but the concessionaire is in charge of financing the expansion and the rehabilitation of the network. As in the lease contract, users are direct clients of the private contractor. The duration of the contract ranges between 25 and 30 years. At the end of this period, the private operator hands over the installation to the state.

Under a joint venture contract, the state or municipality and a private operator, co-owns the water operator. The two shareholders share responsibilities and benefits. Even if this agreement seems to adapted to the politically-sensitive case of water supply, such kind of contract can be very unstable.

The last form of private sector participation in water supply is the full divestiture. Under this arrangement, assets are entirely sold to the private sector. The private operator is in charge of financing, operation, management and bears all the risks. However, these private monopolies remain overseen by the public sector and independent regulatory agencies.

Besides the full divestiture, all forms of public-private partnership previously described are represented in the southern Mediterranean area.

Morocco is the most active country in outsourcing water supply. It is the only country in the area that has awarded concession contracts. The duration of the contracts varies between 20 to 25 years. In Jordan, private water provision is more important in percentage, but the state delegates less responsibilities to the private sector by awarding management contracts for five years.

After a few years' experience with service contracts, Algeria signed a BOT contract for a desalination plant in 2001 for the first time, and outsourced the water supply of Algiers by awarding a management contract to Suez in 2005. After the first five years, more responsibilities might be delegated to the private sector and the contract could turn into a concession contract.

Besides geopolitical problems, Lebanon and Palestine are also starting to outsource water supply. A management contract was awarded in 1996 for water supply in Gaza and two others were awarded in Lebanon for water supply in Tripoli and Baalbeck.

In Tunisia, private sector participation concerns only wastewater with limited service contracts. In Egypt and Turkey, private sector participation is also very restricted, but should increase in the coming years.

Table 1 presents details of the major contracts in water treatment, supply and sanitation in the southern Mediterranean region.

3. Water Institutional Arrangements in Selected Mediterranean Countries

Whether or not the water is publicly or privately delivered, experience shows that institutional arrangement matters the most.

The southern Mediterranean area consists of heterogeneous group of countries with significant economic, political and cultural differences. Thus, rather than providing an overview of institutional arrangements of the water sector for each country of the region, the focus is on a more

Table 1: Detailed outlook of private sector participation in water treatment, supply and sanitation in the MEDA region

Country	Location	Sector	Type of contract	Date	Private contractor
Algeria	Oran	WSD	Service Contract	1999–2004	Saur
Algeria	Algiers Ouest	WSD	Service Contract	2000–2004	Someden (SEM)
Algeria	Constantine	WSD	Service Contract	2005–2008	Someden (SEM)
Algeria	Beni Haroun	Water pumping station	Build-Operate-Transfer	2002–	Alstom/Dragados
Algeria	Arzew	Desalination	Build-Operate-Transfer	2001–	Black and Veatch
Algeria	Bredeah	Desalination	Build-Operate-Transfer	2001–	Degremont (Suez)
Algeria	Algiers	WSD	Management Contract	2005–2010	Suez
Algeria	Taksbet	WT	Design Build Operate	2006–2011	Degremont (Suez)
Algeria	Athmania	WT	Design Build Operate	2006–2011	Degremont (Suez)
Egypt	Toshka	Irrigation	Build-Operate-Transfer	2002–	N/A
Egypt	Cairo	WWT	Management Contract	1992–1996	Joint-Venture Biwater (UK)/ECD (Egypt)
Egypt	Suez Special Economic Zone	WWT	Build-Operate-Transfer	2001–2002 (suspended)	SNC Lavalin
Jordan	Amman	WSD	Management Contract	1999–2006	LEMA Consortium (Suez)
Jordan	Al-Samra	WWT	Build-Operate- Transfer	2002–2027	Consortium Degremont (Suez)/ Morganti
Jordan	Ramtha	WWT	Build-Operate-Transfer	2001–	Veolia
Lebanon	Chekka	WWT	Design Build Operate	2003–2008	Ondeo (Suez)
Lebanon	Batroun	WWT	Design Build Operate	2003–2008	Ondeo (Suez)
Lebanon	Jbeil	WWT	Design Build Operate	2003–2008	Ondeo (Suez)

(Continued)

Table 1: (*Continued*)

Country	Location	Sector	Type of contract	Date	Private contractor
Lebanon	Nabatieh	WWT	Design Build Operate	2003–2008	Veolia
Lebanon	Chouf	WWT	Design Build Operate	2003–2008	Veolia
Lebanon	Tripoli	WWT	Design Build Operate	2003–2006	Suez
Lebanon	Tripoli	WSD	Management Contract	2003–2005	Suez
Lebanon	Baalbeck	WSD	Management Contract	2003–2006	N/A
Morocco	Rabat	WSD/WWT	Concession Contract	1999–2029	Redal (Veolia)
Morocco	Casablanca	WSD	Concession Contract	1997–2027	LYDEC (Suez)
Morocco	Tetuouan and Tangiers	WSD/WWT	Concession Contract	2002–2027	AMENDIS (Veolia)
Morocco	Marrakech	WWT	Design Build Operate	2006–2011	Degremont (Suez)
Tunisia	Tunis South	WWC	Service Contract	2001–2005	SRA/SAVAC/SOMEN
Tunisia	Tunis North	WWC	Service Contract	2002–2006	SOMEDEN (SEM)
Tunisia	Ariana Governorate	WWC	Service Contract	2002–2006	SOMEDEN (SEM)
Tunisia	Tataouine City	WWC	Service Contract	2002–2006	SRA/SAVAC/SOMEM
Turkey	Izmit	N/A	Build-Operate-Transfer	1996–	RWE
West Bank & Gaza	Bethlehem and Hebron	WSD	Management Contract	1999–2003	GEKA (Veolia)
West Bank & Gaza	Gaza	WSD	Management Contract	1996–2000	LEKA (Ondeo-Suez)

Notes: WSD: Water Supply Distribution
WT: Water Treatment
WWT: Wastewater Treatment
WWC: Wastewater Collection
Source: Perard (2007). Based on Grover 2002, Institutional Communication of Suez, Degremont, Veolia, Societe Des Eaux de Marseilles, Press Releases.

homogenous group of five countries: Tunisia, Algeria, Egypt, Morocco and Jordan.

3.1. *Tunisia*

Tunisia has very limited water resources. The amount of renewable freshwater available per inhabitant is 50% below the water scarcity standard. Moreover, this situation is exacerbated by irregular annual precipitation. In addition, water supply is confronted by two major constraints: the remote location of water resources and the low-quality of water. The remoteness of water resources from consumption centres results in heavy water transfer infrastructure investments and the low-quality of water resources with high-salinity increases the cost of water treatment. Thus, Tunisia has made water management one of its first priorities and so far, the strategy adopted has been successful.

In Tunisia, water and sanitation sectors are totally public and are managed by two centralized government agencies:

Societe Nationale d'Exploitation et de Distribution des Eaux (SONEDE) the autonomous national public water supply utility is responsible (since 1968) for delivering potable water in Tunisia, including construction, operation and maintenance of infrastructure. While its mandate traditionally focused on urban areas, in recent years SONEDE has been expanding its operations in rural areas as well. SONEDE employs more than 6,900 people and delivers water to about 8 million people. SONEDE is overseen by the Ministry of Agriculture and Water Resources, which formulates water sector strategies and coordinates investment planning and the allocation of the resources.

Office National de l'Assainissement (ONAS) the autonomous national public sewerage utility is responsible (since 1974) for sewerage collection, treatment and disposal in about 152 urban agglomerations, industrial and tourist zones. Since December 2004, ONAS has been overseen by the Ministry of Environment and Sustainable Development, which sets policies and investment priorities for the sanitation sector. Moderate private sector participation has been introduced recently as service contracts for sewerage and with BOT contracts in June 2006.

In addition to these two major national agencies, the Direction Générale des Grands Travaux Hydrauliques is responsible for the construction of large dams and irrigation infrastructure, and the Direction Générale du Génie Rural et de l'Exploitation des Eaux is responsible for water resources management, irrigation supply, as well as of drinking water supply and sanitation in dispersed rural areas not covered by SONEDE or ONAS.

Water management in Tunisia is centralized and politicized. SONEDE and ONAS are committed through Contract-Programme to achieve specific service and infrastructure goals. Their tariffs are revised periodically but not systematically, on an as-needed basis. Tariff adjustment requests are submitted to the oversight ministry, which has the option to transmit it for evaluation to a Ministerial Council headed by the Prime Minister. The tariff adjustment decision does not always follow economic rationality and does not respect prior formal commitments either.

However, the performance of these agencies has been impressive by a number of criteria. For example, Tunisia has one of the lowest rates of unaccounted water in the region. Unaccounted water was about 30% in 1987, and decreased to 21% in 1997 and to 18.2% in 2004 (World Bank, 2005a). In addition, 100% of urban residents have access to safe drinking water with household connection rates of 98%. Contrary to other cities of the southern Mediterranean region, Tunisian cities usually have continuous water supply. The bill collection rate of SONEDE, which is also in charge of the billing activity of ONAS, is very high at over 99%.

Nevertheless, operational results of SONEDE and ONAS have recently deteriorated because of deferred tariff adjustments and an ambitious capital programme for rural service expansion. Since 2001, the operating ratio of SONEDE remained consistently below 100%.

Furthermore, the tariff system in Tunisia does not seem to be sustainable in the long-term. Contrary to other countries in the region, water and sanitation tariff structures are applied uniformly across the nation. Thus, they do not reflect the real economic cost of water and differences of cost from one region to another.

The second pricing problem is the high-level of cross subsidies among customers. SONEDE tariff structure has two components: a fixed component and a variable component, which is proportional to consumption. There are five blocks of tariffs (Tables 2 and 3).

Differences of price are very important between blocks and levels of fixed charge. The last tariff represents about six times the first one and three times the second one. The last level of fixed charge is 66 times greater than the first one. Thus, 10% of customers pay for more than 80% of the population and only 3% of customers generate 65% of SONEDE revenues (Fig. 2). In fact, 90% of users pay water prices below the real economic cost (SONEDE, 2007). This tariff structure represents a risk that large customers could switch to independent private water systems. Such levels of cross subsidies do not seem viable in the long-term.

3.2. *Algeria*

Algeria faces crucial water scarcity and it has the lowest renewable water resources of North Africa (373.2 cubic metres of renewable freshwater per capita per year). This problem is aggravated by the poor condition of the water pipes network. The water and sewage networks, built in the 1980s, have been allowed to deteriorate badly. In some cities, such as Algiers, upto 40% of the water carried by the network is lost. The technical losses are around 32%, the other 8% is lost due to illegal consumption. As a result, water rationing and shortages are common in Algeria.

Table 2: Tariff of water supply in Tunisia in 2007 in Tunisian Dinars per m3

0–20 m3 per quarter	21–40 m3 per quarter	41–70 m3 per quarter	71–150 m3 per quarter	more than 150 m3 per quarter
0.14	0.24	0.3	0.545	0.84

Source: SONEDE, March 2007. http://www.sonede.com.tn/.

Table 3: Fixed charges for water supply in Tunisia in 2007 in Tunisian Dinars per quarter

Pipe Diameter	15	20	30	40	60	80	100	150
Dinars per quarter	3.300	5.830	10.740	20.570	53.460	53.460	82.810	220.670

Source: SONEDE, March 2007. http://www.sonede.com.tn/.

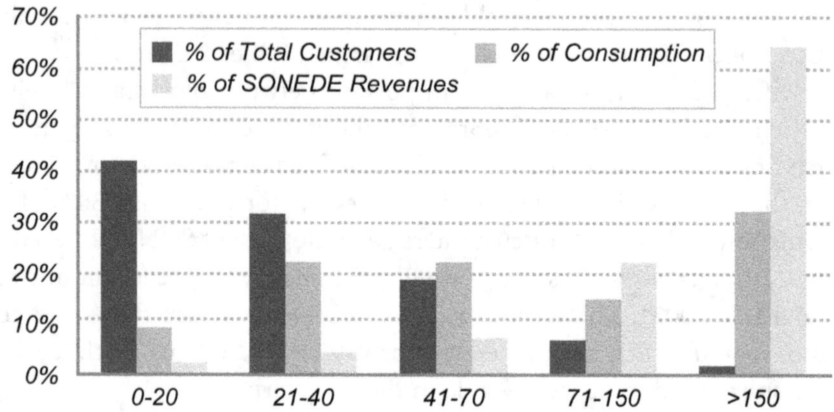

Figure 2: High-level cross subsidies among Tunisian customers

Source: World Bank 2005, Official Project Appraisal Document on a Proposed Loan to SONEDE for an Urban Water Supply Project.

Algeria decided that important institutional reforms were necessary in 2001; the process has been accelerated by the exceptional drought in Algiers in 2002. Water treatment, supply and sanitation have been reorganized as part of the reforms. These operations now depend on four public agencies and the territory is divided into the following five regional basins:

The "Agence nationale des barrages" (ANB), the National Agency for Dams, is in charge of the construction of dams, reservoirs, pumping and water treatment stations and connection pipes.

The "Algerienne des Eaux" (ADE), the national water supply agency, created in 2001, is legally independent and has financial autonomy. It is in charge of 26 public water operators in the most urban areas of the country. The ADE is also in charge of five regional agencies, one for each basin. Each regional agency is subdivided into geographic zones and each zone into functional units. For example, the regional agency of Algiers is subdivided into four zones: Algiers, Setif, Tizi Ouzou and Medea. There are three units in the zone of Algiers: production, supply and management.

The "Office National d'Assainissement" (ONA) (National Bureau for Wastewater) was also established in 2001 after it was found that there was a complete lack of interest in the matter of waste water management within the government. This led to a damage to the environment and wasting a resource that could be re-used. An important task of the ONA is to develop a policy of re-utilization of treated wastewater.

The Agence Nationale de Realisation et de Gestation des Infrastructures Hydrauliques pour l'Irrigation et le Drainage (AGID) is in charge of irrigation and drainage.

In order to rationalize and centralize the management of water, these four entities ANB, ADE, ONA and AGID will be combined under a single agency in the future.

In 2005, Algeria further pursued its effort in reforming the water sector and implemented an ambitious water law. This new code emphasizes private sector participation in water and encourages public water and sewerage services to delegate their activities under a concession contract. Service contracts, management contracts, lease contracts and concession contracts were legalized as early as 1995 in the Water Code (Code de l'Eau). However, so far, concession contracts have not been used.

The new law also proposes that municipalities create and delegate water supply to financially independent public operators ("régie publique"). Corporatization is essential to increase efficiency of public operators and to promote true competition between public and private provision of water.

In addition, article 65 of the law of 2005 calls for an independent regulatory agency in charge of monitoring public and private water provision and setting tariffs. The final decision for creating a regulatory agency still needs to be approved in a specific law. Such a decision would strengthen the institutional framework, lower financial risks in the sector and thus contribute to attract private investors.

The recent reform also concerns water tariffs. There used to be a flat fee for water supply, but this system is being abandoned. The law of 2005 proposes a new progressive tariff system (Table 4). Users can now choose between a flat fee, which is set rather high, and a bill against a metered supply. Although users are not formally obliged to accept a water meter, the fixed fee has been increased strongly to a level at which it is advantageous for virtually all users to have a water meter installed. The aim of this, among others, is to reduce demand. In practice, the first 25 cubic metres per trimester are sold at a low-rate (DZD 3-4 per m3) but higher

Table 4: Tariff of water supply in Algeria in 2007 in Algerian Dinars (DZD) per m3

	0–25 m3 per quarter	26–55 m3 per quarter	56–82 m3 per quarter	more than 83 m3 per quarter
Biskra, Djelfa, El Oued, Ghardaia, M'Sila, Tébessa	3.6	11.7	19.8	23.4
Ain Defla, Mostaganem, Oran, Relizane, Tipaza	3.6	11.7	19.8	23.4
Batna, Constantine, Jijel, Khenchela, Mila, Sétif	3.6	11.7	19.8	23.4
Béchar, El Bayadh, Naâma	3.6	11.7	19.8	23.4
Alger, Blida, Boumerdès	3.8	12.35	20.9	24.7
Annaba, El Tarf, Guelma, Oum El Bouaghi, Skikda, Souk Ahras	3.6	11.7	19.8	23.4
Adrar, Laghouat, Ouargla, Tiaret	3.7	12.025	20.35	24.05
Ain Témouchent, Mascara, Saida, Sidi Bel Abbès, Tlemcen	4	13	22	26
Béjaia, Bouira, Bordj Bou Arréridj, Chlef, Médea, Tissemsilet, Tizi Ouzou	4.3	13.975	23.65	27.95
Illizi, Tamenrasset, Tindouf	4.5	14.625	24.75	29.25

Source: Ministère des Ressources en Eau d'Algerie, February 2007.

consumption is charged at higher prices. Tariffs vary according to the territorial zone and cover the actual costs of renovating and expanding potable water infrastructures.

3.3. *Egypt*

Water is a fundamental issue in Egypt. Indeed, 95% of its water comes from the River Nile and Egypt has to share this resource with nine other states living upstream (the 10 countries of the Nile Basin include Burundi, Congo, Egypt, Eritrea, Ethiopia, Kenya, Rwanda, Sudan, Tanzania and Uganda). Moreover, Egypt is a country that has the largest consumption of the reserve. These circumstances engender political tensions in the region.

In addition, water stress, over withdrawal problems, high-urban population growth and uncertain impact of climate change make this situation particularly concerning.

Municipal water supply and sanitary services are carried out by a set of economic authorities affiliated with the Ministry of Housing, Utilities and New Communities (MHUNC). Under MHUNC, the National Organization for Portable Water and Sanitary Drainage (NOPWASD) is responsible for planning, design and construction of municipal drinking water purification plants; distribution systems; sewage collection systems and municipal wastewater treatment plants throughout Egypt with the exception of some urban areas. The NOPWASD is responsible outside of Cairo, Alexandria and the Suez Canal cities. For Cairo, Alexandria and the Suez Canal area, the responsibility is on the General Organization for Sanitary Drainage in Cairo (GOSDC), the General Organization for Greater Cairo Water Supply (GOGCWS), the Alexandria General Organization for Sanitary Drainage (AGOSD), the Alexandria Water General Authority (AWGA) and the Suez Canal Authority respectively.

Operational and maintenance responsibilities are delegated to local agencies, which are classified into economic/general authorities and public/private companies or utilities in nine Governorates. A central organization, the General Authority for Potable Water and Sanitary Drainage (GAPWSD) supervize these governorate entities.

In 2004, Egypt decided to rationalize the organization of the public water sector and centralize all water activities. The presidential decree 135 for 2004 regroups all drinking water and sanitation entities of the country under one single holding company. The company counts 70,000 public workers and its debt is estimated at EGP 13.8 billion. Thus, its first mission is to seek new financial resources to sustain the operation and management budget and to relieve the burden on the government.

Anticipating private sector participation and a possible privatization of the holding company in the coming years, the government has also created a regulatory agency, the "Central Authority for the Drinking Water and Sanitation Sector, and Protection of the Consumer" (Presidential Decree, 136 for 2004). This regulatory agency reports to the Minister of Housing, Utilities and Urban Communities, and is the liaison body between the government, the society and the holding company to ensure that national policies and regulations are followed. However, this newly-created regulatory agency is not autonomous. Indeed, the Minister of Housing heads the Governing Board and the Ministries of Finance, Health and Population and of the Environment are also represented on the governing board.

Concerning the financing of water, almost 90% of the development, operation and maintenance costs of water services in Egypt are currently funded by public sources. Primary financing of the water sector comes only through three principal sources: sovereign sources and general-tax system, agricultural user-fees and municipal and industrial user-fees.

The lack of financing reforms is a concern since costs have increased significantly. The expenses for drinking water and sanitation grew from EGP 4.73 billion in 1997/98 to EGP 8.45 billion in 2003/04. During the period 1982–2004, EGP 25.0 billion have been spent for potable water supply services and EGP 40 billion have been invested in sanitation services. According to the Ministry of Water Resources and Irrigation (World Bank, 2005b), the costs for water services for the next 15 years will be more than triple that of the current expenditures. Future allocation of such high-costs presents a heavy burden for the state budget. Alternative scenarios for financial sustainability of the water sector need to be addressed.

Moreover, revenues cover only 40% of costs because of subsidies, inefficiency, high-levels of leakage and non-paying state customers. The tariff system has not been reformed and prices are set very low: EGP 0.30/m3 for domestic use in Cairo (Ambassade de France en Egypte, 2005). Cost recovery problems and low tariffs discourage financial investors and private sector participation.

In addition to that, there is an important problem of centralization in tariff setting. In theory, tariffs are set in accordance with local authorities. However, in practice, water supply administration in Egypt is centralized; local governments have neither technical competences nor budgets to manage water services.

3.4. *Morocco*

In Morocco, the amount of renewable freshwater available per inhabitant stands just below the scarcity line with 964.4 cubic metres per capita.

Because of drought and population growth, several studies predict that the amount of renewable freshwater per inhabitant would drop to 500 cubic metres per capita (Ambassade de France au Maroc, 2005).

All major population centres in Morocco have central water supply systems consisting of reservoirs, treatment works and distribution networks. However, many of these are in a poor state of repair. Until recently, an estimated 40% of water was lost through leakage and other problems. In rural areas, where 42% of the population lives, only 56% have access to improved water source (WHO/UNICEF, 2004). Wastewater and sewerage systems have not been developed as widely as the water supply systems. Respectively, 83% and 31% of urban and rural population has access to improved sanitation facilities (Office National de l'eau potable, 2007). Sewage systems exist in most large- and medium-sized cities; however, they are often inadequate. In most parts of the country, wastewater is disposed directly into rivers or the sea. Some major cities have no wastewater treatment systems at all. Thus, water supply and sanitation are considered by the Moroccan government as a strategic issue for development.

Contrary to the high-level of centralization of the Moroccan state, water administration is relatively more decentralized and specialised by function:

- The Directorate General of Hydraulics plans and develops water resources.
- The nine Regional Authorities for Agricultural Development (RAADs) develop and maintain water distribution networks, acquire and distribute water, collect water charges and provide farm inputs and extension services.
- The National Office of Potable Water (ONEP), created in 1972, acquires and distributes water on a retail basis to households and industries and on a bulk supply basis to municipal/provincial governments. As in Tunisia, the National Office of Potable Water is legally and financially independent. It no longer receives subsidies, and is now developing the capacity to finance itself, in addition to which it can borrow to finance system extensions and renovations. It is the major water producer and distributes water to 416 urban centres, 3,656 "Douars" and 198 small rural centres.

The new Water Code of 1995 has led to significant changes. It has created River Basin Organizations, covering one or more RAADs, as nodal agencies for water administration at the regional-level. As the ONEP, these River Basin Organizations are legally- and financially-independent. Their mission and financing mechanism is very similar to French Basin Agencies. They are financed through users' fees ("redevance") and they can lend money for different local investment programmes in water. The first River Basin Organizations were created in 1997.

In 2002, The Moroccan government pursued the decentralization movement by giving the full responsibility of water supply and sanitation services to municipalities. Therefore, municipalities have four options:

- they can manage water services directly;
- they can create an independent public provider and delegate the management of water services;
- they can also delegate the management of water services to the ONEP;
- they can delegate the management of water services to private firms.

Thus, the country counts 13 independent public operators ("regie") and 4 private operators under a concession contract. The first concession, for Casablanca, was awarded in 1997 to Lydec (Suez), by direct negotiation. The second concession, for the capital, Rabat, was awarded in 1999 to Redal (Veolia), also by direct negotiation. However, with time, the process evolved to become more transparent, involving public tendering. This procedure resulted in concessions being awarded to Amendis (Veolia) for two other major cities (Tangiers and Tetouan) in 2002.

Morocco is the only country in the Mediterranean region that has introduced concession contracts for water supply. After a few years of operation, the results of the first concession in Casablanca are relatively satisfying. The private operator has made major investments; between 1997 and 2002, the number of people served increased from 440,000 to 590,000; and unaccounted water dropped from 38.9% to 27.7%, while it is about 25% in cities managed by the ONEP (ONEP, 2007). However, tariffs have increased by 20% over this period and are slightly higher than those applied in other cities where water is managed by the ONEP (Table 5).

Table 5: Tariff of water supply in some Moroccan cities in 2007 in Dirham per m3

		0–6 m3 per month	6–20 m3 per month	20–40 m3 per month	over 40 m3 per month
ONEP (Public)	El Jadida	3.09	7.78	11.86	11.91
	Agadir	2.95	7.77	9.58	9.63
	Safi	3.32	7.88	13.12	13.17
	Marrakech	1.70	6.37	9.36	9.41
	Oujda	3.81	10.11	14.72	14.77
	Fes	1.95	7.07	8.79	8.84
	Nador	2.13	6.01	8.51	8.56
	Settat	2.63	6.86	7.53	7.58
	B.Mellal	2.61	6.51	10.14	10.19
	Kenitra	2.32	5.25	6.59	6.64
	Larache	1.74	5.31	6.06	6.11
	Meknes	1.30	3.88	4.45	4.51
	Taza	2.15	6.00	8.92	8.97
LYDEC (Private)	Casablanca	2.92	9.69	13.20	13.25
	Mohammedia	2.53	8.15	11.68	11.73

Source: ONEP and LYDEC, March 2007.

As in other Mediterranean countries, Morocco has adopted a progressive tariff structure. The definition of the block system is set nationally for both private and public suppliers. However, the price of a cubic metre of water within each block is set locally and tends to reflect the effective cost of water in some form, as it is emphasized in the water law of 1995.

3.5. *Jordan*

Jordan is facing a future of very limited water resources; it has among the lowest-level of water in the world on a per capita basis (165.1 cubic metres per capita per year). Water scarcity is the single most important natural constraint to Jordan's economic growth and development. Jordan's water resources primarily consist of surface and ground water and for several years now, renewable ground water resources have been withdrawn at an unsustainable rate in order to meet the increasing demand. In addition, surface and ground water quality in some areas is deteriorating.

Despite scarcity, water use is not efficient: unaccounted water reaches 47% in the Amman region (GTZ, 2006). Agriculture uses more than 60% of water resources, while it contributes only 2.8% to GDP. Connection rates to the municipal network are high, at more than 90%, but water supply is intermittent.

The institutional framework of the water supply sector in Jordan consists of four entities: the Ministry of Water and Irrigation (MWI), the Water Authority of Jordan (WAJ), the Programme Management Unit (PMU) and the Jordan Valley Authority (JVA).

The MWI was established in 1992 in response to the need for an integrated approach to national water management. It is the official body responsible for the formulation of national water strategies and policies, the monitoring of the water sector, planning and management and procurement of financial resources.

The WAJ and the PMU carry out regulatory tasks. The WAJ was established in 1983 as an autonomous centralized corporate body, with financial and administrative independence linked with Minister of Water and Irrigation. WAJ is fully-responsible for public water supply and wastewater services, as well as for water resources planning and monitoring, construction, operations and maintenance.

The PMU was established within the WAJ in 1996. It carries out the responsibility for regulating water supply and wastewater utilities under private management. The PMU operates under the supervisory control of an Executive Management Board, which is headed by the Minister.

The JVA was founded in 1973. It is responsible for the development and utilization of water resources in the Jordan Valley for irrigated farming, municipal, industrial and tourism purposes. The JVA is also responsible for the dams and reservoirs in the country.

The existing organizational structure does not show clear separations between political, strategic, regulatory and operational tasks. The management of the water sector is centralized and political interference is usual. Autonomous water agencies are headed by the Minister and thus are not independent. Regulatory functions remain limited to the monitoring of the water sector.

Due to the increase in water demand, the MWI adopted, in 1997, a water strategy emphasizing the need to give a major role to the private sector. Thus, the government decided, in 1999, to contract out the operation and management of water and wastewater services in Amman to the Lema consortium (Ondeo, Montgomery Watson and Arab-tech). The contract term was initially five years but was extended until December 2006. While service provision is still not satisfactory, private sector participation in Amman resulted in significant improvements in water supply. Tariffs did not particularly increase, the workforce decreased by 400 staff and the duration of supply increased from 36 hrs per week at the start of the contract to an average of 75 hrs per week in 2004 (LEMA, 2006). After a transition period, the management of water supply of Amman was handed over to the state and transferred in July 2007 to a corporatized public entity, Miyahuna.

Finally, the major problem of the Jordanian water sector resides in the inefficient pricing policy. The water charges are set locally by the MWI. Jordan has adopted a well-defined, progressive tariff structure with subsidies for the poorest communities. However, prices are set too low to be sustainable and disparities among users are too important. The amount paid for water in the Jordan Valley is very low compared to the urban and industrial water tariffs. The average JVA tariff billed in 2000 was USD 0.008/m3, while the average 2001 urban water tariff in Jordan was USD 0.54/m3 and industrial water users were charged USD 1.42/m3 (World Bank, 2004).

4. Water Sector Scorecard

4.1. *Determinants of the Scorecard*

The purpose of the scorecard, developed in this part of the study, is to understand the scope of water-related issues, to monitor institutional reforms in the water sector and to assess the future of private sector participation in the water sector. The scorecard is based on 9 dimensions and 43 indicators. The methodology of the scorecard, developed in this study, has been adopted and expanded at the OECD to create the database "OECD Water At Glance" which examines water supply and sanitation infrastructure in developing countries.

The 9 dimensions, presented in the scorecard, are (1) the water resource; (2) the water use; (3) the management of water; (4) the water pricing policy; (5) the water institutional framework; (6) the private sector participation in water supply; (7) the projected investments in water and wastewater services; (8) the demography; and (9) the economic and business conditions.

The first three dimensions of the scorecard describe problems of (1) water resource; (2) use; and (3) management. The question of management of water supply is not necessary linked with water resource and use. However, (1.1) water scarcity; (1.2) over withdrawal practices; and (1.3) foreign dependency can emphasize the importance of water supply problems.

Moreover, in arid countries the allocation of water between different users: (2.1) agriculture; (2.2) domestic; and (2.3) industry is also to be taken into account.

Managing access to water in urban areas is usually illustrated by the percentage of population with safe access to water (3.1). While this information is useful, it cannot give a complete outlook of the situation. In order to evaluate the quality of water better management in the country, the scorecard also includes five other variables: (3.2) the percentage of population with a household connection to water; (3.3) the continuity of water supply; (3.4) the number of hours of access to tap water; (3.5) an estimate of unaccounted water; and (3.6) the operating cost coverage ratio.

The pricing policy of water is the fourth component of the scorecard (4). An efficient water pricing policy needs to assess the differences of cost of water from one region to another. Water charges are not equal in arid areas and in cities; prices need to be set in consequence. Tariffs need to be set locally (4.1). However, it is essential to keep water affordable for everyone. According to most experiences of tariff reform in the world, one of the easiest ways to subsidize water for the poorest seems to be through a progressive block tariff structure (4.2). Prices of water are displayed in (4.3) and (4.4). Nevertheless, tariffs need to be set at a level viable enough to keep operations running and finance the capital (4.5). Water charges also need to take into account the individual consumption; individual water metering is essential (4.6).

The fifth dimension is the institutional framework (5). Without adequate institutional arrangements, delegating water services to private operators do not necessarily improve efficiency. Thus, the design of a regulatory system is the most essential step in the process of reforming the water sector. The first two elements of this issue concern the presence of a regulatory agency (5.1) and its effective independence (5.2). An independent regulatory agency is a valuable tool, which provides political stability and safe economic environment for both private and public water operators. Often countries create an autonomous water regulatory agency. However, in practice; these agencies are rarely-independent from governments and are thus not very useful. The third component is the separation of powers (5.3). As in a corporate environment, the separation of roles — political, strategic, regulatory and operational — is a condition of efficient management. Another important reform is the corporatization of local water operators (5.4). Establishing legal and financial independence of water operators reduces administrative burden and political interference. It guarantees the transparency of costs and financial flows. It also ensures a fair and fruitful competition among water operators, public or private. The last two indicators of the institutional framework concern the decentralization of the public administration of water. Countries can create river basin organizations (5.5), which are funded through users' fees and aim to finance local water projects. Thus, part of the public responsibility is delegated to the regional-level, which is able to evaluate needs more precisely. This system also reduces the fiscal and administrative burden of the central state. Without creating basin agencies, the administrative burden can also be moderated by decentralizing parts of water policy to regions (5.6).

The sixth dimension is the involvement of the private sector in water supply (6). Introducing private sector participation in a well-defined, institutional environment and establishing a reasonable level of competition between the public and private water sector can improve management efficiency. In order to evaluate the scope of private sector participation properly, the five sub-indicators presented in this section are: (6.1) the presence of private water operators in the country; (6.2) an estimate of the percentage of population delivered by the private sector; (6.3) the location of private contracts; (6.4) the types of contracts; and (6.5) the year of introduction of private sector participation in the country.

The seventh dimension of the scorecard is the projected investments in water and wastewater services. In order to face important water investment costs in the near future, countries will need to tap the private capital market. Forecasted portable water and wastewater investments by 2015 are presented in value (7.1 and 7.2) and as a percentage of the GDP (7.3, 7.4 and 7.5).

The eighth and ninth components of the scorecard, the demography (8) and the economic and business environment (9), are not specific to the water sector. However, the evolution of the demography provides a good estimation of the water market growth and the analysis of national economic and business conditions allow better assessments of the potential for private sector participation in the water sector. For the demographic component, the sub-indicators are (8.1) population growth; (8.2) urban population growth; (8.3) the percentage of urban population in 2005; and (8.4) the projected percentage of urban population in 2015. The economic and business conditions are analysed in five sub-indicators published by the World Bank in "Doing Business in 2007." The first one is the Ease of Doing Business Rank (9.1). Then, the legal rights index (9.2) measures the degree to which laws protect the rights of borrowers and lenders and thus facilitate lending; the index ranges from 0 to 10, with higher scores indicating that laws are better designed to expand access to credit. The third one is an investor protection index (9.3), the index ranges from 0 to 10, with higher values indicating better investor protection. The fourth one is the time for enforcing contracts (9.4) and the last one is the scope of the informal economy (9.5) as a percentage of the Gross National Product.

Lastly, an assessment is proposed (10) on the development (10.1) and possible forms (10.2) of private sector participation in the water sector in the near and medium term. This judgment is based on the analysis for each country of the water resource (1); the water use (2); the management of water (3); the pricing policy (4); the institutional framework (5); the current private sector participation (6); the projected investments (7); the demography (8); and the economic and business conditions (9).

The scorecard is presented in Table 6.

Table 6: Water sector scorecard for countries of the Mediterranean region

Indicators	Sub-Indicators	Algeria	Egypt	Jordan	Morocco	Tunisia	Source of data
1. Water resource	1.1. Water scarcity (Total renewable freshwater per capital)	373.2 m3/ inhab/ year	826.9 m3/ inhab/ year	165.1 m3/ inhab/ year	964.4 m3/ inhab/ year	472.3 m3/ inhab/ year	FAO/World Resources Institutefor the last year available 2000
	1.2. Over withdrawal (Total water withdrawal as percentage of total renewable water resources)	52.03%	117.20%	114.80%	43.45%	57.45%	
	1.3. Foreign dependency ratio (percentage of total renewable water resources originating outside the country)	3.60%	96.91%	22.73%	0.00%	8.71%	
2. Water use	2.1. Agriculture withdrawal	65%	78%	75%	87%	82%	
	2.2. Domestic withdrawal	22%	8%	21%	10%	14%	

(*Continued*)

Table 6: (*Continued*)

Indicators	Sub-Indicators	Algeria	Egypt	Jordan	Morocco	Tunisia	Source of data
	2.3. Industry withdrawal	13%	14%	4%	3%	4%	
3. Water management	3.1. Improved Drinking Water Coverage in Urban Areas (Total)	88%	99%	99%	99%	99%	WHO-UNICEF 2004
	3.2. Improved Drinking Water Coverage in Urban Areas (Household Connection)	85%	99%	96%	86%	94%	
	3.3. Continuous water supply	No	No	No	Yes	Yes	Algeria: World Bank 2007; Jordan: GTZ 2006; Morocco: World Bank 2007; Tunisia:World Bank 2007.
	3.4. Average hours of access to tap water (hours/day)	12 hours in Algiers	12 hours	12 hours	24 hours	24 hours	World Bank 2007

(*Continued*)

Table 6: (*Continued*)

Indicators	Sub-Indicators	Algeria	Egypt	Jordan	Morocco	Tunisia	Source of data
	3.5. Estimate of unaccounted for water	40%	50% in Alexandria and Cairo	47% in Amman	Around 25–30%	Around 20%	Algeria: Institutional communication 2007; Egypt: World Bank 2005c; Tunisia: World Bank 2005a; Jordan: GTZ 2006; Morocco: ONEP 2006, Lydec 2006.
	3.6. Operating cost coverage ratio	82%	40%	70%	110% in Casablanca and Rabat	87%	Algeria: Ibnet; Egypt: Ibnet; Jordan: Stone and Webster 2004; Morocco: World Bank 2006; Tunisia: World Bank 2005a.
4. Water pricing policy	4.1. Geographical tariff setting	Tariff set locally	Tariff set locally	Tariff set locally	Tariff set locally	Tariff set nationally	Institutional communication
	4.2. Progressive tariff structure	Yes	Yes	Yes	Yes	Yes	

(*Continued*)

Table 6: (*Continued*)

Indicators	Sub-Indicators	Algeria	Egypt	Jordan	Morocco	Tunisia	Source of data
	4.3. Price of domestic water in the lowest block tariff category in 2006–2007	Between 0.050 $/m3 and 0.062 $/m3	0.040 $/m3 in Cairo	0.14 $/m3 on average in Amman	Between 0.155 $/m3 and 0.454 $/m3	0.109 $/m3	Algeria: Ministère des Ressources en Eau d'Algerie 2007; Egypt: Institutional communication 2007; Morocco: LYDEC and ONEP 2007; Tunisia: SONEDE 2007
	4.4. Price of domestic water in the highest block tariff category in 2006–2007	Between 0.327 $/m3 and 0.409 $/m3	0.122 $/m3 in Cairo		Between 0.537 $/m3 and 1.76 $/m3	0.652 $/m3	
	4.5. Sustainable level	No. But tariff reform is on track, prices increased in 2005	No*	No, extreme subsidies of water for agricultural use.	Yes	Yes overall, but the high-level of cross subsidies does not seem sustainable.	Institutional communication
	4.6. Metering practice	Yes	Yes	Yes	Yes	Yes	

(*Continued*)

Table 6: (*Continued*)

Indicators	Sub-Indicators	Algeria	Egypt	Jordan	Morocco	Tunisia	Source of data
5. Water institutional framework	5.1. Presence of regulatory agency	Not yet. However, it has been planned in the article 65 of the new water law of 2005	Yes, since the Presidential Decree 136 of 2004	Yes (Water Authority of Jordan and Programme Management Unit)	No	No	Official communication, laws and decrees.
	5.2. Real independence of he regulatory agency		No, agency headed by several Ministers	No, agency headed by the Minister of Water and Irrigation			
	5.3. Separation of powers	Yes	Important political interferences	Important political interferences	Yes	Some political interferences	
	5.4. Corporatization of local operators	Possible since 2005	Yes, since the Presidential Decree 135 of 2004	Yes, launch of Miyahuna in 2007	Possible since 2002	No	
	5.5. Basin Organizations	No	No	No	Yes since 1997	No	

(*Continued*)

Table 6: (*Continued*)

Indicators	Sub-Indicators	Algeria	Egypt	Jordan	Morocco	Tunisia	Source of data
	5.6. Centralisation versus decentralization	Relatively more decentralized.	Decisions are centralized. Decentralization process should be on track in the coming years.	Centralized	Relatively more decentralized.	Centralized	
6. Private sector participation in drinking water*	6.1. Presence of private operators	Yes	No	Yes	Yes	No	Institutional communication and press releases (Excludes service contracts)
	6.2. Estimate of the percentage of population delivered by the private sector	Between 10% and 20%		Around 40%	Between 20% and 30%		
	6.3. Location	Algiers, Taksbet, Athmania, Arzew, Bredeah, Beni Haroun.		Amman	Rabat, Casablanca, Tetuouan and Tangiers.		
	6.4. Types of contract	Management contract and BOT		Management contract and BOT	Concession contracts and BOT		

(*Continued*)

Table 6: (*Continued*)

Indicators	Sub-Indicators	Algeria	Egypt	Jordan	Morocco	Tunisia	Source of data
	6.5. Year of introduction of private sector participation	2001 (legalised in 1995, first management contract in 2005)		1999	1997		
7. Projected investments in water and wastewater services	7.1. Forecasted potable water investments between 2005 and 2015	\$8,630 million	\$7,270 million	\$910 million	\$4,090 million	\$455 million	Gulf Capital (2007)
	7.2. Forecasted wastewater investments between 2005 and 2015	\$1,360 million	\$5,900 million	\$455 million	\$2,725 million	\$680 million	
	7.3. Average annual potable water investments between 2005 and 2015 as a percentage of the 2006 GDP	0.94%	0.86%	0.65%	0.72%	0.14%	Author's calculation based on estimates in Gulf Capital (2007)

(*Continued*)

Table 6: (*Continued*)

Indicators	Sub-Indicators	Algeria	Egypt	Jordan	Morocco	Tunisia	Source of data
	7.4. Average annual wastewater investments between 2005 and 2015 as a percentage of the 2006 GDP	0.15%	0.70%	0.32%	0.48%	0.21%	
	7.5. Average annual potable water and wastewater investments between 2005 and 2015 as a percentage of the 2006 GDP	1.08%	1.56%	0.97%	1.20%	0.34%	
8. Demography	8.1. Population growth 2005–2015	15.9%	19.1%	22.0%	14.8%	10.3%	UN population estimates
	8.2. Urban population growth 2005–1015	26.2%	26.4%	24.7%	26.6%	16.6%	
	8.3. Urban population in 2005	60.0%	42.3%	79.3%	58.8%	64.4%	

(*Continued*)

Table 6: (*Continued*)

Indicators	Sub-Indicators	Algeria	Egypt	Jordan	Morocco	Tunisia	Source of data
	8.4. Urban population in 2015	65.3%	44.9%	81.1%	64.8%	68.1%	
9. Economic and business environment	9.1. Ease of Doing Business Rank	116	165	78	115	80	Doing Business In 2007. World Bank and IFC
	9.2. Legal Right Index	3	1	5	3	3	
	9.3. Investor Protection Index	5.3	4.3	4.3	4.3	3.3	
	9.4. Time for enforcing contracts	397 days	1010 days	342 days	615 days	481 days	
	9.5. Informal economy estimate (% GNP)	34.1%	35.1%	19.4%	36.4%	38.4%	

(*Continued*)

Table 6: (*Continued*)

Indicators	Sub-Indicators	Algeria	Egypt	Jordan	Morocco	Tunisia	Source of data
10. Future of private sector participation in water supply	10.1. Development of private sector participation in water supply in the near and medium-term	Strong development in the near term.	Moderate development in the near term. Stronger in the medium long-term.	Moderate development.	Strong development.	Moderate development.	Author's assessment based on the analysis of water resource, water use, water management, pricing policy, institutional framework, current private sector participation, projected investments, demography and economic and business environment.
	10.2. Forms of private sector participation	BOT desalination contracts and management contracts in the near term. Concession contracts in the medium-term.	BOT and service contracts in the near term.	BOT and management contracts.	BOT and concession contracts.	BOT and service contracts.	

Note: NB. $ refer to USD.
*As of January 2007.

5. Institutional Reforms and Future of Private Sector Participation in Water Supply

5.1. *Tunisia*

With only 472.3 cubic metres of water per inhabitant per year, Tunisia is a water scarce country. In such an arid land, the question of the allocation of water between different users will certainly need to be addressed in the short-term. Indeed, 82% of water is used for agriculture, while this sector contributes to 12.6% of the GDP of the country.

The national Tunisian water operator, SONEDE, is very efficient in comparison with others in Mediterranean countries. It boasts a drinking water household connection rate of 94% in urban areas, continuous water supply and an unaccounted for water ratio of 18%, which is in line with OECD countries. This good performance is due to the strong commitment of the Tunisian government for more than thirty years. Nevertheless, the operating cost coverage ratio has deteriorated for several years and stands at 87%.

Two areas of improvement lie in tariff setting policy and institutional arrangements. Prices of the first blocks of consumption are set very low, while prices for large consumers are particularly high. About 3% of SONEDE clients generate 65% of the revenue. This pricing policy is not sustainable in the long-term; important customers could switch to independent private operating systems. Moderate increases to the prices of the first blocks of consumption seem unavoidable; it would improve the operating cost coverage ratio and secure SONEDE's financial future. The second tariff reform concerns the geographical setting policy; Tunisia is the only country of the region, which applies one uniform tariff to the entire state. An efficient pricing policy would take into account local differences of the cost for providing services. These two reforms should be carried out in the near term.

The second area of improvement is the institutional framework. In Tunisia, the governance of water is centralized and political interferences are usual. In the long-term, the organization of the sector could be improved by decentralizing the management of water and corporatizing local operators.

In the near and medium term, private sector participation is expected to increase moderately. Even if the general economic and business environment is favourable, current institutional arrangements are not particularly suitable to an important development of private sector participation in water supply. Moreover, urban population growth (expected to be over 16% during the next 10 years) is under control and the relative good performance of SONEDE does not push towards delegating water supply services to others.

However, it is expected that Tunisia will more than double its desalination capacity. To face the projected investments, the country will need to tap private finance capital. It is very likely that desalination treatment will be outsourced as BOT contracts. In addition, private sector participation is also expected to continue in wastewater under service contracts.

5.2. *Egypt*

With 826.9 cubic metres of water per inhabitant per year, Egypt is a water stressed country; it faces over withdrawal problems and foreign dependency (95% of water comes from the Nile River). Considering these elements, the repartition of water among users in favour of the agriculture sector (78%) does not seem sustainable in the long-term.

Besides the high connection rate in urban areas, the performance of water management is relatively poor. Water supply is discontinuous (about 12 hrs per day), unaccounted water is very high (50% in Alexandria and Cairo) and the operating cost coverage ratio is very low (40%).

The two areas of improvement are pricing policy and institutional reform.

Egypt has adopted a progressive tariff structure; however, prices of all blocks of consumption are too low to be sustainable. This issue needs to be addressed in the short-term. Nevertheless, any potential increase of water tariffs to a viable level is limited by the strong opposition of the population.

Some progress could also be made by reforming the institutional framework. Water governance in Egypt is characterized by a high-level of political interference and centralized planning. The decentralization process is on track, but takes time to be implemented. The corporatization of more local operators would constitute an important step.

Current institutional arrangements do not seem to be favourable to the development of private sector participation in water supply. Thus, in the near term, without significant institutional reforms, it is likely that private involvement in water supply will be limited to BOT and service contracts.

5.3. *Morocco*

Morocco is just below the limit of water stressed situation (964.4 cubic metres of water per inhabitant per year); the country holds twice more water per inhabitant than Algeria and Tunisia. Agriculture contributes to 15.9% of the GDP, but it uses 87% of water, leaving only 3% to industry, which contributes to 30.4% of the GDP. The allocation of water will need to be reformed in the long-term.

The performance of water supply is relatively good as 99% of people have access to improved drinking water in urban areas. However, 14% of them do not have household connections. Water is supplied continuously and the unaccounted water is at a reasonable level, about 25–30%. Moreover, Morocco is the only country of the Middle East and North African region, which covers operational cost of delivering water (World Bank, 2007). The operating cost coverage ratio is of 110% in Rabat and Casablanca. Indeed, the price of water is much higher in Moroccan cities than in other cities of North Africa.

The reorganization of the water supply sector in Morocco started ten years ago, the institutional framework is now well-defined. The governance of water has been relatively decentralized, some local operators have been corporatized and political interferences are being reduced. Basin Organizations have existed for 10 years.

Private sector participation in water supply has been introduced as early as 1997 and the private sector delivers now water to 20–30% of the population. Morocco is the only country of the region, which has awarded concession contracts.

With 10 years of experience of private delivery, a favourable institutional framework, more than US$4 billion of projected investments in potable water over 10 years and an important urban population growth of 26.6% expected over the next 10 years, private sector participation in water supply is expected to increase in the near term. Potential forms of private involvement are concession contracts as in Rabat, Casablanca, Tangiers and Tetouan, and BOT contracts for some water desalination plants.

5.4. *Algeria*

Algeria is the most arid country of North Africa with 373.2 cubic metres of water per inhabitant per year. Thus, the consumption of water by the agricultural sector is less important than it is in other countries of the region. However, it still represents two-thirds of total freshwater available for a contribution to the GDP of less than 10%, while the industrial sector withdraws 14% of freshwater and contributes to more than 56% of the GDP. In the medium-term, it is probable, that agricultural consumption will naturally decrease in favour of the industrial consumption, as is the case in OECD countries.

The overall performance of water supply in Algeria is low. The household connection rate is only 85% in urban areas; water shortages and rationing are common. The unaccounted water ratio reaches 40%. This situation is due to the lack of political concern and investments for more than 20 years, until 2001, when Algeria started important institutional reform. The country pursued its effort and implemented an ambitious water law in 2005. The governance of water is relatively decentralized, local operators can now be corporatized and political interferences are being reduced.

The price of water is too low to be sustainable, but the tariff reform is on track. On the positive side, the tariff structure is progressive and is set locally. In addition, the metering practice is expanding.

The private sector provides water to more than 10% of the population. The first management contract was awarded for the water supply of Algiers in 2005. In the near term, it is expected that private sector participation will increase at a significant pace. Three combined factors can explain this anticipation: investment needs for renewing water infrastructures are particularly important (US$8 630 million over 10 years); as detailed previously, the institutional framework is well adapted to private sector participation; and lastly, urban population is expected to increase drastically (by 26.2%) over the next 10 years. The economic and business environment could of course be improved, but the level of protection of investors is correct.

In the near term, possible forms of private involvement are management contracts as in Algiers and BOT contracts for desalination treatment since desalination capacity is expected to double by 2015. In the medium-term, if the experience with management contracts is positive, it is very likely that Algeria will opt for a higher degree of private sector participation with concession contracts as in Morocco.

5.5. *Jordan*

Jordan is the most water scarce country of the Mediterranean area with only 165.1 cubic metres of water per inhabitant per year. Considering the water scarcity and over withdrawal problems, allocation of water in Jordan is a critical issue. However, 75% of water is used for agriculture, while it contributes to only 2.8% of the GDP. The low pricing policy in favour of agriculture needs to be revised in the near term.

The performance of water supply is not satisfactory. While 96% of urban population has household connections, water is rationed and is available for only a couple of days per week (about 75 hrs per week). Unaccounted water is very high at 47% and prices cover only 70% of operating costs.

One of the main problems lies in tariff setting. On the positive side, tariffs are progressive and set locally. In addition, the metering practice is very well developed. On the negative side, tariffs are set too low in general and water for agriculture is significantly subsidized.

The second problem resides in the institutional framework. Water governance is centralized, political interferences are abundant and corporatized operators are not fully independent.

Private involvement in water supply is important. About 40% of the population's water is delivered by private operators. Considering the urban population growth (expected to be around +24.7% over 10 years), the good economic environment, the development of a desalination market and the already relatively high-level of private involvement, private sector participation in water supply should moderately increase in the near and medium-term.

It is likely that the form of development will be the management contract. The institutional framework does not seem favourable for a higher degree of private involvement, such as concession contracts. Since desalination capacity is expected to be multiplied by 10 over the next 10 years, BOT contracts for desalination will also be awarded.

6. Conclusion

The study has shown that governments of Mediterranean countries are well aware of the urgency of reforming the water supply sector. Some countries started to restructure the organization of the sector a long time ago; others are still at the beginning of the process.

The Moroccan experience with institutional reform and private sector participation in water services over the last 10 years provides a good example for other countries of the region. Algeria is also well on track to successfully reorganize the water supply sector. In these two countries, private involvement in drinking water is expected to increase strongly in the near term.

The experience of Tunisia reveals that countries can also opt for public delivery and manage water supply very efficiently. However, some public sector reforms, such as corporatization of local operators and decentralization, could improve the service.

In other countries, Jordan and Egypt, the situation is a greater concern; governments need to pursue their efforts in reshaping the institutional framework of the water supply sector and should address the problem of unviable tariffs.

Overall, the study has shown that institutional arrangements and pricing policy seem to be the two factors that matter the most in improving water supply.

Acknowledgement

This chapter is based on a research project funded by the European Commission within the sixth framework programme (FP6) and conducted under the scientific direction of the OECD Development Centre. It is part of the International Research Project "Understanding Privatization Policy: Political Economy and Welfare Effects — UPP Project" co-ordinated by Fondazione Eni Enrico Mattei (FEEM, Italy). The full-length version of the research project was published as Working Paper by the OECD Development Centre in January 2008, it is available at: http://www.oecd.org/dataoecd/16/38/39922177.pdf.

The author is very grateful to Andrea Goldstein and Federico Bonaglia for excellent guidance. The author would also like to particularly thank Peter Borkey, Claude Ménard and Susanne Szymanski for their very useful comments. The usual caveats apply. In particular, the opinions expressed are the sole responsibility of the author and do not necessarily reflect those of the OECD, the OECD Development Centre or the governments of their member countries.

Appendix

Update on Recent Private Activity (2007–2009) in the Water Sector in Mediterranean Countries

Since this research project was conducted in 2006–2007, this part of the study presents an update on recent developments from 2007–2009 in the water sector in selected Mediterranean countries.

Over the period 2007–2009, the evolution of the water sector in the Mediterranean region has been in line with the previous analysis.

In Tunisia, private sector participation is still very limited. As of January 2009, only a few service contracts were awarded. Two BOT contracts for desalination plants are expected to be awarded during 2009: the Djerba desalination plant and the El Alles desalination plant.

As forecasted in the previous analysis, private sector participation in water supply in Algeria has developed strongly during the last two years. Since 2007, the Algerian government awarded three 5-yr management contracts for water supply in Oran, Constantine and Annaba and El Tarf, as well as five BOT contracts for desalination plants in Souk Tleta, Tlemcen Hounaine, Tenes, Mostaganem and Fouka. The Algerian government intends to evaluate the results of the management contracts over a couple of years before delegating water services in more cities. Thus, no new management contracts are expected for a couple of years. On the other hand, at least five other BOT contracts for desalination plant are expected to reach financial closure in the near future. As of January 2009, about 30% of the Algerian population was receiving water from a private operator. This percentage is expected to grow significantly in the next five years.

In Egypt, no major development was reported. A few service contracts were awarded and two BOT contracts for wastewater treatment (New Cairo and Abu Rawash wastewater treatment plants) should be signed in 2009.

In Morocco, experience with private sector participation continues to be satisfactory. Over the last 10 years, Moroccan authorities have learned from international private providers. Thus, in 2007, the National Office of Potable Water (ONEP) started acting as an international private operator abroad. In December 2007, ONEP was awarded its first management contract for the water supply of Cameroon under a 10-yr lease-affermage agreement.

In Jordan, the management contract for the water supply of Amman concluded in December 2006. The experience with private provision was considered as relatively positive. Therefore, it is expected that more private water contracts will be signed in the medium-term. However, for the time-being, no new water contracts have been awarded.

References

Ambassade de France en Egypte - Mission Economique (2005). L'eau en Egypte.

Ambassade de France au Maroc - Mission Economique (2005). Le secteur de l'environnement au Maroc.

FAO/World Resources Institute. Available at http://earthtrends.wri.org/pdf_library/data_tables/wat2_2005.pdf.

Gulf Capital (2007). Banking on water. Research Report. Available at www.gulfcapital.com/News_Resources/Research_Reports/.

GTZ (2006). Regulation and Supervision in Water Supply and Sanitation. Focus: Jordan. Available at http://www2.gtz.de/dokumente/bib/06-0644_I.pdf.

Ibnet database. Available at www.ib-net.org.

LEMA (2006). Available at http://lema.com.jo/index.php?ID=64.

Lydec (2007). Available at www.lydec.ma.

Ministère des Ressources en Eau d'Algerie, February 2007, http://www.mre.gov.dz/.

Perard, E (2006). Private sector participation and regulatory reform in water supply in the North African region. In Presentation at the AfDB-OECD Expert Meeting on Financing Water Supply, Paris, December 2006.

Perard, E (2007). Private sector participation and regulatory reform in water supply in the Middle East and North African region. Presented at the world water week 2007, Stockholm, August 2007.

Perard, E (2008). Private sector participation and regulatory reform in water supply: The southern Mediterranean Experience. OECD Development Centre Working Paper No. 265.

SONEDE, March 2007. http://www.sonede.com.tn/.

United Nations Department of Economic and Social Affairs (2006). United Nations World Population Prospects 2006: Population Database. Available at http://esa.un.org.unpp.

United Nations (UN) Millennium Project (2005). Health, dignity, and development: What will it take? UN Millennium Project Task Force on Water and Sanitation. Available at http://www.unmillenniumproject.org/documents/WaterComplete-lowres.pdf.

WHO/UNICEF Joint Monitoring Program (2004). www.wssinfo.org.

World Bank. *Doing Business database.* Available at www.doingbusiness.org/

World Bank (2004). Jordan: An Evaluation of Bank Assistance for Water Development and Management. Available at http://lnweb18.worldbank.org/oed/oeddoclib.nsf/DocUNIDViewForJavaSearch/9C37F2F7859A103485256EAC006171F9/$file/jordan_cae_water.pdf.

World Bank (2005a). Official Project Appraisal Document on a Proposed Loan to SONEDE for an Urban Water Supply Project.

World Bank (2005b) The Integrated Water Resources Management Plan For Egypt. Available at http://www-wds.worldbank.org/servlet/WDSContentServer/WDSP/IB/2005/11/09/000160016_20051109091008/Rendered/PDF/341800EGY0whit11public10Action0Plan.pdf.

World Bank (2005c) Cost-Effectiveness and Equity in Egypt's Water Sector. Egypt Public Expenditure Review. Draft, Rural Development, Water and Environment Department, Middle East and North Africa Region, World Bank, Washington, DC.

World Bank (2006). *Maroc: Etude des Flux et Mécanismes de Financement du Secteur de l'Eau, Résultats intermédiaires.* Washington, DC: World Bank.

World Bank (2007). *Making the Most of Scarcity: Accountability for Better Water Management Results in the Middle East and North Africa.* Washington DC: The World Bank.

CHAPTER 18

Tempered Responsiveness through Regulatory Negotiations in the Water Sector: Managing Unanticipated Innovations Emerging from Participation Reforms

Boyd Fuller[*] *and Sunil Tankha*[†]

[*]*LKY School of Public Policy, National University of Singapore*
[†]*Institute of Social Studies, Erasmus University Rotterdam*

Many governments are encouraging participation, but what happens when the participatory group one government agency encourages develops a solution that places unanticipated regulatory burdens onto another agency? In the two water infrastructure cases analyzed here, government agencies in Brazil and Thailand promoted the creation of a participatory group that then developed an innovative solution to its problems. In both cases, however, that new solution required the permission of another agency in the same government, and that permission was initially withheld. The initial rejections were reasonable, given the mandate of the agencies involved, and yet they threatened the success of the participatory programs that the two governments had initiated to supplement their traditional service delivery. Luckily, in both cases the participatory groups were able to (a) apply sufficient pressure to bring the resisting agencies to the table for negotiations and (b) negotiate the implementation of their solution. Based on our analysis, this paper argues that developing country governments need to promote "tempered responsiveness" to balance its efforts to encouraging local stakeholder participation in water infrastructure development and its responsibility to protect the public interest. Tempered responsiveness requires regulators to consider and respond to stakeholder innovations while also encouraging stakeholders to be aware of and responsive to the needs and limitations of the regulatory system. Negotiations played a crucial role in enabling these successful negotiations and we argue that they will continue to do so if tempered responsiveness is to be implemented in the water sector. While more research is needed on these negotiations in developing countries, the effectiveness of these processes can, in the meantime, be improved by drawing upon the literature on public dispute resolution and negotiated rulemaking.

1. Introduction

Many governments now encourage stakeholder participation for infrastructure, but in some cases the participation encouraged by one agency may place unexpected regulatory burdens onto another. Water is one infrastructure sector where participation reforms are being touted as essential for successful development. Participation reforms can help mobilize new ideas and resources from local actors (private and public), but regulating agencies, as the cases show here, may have strong incentives to reject solutions that participatory reforms produce. And yet, stakeholder innovations cannot be discouraged without good reason and so water sector regulatory systems must walk a fine line between encouraging such innovation on the one hand and protecting the public interest and respecting scientific norms on the other. In this article, we argue that water agencies performing regulatory functions must adopt a "tempered responsiveness" to innovations proposed by stakeholders and that negotiations between stakeholders and government agencies are one important, and likely inevitable, means of gaining the legitimacy necessary for that approach.

The literature on participation highlights the ability of participatory processes to, more or less successfully, empower citizens, generate new ideas, and legitimize actions and decisions (Arnstein, 1969; Beierle and

Cayford, 1999; Fung, 2006). In the case of water infrastructure management and policy, the convenors and participants in these processes hope that new ideas about how to design, build, implement, and manage infrastructure may emerge (Kenney, 2000; Tankha and Fuller, 2010; William, 2006). Moreover, experience has shown that participation can also increase legitimacy for water sector decisions, especially those which require tariff increases for hitherto free or heavily-subsidized public services.

Whether or not one agrees with the benefits of participation, more and more stakeholders expect more frequent and more empowering participation opportunities. In the water sector, we see two trends in participation that are encouraging innovative solutions for water problems: (a) the increased emphasis on project-related participation for infrastructure development (Bingham, 1997; Creighton, *et al.*, 1998; Dorothy, 2007; Dubash *et al.*, 2001; Kenney, 2000); and (b) the increased support for broader participation efforts, like community-based research,[1] that support local actors in identifying water and other problems for analysis and problem-solving. The case studies analyzed in this chapter emerge from the latter trend while the literature focuses mostly, if not completely, on the former. In each case, there was government support that helped to create a participatory initiative that produced an innovative solution to a water problem and one water sector agency that was required to regulate that innovation.

Little research has been performed that considers how the participation efforts, supported for purposes other than designing and implementing specific infrastructure or policies, impact regulatory systems for water infrastructure. This is the situation for our case studies presented here. Water sector agencies found themselves in unexpected and ad hoc negotiations with stakeholders who, empowered by newly-established

---

[1] Community-based research is conducted by communities in collaboration with others (researchers, other organizations, and so on) to identify community problems and challenges and promote solutions and change. It is premised on the belief that communities are capable of running and participating in their own research. See also Hills and Mullett (2000), Wilmsen *et al.* (2008) as well as http://www.communitybasedresearch.ca/Page/View/CBR_definition.html

participatory processes, generated innovative and tailor-made solutions to their local water problems and wanted government permission and support to implement them. The water regulatory systems were unprepared for these initiatives and their reflex action was to withhold the necessary approvals. By doing so, they risked destroying the very benefits — such as innovative and context-specific problem-solving, empowered stakeholders, and increased trust in the government — that the governments had been trying to create with the participatory reform. These examples show us how regulatory systems, and especially the government, may need to be better prepared to deal with such non-uniform and unpredictable activities so that they can (a) negotiate with stakeholders effectively and work with them to design solutions that meet local and regional needs using the best knowledge of both periphery and centre; (b) make rapid and timely decisions that are aware and tolerant of uncertainty and risk; and (c) capture the innovations produced by stakeholders so that they can be applied to other similar contexts around the region or country.

We identified these concerns tangentially. This chapter emerged from separate research studies conducted to examine participation reforms in the water and energy sectors in Brazil, India, and Thailand. We were interested in understanding how successful examples of participation were occurring inspite of imperfect institutional environments. From these examples, we sought to answer the question, how do reformers in developing countries "get reforms done" in practice. Our lessons for that question in Brazil and India are covered in two other papers, one for the water sector (Tankha and Fuller, 2010) and another for the electricity sector (Tankha *et al.*, forthcoming). In assessing those participation reforms, we came to realize that some of them were having unexpected and sometimes dramatic impacts on the regulatory systems in question. This chapter seeks to introduce those intriguing and surprising insights into the practice and meaning of regulation, with a focus on how getting participation done may have an impact on how governments get regulation done.

Our analysis, based on key informant interviews, focus group discussions, observation of government agencies in action and archival research, is organized as follows: We first explain how mainstream approaches to regulation and improving regulatory capacity in developing countries are only partially adequate for the task in developing countries. We then introduce our two cases, in which government agencies had to cope with empowered local stakeholders who, having organized themselves with support from other government actors and initiatives, are negotiating and influencing the agencies to support solutions beyond those imagined and evaluated previously. We analyze the regulatory dynamics of these cases in Sec. 4, discussing the implications of the findings on the regulatory system, how we might evaluate its effectiveness, and how governments can respond better to the difficult-to-predict impacts of participation reforms. In Sec. 5, we conclude with some policy-relevant lessons and an agenda for further research.

2. Regulation

Regulation is the fallible practice of altering the behaviour of targeted actors to improve the public interest. Regulations generally appear when markets are distorted or do not respond to public values, because there is market power, informational asymmetries, or ethical concerns. All three are found in the water sector. It is important from the beginning to acknowledge that regulation, even in the best of circumstances, is vulnerable to error and subject to competing political pressures. Regulators often (a) have less information than the regulated; (b) make mistakes; and (c) do not want to or are unable to work towards the public good. The first, information asymmetry presents an enduring problem. Regulators need the information that the regulated have and the regulated have incentives not to share it. The second, fallibility, points to the limit of science in understanding and being able to make predictions about our complex world. Regulators with the best intentions can, and sometimes will, make mistakes (because they are human, because the science is incomplete or incorrect, because the data is incorrect or does not apply to all contexts, and so on). Finally, regulators may be captured by special interests or simply may not know what the public's interests are. The latter is not trivial, as experience has shown time and time again that the definition of the public interest is uncertain and contested, especially in the water sector with its value-laden politics. To overcome these issues, regulatory systems have traditionally been conceived as a technical task which needs to be insulated from political pressures, but that solution has not resolved the knowledge and human error components nor consistently generated the necessary legitimacy for water infrastructure projects.[2]

These challenges are compounded when we look at the water sector in developing countries. To begin with, they have to do more with less. They have fewer resources, and of lesser quality than advanced industrialized societies: manpower, capacity, expertise, training, professionalism, and experience (both personal and institutional). They have a broader and a longer task list: more legislation to enact, more oversight of public and private actors, and most importantly, more innovation in order to discover cheaper and more appropriate ways to get things done. In this vein, it is a self-evident truth that developing countries have lesser regulatory capacity than those industrialized countries whose governance systems they aspire to emulate in both form and function. At the same time, the global tendency is to avoid growing the state, especially in terms of manpower. This has led to two increasing tendencies: (a) outsourcing core state functions; and (b) overburdening regulatory functions to the point that tasks are often performed perfunctorily.

The first tendency, outsourcing, is followed by governments seeking an alternative to an incompletely capable state and to leverage private or community resources and efficiencies for providing public services which were traditionally provided by public sector agencies. In this vein, one response by governments has been to privatize or contract out a number of public services like water infrastructure to profit-seeking entrepreneurs. Another response has been to initiate various kinds of participation reforms through which they encourage stakeholders to play a greater role in solving their own problems by using local resources and knowledge of the specific contexts. Such reforms are encouraged by demands from local, national, and international actors for greater stakeholder participation in a variety of public tasks. In turn these demands are, motivated by ideals of democratic governance based on respect for the autonomy, vitality, and problem-solving capabilities of communities. Both these responses create the need to establish regulatory agencies

---

[2] See, for example, Kahan *et al.* (2007) and Kahan and Braman (2006).

where they do not exist, or create additional tasks for regulatory agencies where they exist.

These demands, unfortunately, often lead to the second tendency, overburdening regulatory functions so that they perform perfunctorily. This tendency can restrict the innovation generated by participation (and other private sector-orientated) reforms as regulators refuse to or do not have the ability to evaluate ideas beyond the familiar. Participation reforms place additional burdens on agencies because they require the government to take on the additional task of encouraging and providing support for participation, as well as regulating some of the innovative ideas produced by empowered groups, often well before government agencies have a well-established capacity to do so (Tankha and Fuller, 2010).

Resistance to certain forms of innovation is also increased when governments seek to outsource government functions to private sector participants in the water sector. Profit-motivated corporations demand an (politically-) independent, technically-capable, and a stable regulatory system, a "technicist" model of regulation. The ideal forms of regulatory governance are conceptualized as those in which insulation from societal pressures, most commonly expressed through political processes, is considered as a virtue. However, the independence of regulatory agencies and their reliance on universalistic concepts and data to create predictable rules and regulations leaves little room for responding to local needs and ideas based on the knowledge of unique, specific contexts and it risks destroying other virtues inherent in community-based and participatory approaches. We will discuss the latter point in Sec. 4.4 when we consider the implications of our findings on measuring regulatory effectiveness.

Both the technicist and responsive approaches to regulatory governance place burdens on developing country governments, a burden that can double when governments are pushed to do both by various local and international actors. This is certainly the case even in advanced industrialized countries such as in the United States, where, for example, regulatory agencies must practice "good science," which often is difficult in the face of technical and legal challenges from stakeholders who have multiple entry points during the rule-making process created to serve public participation values (Jasanoff, 1990; Jasanoff and Wynne, 1998). In practice, the

United States struggles to keep up with the demands of this system, with the process often prolonged for years (Fiorino, 1988; Kim, 2007). In developing countries, the combination of overwhelming and competing burdens as well as inadequate capacity can lead to the state performing its tasks perfunctorily or outsourcing its core state functions. Well-intentioned reforms do not achieve their goals, and analysts bemoan a lack of political will and corruptions. Trying to do more with less sometimes results in doing less with less.

In the light of these pressures — (a) to do more with less; (b) to be more responsive while encouraging community initiative and innovation and (c) to be stable and technically- competent to encourage private sector participation in the water sector, often as a condition for receiving indispensable aid money — new insights are required into how participation reforms and regulatory systems interact with, and aid and hinder, each other. This chapter seeks to do so by looking at two water sector cases in which stakeholders, empowered by government policies designed to encourage participation and local problem-solving, presented innovations to the regulatory system. From these cases, we learn a lot about the tensions that government agencies face when regulating stakeholder innovation, and how they might be better managed.

3. The Cases — The Unexpected Regulatory Impacts of Participation

The two cases we present in this chapter, the Lagos São João in the Brazilian state of Rio de Janeiro and the community of Phrak Nam Daeng in Thailand, highlight the unexpected, and difficult to anticipate challenges and opportunities that participation reforms can pose to the regulatory system. In both these cases, the stakeholders worked through participatory forums to analyze the problem that the community faced and generate innovative solutions for addressing them. Once they had devised solutions, the participatory groups discovered that they needed government permission to implement their innovation. The local stakeholders in both countries felt that their needs and knowledge needed to be considered, and they were able to lobby and negotiate successfully to obtain the needed exemption or permission to proceed with their solution. In Brazil, that challenge involved convincing the state agency that regulated water services to grant an exemption to the standard codes that governed sewerage systems while in Thailand, the innovative idea by the community prompted the irrigation department, which was not traditionally a regulatory agency, to examine, initially reject, and finally reluctantly accept a new design for a small dam gate.

We start with the case of sanitation and environmental protection in the Lagos São João region of Brazil. We then introduce the case of Phrak Nam Daeng, Thailand.

3.1. *Region of the Lakes, Brazil*

The Região dos Lagos, or the Region of the Lakes in the Brazilian state of Rio de Janeiro has long been a preferred tourist destination for Brazilian and international travellers. In the 1960s, one of the most picturesque towns in the region caught the legendary Brigitte Bardot's fancy and following in her footsteps came scores of European tourists. With tourism came prosperity, but also pollution that threatened to wipe out the region's distinctive character and signature beauty. Untreated sewage from the region's numerous towns began to fill up the region's lagoons, killing the fish that provided sustenance to the areas fishing industry as well as degrading the aesthetics of the region.

Meanwhile, the Region's growing population increased demand for water and sewerage services and in 1998, the municipalities in the region gave out the concession for providing water and sewerage services to a private investor group from Portugal. At that time, the towns' immediate concern was to ensure sufficient water for residents and tourists, and so the concessions contracts called upon the company to increase water distribution. Sewerage collection and treatment were, unfortunately, not emphasized likewise.

The deteriorating environmental quality of the region raised several issues and preoccupied a number of stakeholders. In one such case, concerned about the effects of growth and pollution on the habitat and survival of a small local primate species, local activists partnered with the World Wildlife Fund to establish a multi-stakeholder forum and seek solutions to the region's environmental problems. This process eventually metamorphosed into an Inter-municipal Consortium of the Lagos São

João (IMC), a forum to tackle regional environmental and quality of life problems which included representatives of local environmental groups, state agencies' representatives of region's 12 local governments in 1999 (Pereira, 2007).

The IMC began by organizing a seminar in April 2000 to (a) present an environmental diagnosis of the region; (b) promote a greater interaction amongst the various stakeholders; and (c) establish several working groups to execute conservation programs. In the seminar, the multi-stakeholder participants identified sewerage discharge into the lagoon as the major cause of environmental problems. However, the solution was not immediately apparent, because the new water and sanitation concessionaires' contracts with the municipalities did not require them to provide the higher-level of sanitation necessary to protect the region's water bodies.

The negotiations between the IMC and the concessionaire made it clear that, while constructing sewage treatment stations was feasible, transporting the sewage to the treatment stations would require a network of drains, which is a costly undertaking. For the concessionaire, there was little clarity in the concessions contract on how these investments would be remunerated. After several sessions of negotiation, the IMC proposed that the storm water collection network be used to transport the sewage to treatment stations. This was technically-possible since the region does not receive much rain, approximately only 700mm per year, which meant that the storm water collection system is dry and unused for most of the year. The IMC proposed that the existing network of drains be used to collect sewerage to transport to the treatment stations during the dry months, while shutting off collection and treatment during the wet months. According to the IMC's calculations, using the storm water collection system to handle the additional sewage requirements would require about 30% of the investment that a traditional system would require. As the IMC would later present the idea to others, it was a choice between treating 80% of the sewage around 95% of the time (i.e., during the dry period) or treating 10% of the sewage throughout the year.

While the new idea seemed technically-feasible, state regulations prohibited using the storm water network to transport sewage. As such, Rio de Janeiro's energy and sanitation services regulatory agency

(AGENERSA) was initially inclined to reject the proposal. However, the IMC was headed by a bureaucrat on secondment from the state's environment agency. He was able to arrange a series of meetings with AGENERSA and eventually they reached an agreement which allowed an exception to be made in the case of the Região dos Lagos.

The concessionaire was reluctant to engage in this experiment as its concessions contract with the municipalities did not contain any provision for the required investments to be remunerated. Here, the IMC played a critical role first in convincing the community that it was necessary to pay an increased tariff for the enhanced sewage treatment services to be provided by the concessionaire, second, in forcing the initially-reluctant concessionaire to agree to provide these services, and third, in persuading AGENERSA to formalize this arrangement. After 27 months of continuous community pressure and agitation, and the sale of the concession by its Portuguese owners to a Brazilian firm, the new investors promised spend US$38.5 million to establish treatment stations.

However, that agreement hinged upon AGENERSA allowing the concessionaire to increase tariffs for its services. Again, the agency initially resisted allowing this as it was reluctant to approve a tariff increase. The IMC, recognizing that it would be impossible to force the concessionaire to make the investments without a feasible plan of remuneration lobbied the regulatory agency till the latter finally approved the necessary tariff increase. As a result of these activities, several treatment stations were built and began operating in 2004.

The success of the negotiations with the concessionaires and the state regulatory agency inspired even more work by the IMC. In 2004, following the directives established by Brazil's 1997 Water Law, a River Basin Committee was established in the region, counting amongst its participants over 50 civil society groups and an array of local and state government representatives and the water and sanitation concessionaires. New works were undertaken, such as retrofitting a local dam, Juturnaiba, with a US$400,000 fish ladder, and decommissioning a bypass canal to restore the São João River's natural course at a cost of US$700,000. A payment for environmental services scheme was also developed to fund unemployed residents of the region to restore riparian forests, thereby protecting a species of local primate. A second and third phase of investments was negotiated with the concessionaire to collect all sewerage by 2009 and to separate the storm water network from the sewerage network by 2013.

In this case study, we see how a multi-stakeholder IMC ended up negotiating and lobbying successfully for not just one, but two regulatory adjustments as it sought solutions to a local water and environment problem. These regulatory adjustments were not part of the IMC's initial plan; instead, IMC's deliberations produced the innovative idea which required them. The innovation itself was based on the particular knowledge of the local stakeholders who came to realize that the broad, universal regulation on the use of storm water drainage systems was in conflict with a context-specific and technically-feasible solution to a local problem.

This case study provides several key observations. First, it reminds us of the limits of regulations based on universalistic science that is often based on assumptions and understandings not relevant to all contexts.[3] Second, it shows how participatory reforms supported by other government actors can create unanticipated work for regulatory agencies. Third, we see how the IMC used lobbying to draw reluctant regulatory agencies into negotiations in which the new solutions were considered and eventually permitted. Fourth, it demonstrates how successful participatory exercises can help stakeholders build networks and self-confidence, which in turn inspire them to identify new problems and create new solutions beyond the ones for which they were initially convened. Finally, the experience shows how interstitial actors, such as the bureaucrat on secondment to the IMC, play key roles in bringing together actors and agencies, especially in developing countries where the gap between the government and the governed or the regulators and the regulated is often quite large.

3.2. *Phrak Nam Daeng, Thailand*

In the 1970s, the Mae Klong River's freshwater flows were severely reduced and altered in timing and quality because of (a) the construction of a new upstream dam; (b) the new *Thonburi-Paktor* highway which cut across the

[3] For more on the interplay of science and local knowledge, see Corburn (2005) and Fuller (2009a).

land, also acting as a dam; (c) the pollution from an industrial plant; and (d) a severe drought. This was a disaster for the Phrak Nam Daeng community, which depended on the freshwater for its economic activities. The community needed to find a way to get more and cleaner water at the right time. The community leader appealed to the Royal Irrigation Department (RID) for help.

In response, RID did what it usually did, constructing water gates in the Thonburi-Paktor highway so that water was stored behind the road for agriculture. Unfortunately, in this instance, the new structure created more problems than it solved, because it forced a dramatic change in downstream economic activities. With the decrease in freshwater flows due to the water gates in combination with the highway and upstream dams, the water downstream became too saline for agriculture. The community switched to shrimp farming, salt harvesting, and other activities more appropriate to the saline, estuarine environment. However, not all were able to adjust. Some had to sell their land to outsiders and leave.

The dam had other effects besides changing the salinity of the two regions. Debris and pollutants, including pesticides from rice production and chemicals used by upstream industries, also accumulated behind the dams. When the dam's gate was lifted to release water (usually to prevent or reduce the impacts of rainy season flooding), the polluted water would flow into the downstream community's lands, sometimes dramatically hurting agricultural production downstream.

Thus, the upstream community wanted to time water releases to mitigate flood events while downstream communities was more worried about timing water releases to manage salt and pollution concentrations in the estuary. Unfortunately, these different needs and the communities' inability to negotiate tradeoffs increased conflict over the next decade, leading to frequent quarrels and then to long-term mistrust. Towards the end, it was so bad that one member of the upstream community said, "When members of the different communities met in markets or other areas, they would not, or could not, look at each other in the eye!"

Fortuitously, one of the leaders of the downstream community learned about community-based research from The Thailand Research Fund. The Thailand Research Fund began funding community-based research in 1999. The fund promoted and supported community-based research as a means of helping communities to engage proactively with their problems. The research fund supported the community to engage in a participatory Research process in which they would identify what problems were the most important to solve and what were the options to address them. Phrak Nam Daeng was to become one of their early and best success stories.

With the help of Thailand Research Fund staff, the Phrak Nam Daeng community engaged in community-based research through which they identified the key problems facing upstream and downstream farmers. As they became more familiar with the problem and its dimensions, they sought advice from various experts and local officials. Finally, they developed a new design for the gate portion of the dam, which was based on their experience with smaller water gates already used in downstream farms to regulate water flows in and out of individual farms.

At this point, the community needed funding to build the dam. They sought it from the local staff of the RID. Unfortunately, they not only refused their request for funds, but also told them that they could not approve the design. Appeals to the central office of the RID also proved to be fruitless at first.

The community found other funds to build the first gate using their design. The community's gate worked, but not as well as the community thought it would. Moreover, the RID soon replaced it with one that they built, a modified version of the community's design. Unfortunately, the RID staff were not very familiar with the saline conditions of the region or the needs of the community that were driving the design. For example, they constructed the gate out of metal that soon rusted under the saline conditions, and they included gates at the bottom of the gate that allowed trash and pollutants to freely flow through the gates, which the community's design had been designed to avoid.

While the Phrak Nam Daeng community and then the RID were each designing and installing their gates, the former continued pressing latter to be more responsive. In this, the community found allies within and outside the agency. State-level politicians and non-government organizations looked for opportunities to influence the decision-makers in the RID, and in time, they were able to arrange for the Royal advisor on irrigation to meet the community. At the same time, a RID staff trained in mediation heard about and visited the case, after which he began to lobby from within for a more receptive response.

In the end, the RID and the Phrak Nam Daeng community worked together to design and construct a third water gate that satisfied both the engineering specifications of the RID and the needs of the community. However, their relationships and cooperation remain poor. For example, RID wants to use the improved gate design in other locations. However, miffed by Department's apparent uncooperativeness, the community is insisting that it has a copyright on the design and that it wants royalties. Furthermore, there are multiple other water gates along the highway that could benefit from the technology. So, while the negotiations did lead to the proper design of one gate, the poor quality of them has slowed down the implementation of the design as well as the relationships between and regulatory learning of RID and the community.

At the same time, based on its learning from this project and other experiences, RID has recently opened up its Office of Public Participatory Promotion. This Office has already supported several communities in their own community-based research. One of the key figures in the Office is the same mediation-trained insider who visited the Phrak Nam Daeng community.

The Royal Irrigation Department's initial actions were driven by regulatory concerns, especially because they were the technical experts and because their engineers are also responsible to the Council of Engineers' codes, the professional body that accredits professional engineers. Their local staff, the first approached by the community, could not approve the design because they were not professional engineers. The engineers at RID's central office did not have a strong faith in the community's ideas, and preferred to work with designs created and vetted internally. The RID staff were also not familiar with regulatory processes that might be employed to address and integrate outside ideas with central rules and regulations.

As in Brazil, this case study shows how participation reforms can create unanticipated work for government agencies applying universalistic regulations and how the regulating agency had to be lobbied and influenced before it would enter into productive discussions. However, the regulating government agency in Thailand, i.e., the RID, is traditionally a service-delivery agency and it does not have the same kind of mandate, capacities, and norms and procedures for managing regulatory tasks. In fact, the regulation of designs is largely self-regulation, with RID using established designs that were created by following professional engineering norms and designs, and enforced and overseen by professional engineers at RID and the professional engineering association, Council of Engineers Thailand. The community's innovation (and the participation reform that encouraged it) required RID to adopt a relatively new role of regulating a community design.

4. Responding to the Challenge: Initial Analysis and Future Research

In the cases presented here, the communities were able to succeed in large part due to their ability to persist in the face of significant government resistance by (a) mobilizing allies and resources to influence government agencies; and (b) the assistance of interstitial actors that facilitated penetrating the agencies. Many other stakeholder initiatives never take off because communities consider the obstacles too great or the likely benefits too little (Tankha and Fuller, 2010). In Sec. 4.1, we argue that the reasons that government agencies and actors initially resist engaging with stakeholders and their ideas and needs are largely legitimate, desirable, and need to be understood if they are to be worked through in order to not derail participation reforms. Understanding the reasons for the initial resistance of government agencies and the challenges these reasons pose for the governance of developing countries seeking to both encourage local stakeholder participation in governance and establish technicist regulatory systems is important to finding ways of improving both participation reform and regulation performance. In Sec. 4.2, we propose that regulating agencies need to adopt a "tempered responsiveness" which walks the middle ground between responsive willingness and technicist resistance. Negotiations such as the ones in the cases provide one forum for this tempering of two concurrent trends in governance as well as local needs and the public interest. Furthermore, even when stakeholders do persist and are able to negotiate with government agencies, the outcomes are not always optimal. While the outcome in the Região dos Lagos case was generally satisfactory, the Royal Irrigation Department and Phrak Nam Daeng community currently share a poor relationship which is delaying the dissemination of the community's innovative water gate design to other communities who could benefit from it. In Sec. 4.3, we explore the literature on public dispute resolution, consensus building, and negotiated rulemaking to elicit lessons about how these negotiations can be managed more effectively to produce tempered responsiveness and better outcomes. Finally, in Sec. 4.4, we discuss how regulatory approaches may be evaluated if we incorporate stakeholder participation as an explicit value-creating activity.

4.1. *Resistance: Reasons and Challenges*

In Sec. 2, we already discussed some of the reasons why regulatory agencies might not want to consider local stakeholder needs and ideas. Here, we examine and develop our understanding of this resistance through the cases. This resistance is, unfortunately natural and fortunately desirable. In Brazil and Thailand, no one prepared the agencies to handle ad hoc regulatory requests like the ones described in this chapter, in large part because these situations were unanticipated. They also lacked key data and in Thailand, the RID had little experience with the regulatory process. Imagine, for instance, that more and more stakeholder groups also start pressing for exemptions from existing regulations or even the creation of new ones based on their innovations for each of their unique conditions. On the principles of fairness, the agency may then be forced to consider each and every request, a potentially massive use of resources on just one regulatory issue.

Regulating agencies and staff also have to consider how they are being assessed. As stakeholders pushed the agencies to permit local innovations, they were also asking the regulating agencies to consider local interests alongside the public interest and to accept and use local (sometimes unscientific) knowledge as the basis for analysis and decision-making. At the same time, the performance of regulating agencies was being monitored by others (e.g., the public, professional associations, legislators, etc). Some of these actors regulating the regulators are concerned with transparency and regulatory capture. Others wonder what impacts the innovations will have on their own community and the public interest. Legislator and other stakeholders can worry about the efficiency of these ad hoc negotiations and regulatory analyses. Professional colleagues and associations are wary of unscientific knowledge and concerned about protecting the reputation of their field.

Finally, professional associations and scientific colleagues expect that decisions be based on "good science," which is usually legitimated by the use of certain methodologies and language (Jasanoff, 1990; Jasanoff and Wynne, 1998). The local knowledge used by the Phrak Nam Daeng community was not tested by scientific methods, although the community did invite experts of various sorts to provide ideas and support. Instead, the main ideas for the water gate were derived from the community's agricultural practices and experience with their setting. Scientific knowledge's credibility is largely derived from the processes that are used to create it ("the scientific method"), and so using local knowledge without vetting it through a scientific process could easily be considered irresponsible by professional associations such as Thailand's Council of Engineers as well as illegitimate by the scientific communities who set the standards for the science used in regulation.

Considering all of the above, plus the risks that can arise to careers from entrepreneurial actions, and the agencies' hesitation seems quite understandable *and desirable.*[4] We depend on the regulatory system to protect us from harm or at least to manage the risks we are exposed to (Beck, 1992). While the idea of a responsive regulatory system makes intuitive sense, we want that responsiveness also to be responsible, in sense that the agencies should continue to either protect or manage the risks from innovation to public welfare, the environment, and other elements of the public interest. This is especially true for the RID in Thailand, which was pushed into playing an unfamiliar role and has, despite the difficulties of the discussions, learned from the experiences and developed its own community-based research program.

Based on this understanding, the next section introduces the idea of "tempered responsiveness" and propose that negotiations among

[4] The difficulties might mount if we also considered professional pride and face here.

regulating agencies and stakeholders is one means by which it can be encouraged and nurtured.

4.2. *"Tempered Responsiveness"*

The participation reforms in Brazil and Thailand are meant to tap into local capacities and resources to solve their own problems. However, many communities choose not to invest time and resources into participatory problem-solving because they believe that the government will not readily accept their ideas and needs. To enable stakeholders' initiative, the regulatory system needs to demonstrate its willingness and ability to receive, consider, and improve the innovations. To promote private sector investment, protect the public interest, and otherwise maintain its legitimacy, the government must temper its responsiveness with its responsibility to the public interest, other stakeholders' needs, and the norms of professionalism.

Responsiveness as we define it here means that (a) agencies consider local needs and knowledge as well as the public interest and science in their analysis and decision-making; and (b) stakeholders believe that they are doing so in good faith. Both components are important factors in both encouraging more stakeholder initiatives and in creating overall legitimacy for the regulatory system and its decisions. In using responsiveness here, we are inspired by the concept of "responsive regulation" posed by Ayres and Braithwaite (1992) and Braithwaite (2006). However, this concept focuses on regulating behaviour, which is not an issue in our cases. Instead, the question faced by parties in our cases is about how to combine and make tradeoffs between local needs and the public interest, and how to make decisions that not only protect the public interest but also encourage stakeholder innovation and do so by managing the increased uncertainties that arise from combining local knowledge with science.

Responsiveness requires willingness, which occurs when the targeted parties accept that they must work towards the implementation of a program or policy. To build willingness, participation reforms are often accompanied by capacity building programs that educate and improve the ability of government actors and organizations to work with communities.

The first lesson from our cases is simple; the target group for such programs should include agencies that may have to regulate the solutions that the participatory processes identify and create.[5]

However, this is a large task. In developing countries, many participatory efforts are undertaken partly because governments lack adequate resources, information, motivation, and capabilities to identify problems, formulate solutions, and implement them for all contexts. In such cases, communities are expected to contribute in terms of ideas, resources and motivation to perform public service tasks which in other contexts would be performed by public sector agencies or regulated private sector agents. Given the resource limitations, a comprehensive approach to building and deploying capacities to prepare the regulatory system for stakeholder innovations and requests such as those described in this chapter is likely far beyond what developing country governments are currently capable of.

Given the unlikelihood that capacity building programs can fully prepare agencies for ad hoc innovation, we begin to explore how regulatory systems may take the path towards a future, long-term transformation by breaking it into smaller, experimental steps that balance as best as possible innovation and risk-taking with protecting the public and the legitimacy of the regulatory system.

We proceed with two assumptions. First, we believe that it is inevitable that the regulatory system will continue to muddle through these situations, and that this ad hoc, imperfect, learning and problem-solving process is not a poor path to take towards improving performance (Lindblom, 1959). In fact, even in developed countries, regulations are often designed and promulgated on imperfect information, leading to call for a more deliberate process of design, implementation, monitoring, and adaption (Holling, 1978; Lee, 1993). Second, we assume that willingness will be built through a more entrepreneurial path. In Tankha and Fuller (2010), we proposed that government agencies could pursue two paths in implementing participation reforms: bureaucratic and entrepreneurial. The

[5] We have covered the need for and paths of this government capacity building in a previous paper (Tankha and Fuller, 2010), though this chapter now extends the argument to include all agencies.

former builds up capacity, with motivation to follow afterwards. The latter builds capacity through experiments undertaken by motivated entrepreneurs (who can be inside or outside government) in which motivated actors take, or are pushed into taking, risks to promote reforms and achieve their intended benefits.

However, willingness is not sufficient for effective regulation in these cases, efforts must be made to protect the public interest, preserve the regulating agency's legitimacy, and maintain a climate conducive to private sector investment. Thus, we suggest that a "tempered responsiveness" must be promoted within regulating agencies, especially in developing countries where full capacity building is improbable. Tempered responsiveness starts with a commitment by regulating actors and stakeholders to consider innovations honestly and with respect, using community needs, the agency's mandate, and the broader public interest as the criteria for that consideration. Furthermore, in light of the incompleteness and uncertainty in both scientific and non-scientific knowledge, tempered responsiveness calls on regulatory system actors and stakeholders to be open to innovations and the opportunities that they represent while keeping in mind, and being transparent about, the burdens and uncertainties that they may place not only on the agencies, but also the public interest (e.g., by externalities imposed on other communities or the environment, by distracting public funds from more urgent matters, and so on).

We emphasize tempered responsiveness because we believe more recognition must be given to the multiple reasons why agencies and staff may choose not to follow through on stakeholders' innovations. Generally, we cannot ask actors in the regulatory system to be responsive to new ideas unless those holding them accountable are also willing to be responsive to the uncertainties and unknowns that make regulatory analysis and decision-making imperfect.

We have already stated our presumption that negotiation among stakeholders and government actors will be a primary method through which the regulatory system's response to innovations will be managed. Luckily, such negotiations can also build the tempered responsiveness that can balance developing countries' competing needs. To start with, they can help build the legitimacy that developing country governments need in the face of incomplete capacity and institutional weaknesses. Proponents of public dispute resolution have long claimed, with little opposition, that negotiations among stakeholders and government actors can increase the legitimacy of the eventual decisions. This presumes that stakeholders see that decision-making takes the results of the negotiation into account. Such negotiations are never intended to replace the government's decision-making role; however stakeholders and government often expect each other to implement (or at least not to hinder the implementation of) the recommendations they jointly agree upon (Susskind *et al.*, 1999). Also, as the cases analyzed here demonstrated, recently empowered stakeholders will not take rejection easily unless they understand which the reasons for it clearly and believe that the process taken to arrive at the decision was legitimate. Focused capacity building can also provide crucial support. For example, governments could establish protocols for how it processes the proposed innovations and guidelines for acceptable uncertainty and risk. Both these would then create room for agency staff to support innovations by protecting them from recrimination should the innovation go wrong. These protocols and guidelines would be based on the presumption of "good faith" on the part of agencies and their staff, which seems appropriate since those actors are asked to treat innovators in the same fashion as part of being responsive. It assumes that the regulatory system is willing and able to establish standardized guidelines for *legitimately* measuring and judging the acceptability of uncertainty and risk for the diverse array of possible innovations.

In promoting tempered responsiveness through negotiation, we recognize that the regulatory system needs to improve the wisdom of how it processes stakeholders' requests. However, wisdom, which we define as the likelihood that regulations produce intended benefits, is difficult to achieve in the situations like those described in this chapter, where (a) the agencies involved will have only partial information about the local conditions; (b) extracting local knowledge for scientific analysis is difficult (otherwise, there would have been no need for participation reforms)[6]; and (c) vested interests in weak-capacity environments might use the same path to seek undeserved exemptions. In fact, as Stiglitz

[6] The literature identifies multiple challenges that make the uptake and use of local knowledge (Corburn, 2005; Fischer, 2000; Fuller, 2009a).

(2009) points out, wisdom is often problematic even in developed countries.[7]

Luckily, negotiations can also be managed to increase the wisdom of decisions. In the next section, we move to the literature on regulatory negotiation, public dispute resolution, and consensus building and what it has to say about how negotiations about regulatory matters can be made to increase legitimacy and wisdom. In introducing this literature, we are not arguing that negotiated processes are better for making regulations. Indeed, the relative merits of traditional and negotiated processes have not been sufficiently analyzed for a conclusive judgement.[8] Instead, we draw from the literature to show how the negotiations that are happening can be conducted more effectively to increase legitimacy and wisdom.

4.3. *Improving Negotiations*

In this section, we explore how governments can better prepare for and improve the wisdom of ad hoc negotiations such as those introduced in this chapter. This wisdom certainly cannot be taken for granted. For example, consider the Thailand case. The parties have much to offer each other and yet their negotiation was slow and acrimonious, resulting in a sub-optimal outcome: a poor relationship and a design that cannot be currently shared to other communities.

Neither the communities nor the agencies had much experience in working together towards evaluating, improving, and implementing innovations. To effectively convene and manage a process among government and non-

---

[7] Stiglitz argues that regulatory structures and systems generally have to be designed by understanding that regulators may (a) have less information than the regulated; (b) make mistakes, which is inevitable; and (c) not want or be able to work towards the public good.

[8] For example, currently there is debate within the literature about the benefits of regulatory negotiation, although we proceed in this chapter on the assumption that the regulatory system will find it difficult in the short-term to avoid negotiations with the innovative groups being empowered by participation reforms. Coglianese (1997) found that there were regulatory negotiations which did not reduce the number of lawsuits, while Langbein and Kerwin (2000) found that parties were generally more satisfied after regulatory negotiations, but that, there were issues of equity and efficiency that needed further study.

government stakeholders, careful consideration must be given to various factors, including, but not limited to, the different cultures of the groups, the nature of their relationship, and the politics, processes, and institutions of the policy-making environment within which the negotiation will take place (Fiorino, 1988; Fuller, 2009b; Kim, 2007; Susskind *et al.*, 1999; Susskind *et al.*, 1985).

To improve the negotiations, we draw on the cases and the literature on public dispute resolution. The literature on public dispute resolution and regulatory negotiation provides insights for how many of these tasks can be done, though it is mostly based on developed, Western experiences. Kim (2007) is one notable exception. This work describes regulatory negotiations in Korea, a country which has recently transitioned into high-income status. To start with, negotiated processes first and foremost rely on identifying and working with stakeholders' different interests, which are understood to be the different concerns, wants, and needs that underlie the public positions stakeholders take (Fisher and Ury, 1991). Once interests are identified, the parties look for solutions that meet them, as best as possible. Common interests can be pursued together, trades can be made across competing and differently prioritized interests, and objective criteria can be used to fairly distribute value.

However, identifying interests and how to meet them is often difficult to effectively convene and manage a process among government and non-government stakeholders, careful consideration must be given to various factors, including, but not limited to, the different cultures of the groups, the nature of their relationship, and the politics, processes, and institutions of the policy-making environment within which the negotiation will take place. Process design and management are key for achieving better outcomes and many basic principles have been established in Western contexts,[9] but they

[9] Typical advice includes: (a) hiring neutral, professional facilitators whose presence and skills can produce a safe and impartial space for authentic dialogue; (b) assessing the conflicts (or disagreements) beforehand to improve process design and stakeholder selection; (c) establishing ground rules that create a safe and effective space for dialogue; (d) pursuing joint fact-finding to establish a common base of scientific data to inform the deliberations; and (e) designing strategies to implement agreements, so that the parties make agreements that are more likely to produce tangible results (Fuller, 2009b).

have not been extensively tested and researched in developing countries. Other factors such as the institutional environment, the different types of knowledge required, and the values and cultures must also be given careful consideration both for the negotiations and the implementation of any agreements.

Looking at our two cases, one specific finding is that government officials supporting the participation reforms can play a key role in educating actors about the possible benefits of negotiating and mediating between the various sides. In Brazil, this actor worked for a government agency and was seconded to the participatory group while in Thailand there was an insider within the Royal Irrigation Department and other allies who helped to bring the parties together for negotiations. In our cases, these actors were familiar with the participatory reforms and with the agencies approached by stakeholders. They were also familiar with participatory processes. In Brazil, the key official was seconded to the participatory group that developed the innovation. In Thailand, the Royal Irrigation Department staff person had received training in public dispute resolution and some of the other key persons had provided him that training.

As we have discussed earlier, the use of purely technical measures to evaluate performance can dampen the ability of the regulatory system to respond to stakeholder innovations in ways that promote government objectives of promoting local problem-solving capacity. In the next section, we discuss the challenges of measuring the effectiveness of the regulatory system given these new situations.

4.4. *Measuring Regulatory Effectiveness*

Sen (1999) argues that development needs to take ideals about equity and democracy as much as or more than meeting physical needs into account. Impersonal, generalized outcome measures such as costs and benefits speak little to the desires of some for freedom and equality in the face of significant poverty, inequalities in wealth, and insufficient opportunities to influence the direction of one's own life. The political independence of regulatory agencies, which analysts regularly recommend to improve regulatory performance in developing countries, may unintentionally suppress the expression of such concerns if they are seen as being unresponsive to non-standard concerns and ideas. In cases where the conflict between "independent" regulation and politics is deep and unresolved, this may lead to the total collapse of the regulatory bargain.

Recent trends towards hybrid approaches to economic organization, social decision-making, and their regulation also complicate the measurement regulatory success. Traditionally, the language of policy analysis and regulation has been the language of economics, and often financial economics. The desirability of decisions is couched in terms of monetized costs and benefits and time discounting. From this perspective, participation incurs costs and creates value but both the costs incurred and the value generated by participation are rarely calculated, quantified, monetized or incorporated in any feasibility analyses. Participation engenders positive externalities, which creates value in addition to the sum of the private values incorporated in the solutions generated through participatory approaches. These externalities take the form of increased social and/or institutional capital which enhances capabilities for solving other local problems. They also create value in sense that democratic processes increase legitimacy of decisions, thus reducing transactions costs. By doing so, they also facilitate a greater exchange of economic and political goods than would be possible under mainstream market arrangements, thus increasing the efficiency of allocation. In this context, we must ask ourselves, if the act of participation itself creates value, then how is this value to be incorporated into regulatory calculations so that these externalities may be internalized into any implicit cost-benefit analyses that are conducted by the regulatory agencies? The identification of values added and costs incurred, defined beyond their narrow financial conceptualizations is urgently required. However, the task is difficult. In fact, the monetization of many values is quite difficult and often contested, especially when considering values such as social capital, community pride, environmental quality, and others about which stakeholders disagree and fight passionately. Science cannot easily resolve such disagreements either, especially where it is uncertain, incomplete, and contested, a common situation in all countries let alone developing ones.

Where it is not easy to find an easily applied, shared set of criteria for making collective decisions, another method must be found by which a regulation is judged by its merits across multiple perspectives. Negotiation is, by definition, one such process since any decision must be acceptable to all who are represented. However, the quality of that representation and the "measuring" of solutions depends on effective process design and management as well as skills and knowledge, as we have discussed in the earlier sections. Our explanations are incomplete, we acknowledge, but our proposals are aimed more at initiating a dialogue around these issues rather than providing a complete package around which a new evaluative framework can be built.

5. Conclusion

Participatory reforms can change who does the regulatory work and how the regulatory system does business. Sometimes, the participatory problem-solving encouraged by are government agency can place unexpected, regulatory burdens onto another agency. Regulatory systems must begin to think more systematically and effectively about how to engage with ad hoc, location-specific innovations and interests. Our study reveals that "tempered responsiveness" through negotiations among stakeholders is one important way that such adaptation will follow.

From our investigations of participatory initiatives in Brazil and Thailand and their unanticipated impacts on the regulatory system, we found four concurrent trends:

Our first finding is that, participation reforms place additional and sometimes unusual burdens on regulatory systems and that these are understudied. The agencies approached by stakeholders in Brazil and Thailand were not expecting or prepared for these bottom up initiatives, even though these initiatives were being encouraged by other government agencies, policies and programs. For the Royal Irrigation Department in Thailand, which is a service delivering rather than a regulatory agency, these stakeholder initiatives created particularly unusual burdens. In addition to studying how these burdens develop, governments need to develop explicit instructions, guidelines and protocols about dealing with and evaluating stakeholder generated proposals, and also determine and provide for the additional financial and human resources that will be required to perform these tasks.

Our second finding is that the agencies who find themselves being requested, or actively pressured, to make regulatory evaluations and decisions of local innovations have legitimate reasons for avoiding them. While other government agencies are being tasked to encourage participation, regulatory agencies are being encouraged, and often required, to insulate themselves from community pressures by using rules-based, technicist approaches for regulation, often to provide a stable environment for private investment in infrastructure. At the same time, professional staff are also held accountable to good scientific practice by their peers and professional associations. Furthermore, the evaluations of these actors' performance will not typically include whether participation's intended benefits were achieved. In this context, agencies and their staff can believe that it is indeed risky to respond to ad hoc initiatives and innovations by place-specific stakeholder using local knowledge, whose legitimacy is often doubted. For this reason also, explicit instructions and protocols should be developed in order to provide guidance to regulating staff.

Our third finding is that negotiations like the ones which occurred in Brazil and Thailand are not only inevitable, but also necessary so that agencies can adopt "tempered responsiveness." Negotiations can provide legitimacy that complements standard norms of following rules and professional norms. They also provide a means through which local innovations can be tested for how they meet other interests, including the public interest as well as those of other possibly impacted stakeholders and experts who are accountable to scientific practices. The literature on public dispute resolution provides a series of recommendations for how the effectiveness of such negotiations can be improved; however, much more research is necessary to understand how such ideas can be used in developing country contexts. However, a greater emphasis on developing the necessary negotiation skills and networks is also required to facilitate these exercises.

Finally, the cases also demonstrate to us, how government staff familiar with participation reforms and methods, can play a crucial mediating role in bringing government and non-government parties together and improving communications among them. This role seemed especially important in our cases because (a) the negotiations were unanticipated and ad hoc; (b) the parties involved were placed in unfamiliar, and sometimes new, roles; and (c) their knowledge, norms, and practices are different. The mediation training program in Thailand, and the creation of the Office for Public Participatory Promotion in which one of the trained mediators plays a key role, are together an interesting example of how government officials can learn and then use mediation and negotiation skills to promote and temper stakeholder innovation. Government officials trained in consensus building and mediation skills can ease the burdens of tempered responsiveness and generally improve the coordination across multiple actors that participation reforms and broader decentralization encourage.

References

Arnstein, S (1969). A ladder of citizen participation. *Journal of the American Insitute of Planners*, 35, pp. 216–224.

Ayres, I and J Braithwaite (1992). *Responsive Rregulation: Transcending the Deregulation Debate.* Oxford University Press, New York.

Beck, U (1992). *Risk Society: Towards a New Modernity.* London, Newbury Park, CA: Sage Publications.

Beierle, TC and JC Cayford (1999). *The Determinants of Successful Public Participation in Environmental Decision-making. Resources for the Future.* Washington, DC.

Bingham, G (1997). Seeking Solutions: Alternative Dispute Resolution and Western Water Issues. Report to the Western Water Policy Review Advisory Commission, Denver, CO.

Braithwaite, J (2006). Responsive regulation and developing economies. *World Development*, 34(5), pp. 884–898.

Coglianese, C (1997). Assessing Consensus: The promise and performance of negotiated rulemaking. *Duke Law Journal*, 46, pp. 1225–1348.

Creighton, JL, JD Priscoli and CM Dunning (eds.) (1998). *Public Involvement Techniques: A Reader of Ten Years of Experience at the Institute for Water Resources.* IWR Research Report-R1, Institute for Water Resources, US Army Corps of Engineers.

Dorothy, MD (2007). Citizen groups and scientific decisionmaking: Does public participation influence environmental outcomes? *Journal of Policy Analysis and Management*, 26(2), pp. 349–368.

Dubash, NK, M Dupar, S Kothari and T Lissu (2001). *A watershed in global governance? An independent assessment of the World Commission on Dams.* World Resources Institute, Washington, D.C.

Fiorino, D (1988). Regulatory negotiation as a policy process. *Public Administration Review*, July/August, pp. 764–772.

Fuller, B (2009a). Local Knowledge and Consensus Building: From Access to Impact. *LKY School of Public Policy Working Papers, SPP09–08.*

Fuller, B (2009b). *Moving Through Value Conflict: Consensus Building and Trading Zones for Resolving Water Disputes.* VDM Verlag Dr. Mueller e.K., Wiesbaden.

Fung, A (2006). *Empowered Participation: Reinventing Urban Democracy* (1st paperback edn.) Princeton, N.J., Woodstock: Princeton University Press.

Hills, M and J Mullett (2000). *Community-Based Research: Collaborative Action for Health and Social Change.* Community Health Promotion Coalition, University of Victoria, Victoria, B.C.

Holling, CS (1978). *Adaptive Environmental Assessment and Management.* New York: John Wiley and Sons.

Jasanoff, S (1990). *The Fifth Branch: Science Advisers as Policymakers.* Cambridge, Mass: Harvard University Press

Jasanoff, S and B Wynne (1998). Science and Decision-making. In *Human Choice and Climate Change*, Rayner, S, EL Malone (eds.), pp. 1–87. Columbus: Battelle Press.

Kahan, DM and D Braman (2006). Cultural cognition and public policy. *Yale Law & Policy Review*, 24(147).

Kahan, DM, D Braman, P Slovic, J Gastil and GL Cohen (2007). The Second National Risk and Culture Study: Making Sense of — and Making Progress In — The American Culture War of Fact. *SSRN eLibrary.*

Kenney, DS (2000). Arguing About Consensus: Examining the Case Against Western Watershed Initiatives and Other Collaborative Groups Active in Natural Resources Management. Natural Resources Law Center, University of Colorado School of Law, Boulder, CO.

Kim, D-Y (2007). *The Challenges of Consensus Building in a Consolidating Democracy: Diesel Vehicles and Urban Air Pollution in Korea.* VDM Verlag Dr. Mueller e.K., Saarbruken.

Langbein, LI and CM Kerwin (2000). Regulatory negotiation versus conventional rule making: Claims, counterclaims, and empirical evidence. *J Public Adm Res Theory*, 10(3), pp. 599–632.

Lee, KN (1993). *Compass and Gyroscope: Integrating Science and Politics for the Environment.* Island Press, Washington, D.C.

Lindblom, C (1959). The science of muddling through. *Public Administration Review*, 19.

Stiglitz, JE (2009). Regulation and Failure. In *New Perspectives on Regulation*, Moss, D, J Cisterino (eds.), pp. 11–23. Cambridge, MA: The Tobin Project.

Susskind, L, S McKearnan and J Thomas-Larmer, (eds.) (1999). *The Consensus Building Handbook: A Comprehensive Guide to Reaching Agreement.* Thousand Oaks, CA: Sage Publications.

Susskind, L and G McMahon (1985). The theory and practice of negotiated rulemaking. *Yale Journal of Regulation*, 3, pp. 133–165.

Tankha, S and B Fuller (2010). Getting things done: Bureaucratic and entrepreneurial approaches to the practice of participatory water management reforms in Brazil and India. *Water Policy*, 12(Supplement 1), pp. 84–103.

Tankha, S, B Fuller and AB Misal (forthcoming). Getting reforms done in inhospitable institutional environments: Untying a Gordian Knot in India's power sector. *Energy Policy*.

William, DL (2006). Collaborative public management and democracy: Evidence from western watershed partnerships. *Public Administration Review*, 66(s1), pp. 100–110.

Wilmsen, C, W Elmendorf, L Fisher, J Ross, B Sarathy and G Wells 2008. *Partnerships for Empowerment-Participatory Research for Community-based Natural Resource Management*. London: Sterling.

Index

www.ingramcontent.com/pod-product-compliance
Lightning Source LLC
LaVergne TN
LVHW010636300926
849161LV00005B/956
* 9 7 8 9 8 1 4 3 3 5 7 3 7 *